German History
in Marxist Perspective

WILLIAM

German History
in Marxist Perspective
THE EAST GERMAN APPROACH

Andreas Dorpalen

WITHDRAWN

WAYNE STATE UNIVERSITY PRESS

DETROIT 1985

*Grateful acknowledgment is made to The Ohio State University for
assistance in bringing this volume to publication.*

Library of Congress Cataloging-in-Publication Data

Dorpalen, Andreas.
German history in Marxist perspective.

Bibliography: p.
Includes index.
1. Germany—Historiography.   2. Marxian historiog-
raphy—Germany (East)   I. Title.
DD86.D67   1985   943'.0072   85-17881
ISBN 0-8143-1804-5

FOR
Rose-Marie

Contents

Foreword

THE PRESENT WORK on the interpretation of German history by historians in the German Democratic Republic was completed shortly before the author's death in December 1982. It represents fifteen years of intensive study—between 1968 and 1982, Andreas Dorpalen published, in key American and German historical journals, a number of important essays on historiography in the German Democratic Republic. This book also constitutes Dorpalen's most comprehensive work, comprehensive both in dealing with the whole span of German history and in examining the mass of historical writing in the German Democratic Republic since reestablishment of a historical profession after 1945. The work is not merely a report but involves a critical, although by no means hostile, assessment of German Democratic Republic interpretations in terms of international scholarship. It represents a herculean task and the culmination of a productive scholarly career. It opens up to the Western reader a historical literature that until now has been largely neglected by English-speaking scholars and that has been approached by West German scholars largely from the perspective of ideology.

Andreas Dorpalen was born in Berlin on May 2, 1911, into a well-to-do upper-class family. His father was a gynecologist. Dorpalen studied at the famous Französische Gymnasium. Not a historian by training, he studied law at the universities of Freiburg and Munich and received his degree from the University of Bonn in 1933. He was unable under the Nazis to pursue a career in law and worked instead in his uncle's banking firm. In 1936 he immigrated to the United States. His future wife, Rose-Marie, to whom he was engaged, left Germany for Great Britain in the same year. They were married in 1942 when she was able to join him; they had two sons, Peter and Bruce. In the late 1930s in New York City, he worked as a freelance writer for various newspapers and magazines and as an editorial assistant with the *Columbia Encyclopedia*.

Dorpalen's early historical publications dealt with the political influence of the German element in America in the colonial and early national period. His first important article, which concerned the political position of the German ethnic voters on the eve of the American Civil War, was published in 1942 in the *Mississippi Valley Historical Review*, then the leading journal in American history; it was later republished.

With *The World of General Haushofer: Geopolitics in Action*, also published in 1942, Dorpalen entered the field of German studies. Although the work was sufficiently significant to be republished in 1966, it was essentially, as Dorpalen stated in the prefatory note, a book for the time—a "modest contribution" to the defeat of the Nazis at a dark moment in the war. The book is not a work of history in the sense in which all Dorpalen's subsequent works are, including the study of Treitschke. Instead, the work combines an analysis of the doctrines of geopolitics with a reproduction of important selections not only from Haushofer but also from earlier theorists—Germans such as the geographer Friedrich Ratzel and non-Germans such as the British geographer Sir Halford Mackinder and the Swedish Germanophile historian Rudolf Kjellen, who combined an advocacy of imperialist expansion with geographical theory. Dorpalen wanted both to explore an important aspect of Nazi ideology and to deal with a much broader theme, the intellectual presuppositions of imperialism in European, American, and Japanese thought in the first third of the twentieth century. Despite these broader connotations, the book has a relatively specialized focus on geopolitics. Haushofer's thought is related to the geographers and the theorists of naval power, such as Alfred Mahan, but Dorpalen does not try to link these geopolitical ideas to more extensive currents in Western intellectual or political history.

Dorpalen's teaching career began in 1943, when he was asked by the U.S. Army to give courses in German history in its specialized training program at Kenyon College. The following year he joined the faculty of St. Lawrence University, where he taught German and European history. In 1958, he accepted an appointment at The Ohio State University, where he served until his retirement in 1978. Between 1948 and 1957 a number of important articles appeared, all of which, except "Tsar Alexander III and the Boulanger Crisis in France" (1951), concentrated on German history from the Bismarck period to Hitler. With the exception of one review article—"The German Historians and Bismarck" (1953)—all of these articles dealt with political history. Dorpalen's work at this time reflected a historian in the traditional sense of historical scholarship—committed to his sources, concerned primarily with the centers of political power, and telling a narrative involving the leading political personalities, such as Bismarck, Emperor Friedrich III, and Wilhelm II. The historian of the 1980s may be struck by the absence of concern for social factors or structural analysis. Dorpalen's emphatic tone of scholarly detachment and political neutrality is also striking, although he is clearly committed to political democracy. In a sense the Haushofer volume, as well as the studies of Treitschke and Hindenburg, all touch on the problem of what went wrong in the course of modern German history. The articles are, however, all marked by a classical abstinence from theory, a rigorous insistence on impartiality, and an earnest desire to reconstruct the past, wie es eigentlich gewesen. In a sense, Dorpalen's choice of topics always reflected his deep concern with the calamities that befell democracy in modern Europe. In his private life in the United States he was very much a liberal, involved in many humanitarian concerns. Yet his commitment to objectivity forced him to be judicious even with historical figures, such as Paul von Hindenburg, whom he could little abide.

The traditionalism of these studies was transcended in the magnificent study *Heinrich von Treitschke,* published in 1957. This is one of the best biographies of a historian I have read and a marvellous work of intellectual history. There is no attempt to cast Treitschke as a forerunner of Nazism. As Dorpalen points out, "as the protagonist of a state founded on monarchy, army, and bureaucracy rather than on Führer and race, he remained controversial in the Nazi era too" (p. viii). Dorpalen succeeds, however, in blending Treitschke's biography with the crisis of a broad segment of liberal opinion. The stress is not on the historian but on the political figure; the two are inseparable. Dorpalen presents not merely a chapter in the intellectual history of the nineteenth century but the setting of politics and society in which these intellectual developments take place. The tragic transformation of liberalism—and Treitschke too began as a liberal—into a socially conservative chauvinism emerges in the course of the biography. Again Dorpalen wisely stops short of positing a continuity in German history. In a "Post Mortem," however, he writes a masterful essay on the mentality of German conservatives in the years preceding and following the First World War.

In *Hindenburg and the Weimar Republic,* which appeared in 1964, Dorpalen presented the first careful analysis of the crucial role of Hindenburg in the Weimar Republic. Dorpalen eschews any theoretical explanation for the rise of Nazism. In the best tradition of German Historismus, Dorpalen seeks to let the sources tell their own stories and to reconstruct the actual course of political events. He sees no inevitability in the destruction of the Weimar Republic. Nevertheless, he portrays the social tensions that prevented any consolidation of the Weimar Republic. He seeks to do justice to Hindenburg, who, despite his monarchist preferences, served the republic loyally. Dorpalen rejects the traditional picture of Hindenburg as a senile old man manipulated by the ultra-right forces represented by Papen. Hindenburg is seen as determinedly opposed to Hitler until the point on January 30, 1933, when he saw no parliamentary alternative.

Hindenburg and the Weimar Republic represents one of the best accounts of the history of the Weimar Republic from Hindenburg's election in 1925 to the consolidation of Hitler's powers in the "Röhm Putsch" in 1934; it is certainly the best of the accounts centering on the role of the president. It was almost immediately translated into German.

Dorpalen was disappointed in the lack of attention received by his book *Europe in the 20th Century*, which was published in 1968. Regarded as a textbook, it failed to receive reviews in the major scholarly and literary journals and arrived shortly before undergraduate history enrollments began to decline. A textbook, particularly of recent times, tends to become dated much more quickly than a specialized monograph. Despite sections on the social and cultural scene, *Europe in the 20th Century* is essentially a political history, with stress on the politics of the separate nation states, both domestically and in their foreign relations, rather than on broader trends common to Europe as a whole. It is an event-oriented history, not one that analyzes changing social structures, despite the attention given to the new authoritarian regimes in Fascist Italy, Nazi Germany, and Soviet Russia. Dorpalen wisely avoids the term *totalitarianism*, then fashionable, and refrains from broad generalizations regarding the political order in the various authoritarian states. Unfortunately, although the Stalin purges and Nazi political control are discussed, Dorpalen does not fully recapture the atmosphere of terror in these regimes. Similarly, too little attention is given to Nazi genocidal practices beyond one brief paragraph on the destruction of the Jews (p. 385).

With the completion of his history of twentieth-century Europe, Dorpalen turned to his study of the historiography of the German Democratic Republic. His interest in historiography was not new. The Treitschke book, of course, had dealt with a major historian, even if the main concern had been on the politics of history. In 1962, he published a perceptive essay on Gerhard Ritter, which in a revised form was republished in German in Hans-Ulrich Wehler's important collection, *Deutsche Historiker*. In this essay, Dorpalen critically examined the reorientation of Ritter's historical views after 1945 and concluded that despite Ritter's new Europeanism, his historiography remained apologetic of the Prusso-German past, of Prussian militarism, of Frederick the Great, and of Bismarck. This essay was important at a time when Ritter, the dean of West German historians, led the bitter attack against Fritz

Fischer's critical reexamination of Germany's role in the outbreak of World War I and its war aims.

The scope and limits of Dorpalen's book on historiography in the German Democratic Republic (DDR) need to be discussed. Dorpalen's work is the most comprehensive study of historical scholarship in the DDR to have appeared in any language, if one excludes the relatively unanalytical decennial compilations of the *Zeitschrift für Geschichtswissenschaft* on DDR scholarship. At the same time, it is neither history of historical scholarship in the DDR nor a study of the historical profession. Western analyses of the conditions of historical scholarship in the DDR do exist, the best probably being Gunther Heydemann's recently published German-language comparative examination of historical studies in the two Germanies.[1] Dorpalen's study is concerned specifically with the way in which DDR historians have interpreted the German national past from the early Middle Ages to the present. Here again, the central interest is in political history, understood in a relatively traditional way as the history of the state and, to an extent, of political parties. An introductory chapter effectively describes the institutional framework of party, academies, and universities in which scholarly activity takes place. He carefully examines the theoretical presuppositions of Marxism-Leninism as an ideology that guides such scholarly activity, with stress on the predictable, "lawful" development of society in the "scientific" sense. Dorpalen insists that the DDR interpretations of German history are rigorously determined within this conception of history, as expressed in the resolutions of the party congresses. Historical studies are centrally directed in the DDR and reflect the official position of party and state.

Dorpalen is interested in the official interpretation of the German past. There is relatively little discussion of methodology and sources. What matters to him is the interpretation of history, which is developed collectively. The work thus gives relatively little attention to individual historians, who are interesting to Dorpalen only insofar as they give expression to the official interpretation. This focus leads Dorpalen to a picture of historical scholarship that is relatively uniform throughout the profession and that has changed relatively little since the constitution of a Marxist-Leninist historiography in the early 1950s.

This stress on the uniformity of a scholarship directed by party and state naturally raises the suspicion that this work re-

---

[1]Gunther Heydemann, *Geschichtswissenschaft im geteilten Deutschland. Entwicklungsgeschichte, Organisationsstruktur, Funktionen, Theorie- und Methodenprobleme in der Bundesrepublik Deutschland und in der DDR* (Frankfurt a.M., 1980).

flects attitudes of the Cold War. This is by no means the case,
however. Dorpalen's approach in this work reflects the detachment
and the commitment to an ideal of objectivity that pervades all his
writings. His rejection of Marxism-Leninism is as clear as his ideological distance from Treitschke and Haushofer in his earlier writings. On the other hand, Dorpalen does not reject DDR interpretations of the past outright, but takes them seriously. Throughout
the book he examines the conclusions of DDR historiography in
the light of the existing literature in the East and the West and
more than once sides with the DDR historians. As he points out,
Western historical interpretations too often reflect political biases,
from Bosl's untenable picture of a harmonious medieval society,
free of serious conflict, to the one-sided West German conservative
interpretations of the resistance against the Nazis, which ignore
the rank and file opposition of Communists and Social Democrats.
At the same time, Dorpalen does not hesitate to refute as simplistic the DDR explanation of the Nazis as a function of "monopoly
capitalism." The constant and balanced reference to the Western
literature is one of the strengths of the book.

The emphasis in Gunther Heydemann and Christina von
Buxhoeveden's[2] studies on the reorientation in DDR interpretations with changing political conditions is in sharp contrast to
Dorpalen's view of a relative stability over the years. Dorpalen
recognizes one great reorientation in DDR interpretations of German history, a reorientation that took place relatively soon, in the
early 1950s. This was the rejection of the conception that German
history was a continuous story of political and ideological "misery" (Misere) marked by the preponderance of authoritarian and
antidemocratic traditions; this conception was maintained by the

---

[2]Christina von Buxhoeveden, Geschichtswissenschaft und Politik in der DDR.
Das Problem der Periodisierung (Köln, 1980).

party in the periods during the Nazi regime and immediately following World War II and was elaborated by Georg Lukács[3] and Alexander Abusch.[4] The break with this conception coincided with the attempts by the nascent East German state to define itself as the heir of a progressive, democratic heritage. Dorpalen shows that the recent positive revaluation of Luther, Frederick the Great, and Prussia had its sources much earlier in DDR historiography than has generally been recognized.

Some important aspects of DDR historiography do not fall within the scope of this volume. Some of the great contributions of DDR historical studies have been in the areas of social and economic history, which were relatively neglected in Germany until 1945 and which continued to be neglected in the Federal Republic even after 1945. Much sooner than in the Federal Republic, historians in the DDR broke through the event-oriented, narrative approach that was dominant in much West German scholarship and combined empirical work and theory in the study of social transformation, particularly the impact of industrialization. Certainly the questions were informed by Marxist-Leninist conceptions, but this did not necessarily invalidate the results of empirical studies that derived from these questions.

The controversies surrounding the questions of the rise of capitalism, industry, and the working class are referred to only marginally in this book, because they do not relate directly to political development (although, of course, the two are related in a fundamental sense). These controversies also raise the question of the place that the German development occupies in the broader history of the Western world. Dorpalen recognizes this question in the abstract form of the DDR formulation of a law of stages, but he does not do justice to the specific works in the DDR—whether those of Hans Mottek[5] in the 1950s and 1960s or those of Hartmut Zwahr[6] in the 1970s and 1980s—that deal empirically with the industrial transformation of Germany and the emergence of a working class. The seminal role of Jürgen Kuczynski in the debates since the 1950s is touched on only briefly. Concerned with the lower classes, DDR historians have made important contributions to the study of everyday life, both in its material and its cultural aspects. The *Jahrbuch für Wirtschaftsgeschichte*, which has become an international forum for questions of economic theory as they relate to history and

[3]Georg Lukács, *Die Zerstörung der Vernunft* (Berlin, 1954).
[4]Alexander Abusch, *Der Irrweg einer Nation* (Berlin, 1946).
[5]Hans Mottek, *Wirtschaftsgeschichte Deutschlands. Ein Grundriss*, 2 vols. (Berlin, 1957–64).
[6]Hartmut Zwahr, *Zur Konstituierung des Proletariats als Klasse. Strukturuntersuchung über das Leipziger Proletariat während der industriellen Revolution* (Berlin, 1978).

for empirical studies in economic history, contrasts in the openness of its discussions with the much more closely ideologically defined and politically oriented *Zeitschrift für Geschichtswissenschaft*. The latter journal receives greater attention in Dorpalen's research, understandably so from his perspective.

This work is not the final word on the historiography of the DDR. Nor, it should be repeated, was it intended to be. Dorpalen's aim was much more modest. As the chapter headings, and thus the periodization, suggest, he was interested primarily in the DDR interpretations of the political history of Germany. To be sure, this history included religious and economic events, such as the Reformation or the process of industrialization, insofar as these were important for the understanding of the history of German politics. From the perspectives of a new generation of social historians, additional aspects of DDR historiography will appear significant. Nevertheless, this is the most important analysis of the DDR Geschichtsbild that we possess. In addition, it reflects the two great qualities that characterize all of Dorpalen's writings—a scholarly detachment that despite a deep attachment to democratic values seeks to maintain judicious impartiality, and the desire and ability to relate politics and ideas.

Georg G. Iggers

Preface

MARXIST-LENINIST HISTORIOGRAPHY has not aroused much interest in this country. What work has been done in this area—especially in Soviet historiography—has been mainly of a polemical nature; attention has focused in particular on inaccuracies and misinterpretations and on the impact of the changing Communist party line on historical research analyses. Few attempts have been made to explore Marxist interpretations on their own terms, least of all on a comprehensive scale that takes in more than an isolated event or development.

This study attempts to analyze East German interpretations of German history on their own Marxist-Leninist terms. Although this approach will be a critical one, criticism will not be its main, let alone its sole, purpose. It will be equally concerned with exploring the Marxist thought processes, which provide an indispensable key to an understanding of Marxist historical conceptions and interpretations. At the same time, these processes can also throw light on present-day Marxist political conduct and attitudes, at least of the East German kind. All in all, Marxist studies and critiques of the past are not necessarily invalidated by the fact that Marxist solutions to present problems hold little attraction. East German historiography thus warrants a systematic examination.

Many friends and colleagues have provided help in one form or another. I am particularly indebted to the late Fritz T. Epstein, Felix Gilbert, Frederick G. Heymann, Georg G. Iggers, James M. Kittelson, Joseph H. Lynch, Hans Rosenberg, Hans Schleier, and Luitpold Wallach. I need hardly add that errors in fact and conclusion are solely mine, the more so as I did not always take the advice I received.

I also had the good fortune of enjoying the stimulating hospitality of the Institute for Advanced Study for a term in 1969 and that of the *Historische Seminar* of the Rheinische Friedrichs-Wilhelms-Universität in Bonn for several months in 1971. My stay in Bonn was made possible in part by a research grant from the American Philosophical Society.

I am also most grateful to The Ohio State University for several extended research leaves and to the many secretaries in the Department of History who, under the ever-helpful guidance of Phyllis R. Tietzel, the Assistant to the Chairman, typed and retyped the various versions through which this book went.

My gratitude to my wife, Rose-Marie, is especially heartfelt in the case of this study, whose gestation period extended over many years and whose writing claimed my attention far beyond what wifely forbearance is normally willing to tolerate.

Abbreviations

Abriss	*Geschichte der Sozialistischen Einheitspartei Deutschlands: Abriss*, ed. Gerhard Rossmann et al. (Berlin [East], 1978)
ADAV	Allgemeiner Deutscher Arbeiterverein (General German Workers Association)
AHR	*American Historical Review*
BzG	*Beiträge zur Geschichte der (deutschen) Arbeiterbewegung*
CEH	*Central European History*
DDR	Deutsche Demokratische Republik (German Democratic Republic)
Holborn	Hajo Holborn, *A History of Germany*, 3 volumes (New York, 1959–69)
HZ	*Historische Zeitschrift*
GdA	*Geschichte der deutschen Arbeiterbewegung*, ed. Institute of Marxism/Leninism at the Central Committee of the Socialist Unity party, 8 volumes (Berlin [East], 1966)
Gebhardt	Bruno Gebhardt, *Handbuch der deutschen Geschichte*, 4 volumes (Stuttgart, 1970)
Grundriss	*Klassenkampf, Tradition, Sozialismus: Von den Anfängen des deutschen Volkes bis zur Gestaltung der entwickelten Sozialistischen Gesellschaft in der Deutschen Demokratischen Republik: Grundriss*, ed. Ernst Diehl et al. (Berlin [East], 1978)
GWU	*Geschichte in Wissenschaft und Unterricht*
HbDtWSG	*Handbuch der Deutschen Wirtschafts- und Sozialgeschichte*, ed. Hermann Aubin and Wolfgang Zorn, 2 Volumes (Stuttgart, 1971–76)
IMT	International Military Tribunal, *Trial of the Major War Criminals* (Nuremberg, 1947–49)
JfG	*Jahrbuch für Geschichte*
JMH	*Journal of Modern History*

JWG	*Jahrbuch für Wirtschaftsgeschichte*
KPD	Kommunistische Partei Deutschlands (Communist Party of Germany)
Kuczynski, *Geschichte*	Jürgen Kuczynski, *Geschichte der Lage der Arbeiter unter dem Kapitalismus*, 37 volumes (Berlin [East], 1960–72
MEW	Karl Marx/Friedrich Engels, *Werke* (Berlin [East], 1956–68)
Mottek (et al.)	Hans Mottek, *Wirtschaftsgeschichte Deutschlands* (Berlin [East], 1964–72). Vol. 3 with Walter Becker and Alfred Schröter.
SAPD	Sozialistische Arbeiterpartei Deutschlands (Socialist Workers Party of Germany)
SDAP	Sozialdemokratische Arbeiterpartei (Social Democratic Workers Party)
SDG	*Sowjetsystem und Demokratische Gesellschaft: Eine vergleichende Enzyklopädie*, ed. C. D. Kenig et al., 6 volumes (Freiburg, 1966–72)
SED	Sozialistische Einheitspartei Deutschlands (Socialist Unity Party of Germany)
SPD	Sozialdemokratische Partei Deutschlands (Social Democratic Party of Germany)
Streisand	Joachim Streisand, *Deutsche Geschichte in einem Band* (Berlin [East], 1974)
Swb	*Sachwörterbuch der Geschichte Deutschlands und der deutschen Arbeiterbewegung* (Berlin [East], 1969–70)
TWC	*Trials of War Criminals before Nürnberg Military Tribunals* (Washington D.C., 1947–49)
Unb. Verg.	*Unbewältigte Vergangenheit: Kritik der bürgerlichen Geschichtsschreibung in der BRD* (Berlin [East], 1977)
USPD	Unabhängige Sozialdemokratische Partei Deutschlands (Independent Social Democratic Party of Germany)
VfZ	*Vierteljahrshefte für Zeitgeschichte*
VKPD	Vereinigte Kommunistische Partei Deutschlands (United Communist Party of Germany)
VSWG	*Vierteljahresschrift für Sozial- und Wirtschaftsgeschichte*
Wörterbuch	*Wörterbuch der marxistisch-leninistischen Soziologie* (Berlin [East], 1969)
WZ	*Wissenschaftliche Zeitschrift der Universität . . . Gesellschafts- und sprachwissenschaftliche Reihe*
ZfG	*Zeitschrift für Geschichtswissenschaft*

The Marxist-Leninist
Concept of History

MARXISM-LENINISM is a history-minded *Weltanschauung.* In the words of one East German scholar, it is "the unified materialistic theory of social development. . . . Marxism-Leninism is, therefore, inseparably connected with the scientific exploration of history, it develops unceasingly as the result of the exploration of past and especially present history."[1] History permeates Marxist studies from the earliest writings of Marx and Engels to the work of present-day Marxist-Leninist authors.[2]

History in the Marxist view is not merely concerned with the past; it is perceived as a developmental process of which, as is said above, the present is an integral part. Moreover, because this process is considered subject to ascertainable laws, its future course is viewed as a predictable extension of past and present developments and as such is also a legitimate concern of the historian. The task of the Marxist scholar consists in tracing this social process from man's transcendance of the animal kingdom to the present and beyond as the "lawful [i.e., scientifically predictable] process of mankind's advance toward communism." If many non-Marxists question the purposefulness of history, no such doubts beset the Marxist historian.[3]

---

[1]Peter Bollhagen, in *Einführung in das Studium der Geschichte,* ed. Walter Eckermann and Hubert Mohr (Berlin [East], 1966), p. 37.
[2]The terms *Marxist* and *Marxist-Leninist* are used interchangeably in this study, with *Marxist* serving as an abbreviation of *Marxist-Leninist,* that is, Marxism as modified and expanded by Lenin's teachings. On the other hand, the term *Leninist* will be used whenever a specific contribution of Lenin to Marxist theory or practice is to be stressed. This usage follows the Soviet and East German practice.
[3]"Geschichte," *Swb,* vol. 1, p. 673; Peter Bollhagen and Gerhard Brendler, in Eckermann and Mohr, *Einführung,* pp. 30–31; Alfred Loesdau, "Der Präsentismus in der bürgerlichen Historiographie der U.S.A.," *ZfG* 14 (1966): 1075; Frank Rupprecht, "Bestimmung und Erforschung des sozialistischen Geschichtsbewusstseins," ibid., 15 (1967): 837.

The Basic Role of Production

In the Marxist perspective, human progress has followed a definite pattern. Because man's most immediate concern has always been the meeting of his material needs, "mankind," in Friedrich Engels' famous words, "must first of all eat, drink, have shelter and clothing before it can pursue politics, science, art, religion, etc." Yet what distinguishes humans from animals, who too need shelter and food, are the skills and tools they developed in order to *produce* what they need. Work, production, and the interchange with nature, Marx and Engels point out, ended man's total dependence on nature and raised him above animals: production, they concluded, thus constituted the central element in human history. Correspondingly, improved production was also the key to man's rise from the primitivity of his early beginnings to his present stage; ultimately, such production will make possible the communist order in which all essential human needs will be met.[4]

This view of the fundamental importance of material production is reinforced by the conviction that production shaped man into the social being he is: based on cooperation, production brought forth human society—a process that derived further momentum from the increasing division of labor. Marxism thus sees human societies as systems based on the relations men enter into with one another, knowingly or unknowingly, in the production process. These relations also condition man's way of thinking and living, for that way, too, arises "from the need, the necessity, of intercourse with other men" (*German Ideology*). Politics, justice, religion, and other ideas and institutions are viewed, at least in an ultimate sense,[5] as being fashioned by this material foundation; they constitute the ideological superstructure. Therefore, there can be no abstract society, only *concrete-historical systems* whose social structure is shaped by their specific modes of production. Accordingly, history is divided into *socioeconomic formations*—the primitive-communal system, the slaveholding system, the feudal system, the capitalist system, and the socialist/communist system.[6] These for-

---

[4]Engels, in MEW, vol. 19, pp. 335–36. The classic analysis of the significance of production is, of course, found in *The German Ideology*, ibid., vol. 3, pp. 28ff. See also *Grundlagen der marxistischen Philosophie* (Berlin [East], 1961), pp. 411–12.

[5]As Engels already pointed out, Marxist theory does not claim that every thought and action can be traced back to a *direct* material causation. See Engels' letters on historical materialism in MEW, vol. 37, pp. 436–37, 463–65, 488–94.

[6]Socialism in the Marxist scenario is a preliminary phase of the communist order, in which all major means of production have been socialized, but some class differences remain, some private enterprise survives, and goods and services are available only according to work done. Socialism is to be superseded by communism, in which there will be full social equality and in which productive abundance will make possible the equitable satisfaction of human needs.

mations, each more productive than the preceding, follow one another as the productive forces keep growing: history is thus "above all the history of the development of production, the history of the modes of production. . . ." This materialist concept of history is contrasted with its idealist counterpart, which is described as finding the wellsprings of human history in ideas and theories and as attributing change to individuals ("great men") propelled by their subjective motives within this framework of ideologies, religions, or some undefinable world spirit, as propounded by Hegel.[7]

Because Marxists consider the mode of production the key to the spirit and structure of any society, they devote special attention to the analysis of the production process. In accordance with Marx's outline of his social theory in the preface to his *Contribution to the Critique of Political Economy*, they divide the production process into two elements—productive forces and production relations. The productive forces consist of human labor, management, science and technology, tools, machines, and natural resources, to the extent that the latter are being utilized. Production relations are those that exist between men within and as a result of the production process. These relations are determined by the ownership and control of the means of production, the relations evolving out of the division of labor, the forms in which labor is used (slave or hired labor), how products of labor are exchanged (barter or money economy), and other relationships generated by the production process.

The production relations, in particular the manner in which the fruits of production are appropriated, are seen as determining the character of a society at a given moment, but in this view it is the productive forces that account for the society's continuing development and for its eventual replacement by another socioeconomic formation. Societies grow and expand as means of production are improved and increased, new skills and techniques adopted, and new natural resources found or harnessed.

There comes a point in this process at which the prevailing production relations—the particular kind of ownership of the means of production, the specific utilization of labor—impede the further development of the productive forces. The ensuing confrontation between productive forces and production relations mani-

---

[7]*Grundlagen des Marxismus-Leninismus: Lehrbuch* (Berlin [East], 1960), pp. 139ff. (quotation on p. 141); "Gesellschaftsformation, ökonomische," *Wörterbuch der marxistisch-leninistischen Soziologie* (Berlin [East], 1969), pp. 152ff.; also Rugard-Otto Gropp, "Die Begründung des historischen Materialismus—eine Revolution in der Geschichtswissenschaft," in *Studien zur deutschen Geschichtswissenschaft*, ed. Joachim Streisand (Berlin [East], 1962), vol. 1, pp. 203ff. On idealist historiography, see *Swb*, vol. 1, p. 802.

fests itself in the growing intensity of social conflicts—in the escalation of the class struggle.[8] It is resolved by social revolutions, which open the door to new production relations that provide scope to the growing productive forces. Revolutions thus are not deplored as catastrophes, but are welcomed as salutary constructive events, accelerating needed socioeconomic developments; Marx called them the "locomotives of history."[9]

Such revolutions are not necessarily violent ones; thus, the transition from capitalism to socialism in East Germany, it is explained, could be effected peacefully, thanks to the help provided by the "socialist brotherland." What matters is that the revolution deprives the old ruling class of its power and enables the ascending class to seize power, which means that to be effective, a social revolution must at the same time be a political one. Changes that are not accompanied by such an exchange of ruling classes, according to Lenin, are mere reforms, ever at the mercy of the old rulers.[10]

Given the significance attributed to the productive forces, a large number of studies have been devoted to their development as the key to the course of history.[11] When the economic historian Jürgen Kuczynski suggested some years ago that men made history primarily on the plane of the superstructure, that is, on the political and ideological level, he was sharply rebuked by his colleagues. Men made history above all as a productive force, he was told; shifting the focus of their historical role to the superstructure meant draining materialism out of history. In practice, however,

---

[8]Social conflicts are attributed to the growing incompatibility of productive forces and productive relations, which explains why the inclusion of management among the productive forces, although now supported by most DDR historians, has been a matter of controversy: it places the owners, or those in control of the means of production on behalf of the owners, among those very forces that are to challenge the existing productive relations, including the private ownership of the means of production ("Produktivkräfte," Swb, vol. 2, p. 299; "Leitung," Wörterbuch, pp. 267–68; Wolfgang Jonas, Valentine Linsbauer, and Helga Marx, Die Produktivkräfte in der Geschichte [Berlin (East), 1969], vol. 1, pp. 31–33; Georg Klaus and Hans Schulze, Sinn, Gesetz und Fortschritt in der Geschichte [Berlin (East), 1967], pp. 160–61). Yet if management's technical functions place it among the forces of progress, its social role as capitalist management—which is ultimately decisive and which by definition, as it is seen, identifies it with exploitative, repressive, and manipulatory objectives—assigns management to the antiprogressive camp and to the defense of the existing production relations ("Leitung," pp. 267–68).
[9]"Produktivkräfte," Swb, vol. 2, p. 299; "Leitung," Wörterbuch, pp. 267–68; GdA, vol. 1, pp. 50–51; Marx, in MEW, vol. 7, p. 85.
[10]See Lenin, "Revolution," Swb, vol. 2, p. 382; Günter Benser and Heinz Heitzer, "Die Gründung der DDR-Ergebnis einer erfolgreichen Volksbewegung," ZfG 26 (1978): 210. On the Marxist interpretation of the revolutionary changeover in East Germany, see also chapter 9.
[11]There exists in the DDR a special research group (Arbeitskreis) called Geschichte der Produktivkräfte, much of whose work is published in the Jahrbuch für Wirtschaftsgeschichte.

Marxist historiography has not followed its own rules. General histories pay far more detailed attention to developments in the superstructure than to the changing modes of production in the basis. "Of all forms of social practice, even though it is founded on the production process," Ernst Engelberg, the dean of the East German historians, points out—more circumspectly than Kuczynski, however—"the political struggle is of special importance to the historian."[12]

The concern with political matters is significant also that it indicates the importance Marxists attribute to the superstructure of social systems and to the realm of ideas. The emphasis on material production as the foundation of all social life, then, is not to suggest that ideas play only a minor role in the Marxist view. What it does mean is that ideas are seen, not as developing on their own in individual minds, but as reflecting—if ever so indirectly, by way of ideology or politics—the material environment in which they originate. Again, this is not to imply that ideas must revolve around material concerns; although the material environment conditions ideas, it does not necessarily motivate them, and their motivation may thus be found in the quest for nonmaterial objectives. Once generated, moreover, ideas may develop a momentum of their own and may in turn have a strong impact on their environment, accelerating or retarding the march of progress.[13]

The focus on the modes of production as the crucial element of the historical process lends to Marxist historiography a supranational and even global perspective. In this approach, German history becomes a part of both a European and, in a more general sense, a worldwide process. Its course, like that of other national histories, is determined by the development of its productive forces, and this development, whatever its national or regional variations and particularities, is everywhere subject to the same historical laws. Although the traditional approach has been to stress the differences between Germany's history and that of other nations, the emphasis here is on the common features, with results that not only have produced novel historical conclusions, but also have had their impact on the social and political plane.[14]

---

[12]See Jürgen Kuczynski, "Der Mensch, der Geschichte macht," *ZfG* 5 (1957): 1ff. and the ensuing discussion in ibid., 5 (1957) and 6 (1958). For Kuczynski's changed view, compare his *Geschichte*, vol. 1, p. 87 and *JWG* 1 (1971): 15. Engelberg's quotation is found in *Probleme der marxistischen Geschichtswissenschaft*, ed. Ernst Engelberg (Cologne, 1972), p. 121; on this same point, see also Ernst Diehl, "Aufgaben der Geschichtswissenschaft der DDR nach dem IX. Parteitag der SED," *ZfG* 25 (1977): 271.

[13]Gottfried Stiehler, *Gesellschaft und Geschichte* (Berlin [East], 1974), p. 152; also Helmut Fleischer, *Marxismus und Geschichte* (Frankfurt, 1969), pp. 58–60.

[14]*Grundlagen*, p. 146; Horst Bartel et al., in *ZfG* 18 (1970): suppl., 29; Engelberg, "Zu methodologischen Problemen der Periodisierung," *ZfG* 19 (1971): 1220; and

Classes and Class Struggle

Although production is a cooperative process, it has not been performed on an equal basis, Marxists point out, since the time of the primitive-communal society. That classless system of social equality was superseded by a series of socioeconomic formations that were divided into classes with unequal powers and rights.

By Marxist criteria, the emergence of classes was the most important development in the production process. Classes came into being when men were able to produce surpluses of material necessities, for such surpluses permitted some members of the community to live on the physical labor of others. Thus exploitation of man by man began and classes and class conflicts developed. The classless primitive-communal system gave way to the slaveholding system, with its divisive class structure, and to the formation of states to protect the class interests of the ruling minority. The slaveholding system, in turn, was replaced, successively, by the feudal and capitalist class societies. In all these social systems, the individual's place in the production process was determined by his ownership or nonownership of the means of production, his role in the social organization of work, and the manner in which and the extent to which he shared in the available social wealth. In the Marxist view, it is the individual's place, based on objective criteria, that assigns him to one or another class. Class status thus cannot be established by subjective decision; the worker who considers himself a member of the bourgeois middle class merely indulges in illusionism. On the other hand, because the class concept is derived from objective criteria and not from subjective assessments, it can be applied to times that did not yet know that concept, such as antiquity or the Middle Ages.

Marxists distinguish between primary classes (Grundklassen) and secondary ones (Nebenklassen). The primary classes are those which have been formed by a given mode of production and on which that mode rests—slaveowners and slaves in the slaveholding system, feudal landlords and peasants in the feudal system, bourgeois capitalists and workers in the capitalist order. The secondary classes are either remnants of an earlier system or harbingers of a future one—peasants and artisans in the slaveholding system, urban burghers in the feudal order, landowners and peasants under capitalism. Finally, there are social strata (Schichten) that have differing relationships to the means of production and hence have

---

Diehl et al., "Erfahrungen und Erfordernisse," *BzG* 14 (1972): 367. See also Wolfgang Küttler, who stresses the wide variations in the worldwide historical process in his "Methodologische Kriterien historischer Formationsbestimmung," *ZfG* 23 (1974): 1041, 1047–48.

varying class affiliations. Without a separate role in the production process, these social strata are considered too weak to act independently but can be useful allies of a primary class; one such stratum is the intelligentsia in the capitalist system. Given the key role of classes, their rise and decline and their relationship to society as a whole and to other classes are foremost subjects of scholarly investigation, and East German journals are filled with continued discussions of their role and impact on the various phases of social development. "Within the structural ramifications of social totality, classes—both as an economic and a social category—are the connecting link between basis and superstructure," Ernst Engelberg sums up their role; "they determine the relationship between society and individual; as a social category they also provide the key that enables us to understand the social function of all areas of the ideological superstructure."[15]

As much as they deplore the inequities of the various class systems, Marxists grant that these systems served a historical purpose: they allowed a minority who no longer had to be material producers themselves to direct production, attend to public affairs, and promote art and science. In doing so, these class societies helped incease productivity. Whatever the injustices they entailed, these societies thus became agents of progress, at least for a time, and moved mankind closer to the socialist order. As Engels wrote in a much-quoted passage of his *Anti-Dühring,*

> Only slavery made possible the division of labor between agriculture and industry on a larger scale, and with it the flower of the ancient world—Greekdom. Without slavery no Greek state, no Greek art and science; without slavery no Roman empire. And without the foundation of Greekdom no modern Europe either. We should never forget that our entire economical, political, and intellectual development is based on a condition in which slavery was necessary and was accepted as such. In this sense we are entitled to say: without slavery no modern socialism.

Even the enslaved, he felt, were better off in the slaveholding system than their counterparts had been in the primitive-communal order, for in the latter order, captured enemies were killed (and earlier, even eaten) rather than used as laborers.[16]

---

[15]"Klassen," *Swb*, vol. 1, pp. 918–19; "Klasse, soziale," *Wörterbuch*, p. 238; Engelberg, "Über Gegenstand und Ziel der marxistisch-leninistischen Geschichtswissenschaft," *ZfG* 16 (1968): 1129. On some of the discussions, see chapter 2, pp. 93–95 and chapter 3, p. 103. One difficulty that was never resolved satisfactorily concerns the status of the petty bourgeoisie, whose elusive position was already deplored by the *Communist Manifesto*. See also *Grundlagen*, p. 181, and Rolf Weber, *ZfG* 21 (1973): 447. Lenin spoke of the petty bourgeoisie as "two-faced by its very nature."

[16]*Grundlagen*, pp. 149–50; Engels, in MEW, vol. 20, pp. 167–69.

However, as a product of history, Marxist scholars also point out, the class society will continue only as long as it remains socially useful. The time has now come, they maintain, when the private ownership of the means of production, the mainstay of all class societies and the tool with which a minority exploits the majority, no longer promotes social progress, but rather obstructs it. The capitalist system must therefore be replaced by the socialist order, which will give free rein to production by the abolition of private ownership of the means of production and the resulting liquidation of the exploiting classes.

This changeover is being achieved by the class struggle and its ultimate weapon, social and political revolution. By these means, the exploited throughout history have bettered their lot and brought about the replacement of antiquated social orders by more adequate ones. Such efforts are indispensable because discrepancies between productive forces and production relations cannot by themselves achieve changes: these discrepancies can be resolved only through human action. Class struggles thus become the motor power of history. "History," in the famous words of the *Communist Manifesto*, "is the history of class struggles." (There is no incompatibility between this definition of history and the one given earlier: the *Manifesto* emphasized the means by which history is made; the definition centering on the modes of production focuses on the substance of the historical process.)

The makers of history are found in the popular masses—a force encompassing all toiling classes and strata. This claim to the history-making role of the masses rests on the argument that the masses not only sustain the material existence of any society as "direct" producers of all vital necessities but also are the actual originators of improved production techniques—an argument that is based on the assumption, equally cavalier, that all such improvements ultimately grow out of the experiences and activities of the toilers. In this manner, the masses are credited with bringing about those conflicts between productive forces and production relations that ultimately can be resolved only by revolutions and that are thus the stepping-stones toward progress. The revolutions in turn can be successful only if they have the support of the masses—a support that is assured by the need of the masses for social and economic improvement. The history-making role of the masses thus is derived from their key role, both qualitatively and quantitatively, in the production process and the class struggle, the two foci of the Marxist scenario.

With industrialization, the urban working class, or proletariat, becomes the most important component of the masses, because of its indispensable role in industrial production; its physical concentration, which facilitates concerted action; and the scientific guidance provided to it by Marxism. At the same time, the dissolution of all patriarchal relationships and the dropping of all religious pretenses points up the full extent of the wretchedness of the proletariat—a condition that, if it is now admittedly no longer absolute, is still assailed as a relative or "tendential" one. Moreover, by liberating itself from capitalist exploitation through the seizure and socialization of the means of production, the working class will liberate all mankind from repression and exploitation. "All previous historical movements," states the *Communist Manifesto*, "were movements of minorities or launched in the interest of minorities. The proletarian movement is the self-reliant, independent movement of the immense majority."[17]

Given the importance attributed to the masses, Marxist historiography pays special attention to their concerns and activities. It takes pride in its partisanship (Parteilichkeit) on behalf of the masses as the historical agents of progress. This is a partisanship, DDR authors stress, that takes the side of the lawful, historically determined trends of social reality and that thus has a scientific foundation—unlike bourgeois historiography, which, contrary to its disclaimers, also has always been partisan but which sides with the opponents of progress and therefore arrives at erroneous results.[18] Yet even this kind of circular reasoning, in which premise and conclusion blend into one,[19] does not shield the Marxist historian from facing a historical record that accords to the masses a far more modest role in the historical process than he sees them play.

For a time this discrepancy between claim and reality was blurred by a simplistic identification of all progressive forces with the popular masses; as a result, all progressive elements—including merchants, manufacturers, clerics, and noblemen who sided with

---

[17]*Grundlagen*, pp. 204ff.; *Swb*, vol. 1, p. 836, vol. 2, pp. 753–54, 777–78; *Wörterbuch*, pp. 498–99, 330; Klaus and Schulze, *Sinn, Gesetz und Fortschritt*, p. 8; Brendler, "Zum Prinzip der Parteilichkeit . . . ," *ZfG*, 20 (1972): 279–80. On the immiseration of the masses, see *Swb*, vol. 2, p. 702; *Grundlagen*, pp. 276–78; Gottfried Stiehler, *Geschichte und Verantwortung* (Berlin [East], 1972), p. 24; see also Kuczynski, *Geschichte der Lage der Arbeiter unter dem Kapitalismus* (Berlin [East], 1961), which through its thirty-eight volumes deals specifically with this problem.

[18]"Parteilichkeit," *Swb*, vol. 2, pp. 255–56; "Parteilichkeit," *Wörterbuch*, pp. 331–33; Bollhagen, in Eckermann and Mohr, *Einführung*, p. 88; Engelberg, "Parteilichkeit und Objektivität in der Geschichtswissenschaft," *ZfG* 17 (1969): 75.

[19]Gerhard Brendler uses such circular reasoning when he warns against gearing historical research to "desired" answers but at the same time enjoins historians to anchor their work in "objective reality"—that is, in the progressive role of the working class as a frame of reference beyond subjectivist arbitrariness (Brendler, "Zum Prinzip," pp. 286, 293).

the forces of progress—were considered part of the masses.[20] More recently, however, most DDR scholars have included among the masses only the toilers and the exploited, in accord with their role as material producers. At the same time, it is granted that the ruling classes, either in pursuit of their own interests or in response to the thrusts of the masses, have made contributions to progress even while seeking to uphold the existing order.[21] In the case of revolutions that challenge the feudal order, moreover, bourgeoisie and masses are found to have been mutually dependent upon each other, with the masses removing the obstacles blocking progress and the bourgeoisie taking the lead in reorganizing society. And if it is now accepted that some forces outside the masses have striven for social progress at one time or another, it is also conceded that there were elements among the masses, as in the Vendée, that sided with antiprogressive, counterrevolutionary endeavors.[22]

Although these shortcomings of the masses are now commonly recognized (and variously attributed to apathy, despair, or credulity), the thesis of their decisive history-making role has not been abandoned. Only Jürgen Kuczynski has challenged it and has asked what the masses had been fighting for all this time if all along they had been the main force of history and had determined its course. "Was it they in their capacity as 'creator and main force' who determined that they were to live in the utmost misery, suppressed and despoiled?"[23]

Kuczynski exempts the working class from this challenge, but the question might well be raised in regard to the latter as well. No less a Marxist than Lenin indeed did raise that question; he concluded that the working class was unable to develop on its own that self-confident class consciousness that would enable it to fulfill its revolutionary mission. The proletariat required leadership by men able to apply Marxist theory to political practice and organized in a tightly structured centralized party that would shield

[20]See "Volkmassen," *Wörterbuch*, p. 498; Bernhard Töpfer, "Volksbewegungen . . . [im] entwickelten Feudalismus," *ZfG* 25 (1977): 1158–59. Additional references are cited by Brendler and Küttler, in *ZfG*, 26 (1978): 804.

[21]See Joachim Herrmann, in *Die Volksmassen in der Geschichte der vorkapitalistischen Gesellschaftsformationen*, ed. Hermann and Irmgard Sellnow (Berlin [East], 1975), p. 18; Manfred Kossok, "Volksbewegungen im bürgerlichen Revolutionszyklus," *ZfG* 26 (1978): 598; Brendler and Küttler, 814–16. Additional references are cited by Adolf Laube, in *ZfG* 26 (1978): 611 n. 33. On ruling classes, see Töpfer, "Volksbewegungen," p. 1160.

[22]Kossok, "Volksbewegungen," pp. 598–99, 597 (quoting Lenin); Brendler and Küttler, 816–17.

[23]Kuczynski, "Der Mensch," 1ff.; Kuczynski, review, *JWG* 4 (1976): 163ff. (quotation on p. 169); also Klaus Goessler, "Der historische Materialismus und der Mensch der Geschichte macht," *ZfG* 5 (1957): 1239.

the workers against the corrupting reformism to which the proletariat was succumbing in the Western European countries. The subsequent socialist revolutions were accordingly launched by Leninist parties, and the demotion of the masses from subjects to objects of history culminated in the totalitarianism of the Stalinist revolutions "from above."

Yet no deviation from the original Marxist doctrine is admitted: the "new-type" Bolshevik party is described as a child of the working class, drawing its inspiration and strength from that class, responsible to it, as always removable by the latter should it not live up to its tasks—an argument hard to reconcile with the alleged political inadequacy of the working class that led to the creation of the Leninist parties in the first place.[24] Marxism, which had drawn its original inspiration from the French Revolution and had envisaged the creation of a society free from obsolete political and social shackles—and one in which the (temporary) dictatorship of the proletariat would be a self-governing one—thus became the foundation of all-embracing totalitarian dictatorships. Yet the distance between Marx/Engels and Lenin/Stalin—or, for that matter, the East German leadership—ought not to be overestimated. The potential for totalitarianism existed in the original theory—in Marx's Hegel-derived all-inclusive rationality of the historical process and in Engels' unwitting encouragement of a mechanistic determinism, from which Marx did not dissociate himself and which, indirectly at least, he seemed to approve.[25] As the dissident East German critic Rudolf Bahro has noted, these totalitarian seeds were recognized even in Marx's time by the Russian anarchist Mikhail Bakunin. With remarkable foresight, Bakunin warned that Marx's dicta-

---

[24]On this question, see also the circular reasoning of *Grundlagen der marxistischen Philosophie*, p. 690; Manfred Weissbecker, "Extrem reaktionäre Organisationen des Imperialismus und werktätige Massen," *ZfG*, 25 (1977): 293. Joachim Streisand has frankly explained that conditions are much too complex to be understood by the average individual and that for this reason that individual requires guidance by a Marxist-Leninist party (Streisand, "Geschichtsbild und Geschichtsbewusstsein . . . ," *ZfG* 17 (1969): 41). A West German historian, Dieter Riesenberger, notes that similar views on the part of West German authors have been attacked as elitist by DDR critics (Reisenberger, *Geschichte und Geschichtsunterricht in der DDR* [Göttingen, 1973], p. 10). He refers specifically to Rudolf Hub, in Engelberg, *Probleme*, p. 276. Dieter Fricke has made the same charge, in *ZfG* 25 (1977): 139–40. The most determined attempt to give the masses access to power was made by Mao Tse-tung's Cultural Revolution, with results that were hardly encouraging.

[25]On Marx's ambiguous attitude see George Lichtheim, *Marxism: An Historical and Critical Study* (New York, 1966), pp. 236–38, 241ff. and Fleisher, *Marxismus und Geschichte*, pp. 37ff.; Fleisher points out in particular that Marx lent support to the theory of an automatic determinism by quoting approvingly a reviewer of *Capital* who attributed to him the view that history was a natural process dominated by autonomous laws (MEW, vol. 23, pp. 26–27); see also "Marxismus," *SDG*, vol. 4, p. 334.

torship of the proletariat would result in the despotism of an elitist minority that would abuse the concept of "scientific socialism" to claim that it understood the interests of the people better than the people themselves did.[26]

The emphasis on the central role of class struggle points up another basic tenet of the Marxist doctrine—the dialectical nature of all development, including the historical process. Dialectics, the theory of the interplay of interdependence and conflict in all phenomena and processes, holds that all forces generate countervailing forces and that all developments derive their thrust from the struggle of these opposites. Stability, on the other hand, is a relative and temporary condition. The opposites can be "antagonistic"—that is, irreconcilable—as are the conflicting class interests in a class society, and the conflicts between them must be resolved by revolutions opening the door to a new social order. They will become "nonantagonistic" and hence reconcilable in a socialist society as its members divest themselves of their class interests and will be fully so in the community order in which there will be no classes at all. Because of the dialectical nature of historical developments, these developments do not evolve straightforwardly but are diverted into by-paths or forced into temporary retreat and thus can progress only in tortuous ways.[27]

The Laws of History

If historical developments are nonetheless found to be progressive even in class societies, advancing through ever higher, more productive socioeconomic formations to the socialist and ultimately the communist order, the explanation is that the course of history is subject to laws that assure such ascendance. The concept of historical laws has had a varied history in the development of Marxism. Marx and Engels alluded to such laws in their early writings, viewing history as a natural process and looking upon it as a chain of cause-and-effect relationships in which "objective" conditions force men, or rather classes, to take certain actions. As Marx and Engels wrote,

> It does not matter what this or that proletarian or even the entire proletariat *conceives* presently as its goal. What matters is what the proletariat *is* in reality and what in accordance with this *being* it will be forced to do historically. Its goal and its historical action are

[26]Rudolf Bahro, *Die Alternative* (Cologne, 1977), pp. 46ff.
[27]*Grundlagen*, pp. 84ff. See also Peter Christian Ludz, *Ideologiebegriff und marxistische Theorie* (Opladen, 1976), pp. 253ff.

determined clearly and irrevocably by its own life-situation as by the entire organization of present-day bourgeois society.

Its growing misery will compel the working class to overthrow the capitalist system, which rests on the private property of the means of production, the source of the workers' exploitation, and will replace it with the socialist order, in which means of production will increasingly be owned socially and classes will gradually be erased. Eventually, when the last vestiges of a restrictive class society have been erased and productivity has attained its full potential, that order will grow into the communist one, in which individual needs can be met equitably and man will attain genuine freedom to develop his faculties fully.

In his early years, Engels, like Marx, envisaged this development as a historical process that men, driven by their misery, would keep advancing (historical materialism); in later years, however, correlating society and nature, Engels saw societal development as an overarching process of which history was but a part and which was as such subject to a universal dialectic and propelled by laws that operated autonomously (dialectical materialism). Whereas in Engels' earlier view, men suffering from capitalist exploitation were driven by their misery to the overthrow of the capitalist system, he later came to view that system as doomed by an irreversible process. With the laws assuming, as it were, the role of revolutionary action and with revolution a distant prospect in the industrialized countries of Western Europe, Marxists came to rely on evolution—and reforms—to attain their revolutionary goals. The "Revisionist" school of Eduard Bernstein went even further; rejecting the rigid determinism of Engels and his influential disciple Karl Kautsky, it denied that socialism was the indispensable precondition of human freedom and concluded that men could determine their future, introducing socialism by continuing on the reformist path that had already produced a measure of social security, labor unions, and other social advances.

This approach was challenged by Lenin and others (Rosa Luxemburg, among them) on the grounds that it could but uphold the capitalist order and that historical laws as relationships between existing conditions and necessary consequences could become operative only through sustained revolutionary activity. Yet Lenin and Stalin and their Soviet and East German disciples, while reverting to the original Marxist activism, also retained Engels' dialectical materialism, whose emphasis on the inevitability of the Marxist prognosis gave it a special thrust. They could do so partly because they could claim with some justification that Engels himself had never meant to renounce all revolutionary action. Empirical confirmation of the inevitability of historical trends was also found in the fact that the need to replace one mode of production with another had been recurring over the centuries, that it arose independently of men's will and consciousness, and that there had almost always appeared social forces whose interests drove them to meet this need by overthrowing the old order and making way for a new one more responsive to the developmental stage of the productive forces.[28]

Thus, in the words of the East German philosopher Gottfried Stiehler, historical laws are "both causes and products of human activity." With their operation depending on human will and ability, historical laws merely present opportunities for actions that, inevitably, are in accordance with such laws. The effectiveness of historical laws may be reduced through human error, lack of decisiveness, or accidental events; it may also be neutralized by countervening forces, such as a bourgeoisie propelled by its quest for profits and property and thus fighting hard to block social progress. Although the laws that promote progress are expected ultimately to prevail over all antiprogressive counterforces, they must do so only after having overcome a myriad of obstacles. "We know," Stiehler quotes a Soviet author, "that ultimately our cause will win by historical necessity, but the success of our struggle is not predetermined in every single encounter even if all objective conditions are present." However, knowledge of the laws can also block counterforces and accelerate progress: although capitalist imperialism is presumed to be by necessity a breeder of wars, the socialist states, impelled by the necessity to preserve peace, are expected to prevent the imperialist West from plunging the world into war. Similarly, the laws governing the capitalist system can be annulled altogether by the abolition of private ownership of the means of production. On the historical plane, knowledge of historical inevitability enables the historian to pinpoint erroneous decisions and missed opportunities and to develop alternative solutions within the context of given conditions—a major concern of Marxist historians for both scholarly and political reasons (see below, pages 57–59).[29]

Marxist scholars are aware that societies have not always progressed and that some have perished. In these instances, it is explained, the historical laws did not prevail because no class arose

---

[28]See Marx and Engels, in MEW, vol. 2, p. 38. (Note the use of the term *historical* in the sense of *developmental*.) See also *Grundlagen*, pp. 157–58; Stiehler, *Geschichte*, pp. 18–19, 31–32. Based on a concrete rationale, Marxist historical laws are contrasted with the unfathomable "divine" and "eternal" laws that post-Hegelian contemporaries of Marx and Engels postulated (see Hans Schleier, *Sybel und Treitschke* [Berlin (East), 1965], pp. 263–65).

[29]*Grundlagen*, pp. 158–59; Stiehler, *Geschichte*, pp. 19–21, 23, 26, 36–37.

to adjust the outdated production relations to the burgeoning productive forces. However, such cases are considered atypical. "What
is typical and hence lawful is the upward development of the productive forces, the progressive development of human society."
Still, given the problems of such an ascending development, Marxist historians allow, as did Marx and Engels, that historical laws
should more accurately be described as mere "tendencies."[30]

Whatever the specific effectiveness of the laws, the reliance
on them serves as a basis for the claim that only the Marxist
approach raises history to the level of a science. As a science,
Marxist historiography is concerned with that which keeps recurring and hence is generally valid. This approach is contrasted with
"bourgeois" historicism, which looks on historical developments
as unique and unrepeatable rather than as part of a scientifically
predictable process. The bourgeois historian thus is taken to task
for being guided by subjective intuition or inspiration in his approach to history and not by objective social reality, which alone
can provide the basis for any scholarly interpretation of history.
Accordingly, DDR historians reject the concept of a non-Marxist
Geschichtswissenschaft and classify non-Marxist historical scholarship as mere Geschichtsschreibung.

The idea that Marxist historical science resembles the natural
sciences in emphasizing the recurrence of patterns accords with the
Marxist axiom that the historical process is rooted in man's confrontation with nature and his harnessing and utilization of nature's
forces and resources by way of successive modes of production. Accordingly, like the natural sciences, Marxist historical science
probes the origins, evolution, and replacement of structures—in this
case, socioeconomic formations. The very term *socioeconomic formation* is borrowed from the vocabulary of geology, and the definition of the task of the historian as the "reproduction of concrete
historical reality" underscores the view of man's history as a "process of natural history," as the "uninterrupted evolution and movement of the highest and most complex existential manifestation of
matter."[31]

The belief in the scientific nature of history is buttressed by
the insistence that in the concept of *production* (in the widest
meaning of the term, including above all *human* productive forces)
Marxism has an "objective" standard by which historical processes

---

[30]Karl Lärmer, "Triebkräfte der Produktivkräfte," *JWG* 1 (1960): 177; Streisand,
"Geschichtsbild-Geschichtsbewusstsein-Geschichtswissenschaft," *ZfG* 15 (1967):
825–26; Stiehler, *Geschichte*, pp. 23ff.

[31]Wolfgang Küttler and Gerhard Lozek, in Engelberg, *Probleme*, pp. 34, 42–43;
Brendler, in ibid., p. 109; *Unb. Verg.*, p. 145; Brendler and Küttler, "Die histo-
rische Analyse ökonomischer Gesellschaftsformationen," *ZfG* 21 (1973): 6–7;
Klaus and Schulze, *Sinn, Gesetz und Fortschritt*, pp. 7ff.

can be measured with scientific precision. Progress in particular is measured in terms of the development of the productive forces, and the ascending line in the succession of socioeconomic formation is traced in the greater productivity each system attained compared to its predecessor. Marxist historians thus pride themselves in not reading into history a "subjective" meaning through recourse to external value criteria, but instead analyzing it "objectively" by deriving meaning from the historical process itself. Correspondingly, facts acquire historical meaning only within the framework of a particular socioeconomic formation, and they can be evaluated in relation to the structure and movement of such a formation.[32]

Yet this approach is not without its own problems. For example, much is made of the idea that Marxist periodization is scientific because it is based on the socioeconomic formations through which societies pass. This is contrasted with non-Marxist historiography, which has arbitrarily chosen certain dates to divide antiquity from the Middle Ages and the latter from the modern period.[33] Instead of such abrupt incisions, Marxist periodization recognizes periods of transition; however, as a West German historian, Jürgen Kocka, has pointed out, these periods are exceedingly lengthy. The transition from feudalism to capitalism, for example, extended for more than 500 years in Germany, which makes it chronologically useless. On the other hand, the capitalist age itself, supposedly one of the main historical periods, lasted less than a century in Germany by Marxist reckoning, because the Bolshevik revolution of 1917 ushered in the transition from capitalism to socialism. Apart from these disparities the determination of subdivisions of these periods also has given rise to spirited debates, once again raising questions about the precision of the Marxist approach.[34]

Even the import of some of the socioeconomic formations has been questioned. Thus, it is now recognized by DDR scholars that the slaveholding system did not play the worldwide role that Lenin and Stalin (rather than Marx and Engels) had attributed to it. Neither was the slaveowner-slave relationship as central to the socioeconomic order of the time as had been assumed: during the greater part of the period, the most numerous and crucial class

[32]*Grundlagen*, p. 147; Klaus and Schulze, *Sinn, Gesetz und Fortschritt*, pp. 135ff., 241; Bollhagen, in Eckermann and Mohr, *Einführung*, p. 39; Gerhard Bartsch et al., *Geschichte als gesetzmässiger Prozess* (Berlin [East], 1976), pp. 43ff.; Engelberg, in Engelberg, *Probleme*, p. 12.
[33]Bollhagen and Brendler, in Eckermann and Mohr, *Einführung*, pp. 81ff.; Engelberg, in Engelberg, *Probleme*, p. 121.
[34]Jürgen Kocka, "Zur jüngeren marxistischen Sozialgeschichte," *Kölner Vierteljahrsschrift für Soziologie und Sozialpsyschologie* 16 (1972): suppl., 514 n. 72.

struggles in Rome were those between patricians and free plebeians (as Marx already knew).

DDR historians do not see in such defects a fundamental challenge to the concept of history as a succession of socioeconomic formations. As they emphasize, this approach does not establish a fixed worldwide pattern but simply states that societies organize themselves in such systems without excluding variations in the sequence and form of these systems. In the late 1960s and early 1970s the pages of the *Zeitschrift für Geschichtswissenschaft, the Ethnographisch-Archäologische Zeitschrift,* and the *Jahrbuch für Wirtschaftsgeschichte* were filled with a spirited debate about the actual number and sequence of such formations—in the end, most participants held that the five formations mentioned earlier constituted the most meaningful reconstruction of history in the sense that they represented the main line (Hauptlinie) of developments in the key areas of world history. Yet, as was also acknowledged, that sequence was not rigid either, and some societies are found to have even skipped an entire formation. (The Germans, for example, never had a slave-holding system.[35])

Similarly, when Marx's definition of socialism as a transitory preliminary phase of communism proved unrealistic, it was modified for a time. The revised definition described socialism as a "relatively independent" system, in accordance with the expectation that the sweeping social and economic transformation on which the communist order is predicated was still far off, as was the abolition of all vestiges of the class society and the organization and growth of production that would inspire everyone to work according to his ability and assure the satisfaction of his essential needs. This reassessment has since been abandoned again as a "distortion" of Marxist-Leninist theory. The fear apparently was that the increased focus on socialism might lead the nation to lose sight of the ultimate goal. Of course, Communism does not constitute a

---

[35]See Töpfer, "Zu einigen Grundfragen des Feudalismus," *ZfG* 13 (1965): 787, 807; Rigobert Günther, "Die Klasse der Sklaven und ihr Klassenkampf," ibid. 8 (1960): 109–10, 112; Engelberg, "Probleme der gesetzmässigen Abfolge der Gesellschaftsformationen," ibid., 22 (1974): 171; Küttler, "Methodologische Kriterien historischer Formationsbestimmung," ibid., 1042. On this problem see also the well-documented critique of a West German historian, Friedrich Vittinghoff, "Die Theorie des historischen Materialismus über den antiken Sklavenhalterstaat," *Saeculum* 11 (1960): 89ff.; "Sklaverei," *SDG,*vol. 5, pp. 878–80. Questions have also been raised concerning the validity of the primitive-communal society as a socioeconomic system (Vittinghoff, *Theorie des historischen Materialismus,* pp. 97ff). On the other hand, the introduction of an additional formation based on Marx's "Asian" mode of production has also been discussed ("Periodisierung," *SDG,* vol. 4, pp. 1148–50). Evidently because of these uncertainties the politburo of the SED made the study of early history (Ur- und Frühgeschichte) a primary assignment for historians in the Central Research Plan for 1976–80 (*Einheit* 30 [1975]: 1048). The discussion is summed up in Bartsch et al., *Geschichte,* pp. 51ff., 59ff.

fixed social condition either, but rather a continuing developmental process—the perspective of a society in which—in ways that cannot be specified at this point—the full emancipation of mankind will be attained.[36]

The problems that have arisen here are the results of a methodology that does not start out by ascertaining facts and then interpreting them but instead takes as its point of departure a historical model, against which the facts are evaluated. Facts, then, are used in order to confirm the historical laws; if they fail to do so, they must help to explain why the laws were not operative in that particular case. The results of the research thus are anticipated, which accords with the basic assumption that history—as a lawful process—is basically rational, because the laws of history express logical necessities. Indeed, Marxist authors keep stressing that history *is* logical. It is not surprising that this a priori approach tempts the Marxist historian to make do at times with evidence the non-Marxist would not find conclusive. In the same vein, when no evidence is found to indicate that events followed the predefined historical model, the conclusion has repeatedly been, not that there was no such evidence, but that future research would have to uncover it. On the other hand, because the available sources do not necessarily tell the whole story, this approach can also raise questions that might otherwise not be asked.[37]

Because, according to historical laws, mankind's progress can be accomplished only through the action of social classes, classes victimized by existing conditions are expected to bring about needed changes. Once objective conditions have put such changes on the "historical agenda," failure to act or prepare for action becomes a dereliction of duty. Classes that fail to fulfill their "historical mission" are accordingly taken to task, but the severity of the reprimand varies, in keeping with the principle of partisanship. Inaction on the part of the peasantry or the working class when action was called for "objectively" is generally blamed on the leadership or attributed, as mentioned before, to despair, apathy, or illusionism (which again casts doubts on the "historical creativity" of the masses). Censures of the bourgeoisie, on the other hand, are

---

[36]"Sozialismus," *Swb*, vol. 2, p. 511; Ernst Hoffmann, "Zur geschichtlichen Entwicklungsfolge fortschreitender Gesellschaftsformationen," *ZfG* 16 (1968): 1274ff.; Diehl, "Aufgaben der Geschichtswissenschaft," p. 268; Brendler and Küttler, "Historische Analyse," pp. 17ff.; Bartsch et al., *Geschichte*, pp. 103–5.
[37]Hans-Peter Jaeck, in Engelberg, *Probleme*, pp. 91 n. 45, 94; Gerhard Schilfert, "Die Geschichtswissenschaft im System der Gesellschaftswissenschaften," *ZfG*, 13 (1965): 595; Bollhagen and Brendler, in Eckermann and Mohr, *Einführung*, pp. 70, 242; Erika Herzfeld, review, *ZfG*, 8 (1960): 194; also Helmut Bleiber, "Bourgeoisie und bürgerliche Umwälzung," ibid., 25 (1977): 311; Schilfert, *Deutschland von 1648 bis 1789* (Berlin [East], 1975), p. 17.

not mitigated by a similar empathy; they bristle with charges of opportunism, treachery, and cowardice. For the cause of lawful progress, the bourgeoisie is even expected to help dig its own grave, in addition to producing its own gravediggers, as the *Manifesto* predicted.[38]

The stipulation of historical laws and the concomitant stipulation of historical tasks does not, however, eliminate all freedom of decision on the part of classes and individuals. In the Marxist view, men have no freedom and are the instruments of these laws only as long as they are unaware of the laws and obey unconsciously the dictates of historical necessity. Once men understand the inevitable course of their destiny and, under the leadership of a Marxist-Leninist party, are guided by it, they do have meaningful choices—they may pursue their destiny in one way or another, head-on or in roundabout ways, with greater or lesser intensity. The decisions that are now made are free ones, because they are guided by knowledge of the underlying laws and necessities and will increasingly produce the desired results. Freedom, in Engels' words, is the comprehension of necessity.

This concept governs the policies of all socialist states. It serves to justify the nature of their regimes, and this ideological justification is reinforced by political arguments pointing to internal and external threats to the socialist order. In the case of East Germany there is the additional concern about the West German state, which insists on the continued existence of one German nation, linking both German states and thereby challenging the independence of the German Democratic Republic. Thus, even though in the socialist system now attained in the DDR the nationalized economy can be rationally organized and no longer is at the mercy of the planless market economy, and even though classes have been largely eliminated, the realm of freedom that

---

[38]See Bollhagen, in Eckermann and Mohr, *Einführung*, pp. 262–63; *GdA*, vol. 1, pp. 44–45; Max Steinmetz, *Deutschland von 1476 bis 1648* (Berlin [East], 1965), pp. 129, 156; Schilfert, *Deutschland*, pp. 28, 30. See also the revealing statement that by 1848 the Prussian Junker class had been "condemned to disappearance by history" (Manfred Kliem, in *ZfG* 17 [1969]: 311). On the censure of the bourgeoisie, see Andreas Dorpalen, "Die Revolution von 1848 in der Geschichtsschreibung der DDR," *HZ* 210 (1970): 335–37. Also see the responses of Walter Schmidt, in *ZfG* 21 (1973): 302; Schleier, *Die bürgerliche Geschichtsschreibung in der Weimarer Republik* (Berlin [East], 1975), p. 192 n. 22; and, less consistently, Bleiber, "Bourgeoisie," 313 with 318–19; also chapter 5. On the understanding attitude toward the working class, see below and chapters 6–9. The concept of the assignment of historical tasks is not wholly unknown to non-Marxist historians, but in their case it is they rather than "history" that assign these tasks; see Franz Schnabel, *Deutsche Geschichte in neunzehnten Jahrhundert* (Freiburg, 1949), II, 94; Werner Frauendienst, quoted in *Das kaiserliche Deutschland*, ed. Michael Stürmer (Düsseldorf, 1970), p. 73 n. 18.

Marx envisaged as the final goal has not been brought noticeably closer.

Also contrary to Marx's vision, the ultimate communist order is viewed primarily as a system that, under the leadership of the Marxist-Leninist party, will create a society of abundance and do away with any remaining social inequities. In the words of the program of the DDR's ruling Socialist Unity party, "Steady social progress, material and cultural goods for each member of society corresponding to his growing needs, individual claims and inclinations—that is the goal of communist production." No longer is any mention made of individual freedom or of the full unfolding of man's potentialities; in the context of communism, production work is expected to become truly creative, a source of joy, with menial jobs taken up by machines and mental and physical labor put on an equal footing. Freedom, then, as Stiehler has put it, is a "social category and its essence . . . the socially established control of man over nature and the social processes." It means freedom from the economic and political servitudes of the capitalist system, the right to work, to social security, to a comprehensive education, and to active participation in the exercise of state and political power in accordance with the historical laws and necessities.[39] As a social category this concept of freedom does not include individual civil liberties, and Marxist constitutions hence grant the right to free speech, press, and assembly only on behalf of the socialist cause. Correspondingly, the Marxist concept of democracy focuses not on individual rights and choices but on the social, economic, and cultural needs of the masses.

By maintaining that man can and must attain the socialist/communist goals by his own efforts, Marxism proclaims him the master of his destiny. Correspondingly, it rejects resignation and fatalism and insists that man must assume responsibility for his destiny and cannot blame setbacks on an angry god, an inscrutable fate, racial insidiousness, or other mystical or imaginary forces. Although earthquakes, famines, a poor soil, or harsh climate may have their impact on social progress, in the last analysis humans are held accountable for their situation. This approach has yielded

---

[39]Stiehler, *Geschichte*, pp. 19–23, 40, 46, 60; Wolfgang Eichhorn II, in *Objektive Gesetzmässigkeit und bewusstes Handeln in der sozialistischen Gesellschaft*, ed. Wissenschaftlicher Rat für marxistisch-leninistische Philosophie am Institut für Gesellschaftswissenschaften beim ZK der SED et al. (Berlin [East], 1975), pp. 124–25; also Marek Fritzhand, in ibid., pp. 142–43; G. Fiodorov, "Der dialektische Materialismus über Freiheit und Notwendigkeit," *Sowjetwissenschaft*, Gesellschaftswissenschaftliche Abteilung (1955):448ff.; Marx, in MEW, vol. 25, p. 828, vol. 13, p. 9; "Kommunismus," *Swb*, vol. 1, pp. 955ff.; "Freiheit," *Wörterbuch*, pp. 130–32.

valuable new insights historically and has led to significant revisions of traditional views.[40]

It remains to determine the place of the individual, of "great men," in the Marxist scenario. Although Marxists deny that history is "made" by great men, they do acknowledge the historical impact of outstanding individuals—not in their own right, but as the spokesmen of their respective classes. Indeed, each class must have leaders to organize it, give expression to its needs, and guide its actions; such leadership constitutes an "objective necessity" and emerges inevitably, following historical laws. Yet the leaders, far from creating history, are merely credited with giving form to the thrusts of social groupings and classes, and their activities must be assessed within this context. When the author of a biography of Ernst Thälmann, the head of the German Communist party in Weimar days, discussed Thälmann's stand in the Nazi era as Thälmann's own rather than as that of the German Communist party and working class, he was sharply rebuked for his individualistic approach. Thus, Marxist historical accounts do have heroes, but the heroes are mouthpieces rather than profiled individuals. Even as subjects of biographies, outstanding personalities rarely are brought to life, but are depicted primarily in terms of their social functions. The ultimate hero is always the exploited but struggling masses, and above all the industrial working class.

Marxist scholars maintain that by attributing to significant personalities a derivatory role, as it were, they reinforce also the scientific character of their work. It would be unscientific to explain events in terms of the nondeterminist, changing intentions of individual "great men," because such individual causations lack the generality and hence the evidential value of social classes. The preoccupation with individuals for themselves, outside their class contexts, would also divert attention from those social forces that are the actual driving forces behind them. Moreover, in a concept of history in which actions are measured in terms of their contribution to or detraction from social progress, individual intentions are irrelevant, and only the results count. Empathy with individuals can only cloud the issue. For the same reason, Marxist historians reject psychological interpretations and dismiss them as apologetic attempts to evade rational explanations. For them, there can be no question but that history is a social science, not one of the humanities.[41]

---

[40]Fiodorov, "Dialektische Materialismus," p. 450; Bollhagen, in Eckermann and Mohr, *Einführung*, p. 39; Kurt Holzapfel and Walter Markov, review, *ZfG* 11 (1963): 1373–74; Dietrich Eichholtz and Gerhard Hass, "Zu den Ursachen des zweiten Weltkrieges . . . ," ibid., 15 (1967): 1155–56.

[41]See *Grundlagen*, pp. 210ff.; Bollhagen, in Eckermann and Mohr, *Einführung*, pp. 54–55; illustrations in Hans Schulze, in *ZfG* 11 (1963): 834; Helmut Kolbe, in ibid., 16 (1968): 1335; Kuczynski, *Geschichte*, vol. 1, pp. 51, 53, S. B. Kahn, in *ZfG*

This certitude also accounts for Marxist historians' uncompromising rejection of all non-Marxist methods. The historian who claims to have found the key to history through the application of objective historical laws and standards of measurements cannot admit the validity of any other approach. "The Marxist doctrine is all-powerful," Lenin once summed up this position, "because it is true."[42]

The inflexibility displayed toward non-Marxist scholarship does not extend to the Marxist's own work. His own criteria give him considerable flexibility to adjust his conclusions to the reality of the facts. Laws are reduced to tendencies, and the dialectic of history allows for the operation of antiprogressive forces that explain the (temporary) noneffectiveness of the laws of progress. The formations themselves are variable constructs whose components—economics, government, culture, and others—are relatively independent of one another and interact with one another in different ways, with correspondingly different results. Similarly, transitions from one system to another are subject to wide-ranging variations, depending on the relative dynamism of the productive forces, individual events, accidents, and other factors. The theses and tenets of dialectical and historical materialism thus provide merely a framework within which concrete historical events and developments still must be researched, analyzed, and interpreted and are subject to discussion, refinement, and revision. Conversely, it is also part of the historian's assignment, as mentioned earlier, to find the required data to document a development that according to historical law *must* have occurred.[43]

There are limits, however, to this autonomy. These limits are set by the axioms of dialectical and historical materialism concerning the central role of production, the class struggle, and the decisive history-making role of the popular masses. Other limitations

---

3 (1955): 259–60; Günter Vogler, in ibid., 10 (1962): 1143. See also the critique of the Thälmann biography by Walter Bartel, *Ein Held der Nation* (Berlin [East], 1961), in *ZfG* 10 (1962): 281–82. For a somewhat different view of the role of the "historical personality," see Manfred Bensing, *Thomas Müntzer und der Thüringer Aufstand* (Berlin [East], 1966), p. 251. A suggestion by Kuczynski some years ago that in exceptional moments an individual may outgrow his environment and, on his own, touch off progressive developments was sharply rejected in an avalanche of articles *ZfG* 5 (1957): 14ff. and *passim*.

[42]Lenin, "The Three Sources and Three Component Parts of Marxism," in *The Lenin Anthology*, ed. Robert C. Tucker (New York, 1975), p. 640.

[43]See Bollhagen, in Eckermann and Mohr, *Einführung*, p. 39 and Kocka, "Jüngeren marxistischen Sozialgeschichte," p. 493. For discussions and refinements or revisions of earlier views, see the debates on the origins of the first German state (chapter 2), the more recent assessments of the Reformation (chapter 3), the beginnings of the Industrial Revolution (chapter 5), and the different analyses of Nazism (chapters 7 and 8).

result from explicit stands taken by Marx, Engels, and Lenin on specific questions, although historians may make criticisms and modifications, called "creative utilization" (schöpferische Auswertung), of their teachings. In this vein, Ernst Engelberg has even warned against too rigid an application of their theoretical statements, which he says should be treated merely as guideposts in the analysis of historical data within their respective structural and developmental context; this advice, however, has not been followed in practice.[44]

Another limitation is imposed on the Marxist historian by the demand that his work be politically relevant. As has been said, his task is to explain the inevitable process of the ascent of societies to the Communist order and to contribute, by his research and findings, to the solution of problems impeding such an ascent. Accordingly, his work is geared to these objectives: although DDR scholars have explored at great length the socioeconomic functions of the medieval manor and the Nazi concentration camp, they would not describe social life in a manor or conditions in a concentration camp for their own sakes. In the same vein, unduly minute topics are frowned upon. Because individuals as such are of no historical interest either, no East German historian would concern himself with the fact that Emperor William II had a withered left arm or that Hitler may have been partly Jewish.[45] What is called for instead are answers to questions concerning the successes and failures of the masses to achieve social progress; the ability of slaveholders, feudal nobility, and great bourgeoisie to frustrate such efforts; or the effectiveness of Marxist-Leninist revolutionary theory in clearing the road to power for the industrial working class.[46]

Finally, important restrictions result from the ideological function of the Marxist historian and from the special social and political role he assumes in his capacity as a historian in a Marxist-Leninist state, especially in one as exacting as the German Democratic Republic.

---

[44]See Kocka, "Jüngeren marxistischen Sozialgeschichte," pp. 493–94; Engelberg, in Engelberg, *Probleme,* p. 147; Engelberg, "Über die Revolution von oben," *ZfG* 22 (1974): 1191. Examples of criticisms and "creative utilizations" of Marx, Engels, and Lenin are found in *ZfG* 6 (1958): 191; ibid. 11 (1963): 147, 152; ibid. 13 (1965) 798 n. 52; ibid. 15 (1967): 56–57, 777, 1020, 1022, 1191; Ernst Werner, *Pauperes Christi* (Leipzig, 1956), p. 11; Klaus and Schulze, *Sinn, Gesetz und Fortschritt,* p. 46. The list could easily be extended.

[45]The fact that the historian Heinrich von Treitschke was totally deaf from early manhood, which by all accounts had a strong impact on his personality and intellectual development, is mentioned in passing in a half-sentence in an East German monograph on him and his fellow historian Heinrich von Sybel (see Schleier, *Sybel und Treitschke,* p. 36).

[46]Editorial statement in *BzG* 11 (1969): 378, 381.

The DDR Historian and the Socialist Unity Party

In a system that views class struggles as the motor power of history, the historian cannot and must not stand apart from these struggles. In fact, he is given a role of considerable importance in them. His very involvement in historical work postulates his participation in one way or another in the settlement of those social and political problems, all of them based in history, that call for solutions. As the philosopher Peter Bollhagen notes:

> Regardless of whether the historian assumes a progressive or reactionary position on these questions, historical conditions—both objective and subjective ones—especially major questions of social development, are somehow reflected in his work and pervade and influence it. Conversely the work of the historian serves society, its various classes and strata, as a historical underpinning for their interests, enables them to take a position, and guides them through the historical process.

Historiography is assessed, therefore, not as the product of detached contemplation, but as a social process shaped by the class interests and affiliations of the individual scholar. Thus, given the close relationship between historical work and fundamental issues of Weltanschauung, Bollhagen concludes, "there can be no ideological neutrality. [Research and teaching] are always part of the basic ideological struggle between materialism and idealism, between scientific and unscientific thought, and must take sides in this struggle." Any pretense at neutrality would deny the existence of objective truth, lose itself in relativism, and accord equal validity to religious, fascist, and scientific-materialist interpretations.[47]

Because Marxism views theory and practice as one—neither having meaning without the other—the social effects of historical work are a matter of special concern. Any genuine historical problem, given the continuity of the historical process, thus has some bearing, no matter how indirect, on present social and political practice. As Ernst Engelberg notes, historiography does not merely reflect substantive interests, but functions as an active history-making political force on behalf of different classes and groups. He points to German "bourgeois" historiography as a characteristic example of such a "class approach": since Ranke's days, Engelberg states, historiographical research done by the bourgeois had been limited mainly to the top governmental and political strata—which was true at the time the statement was made (1958). "On the other hand, it [bourgeois historiography] faces the struggle of the people in uncomprehending hostility; not infrequently it falsi-

---

[47]Bollhagen, in Eckermann and Mohr, *Einführung*, pp. 31–33; also Brendler, in Engelberg, *Probleme*, pp. 109–10.

fies historical facts in the interest of the exploiting system." Other
East German historians have seen this preoccupation with rulers,
ministers, wars, and diplomacy as a deliberate attempt to keep the
masses from realizing that they ever exerted any influence on the
course of events and could do so again. If Marxist historians for
their part take up the cause of the working class, they maintain
that rather than injecting a new element into history they are
merely pursuing the established practice of making history serve
specific class interests. Far from staying aloof of the class struggle,
historiography is viewed as having been always a major ideological
weapon.[48]

In this perspective, the work of the historian is of immediate
political significance, and the leadership of the German Communist party (KPD) and of its successor, the Socialist Unity party
(SED), concerned itself with historical activities in East Germany
from the moment the first Communists returned from their Moscow exile in 1945. Indeed, the exiles returned to their homeland
equipped with carefully made plans for the reinterpretation of German history from the Marxist perspective and for the propagation
of this revised history in the schools, the press, and elaborate programs of publication. This approach was considered all the more
important because the political program of the KPD was derived in
large measure from the lessons of history as perceived through the
prism of dialectical and historical materialism. These lessons could
be presented convincingly, however, only after the traditional concepts of history had been eradicated. "History as a science for society's guidance thus was combined with its function as a source of
society's self-understanding."[49]

The first task was to enlighten the nation about the real—that
is, reactionary—nature of Nazism. Accordingly, historians in the
Soviet occupation zone were asked in 1945 to uncover the roots of
"Hitler fascism" as the creature of monopolists, Junkers, and militarists and to destroy the myth of Nazism as the creation of a
"mob of petty bourgeois fanatics on a rampage." Early studies dealt
in particular with the ruinous role of German heavy industry, the
impact of Prussian militarism, and the fraudulent claims of an
alleged German socialism. (On the latter topic one of the party
leaders, Walter Ulbricht, published a manual, *Die Legende vom*

[48]Engelberg, "Politik und Geschichtsschreibung," *ZfG* 6 (1958): 469; Gerhard Lozek
and Horst Syrbe, "Die moderne Epoche, die Perspektive der deutschen Nation
und die Sorgen imperialistischer westdeutscher Historiker," *ZfG* 11 (1963): 1237;
Heinrich Scheel et al., ibid. 18 (1970): suppl., 381; Helmut Bock, review, *BzG* 3
(1961): 187–88.
[49]For details, see Werner Berthold, *Marxistisches Geschichtsbild: Volksfront und
antifaschistisch-demokratische Revolution* (Berlin [East], 1970); quotation on pp.
156–57.

deutschen Sozialismus.) In the same vein, events such as the revolutions of 1848 and 1918 were described as triumphs of the reactionary forces—triumphs that, it was pointedly added, had not been inevitable. The purpose was to emphasize the mistakes that had been made in order to make the nation more receptive to Marxist guidance.[50]

Yet once this task has been completed, historians were urged to turn their attention to the positive aspects of German history. At its party congress in 1950 and in a series of subsequent resolutions, the SED called on the historical community to abandon the "misery concept" of German history, stressing instead its progressive and liberating trends. Greater attention was to be paid to the numerous revolutionary movements in Germany's history whose significance had so long been neglected or misrepresented for "class" purposes— the German Peasants War, the struggles for German unity against feudal small-state parochialism (Kleinstaaterei), and the history of the German and international labor movement. By tracing a democratic-revolutionary strand through German history, historians would also show that the German Democratic Republic embodied a historical heritage reaching far back into Germany's past, thus attesting the legitimacy of the new state. Similarly, the association of these revolutionary traditions with the struggle for German unity would strengthen the case of the DDR government for the reunification of Germany on its own terms rather than on West German terms. The social historian Alfred Meusel summed up this enlistment of the historians in this campaign as follows:

> The thema probandum of German historical research and teaching must be the struggle for German unification. We have to show that at all turning points of German history—at the time of the Reformation and the great Peasants' War, at the time of the Wars of Liberation, in the Revolution of '48, in the November Revolution of 1918 and during the following years, and again, now after [our] liberation from fascism by the Soviet Army—there existed serious democratic forces which fought for a united Germany in the form of a peace-loving, democratic, and sovereign national state.[51]

At the same time, the SED provided substantial technical facilities to implement its directives—among them the establishment of historical research institutes at the German Academy of

---

[50]See ibid., pp. 159ff., 191–93. For representative negative assessments of the revolutions of 1848 and 1918, see Jürgen Kuczynski, *Die Bewegung der deutschen Wirtschaft von 1800 bis 1946* (Berlin [East], n.d.) pp. 67–69, 120–21.

[51]See Berthold, *Marxistisches Geschichtsbild*, pp. 261ff.; Alfred Meusel, "Die wissenschaftliche Auffassung der deutschen Geschichte," *Wissenschaftliche Annalen*, 1 (1952): 405 (note the new emphasis on the democratic aspects of the revolutions of 1848 and 1918); Helmut Heinz, "Das Lehrbuch der Politischen Grundschulen der SED von 1951," *ZfG* 24 (1976): 1370, 1381.

Sciences in East Berlin and at the universities of East Berlin and Leipzig. It also appointed a group of historians (Autoren-Kollektiv) to prepare a Marxist-Leninist textbook on German history and directed another collective, headed by Ulbricht, to write a history of the German working-class movement. Several SED-controlled research institutes—the Institute for Marxism-Leninism and the Institute for Social Sciences, both attached to the party's central committee—and a training school for party leaders, Parteihochschule Karl Marx, also had elaborate historical sections. In addition, the party concerned itself with the training of Marxist historians, of which there were only a few at first. "Cadres" of aspiring historians were hastily taught the fundamentals of Marxism-Leninism and of history as viewed from the Marxist perspective and were then given teaching assignments to replace non-Marxist professors, who had been dismissed or had left on their own. (Some non-Marxists, however, who were giving their due to the social and economic components of history, retained their chairs; the last of them retired in the early 1960s.) Not infrequently, teaching assistants were put in charge of major courses to assure a "progressive" presentation. Because of the lack of adequate German-language materials, the party sponsored translations of Soviet textbooks and monographs. Similarly, Soviet ideological and methodological approaches were adopted as products of a society that had acquired a great deal of experience in the application of Marxist history to historical problems.[52]

The SED tightened its grip on historical activities during the following years. At the first state-wide meeting of DDR historians in 1952, Kurt Hager, head of the propaganda department of the SED's Central Committee, demanded that all historians "master" historical materialism and take up systematically the study of Marx and Engels. A politburo resolution in July 1955 made further provisions for the "improvement of historical research and teaching in the DDR." It called for the refutation of a then-current West German thesis that viewed Germany as part of the Christian West (christliches Abendland), as opposed to the pagan East.

In the East German view, this preoccupation with false supranational ties was meant to undermine the reunification of the two German republics on democratic, that is, Marxist-Leninist, terms. Instead, historians were to be guided by the concept of proletarian internationalism and the solidarity of all workers throughout the world. Their research was to uncover the historical roots of the

---

[52]Berthold, *Marxistisches Geschichtsbild*, pp. 262–64, 250–51; Brendler and Küttler, "Historische Analyse," p. 10; Heinz, "Die erste Zentrale Tagung der Historiker der DDR 1952," *ZfG* 26 (1978): 394; Ruge, review, ibid., 450.

friendship between the German people and the peoples of other capitalist countries, with particular emphasis on their joint anti-imperialist struggles across national boundaries. In the same vein, scholars were asked to analyze the history of the international workers movement in its struggle against imperialism and militarism—an assignment that was deemed the more pressing because the Federal Republic had just become a member of NATO.

Now that Marxist-trained historians were available in greater numbers, the politburo resolution concerned itself also with more basic problems. There had been complaints about inadequate Parteilichkeit on behalf of the working class and the indiscriminate use of documentary materials without regard to their "class origin." Similarly, it was charged that the overall approach of historians was still too subjective in many cases, confining itself to the political superstructure and neglecting the socioeconomic foundations—all failings attributed to the prevalence of bourgeois historians during those early years. The need for increased research into the operations of the objective economic laws (ökonomische Gesetzmässigkeiten) was stressed. Such research was to trace the development of the productive forces and the nature of the production relations through the various periods of German history in order to demonstrate the lawful advance of that history. The overall purpose of these directives was, Engelberg and Rolf Rudolph point out, to broaden the historical perspective from a democratic to a socialist one: with this resolution, "Marxist historical studies moved forward on a broader front in the DDR."[53]

Political and ideological needs have continued to give direction to historical teaching and research, in keeping with the concept of history as a major class-struggle weapon. Commenting on resolutions of the SED party congress of 1958, Gerhard Schilfert has aptly described the functions of history and historians in the DDR:

> Because of the historical necessity to check West German imperialism and militarism and to show that the DDR is the only legitimate German state—and one whose formation and development is historically lawful—the criteria by which historical research in the DDR must be assessed could now be established with scientific precision: to what extent have historians done justice to these basic demands and acted upon them in order to raise the scientific level of their work? In this context modern history must keep in mind that it finds itself in a sense in the front line against the imperialist world order.

[53]Heinz, "Erste zentrale Tagung," pp. 391–92, 398–99; Schilfert, ZfG 8 (1960), suppl., 532–34; Engelberg and Rolf Rudolph, ibid., 16–18; also Riesenberger, Geschichte, pp. 13–14.

In order to intensify work in these strategic areas, specially qualified "scientific cadres" were assigned to the various research institutes. The institutes also agreed on a division of labor, with each institute concentrating on a specific field. Similarly, work schedules were arranged and deadlines set. Yet as recurrent complaints revealed, historians did not always follow the party's instructions, and not a few continued to undertake research not sufficiently geared to the needs of the young socialist state and its confrontation with the imperialist West. In consequence, in 1964 a special department was set up at the Academy of Sciences in East Berlin to coordinate all historical research, supervise research plans, deal with questions of overall functions and purposes (*Perspektivfragen*), initiate the discussion of important scientific and ideological questions, and promote the collaboration of DDR historians with their counterparts in the other socialist countries, especially the U.S.S.R. A few years later these functions were transferred to a Council for History (Rat für Geschichtswissenschaft), attached to the SED's Institute for Marxism-Leninism. Since 1964, historians have also received overall assignments by way of a Zentraler Forschungsplan, worked out jointly by the SED and social scientists to give to historians' work a direction most in accord with the political, social, and other needs of the country.[54]

New emphasis has also been placed on collective research projects. Whereas earlier such projects had been sponsored in order to expedite the reinterpretation of history from the Marxist point of view, collaboration was now called for also as a working technique that fostered a socialist attitude and made it easier to overcome subjective, individualistic, and antidemocratic positions. Finally, on the grounds that the class struggle with the West was intensifying, historians were also officially enjoined to monitor and refute non-Marxist and especially West German historiography—a task to which they had actually devoted themselves from the beginning and which has always been considered an important assignment in the ideological confrontation with the bourgeois West.[55]

[54]See Schilfert, *ZfG* 8 (1960), suppl., pp. 533–34. On the fields of specialization of the various research institutes, see Eckermann et al., in Eckermann and Mohr, *Einführung*, pp. 9ff. On complaints, see Diehl, "Die Aufgaben der Parteihistoriker . . . ," *Bzg*, 2 (1960): 7; Rudolph, "Die nationale Verantwortung der Historiker der DDR," *ZfG* 10 (1962): 273–74; Ulbricht, ibid., 1265–66. On the historical division of the academy, see Hannes Hörnig, "Ein neuer Abschnitt in der Geschichtswissenschaft," ibid., 12 (1964): 385–86; Engelberg, "Die Aufgaben der Historiker der DDR von 1964 bis 1970," ibid., 400–402.
[55]See Rudolph, *Nationale Verantwortung*, pp. 273–74, 284; Engelberg, "Aufgaben," pp. 393–94. In addition to monographs, symposia—among which *Unbewältigte Vergangenheit* (Berlin [East], 1970, 1971, 1977), issued under the auspices of the Central Committee of the SED, the Academy of Sciences of the DDR, and the

Subsequent party directives called on historians to prove that the socialist transformation of the East German state was in accordance with established historical laws. In this manner they were to help strengthen the confidence of the DDR citizenry in the victory of the working class and of socialism over bourgeois imperialism. At the same time, party directives and the various Zentrale Forschungspläne paid much attention to the position of the DDR in the socialist camp, to its developing socialism as part of a worldwide revolutionary process, and to the commonality of historical features and interests the DDR shares with the other socialist countries. "In all its work," the Zentrale Forschungsplan of 1972 stipulated, "historical scholarship takes as its point of departure that the socialist world system gathered around the Soviet Union is the inevitable result of the entire course of world history and that the DDR is the legitimate heir to all the revolutionary, progressive, and humanistic traditions of German history and above all of the German workers' movement." The main concern of these plans thus was to establish a historical underpinning for the clear demarcation (Abgrenzung) of the DDR from the Federal Republic. Similarly, the breakup of the one-time German nation into the DDR's "socialist" nation and West Germany's "bourgeois" one was to be shored up historically.[56] Occasionally the party would also take a stand, directly or indirectly, on specific historical interpretations that raised politically sensitive issues. Some of these—on the lessons of the Revolution of 1848, the role of the German working class at the outbreak of World War I, the character of the revolution of 1918, and the role of the Communist party leadership during the Nazi era—will be discussed in subsequent chapters.[57]

The increased direction and supervision of all historical work had the desired results. If earlier historians did not always abide by the directives of the SED, there has been no similar lack of respon-

---

Karl-Marx-Universität at Leipzig, deserves special mention—and periodical analyses of Western and especially West German historiography in the various historical journals, a special paperback series, Zur Kritik der bürgerlichen Ideologie, is being published. See also Dorpalen, "History and Politics: An East German Assessment," CEH 12 (1979): 83ff.

[56] See Horst Bartel et al., ZfG 18 (1970): suppl., 22; Karl Reissig, "Der VII. Parteitag der SED . . . ," ibid., 15 (1967): 773; Horst Bartel and Schmidt, "Neue Probleme der Geschichtswissenschaft in der DDR," ibid., 20 (1972): 797ff., especially 814ff.; Heitzer, "Neue Probleme der Erforschung der Geschichte der DDR," ibid., 954ff; Zentraler Forschungsplan of 1972, in Einheit 27 (1972): 169ff. (quotation on p. 180); Plan of 1975, in ibid. 30 (1975): 1056ff. On the historical background of the two-nations concept see Dorpalen, "Marxism and National Unity: The Case of Germany," Review of Politics 39 (1977): 505ff.

[57] On the SED's active participation in the preparation of the Geschichte der deutschen Arbeiterbewegung, see GdA 1 38*–39*. On the party's stand on specific issues, see chapter 5, pp. 50–51, chapter 6, pp. 50ff., chapter 7, pp. 15ff., chapter 8, pp. 31–32, 108 n. 101.

siveness since the mid-1960s. By then the ideologically unreliable and the incompetent had been eliminated, and university faculties and research institute staffs consisted of thoroughly trained historians of the Marxist-Leninist school. As Marxists, these historians readily accept the principle of the unity of theory and practice and the right of the party, as the leader in the class struggle, to establish priorities and issue assignments, for such assignments enable the historian to render aid more effectively in this struggle. "The issue," Ernst Hoffmann explains, "is not a dogma of infallibility on the part of the party or a substitute for the independent work of the professional historians. The issue is a better organization of these joint endeavors."

The DDR historian finds it all the easier to submit to the political leaders because the latter, as Marxists, also are guided by the lessons of history in evolving their policies. "Well-being and hardship, victory and defeat, rapid progress or stagnation depend to a large extent on a correct scientific analysis . . . ," Hoffmann notes. "Historical scholarship thus is a precondition of the continued existence of every Marxist party, one of the laws by which alone it can live. And a Marxist party that would neglect history, that would not engage in the constant scientific exploration of historical developments, would be self-destructive and would undermine one of its existential foundations." Politics, Engelberg sums up, is the art of doing what has been found to be historically necessary: "Bismarck . . . spoke of politics as the art of the possible; it never occurred to him that politics must have a scientific foundation."[50]

The directives of the SED to the historians, the research plans, and the assignments are worked out in cooperation with historians, who do much of the preparatory work. This cooperation has proven mutually beneficial. If the political leaders have had the support of the historians in their plans and policies, the latter in turn have received generous material and institutional aid. The support that historical research receives from the state in the DDR, as well as the number of historians engaged exclusively in research (rather than in both research and teaching), far surpasses that in the Federal Republic or other Western countries. As a result, DDR historians have been able to produce an astonishing amount of monographic and periodical literature. Moreover, through large-

[58]Ernst Hoffmann, in Eckermann and Mohr, *Einführung*, pp. 94–95; Hoffmann, "Zur Bedeutung der Beschlüsse der SED über die neueste deutsche Geschichte für die Geschichtswissenschaft," *BzG* 7 (1965): 440ff. (quotations on pp. 422–43); Engelberg, *Probleme*, pp. 121–22, 124; Engelberg and Rudolph, *ZfG* 18 (1970): suppl., 13–14 (quotation on p. 13); also generally Bollhagen, in Eckermann and Mohr, *Einführung*, pp. 37ff.

scale collective ventures, drawing on great numbers of collaborators, they have been able to publish multi-volume histories of the
two World Wars that their West German counterparts are only
now beginning to match.[59]

Thus led and aided by the SED, the East German historians
are playing their assigned role in the ideological class struggle.
They are living up fully to their mandate, which Engelberg has
described, in a paraphrase of Marx's famed Feuerbach thesis, as not
merely interpreting the world, but changing it, too.[60]

The DDR Historian as Scholar

By Marxist criteria, the political nature of history does not affect
its scientific standing. "Science," in that view, "grows out of the
practical life process of society and is irretrievably tied to it; as the
product of man's perceptive activity [Erkenntnistätigkeit] it is a
continuously developing system of perceptions about the laws of
nature, society, and human thinking. . . . It serves the *conscious
changing of reality*. . . . Given its social function, it is a productive
force of society and is the basis of [man's] control over the laws of
nature and society and over [his] planning and directing of social
processes; it is also the basis of social prognoses."[61] Like any other
human activity, science thus is seen as rooted in the soil of materialism, and history, like all scientific disciplines, can obtain scientifically valid answers only on that basis.

The scientific task of the Marxist historian, as mentioned
before, consists in explaining the operation of historical laws.
Above all, historical science has to prove that the course of human
history, in its core, leads inevitably toward socialism and communism. . . . A scientific concept of history is needed in order to
develop the correct perspective of mankind's communist future
and to build consciously the socialist and communist society"
(Bartel/Schmidt). The specific assignment is and has been to show
how the forces of progress asserted themselves against the counter-

---

[59]See *Deutschland im ersten Weltkrieg*, ed. Fritz Klein et al., 3 vols. (Berlin [East],
1968–69); *Deutschland im zweiten Weltkrieg*, ed. Wolfgang Schumann and Gerhart Hass, 4 vols. (Berlin [East], 1974–81). See also Andreas Hillgruber, "Deutschland im Zweiten Weltkrieg—Zur Forschungssituation in der Bundesrepublik vor
der 'Herausforderung' durch die DDR-Historie," in *Tradition und Neubeginn:
Internationale Forschungen zur deutschen Geschichte im 20. Jahrhundert*, ed.
Joachim Hüttler et al. (Cologne, 1975), pp. 235ff.
[60]See Engelberg, "Über Gegenstand und Ziel," p. 1143. How well historians have
acquitted themselves of their task is explored in a history of DDR historiography;
Diehl, "Aufgaben," pp. 274–75.
[61]*Wörterbuch* pp. 515–16. (Italics in the quotation are mine.)

forces of reaction in order to meet the "objective developmental needs of society in our nation." In this manner, the "deformed picture of German history, the product of a purposeful reactionary historiography," would be replaced by a scientifically correct picture that would pay tribute to the democratic and humanistic traditions of the German people. Such a picture would also show that socialist ideology grew out of these progressive traditions and that the German Democratic Republic was the lawful executor of this heritage. This meant uncovering long-forgotten traditions that were buried or falsified by the ruling classes and rewriting and reinterpreting history as propelled forward by the class struggle. It also meant supporting the idea that the workers' movement, under Marxist-Leninist leadership, was drawing on the liberating, democratic strands of the German past to lead the nation into a happier future.[62]

Such a preconceived approach to history is not considered to be in conflict with the standards of scholarship on the grounds that the approach itself is scientific because it takes as its point of departure social reality and the inevitability of historical developments. Yet, as mentioned before, the confirmatory nature of historical research has tempted researchers into making do with inadequate evidence, or in some cases with none at all, and on occasion this has been acknowledged.[63] Still, this approach has produced important new findings, too, fully borne out by the evidence and carefully analyzed.[64]

The fact that this approach serves political purposes is in turn taken as proof that these purposes, too, are scientifically valid. Actually, it is noted, historical scholarship has never been divorced from social and political premises. "The historian," writes Gerhard Brendler,

> can describe past social reality, irrevocably gone in its concrete manifestations, only from the conceptual premises of his time and the consciousness of his class. Perceptions of history always include a politics-oriented perception of the present and vice versa. The conceptual premises of any given time just as the state of consciousness

---

[62]Bartel and Schmidt, "Neue Probleme," pp. 801–2; Marion Einhorn and Heinz Habedank, "Das Programm des Sozialismus und die Aufgaben der Historiker der DDR," *ZfG* 11 (1963): 251, 253; Leo Stern, *Gegenwartsaufgaben der deutschen Geschichtsforschung* (Berlin [East], 1952), pp. 52–53; Schmidt, "Über die Aufgaben der Geschichtswissenschaft bei der sozialistischen Bewusstseinsbildung," *ZfG* 17 (1969): 58.

[63]See Klein et al., *Deutschland im ersten Weltkrieg*, vol. 2, pp. 60–61; Klein, *ZfG* 23 (1975): 488. The problem was particularly acute in the early years of East German historiography, when it seemed more important to spread the Marxist view of history than to worry about adequate proof. On this "Wissenschaftliche," see also Meusel, p. 396.

[64]Chapter 5, pp. 28–29, 37–38; chapter 7, pp. 6ff., 78ff.

of its classes are products of history. Thus concern with the past starts from the present, as shaped by history.[65]

The alignment of history with political needs is indeed not novel, although the connection has rarely, if ever, been established as openly and systematically as in Marxist societies. Politically oriented historians—the Mommsens and Treitschkes, the Guizots and Michelets, Macauley and Carlyle—have long been part of the historiographical landscape.[66]

In their case, DDR historians consider such Parteilichkeit wholly compatible with scholarly standards, because their Parteilichkeit, as noted before, aligns itself both with objective law-governed progress toward the socialist/communist order and with the working class, which is the force propelling society toward that order. "For this reason," *Sachwörterbuch der deutschen Geschichte* states, "proletarian partisanship not only goes hand in hand with genuine objectivity, but actually constitutes a precondition for the correct understanding of social relationships." Parteilichkeit, like ideology, thus is not a peripheral attribute of Marxist historical work that can be discarded at will, but an existential part of that work. Complaints of Western critics that Marxist authors refuse to divest themselves of their ideological preconceptions are therefore pointless, for these critics misunderstand the very nature of Marxist historiography.[67]

If the East German historian is partisan on behalf of the cause of progress, he just as openly deprecates the antiprogressive forces of history. The concept of "listening to the other side" is rejected as "bourgeois objectivism" that will not take a progressive critical stand and in effect explains away everything. In the same vein, several authors have stated that "the struggles for historical progress on the part of the popular masses and above all the working

---

[65]See Brendler, *Das Täuferreich zu Münster 1534/35* (Berlin [East], 1966), p. 9. The statement recalls H. T. Buckle's comment that "there must always be a connection between the way in which men contemplate the past and the way in which they contemplate the present; both views being in fact different forms of the same habits of thought, and therefore presenting in each age, a certain sympathy and correspondence with each other." Quoted in Fritz Stern, *The Varieties of History* (New York, 1956), p. 15.

[66]For some striking examples of the use of history for political purposes see Schleier, "Zur Auswirkung der Reichsgründung auf historisch-politische Konzeptionen der bürgerlichen Geschichtsschreibung bis 1914," in *Die grosspreussisch-militaristische Reichsgründung 1871*, ed. by Horst Bartel and Engelberg (Berlin [East], 1971), pp. 517ff.; Schleier, *Bürgerliche Geschichtsschreibung*. On the other hand, the political neutrality most non-Marxist historians seek to maintain is dismissed as tacit support of the existing system ("Parteilichkeit," *Swb*, vol. 2, p. 256).

[67]See "Parteilichkeit," *Swb*, vol. 2, pp. 255–56; *Grundlagen*, pp. 401–2; Brendler, "Prinzip," pp. 298–99. On the relationship between Parteilichkeit and objective truth in East German philosophical discussions, see Rüdiger Thomas, in *Wissenschaft und Gesellschaft in der DDR*, ed. Thomas (Munich, 1971), pp. 62ff.

class—struggles that have been successful, on the whole, despite all defeats and setbacks—are the determining element of the history of the German people, not the antipopular and reactionary activities of the exploiting classes, with their disastrous consequences." The perspectives of exploiting classes, their efforts to safeguard their own interests, are thus of concern to the Marxist historian only insofar as such endeavors impinge on the interests of society, especially those of the toilers. Similarly, when progress is the only valid criterion, it is always results that matter, never intentions; the sincerity, logic, or justification of an action by itself is irrelevant. Communists who pursued a strategy that proved ineffective or that was subsequently censured by the KPD leadership or the Comintern were ignored on the grounds that to pay attention to them would merely confuse the issues. (This of course applies equally to those party members who, by deviating from the officially sanctioned party line, assumed an "antiprogressive" stance.) What Kuczynski has said of the less savory aspects of the French Revolutionary wars—that they were historically less important— can be applied to all factors and forces impeding what constitutes progress in the Marxist-Leninist view.[68]

Substantively, one of the major concerns of East German historians has been to demonstrate the key role that the popular masses, and in more recent times the working class within these masses, are claimed to have played. Thus, special attention is paid to all manifestations of social or political activity among the medieval peasantry and urban poor, or more recently to the industrial working class and its allies. As the vanguard of progress, the revolutionary Marxist party in its various phases holds the center of interest. (Correspondingly, in the hierarchy of archival sources, materials concerning the Communist and Socialist Unity parties and, next to them, sources relating to the German and international labor movement rank before all other materials.)[69]

DDR historians pride themselves in developing a truly "national" history in which the working class is accorded its due place in history. This approach, as mentioned before, is contrasted with the traditional one of German historians who confined their research to wars, diplomacy, and the politics of the upper classes. It

[68]See Jan Solta, in *JWG* 1 (1960): 326; Horst Bartel et al., *ZfG* 18 (1970): suppl., 27–28 (with quotation). On "rightist-opportunist" and "ultraleftist" offenders of Weimar days whose role is being minimized, see *GdA*, vol. 3, pp. 321–22, 383, vol. 4, p. 26. On the blurred treatment of the controversy over the deviationist Heinz Neumann, see chapter 7, pp. 81–82. See also Kuczynski's statement in his *Geschichte*, vol. 1, p. 45.
[69]See Botho Brachmann, in Engelberg, *Probleme*, pp. 224–26. Brachmann also calls for the ordering of sources according to partisan, scientific rather than "technicist," principles (ibid., pp. 231–32).

is recognized that for some time now West German scholars have shown an increasing interest in the history of workers and peasantry, but rather than welcome this broadened approach, East German historians dismiss it as an abuse of progressive historical traditions, meant to deceive the toilers. DDR authors consider it now their task to show that only the East German view of history is derived from the great traditions of humanist progress brought forth by the German people. "We must not yield *one* progressive thinker or poet, not *a single one,* to our opponents," Kurt Hager, a politburo member, admonished a gathering of social scientists. "History must be written in such a way that it becomes clear that the DDR is the socialist state in which all great progressive and revolutionary traditions of our people are being preserved."[70]

As Marxists, however, East German historians are concerned with more than giving their due to those whom they view as the makers of history—that is, the masses, the working class, and the latter's revolutionary parties. Because history is a story not only of achievements but also of failures, DDR scholars consider it part of their task to ascertain whether those failures were inevitable (because "objective conditions" were not yet "ripe") or whether a different strategy might have produced more constructive results. The search for alternatives, as noted before, is an integral part of East German historiography, partly because such searches enable "objective reality" to be recreated as completely as possible but also because the determination of available alternatives is considered of great educational and inspirational value. The assumption is that the nation's self-confidence would be strengthened if it were shown that earlier failures of progressive endeavors were due to ignorance of historical laws and of man's role in the action of these laws; with proper regard to objective conditions and laws and through informed, conscious action, man could have mastered his destiny then as he can now. A contemplative, stock-taking approach, on the other hand, is rejected as merely encouraging acquiescence in the world as it was and is—a fatalism that runs counter to the very essence of Marxism-Leninism. Thus, the historian who offers alternatives and encourages confidence in the attainment of democratic and socialist objectives fulfills his mandate of not merely interpreting but also changing the world, and becomes himself a "maker of history."[71]

---

[70]See Peter Schuppan, *ZfG* 8 (1960): suppl., 202; Bock, review, *ZfG* 3 (1961): pp. 185–86; Weber, ibid. 10 (1968): 370; Horst Bartel and Schmidt, "Neue Probleme," p. 817, with Hager quotation (italics in original); also, for additional data, see Dorpalen, "History and Politics," pp. 85ff.

[71]Stiehler, *Geschichte und Verantwortung,* pp. 75ff.; Klaus and Schulze, *Sinn, Gesetz und Fortschritt,* p. 86; Engelberg, "Gegenstand," pp. 1140–41, 1143; Engelberg, *Deutschland von 1849 bis 1871* (Berlin [East], 1962), p. xxiii.

The search for alternatives also serves to satisfy the demands of socialist humanism. Although social progress, being predetermined by historical law, is viewed as inevitable, it has nonetheless been costly most of the time. Alternatives reveal that progress need not have been purchased at the high price of war or interminable social misery and that the sacrificing of millions of human beings for the benefit of an abstract "mankind" can be prevented. There is no need, the historian must prove, to attain social progress without regard for the cost in human lives and happiness; so far research in such areas has been applied only to the history of the nonsocialist world.[72]

The task the historian faces in his search for alternatives is difficult, however, for realistic alternatives are not easily found. Many of those that have been proposed by DDR scholars have not been convincing.[73]

The DDR Historian as Propagandist

Historical scholarship is of no social use unless its findings are passed on to the public. This imposes additional tasks on East German historiography, which is considered a social science not only because it deals with society, but also because it is meant to help mold society. To be socially useful, historical findings must also be propagated, and propaganda in this sense of disseminating historical knowledge is an important function of the historian. The original call for the organization of the Deutsche Historiker-Gesellschaft, the professional association of East German historians, emphasized that the society would consider it one of its main responsibilities to further socialist education and the "development of a socialist consciousness" (sozialistische Bewusstseinsbildung). The importance of this task has been reiterated at every historical meeting, for such consciousness enables men to identify with the Marxist socialist order as the logical solution to society's problems. Equally important, such consciousness conveys to them the necessity of their doing the job that is assigned to them by the laws of

---

[72]Stiehler, *Geschichte und Verantwortung*, p. 75; Horst Köpstein, review, *ZfG* 10 (1962): 1699.

[73]See, for example, chapter 2, pp. 10–11; chapter 4, pp. 15–16; chapter 5, pp. 71–72; and chapter 7, pp. 90–91; also see Stiehler, *Geschichte und Verantwortung*, pp. 83ff., who himself all but demolishes one of his proposed alternatives (concerning the stance of the Social Democratic party in 1932). Other of his alternatives also raise serious questions.

history to help attain, develop, and defend the Marxist socialist order.[74]

The task of the historians is facilitated by the demands of Parteilichkeit which compel DDR authors to play down or depreciate antiprogressive forces and developments or to ignore them altogether. By thus streamlining their presentations, East German historians are able to convey a self-confident certitude that contrasts sharply with the relativism, qualifications, and unanswered questions of non-Marxist authors. This confidence derives further strength from the basic optimism that follows from the Marxist conviction of the inevitability of social progress. Moreover, research has detected such progress even in periods traditionally viewed as stagnant and uneventful, such as the late seventeenth century. Such findings, too, add to the persuasiveness of the Marxist claims for the future.[75]

As a "political" science, history must provide ideological orientation. The importance of this task is constantly stressed: Kurt Hager, of the SED's politburo, finds that the development of socialist consciousness is tied to the imparting of a Marxist-Leninist picture of history; Walter Schmidt, of the Institute of Social Sciences at the party's Central Committee, calls history a "constituent element of socialist ideology." What the historian therefore must propagate is not the spirit and values of those times he has recreated—this might have the kind of restorative effect to which Marxists are wholly opposed—but the Marxist perceptions of that past and their relevance to the present. The editors of one historical journal have succinctly summed up this position: "The findings that [history] offers are statements on politics." In this spirit, Heinz Heitzer stated, in the introduction of a book he wrote on anti-Napoleonic resistance movements in post-Jena Germany, that the book was meant to "contribute to the present national struggle of the German people by providing the working people with information likely to raise their national consciousness, their patriotic initiative, pride in the progressive traditions of the history of the German people." Similar observations can be found in the prefaces to most historical accounts whose current significance may not be obvious, and their present-day relevance is underlined by appropriate comments throughout the body of these studies. The obligation of the historian—whether a medievalist, a nineteenth-century scholar, or a specialist in contemporary history—to help strengthen the national consciousness of the DDR citizenry and thus aid in

---

[74]Günter Kröber, *Wissenschaft im Sozialismus* (Berlin [East], 1973), pp. 42–43; editorial statement in *BzG* 11 (1969): 375; call for *Historiker-Gesellschaft* in *ZfG* 6 (1958): 218.
[75]"Dialektischer und historischer Materialismus," *Swb*, vol. 1, p. 479; Lozek and Syrbe, *Moderne Epoche*, p. 1247. See also chapter 4, pp. 1ff.

stabilizing its socialist order is an ever-recurring theme of East German historical literature.[76] Beyond this "domestic" assignment, the propagation of the findings of DDR historians is intended also to convert the West German working class and other sympathetic elements to the socialist cause.[77]

Because the historian is to assist in the solving of current social and political tasks, his choice of topics and his assessments are subject to change and must be reappraised and reformulated in keeping with shifting political needs and objectives. "This is not simply an accommodation, but an objective necessity that derives from the partisan demand for social effectiveness, for keeping-in-step with social needs, thinking ahead toward the future, and the rejection of an art-for-art's-sake kind of history."[78] A striking shift of this type has taken place in the determination of Germany's politico-cultural position vis-à-vis her neighbors. In the 1950s and early 1960s, when reunification still seemed a possibility, DDR historians kept attacking the West German concept of a "Christian West" (*christliches Abendland*) as opposed to the pagan uncivilized East on the grounds that it was meant to widen the gap between East and West Germany. Since the late 1960s, on the other hand, the emphasis has been on the communality of East German and other East European developments after World War II as part of a worldwide revolutionary process—an approach that was intended to help integrate the DDR further into the socialist camp and at the same time provide a historical underpinning for the policy of demarcation against the West.[79] Such subjection to the demands of politics seems to move the historian close to the political publicist, a conclusion with which DDR historians do not quarrel.[80]

Given this affinity, the colorless tenor of East German histori-

[76]Brendler, "Zum Prinzip," p. 294; Hager, quoted in *BzG* 11 (1969): 385; Schmidt, in *Geschichtsbewusstsein und sozialistische Gessellschaft*, ed. Helmut Meier and Schmidt (Berlin [East], 1970), pp. 8–9, 15ff., 30ff.; Schilfert, "Geschichtswissenschaft," p. 585; Fricke, "Die Bedeutung des Leninismus für die nichtproletarischen demokratischen Kräfte . . . ," *ZfG* 18 (1970): 999–1000; editorial statement, *BzG* 11 (1969): 375; Heitzer, *Insurrectionen zwischen Weser und Elbe: Volksbewegungen gegen die französische Fremdherrschaft im Königreich Westfalen (1806–1813)* (Berlin [East], 1959), p. 14.

[77]*GdA*, vol. 1, p. 11*; Meier, "Geschichtsbewusstsein in der Systemauseinandersetzung," in Meier and Schmidt, *Geschichtsbewusstsein und sozialistische Gesellschaft*, pp. 56ff; Lothar Berthold, "Über . . . die Aufgaben der Geschichtswissenschaft . . . ," *BzG* 11 (1967): 199–200.

[78]Brendler, "Zum Prinzip," p. 295; also editorial statement, *BzG* 11 (1969): 378, 381.

[79]On this, see also a West German study by Hans Georg Wolf, "Geschichtsbewusstsein und Geschichtsunterricht in der DDR," *GWU* 28 (1977): 65ff.

[80]Brendler, "Zum Prinzip," pp. 295–96. Adjustments to shifting political concerns also occur, of course, in non-Marxist historiography. Present-day West German historiography, as compared to the Prussian, Imperial, Weimar, and Nazi varieties, provides a striking example, and corresponding examples can be cited for any other Western country. Yet these realignments have rarely been as systematic and all-pervasive as those in the DDR.

cal accounts may seem surprising. Yet the very exigencies of politics and ideology and the dictates of democratic centralism—that is, the unquestioning acceptance of party resolutions—place great restraints on DDR authors.[81] Their methodological approach imposes further limitations upon them. A historiography that is concerned with the individual as a social being, historically important only in his relationship to society, and that considers personal traits, psychological problems, and human-interest data as irrelevant must find it difficult to inject life into its presentations. Nor does the historian who must find his way through the dialectic of object and subject, appearance and substance, inevitable occurrences and accidental events, retain much scope for literary distinction. The scientific nature of history, the priority of analysis over narrative, rule out any substantive kinship with art. Where art is conceded a place, as in the manner of presentation, it is rarely found. *Geschichte der deutschen Arbeiterbewegung* praises the brilliance of Franz Mehring's style and quotes approvingly Mehring's statement that "all historiography is both art and science," but its own uninspired, cliché-ridden prose fails to live up to this stipulation.[82] All in all, DDR authors have produced few well-written studies, even among those aimed at a broader audience.

DDR authors are, of course, aware of the fact that history, in order to fulfill its educational and inspirational role, must have an emotional impact. One answer has been to invoke moral judgments for the "consciousness-forming effect" of such judgments. For the rest, polemics has often served as a substitute.[83]

Given their political purpose and their polemical style, East German historical studies are clearly briefs—and are meant to be such in the ideological class struggle. They are briefs either for the prosecution or for the defense, depending on their particular subject matter. Even briefs, however, if read carefully, can contain valuable information, analyses, and conclusions. They can also tell a great deal about their authors.

[81]The principles of democratic centralism apply also to Marxist scholars as such, whether or not they are members of the Socialist Unity party (see Kröber, *Wissenschaft im Sozialismus*, p. 229).

[82]Klaus and Schulze, *Sinn, Gesetz und Fortschritt*, pp. 50ff., 76–77; *GdA*, vol. 1, p. 22*; Jaeck, in Engelberg, *Probleme*, p. 98.

[83]Schilfert, "Geschichtswissenschaft," p. 585; "Geschichtsbewusstsein," *Swb*, vol. 1, pp. 676–77. On moral judgments, see Brendler, "Zum Prinzip," pp. 296–97, but also see Klaus Vetter's warning against "moralizing" ones in *ZfG* 22: 638. On polemics, see Jaeck, in Engelberg, *Probleme*, pp. 98–99. See also the revealing comment of Kuczynski on the magnum opus of his father, René Kuczynski, *A Demographic Survey of the British Colonial Empire* (Oxford, 1948–1953): "This standard work of 2,300 pages contains not a single word of agitation; most of the time it even forgoes any propagandistic commentary." (Kuczynski, *René Kuczynski: Ein fortschrittlicher Wissenschaftler in der ersten Hälfte des 20. Jahrhunderts* [Berlin (East), 1957], p. 127.) On the other hand, one reviewer described Brezhnev's memoirs as a "model example of mass-effective historical propaganda" (Fritz Zimmermann, *BzG* 21 [1979]: 457).

2

The Middle Ages

The Age of the Feudal System

The Origins of the Feudal System

G ERMAN HISTORY AS A "national" history has its beginnings in the Middle Ages, or, in the Marxist blueprint of periodization, during the socioeconomic formation of feudalism.[1] Its roots, however, reach back much farther, and no one is more aware of this fact than Marxist historians. Because of their conception of history as essentially a succession of modes of production, East German historians have devoted considerable attention to these socioeconomic beginnings. In fact, they have analyzed these early phases in greater specificity than have most non-Marxist scholars.

Because the production of his material necessities is acclaimed by Marx as man's "first historical act," Marxists do not require written sources to write "history." Archaeological finds provide immediate authentic information on production activities; settlement patterns, fortifications, and tombs supply additional data; and the "laws of history" offer overall guidance. Most Marxist historians thus do not distinguish between history and prehistory. They consider the appearance of written sources significant in another context, however: writing skills were developed at that higher level of social organization at which Marxists see classes emerge. Written records thus become an attribute of class society; their appearance coincided with the demise of the classless primitive-communal society.[2]

The history of the primitive-communal society from which

---

[1]The term *Middle Ages* is now used in the traditional sense by East German historians, referring to the period from the fifth century to the latter part of the fifteenth century. Earlier some DDR scholars applied the term to the entire "feudal period," that is, through the eighteenth century. For example, see Eckermann and Mohr, *Einführung in das Studium der Geschichte*, p. 82.

[2]See Karl-Heinz Otto, *Deutschland in der Epoche der Urgesellschaft* (Berlin [East], 1961), p. 2; Otto, *Aus Ur- und Frühgeschichte* (Berlin [East], 1961), pp. 19–20; also Joachim Herrmann, *ZfG* 18 (1970): suppl., 293. On the other hand, Streisand (p. 16) still distinguishes between prehistory and history. The identification of written history with class history was first made by Engels in an editorial note to the 1888 edition of the *Communist Manifesto*.

all East German surveys of German history take their departure is
presented as that of a social order that, by means of improved
production techniques and divisions of labor, moved from communal beginnings to hierarchical structures, private property, and a
class society. Clans, families, and tribes are viewed first of all as
production units and only secondarily as groupings providing military protection and maintaining internal peace. As wars occurred
more frequently, military aristocracies and eventually kingships
evolved. These leadership groups were subject to the decisions of
popular assemblies (Engels spoke of "military democracies"), but
they also acquired special landholdings, possibly as tenants rather
than owners, and others worked these lands for them; they also
began to assemble followings (Gefolgschaften) who were loyal to
them rather than to the people. Thus the rudimentary elements of
classes began to appear, and the foundations were laid for future
states. Despite the scarcity or lack of clarity of evidential materials, DDR authors present these analyses with considerable assurance. Only occasionally are doubts voiced concerning the certainty
of these findings.[3]

For the Marxist historian, the significance of this period lies
in its implications for present and future developments. The continued predominance of communal landownership and the resulting
check on irreconcilable class differences is proof to him of his
claim that private property and a class society based on such property have not always been and need not forever remain the basis
of social relations. Hence he rejects any theories that seek to confine the existence of communal property arrangements to the earliest times of human existence. The contrary view that the early
Germans were independent landowners living on the labor of unfree peasants is dismissed as a bourgeois obfuscation that tries to
present class divisions as something permanent and unchangeable.
Yet the very author who makes this charge also admits that although the early Germans had no comprehesive slaveholding system on the Roman model, some at least did have unfree peasants,
more akin to serfs than to slaves, whom they "exploited."[4]

[3]See Streisand, pp. 15ff.; Grundriss, pp. 19ff.; Otto, Aus Ur- und Frühgeschichte,
pp. 4ff., 172–74. Doubts are expressed by Hans Mottek in his Wirtschaftsgeschichte Deutschlands, vol. 1, pp. 41–46, 52–53; Herrmann, ZfG 8 (1960): 143–
45. The concept of military democracies, if not that term, was originally used by
non-Marxists also, but was more recently abandoned in favor of an interpretation
that defines the then-existing political system as that of an aristocratic rule—a
description that DDR scholars accept only for a later time (Eckhard Müller-
Mertens, Deutsche Literatur-Zeitung 80 [1959]: 413ff.; Karl Bosl, in Gebhardt,
vol. 1, p. 708 n. 5; Herbert Jankuhn, in HbDtWSG, vol. 1, p. 74).
[4]See Mottek, Wirtschaftsgeschichte Deutschlands, vol. 1, pp. 47–49. In support of
his charges, Mottek cites only some publications (not accessible to me) by Werner
Wittich and Wilhelm Fleischmann, dating back to 1896 and 1911, respectively.

Concerning the confrontation between the Germanic tribes and the Romans, the East German accounts assume hardly more of a "national" flavor. It is stressed that these tribes did not differ biologically or ethnically from other such groups, but were held together by economic, linguistic, and cultural ties.[5] As before, socioeconomic conditions receive special attention, and stress is laid on the collectivist features of the economy and the resulting mitigation of social differentiations, in disregard of any findings that challenge such a categorical stand. In this vein, DDR scholars hail the victory of the Germanic tribes over the Romans in the famous battle of the Teutoburg Forest in 9 A.D. as a success won over an oppressive slave-holding state by free men whose communal landownership had kept alive their spirit of independence. Some authors add, perhaps for the benefit of peoples fighting for their liberation at the time of writing, that the rebelling Germanic tribes also drew strength from the fact that they were struggling to free their homeland.[6]

Subsequent developments are considered important as evidence of the process by which antiquated production relations were replaced by more adequate ones. It was no simple matter, however, to reconcile the transition to feudalism with the accepted development model (see Chapter 1). There were no expanding productive forces colliding with antiquated production relations and touching off a social revolution as the gateway to feudalism. Explanations of what occurred vary; the gist of the most widely accepted views may be summed up as follows.

In the Germanic territories that had warded off Roman rule, communal landownership gave way to private holdings as the leaders appropriated communal lands. To assure increased food production for themselves and their followers, the leaders had peasants cultivate these lands; unlike slaves, however, the peasants, as an incentive, retained part of what they produced. The improved production techniques led to substantial population in-

---

Actually, Western historians are divided on the question of whether communal landholdings survived into the early Middle Ages among the Germans: see Josef Kulischer, *Allgemeine Wirtschaftsgeschichte des Mittelalters und der Neuzeit* (repr. ed., Berlin [East], 1954), vol. 1, pp. 8ff.; Alfons Dopsch, *Wirtschaftliche und soziale Grundlagen der europäischen Kulturentwicklung* (repr. ed., Aalen, 1961), vol. 1, pp. 53ff.; "Eigentum," *SDG* 2: 41ff.; Bosl, in Gebhardt, vol. 1, pp. 703–4.
[5]Otto, pp. 104–6; Streisand, p. 25.
[6]See Otto, pp. 116ff.; Streisand, pp. 26–27; *Grundriss*, pp. 41–42. Compare Bruno Krüger, "Der Freiheitskampf germanischer Stämme während der römischen Offensive in den Jahren 12 v. u. Z. bis 16 u. Z," in *Die Rolle der Volksmassen in der Geschichte der vorkapitalistischen Gesellschaftsformationen*, ed. Joachim Herrmann et al. (Berlin [East], 1975), pp. 159ff. with Bosl, in Gebhardt, vol. 1, p. 703. On the complex question of Germanic landownership, see Friedrich Lütge, *Deutsche Sozial- und Wirtschaftsgeschichte* (Berlin [West], 1952), pp. 16, 20–22.

creases, and these in turn drove the Germans to invade the Roman Empire in their quest for new lands. Rome's slaveholding society, weakened by slave revolts and its own inefficiency, was swept away as the invaders brought with them their superior mode of production. The institution of serfdom was further strengthened when free peasants, ruined by war and other disasters, surrendered their land and accepted serf status in return for protection.

Essentially, then, production relations were adjusted to stimulate the stagnating productive forces, and the result was the rise of a new mode of production—in its dimensions a revolutionary change, even if it was not brought about by social risings. Thus the feudal order emerged as the first fully developed class society on German soil. It is defined as a "socioeconomic order" in which the "chief means of production is the land, the property of secular and ecclesiastical feudal lords, while the direct producers, the peasants, work the decisive share of the soil with their own implements and are forced by noneconomic means [personal physical force, judicial authority, policy, military] to deliver the feudal rent."[7]

Given its antagonistic class conflicts, its repression, and its exploitation, East German historians consider feudalism a setback compared to the classless primitive-communal society. In terms of productive efficiency, however, the feudal order is viewed as progressive, because it introduced improved agricultural techniques and furthered an increasing division of labor (of which the rise of the towns was the most spectacular symbol).[8] All in all, developments are seen as centering on a new growth of productivity sparked by the replacement of two outdated social orders—the primitive-communal society and the slaveholding order—by a more efficient one—the feudal system. The rapacity of individual kings and other military leaders may have touched off many of the wars and migrations that brought about these changes, but these men merely accelerated a process that was historically inevitable.[9]

Feudalism took root more rapidly and more thoroughly in the Frankish kingdom than in any other part of Germania. As that

[7]Mottek, *Wirtschaftsgeschichte Deutschlands*, vol 1, pp. 57ff.; *Grundriss*, pp. 46ff.; Stiehler, *Gesellschaft und Geschichte*, pp. 222ff.; Herrmann, "Der Prozess der revolutionären Umwälzung zum Feudalismus in Europa...," *ZfG* 20 (1972): 1228ff.; Herrmann, "Die Rolle gentilgesellschaftlicher Stämme... bei der Herausbildung... vorkapitalistischer Gesellschaftsformationen," ibid. 25 (1977): 1149ff.; see also the discussions in ibid. 20 (1972) and 22 (1974). The quotation is from *Swb*, vol. 1, p. 582.

[8]"Feudalismus," *Swb*, vol. 1, p. 583; Herrmann, "Frühe klassengesellschaftliche Differenzierungen in Deutschland," *ZfG* 14 (1966): 418; Horst Gericke, "Zur Dialektik von Produktivkraft und Produktionsverhältnis im Feudalismus," ibid., 919–21.

[9]Leo Stern and Hans-Joachim Bartmuss, *Deutschland in der Feudalepoche von der Wende des 5./6. Jh. bis zur Mitte des 11. Jh.* (Berlin [East], 1965), pp. 8ff.

kingdom expanded, it stimulated the growth of productive forces in those parts of central, western, and southern Europe that came under Frankish control. "To have furthered this development," *Grundriss* states, "constitutes the historical significance of the Frankish Empire."[10]

Political developments in the Frankish kingdom and empire are assessed against this background of progressing feudalization. In both forms the Frankish state is seen as the tool of the feudal nobility. At times one noble family would assume dominion over the others—thus at the end of the fifth century, the Merovingians established the Frankish kingdom, and in the eighth century the Carolingians rose to power and Charlemagne established a more centralized government that served as the basis for the expansion of the kingdom into the empire. Even then, centralization was limited; as Hans-Joachim Bartmuss points out, the feudal lords managed to retain or seize local and administrative and judicial powers, and this counter-trend gathered further momentum as the Carolingians enfeoffed land holdings to nobles in return for the latter's military service.[11]

For a time, East German historians placed special emphasis on the unintegrated nature of the Carolingian empire; they hoped thus to refute the West German thesis of Germany's Western background (*Abendlandideologie*), which rested on the union of Germanic and Romanic components in the Frankish state. They dismissed this claim as a historical fraud that merely served as a smokescreen for West Germany's membership in NATO and similar "imperialist" agencies and as a pretext for attempts to detach the DDR and other socialist countries from the socialist camp. In more recent publications, this point no longer is made—possibly because the complete separation of East and West Germany and of Eastern and Western Europe has deprived the issue of its political relevance.[12]

If enfeoffment contributed to the decentralization of the Frankish empire, it also had progressive aspects in the Marxist view. The newly created vassals strengthened the feudal nobility as a class and thus advanced the growth of the feudal system. The

---

[10]*Grundriss*, p. 65.

[11]See Streisand, pp. 33–35; Stern and Bartmuss, *Deutschland*, pp. 79–82 (with quotation), 112, 142; Mottek, *Wirtschaftgeschichte Deutschlands*, vol. 1, pp. 77–78. See also, from a non-Marxist perspective, Marc Bloch, *Feudal Society* (London, 1961), pp. 443ff.

[12]See Stern and Bartmuss, *Deutschland*, p. 116, as compared with *Grundriss*, pp. 65–66. On *Abendlandideologie*, see Theodora Büttner, " 'Abendland' ideologie und Neo-Karolingertum im Dienste der Adenauer-CDU," *ZfG* 7 (1959): 1089ff.; Leo Stern, "Die klerikal-imperialistische Abendlandideologie im Dienste des deutschen Imperialismus," ibid. 10 (1962): 286ff.

growth of the feudal nobility is considered more significant in the long-range perspective than is the weakening of the Carolingian empire which follows from the proposition that the decline of the Carolingian rulers and the corresponding rise of the feudal lords constituted merely a shift of power within the same ruling class. Essentially the Frankish kings and emperors are considered feudal lords too, though endowed with greater powers and special prerogatives. Similarly, the state that they ruled is viewed as as instrument through which the feudal exploiters, whether kings or nobles, imposed their will upon the exploited (thus expanding their dominion and protecting it from outside attack). Whether governmental power was exercised by a central government or by local lords, the peasantry was oppressed with an iron hand.

For the Marxist, then, the chief dividing line in medieval society runs between landlords and peasants rather than between kings and nobles. (Correspondingly, the Marxist concept of feudalism relates to the lord-peasant relationship, known in the West as the manorial system, rather than to that between lord and vassal.) As Hans-Joachim Bartmuss points out, "the entire pyramid of [lords, vassals, and subvassals] weighed on the productive class, the unfree peasants; in the feudal system all members of the ruling class were living at their expense." As the main material producers, the peasants thus fulfilled a central function in the medieval order, and the peripheral role, at best, that is allowed them by non-Marxist historians is rejected as wrong.[13]

Because of their basic role in the production process, the peasants rank as one of the two main classes in the feudal system; the nobles who owned or controlled the land, the chief means of production, constituted the other main class. That the concept of classes was unknown to the Middle Ages is immaterial in this perspective: the class status of peasantry and nobility is derived from "objective" criteria, such as their respective relationship to the means of production, their role in the production process, and the manner and extent of their sharing in the produced social wealth. By these same criteria, the two classes face each other in an "elementary class antagonism," in the words of Bartmuss. "The entire feudal period," he adds, "is characterized by the embittered struggle between the exploiting feudal lords and the exploited." However, he also notes, somewhat inconsistently, that "this class struggle was not at all times equally intensive and effective."[14]

[13]See Stern and Bartmuss, *Deutschland*, p. 82; Eggert, "Rebelliones Servorum," *ZfG* 23 (1975): 1147–48, with quotations from West German authors. Not all non-Marxist authors have discounted the significance of the peasantry; Karl Lamprecht, Alfons Dopsch, and Marc Bloch are important exceptions; see also Karl Bosl, in *HbDtWSG*, vol. 1, p. 160.

[14]Stern and Bartmuss, *Deutschland*, pp. 82, 127.

The peasants are acclaimed for having made history in these struggles. By resisting exploitation, it is pointed out, they obtained reductions of taxes and services and other concessions. These alleviations in turn induced them to increase their production, because increased production would now redound to their benefit. Increased production, however, meant social progress.[15] Because feudalism up to the thirteenth century was still in its "progressive" phase and had not yet exhausted its productive potentialities, this was all the peasants could hope to achieve and there was no question as yet of replacing the system as such. "No social order ever perishes," Marx has taught,

> before all the productive forces for which there is room in it have been fully developed, and new higher relations of production never appear before the material conditions of their existence have matured in the womb of the old society. Therefore mankind always sets itself only such tasks as it can solve; for, looking at matters more closely, it will always be found that the task itself appears only when the material conditions for its solution exist already or at least are developing.

Therefore, peasant resistance during that early phase of the feudal era was no less a class struggle because it had no political goals.[16]

Given the significance East German historians attribute to peasant resistance, they have made great efforts to assemble whatever evidence they could find of peasant struggles. Following the pioneering work of the Soviet historian B. F. Porshnev, they see manifestations of such struggles in the refusal of services and payments of dues, in the defiance of seigniorial orders, and in escapes from the land.[17] The "highest" form of the class struggle was the peasant revolt, one of which—the Stellinga rising in Saxony in 842–843—grew into a major insurrection; King Louis the German had to intervene with his army to help subdue this rebellion.[18]

Actually, the history-making effect of these activities was

[15]*Grundriss*, pp. 66–67, 74, 81–82.

[16]See Stern and Horst Gericke, *Deutschland in der Feudalepoche von der Mitte des 11. Jh. bis zur Mitte des 13. Jh.* (Berlin [East], 165), p. 59; Marx, in MEW 13: 9; Kuczynski, *Geschichte*, vol. 1, p. 119; Töpfer, review, ZfG 17 (1969): 1359. One Soviet historian, A. R. Korsunskij, maintains, however, that resistance without political goals is not a genuine class struggle (Korsunskij, *Rolle der Volksmassen*, p. 195).

[17]B. F. Porshnev, "Formen und Wege des bäuerlichen Kampfes gegen die feudale Ausbeutung," *Sowjetwissenschaft*, Gesellschaftswiss. Abteilung, 1952, pp. 440ff.; Stern and Bartmuss, *Deutschland*, pp. 127ff. with 268–69; Stern and Gericke, *Deutschland*, pp. 42ff.; Mottek, *Wirtschaftsgeschichte Deutschlands*, pp. 130–31; Siegfried Epperlein, *Herrschaft und Volk im karolingischen Imperium* (Berlin [East], 1970).

[18]The Stellinga rebellion has been the subject of many East German studies. For a survey of the literature and a suggestive analysis see Eggert, "Rebelliones Servorum," pp. 1154ff.

rather limited. On the DDR historians' own showing, peasant resistance seems rarely to have led to an alleviation of peasant burdens and hence to have sparked increased productivity. On the contrary, as many of these same authors show, the significant increases of productivity were attained by technical improvements—three-field rotation, construction of water mills and of roads and bridges—for which credit must go to the landlords, or rather, their administrators, and above all to the monasteries.[19]

Peasant resistance has also been credited with having led to the formation of the first German state in 919. If the nobles agreed to create a new central power after the final demise of the Frankish rulers, they did so, Eckhard Müller-Mertens contends, because by themselves they were neither strong enough to keep the enserfed peasants oppressed nor able to subject the remaining free peasants to their control. Others have challenged this view, however, and have attributed the creation of this new state to the debilitating effects of noble rivalries (Bartmuss) or to expansionist plans of the nobles (Töpfer). All DDR authors are, however, agreed on the primacy of socioeconomic causations; the hope to fight off Hungarian and Norman invaders more effectively with the help of a central government is considered at best a secondary objective.[20]

One problem that besets these analyses, as it besets all such investigations, is the scarcity of concrete data on peasant activities. Despite these limitations, however, East German medievalists who proceed from their model rather than from the sources have no qualms about introducing the peasants as major actors on the historical stage. The model centers on the dialectic of the production process and is personified in the struggle between exploiters and exploited. On this basis, DDR scholars can argue that if the sources have little to say on the class struggle of the peasants, the reason is that almost all contemporary chroniclers were members of the feudal nobility. As such, they were concerned with the world of the ruling class—kings, nobles, and church dignitaries—and paid little attention "to the sphere of material production and production relations, and resistance of the popular masses against repression and exploitation received short shrift." Similarly, it has been

[19]See Stern and Bartmuss, *Deutschland*, pp. 128ff. On the achievements of the landlords, see Mottek, *Wirtschaftsgeschichte Deutschlands*, vol 1, p. 100; *Grundriss*, pp. 68, 72,; Ernst Münch, "Die Grundherrschaft des vollendeten Feudalismus im Prozess des gesellschaftlichen Fortschritts," *ZfG* 27 (1979): 145–46.

[20]See Eckhard Müller-Mertens, "Vom Regnum Teutonicum zum Heiligen Römischen Reich Deutscher Nation," *ZfG* 11 (1963): 325–28; Stern and Bartmuss, *Deutschland*, pp. 162–63; Bartmuss, *Die Geburt des ersten deutschen Staates* (Berlin [East], 1966), pp. 150ff., 261ff.; Töpfer, review, *ZfG* 13 (1965): 1087ff.; Herrmann, "Sozialökonomische Grundlagen und gesellschaftliche Triebkräfte für die Herausbildung des deutschen Feudalstaates," ibid., 19 (1971): 773–74, 788. Streisand, pp. 36–37, has a partial summary of the debate.

charged that, for political reasons, the contemporary records purposely minimized the class struggles of the popular masses, sometimes depicting them as tribal rather than social risings. Some
evidence has been found to support this thesis.[21]

Nonetheless, the East German approach has not avoided the
pitfalls inherent in the deductive start from a preconceived thesis.
Many conclusions admittedly rest on conjecture; data supposedly
attesting to peasant resistance do not always do so; in other cases
the evidence is inadequate.[22] Still, that approach has produced
enough proof to confirm the fact, established earlier already by
non-Marxist medievalists, such as Alfons Dopsch, Marc Bloch, and
the literary historian Fritz Martini, that the period was not as socially quiescent as has traditionally been assumed. Even if one
cannot accord the peasants the same place as history-makers that
rulers, nobles, and high churchmen could claim, it is clear that
historically relevant actions did take place on both planes. This
conclusion can also draw support from a source that DDR scholars,
too, have used—the literature of the times. As Martini has pointed
out in terms not unlike those used later by East German scholars,

> The medieval doctrine of the estates did not succeed, even with the
> help of its ideational underpinning, in pacifying society, as had been
> hoped. At an early date the contemporary literature indicates an
> inner unrest, propelled primarily by the peasant. The burden of the
> system of the estates weighed on him, and he was not protected in
> the rights that he claimed for himself in his simple, strong inner
> consciousness. He tried to preserve them and with them himself by
> keeping up this resistance. What knightly poets regarded as aping,
> presumption, and rudeness was in reality the defiance of the peas-
> antry defending their own living space and claims, and striving for
> the free development of their potential.[23]

Confronted with these findings, West German historiography,
too, has begun to abandon its view of the medieval world as a
"harmonious-patriarchal community" in which "the rural population basically ha[d] no history." Thus Karl Bosl, the Munich medievalist who earlier made that statement, now accords medieval

---

[21]Eggert, "Rebelliones," p. 1148ff., 1152ff., 1164; also Herrmann, *Sozialökonomische Grundlagen*, p. 772.
[22]Eggert admits the speculative nature of some of his arguments in "Rebelliones,"
pp. 1149, 1164. I am indebted to my colleague Joseph H. Lynch, Ohio State
University, for having pointed out to me that the data assembled by Stern and
Bartmuss (*Deutschland*, pp. 268–69) in many cases do not bear out the claims of
the authors. That the evidence in other cases is also inadequate has been noted by
the East German historian Waltraud Bleiber, in *ZfG* 19 (1971): 1214.
[23]Fritz Martini, *Der Bauer im deutschen Schrifttum von den Anfängen bis zum 16.
Jahrhundert* (Halle, 1944), p. 27. See also Gericke, "Der Hauptklassengegensatz in
der feudalen Gesellschaft im Spiegel einiger literarischen Zeugnisse des 11. bis 13.
J[ahr]h[underts]," *ZfG* 10 (1962): 889ff.

peasantry a "significant economic and social role in the historical process."[24]

The Church: "Bulwark of Feudalism"

The Church, whose influence spread as the feudal order expanded, was in the Marxist assessment an integral part of the feudal order. Marxists do not deny the reality of religious faith, and they acknowledge that kings and nobles accepted its power as readily, if perhaps not as sweepingly, as the popular masses. The fear of eternal damnation was shared by both lord and serf, and both strove anxiously for their souls' salvation. Yet salvation was predicated on the acceptance of the divine ordination of the secular world as it was, with its social differentiations and disparate burdens. Such acceptance, Gerhard Zschäbitz points out, did not grow out of an a priori religious need, but was part of the social education by which the ruling class imposed its own world view on the masses—a view in which it fully believed, and in which it also played the dominant role.[25]

The medium through which this view was disseminated was the Church. By teaching the masses submissiveness to their masters and acceptance of their low status, the Church helped to strengthen the feudal order. Of equal importance, DDR authors note, were the worldly ties that linked the Church to the feudal order. The Church furthered its consolidation by providing the organizational framework and the trained personnel for the administration and integration of the expanding Frankish domain. Moreover, because it was compensated for this work with large tracts of land and because it acquired much landed property from individuals in search of salvation, the Church became itself a large landowner, sharing the concerns of the feudal nobility. This parallelism of interests was strengthened by the social homogeneity of Church hierarchy and nobility. An alliance with the papacy, culminating in the pope's coronation of Charlemagne as emperor, further reinforced these ties and provided the ideological underpinning for continued expansion. In the face of these facts, the subjective concepts of individual rulers or churchmen concerning the role of the

---

[24]See Stern and Gericke, *Deutschland*, pp. 58–59, 255 n. 125–26; also see Karl Bosl, in Gebhardt, vol. 1, p. 706. Compare that work with Bosl's work in *HbDtWSG* (vol. 1, p. 160).

[25]Gerhard Zschäbitz, *Zur mitteldeutschen Wiedertäuferbewegung nach dem grossen Bauernkrieg* (Berlin [East], 1958), pp. 19–20.

Church are considered irrelevant—it was the objective reality that determined its functions.[26]

This linkage of the Church to the feudal order is not viewed as necessarily bad, however. Socioeconomically, the Church is regarded as a progressive force, because it helped replace communal and slaveholding systems with the more advanced feudal order. Culturally, it is credited with keeping alive parts of the Greco-Latin inheritance. Once the Church had helped the Frankish and German rulers bring ethnically and linguistically related tribes under their control, however, the Church's role in aiding and even instigating further expansion is no longer considered progressive. In fact, the Crusades are deplored as a ruinous undertaking, diverting the German kings from the tasks that required solution at home. Similarly, the Holy Roman Empire appears as an unending source of difficulties, and it is stripped altogether of its religious components.[27]

The religious reform movements that spread from the monastery of Gorze in Lorraine and that of Cluny in Burgundy in the tenth century fit readily into the conception of religion as serving the social and economic concerns of rulers and placating those of the ruled. Again, the religious element that touched off these movements is acknowledged—the need to lead clergy and monks back to the old ideals of self-discipline, modesty, and dedication lest a sinful clergy jeopardize the chances of eternal salvation. It is also noted, however, that a clergy that neglected its duties and indulged itself was losing its hold on the masses and could no longer control them on behalf of the ruling class. In their disenchantment the masses were turning to religious heretics who not only questioned the effectiveness of the sacraments administered by unworthy priests but also assailed the hierarchy and called on their followers to withhold the tithe. Such assaults, Ernst Werner points out, addressed themselves not just to their immediate eccle-

[26]See *Grundriss*, pp. 56–57, 63ff.; Stern and Bartmuss, *Deutschland*, pp. 58ff., 108ff.; Mottek, *Wirtschaftsgeschichte Deutschlands*, vol. 1, p. 66, 85–86, 91. In a less categorical form, some of these views have also been voiced by non-Marxist historians; see Heinrich von Eicken, *Geschichte und System der mittelalterlichen Weltanschauung* (Stuttgart/Berlin, 1913), pp. 345–46: "The Church, by taking possession of the world and its riches, became itself part of the world. . . . The Middle Ages could not solve this contradiction, because it was not the willful handiwork of a few individuals, but the logical result of the system. Its resolution would have meant the repudiation of this system. Hard as the Middle Ages tried to escape from this vicious circle, such attempts could not be successful as long as they did not transcend that system." Similarly, the West German medievalist Franz Steinbach speaks of a "supraethnic [übervölkische] community of interests of magnates, rulers, and Church (*Handbuch der deutschen Geschichte*, ed. Leo Just et al. [Stuttgart, 1956], vol. 1, pp. ii, 21; see also Martini, *Bauer im deutschen Schrifttum*, pp. 17ff.).

[27]*Grundriss*, pp. 82–84.

siastical targets but to the feudal system as well; for this reason
they were denounced as heretical rather than acquiesced to as
merely reformist. Beyond that, poorly administered monasteries
suffered reductions in productivity, reducing the revenues of their
feudal lords. Rulers and nobles therefore supported the monastic
reforms as much for social and economic reasons as from religious
conviction.[28]

The German kings, it is argued, could sponsor these reforms
more readily because the reforms launched in Germany were Gor-
zian ones that, unlike the Cluniac reforms, did not challenge the
supremacy of the secular power. The Cluniac reforms, on the other
hand, made the monasteries affected by them directly subordinate
to the pope and thus helped strengthen Rome's prestige and authority vis-à-vis the secular powers. Ultimately, however, this resurgence of papal power affected Germany, too. In the latter half of
the eleventh century it culminated in Pope Gregory VII's challenge
of the right of investiture of the German rulers—that is, of their
right to appoint the Empire's bishops and abbots. Because the bishops, as territorial lords, were also vassals of the monarch, this was
an eminently political question.

In the Marxist view, the struggle between kings and popes
was fought out within the ruling class. Yet, it also had its class-
struggle aspects. In addition to the higher nobility, most of whom
came to the aid of the Church in the hope of weakening the central
power, contingents of free peasants were mobilized by the king;
these peasants hoped to shake off the exactions imposed on them
by their feudal lords. The monarch also secured some help from
the newly emerging towns, which also were fretting at their subordination to the feudal nobility. (The pope, for his part, made use of
the communal movement in some of the Italian cities to force out
bishops supporting Henry IV.) Essentially, though, the struggle is
viewed as an intraruling class contest. On that plane, as Marxists
and non-Marxists both have concluded, it was neither king nor
pope but rather the German princes who emerged as the winner.
Because of the investiture contest, the German princes grew more
independent at the expense of the central power.[29]

As a conflict within the ruling class, the investiture contest is
of less interest to DDR authors than are challenges to the Church
from external social forces. The misery and unrest generated by

[28]See Ernst Werner, *Die gesellschaftlichen Grundlagen der Klosterreform im 11.
Jahrhundert* (Berlin [East], 1953); Stern and Gericke, *Deutschland*, pp. 73ff., 80–
81; Töpfer, *Volk und Kirche zur Zeit der beginnenden Gottesfriedensbewegung
in Frankreich* (Berlin [East], 1957), pp. 86–87. Again these points are not wholly
novel; see Albert Hauck, *Kirchengeschichte Deutschlands* (Leipzig, 1904–1913),
vol. 3, 443ff.; Eicken, *Geschichte und System*, pp. 228–29.
[29]Stern and Gericke, *Deutschland*, pp. 80ff., 101ff.; *Grundriss*, pp. 96ff.

such challenges are seen as threats to the feudal order as such. The Church contended with this burgeoning class conflict by proclaiming "peaces" and "truces of God" that created sanctuaries in churches and monasteries, shielded some segments of the population—women and children, peasants and traders—from the incessant fighting, and suspended all fighting during parts of the week or over limited periods of time. What gave these efforts their special significance in the Marxist perspective was that they enabled the Church to check the unrest of peasants and townsmen. By putting an end to the spreading unrest, the Church imparted new strength to the feudal order.[30]

DDR scholars see another and even more serious threat to that order in the heretical movements of the Cathari and Waldensians that arose during the twelfth and thirteenth centuries. Unlike the localized activities of individual heretics, these were major movements that spread across large parts of Germany. Again, it is granted that those who joined these movements were driven to them by religious motives. At the same time, all DDR authors maintain that in the last analysis it was the exploitation they suffered that made people receptive to heretical thoughts.[31]

The concept of heresies as being class struggles in religious guise is maintained despite the presence of nobles and prosperous townsmen among the heretics and in the face of the dominance of such privileged people among the "activists" in the heretical sects. As a West German historian, Herbert Grundmann, has shown, few members of the lower classes entered the inner circle of the Cathari and Waldensians and became *perfecti*; they were mostly to be found among the *credentes*, the "believers" or followers. Grundmann does not claim that the heretics were completely divorced from their social and economic environment, but he sees them reacting, as their teachings make clear, against the excessive preoccupation with material concerns rather than calling for social changes and material improvements. DDR medievalists dismiss these facts as irrelevant on the grounds that the more well-to-do also turned to heresy for "class" reasons—some because they thought their social standing within the ruling class threatened, others because they hoped to appropriate some of the Church's lands. No evidence is offered to support these claims; perhaps for this reason the most recent DDR survey of German history, *Grundriss*, passes over this issue in its discussion of the heretical move-

[30]Stern and Gericke, *Deutschland*, pp. 108ff.; Werner, *Gesellschaftliche Grundlagen*, pp. 11–12; Erbstösser, *ZfG* 8 (1960): suppl., 106.
[31]See Stern and Gericke, *Deutschland*, pp. 77ff., 87; Gottfried Koch, *Frauenfrage und Ketzertum im Mittelalter* (Berlin [East], 1962), pp. 13ff. See also, from a non-Marxist perspective, Arno Borst, *Die Katharer* (Stuttgart, 1953), pp. 226ff.

ments. Again, although it is regretfully noted that these movements contented themselves with a religious approach and did not arouse the masses to revolutionary activities, this failure is not perceived as arguing against the class-struggle thesis. One East German scholar, Bernhard Töpfer, hails such movements as furthering antifeudal ideologies and thus paving the way for subsequent revolutionary changes.[32]

The Church, for its part, fought back with inquisition, burnings at the stake, and the creation of orders of begging friars who, by their asceticism, were to restore faith in the spiritual integrity of the Church. In this manner, Gericke notes, "the Church could contain the religious manifestations of the extant social tensions and channel them into directions that did not threaten the continued existence of feudal society." In fact, he finds the Church so strengthened by its reforms and innovations that it became for some centuries the fulcrum of the feudal system of Western and Central Europe.[33]

The German State and the Holy Roman Empire

East German analyses of both the German kingdom and the Holy Roman Empire resemble the traditional studies in the questions they raise and the emphases they apply. The point of departure, however, is always the probe of socioeconomic conditions. The formation of the first German state is related to needs that grew out of the feudal system; the ability of King Otto I (936–973) to extend German power to Italy, in turn, is attributed to the rapid growth of the productive forces in Germany. Population increases, the opening up of new arable land, improved agricultural tools and techniques, and not least the presumedly constructive effects of the class struggles between peasants and lords are credited with producing an amount of social wealth that raised the German kingdom to the foremost power in Europe and enabled it too set out on its expansionist ventures.[34]

---

[32]Stern and Gericke, *Deutschland*, pp. 77–78, 214; Koch, pp. 156ff.; compare those works with Herbert Grundmann, *Religiöse Bewegungen im Mittelalter* (Berlin, 1935), pp. 29ff., 157ff., 188ff., 194ff., and 476ff. In addition, see Grundmann in *Archiv für Kulturgeschichte* 37 (1955): 163ff.; Borst, *Die Katherer*, pp. 92 n. 13, 104; *Grundriss*, p. 107; Töpfer, "Volksbewegungen und Gesellschaftlicher Fortschritt im 14. und 15. Jahrhundert in West- und Mitteleuropa," *ZfG* 26 (1978): 729.

[33]Stern and Gericke, *Deutschland*, pp. 79–80, 84ff. (quotation on p. 87).

[34]See *Grundriss*, pp. 81–82. The systematic correlation in *Grundriss* of the changes in production—the material foundation—with political developments—the ideological superstructure—is indicative of the efforts DDR historians are making to

Although socioeconomic conditions are accorded primary consideration, East German medievalists do not ignore other factors that went into the making of the German state. Thus, they have also explored the ethnic origins of that state, and a considerable literature has evolved around this particular issue.[35] In this context, special attention has been paid to the impact the feudal system had on the emergence of a sense of community through its sponsorship of collective activities—the clearing of forests and the establishment of new settlements—and through the common living standards and styles that were evolved within the system. Even shared experiences in the class struggles are claimed to have strengthened these ties, as did the common defense against Norman and Hungarian invaders. At a later date, concomitant with the growth of the towns, trade relations also are held to have furthered this sense of cohesion.[36]

Some East German authors also find cultural influences at work in this coalescence. In this context, the beginning formation of the German language has received some attention. Although it is granted that the German language was little more than a loose aggregation of regional dialects at this stage, these dialects are found to have shared traits that distinguished them from their Romance counterparts. There is some difference of opinion, however, as to how far this sense of commonality extended. Whereas Bartmuss sees it as being confined to the ruling class, *Grundriss* looks upon it as the foundation of an emerging people. Whatever the extent of these cultural bonds, they are considered significant as prefigurations (Vorformen) of a national consciousness. As such, they serve as additional proof of Germany's separateness from an alleged Western community.[37]

What has also been of concern to DDR scholars is the question of whether the state of the Saxon kings was structurally a novel creation or simply the renamed East Frankish kingdom—a question that has long preoccupied non-Marxists as well. Bartmuss has argued that the state of Henry I rested on a different material foundation—a more advanced feudal foundation—than the preceding East Frankish kingdom and was therefore a novel creation.

---

improve their methods and come closer to fulfilling the tasks they have set themselves. Stern and Bartmuss (*Deutschland*) and Streisand still fail to develop such a direct correlation between basis and superstructure.

[35]Müller-Mertens, "Regnum," pp. 321–22; Bartmuss, *Geburt*, pp. 94ff.; Wolfgang Eggert, *Das ostfränkisch-deutsche Reich in der Auffassung seiner Zeitgenossen* (Vienna, 1973); *Grundriss*, pp. 75–76.

[36]*Grundriss*, pp. 75, 80; Mottek, *Wirtschaftsgeschichte Deutschlands*, vol. 1, pp. 67–78.

[37]Müller-Mertens, "Regnum," p. 323; *Grundriss*, p. 80; Stern and Bartmuss, *Deutschland*, pp. 164–65; Töpfer, review, *ZfG*, 13 (1965): 1089–90.

Joachim Herrmann and Wolfgang Eggert have rejected this thesis on the grounds that there was no change in the foundation and that whatever changes occurred were merely shifts in political power. Although *Grundriss* uses some of Bartmuss' arguments, it does not take an explicit stand on the issue.[38]

To DDR authors, this question was at first not only a historical one but also one fraught with political implications. In taking it up, they saw themselves as the authors of a genuinely national historiography, in contrast to West German historians, whose "Western-oriented, all-European" approach led most of them to regard such questions as irrelevant. Whether or not this was true in the early post-World War II period, West Germans have since dealt at length with this problem, and recent West German surveys of the period agree with the prevailing East German view that the German state evolved out of the East Frankish one. Perhaps because the issue has lost its political import, the authors of *Grundriss* did not deal with it in their survey.[39]

Under Henry I and his successor, Otto I, the central power was strengthened and the reins of government tightened. DDR historians view this consolidation as "progressive" and in accord with the historical trend. They deplore therefore the efforts of Otto and his successors to expand their domain into Italy. This, of course, is a question that has long occupied German historians. In the East German view, the Italian campaigns merely diverted the German rulers from their "historical task" of strengthening their power at home (as did the English and French kings). The creation of the Holy Roman Empire thus is viewed as but the outgrowth of Otto I's greed for booty and power and his desire to consolidate his Italian conquests by establishing his ascendancy over the Church. Yet these same authors acknowledge that Otto first moved into Italy to forestall attempts by the dukes of Bavaria and Swabia to strengthen their own territorial power by seizing Italian lands. Had the two princes done so, such territorial aggrandizement would have weakened the central power in Germany. At the same time, Otto's alliance with the papacy strengthened his ties with the Ger-

[38]See Bartmuss, *Geburt*; Bartmuss, in Stern and Bartmuss, *Deutschland*, pp. 162ff.; Herrmann, "Sozialökonomische Grundlagen," pp. 787–89; Eggert, *Ostfränkisch-deutsche Reich*; *Grundriss*, p. 75–76. See also Müller-Mertens, *Das Zeitalter der Ottonen* (Berlin [East], 1955), pp. 31ff. Müller-Mertens was the first East German medievalist to see the German state evolving out of its East Frankish predecessor. In a more recent study he argues that a "German" state did not come into being until after the struggle of the investitures; see *Regnum Teutonicum* (Berlin [East], 1970).
[39]See Bartmuss, *Geburt*, p. 88; Müller-Mertens, *Zeitalter*, pp. 11–12. For recent West German views see Joseph Fleckenstein, in Gebhardt, vol. 1, pp. 225–26; Bosl, in ibid., vol. 1, pp. 762–63. See also Geoffrey Barraclough, *The Origins of Modern Germany* (New York, 1963), pp. 23–26.

man hierarchy, that major support of his government. It can thus be argued—as Geoffrey Barraclough, the Anglo-American medievalist, has done—that Otto's intervention in Italy benefited rather than impaired German interests. Barraclough has also shown that the involvement in Italian affairs of Otto's immediate successors, Otto II and Otto III, furthered rather than harmed German interests. On the other hand, when their successors, preoccupied with German concerns, neglected their Italian commitments, the papacy was able to reassert itself. By allying itself with the German princes, it successfully challenged the German kings on their home ground.[40]

The investiture contest, in turn, led to prolonged intervention in Italy, because to the German kings the right to ecclesiastical investiture was of crucial political import. After having been a mainstay of the Ottonian empire, the German bishops had, in the Salic era, become more concerned with consolidating their position in their own territories than with supporting the central power. To lose control over ecclesiastical investitures meant therefore a serious political threat to the German rulers, whose authority was already being assailed by the lay princes. The German situation thus differed sharply from conditions in England and France, where the emerging central power was looked upon by the hierarchy as a bulwark against political anarchy. For this reason, the unfavorable comparisons DDR authors make between the German expeditions to Italy and the stay-at-home policies of the English and French kings are rather pointless. They ignore the fact that the English and French rulers could give up their investiture rights without weakening their political power, whereas the German monarchs could not. Although Gericke, for one, is aware of this crucial difference, he nonetheless fails to draw the corresponding conclusions.[41]

If the German kings ought not to have gone to Italy to recover their power, where (in the East German view) should they have looked for support? DDR scholars insist that Henry IV ought to have allied himself with the towns and the peasants who constituted also the forces of progress. Gericke and others note with approval that Henry IV did try to find allies among the peasants and towns, but they also complain that he never made adequate use of these allies. Gericke suggests that this failure might be attributed to Henry's class status as a feudal lord, which made it impossible for him to wholeheartedly ally himself with his "class enemies." The fact was that neither peasants nor townsmen were as

[40]Streisand, p. 38; Stern and Bartmuss, *Deutschland*, pp. 186–88; *Grundriss*, pp. 82–83; Barraclough, *Origins*, pp. 49ff., esp. 65ff.

[41]Stern and Gericke, *Deutschland*, p. 116; Heinz Köller and Bernhard Töpfer, *Frankreich* (Berlin [East], 1969), vol. 1, pp. 81–82.

yet a match for the knightly horsemen and hence were not very effective allies. Henry, in turn, as Gericke and Mottek also point out, was often hard pressed by his many enemies and could not always provide help to the towns in their struggles with the feudal nobility. In consequence, the latter at times would side with the princes.[42]

Ultimately, Henry IV's efforts to restore a strong central power led to his overthrow by his son, Henry V, in league with the princes. Thus the "conflict within the ruling class" ended with the victory of the princes. The autonomous position of the latter, both lay and ecclesiastical, was not impaired when Henry V finally reached a compromise agreement with the papacy in the Concordat of Worms. In Gericke's words, the princes had become a "third power, equally independent of emperor and pope," and strong enough now to proceed with the consolidation of their territorial domains at the expense of the central power.[43]

One East German medievalist, Eckhard Müller-Mertens, has welcomed this outcome of the investiture contest on the grounds that a strong central government would not have corresponded to the realities of the feudal order. In Müller-Mertens' opinion, the opposition of the higher nobility to Henry IV was progressive because it led to the formation of regionally administered territories (*Landesherrschaften*) that served the needs of the feudal system more efficiently than a centralized state could. "What was at stake was not the question of centralism or particularism in the German constitution, but the ending of the feudal dismemberment that had taken place in the early Middle Ages—a centralization within the existing decentralization." Similarly, Hans Mottek has argued that decentralization and the continuing clashes among the feudal ruling class made it easier for the German towns during the twelfth and thirteenth centuries to expand and achieve independence and thus contribute to the rapid increase in productivity during that period. The peasants, too, Mottek claims, benefited from this decentralization, because it strengthened their position in their class struggles and helped them improve their condition. In this view, the weakness of the central government became harmful only at a later date, when the socioeconomic needs of the urban bourgeoisie required a strong central power. [44]

These arguments have more recently been refined by Bern-

---

[42]Stern and Gericke, *Deutschland*, pp. 16ff., 98, 111ff., 115; Mottek, *Wirtschaftsgeschichte Deutschlands*, vol. 1, pp. 166–67; *Grundriss*, pp. 97–98. Also see Barraclough, *Origins*, p. 136.

[43]Stern and Gericke *Deutschland* p. 119; also *Grundriss*, p. 98.

[44]Müller-Mertens, "Regnum," pp. 328ff. (quotation on p. 335); Mottek, *Wirtschaftsgeschichte Deutschlands*, vol. 1, pp. 124–25.

hard Töpfer. Töpfer points out that the princes derived their increasing power not only from the weakness of the kings/emperors, but also from changes in the socioeconomic "basis" of German feudal society. These changes resulted from the growing productivity of the towns, which affected the economy of the rural areas as well. To buy the goods the towns had to offer, the peasants sought to produce and retain more of their "surplus product," while the lords increased their exactions. In this contest the peasants were in a stronger position: they could escape to the towns or migrate to regions where their obligations would be less demanding. Economic and legal concessions thus had to be granted to them. Because such concessions could be afforded more easily by the wealthier feudal lords than by minor ones, the feudal magnates were able to take over properties of the lesser nobility and thus increase their own power.

Given this inevitable trend, Töpfer argues, it was not the immediate task of the German rulers to crush the power of the princes. Rather, their main concern should have been to adjust to this process of regional concentration and build up their own landed holdings—the crucial source of strength for any lord in the feudal system. Only by expanding their own territory in Germany could the kings/emperors have redressed the balance of power and outdistanced the princes.[45]

Whatever their views on these matters, DDR scholars give but grudging approval to Frederick I (Barbarossa) (1152–1190) for what traditionally has been hailed as a great achievement—the stabilization once more of the central power. Gericke and others complain that this stability was attained at the price of further concessions to the princes, in dissociation from the towns, and was therefore only a "relative" one. Töpfer, whose overall judgment of Frederick is somewhat more favorable, regrets that the monarch, after some auspicious beginnings, did not enlarge his territorial holdings in Germany as much as he might have. All are agreed that Frederick ought not to have undertaken his Italian campaigns in his quest for the riches of the northern Italian cities. Because of their economic superiority, these cities could put armies into the field that fought off all of Frederick's attempts to subjugate them.

Frederick II (1215–1250) in turn is rebuked by DDR historians, as he is by non-Marxist scholars, for residing in Italy and neglecting his German duties. What is seen as especially reprehensible is Frederick's intervention against his son, Henry VII, when the latter, as regent in Germany, sought to win the support of the

[45]Bernhard Töpfer and Evamarie Engel, *Vom staufischen Imperium zum Hausmachtskönigtum* (Weimar, 1976), pp. 67, 83–84, 86ff., 95ff., 106–7, 109.

towns against the princes. In the end, by turning over to the princes full control of the towns and granting them judicial and administrative sovereignty in their territories, Frederick "legalized" princely particularism. With this measure, Gericke comments, "the central power gave itself up."[46]

Along with other East German historians, Gericke sees these conclusions confirmed in the subsequent course of events. In a circular reasoning not uncharacteristic of their a-priori approach, these authors note that when the German towns joined forces against the princes during the rulerless Interregnum after the death of Frederick II, there was no central government around which the towns could have rallied. At that, Erhard Voigt concludes, the attempt of a central power to subdue the princes with the help of the towns would at best have not been "a hopeless struggle" (kein aussichtsloses Ringen). Because the towns did not act "out of a deeper understanding of the objective laws of feudal society," Voigt also wonders how many towns would have been willing to side with the king, who had little to offer them. In his textbook, published a few years later, Voigt judges the possibility of such an alliance somewhat more positively in two passages, less so in a third. He and others also point out, however, that in any alliance between king and towns the latter would no longer have accepted the king's unlimited power of taxation and other royal prerogatives. Rudolph von Habsburg, the first recognized ruler after the Interregnum, found this out when he imposed heavy levies on the towns after they had helped to secure his election. Any permanent coalition between central power and towns thus would have provided but limited help to that power.[47]

Töpfer and his school, on the other hand, again find the increase in princely strength a process in keeping with socioeconomic developments. Although they too deplore Frederick II's intervention against his son when the latter sought a rapprochement with the cities, they blame Frederick primarily for his failure to expand his territorial holdings in Germany as a basis for the eventual establishment of a national monarchy. Less speculative than

[46]See Stern and Gericke, Deutschland, pp. 137–38, 142–43, 147ff., 163ff. (quotation on p. 164); Müller-Mertens, Zeitalter, pp. 337–38; Grundriss, pp. 105, 107–8; Erhard Voigt, "Zum Charakter der 'staufischen' Städtepolitik," in Die Volksmassen: Gestalter der Geschichte, ed. Bartmuss et al. (Berlin [East], 1962), pp. 19ff.; Töpfer and Engel, Imperium, pp. 124ff., 136–37. Significantly, Streisand mentions neither Frederick I nor Frederick II.
[47]Stern and Gericke, Deutschland, pp. 166–67; Voigt, pp. 52–53; Stern and Voigt, Deutschland von der Mitte des 13. bis zum ausgehenden 15. J[ahr]h[undert] (Berlin [East], 1965), pp. 5, 78, 82, 206; also Müller-Mertens, Zeitalter, pp. 338–40; Siegfried Epperlein, "Städtebünde und Feudalgewalten im 13. Jahrhunderts," ZfG 20 (1972): 704, 708, 718.

Gericke's thesis, this argument too seems hard to fit into the existing conditions.[48]

Because the Holy Roman Empire receives attention only insofar as it affected German developments, only one question that transcends its impact on Germany needs to be touched upon here. With its religious underpinning, professing to represent a universal idea, did the Empire plan to embrace the entire world? Like their non-Marxist counterparts, most East German medievalists deny such intentions. They conclude that the concept of a holy empire (*sacrum imperium*) served merely to establish the divine nature of the Empire and to legitimize the imperial policies of the German monarchs and their aggressive moves against their immediate neighbors.[49] DDR authors also reject as unhistorical, however, attempts of West German authors to present the Holy Roman Empire as a forerunner of current endeavors to unite Western Europe—indeed an untenable analogy, given the suspicions the Empire aroused among the other countries of Europe. Similarly, East German medievalists dismiss claims of a special civilizing or "Occidental" (*abendländisch*) mission on behalf of the Empire. Such assessments are scorned as hypocritical attempts to conceal the aggressive character of the policies of the emperors.[50]

The claim to a civilizing mandate has traditionally served to justify Germany's eastward expansion in the twelfth and thirteenth centuries. DDR scholars, on the other hand, view this "thrust to the east" as but another manifestation of feudal aggressiveness. As *Grundriss* explains it, feudal lords found it profitable, because of the growth of commerce and a burgeoning money economy, to expand their holdings in order to appropriate the "surplus product" of additional peasants. For this purpose, they called on German peasants to settle on the newly acquired lands east of the Elbe river. They were seconded by the Church, which was itself, as is stressed, a main beneficiary of these conquests. The Church held out the prospect of eternal salvation to all those who by settling among the heathen Slavs would help to Christianize these lands. Large numbers of peasants, attracted by promises of lighter payments and services to their lords, migrated east. So did merchants and artisans who wished to escape oppression at home.

[48]Töpfer and Engel, *Imperium*, pp. 200ff., 210–11, 235–36, 309ff.
[49]See Koch, "Die mittelalterliche Kaiserpolitik im Spiegel der bürgerlichen Historiographie des 19. und 20. J[ahr]h[underts]," *ZfG* 10 (1962): 1837ff.; Koch, "Sacrum Imperium," ibid. 16 (1968): 596ff.; Töpfer, "Reges Provinciales," Ibid. 22 (1974): 1348ff.; Töpfer and Engel, *Imperium*, pp. 117, 130. Compare these works with Stern and Gericke, (*Deutschland*, pp. 151–52, 270 n. 2), who impute aspirations on the scale of the Roman Empire to the emperors.
[50]Koch, in *Kritik der bürgerlichen Geschichtsschreibung: Handbuch*, ed. Werner Berthold et al. (Cologne, 1973), pp. 121ff.; also Büttner, " 'Abendland'ideologie," pp. 1089ff.; Stern, "Klerikal-imperialistische Abendlandideologie," pp. 286ff.

East German analyses of this eastward advance also differ from traditional ones in regard to the methods of *Ostexpansion*. Unlike Western historians, DDR scholars view it as essentially violent, the product of wars and forcible occupation. Western medievalists acknowledge that the Germans waged wars in some areas but maintain that the greater part of the eastward expansion proceeded at the invitation of Slav princes and nobles who welcomed the more productive and industrious Germans. Most East Germans, in turn, condemn the treaties concluded by German and Slav landed proprietors as endeavors of the Slav feudal lords to strengthen their class position vis-à-vis their own peasantry. DDR historians find further manifestations of this class struggle in the resistance to the German advance put up by the Slav peasants. Yet, whether that resistance was in fact class-oriented and antifeudal and, if so, how widespread it was is not clear from the evidence that is offered.[51]

The emphasis East German scholarship places on the aggressive and violent nature of Ostexpansion has raised some awkward political questions. The land that was conquered between the Elbe and Oder rivers constitutes in its larger part the territory of the present-day German Democratic Republic. Thus the question arises whether this territory is historically Slav and might thus be claimed by Poland; for these and other reasons, after World War II, Poland claimed as historically hers the German lands east of the Oder and Neisse Rivers. The East German answer has been that Germans have earned their claim to the DDR territory by helping develop it, as they did not do for the land in Italy, where no Germans settled; this argument, of course, could also be applied to the formerly German lands east of the Oder-Neisse line. (Unlike their Polish counterparts, DDR historians do not justify that transfer of land to Poland on historical grounds; see chapter 9). At the same time, to avoid any semblance of national superiority, it is acknowledged that the Slavs also made significant contributions to the development of that area. And in being absorbed into their German environment, they are credited, too, with having infused a Slav strand into German ethnicity ("Ethnogenese").[52]

[51]Streisand, p. 41; Stern and Gericke, *Deutschland*, pp. 168ff.; *Grundriss*, pp. 103–4; Epperlein, *Bauernbedrückung und Bauernwiderstand im hohen Mittelalter* (Berlin [East], 1960), pp. 139ff., 154–55; Koch, in Berthold et al., *Kritik*, pp. 127–28; compare with Barraclough, *Origins*, pp. 249ff.; Herbert Grundmann, in Gebhardt, vol. 1, 579ff.

[52]Boleslaw Wiewora, *The Polish-German Frontier in the Light of International Law* (Poznan, 1964), p. 61; Mottek-Stern exchange, in *ZfG* 3 (1955): 222–23; Stern and Gericke, *Deutschland*, p. 168; Mottek, *Wirtschaftsgeschichte Deutschlands*, vol. 1, p. 126; *Grundriss*, p. 104; Herrmann, *ZfG* 18 (1970): suppl., 307. For a more differentiated account, see Töpfer and Engel, *Imperium*, pp. 211ff.

An ambiguity remains, however. It is reflected in recurring complaints that the process of Germanization created class divisions along ethnic lines, with German nobles controlling much of the land and German merchants forming a ruling patriciate in many cities. Thus, socioethnic tensions are found to have burdened German-Slav relations over the centuries, the implication being that these relations were set on their proper course only recently with the removal of the German minorities from the countries of eastern Europe and the concomitant creation of socialist societies in that same area.[53]

DDR authors do not regard Ostexpansion as an unmitigated blessing for Germany. Like the expeditions to Italy, Ostexpansion weakened Germany's central power—in this case by vastly increasing the territorial holdings of princes and nobles and thus rendering them even more independent of the central authority. The rulers, for their part, took no direct part in the eastward advance and derived but limited gains from these conquests. In fact, Gericke argues that Ostexpansion was undertaken in part to increase the independence of the feudal magnates. As a further result, the center of political gravity in Germany shifted toward the east, where the kings owned few lands and thus were weakest.[54]

The decline of the central power continued during the following centuries. In the factual assessment of this decline, East German analyses do not differ from non-Marxist ones. Yet, in keeping with the didactic mandate of the Marxist historian, DDR medievalists are concerned not merely with failures and setbacks (and occasional advances) but also with opportunities used or missed to save Germany from her fragmentation. Many authors maintain that a consistent policy of building up the royal domain could still have restored the strength and authority of the central power. Instead of acquiring territory in Germany, however, the kings/emperors moved into Poland and Hungary, compounding the difficulties they invited by their continued expeditions to Italy. It is pointed out, too, that the drive for territorial gains was bound to be futile as long as the monarchy was not transformed from an elective to a hereditary one. Because the electing princes controlled the choice of the German monarch, they often chose successors from a family other than that of the last incumbent to keep the central power from becoming too strong. Such successors did not inherit the holdings of their predecessors and had to try to enlarge their own territories. Given the uncertainties of succession, the territorial

[53]Stern and Gericke, *Deutschland*, pp. 185, 191–92, 205–8; Streisand, p. 41; *Grundriss*, p. 104; Töpfer and Engel, *Imperium*, pp. 222ff.
[54]Stern and Gericke, *Deutschland*, pp. 178–79, 206–7; *Grundriss*, p. 104; Töpfer and Engel, *Imperium*, p. 224.

policies of these rulers frequently were determined by fleeting family interests rather than by the enduring concerns of the central power, with results that were often disastrous for Germany.[55]

By the fourteenth century, the feudal order had reached its full potential. Even those authors who see the princely decentralization of earlier days as "progressive," on the grounds that it furthered the development of the feudal system, are agreed that by the fourteenth century a strong central power was needed to deal with the changing demands of production. The centers of productive growth now were the cities, and it should have been the concern of the central power to protect them from princely intrusions. Many East German historians still consider it the gravest mistake of the German rulers that they did not ally themselves with the cities, which could have helped them. Representing the forces of progress, the cities were more than ever the "natural" allies of the kings/emperors against their "relentless" opponents, the princes (Müller-Mertens).

DDR historians find particularly deplorable the unwillingness of Louis IV ("The Bavarian") (1314–1347) to take advantage of the antipapal movement which was spreading through Germany during his reign and in which the urban centers played an especially active role. Repudiated by Pope John XXII as a usurper and abandoned by most German princes, Louis ought to have allied himself with the cities in their feud with the papacy. The cities objected to the pope's interference as a danger to peace and to the orderly conduct of business; they were also resentful of the Church's financial exactions, tax exemption, and commercial and manufacturing competition. These grievances exploded into open rebellion, with cities expelling bishops and priests and withholding their payments. "It would have been the task of the king," Voigt maintains, "to put himself at the head of the spontaneously growing antipapal movement and with its help compel oppositional princes to either join him or remain neutral, force the pope to rescind his [measures against Louis], and strengthen the authority of the crown." At the same time, Voigt concedes that such a fight would have been lengthy and difficult. As to its outcome, he again can only assume that the struggle would have been "by no means without a chance of success."[56] Yet, quite apart from these uncertainties, one wonders why a Marxist historian would expect the kings/emper-

[55]Stern and Voigt, *Deutschland*, pp. 77ff.; *Grundriss*; pp. 111–12, 119–20; Müller-Mertens, "Regnum," pp. 341–42; Töpfer and Engel, pp. 295ff., especially pp. 301–2, 341–42; Streisand, p. 45.
[56]Müller-Mertens, *Zeitalter*, p. 337; Stern and Voigt, *Deutschland*, pp. 205ff. (quotation on p. 206), 216–17; *Grundriss*, p. 118; *Kaiser, Volk und Avignon: Ausgewählte Quellen zur antikurialen Bewegung in Deutschland in der ersten Hälfte des 14. Jahrhunderts*, ed. Otto Berthold et al. (Berlin [East], 1960).

ors, who are regarded as essentially feudal lords in the Marxist view, to side with the cities against their fellow lords. Gericke, it may be recalled, did raise this question in another context, but he did not raise it here.

In chiding the kings for bypassing the cities, DDR authors also ignore the cities' reluctance to ally themselves with the kings. As these same authors are forced to admit, the cities had reservations about a strong central power, despite their occasional cooperation with that power. They had not found the German rulers reliable partners in their occasional coalitions and preferred therefore to deal with the princes. Perhaps that was why they never tried to expand their regional leagues into a nationwide one to establish a central power on their own terms. During the fourteenth and fifteenth centuries, they flourished as never before, outdistancing their counterparts in the more centralized English and French states. Moreover, if the English and French experience taught them anything, it was that demands imposed by a strong central power would have proved far more burdensome and less easily circumvented than those imposed by the princes. Although this is acknowledged in East German literature, no explanation is provided for why an alliance between kings and cities would have nonetheless been a realistic alternative. The point of these analyses, however, is not merely to find solutions within the existing context but also to show what could have been done, had the laws of history as uncovered by Marx been known and applied at that time. Yet, as the controversy between the Gericke and Töpfer camps shows, even knowledge of these laws and the wisdom of hindsight do not always provide clear-cut answers.[57]

Preoccupation with the fate of the central power is evident also in the accounts of later developments. Thus the antipapal movement that joined with the cities to rally peasants, lower nobility, a few princes, and even some bishops and priests against Rome is hailed as the first national movement in Germany. On the other hand, the Golden Bull (1356) is seen primarily as perpetuating German particularism. Yet that document declared the king's election by the German electoral princes as sufficient to establish his imperial authority, thus dispensing with the pope's confirmation. What concerns DDR scholars most, however, is the acknowledgment in the Bull of the electors' privileges of judicial

---

[57]Stern and Gericke, *Deutschland,* p. 98; Stern and Voigt, *Deutschland,* pp. 174ff., 182ff., 78, 216, 251, 347 n. 56; Mottek, *Wirtschaftsgeschichte Deutschlands,* vol. 1 pp. 167ff., 186ff.; *Grundriss,* p. 126; Müller-Mertens, "Regnum," pp. 338–39; Brigitte Berthold et al., "Die Stellung des Bürgertums in der deutschen Feudalgesellschaft . . . ." *ZfG* 21 (1973): 211ff., 217; Epperlein, "Städtebünde," pp. 695ff., especially pp. 704, 708, 716–18.

sovereignty, coinage, and mining in their territories: by thus assuring the electors of their electoral independence, the Golden Bull
gave new legal sanction to the fragmentation of Germany.[58]

The analyses of the popular antipapal movement as a national
movement and of the Golden Bull as (at least by implication) an
antinational one, despite its emancipatory anti-Vatican thrust, are
indicative also of the Marxist concept of the nation as primarily a
social unit and only secondarily a political one. The popular antipapal movement is praised for rallying various classes and strata into a
coalition that represented the true interests of what eventually became the nation. The Golden Bull, on the other hand, deepened the
cleavages within the empire by endowing the princes/electors with
new privileges. By Marxist criteria, it had a disuniting, anti-
"national" impact.[59]

Even though East German medievalists condemn the Golden
Bull as, in Marx's words, the "Basic Law of German Vielstaaterei,"
they insist nonetheless that the decline of the central power could
still have been halted by the expansion of the royal domain within
Germany. Because he pursued such a territorial policy, Charles IV
(1347–1378) receives high marks, even though he issued the Bull,
for pursuing such a territorial policy. He is taken to task, on the
other hand, for reaching for the crowns of Poland and Hungary—
moves that diverted him and his successors from their German
tasks and accounted in part for the rapid diminution of their territorial possessions both in Germany and outside. As a result, King/
Emperor Sigismund (1410–1437) was left with hardly any lands of
his own within the empire except for Bohemia, and Bohemia he did
not control until the last three years of his reign, because the
Hussite movement kept him from taking it over.[60]

Altogether, the fifteenth century, with its unending interne-
cine wars, presented a melancholy picture of imperial decline.
Even the most persistent DDR critics of the emperors' policies are
forced to admit that by then the central power could no longer be
rehabilitated by a change in those policies. Its only chance of survival lay in a fundamental restructuring of the empire's constitutional system. East German historians have therefore paid considerable attention to various contemporary plans which sought to
strengthen the central power. One in particular, known as the *Re-*

[58]See Stern and Voigt, *Deutschland*, pp. 210ff.; *Grundriss*, pp. 118–19. On the
"national" perspective of the Golden Bull, see Holborn, vol. 1, p. 28; Barraclough,
Origins, pp. 315–17.
[59]Alfred Kosing, *Nation in Geschichte und Gegenwart* (Berlin [East], 1976); also
Andreas Dorpalen, "Marxism and National Unity: The Case of Germany," *Review of Politics* 39 (1977): 506–8.
[60]Streisand, pp. 46–47; Stern and Voigt, *Deutschland*, pp. 215ff., 246, 251ff.; *Grundriss*, pp. 119–20, 125–26.

formatio Sigismundi, has fascinated DDR scholars. It not only called for the curbing of princely and ecclesiastical powers but also proposed social and economic reforms that aimed at the very foundations of the feudal order. The anonymous author demanded an end to serfdom, the secularization of all Church-owned lands, the abolition of guilds, and strict control of commercial activities; he also warned that the common people would resort to force if they could not achieve their goals otherwise.[61]

The *Reformatio* was published shortly after the end of the Hussite Wars, the "culmination of class struggles . . . in the early part of the fifteenth century" (*Grundriss*). By adopting some Hussite demands, the *Reformatio* helped channel the revolutionary impulses of that movement into Germany's social unrest. With its attacks on the Church, that bulwark of feudalism, and on the profiteering of merchants, Voigt observes, "the *Reformatio Sigismundi* has rightly been called the 'trumpet of the Peasants' War.' " It reflects the realization that the ruling circles were everywhere pursuing egoistical policies and that only the "common man," the popular masses—under the leadership of a "people's emperor" who would arise from among the people, as the *Reformatio* envisions it—could bring about a revolutionary change in Germany." The continuing unrest in town and country throughout the fifteenth century seemed proof that the masses were working at their "historical task."[62]

The Peasantry

Because the peasants rank as a "main" class of the feudal order, their role as makers of history is a central topic of East German research. The peasants are credited not only with sustaining feudal society as producers—in itself a major historical contribution—but also with having made possible, by providing ever-larger food surpluses, the increased division of labor that led to the rise of the towns. Similarly, deforestation and the procurement of new arable land are viewed as achievements of peasants rather than of lords, as has traditionally been the case.[63]

Another topic of central significance to DDR scholars is the

[61]Stern and Voigt, *Deutschland,* pp. 169ff., 231ff., 246–48, 251–53, 255ff.; *Grundriss,* pp. 123ff.

[62]Stern and Voigt, *Deutschland,* pp. 172–73, 257–58 (quotation on p. 258).

[63]See Stern and Gericke, *Deutschland,* pp. 44–45; *Grundriss,* pp. 86–87; Epperlein, *Bauernbedrückung,* p. 12. On deforestation as a peasant achievement see also the West German historian Wilhelm Abel, in *HbDtWSG,* vol. 1, p. 170.

rural class struggle in its various manifestations and in its impact on political and social developments. Peasant unrest has been considered a major reason for the revival of a central power in the early tenth century, as has already been mentioned. Subsequent efforts on the part of the nobles to reinforce their administrative and judicial authority are similarly explained as reactions to the growing strength of the peasantry. Moreover, work slowdowns by peasants, withholdings of payments and services, escapes to the towns, and migrations to regions offering better working conditions are viewed not just as disturbances of the existing order but also as stimuli to reforms and innovations that helped to develop the feudal system to its highest potential. DDR authors claim that peasant resistance forced the landlords to reduce the peasants' obligations and thus improve their immediate lot. They also maintain that the easing of burdens made increased productivity more attractive, because the peasants now benefited directly from their additional output. Here again, however, cause-and-effect connections are difficult to establish, because no solid evidence is provided; what are claimed to have been hard-won concessions may well have been, in many cases, accommodations for the lords' convenience. More convincingly, Ostexpansion, which raised rural productivity to new heights, has been attributed in part to conflicts between peasants and landlords. Siegfried Epperlein has shown that peasants went east, not primarily because their homeland was overpopulated (it often was not), but in order to escape from oppression and exploitation. Epperlein's materials are too limited to permit firm conclusions, but his thesis clearly deserves further study.[64]

As the "highest" form of the class struggle, the peasant rising receives special attention. Few risings occurred between the tenth and fourteenth centuries, but these few have been analyzed at great length, among them the two most important ones—the Saxon peasant rebellion of 1075 and the Stedinger revolt in northwestern Germany, which continued for some thirty years in the 13th century. At best, these risings secured to the peasants an easing of their economic burdens; none preserved for them the political and social rights that they were defending. Such nonfeudal liberties could not be maintained, it is argued, because the feudal order had

[64]See Stern and Gericke, *Deutschland*, pp. 41, 49–51, 63ff.; Stern and Voigt, *Deutschland*, p. 4; Mottek, *Wirtschaftsgeschichte Deutschlands*, vol. 1, pp. 132–33; *Grundriss*, pp. 101–2; and Epperlein, *Bauernbedrückung, passim*. Epperlein's thesis has been confirmed at least indirectly by the West German historian Abel, in *HbDtWSG*, vol. 1, pp. 198ff. For Western Europe, a clear correlation between peasant freedom and colonization has been established by Bryce Lyon, "Medieval Real Estate Developments and Freedom," *AHR* 63 (1957–1958): 47ff.

not yet exhausted its progressive potential and was still capable of further development.[65]

Nonetheless, DDR authors find these risings significant because they see in them further evidence that the peasants, contrary to West German claims, were no mere pawns in the maneuvers of kings and nobles. It is therefore wrong, Gericke states, to look for the mainspring of social developments on the "seigneurial" side of the feudal order. "The impulses for 'social upward mobility' did not come from above, the peasants did not obtain their liberties by devoted service, but had to fight for them in various ways in bitter struggles. They had to defend them determinedly against the attacks of the feudal lords and were ready and able to do so." This deprecation of service as an avenue to social and economic betterment is directed against the West German medievalist Karl Bosl, who has pointed out the existence of such an avenue, using the rise of a new caste of royal officials, the *ministeriales*, as a prime example. Bosl's thesis challenges the very basis of the Marxist approach, because it attributes this rise to class cooperation rather than to class struggle. Denying the reality of such a path to social improvement is as useless as denying that peasant resistance can sometimes better the lot of the peasantry. What can be said is that, on balance, peasant resistance benefited the peasants as a class, thus improving conditions for larger numbers of them, though on a more modest scale, than did individual service.[66]

As still another manifestation of the class struggle, peasant involvement in heretical movements continues to receive careful attention. Unlike the heresies of the early feudal period, those of the later phases were primarily urban phenomena. Still, where heresies spread to rural areas, they are viewed as evidence of the growing significance and self-esteem of the peasantry. Even when the heretics' professed objectives were purely spiritual, DDR scholars view their attacks on the Church as a challenge to more than just the ecclesiastical order. Given the importance DDR scholars attribute to the Church's social function, they regard the heresies as threats to the feudal system as well.[67] More recent analyses have

---

[65]Stern and Gericke, *Deutschland*, pp. 97ff., 53ff.; Töpfer, "Volksbewegung, Ideologie und gesellschaflicher Fortschriftt [im] entwickelken Feudalismus," *ZfG* 25 (1977): 1162–63.

[66]Stern and Gericke, *Deutschland*, pp. 58–59; Bosl, *Frühformen der Gesellschaft im mittelalterlichen Europa* (Munich, 1964), pp. 156ff.

[67]See Stern and Gericke, *Deutschland*, pp. 73, 79; Stern and Voigt, *Deutschland*, pp. 165ff.; and Töpfer and Engel, *Imperium*, pp. 47–48, 182, 186. Surprisingly, no attempt has been made to reinforce the thesis of the close relationship of Church and the feudal system by pointing to the Church's practice of excommunicating peasants delinquent in their manorial obligations or imposing other religious penalties for offenses against the Church as a feudal lord. The Stedingers, for example, who refused to submit to the seigneurial lordship of the archbishop of

been careful, however, to emphasize the nonrevolutionary nature of the heretical movements—a reflection of the fact, it is noted, that "class contradictions" had not yet sharpened to a degree that made a collision inevitable. "[The] task [of the heresies]," Erbstösser concludes, "lay in their deepening the ideological cleavage between people and feudal church and in the creation of favorable conditions for future revolutionary events."[68]

During the fourteenth century, the lot of the peasants deteriorated. In addition to the crop failures and pest epidemics that swept the country, East German medievalists attribute the crisis to the greater economic strength of the cities, which could dictate prices to the countryside, keeping their own prices up and depressing those for agricultural products. At the same time, feudal lords tightened their hold on the peasantry, exacting increased payments and services from them to compensate for the diminished returns from their own grain sales; following Engels' lead, DDR authors speak of this period as a second serfdom. Finally, heavy indebtedness to urban money lenders also added to the peasants' difficulties.[69]

Peasant resistance to these burdens escalated into armed risings that became especially frequent during the fifteenth century. On the whole, these revolts yielded no benefits to the peasants; suppressed with the help of the princes, most of them left the peasants worse off than they had been before. Perhaps for that reason, these risings have received little attention from non-Marxist scholars. To East German historians they are important, however, because of the antifeudal tenor of some of the demands that were made. Moreover, unlike earlier revolts, these risings were no longer entirely local; some of them touched off upheavals elsewhere. Yet, as is regretfully noted, local parochialism prevented the merger of these various rebellions into one movement. Nor did the peasants join forces with the oppressed groups in the cities, let alone with the burghers, who increasingly lost their autonomy to the princes. Viewed as exploiters by the peasants, the burghers were at times as much the targets of peasant attacks as were their lords. As for the potentialities of such a town-country alliance, DDR authors point to the dynamics of the Hussite movement, which drew its strength from just such a coalition.[70]

Bremen, were branded as heretics, and a crusade was organized against them. See Epperlein, *Bauernbedrückung, passim*; Stern and Gericke, *Deutschland*, p. 56.

[68] Erbstösser, *Sozialreligiöse Strömungen im späten Mittelalter* (Berlin [East], 1970), especially pp. 154ff. (quotation on p. 156); Töpfer, "Volksbewegung, Ideologie," pp. 1164–65.

[69] Stern and Voigt, *Deutschland*, pp. 8ff., 93ff., 104ff., 123ff.; Mottek, *Wirtschaftsgeschichte Deutschlands*, vol. 1, pp. 225ff., 234ff.; *Grundriss*, p. 116; Berthold et al., "Stellung," pp. 211–12.

[70] Stern and Voigt, *Deutschland*, pp. 114–15, 169ff.; Berthold et al., "Stellung," pp. 211–12; *Grundriss*, pp. 123–24.

Underlying these analyses of the peasantry is the conviction that the peasants—as the largest element of the popular masses, ever the ultimate makers of history—must have played an important historical role. One merit of the East German accounts is that they give their due to the peasants as the tillers of the soil and as contributors to increased productivity. Moreover, their dialectical approach to the lord-peasant relationship, even if it focuses one-sidedly on the tensions, does convey a better sense of the interdependence of the two classes and their interaction upon each other than non-Marxist accounts that deal with them as separate rather than as interacting groups.[71]

Yet if one applies Engelberg's and Kuczynski's criteria, by which history, though rooted in the production process, is made primarily on the political plane (see chapter 1), the historical contribution of medieval peasantry appears considerably smaller. Töpfer, for one, has admitted as much. He credits the masses with having touched off changes in the governmental and ideological superstructure, but also notes that the concrete form that these changes assumed was determined by the reactions and interests of the ruling classes. "Here," he concludes, "the limits of the role of the popular masses in feudal society become evident."[72]

The Towns

The emergence of the medieval town marks for the Marxist historian another milestone in the growth of production. In this view, towns developed thanks to the production of surplus food, which made possible the separation of handcrafts from agriculture and the expansion of trade. Most East German medievalists reject what they call the "theory of continuity," which is advanced by some West German scholars who see in the rise of the German medieval town a compound of old Roman and new German elements—"the product of a fertile synthesis of Mediterranean urban traditions and the living style of the German north." DDR scholars do not deny that the sites and structures of towns were often determined by traditions, techniques, and experiences that can be traced back to Roman times, but they consider these aspects of secondary importance. Such "cultural-areal" ("kulturräumliche") views are assailed on the grounds that they ignore the socioeconomic bases of urban growth. What is deemed decisive in the formation of towns is not

[71]For a West German account that pays attention to the element of interaction, see Abel, in *HbDtWSG*, vol. 1, pp. 183ff.
[72]Töpfer, "Volksbewegung, Ideologie," p. 1162.

the new urban life that sprang up among the remnants of old Roman settlements, but the increase of productive forces that made such a revival possible. "The progressing social division of labor [i.e., the division into peasants, craftsmen, and traders] and the expansion of commodity production," Gericke notes, "constituted the economic roots of *all* feudal towns and the mainsprings of their development." Any other explanation would create an "irrational, ahistorical picture of the medieval town and its emergence in order to deny the operation of historical laws and the role of the popular masses."[73]

A major concern of East German medievalists has been to fit the towns' population, the *Bürgertum*, into the class system of the agrarian-oriented feudal order. Reflecting the uncertainties that go back to Marx and Engels, the medieval Bürgertum is defined variously as class, estate, and stratum, to mention only the most frequent and basic classifications.[74] In the early 1970's, the question of the Bürgertum's status was debated at length in the *Zeitschrift für Geschichtswissenschaft* and in the *Jahrbuch für Wirtschaftsgeschichte*.[75] The outcome was inconclusive. A minority of the participants maintained that the urban population was too divided in terms of status within the production process to qualify as a class, but the majority accepted the thesis that the urban citizenry coalesced into a class as a result of its adversary relationship to the feudal powers from the eleventh to the thirteenth centuries, during which time it fought for its freedom from its overlords. This conclusion, however, was qualified by various reservations expressed by some of the thesis' supporters. Moreover, all discussants agreed that even as a separate class the Bürgertum remained integrated into the feudal system, with its merchants serving as the connecting link between the different feudal units. By its economic progress, the Bürgertum injected fresh stimuli into that system, raising it to new levels of productivity.[76]

Still, because urban economic activity was essentially non-agrarian, the Bürgertum could constitute only a secondary class in the feudal order (see chapter 1, pp. 28–29). It retained that status even as the towns attained economic superiority over the countryside which had taken place by the fourteenth century. This ascen-

---

[73]Stern and Gericke, *Deutschland,* pp. 9–11 (italics in original), 18–20; Mottek, *Wirtschaftsgeschichte Deutschlands,* vol. 1, pp. 166ff.; Töpfer, "Volksbewegung, Ideologie," pp. 1163–64, 1167.

[74]For other terms, see Günter Vogler, "Probleme der Klassenentwicklung in der Feudalgesellschaft," *ZfG* 21 (1973): 1183–84.

[75]The debate can be found in *ZfG* 21 (1973) through 23 (1975) and in *JWG* 1973–74. A part of the debate is conveniently summarized in *ZfG* 21 (1973): 1505ff. See also the report on a more recent discussion in ibid. 27 (1979): 1176–77.

[76]Herrmann, "Prozess," p. 1233.

dancy did not lead to the early breakdown of the feudal agrarian order, it is explained, because feudal production methods kept dominating urban manufacture as well. Capitalist techniques were not applied until the fifteenth century, and then only on a limited scale. All in all, for both economic and political reasons, it took several centuries for capitalism—and with it a bourgeoisie that would rank as a primary class—to hold full sway.[77]

Although the towns did not challenge the feudal order as such, they did seek to attain greater freedom of action within that system. As class conflicts, these struggles for independence from feudal overlords have been probed at great length. (Few DDR authors note that some towns did acquire autonomy by peaceful agreement.) The communal movements that were formed to wrest power from the nobility are hailed as another example of the history-making powers of the popular masses. Yet once again the masses served as merely a supporting cast; the "creative" history-making leadership of the communal movement was in the hands of an urban patriciate—a merchant elite whose power, it is stressed, derived not from land ownership but from its mobile property and its money holdings. These men, moreover, were instrumental in creating new economic opportunities by expanding trade and building up capital. Given this record, their dominant role had already had Engels' approval: he saw in these major merchants the "revolutionary element in society which was otherwise stable—stable, so to speak, by heredity." Voigt calls them the "social carriers" of the available capital, which was just then, at the end of the thirteenth century, injecting new impulses into market production. However dubious the business practices of these merchants may have been, their activities "objectively" were "progressive" and their leadership role thus "historically" justified. Nonetheless, the ultimate credit is bestowed on the masses. "The success of the popular masses in the class struggle in town and country," Töpfer points out, "was a major cause of the further development of the productive forces in the upswing of the twelfth and thirteenth centuries. Only on the basis of the high level attained in small-scale production, both in handcrafts and agriculture, could the transition to capitalist practices get under way."[78]

Eventually, the rule of the merchant partriciate was challenged by nonpatrician burghers—guildmasters, lesser merchants, and professional men. The admission of guildmasters to the town governments is considered significant, because it gave the "sphere of production" access to the policy-making process. As a result, the guilds

---

[77]Berthold et al., "Stellung," pp. 212ff.; Vogler, "Probleme," pp. 1196ff.
[78]Stern and Voigt, *Deutschland*, pp. 30–32, 49ff.; Berthold et al., "Stellung," pp. 209–10, 212; *Grundriss*, pp. 114–15; Kuczynski, quoted in Herrmann et al., *Rolle der Volksmassen*, p. 18; Töpfer, "Volksbewegung, Ideologie," p. 1161.

achieved greater autonomy within the towns and production expanded. The increased productivity in turn led to new capital accumulations and the gradual penetration of capital into production—
in mining, metal processing, and textiles. Although this beginning
shift to early forms (*Keimformen*) of capitalist production injected a
disintegrating element into the feudal system, it is not considered to
have been an immediate threat to that system. The available capital
was controlled by merchants rather than manufacturers. Moreover,
merchants shared common concerns with the feudal nobility in
matters of trade and often cooperated closely with the latter and
even sought to identify with the nobility in their life style. A real
threat to the feudal order would materialize only when capitalist
production dominated trade and, by depriving the "direct" producers of all but their labor power, ushered in a new socioeconomic
order. There was evidence of such a shift only in the mining industry in the fourteenth and fifteenth centuries.[79]

The rise of the towns was not, however, a story of uninterrupted progress. Throughout the fourteenth century, towns, like
the countryside, suffered grave economic setbacks. Most assessments of these urban difficulties differ from non-Marxist ones in
that they give little weight to the pest epidemics ("Black Death")
of that period as a cause of the crises. In keeping with their conviction that most crises are man-made, DDR scholars tend to attribute these setbacks to the agrarian crisis, with its resulting social
dislocations, restrictive guild practices, overproduction, and other
such factors.

Basically, the problems are seen as reflections of the "contradictions" developing between the urban economies and the feudal
order and thus generating the "first crisis of the feudal order." Even
then progress could not be stopped altogether; as Voigt puts it,
"symptoms of decay and elements of progress were dialectically
linked to each other, with the latter on the whole in the ascendancy." A large influx of newcomers into the cities, new capital
accumulations, and new business ventures provided fresh impulses
for further expansion.

Yet in the end the ruling feudal class recovered its strength, it
is noted, by countering the new economic developments with new
forms of exploitation and domination. Thus, the territorial princes,
having reinforced their position by creating highly centralized states
that were effectively administered by trained officials, brought the
bulk of the towns under their direct control, and with them the
towns' economic resources. What the imposition of the "second

[79]Berthold et al., "Stellung," p. 210; Werner Mägdefrau, "Die Bedeutung der Volksbewegungen im Thüringer Dreistädtebund," *ZfG* 21 (1973): 1322–24; Stern and
Voigt, *Deutschland*, pp. 182ff.

serfdom" did to sustain the feudal order in the countryside, princely centralization achieved in regard to the cities.[80]

In the context of these developments and as representative of them, the fate of the Hanseatic League has received considerable attention. Like all city leagues, the Hanse is viewed as an "instrument in the class struggle against the feudal nobility"; its economic focus on trade made it the creature of merchant capital. As such, the Hanse could play the important role it assumed in the "first phase" of capital accumulation—protecting, expediting, and expanding trade. Its decline is attributed to the fact that when the Hanseatic cities were unable to maintain their trade monopoly against their more enterprising English and Dutch rivals, most of them had no economic base of their own to fall back on. With their capital invested in money-lending or real estate, few cities had any significant links to production; what capital flowed into manufacture was used mainly to extract profits from existing facilities rather than to create new ones.

Other factors contributed to the Hanse's demise. Divided by factional struggles among its members and weakened by internal fights between the ruling group and a discontented opposition, the league was no match to the growing power of central governments in England, Holland, the Scandinavian countries, and Russia, or to German princes who sought to consolidate their power by incorporating Hanse cities into their territories. Müller-Mertens has therefore concluded that a shift to manufacturing activities could at best have preserved the Hanse on a regional basis, never in its entirety. Even this conclusion is not certain, given the varying fate of such manufacturing centers as Lübeck, Hamburg and Danzig, which did preserve their independence, and of such other centers as Wismar, Rostock, Cologne, and Dortmund, which did not.[81]

All in all, DDR analyses of the Hanse differ little from non-Marxist ones. One aspect that plays some role in the traditional historiography of the league is, however, notably missing from the

[80]See Stern and Voigt, *Deutschland*, pp. 11–12; Werner, in *Städtische Volksbewegungen im 14. Jahrhundert*, ed. Erika Engelmann (Berlin [East], 1960), pp. 11ff.; also Voigt, in ibid., pp. 177–78; Töpfer, in ibid., pp. 183–85; Hans-Heinrich Müller, review, *ZfG* 18 (1970): 423–24; Erika Uitz, in ibid. 21 (1973): 417 n. 78. Mottek (*Wirtschaftsgeschichte Deutschlands*, vol. 1, pp. 193ff.), on the other hand, gives considerable weight to the economic impact of the epidemics. So does Voigt in Stern and Voigt, *Deutschland*, p. 9, contradicting what he says on pp. 11–12, and E. Zöllner, in ibid., p. 97.

[81]Streisand, pp. 48–50; Stern and Voigt, *Deutschlands*, pp. 60ff., 189ff.; Mottek, *Wirtschaftsgeschichte Deutschland*, vol. 1, pp. 218–20, 297–98; Konrad Fritze, in Engelmann, *Städtische Volksbewegungen*, pp. 148–49; Johannes Schildhauer, "Grundzüge der Geschichte der deutschen Hanse," *ZfG* 11 (1963): 733ff. (quotation on p. 733); Müller-Mertens, in *Neue Hansische Studien*, ed. by Fritze et al., (Berlin [East], 1974), pp. x–xi.

East German discussions—how the Hanse's decline was affected by natural causes, such as the migration of the herrings from the Baltic to the North Sea and the silting up of the sea lanc to Bruges, a main outlet of Hanse trade. Again, the emphasis in explaining the league's demise is on man-made factors rather than on nature's intrusions.[82]

The internal unrest that weakened many of the Hanse's cities and that contributed to its disintegration affected other German cities as well. Growing out of protest movements of discontented nonpatrician burghers and pauperizied "plebeian" elements, these eruptions serve as further testimony to the "growing role of the masses" (Czok) and as harbingers of future developments. Even if in most cases the protesting masses were too weak and disorganized to assert themselves and although they confined their demands to economic concessions rather than asking for political changes, by which alone they could have improved their lot permanently, the demand for concrete material improvements is perceived as a distinct advance over the earlier religious movements of indirect protest. What mattered was the growing self-assertion of the "preproletarian" exploited, which would grow as early capitalism gained ground. Still, it is also noted that whatever revolts took place were isolated events, without outside support. For a successful rising, a unifying ideology was needed—one that would fuse local discontent into a nationwide movement.[83]

[82]On the migration of the herrings and the silting up of Bruges' harbor as causes of the Hanse's decline, see Grundmann, in Gebhardt, vol. 1, p. 604, and Holborn, vol. 1, pp. 80–81. On the other hand, Phillippe Dollinger (*The German Hansa* [Stanford, 1971], pp. 239, 314) and Hermann Kellenbenz (in *HbDtWSG*, vol. 1, p. 439) consider these factors of little or no importance.

[83]Stern and Voigt, *Deutschland*, pp. 195ff.; Mottek, *Wirtschaftsgeschichte Deutschlands*, vol. 1, pp. 201ff.; Berthold et al., "Stellung," pp. 215–16; Engelmann, *Städtische Volksbewegungen, passim*, especially Fritze, pp. 153–54, and Karl Czok, pp. 163–64.

3

From Feudalism to Capitalism

The Reformation to the Thirty Years War

The Reformation as Early Bourgeois Revolution

EARLY IN THE SIXTEENTH CENTURY, according to DDR historians, the rural and urban class struggles escalated into a "gesamtgesellschaftliche Krise"—a crisis embracing all classes of German society. Although in this view the basic contradiction was still that between peasants and lords in an essentially feudal society, a new antagonism was developing between the feudal order and the emerging early capitalist forces, accentuating the confrontation between peasants and lords. These new forces, it is claimed, were being blocked in their further growth by feudal impediments: serfdom in the country, which deprived capitalism of the mobile labor force on which it depended; a rigid guild system in the towns, with restrictions on entrepreneurial initiative; and the lack of a unified market on the national plane. As these obstacles disrupted the lawful process of an expanding commodity production, tensions within and between classes intensified, outgrew their local confines, and attained national dimensions.

The antiquated imperial administration, it is noted, was unable to resolve these problems and equally incapable of putting an end to the disintegration of the empire. The weakness of the central power also left Germany vulnerable to the intrusions and financial exactions of the Church; Rome placed much heavier ecclesiastical burdens on the Germans than on the English and French, whose centralized governments could shield them against such abuses. In this situation, DDR authors conclude, there existed the elements of a revolutionary situation—that is, the conditions for the formation of a mass movement drawing on elements from all classes and aiming at the destruction of the dominant feudal order. The Reformation is viewed as this movement: Luther's theological teachings provided the ideological guidance that fused the various class tensions and struggles into a social revolution, with the Peasants' War its violent culmination.[1]

[1]Steinmetz, *Deutschland*, especially pp. 82ff.; *Grundriss*, pp. 131ff.; Streisand, pp. 53ff.

To Marxist scholars, then, the Reformation was not simply a religious and theological reform movement, as a dominant tradition in non-Marxist historiography had long seen it, but a socioeconomic response, in religious guise, to the inadequacies of the feudal system and its ideological mainstay, the Church.[2] Once again, however, the religious element is not ignored; indeed, East German historians pay considerable attention to it, for they acknowledge that Luther's teachings provided the ideological justificaion for what they view as a revolution. As the philosopher of history Gottfried Stiehler explains,

> Religion was the inevitable ideological form in which class interests were expressed at the time, because the entire spiritual life of society was dominated by theology.... The prerequisites for a scientific understanding of the factors determining men's actions did not yet exist; as a rule people tended to associate economic and political questions with questions of religion, of faith. Thus they might often be convinced of fighting for religious ideals while actually economic interests were involved. Politics, judicial decisions, and all the sciences were the offspring, were branches of theology. "The doctrines of the Church were also political axioms, and passages from the Bible had the force of law in every court" [Engels]. It was not a matter of deceiving oneself or others if the struggle between the classes and confrontations within the classes were seen as clashes over religious principles.[3]

Thus, although Marxists do not consider religious beliefs as originating forces sui generis, viewing them rather as products of social education in the widest sense of the term, they allow that once under way, these beliefs may well develop a life of their own and become relatively independent of their material basis. In this view, religion can thus exert that unifying power beyond class barriers that gave the Reformation its social and national impetus. "Marxism does not deny the existence of religion and faith," notes Max Steinmetz, the leading East German Reformation historian, "but Marxism refuses to explain religion and faith solely [!] in terms of religious motivations." The theological approach, he explains elsewhere, results in irrationalism and mystification; blind faith takes over and denies that history is a recognizable, law-determined process.[4]

[2]See *Unb. Verg.*, pp. 226, 228. For a perceptive survey of this issue by a Western historian, see Thomas A. Brady, Jr., *Ruling Class, Regime and Reformation at Strasbourg: 1520–1555* (Leiden, 1978), pp. 1ff.; also see Rainer Wohlfeil, in *Reformation oder frühbürgerliche Reformation?*, ed. by Wohlfeil (Munich, 1972), p. 23. Brady points out that although Western historians are now more concerned with the social context of the Reformation, their approach in many cases is still shaped by religious concepts.

[3]Stiehler, *Gesellschaft und Geschichte*, pp. 139–40.

[4]Streisand, pp. 58–59; Steinmetz, "Die Entstehung der marxistischen Auffassung von Reformation und Bauernkrieg als frühbürgerliche Reformation," *ZfG* 15 (1967): 1181; quotation in ibid. 25 (1977): 863; Gerhard Brendler, *Das Täuferreich zu Münster: 1534–35* (Berlin [East], 1966), p. 73.

In the same vein, Steinmetz perceives Luther as a child of his time and interprets Luther's decision to enter a monastery as an "expression of the general social crisis . . . that did not stop before the psychic domain and greatly affected man's self-certitude. The collision of the old ways with the emerging new forces aroused many a subconscious or even open doubt concerning old venerable traditions; in Luther's case they manifested themselves as qualms of conscience and anxiety about his salvation." Similarly, Gerhard Zschäbitz has "no doubt" that Luther's retreat into a monastery was dictated by the tensions produced by the approaching social crises: "Under its gray wings, fear of hell and death might well have produced anxieties that an individual might find intolerable."

Yet, as these assessments also make clear, East German scholars do not deny the genuineness of Luther's religious experiences. Gerhard Brendler expresses a widely held view when he states that "Luther was concerned about the gospel. One should take him at his word on this without sharing his illusions. The comparative independence of ideological phenomena is here again evident." Historically, however, Luther's subjective motivations are considered irrelevant. What does matter is that his teachings—with their emphasis on faith rather than "good works," the immediacy between individual and God, and the superfluity of a cumbersome ecclesiastical hierarchy—are seen "objectively as the theological expression of the economic and political struggle of the Bürgertum and the popular masses against the papal church directed from Rome and impeding all social progress" (Steinmetz). Summing up Luther's achievements, Steinmetz says that they have not the personal accomplishments of an individual, a "blessed divine," but the articulation of the needs of German society in his time. Luther's importance, then, lay in his ability to serve as the spokesman of the people. The Reformation thus is seen as an integral part of German history—a fact that non-Marxist historians frequently forget in their preoccupation with the religious and theological aspects of that event.[5]

Luther's attack on the Church is significant to Marxist historians not merely because that attack articulated popular needs and wishes. Because they view the Church as the ideological mainstay of the feudal order, DDR authors see the Reformation as directing itself against that system as well as against the Church. As the Reformation challenged the spiritual authority of the Church, it

[5]Steinmetz, *Deutschland*, pp. 88, 90; Streisand, pp. 59–63; Gerhard Zschäbitz, *Martin Luther: Grösse und Grenze* (Berlin [East], 1967), vol. 1, p. 33; Brendler, in *450 Jahre Reformation*, ed. Stern and Steinmetz (Berlin [East], 1967), p. 66; and *Grundriss*, p. 149. Few, if any, non-Marxist historians would today attribute the Reformation to purely religious causes; see Rainer Wohlfeil and Thomas Nipperdey, in Wohlfeil, *Reformation*, pp. 22–24, 207.

challenged as well the religious sanction of feudalism and its carefully nurtured sacrosanct status. Given the widespread hatred of
the rapacious and parasitical Church, it is pointed out, the Lutheran movement assailed the feudal order in the area in which it
was most vulnerable. Because the forces chafing under feudal restraints were still much weaker than the entrenched feudal lords,
this was indeed the only approach open to them. Thus everything
seems to fall into a pattern, and DDR scholars see nothing surprising in the fact that the assault on the feudal system took a religious form. Indeed, for the reasons given, they deem this approach
as "historically necessary." These conclusions are presented with
such forcefulness that some accounts almost seem to suggest that
the attack on the Church was launched specifically in order to get
at the feudal order. Yet, as in Luther's case, the discussions do not
ignore the prevailing concern over a corrupt and demoralized
Church unable to satisfy the spiritual needs of a growing number
of faithful, nor do they question the genuineness of the confidence
that Luther's teaching would renew and strengthen Christianity.
However, they dismiss these attitudes, as in their view they must,
as illusions behind which social reality ultimately asserted itself.[6]

To classify the Reformation, negatively, as an antifeudal
movement presented no problem—the Peasants' War, viewed as an
integral part of the Reformation, provided additional confirmation.
Defining the Reformation in terms of its positive goals, on the
other hand, proved more difficult. At the outset of the debate,
Steinmetz and others saw its "main task" (Hauptaufgabe) as the
creation of a united centralized Germany, with the elimination of
princely particularism and centrifugal feudalism being complemen-
tary aims. During the 1960s, however, DDR scholars came to believe that national unity was not yet a viable issue at the time. In
the transition from feudalism to capitalism, they thought, the
main task of the Reformation was to free the emerging capitalist
forces from its feudal shackles. The centralized nation-state would
materialize from rather than initiate such a development, because
the formation of nations is a lawful result of the capitalist order.[7]

The framework for the social Hauptaufgabe of the Reformation, the strengthening of the emerging capitalist forces, was postu-

[6]Steinmetz, Deutschland, pp. 67, 85; Grundriss, p. 146.
[7]The debate is discussed by Wohlfeil, in Wohlfeil, Reformation, pp. 17–18; Dietrich Lösche, in ibid., pp. 180–81; Günter Vogler, in ibid., pp. 190–93; and Josef
Foschepoth, Reformation und Bauernkrieg im Geschichtsbild der DDR (Berlin
[West], 1976), pp. 57ff. On political centralization as a primary task, see also
Ingrid Mittenzwei, in Die frühbürgerliche Revolution in Deutschland, ed. Brendler (Berlin [East], 1961), pp. 102–103, 106; Karlheinz Blaschke, "Deutsche Wirt-
schaftseinheit oder Wirtschaftspartikularismus?" in ibid., pp. 53ff. On the relationship of nations and capitalism, see Alfred Kosing, Nation in Geschichte und
Gegenwart (Berlin [East], 1976), especially pp. 58ff.

lated by Engels in some of his later writings. He defined the Reformation as "Revolution No. 1 of the bourgeoisie" (others being the subsequent English and French ones). Yet Engels already had to contend with the fact that there was no evidence of a bourgeois role in this supposedly bourgeois revolution. At first he argued that the upheaval was bourgeois in nature because objectively—that is, in terms of its causes, goals, and results—it furthered the interests of that class. Later he came to maintain the position (which he thought was upheld by the studies of Karl Kautsky) that capitalist production had advanced far already in mining at the time of the Reformation and that hence a capitalist bourgeoisie did exist. These findings confirmed to his satisfaction his definition of the Reformation as a bourgeois revolution in religious guise.[8]

Engels' definition bequeathed to his disciples the task of explaining why the bourgeoisie took part only reluctantly, if at all, in the revolution of which it was claimed to be the main beneficiary. For, as all research showed, the capitalist bourgeoisie—bankers, merchants, and large manufacturers—hesitated to join the Lutheran movement, and if they did join they did so mostly under popular pressure. Later, moreover, fearful of the more radical manifestations of the Reformation and the Peasants' War, they turned on both movements and backed their opponents.[9]

These studies also show that capitalist interests were not yet hampered seriously by feudal restrictions. Commerce flourished despite the territorial divisions of the Empire because intra-imperial tariffs were low.[10] The lack of uniform laws was being remedied by the adoption of Roman law, and the lack of a uniform system of weights and measures does not seem to have been a major concern of the burghers: they did not support proposals for an empirewide system in the imperial diet. Neither did they approve of a system of imperial external customs that would have served as a protecting

[8]Originally—in his *Peasants' War*, for example—Engels did not consider the Reformation a revolution. For convenient surveys of his views, see Wohlfeil, in Wohlfeil, *Reformation*, pp. 12–14, and Lösche, in ibid., pp. 163ff. Neither one, however, takes up the ambiguities of some of Engels' statements. On this, see below in the text. The discussion of Engels' position by Abraham Friesen (*Reformation and Utopia: The Marxist Interpretation of the Reformation and Its Antecedents* [Wiesbaden, 1974]) is less satisfactory.
[9]Bernd Möller, *Reichsstadt und Reformation* (Gütersloh, 1962), pp. 25ff.; Brady, *Ruling Class*, pp. 199ff.; Johannes Schildhauer, *Soziale, politische und religiöse Auseinandersetzungen in den Hansestädten Stralsund, Rostock und Wismar im ersten Drittel des 16. Jahrhunderts* (Weimar, 1959), pp. 98ff., 141–142, 159ff.; also Nipperdey, in Wohlfeil, *Reformation*, pp. 215–17.
[10]Karlheinz Blaschke, in Brendler, *Frühbürgerliche Revolution*, pp. 53ff.; Steinmetz, *Deutschland*, pp. 22ff.; Adolf Laube, in *Der Deutsche Bauernkrieg 1524/25*, ed. Brendler and Laube (Berlin [East], 1977), p. 59; see also, from a non-Marxist perspective, Holborn, vol. 1, pp. 67–68; Friedrich Lütge, *Deutsche Sozial- und Wirtschaftsgeschichte* (Berlin [West], 1952), pp. 172–73.

wall against foreign countries and would have brought the various parts of the empire more closely together. Instead, the cities complained about the imperial government, which they, more than the princes, thought burdensome and expensive.[11]

The fact was, as East German historians themselves admit, that at least the banking and merchant capitalists were still faring well under the existing conditions. "They were not a modern bourgeoisie," Gerhard Zschäbitz notes, "which must fight for its political power in order to fend off economic stagnation. Many threads linked them with the dominant feudal powers." Steinmetz, who blames Germany's difficulties on the lack of imperial centralization, grants that trade did not suffer notably under the existing political and legal disunity, and Adolf Laube has noted that a national market and a division of labor transcending territorial boundaries were coming into existence. Steinmetz's claim that the feudal order impeded capitalist production by withholding manpower from manufacturers has been refuted by other East German scholars and by Steinmetz's own implicit admission that capitalist production was still in its early stage and thus had only limited manpower needs. It was more significant from the Marxist perspective that most capital was still being invested in banking and trade rather than in production. Only in the sphere of production, however, could capitalism become "historically progressive" (Zschäbitz).[12] The issue is far from being resolved, and a new approach to it that has recently been suggested will be discussed later in another connection.

Even without the benefit of many of these studies, a Soviet historian, O. G. Tchaikovskaya, had earlier taken issue with Engels' definition of the Reformation as a bourgeois revolution. Tchaikovskaya claimed that the Reformation was no revolution at all, let alone a capitalist one, and the Peasants' War was simply another peasant revolt. The ensuing debate was rendered more difficult by Engels' failure to distinguish clearly between Bürgertum (noncapitalist or small-capitalist) and bourgeoisie (large-capitalist), terms that he used interchangeably. At least partly because of these imprecisions, the debaters could not agree on what Engels

[11]On law, see James Westfall Thompson, *Economic and Social History of Europe in the Later Middle Ages (1300–1530)* (New York, 1960), pp. 487–88; also Blaschke, in Brendler, *Frühbürgerliche Revolution*, pp. 57–58. On weights, measures, and imperial customs, see Karl Brandi, *Deutsche Geschichte im Zeitalter der Reformation und Gegenreformation* (Leipzig, 1941), pp. 152, 154; on general attitudes, see Mottek, *Wirtschaftsgeschichte Deutschlands*, vol. 1, p. 242.
[12]See Steinmetz, *Deutschland*, pp. 20–21. Equally contradictory are *Grundriss*, pp. 140, 147; Zschäbitz, in Wohlfeil, *Reformation*, pp. 126ff.; Mottek, *Wirtschaftsgeschichte Deutschlands*, vol. 1, pp. 224–25; Laube, in Brendler and Laube, *Bauernkrieg 1524/25*, pp. 57–59; Laube, in *Jahrbuch für Geschichte des Feudalismus*, 1 (1977): 281.

had really meant. There is no need here to go into the details of the discussion, which was carried on with notable asperity, replete with charges of willful misinterpretations of Engels' views and the available data. (Actually, all participants departed from Engels' views at one point or another, if only by assigning the Reformation to the Middle Ages.) It is also noteworthy, as the West German Reformation scholar Rainer Wohlfeil has pointd out, that no one would say outright that Engels had been mistaken. The discussion coyly revolved around interpretations of what he had meant to say.

One point, however, deserves to be mentioned, because it was developed further in subsequent East German analyses. In reply to Tchaikovskaya, A. D. Epstein, a Soviet sixteenth-century specialist, argued that because the Reformation movement was antifeudal and capitalist elements did exist, it had to be bourgeois in substance, if not in form. In the absence of a bourgeoisie, the popular masses were the social carriers of the uprising; it was, as he put it, a "bourgeois revolution without bourgeoisie." The argument was taken up by the DDR scholars Ingrid Mittenzwei and other East German historians. In further modification of Engels' views, they spoke of the Reformation as an *early* bourgeois (*frühbürgerlich*) revolution, suggesting that capitalism was still in its initial stage of development, as was the German bourgeoisie.[13]

Not everyone accepted this tortuous argument. The medievalist Bernhard Töpfer objected that the connection between the Reformation and capitalism had been overstressed. He agreed that the Reformation was the result of changing economic conditions and that it in turn had its impact on these conditions, but he maintained that the most important development of the period, the rise of "manufacture capitalism," occurred independently of the Reformation—a conclusion that has been borne out by the studies of two other DDR authors, Gerhard Heitz and Karlheinz Blaschke. However, Töpfer rejects above all the classification of the Reformation as a bourgeois revolution—or, for that matter, an early bourgeois one—in the absence of a substantial capitalist bourgeoisie. He argues that such a revolution presupposes the seizure of power or at least the sharing of it by the bourgeoisie, and this did not happen. In support of his stand, Töpfer invoked the authority of Marx, who did not include the Reformation among the bourgeois revolutions. He could also have called on Engels, who stipulated that "every real [!] revolu-

---

[13]Parts of the Soviet debate have been published in German translation in *Sowjetwissenschaft, Gesellschaftswiss. Beiträge,* 1957 and 1958. A good résumé of the debate and the subsequent East German discussions can be found in Foschepoth, *Reformation und Bauernkrieg;* Mittenzwei, in Brendler, *Frühbürgerliche Revolution,* p. 104; also Zschäbitz, in Wohlfeil, *Reformation,* p. 133. On masses, see *Grundriss,* pp. 146–47; Steinmetz, in Wohlfeil, *Reformation,* p. 157; Lösche, in ibid., p. 183.

tion is a social one inasmuch as it gives a new class access to power and enables it to revamp society according to its own ideas." Unlike the genuinely bourgeois Dutch, English, and French revolutions, Töpfer notes, the Reformation did not achieve any adaptation of state and society to bourgeois-capitalist needs, but merely attained an adjustment of the Church's structure to *bürgerlich* interests. Töpfer concludes that the Reformation was a prelude to, rather than an early phase of, the bourgeois revolutions; as such it had more in common with the Hussite movement and with Wat Tyler's peasant revolt in England (1381), with its Wycliffeian aspirations toward church reform, and ought to be grouped with these risings as part of a sequence of special reformatory movements.[14]

Töpfer's views were rejected by his colleagues, but given the fact that the "early bourgeois revolution" produced no tangible results in terms of social or political changes, it became necessary to redefine the revolutionary content of the Reformation. Some authors followed up on Engels' observation, mentioned earlier, that the European Bürgertum asserted itself against feudalism in three great battles—the Reformation and the English and French revolutions. Viewed in this manner, the Reformation was but a phase in a continuing revolutionary process, in the course of which the Bürgertum threw off, by stages, the shackles of feudalism. The Reformation constituted the early phase of this process, during which capitalist elements were just beginning to form and the bourgeoisie was equally undeveloped. Because of the immaturity of the bourgeois-capitalist forces, the Reformation could not yet abolish the feudal system and turn over power to the bourgeoisie; what it did attain was the breakthrough of bürgerlich standards and values. These received their practical implementation in the Calvinist Reformation, which was inspired by the Lutheran Reformation. Calvinism in turn furthered the rise to power of the bourgeoisie by sparking revolutions in the Netherlands, England, and France, all of them far more advanced capitalistically than Germany. The revolutionary contribution of the Lutheran Reformation thus was made in the religious-ideological domain, by the fostering of bürgerlich qualities.[15]

Zschäbitz, who was the first East German scholar to set forth this thesis, contended that Töpfer, in denying that the Reformation was either frühbürgerlich or a revolution, was merely concerned

---

[14]Bernhard Töpfer, "Fragen der hussitischen revolutionären Bewegung," *ZfG* 11 (1963): 146ff.; Töpfer, in Wohlfeil, *Reformation*, pp. 70ff.; Engels on seizure of power, in MEW, vol. 18, p. 560; Gerhard Heitz, in Brendler, *Frühbürgerliche Revolution*, p. 60; Blaschke, "Frühkapitalismus und Verfassungsgeschichte," *WZ Leipzig* 14 (1965): 439–41; see also Laube, cited in *ZfG* 23 (1975): 1215–17.

[15]Engels, in MEW, vol. 19, pp. 533–34; ibid., vol. 21, pp. 304–5, 402; ibid., vol. 22, pp. 299–300.

with the "necessary" final result of a bourgeois revolution. Actually a frühbürgerlich revolution was a "prebourgeois" (*vorbourgeoise*) revolution that "tended toward forcibly bringing about the participation of a more or less developed bourgeoisie in the exercise of [political] power." To buttress this labored thesis, Zschäbitz pointed to some of the positive effects of the Reformation: on the European plane it helped to prepare for the breakthrough of capitalism by providing a bourgeois ideology in religious guise, which, although largely ineffective in Germany, in its Calvinist form—as Engels had argued—it paved the way for the subsequent bourgeois victories in Western Europe. In Germany, Zschäbitz credits the Reformation (always including the Peasants' War) with more or less ending the further deterioration of the peasants' conditions wherever the latter had risen and fought for their rights. He also welcomes the secularization of ecclesiastical territories as a step toward greater centralization and points to the improved cultural and educational facilities that provided the Bürgertum with "weapons with which under more highly developed conditions it could overcome its servility and blind faith in its rulers."[16]

In a similar effort to bypass Töpfer's objections, Dietrich Lösche observed that "the decisive criterion of a bürgerlich revolution is not the seizure or sharing of power of the bourgeoisie, but any serious struggle launched for the purpose of gaining power, and such a struggle got under way with the Reformation." Because the Church was part of the established power structure, any attack directed against it challenged the feudal system and became a struggle for power. Like Zschäbitz, Lösche too sees the Reformation yield benefits of a bürgerlich nature, such as the destruction of the ideological monopoly of the Roman Catholic Church with its restrictive rules. Again like Zschäbitz, Lösche points to the European dimensions of the Lutheran Reformation and its role as the initiator of a new bürgerlich consciousness as the key to the full appreciation of its revolutionary nature.[17]

More recently, Steinmetz, too, has made these points. He stresses in particular the bürgerlich aspects of the Lutheran Church—its simplicity and frugality (an "inexpensive" [*wohlfeil*] church in Luther's words), the new attitudes toward work and profession, and the new emphasis that was placed on education. Opening up future possibilities for the Bürgertum, Steinmetz notes,

---

[16]Zschäbitz, in Wohlfeil, *Reformation,* pp. 125, 137–38; Engels in MEW, vol. 21, pp. 304–5.
[17]Lösche, in Wohlfeil, *Reformation,* pp. 171–72, 175, 177, 179–82; also Brendler, in *Weltwirkung der Reformation,* ed. Steinmetz and Brendler (Berlin [East], 1969), vol. 1, pp. 179–80.

these bürgerlich achievements of the Reformation and their European reverberations justify its designation as a frühbürgerlich revolution. Altogether most East German historians now view the opening of the door to Bürgerlichkeit in Germany and beyond as the most important result of the Reformation. In this sense, then, the frühbürgerlich revolution is found to have been victorious. And if earlier the Reformation had been dubbed a *Princes' Reformation* (*Fürstenreformation*) on the grounds that the German princes were its main beneficiaries, the term has been dropped now in favor of the designation *Church Reformation* (*Kirchenreformation*), which yielded some significant gains to the Bürgertum, both in Germany and in other countries.[18]

In Germany's case, the facts hardly bear out such conclusions. They ignore the Bürgertum's decline after the Reformation, when towns and cities governed by it were increasingly being absorbed into princely territories. In addition, although education spread and thrift was valued, it has rightly been questioned whether in Germany the Reformation inspired new attitudes toward work and profession—piety and enlightenment would seem to have had more of an impact in that direction. Some East German historians therefore continue to view the outcome of the frühbürgerlich revolution as a defeat for the Bürgertum.[19]

If, then, the substantive identification of the Reformation with Bürgerlichkeit causes some difficulties, proving that the Reformation, seen as a frühbürgerlich antifeudal revolution, was a bürgerlich, as distinct from a bourgeois, undertaking in terms of its protagonists has been even more difficult. Steinmetz attempted to prove its bürgerlich character by pointing out that the leaders—not only the reformers themselves, but also the town councillors and academics and the writers and artists who took up their cause— were all of bürgerlich background. Even among these leaders, how-

---

[18]See Steinmetz, in Wohlfeil, *Reformation*, pp. 152ff.; also Engelberg, "Problemen," p. 1240; Zschäbitz, in *Studien über die Revolution*, ed. Manfred Kosock et al. (Berlin [East], 1969), pp. 42–43; and Brendler, in Stern and Steinmetz, *450 Jahre*, p. 65. This interpretation of the revolutionary nature of the Reformation has been accepted also by a West German scholar, Winfried Schulze, "Reformation oder frühbürgerliche Revolution?" *Jahrbuch für die Geschichte Mittel- und Ostdeutschlands*, 22 (1973): 267–69. On the changing designations, see Foschepoth, *Reformation und Bauernkrieg*, p. 102.

[19]See Holborn, "Der deutsche Idealismus in sozialgeschichtlicher Beleuchtung," *HZ*, 174 (1952): 364–65; Franklin Kopitzsch, in *Der Bauernkrieg 1524–26*, ed. Wohlfeil (Munich, 1975), pp. 198–99; also Holborn, vol. 2, pp. 39–40. On defeat, see Brigitte Berthold et al., "Die Stellung des Bürgertums in der deutschen Feudalgesellschaft bis zur Mitte des 16. Jahrhunderts," *ZfG* 21 (1973): 217; Hildegard Hoffmann and Ingrid Mittenzwei, "Die Stellung des Bürgertums in der deutschen Feudalgesellschaft von der Mitte des 16. Jahrhunderts bis 1789," ibid. 22 (1974): 197.

ever, there were many who joined the reformatory movement only under mass pressure, and they dissociated themselves from that movement when it escalated into what Marxists have termed a People's Reformation (*Volksreformation*), demanding social and political concessions for the lower classes.[20] Steinmetz has since abandoned his efforts to portray the Bürgertum as the social carrier of the Reformation and, like his colleagues, he agrees now that the Bürgertum was too weak and disorganized to provide continued leadership to the movement.[21] This leaves the popular masses—the *Kleinbürger*, the peasants, and the urban "plebeians"—as the propelling force of the Reformation, a conclusion that Marxists have no difficulty in accepting.[22]

The West German historian Josef Foschepoth has pointed out that the masses, in being credited with the alleged breakthrough of bürgerlich values, are being praised for a victory that meant little to them. To Foschepoth this incongruity is indicative of the low esteem in which the masses are actualy held by their Marxist-Leninist champions.[23] Marxists, of course, would challenge this charge. For them, the masses, whatever their subjective intentions, were objectively carriers of social progress that would redound to their benefit, too. To have sparked progress was to have been historically decisive, moreover, and that made the masses agents of history. Yet, even within the Marxist framework, the history-making power of the masses once again turns out to be limited: Steinmetz notes that without bürgerlich leadership, that is, without the leadership of the class that should have assumed this role, the revolution succeeded only in the religious-ideological realm.[24]

This last argument points up the impasse into which the appraisal of the Reformation as a bürgerlich revolution has led Marxist scholars. On the one hand, the Bürgertum is judged to have been too immature and unorganized to stage a revolution; on the other hand, it is blamed for having defaulted (*versagt*) on its leadership task. Even the concept of frühbürgerlich cannot resolve this inconsistency. The one adjustment to it that has been made is that

---

[20]See Steinmetz, in Wohlfeil, *Reformation*, pp. 153–54. See also the material in Foschepoth, *Reformation und Bauernkrieg*, pp. 73–74; Foschepoth brings out well the discrepancies in the East German position. See also the sources cited in note 8.

[21]Steinmetz, "Luther und Müntzer," *WZ Leipzig*, 23 (1974): 444; Steinmetz, "Der geschichtliche Platz des deutschen Bauernkrieges," *ZfG* 23 (1975): 269. See also *Illustrierte Geschichte der deutschen frühbürgerlichen Revolution*, ed. by Laube et al. (Berlin [East], 1974), p. 143, as compared to pp. 171ff.

[22]Steinmetz, in Wohlfeil, *Reformation*, p. 157; Lösche, in ibid., p. 183.

[23]Foschepoth, *Reformation und Bauernkrieg*, pp. 75–76.

[24]Laube et al., *Illustrierte Geschichte*, p. 302; Steinmetz, "Geschichtliche Platz," p. 269.

bürgerlich conduct is no longer castigated as treacherous, as it was in earlier accounts; now it is only thought weak and timid.[25]

DDR historians are aware of these discrepancies, and many of them have admitted that the thesis of the frühbürgerlich revolution still leaves many questions unanswered. As Steinmetz put it some years ago, "we have not yet gotten around during the last fifteen years to proving comprehensively in our field what we have set forth as a thesis."[26] The statement is still valid today. Given these difficulties, it might seem surprising that the thesis has not been abandoned.

It is evident from what has been said that Engels' definition of the Reformation as a bürgerlich revolution sets the framework for the Marxist Reformation debate. As some West German authors have put it, Engels' *Peasants' War* and his other statements on the Reformation and the Peasants' War enjoy canonical or near-canonical authority. This Engels orthodoxy, to be sure, is not wholly inflexible. Töpfer, as was mentioned earlier, did challenge Engels, yet was seriously debated rather than excommunicated as a heretic. Similarly, Dietrich Lösche has wondered why some Marxist scholars would call the Reformation a bourgeois revolution without bourgeoisie "although Engels viewed the situation somewhat more positively . . . and a plethora of more recent publications . . . have confirmed or at least not refuted his view"; thus, Lösche implies that such a refutation was conceivable. On the other hand, it is noteworthy that Töpfer never mentions Engels by name in his rejection of Engels' thesis, just as Soviet historians never criticized Engels directly in the debate mentioned earlier in which they questioned his views.[27]

If there is a modicum of flexibility in the analyses of the Reformation, this follows from Engels' status, in principle, as an expert authority rather than a lawgiver. He was simply the first to perceive that, as Steinmetz has said, "every revolutionary movement must in this phase evolve into a bürgerlich revolution, be-

---

[25]See Steinmetz, in Wohlfeil, *Reformation*, p. 54. Also compare ibid., pp. 49–50 and Steinmetz, *Deutschland*, p. 160 with Steinmetz, "Geschichtliche Platz," p. 255. See also Manfred Bensing, *Thomas Müntzer und der Thüringer Aufstand 1525* (Berlin [East], 1966), p. 140 (compared to p. 234); Engelsing, "Problemen," p. 1240. See also the circular argumentation in Lösche, in Wohlfeil, *Reformation*, pp. 174–76.

[26]See Steinmetz, quoted in Wohlfeil, *Bauernkrieg 1524–26*, pp. 9, 38 nn. 33 and 37 (with quotation); Siegfried Hoyer, cited in *HZ*, suppl. 4 (n.s., 1975): 6; Laube, in Brendler and Laube, *Deutsche Bauernkrieg*, pp. 64–65; Engelberg, review, *ZfG* 21 (1973): 877. On the evidentiary difficulties, see the tortuous arguments of Brendler, " . . . Zu den Vor- und Frühformen der bürgerlichen Revolution," *JfG* 10 (1973): 27–28.

[27]Wohlfeil, in Wohlfeil, *Bauernkrieg 1524–26*, pp. 11–12; Wohlfeil, in Wohlfeil, *Reformation*, pp. 11–12; Nipperdey and Peter Melcher, in ibid., p. 289; Lösche, in ibid., p. 174; Engelberg, "Nochmals zur ersten bürgerlichen Revolution . . . ," *ZfG* 10 (1972): 1286.

cause the bürgerlich revolution constitutes the only possible attempt at a revolutionary solution under the conditions of rising capitalism." This notable example of circular reasoning has its counterpart in an equally peremptory pronouncement by Engelberg. Invoking Engels explicitly as an expert, although not always an infallible one, Engelberg argues that, "however one may assess the extent of the feudal ties of the Bürgertum, their qualitative degree, so to speak, and their quantitative volume, in particular in relationships with the peasants, this class had the objective task of striving and fighting for a new social order."[28] Within these perimeters, then, DDR Reformation historians must marshal their explanations and continue their search for the role of the Bürgertum and the impact of bürgerlich capitalism.

Convinced that this approach is correct and that the facts to bear out that approach are available and need only be found, DDR scholars pursue this search with unflagging energy. Clearly they do not intend to rest until the thesis of the Reformation as a frühbürgerlich revolution has been fully substantiated. The most recent effort, by Adolf Laube, tries to do away with the "still rather fuzzy concept of a general Bürgerlichkeit of the Reformation" and once again directs its attention to the role of the capitalist entrepreneurs. Laube is not concerned, however, with the "monopolist" big bankers and merchants à la Fugger, but with the "nonmonopolist" small and medium-sized mine-owners and manufacturers who, he feels, have been largely neglected in the analyses of the Reformation. Yet he points out that these smaller capitalists, unlike the bankers and traders, did not fit readily into the feudal system and had serious conflicts over their rights and authority with the feudal powers. Laube calls for further research into the role of these groups in the Reformation movement on the chance— and he presents some data to support this assumption—that that role may bear out the assessment of the Reformation as a frühbürgerlich revolution that furthered the beginning transition from feudalism to capitalism.[29]

The attention the Reformation receives derives, however, not only from these historiographical issues. To the DDR historian, Reformation history is also a key battlefield of conflicting world

---

[28]Steinmetz, in Wohlfeil, *Reformation*, p. 153; Steinmetz expressed the same idea, somewhat more cautiously, in *HZ*, suppl. no. 4 (n.s., 1975): 117; Engelberg, "Probleme der gesetzmässigen Abfolge der Gesellschaftsformationen," *ZfG* 22 (1974): 171–72.

[29]See Adolf Laube, "Die Herausbildung von Elementen einer Handels- und Manufakturbourgeoisie und deren Rolle in der deutschen frühbürgerlichen Revolution," *Jahrb. für Gesch. des Feudalismus* 1 (1977): 273ff., especially 288ff. (quotation on p. 303). On the failure so far to establish a link between capitalist production and the Reformation, see Wohlfeil, in *HZ*, suppl. no. 4 (n.s., 1975): 117.

views, and one in which the assertion of the "socialist" viewpoint
and the refutation of the "imperialist" one assumes a special significance. The assessment of the Reformation as a social revolution serves this purpose especially well: when such an assessment
discredits appraisals of the Reformation as a religious movement
and/or as Luther's individual achievement, it points out the ulterior motives of historians who propose such interpretations. Not
only do such non-Marxist appraisals substitute mysticism and irrationalism for precise scientific methods, they also belittle the
masses as spoilers of Luther's work instead of recognizing them as
the driving force of historical progress.[30]

Beyond that, it is considered essential to demonstrate the
"European" nature of the Reformation by presenting it as the first
phase of that chain of bourgeois revolutions that subsequently
swept across Western Europe. (Steinmetz has also pointed out the
European antecedents of the Lutheran Reformation, noting that it
derived much of its inspiration from the Englishman John Wycliffe,
the Czech Jan Hus, and the Dutchmen Wessel Gansfort, John of
Wesel, and Popper von Goch.[31]) It can thus be shown that, contrary
to the claims of German historicism, Germany was part of the
European mainstream and not separated by innate differences from
other nations. If Germany did develop differently, it did so because
of the weakness and timidity of its Bürgertum, which, during the
Reformation as on later occasions, failed to live up to its historical
tasks.[32] At the same time, the incorporation of the Lutheran Reformation into the European revolutions of the sixteenth, seventeenth, and eighteenth centuries also serves to discredit the thesis
of an alleged historical Western community that was irreconcilably
opposed to an alleged corresponding Eastern camp, which now also
includes the DDR and which territorially was the birthplace of
Lutheranism. (Ironically, West German historians, such as the late
Gerhard Ritter, invoked Lutheranism as a mainstay of just such an
anti-Communist Western community.[33])

Above all, however, DDR historians are convinced that they
are making an important political contribution in demonstrating
that the Reformation was a progressive social revolution. As such a

[30]Steinmetz, in Wohlfeil, Reformation, pp. 108ff., especially pp. 117ff., and in Wohlfeil, Bauernkrieg 1524–26, p. 44 n. 108.

[31]Steinmetz, "Luther und Müntzer," pp. 433–34; also pp. 435–36.

[32]Streisand, "Geschichtsbild," p. 42; Steinmetz, in Stern and Steinmetz, 450 Jahre,
p. 50; Brendler, in Steinmetz and Brendler, Weltwirkung, vol. 1, pp. 181–81;
Grundriss, pp. 158–59; Steinmetz, Deutschland, pp. 159ff. Foschepoth (Reformation und Bauernkrieg, pp. 149ff.) sees political influences at work here, but the
"European" approach was initiated prior to the SED party directives to which he
refers. This approach is, moreover, wholly in keeping with Marxist theory; see
chapter 1, p. 27.

[33]Steinmetz, in Wohlfeil, Reformation, p. 118.

revolution, the Reformation serves as evidence of a deep-rooted, centuries-old democratic tradition in Germany, of which the DDR is claimed to be the legitimate heir. The voluminous literature that has grown around the Reformation and the Peasants' War; the ceremonies, conferences, and publications commemorating the 450th anniversaries of Luther's Ninety-Five Theses and the Peasants' War; and the continued references to these events as landmarks of German history are indicative of the significance that is accorded to them and explain the importance, not just for historians, of the East German Reformation debate.[34]

The People's Reformation and the Peasants' War

The frühbürgerlich revolution is subdivided into three phases by DDR scholars. In their view, the early phase (1517–1521) was the anti-Roman one, during which the Reformation movement, under Luther's leadership, fought its battles on the theological plane and established a religious ideology adapted to bürgerlich needs. It was superseded by the so-called People's Reformation (1521–1524), which in turn culminated in the Peasants' War (1524–1525).

The second phase owes its designation as the People's Reformation to the assertion of popular hopes and needs at that time. More radical-minded reformers, backed by peasants and urban masses, strove to introduce those institutional church reforms for which Luther had called but which he had not carried out on the grounds that only the secular authorities were empowered to do so. As a result, the "inexpensive" church that he wished to create had become a church only for the upper classes; they helped themselves to the secularized church property but continued to exact the tithe from the peasants in lieu of the former claimants. DDR scholars also point out that the lower classes, for their part, had all along viewed the Reformation movement as a vehicle for the satisfaction of their social and political grievances, but had found Luther unwilling to take up their cause.[35]

In accounts in the 1950s and early 1960s, Luther was denounced as a traitor and prince's lackey because of his opposition to these demands and because he took the side of the princes against the masses. More recently, however, it has been argued

---

[34]Leo Stern, "Die DDR-Verkörperung der progressiven Traditionen der deutschen Geschichte," *ZfG* 17 (1969): 1108–9; Steinmetz, in Steinmetz and Brendler, *Weltwirkung*, vol. 1, pp. 7ff., 44–46; Horst Bartel, "Der deutsche Bauernkrieg in der Tradition der revolutionären Arbeiterbewegung," *ZfG* 22 (1975): 148ff.

[35]Brendler, in Stern and Steinmetz, *450 Jahre*, p. 67; Laube et al., *Illustrierte Geschichte*, pp. 173–74, 193.

that Luther's was not a personal decision, but one that grew out of his "class" position. Thus, he was not a traitor, a groveler, or a demagogue, but acted as a member of the educated and propertied Bürgertum; as such, he, like his entire class at that time, was unable to understand the true interests of his class or to appreciate the needs of the masses. On the other hand, all DDR authors remain opposed to the "theologizing" approach that holds that Luther's position involved no partisanship and that attributes to his theological approach his lack of concern with the social and political consequences of his teachings. "The self-image of the reformers," Steinmetz notes, "is not identical with their actual historical role."[36]

This more lenient assessment of Luther is partly explained by the acknowledgment that Luther made a major contribution to the frühbürgerlich revolution by providing it with a religious ideology responsive to bürgerlich needs—the one lasting success of that revolution and the step most immediately needed to spark further progress. Beyond that, Luther is given credit for having made possible by his teachings the more radical phase of the Reformation, even if subsequently he was to turn on it with such vehemence. Without his spadework, it is pointed out, his theological interpretation of the evangelical message could not have been given its secular application. Thus Thomas Müntzer, who gave the People's Reformation its religious ideology, set out as an ally of Luther; in dialectical interaction he went beyond Luther by insisting that the kingdom of God could be established on earth and that if the governmental authorities did not act, this perfected realm would have to be established by revolutionary mass action. All in all, then, the People's Reformation and Müntzer's teachings are not considered a break with the Luther-led Reformation, but part of one revolutionary process, which in this new phase attained a higher level. As Gerhard Brendler has put it:

> A Luther had to come to the fore so that a Müntzer could become possible. And the masses, like Müntzer himself, had to hear Luther to attain the maturity to understand Müntzer's sermon. On the other hand, once Luther had spoken, Müntzer could not remain quiet. . . . However bitterly Luther and Müntzer may have fought each other

[36]Steinmetz, Deutschland, pp. 106, 110; Meusel, Thomas Müntzer und seine Zeit (Berlin [East], 1952), pp. 84–85, 97, 104, as compared to Zschäbitz, Luther, vol. 1, pp. 208–9, 223; Brendler, in Stern and Steinmetz, 450 Jahre, pp. 65–66; Laube et al., Illustrierte Geschichte, pp. 153, 276–77. In a sophisticated, carefully researched study—Luthers Weg von der Reformation zur Restauration (Halle, 1964)—Rosemarie Müller-Streisand has traced the theological and political strands to which she attributes Luther's position. Luther's theological approach is discussed in Nipperdey and Melcher, in Wohlfeil, Reformation, p. 299; his views on "theologizing" are discussed in Steinmetz, in Unb. Verg., pp. 228–29.

theologically and politically, historically they belong together. There is no question here of a trivial friend-foe relationship; a genuine historical dialectic is here at work. . . . This is not a question of rendering a belated judgment on history, but of understanding the course of events in their inevitability and of thus doing them justice.

Shifting the argument to the plane of practical politics, Brendler adds that to exclude Luther from the progressive tradition would be to abandon to the bourgeoisie and its historical tradition one of the two main spokesmen of the first great German mass movement.[37]

What especially impresses DDR authors about Müntzer's teachings, as it had Engels, is his apparent anticipation of some of the teachings of Marx. Like Marx, Müntzer believed in the perfectability of human society. He also insisted that man could find salvation not simply through the mercy of God, but by taking an active part in his redemption. Far from being a helpless sinner, man was responsible for his fate and able to change society. He could not do this without or in defiance of God, however, but only in keeping with God's demands, with divine law. The state in turn did not exist above the classes, but was merely an instrument with which God's will was to be carried out. The princes were therefore the mandatories of God; should they abuse their power for their own selfish purposes, power was to be taken from them by the masses. Ultimately the masses were predestined to take up the fight against the godless and to reorder society if princes, nobles, and wealthy burghers were not willing or able to perform this task. "Müntzer thus was one of the first thinkers," Steinmetz notes, "who perceived the role of the masses in revamping and creating a new social life."[38]

Müntzer is found to have anticipated not only Marx, but Lenin as well. Like Lenin, he understood that to be implemented, a revolutionary ideology required a revolutionary organization, a group of specially selected believers. Müntzer also realized that the masses, ignorant and dulled by their poverty, had to be prepared for their mission by education, and he knew, too, that men wholly absorbed in making a living have no time to study the Bible. Reli-

---

[37]See Foschepoth, *Reformation und Bauernkrieg*, pp. 80ff., 105ff.; Steinmetz, "Thomas Müntzer in der Forschung der Gegenwart," *ZfG* 23 (1975): 675ff.; Steinmetz, review, ibid., 25 (1977): 863; Zschäbitz, *Luther*, vol. 1., p. 179; Brendler, in Stern and Steinmetz, *450 Jahre*, pp. 67 (with quotation), 69; Rudolf Hub, in Steinmetz and Brendler, *Weltwirkung*, vol. 1, p. 155. The concern that Luther must not be abandoned to bourgeois historians has its West German counterpart in warnings that the Peasants' War ought not to become the exclusive property of DDR propagandists (Heide Wunder, in *Die Zeit*, October 10, 1975).
[38]Bensing, *Thomas Müntzer*, pp. 45ff.; Steinmetz, "Thomas Müntzer," pp. 678–79; Steinmetz, *Deutschland*, p. 120 (with quotation); Laube et al., *Illustrierte Geschichte*, pp. 199–200, 276.

gious reform, to be effective, thus was inseparably intertwined with social reform.[39]

As in Luther's case, there is general agreement that Müntzer's teachings were inspired by genuine religious beliefs. Nor, it is also agreed, could he have made himself understood by the masses except in religious terms. DDR scholars are also convinced, however, that it was Müntzer's theology, his approach to social problems by way of religion, that led him to set his goals far beyond what was then attainable in terms of social advances. They see as unrealistic his aim of establishing a community-oriented society of freedom and equality at a time when the historical agenda, in keeping with the emerging capitalist order, called for an individual-centered social order propelled by individual egoism. In addition, although Müntzer is praised for having understood that the masses had a historical role to play, he is also criticized for having assigned to them a leadership role that they could not assume at the entry to the bourgeois-capitalist age; they would be ready for that role only in the late phase of that age, when society would be moving from the capitalist to the socialist order. In other words, what is held against Müntzer is that he tried to bypass the capitalist order.[40]

In the Marxist view, however, Müntzer's error does not detract from his importance. He is hailed as one of the great historical figures, because he called for a social order without exploitation and sensed the direction developments would eventually have to take. In the same vein, he is praised for anticipating the role that the workers would play in that process and their ability to create a society of which they would be the masters. The society that Müntzer envisaged, it is constantly stressed, has now been created in the German Democratic Republic.[41] The analogy is not as far-fetched as it may seem, even granted that Müntzer aimed at a spiritual commonwealth that would assure man's spiritual salva-

---

[39]Laube et al., *Illustrierte Geschichte*, pp. 196–97; Brendler, in Brendler and Laube, *Bauernkrieg 1524/25*, p. 83.

[40]See Alexander Kolesnyk, in Wohlfeil, *Bauernkrieg 1524/25*, pp. 95–96; Willibald Gutsche, in ibid., p. 97; Bensing, *Thomas Müntzer*, p. 90; and Steinmetz, "Thomas Müntzer," pp. 680–81, 685. The attempt of an Anabaptist group to establish a "kingdom" of justice and equality in Münster in 1534–1535 is also seen as foredoomed to failure because of its utopian anticapitalism (Streisand, pp. 72–73; *Grundriss*, pp. 160–61). On the other hand, DDR historians have not concerned themselves much with Müntzer's famous statement, "*Omnia sunt communia.*" The community of goods envisaged here is considered either a distant goal (Steinmetz, *Deutschland*, p. 123, and Steinmetz, in *ZfG* 23 [1975]: 683), or an ethical guideline (Hermann Goebke, in Brendler, *Frühbürgerliche Revolution*, p. 100), as it has been by most West German historians.

[41]Brendler, in Brendler and Laube, *Bauernkrieg 1524/25*, p. 87; Steinmetz, "Geschichtliche Platz," p. 253; Steinmetz, "Thomas Müntzer," p. 685; Laube et al., *Illustrierte Geschichte*, pp. 400ff.

tion and that he viewed all social and political reforms as mere means toward that end.[42] The East German state, free and equal by Marxist criteria (see chapter 1) and attuned to the laws of history, has much in common with the exacting theocracy, led by a select and autocratic elite and attuned to divine law, that would have come into being had Müntzer been able to set up his commonwealth of the godly.[43]

Müntzer has also been important to East German Reformation historians as a connecting link between the Reformation and the Peasants' War: he was associated with Luther in the early phase of the Reformation, gave the People's Reformation its ideological underpinning, and played a major role in the Peasants' War.[44] Müntzer thus symbolizes the basic thesis of DDR historiography that the Reformation and the Peasants' War were part of "one unified revolutionary process," with the Peasants' War its lawful culmination. In fact, for some time the thesis of the frühbürgerlich revolution rested primarily on this linkage. The revolutionary character of the Reformation would have been difficult to explain prior to the new interpretation of its bürgerlich substance if the Peasants' War, as a revolutionary struggle for power, had not been considered an integral part of it. Accordingly, DDR scholars have complained that Western denials of that connection were meant to reduce the Reformation to a

[42]This is seen by Zschäbitz, *Zur mitteldeutschen Widertäuferbewegung nach dem Grossen Bauernkrieg* (Berlin [East], 1958), pp. 36–37, 39, 43–44. In a rather oblique way, Zschäbitz dissociates himself from Engels, who viewed Müntzer as simply a social revolutionary. Zschäbitz is, on the other hand, explicit in his rejection of corresponding views of Wilhelm Zimmermann, whose *Allgemeine Geschichte des grossen Bauernkriegs* (1842) was Engels' main source of information, and of the Soviet historian M. M. Smirin, whose massive study *Die Volksreformation des Thomas Müntzer und der Grosse Bauernkrieg* (1956) long dominated the Marxist Müntzer debate. See also Bensing (*Müntzer und Aufstand*), who also acknowledges the priority of Müntzer's religious concerns.

[43]That Müntzer's commonwealth would have evolved into a rigid theocracy is also implied in Bensing's penetrating analysis of Müntzer's acceptance of the role of social revolutionary (Bensing, *Müntzer und Aufstand*, pp. 45ff., 54ff., 249, 251). See also Zschäbitz, *Wiedertäuferbewegung*, pp. 39, 43–44.

[44]See Smirin, *Volksreformation*, pp. 376ff. and, following him, Meusel, *Thomas Müntzer*, p. 162; Steinmetz, in Wohlfeil, *Reformation*, p. 54; Lösche, in ibid., pp. 178–79; Bensing, *Müntzer und Aufstand, passim*; Laube et al., *Illustrierte Geschichte*, pp, 193, 224-26, 242–43, 265ff., although some of these latter are more cautious in their assessment of Müntzer's influence. Of non-Marxists, Peter Blickle (*Die Revolution von 1525* [Munich, 1975], pp. 151, 210) confirms some of Smirin's findings, and so does Torsten Bergsten (*Balthasar Hubmaier* [Kassel, 1961], cited by Blickle, *Revolution von 1525*, p. 210 n. 18. On the limits of Müntzer's influence see also the West German historian Richard van Dülmen's careful study *Reformation als Revolution* (Munich, 1977), pp. 129ff., 137ff. Such limits may also be inferred from Walter Elliger (*Thomas Müntzer* [Göttingen, 1975]), who deals with this question only incidentally (ibid., pp. 382–83, 394, 522, 674, but also pp. 415–16). Most likely, the actual extent of Müntzer's influence will never be fully determined.

purely religious controversy, depriving it of all social and political implications.[45]

More recently, the relationship between the Reformation and the Peasants' War has been seen somewhat differently. As before, both are viewed as part of one integral revolutionary process, but the Peasants' War no longer overshadows the Reformation. Because the Luther-dominated phase of the Reformation is now credited with its own revolutionary achievements, it is accorded a more significant role in the "unified revolutionary process" than it had been before. Correspondingly, the historical task of the Peasants' War is no longer seen so much as the abolition of serfdom, the reduction of feudal dues, the secularization of church property, and other such changes; it is now seen as the "deepening of the progressive reformatory beginnings, their translation into bürgerlich practice, and their consolidation"—the continuation of the Reformation by other means, as Foschepoth puts it. "In its objective effect," Vogler concludes, "the class struggle of the peasants aimed precisely in the direction toward which the new era pointed—toward capitalism. In that respect the peasant risings were more than merely a struggle for peasant concerns: they were an essential propelling force of historical progress as such." In this vague way, never fully explained, the outcome of the Peasants' War can now be presented as something of a success.[46]

Following up on this new approach, Ernst Engelberg has suggested, on the basis of a complex exegesis of Engels, that the era considered to be that of the Reformation should be extended. Because the historical significance of the Lutheran Reformation lies in its promotion of bürgerlich values and its impact on Calvinism and (by way of Calvinism) on the Dutch, English, and French revolutions, it would be more accurate to consider the Reformation era as extending from 1517 to 1536, the year of the "victory of Calvin's Reformation in Geneva," rather than ending with the collapse of the Peasants' War in 1525. Engelberg argues that the end of the Peasants' War did not bring the Reformation to a halt; the latter kept spreading to new towns and cities, mainly at the Bürgertum's instigation. The real climax thus had to be seen in the incorporation of Reformation precepts in Geneva's municipal constitution.

Engelberg's periodization was rejected by Steinmetz, who contended that it reduced the People's Reformation and the Peasants' War to mere episodes of secondary importance. Steinmetz also pointed out that although the Reformation continued to spread, it

---

[45]Steinmetz, in Wohlfeil, *Reformation*, pp. 59–60; *Grundriss*, p. 153.
[46]Zschäbitz, in Kosock et al., *Studien*, p. 43; Vogler, *Die Gewalt soll gegeben werden dem gemeinen Volk* (Berlin [East], 1975), p. 128; Steinmetz, "Geschichtliche Platz," p. 263; also Foschepoth, *Reformation und Bauernkrieg*, pp. 101–2.

lost much of its momentum after the defeat of the peasants and that this defeat at the hands of the princes had a decisive effect on the course of German developments in the seventeenth and eighteenth centuries. In addition, although he granted that there was a connection between the Lutheran and Calvinist Reformations, he felt that it was too weak and too one-sidedly ideological—that is, without an economic or political basis—to justify the periodization suggested by Engelberg.[47]

As for the thesis of the integral unity of the Reformation and the Peasants' War, it has yet to be proved that, as Steinmetz asserts, the latter grew out of the Reformation, carrying on its endeavors and pursuing its goals.[48] In the same paper from which this definition is taken, Steinmetz places the Peasants' War into that succession of peasants' movements which punctuated this period. He sees it differing from previous risings, however, in that it got under way at the emergence of early capitalist developments and was aiming its thrust not only at the feudal powers but also at the undemocratic and burdensome hierarchical system of the Catholic Church. The distinctive feature of the Peasants' War was, he concludes, that "the peasants' class struggle and reformatory endeavors interpenetrated each other on the national level." Similarly, Günter Vogler has written that the Peasants' War was rooted in political, economic, and social conditions that were unconnected with the Reformation, but that the latter provided the peasants with the ideological justification for their demands. In this form, East German analyses of the relationship between the Reformation and the Peasants' War do not differ greatly from most present non-Marxist ones, but they hardly sustain the thesis of the integral unity of these two movements.[49]

[47]See Engelberg, "Problemen," pp. 1238–39; Engelberg, "Nochmals," pp. 1285ff., as compared to Steinmetz, "Geschichtliche Platz," pp. 261, 263; Vogler, "Friedrich Engels zur internationalen Stellung der deutschen frühbürgerlichen Revolution," *ZfG* 20 (1972): 444ff.; Brendler, "Vor- und Frühformen," pp. 29–30. Franklin Kopitzsch has pointed out that if one were to pursue Engelberg's suggestion, it would be more meaningful to select 1541, the year of Calvin's actual victory, rather than 1536, the year of his arrival in Geneva, as the end of the Reformation era (Kopitzsch, in Wohlfeil, *Bauernkrieg 1524–26*, p. 215 n. 201).
[48]See Steinmetz, "Geschichtliche Platz," p. 262. Dietrich Lösche goes even further, claiming that "both the Reformation and the Peasants' War had exactly the same objective—the realization of the Reformation," which was a bürgerlich-antifeudal as well as an ideological, anticlerical movement (Wohlfeil, *Reformation*, p. 178).
[49]See Steinmetz, in ibid., 254–55, 269; Vogler, *Gewalt*, p. 24. For non-Marxist views, see Holborn, vol. 1, pp. 170–71; Walter Peter Fuchs, in Gebhardt, vol. 2, pp. 64, 66; Günther Franz, *Der deutsche Bauernkrieg* (Darmstadt, 1956), pp. 286ff. and *passim*. Some recent non-Marxist studies have raised the question of whether *all* peasant risings in 1524–1525 were sparked by the Reformation (H. C. Erik Midelfort, "The Revolution of 1525? Recent Studies of the Peasants' War," *CEH* 11 [1978]: 201–2). Some clearly were not (see Laube et al., *Illustrierte Geschichte*, pp. 207ff.; also Elliger, *Thomas Müntzer*, pp. 644–45, 647–48; Franz, pp. 100–101; 106ff., 153ff.).

The implicit premise of the Marxist analyses is that the Peasants' War was caused above all by social and economic conditions and that the changes called for by the peasants and their allies in towns, cities, and mines struck at the core of the feudal system. Whatever political demands the peasants advanced are seen as merely implementing the revolutionary social and economic goals. The traditional approach, on the other hand, which viewed the Peasants' War as primarily a political rising,[50] is rejected as a cynical attempt to deny the revolutionary nature of the Peasants' War and to fit it as a merely reformist movement into the existing feudal order. Such an interpretation, it is charged, is simply meant to persuade today's working class that the insurrectionists of the Peasants' War were convinced that if they obtained political rights, they would be assured of a genuine and lasting improvement of their lot, even without changes in the socioeconomic system. By this stratagem West Germany's working class is to be dissuaded from resorting to revolution to improve its own lot and persuaded to accept the present "state-monopolist" system as responsive to its needs.[51] In recent years a number of non-Marxist Reformation scholars, too, have concluded that the Peasants' War, apart from its religious connotations, was primarily a social rather than a political upheaval, but DDR critics still assail them for trying to integrate the rebelling masses into the feudal system rather than viewing their efforts as genuinely revolutionary ones aimed "objectively" at the destruction of the feudal order.[52]

As evidence of the "progressive" nature of the war, the demands of the peasants and their urban allies have received close attention. Such programs as the *Twelve Articles*, emanating from Wuerttemberg, and the *Artikelbrief* of Black Forest Peasants have been carefully analyzed as antifeudal manifestoes that removed obstacles to the rise of capitalism. The *Heilbronn Program*, in turn, one of the few bürgerlich programs, receives credit for its advocacy of a unified judicial system; uniform weights, measures, and currency throughout the empire; and the elimination of all territorial taxes and tariffs. The program's call for the liquidation of all large commercial companies is hailed as an attack on monopolies. Similarly, the assurance of equal judicial protection by the replacement

---

[50]For a convenient survey of this approach, see Herman Vahle, "Der deutsche Bauernkrieg als politische Bewegung im Urteil der Geschichtsschreibung," *GWU* 23 (1972): 257ff. The most influential representative of this view is, of course, Franz (*Deutsche Bauernkrieg*, pp. 286ff).

[51]*Unb. Verg.*, pp. 54ff., 229–30; also Andreas Dorpalen, "History and Politics: An East German Assessment," *CEH* 12 (1979): 83ff.

[52]Blickle, *Revolution von 1525*; essays by Rudolf Endres, Rainer Postel, and Franklin Kopitzsch, in Wohlfeil, *Bauernkrieg 1524–26*, and the critique in *Unb. Verg.*, pp. 230ff.

of feudal law with divine law is greeted as another progressive step. Fault is found, on the other hand, with the program's neglect of all peasant concerns, for it thus cut off the burghers from the very forces that could have helped them to achieve their goals.

Conversely, the *Landesordnung* of Michael Gaismaier, the leader of the Tyrolean uprising in 1526, catered to peasants and miners and was characterized by a strong anticity bias. With its call for a democratic peasant republic, full social equality, and the commonweal rather than divine law as the guiding principle, the *Landesordnung* is considered the "most important attempt to de- velop a new political and social order out of the social and political concepts of peasant communities and miners." On the other hand, the socialized economy it envisaged is dismissed as utopian, be- cause it reaches far beyond the emerging bourgeois-capitalist order, and its social parochialism is found equally unrealistic. Gaismaier is contrasted with Müntzer, the only one who saw the need for a movement embracing both town and country and who, for a brief moment at least, did unite parts of the Bürgertum, urban plebeians, and peasants in a common front in Thuringia.[53]

The lack of a town-country alliance in which burghers, peas- ants, and urban masses would have fought jointly against princes and nobles was of course a major reason for the defeat of the peas- ants. The failure to form such an alliance is blamed on the Bürgertum of the large and medium-sized towns, whose fear of the masses and concern for its property led it to sacrifice its antifeudal interests and side with the princes. Like other such strictures, these are self-contradictory. Because all East German Reformation specialists are agreed that the Bürgertum had not yet matured either objectively or subjectively to the point where it could per- ceive its true interests, it seems specious to blame it for not having displayed what, on the East Germans' own showing, could be called only superhuman foresight. Of course, note is taken of the role of the urban masses, which forced a few of the larger towns to join the peasants, and of the more numerous smaller towns in which local self-interest led to such cooperation. Yet, dictated by mass pressures or opportunism, this help is dismissed as rather ephemeral in most cases.

The peasants, however, are not seen as blameless, either. Their moderate majority is taken to task for its compromises with princes and nobles and its efforts to restrain the revolutionary mi- nority from pursuing the fight with full force. The insurgents are also blamed for their local parochialism and the corresponding lack

[53]Steinmetz, *Deutschland*, pp. 132–34, 141–42, 150–51; Vogler, in Brendler, *Früh- bürgerliche Revolution*, pp. 116ff., especially pp. 124–25; Laube et al., *Illustrierte Geschichte*, pp. 232–34, 242–44, 257–60, 288–90.

of coordination of their activities. Military deficiencies round out the causes to which these analyses attribute the defeat of the peasants.[54]

The results of the war are assessed in the context of the period's transition from the feudal to the capitalist order. Until recently, these assessments were focused on the war's immediate results. The attempt of the peasants to revamp the social order from below was judged a failure; on the whole feudalism remained strong, although the lot of the peasants in the regions involved in the fighting did not deteriorate further. At the same time, the power of the princes increased, consolidating the territorial divisions of the empire and laying the foundation for princely absolutism.[55] Recent West German findings that paint a more positive picture of the lot of the peasants and also question the connection between princely victory and princely absolutism may lead DDR scholars to modify their conclusions. The immediate reaction has been guarded. Vogler feels that compared to the original demands of the peasants, the concessions that were made to them in some regions were rather modest.[56] He and some others, it will be recalled, think that the most positive and historically significant impact of the war was its very occurrence, which supposedly reinforced the trend toward Bürgerlichkeit that the Reformation is claimed to have launched.

If not all DDR historians concur in this judgment, most of them are agreed that the Peasants' War left at least one positive legacy. As they see it, the memory of the rebelling peasants fighting for their rights lived on in Germany and served as an inspiration to generations to come—a beacon pointing to the potential of mass action and democratic regeneration. Here, of course, they follow in the footsteps of Engels, who made this point in his *Peasants' War.*[57]

Yet this picture of the war's inspirational impact also rests on tenuous foundations. A recent study by Horst Bartel notes that only in the nineteenth century, after a long period of distortion and defamation, did the German working class revive and nurture this legacy of the war.[58] Although from then on a great deal was published regarding that event under Social Democratic and Commu-

---

[54]*Grundriss*, pp. 158–59; Steinmetz, "Geschichtliche Platz," pp. 258, 265–66, 268–69; Laube et al., *Illustrierte Geschichte*, pp. 290ff., 260–62, 300–302.

[55]Laube et al., *Illustrierte Geschichte*, pp. 302–3; Streisand, p. 73; Zschäbitz, in Wohlfeil, *Reformation*, p. 138.

[56]Blickle, *Revolution von 1525*, pp. 224ff.; Midelfort, "Revolution of 1525?," pp. 204–5; Vogler, in a review of Blickle's book, in *ZfG* 14 (1976): 105.

[57]Vogler, *Gewalt*, p. 128; Bartel, "Deutsche Bauernkrieg," pp. 133ff.; Steinmetz, in ibid., p. 685. See also Engels, in MEW, vol. 7, p. 329.

[58]Bartel, "Deutsche Bauernkrieg," pp. 133–34.

nist auspices, it is not clear to what extent this rising of *peasants* impressed the *workers* among whom these publications were circulated. (There is no indication that this literature reached and affected the peasantry.) Subsequent efforts made in the DDR to cultivate the memory of the Peasants' War may have been more effective. If nothing else, these endeavors have had some impact in West Germany. Although most West Germans still seem to look on the Peasants' War as a revolt of marauders and arsonists,[59] West German historians, partly in response to the East German concern with the war, have produced a large number of studies endeavoring to do justice to the cause of the peasants.[60] Because these efforts touch on basic ideological issues, the debate on the Peasants' War is not likely to subside.

The Resurgence of Feudalism

Ever concerned with the state of production, accounts of the subsequent period stress the renewed strength of the feudal system and corresponding delays in the growth of capitalism. Peasants were subjected to increased exploitation—mainly, however, in the regions not touched by the Peasants' War. (In areas involved in the risings, it is noted with some satisfaction, the lords had learned to respect the limits of the peasants' endurance.) Special attention is paid to the emergence in northeastern Germany of the *Gutswirtschaft*—a landed estate managed largely by the owner himself, as opposed to the *Grundherrschaft*, which was cultivated by tenants. The formation of the *Gutswirtschaft* serves as a prime example of refeudalization. In the sparsely settled lands east of the Elbe river, large surpluses of cereals and foodstuffs were produced, and the estate owners (Junkers) found it more profitable to grow and dispose of these crops themselves. Because their territorial rulers were weak, the Junkers were able to deprive the propertied peasants of their land and force them to work for them on the *Gut*. They derived further power over the peasants from their police and judicial functions, and as church patrons they enjoyed the support of their Lutheran clergy. With such accoutrements the East Elbian Junkers obtained almost unlimited control over their peasants. Moreover, having been spared the turmoil of the Peasants' War, they had no frightening memories to restrain them in their exac-

---

[59]Heide Wunder, in *Die Zeit*, October 10, 1975.
[60]Franz, *Das Politisch-Historische Buch* 24 (1976): 1ff.; Midelfort, "Revolution of 1525?," pp. 189ff.

tions. "Second serfdom" (see chapter 2, page 92) thus spread rapidly through the regions east of the Elbe river.[61]

The territorial princes, too, are found to have injected new strength into the feudal order: they consolidated their own power through the secularization of ecclesiastical properties, increased control of their subjects, and economic policies that impeded the accumulation and utilization of capital.[62] This last claim, however, remains unspecified and undocumented; the assumption of what must have happened has misled DDR authors into accepting it as the reality that did occur. Detailed West German analyses leave no doubt that there existed no serious *feudal* impediments to capitalist growth at the time. If anything, the evidence shows that the princes were fostering such growth. What obstacles entrepreneurs did encounter resulted not so much from feudal restrictions, such as serfdom or from the lack of a national market as from the shifting of trade routes in the wake of the new geographical discoveries, the influx of silver and other metals from South America, and, above all, their own lack of initiative.[63] In one frequently cited case, in which feudal nobles moved into what might be called the bürgerlich domain—the takeover of grain exports by East Elbian Junkers—the Junkers did so only after the commercial decline of north German cities had been under way for some time.[64]

DDR historians are on firmer ground when they point to the changing social function of Lutheranism as benefiting the feudal order. Lutheranism became increasingly a tool of the Lutheran princes. Making themselves heads of the church organization, they used the church to exert more effective control over their subjects. "The masses," Steinmetz observes, "were no longer the acting subject, but the object. The confrontations that arose were no historical contribution to the formation of the German nation—they were

[61]See Steinmetz, *Deutschland*, pp. 222ff.; Mottek, *Wirtschaftsgeschichte Deutschlands*, vol. 1, pp. 333ff. Steinmetz and Mottek regard this particularly ruthless treatment as a sort of justified punishment of the north German peasants for having failed to come to the aid of their brethren in central and southern Germany in the Peasants' War (Steinmetz, *Deutschland*, p. 225; Mottek, *Wirtschaftsgeschichte Deutschlands*, vol. 1, p. 339).

[62]Streisand, p. 73; Grundriss, pp. 157–58, 161–62; Mottek, *Wirtschaftsgeschichte Deutschlands*, vol. 1, pp. 251ff.; Hoffmann and Mittenzwei, "Stellung des Bürgertums," p. 197.

[63]See Hermann Kellenbenz, in *HbDtWSG*, vol. 1, pp. 414ff.; Wilhelm Treue, in Gehardt, vol. 2, pp. 459ff., 469ff.; Lütge, *Deutsche Sozial- und Wirtschaftsgeschichte*, pp. 268ff.; Hans Hausherr, *Wirtschaftsgeschichte der Neuzeit* (Cologne, 1970), pp. 44ff. See also the ambiguous account in Laube et al., *Illustrierte Geschichte* (pp. 355ff.), which tries hard but fails to uphold the thesis of the blockage of capitalist growth by feudal restrictions.

[64]Mottek, *Wirtschaftsgeschichte Deutschlands*, vol. 1, pp. 298, 337–38; Steinmetz, *Deutschland*, p. 222; Streisand, p. 74. See also Treue (in Gebhart, vol. 2, p. 470), who stresses the lack of bürgerlich entrepreneurial initiative in northeastern and eastern Germany.

power struggles between individual feudal lords and feudal conditions." The Lutheran princes also turned Lutheranism into a political weapon that they wielded against the Catholic central power and the Catholic princes. From a force that had rallied the Germans in an incipient national unity, Lutheranism thus was transformed into a disrupting force, deepening the existing divisions and setting up further obstacles to the development of a bürgerlich nation and, it is charged once again without proof, to capitalist expansion.[65]

The religious cleavage of Germany was institutionalized by the Peace of Augsburg in 1555. This compromise of *cuius regio, eius religio* contributed to the further consolidation of the territorial states at the expense of the central power. In their first analyses of this arrangement, DDR historians viewed the Augsburg accord as a disastrous solution inasmuch as it strengthened the princes, the "most antinational class," in Streisand's words. Steinmetz voiced similar views.[66] More recent accounts find this accretion of strength to the princes less decisive. Even though no other group had a stake in a decentralized empire that could compare with the princes', it is recognized that few people were actively concerned with strengthening the central power. The Reformation itself had been national only in the sense that it sought to shake off the hold of the Roman Pope; in the Peasants' War, too, few programs had called for national unification. Given also the continued extra German preoccupations of Emperor Charles V, who was involved in wars with the French and the Turks and who was anxious to retain and establish bases of power outside of Germany, the Peace of Augsburg did not destroy any genuine chance of creating a more centralized empire. It has even been argued that by consolidating power in their own states the princes furthered the process of centralization. Marx, too, had reached this conclusion when he said of the absolutist regimes that subsequently evolved that their "civilizing activity" lay in their centralizing function. Thus, more recent accounts, although still taking note of the divisive nature of the Peace of Augsburg, no longer see it as a major incision. Streisand, for example, speaks of it, hardly more accurately, as a victory of the "most reactionary" rather than the "most antinational" forces.[67]

[65]See Steinmetz, *Deutschland*, pp. 198–199 and Laube et al., *Illustrierte Geschichte*, pp. 316–18. The change of function of Lutheranism has, of course, also been noted by Western scholars; see, for example, Frederick G. Heymann, "The Hussite Revolution and the German Peasants' War," *Medievalia et Humanistica*, n.s., no. 1 (170): 155.

[66]Streisand (1968 ed.), p. 58; Steinmetz, *Deutschland*, p. 209.

[67]Brendler, in Stern and Steinmetz, *450 Jahre*, pp. 68–69; Helga Schultz, "Bäuerliche Klassenkämpfe zwischen frühbürgerlicher Revolution und Dreissigjährigen Krieg," *ZfG* 20 (1972): pp. 172–73; Marx, in MEW, vol. 4, p. 347; Mottek, *Wirtschaftsgeschichte Deutschlands*, vol. 1, pp. 255–56; *Grundriss*, p. 163; Streisand (1974 ed.), p. 78.

All in all, then, the latter part of the sixteenth century is presented as a period of steady decline on the "national" level. While economic necessity called for centralization on that level, disintegration continued to spread—a trend reinforced by the Catholic Counter Reformation and the adoption of Calvinism in some parts of Germany. The Counter Reformation appears as a product of feudal reaction; Steinmetz points out that it had its economic base in those countries in which feudalism was still most firmly entrenched—Spain, Portugal, the papal state, the Habsburg domain, and Bavaria. Politically it is attacked as an attempt to recreate the old universalist empire at a time when universalism had become obsolete and socioeconomic developments called for the formation of nation-states. The Counter Reformation was nonetheless able to recover considerable ground for the Catholic Church, a success that is attributed to the highly effective political, educational, and missionary activities of the Jesuits and to the disunity of the Protestant camp, which was rent by doctrinal quarrels, rivalries among Protestant princes, and the acceptance of Calvinism in some parts of Germany.[68]

From this perspective, the Jesuits fit well into the feudal "counterrevolutionary" strategy. An elitist group, catering to the upper classes and anxious to suppress all signs of popular self-assertion, they were instrumental in tightening the organizational structure of the Church and restoring Papal absolutism. Through their missionary activities, which extended into Latin America and the Far East, the Jesuits not only expanded the influence of Catholicism but also helped pave the way for the Spanish and Portuguese colonial empires. Marxists see in the order's missionary activities a conscious collaboration with the emerging forces of capitalism and attribute the effectiveness of the Jesuits to their skillful adaptation to the new economic conditions. Specifically, East German historians point to the readiness of the Church to condone the enslavement of blacks, a major source of new wealth, and to the defense of slavery by Jesuit missionaries on the grounds that slavery gave blacks an opportunity for conversion and thus saved them from eternal damnation. This alliance with "progressive" capitalist elements, notes Max Steinmetz, was actually used by the Jesuits to strengthen the position of the forces of reaction—the Catholic Church and the feudal system—because the Jesuits wished to uphold the existing social order.[69]

[68]Steinmetz, *Deutschland*, pp. 227ff., 236; Steinmetz, cited in *ZfG* 10 (1962): 1679; Mottek, *Wirtschaftsgeschichte Deutschlands*, vol. 1, p. 253.

[69]See Mottek, *Wirtschaftsgeschichte Deutschlands*, vol. 1, p. 250, citing Werner Sombart, *Der moderne Kapitalismus* (Munich and Leipzig, 1924), vol. 1, pp. ii, 694; Steinmetz, *Deutschland*, p. 231. Among non-Marxists, in addition to Som-

The Jesuits' impact in Germany is ascribed to their "class-centered" strategy of seeking access to princes and feudal nobility rather than engaging in work with the lower classes. In doing so, the argument runs, they injected a new dynamism into the Catholic camp, which helps to account for the recovery of much lost terrain. This reassertion was aided further by the disarray in the Protestant camp and the divisive effect of Calvinism as a new rallying ground—a Calvinism, moreover, that was molded by its imposition from above in most cases and by the rulers' retention of Lutheran-type organizational and supervisory rights. With the doctrine of predestination dropped from the German Calvinist creed, Calvinism in its German form was also deprived of one of its major activist impulses. "Though more progressive [in matters of education and scholarship]," Max Steinmetz concludes, "Calvinism was to a large extent restrained by the feudal powers and in this manner was diverted from its antifeudal impetus."[70]

This blending of religion and politics has been noted not only by Marxists. Hajo Holborn has shown how Lutheranism, defensive and politically passive, left its impact on northern Germany. Whereas DDR scholars deplore this convergence, Holborn's assessment is positive. "One cannot help being impressed," he writes,

> with how neatly Lutheran social ethics, with its hankering for a static medieval society, without capitalistic enterprises and expansionist power politics, corresponded to the general needs, particularly of central and northeastern Germany. This predominantly agrarian society, not capable of mobilizing large internal resources for external efforts—a measure which would in any case have threatened the precarious balance of internal forces—found in the Lutheran religion and ethics a natural expression of its aspirations.[71]

To Marxists, such an affirmative appraisal merely signifies acquiescence in a system that suppressed and exploited the masses.

DDR historians find equally objectionable the traditional accounts of the politics of the period. Dealing with the struggles between emperor and princes in the empire and between princes and estates in the territories, these studies, it is charged, neglect the concerns of peasants and urban masses and, moreover, ignore

---

bart, Hausherr (*Wirtschaftsgeschichte der Neuzeit*, pp. 54–55) and Clarence H. Haring (The Spanish Empire [New York, 1947], pp. 198ff.) offer some evidence of capitalist proclivities among Jesuits—a kind of "feudal capitalism," as it developed simultaneously among the Junkers of northeastern Germany (Mottek, *Wirtschaftsgeschichte Deutschlands*, vol. 1, pp. 352–53). See also G. Frederici, *Der Charakter der Entdeckung und Eroberung Amerikas durch die Europäer* (Stuttgart, 1925), vol. 2, pp. 161–62, 261.

[70]Steinmetz, *Deutschland*, pp. 241–42; *Grundriss*, pp. 166–67; Streisand, pp. 75–76; see also Barrraclough, *Origins*, pp. 375ff.; Holborn, vol. 1, pp. 259–60.

[71]Holborn, vol. 1, p. 261; also Ernst Walter Zeeden, in Gebhardt, vol. 2, 222–23.

their never-ceasing class struggles—an approach that again accepts the existing order as equitable. Not surprisingly, what little original research East Germans have done for this period has been concerned with the lot of the peasantry which remained the primary class among the exploited in the still mainly agricultural empire.

These studies center on the continuing class struggle even in this period of seeming stagnation and apathy. The so-called lower forms of that struggle—refusal of payments and services, complaints and petitions submitted to the territorial rulers, lawsuits, and escapes—receive special attention as the means resorted to most often by the peasants to check the process of refeudalization. Although such measures admittedly could not stop seigniorial encroachments, it is found that in many cases these actions did set limits to them. The purpose of tracing these manifestations of the less obvious forms of class conflicts is also political, however:

> Only by thoroughly tracing and presenting the class struggle of the peasants in all its forms . . . can we effectively foil the attempts of bourgeois historiography to eliminate altogether from history the class struggle of the peasants in this period as the decisive factor of social development or to separate from the overall process of social development this resistance against refeudalization after the Peasants' War and dismiss it as merely a prelude to the risings after the Thirty Years War. (G. Franz)

Yet the data that DDR researchers have gathered on these class struggles hardly bear out their claim of the decisiveness of these conflicts.

As for the abortive risings that occurred in Austria and southern Germany—areas, it is stressed, that had revolutionary tradition—their failure is attributed to the same causes that brought on the defeat in the Peasants' War: cities and towns without whose leadership the risings could not succeed would not support the peasants. Once again, moreover, the risings were localized and this time lacked even a revolutionary ideology, such as Müntzer's, that might have provided some common objectives.[72]

East German scholars have also found evidence of an open class struggle in the Mansfeld region of central Germany where miners repeatedly rose in protest against low wages, bureaucratic abuses, and defraudations. For Marxists these risings are of special significance as a first indication of things to come. "Apart from germinal forms of proletarian class consciousness," Steinmetz finds, "the miners' movement in the Mansfeld area resort[ed] to

[72]Schultz, "Bäuerliche Klassenkämpfe," pp. 156ff. (above quotation on p. 159; the reference is to G. Franz, *Geschichte des deutschen Bauernstandes vom frühen Mittelalter bis zum 19. Jahrhundert* [Stuttgart, 1970]); Heitz, "Zu den bäuerlichen Klassenkämpfen im Spätfeudalismus," *ZfG* 23 (1975): 769ff.

typically proletarian methods of fighting, such as strikes." There were also occasional acts of sabotage; descent into the mines was blocked by the destruction of ladders and ropes. Perhaps even more significant, a mutual-aid system was set up in order to take care of the needy. All in all, the uprisings of the Mansfeld miners are viewed as foreshadowing the proletarian solidarity and collective action that would eventually be achieved by their descendants. Note is also taken of the discontent of the urban masses, which exploded into risings against the ruling patricians and guildmasters in Cologne (1611) and Frankfurt-on-the-Main (1615), while in Berlin and some other towns religious maneuvers on the part of the rulers sparked bitterness into open upheavals.[73]

DDR scholars are aware of the localized nature of all these risings and of the limited impact they had. What matters to them is that these upheavals were part of an unceasing movement that continued to gnaw at the feudal order. As Hans Mottek points out, the flare-ups of peasant resistance kept alive the fear of a new Peasants' War and, though the peasants were defeated each time, the struggles did nonetheless help to mitigate some abuses. According to Helga Schultz, another positive effect of the risings was that their suppression required the intervention of the territorial rulers, as did the appeals, complaints, and law suits the peasants initiated. Such interventions, she notes, strengthened the princes vis-à-vis the nobility and furthered centralization on the territorial level—a development that Schultz, unlike some of her colleagues, considers progressive.[74] DDR authors thus do not agree with those West German historians who feel that after the Peasants' War the "common man" withdrew from German history and did not reenter it until the nineteenth century.[75]

The Thirty Years War

The Thirty Years War—the climactic crisis of the period—is assessed as another phase in the transition from feudalism to capital-

[73]Steinmetz, *Deutschland*, pp. 218ff., 254ff. (quotation on p. 258); Roland F. Schmiedt, in ibid., pp. 282, 286–87, 290–92; Mottek, *Wirtschaftsgeschichte Deutschlands*, vol. 1, pp. 315ff.
[74]See Mottek, *Wirtschaftsgeschichte Deutschlands*, vol. 1, p. 317, with additional references. Also see Schultz, "Bäuerliche Klassenkampfe," pp. 172–73. In a speech in 1970, the then West German Federal President Gustav Heinemann called attention to one of the peasant risings, that of the Saltpeterers in the Black Forest (1612). Heinemann, too, saw it as a link in a long chain of popular movements in Germany's past and as part of a democratic tradition and deplored that little attention had ever been paid to it.
[75]Franz Schnabel, *Deutsche Geschichte im 19. Jahrhundert* (Freiburg, 1949), vol. 2, p. 95; Fuchs, in Gebhardt, vol. 2, p. 71; Franz, *Deutsche Bauernkrieg*, pp. 299–300.

ism. On the German level, the conflict is indicative to DDR scholars of the incompetence and unwillingness of Germany's feudal
class to respond to the need for a unified country. Anxious to further
their own particular concerns, the German princes hastened the
decline and disintegration of Germany. At the same time, their divisiveness continued to impede the growth of capitalism.

East German historians are convinced that such a decline
would not have occurred if the German people, rather than the
princes, had emerged as the victors from the Reformation and the
Peasants' War. Thus Gerhard Brendler maintains that the defeat of
the masses deprived Germany of the strength and the will to work
for national unity—a conclusion inspired by mystic faith in the
masses rather than borne out by hard evidence. Similarly, Brendler
claims that the Thirty Years War was the "belated result and the
historically determined [i.e., gesetzmässig] consequence of that defeat."[76] In the same vein, Streisand considers the defeat of the early
bourgeois revolution and the victory of the princes an "essential
condition for the outbreak of a European war extending over thirty
years and fought essentially on German soil: in order to attain
their antinational class goals, [the princes] entered alliances with
foreign powers and thus brought the rivalries of these latter right
into Germany." Pursuing this thought further, Roland F. Schmiedt
points out, however, that along with the German princes, foreign
powers—in particular, Sweden and France—had a strong interest
in a weak and divided empire in order to pursue their own power-
political plans. Still, there is general agreement that the political
disintegration of the empire caused the war and was not itself
caused by that conflict.[77]

As these comments also suggest, Marxist historians view the
Thirty Years War from its outset as a European rather than merely
a German conflict; in this war, a Spanish-Habsburg-Catholic coalition fought against an anti-Spanish, anti-Habsburg, anti-Catholic
camp. The Spanish-Habsburg front (Spain, Austria, Bavaria) is depicted as the embodiment of feudal "reaction," supported by the
revitalized Catholic Church, which was equally anxious to turn
the clock back. The opposing alignment consisted of states that are
described as early bourgeois (Netherlands, England) or, though still
basically feudal, as tending to be more progressive than the Habsburg camp (Denmark, Sweden, France). The presence of France in

---

[76]See Brendler, report, *ZfG* 10 (1962): 1677–78; also *Grundriss*, p. 173; Schmiedt, in
Steinmetz, *Deutschland*, p. 280. The East German claim that the Peasants' War
aimed at a strengthened empire—a view propounded also by Franz (*Deutsche
Bauernkrieg*, p. 288)—has been convincingly refuted by Horst Buszello in *Der
deutsche Bauernkrieg als politische Bewegung* (Berlin [West], 1969).

[77]Streisand, pp. 78, 82; Schmiedt, in Steinmetz, *Deutschland*, p. 328; Josef Polisensky, in *Aus 500 Jahren deutsch-tschekoslovakischer Geschichte*, ed. Karl
Obermann and Josef Polisensky (Berlin [East], 1958), pp. 99ff.

this predominantly Protestant coalition and the collaboration of Lutheran Saxony with the Catholic powers are considered proof of the essentially political character of the war, with religious contentions serving as a convenient cover for more mundane concerns.[78]

Socially, in this view, the war grew out of the "basic contradiction" between the feudal nobility and the emerging capitalist forces, yet the facts do not fit easily into this assessment. With the feudal-capitalist transition still in its early stage, that "basic" conflict is found to be as yet largely confined to domestic developments, and even domestically its impact is considered significant only in some of the states. Generally, it turns out, "contradictions" *within* the feudal class dominated the war; they grew out of the expansionist designs of the "historically antiquated" ("historisch überlebt") Spanish monarchy and the equally ambitious Austrian Habsburgs on the one hand and the countermoves of the more advanced feudal monarchies on the other. These latter regimes are characterized as developing toward that national absolutism best suited to the needs of the emerging capitalist system, and the terri torial designs they pursued are explained as protective measures against the Spanish-Austrian threats. After 1630, however, the bourgeois-influenced states—England and Holland—played a rather minor role in the war. In the tortuous words of two Czech historians, Josef Polisensky and Miroslav Hroch, the war, though basically the "expression of a certain level of contradiction between newly developing productive forces and stagnant feudal productive relations, [came] at a time when the larger part of Europe was not yet ripe for a solution of this basic contradiction," i.e., was not ripe for a conversion to bourgeois regimes.[79]

Nonetheless, if the Thirty Years War assumed European dimensions, Marxist historians are certain that this expansion cannot be explained simply in terms of political considerations. With politics a part of that superstructure that rests on the socioeconomic foundation, they conclude that the novel character of the Thirty Years War must have reflected some major change in that foundation. According to Miroslav Hroch, on whose work DDR scholars have heavily drawn, the change lay in the notable growth of produc-

[78]See Streisand, pp. 78–79; Schmiedt, in Steinmetz, *Deutschland*, pp. 272ff., 281; Mottek *Wirtschaftsgeschichte Deutschlands*, vol. 1, p. 254; Herbert Langer, "Neue Forschungen zur Geschichte des Dreissigjährigen Krieges," *ZfG* 16 (1968): 933, 937–38, 940–41, with some non-Marxist references. Among non-Marxists, Walter Platzhoff (*Geschichte des europäischen Staatensystems: 1559–1660* [Munich, 1928], p. 154) and Cicely V. Wedgwood (*The Thirty Years War* [New York, 1961], p. 13) also stress that the war was a European one from its beginning.
[79]Schmiedt, in Steinmetz, *Deutschland*, pp. 278ff. (Polisensky and Hroch are quoted on p. 279); Langer, "Neue Forschungen," p. 942; also Miroslav Hroch, "Der dreissigjährige Krieg und die europäischen Handelsbeziehungen," *Wiss. Z. Greifswald* 12 (1963): 533–34, 541–42; Polisensky, in Obermann and Polisensky, *500 Jahren*, pp. 119ff.

tivity (demonstrated on the basis of admittedly limited evidence), specifically, increased food production and improved preservation of food, expanding mining and metal-processing operations, increased ship construction and improved and enlarged harbor facilities, and other developments aiding long-distance transportation of merchandise. These developments added up to expanded commercial relations and to increased profits to be derived by state governments from taxes and tariffs. Hroch concludes that the growth of production was not yet sufficiently large to cause a rapid increase of capitalist operations and thus threaten the feudal system in its entirety. He sees, however, a direct connection between the range of action of the individual states and the ability of the rising bourgeoisie to influence foreign policy; the socially more advanced English and Dutch states thus ranged farthest in their diplomatic activities and the granting of trade subsidies.

Hroch also notes that as the feudal powers became aware of the potential of commercial activities as a source of state revenue, they raised taxes and duties, sought to direct foreign trade by political and legal means, and strove to secure control over trade routes, harbors, river mouths, mountain passes, and trade centers. "Given this situation, every crisis in an area that was part of the European market naturally created disquiet and direct concern in most other such areas—not only among merchants but among feudal rulers as well. There was but one step from direct concern to direct intervention, provided political conditions were favorable." According to Hroch, this conclusion is borne out by the fact, stressed also by other Marxist historians, that the war not only involved central and western Europe but also had repercussions in Poland and Russia, which both had commercial ties with western Europe; Poland also had political ties with that area.

Hroch also applies his thesis to the struggle for control of the Baltic Sea, on which the Thirty Years War centered for several years. He shows that Sweden's intervention was motivated in part by her Baltic trade interests, as were England's efforts to encourage that intervention. By the same token, Dutch attempts to bring an end to the Swedish campaign by mediating between King Gustavus Adolphus and Emperor Ferdinand II grew out of the fear that a Swedish victory would be just as dangerous to the Netherlands' Baltic Sea trade as would a victory of the Habsburgs. Other clashes, of more indirect bearing on the war, between Sweden and Poland and Sweden and Denmark are also found to have been rooted, in part at least, in such trade rivalries.[80]

[80]See Hroch, "Dreissigjährige Krieg," pp. 534ff. (quotation on p. 536); see also Schmiedt, in Steinmetz, Deutschland, pp. 278–79, 322ff.; Langer, "Neue Forschungen," pp. 934, 936, 940; Polisensky, 500 Jahren, p. 100. Generally, on the economic importance on the Baltic Sea trade, see Hausherr, Wirtschaftsgeschichte

Hroch sees a further correlation between the extension and duration of the Thirty Years War and the growth of production and trade, inasmuch as only this growth enabled the participants to raise the huge sums of money that were needed in order to finance military expenditures and the large subsidies that were paid to allies. In fact, war was the only way, Hroch maintains, in which feudal powers were able to utilize the growth of production. Because they could not use it productively, they spent it in "typically feudal" fashion—financing wars that would lead to the conquest of additional territories, which in turn could be exploited in the same feudal fashion.[81]

Marxist historians admit that too little is known as yet about economic conditions and policies of the period to do more than throw out suggestions and establish the points of departure for further studies. Some earlier non-Marxist investigations have already shown that such studies may well convey a clearer view of the causes and course of the war. One such analysis of Gustavus Adolphus' economic designs established that the Swedish king planned to develop a major market in Germany for Swedish exports. He especially wished Germany to buy Swedish ores by forcing the German states to convert their currencies from silver to copper. Another plan, not carried out in the end because of the monarch's death, aimed at merging the economy of the Swedish-controlled German territories with that of Sweden. In addition, the occupied German states served as a welcome and profitable source of revenue and were burdened with heavy taxes and tariffs.[82]

Marxists, therefore, see Gustavus Adolphus "not as a conqueror for the sake of conquest, nor as a Christian for the sake of

---

der Neuzeit, pp. 241–42; and on the role of that trade in the Thirty Years War, see Friedrich Bothe, *Gustav Adolfs und seines Kanzlers wirtschaftspolitische Absichten auf Deutschland* (Frankfurt/Main, 1910), pp. 51ff., 74ff.; also, on the far-flung economic interconnections, see Friedrich Lütge, in *Sitzungsberichte der Bayerischen Akademie der Wissenschaften*, Philos.-Histor. Klasse, 1964, pp. 26, 56–57; and Hermann Kellenbenz, *Explorations in Entrepreneurial History* 6 (1953): 107ff.

[81] See Hroch, "Dreissigjährige Krieg," pp. 540–41; also Langer, "Neue Forschungen," pp. 947–48. Langer concludes (p. 935) that the inadequacies of feudal production methods also accounted for the overpopulation prevalent in the more backward countries, which thus served as the main source of manpower for the large armies of mercenaries. Consistent with these views, Langer rejects (p. 939) the assertion of the West German economic historian Friedrich Lütge (*Deutsche Sozial- und Wirtschaftsgeschichte*, p. 236) that the war had no economic causes ("[ein] wirtschaftsexogenes Ereignis").

[82] Schmiedt, in Steinmetz, *Deutschland*, pp. 335–36; also Jan Peters, "Über die Ursachen der schwedischen Teilnahme am dreissigjährigen Krieg," *Wiss. Z. Greifswald* 8 (1958–1959): 199ff. On Gustavus Adolphus, see Bothe, *Gustav Adolfs*, pp. 65ff., 78ff., 92ff. In the Marxist view, the king's historical importance in this context consisted, not in imposing his will on the course of events, but in reflecting in his actions and policies the growing importance of the Baltic Sea both as a focal point of the developing European market and in international politics (Hroch, "Dreissigjährige Krieg," p. 540).

the Protestant German principalities, nor as a mixture of both," but as a rather skillful ruler who "to the great satisfaction of the Swedish aristocracy successfully used the favorable opportunity to expand eastward Sweden's economic and political position." (One East German historian has found considerable support in the *Riksradet* protocols of the time for the view that religious considerations played at best a secondary role in the Swedish plans.) Thus Gustavus Adolphus appears as largely the executor of the wishes of Sweden's aristocracy, which at the time had extensive commercial and manufacturing interests and proved extremely efficient in promoting them.[83]

If the Swedish monarch is judged with considerable reserve, the evaluation of Wallenstein is more positive. The general is commended as the one leading actor who tried to strengthen the empire's central authority and who also sought to extricate it from a war from which it had nothing to gain. Wallenstein's shadier traits, his dubious financial manipulations, his ambition and ruthlessness, are not ignored, but what is considered historically relevant is the unifying and peace-making role he is claimed to have played, even if he did so only to further his own concerns. Like Gustavus Adolphus, moreover, Wallenstein receives credit for his grasp of the economic potentialities of the time—an insight nourished by his far-flung interests as a highly successful landowner, manufacturer, and trader with close connections to Dutch banks and merchants.

Wallenstein's ultimate failure is attributed "objectively" to the absence of any "progressive" forces, above all a manufacturing bourgeoisie, that could have provided the social basis for his endeavors. "Subjectively," Wallenstein is seen at fault for not having sought the support of the cities, although it is not explained how they could have helped him effectively and whether they were willing to do so; in another connection, one of his critics, R. F. Schmiedt, even wonders whether the "objective" conditions for any unification existed at all.[84]

Because the Thirty Years War is viewed as part of the transition period from feudalism to capitalism, East German scholars have raised the question whether the conflict's upheavals and dislocations furthered this transition. The answer has been negative. No bürgerlich forces were ready to assume the leadership of the forces of discontent; instead, the old divisions between impo-

[83]Peters, "Über die Ursachen," pp. 200ff.; on the role of religion, see pp. 203–4.
[84]See Schmiedt, in Steinmetz, *Deutschland*, pp. 323ff., 340ff., 346. Streisand (pp. 80ff.) apparently considers an alliance between Wallenstein and Bürgertum as a realistic alternative—a conclusion he bases on a corresponding statement by Schmiedt, which for lack of proper identification I have not been able to verify (Hroch, in *Hansische Studien*, ed. Gerhard Heitz and Manfred Unger [Berlin (East), 1961], pp. 135ff.

tent, diffident townspeople and a parochial peasantry impeded any joint actions, and no "revolutionary crisis" developed. What popular unrest there was grew out of local hardships—debased currencies and inflationary prices in the towns and the ravages of a brutalized soldiery in the country. In most cases, it is noted, the resulting resistance was simply a desperate struggle for survival; only in a few cases did these risings have overtones that in the Marxist view could be called antifeudal in that they caused—or, if successful, would have caused—some material losses to beneficiaries of the feudal system. Thus, peasants rising in the Harz mountains not only fought against the depredations of a merciless soldiery but also ransacked monasteries and feudal estates, as well as homes of the urban rich. The most important of these risings, the Upper Austrian peasant rebellion of 1626–1628, called for the elimination of various manorial dues and other such burdens. Going further, Bavarian peasants revolting in 1633–1634 demanded the cancellation of all manorial services and dues, with some of them seeking also the abolition of all governmental authority and the breakup of all estates. Each of these rebellions was squashed, but those of the 1640s, though minor and local, may have helped to induce the belligerent governments to conclude peace. DDR authors claim this to be a fact, again without factual substantiation; it is at least a plausible possibility that additional research may well confirm.[85]

Non-Marxist historians have, on the whole, paid little attention to these activities, because they considered them either "lost causes" and hence historically irrelevant or as being as lawless and harmful as those of the soldiery and hence not worthy of any special attention. That the long-range impact of the risings was insignificant East German historians do not deny; the revolts contributed little, if anything, to the decline of the feudal system. What does matter to DDR scholars, however, is that the antifeudal forces were not entirely dead and that the class struggle continued even under such adverse conditions.[86]

Marxist analyses of the Peace of Westphalia have not produced any novel insights concerning that treaty. Some Czech his-

---

[85]See Schmiedt, in Steinmetz, *Deutschland*, pp. 352ff.; Streisand, p. 83; *Grundriss*, pp. 171–72; Langer, cited in *ZfG* 23 (1975): 432. Of non-Marxist discussions, Otto Schiff's "Die deutschen Bauernaufstände von 1525 bis 1789," (*HZ* 30 [1924]: 204ff.) offers additional material. The only indication that I have seen of popular pressures having contributed to the speed-up of the peace negotiations can be found in Bedrich Sindelar, "Comenius und der Westfälische Friedenskongress," *Historica* 5 (1963): 96; the statement is based on that author's *Die Böhmischen Exulanten in Sachsen*, which I have not seen. However, the reference in *Historica* does make it clear that the events referred to, but never spelled out, occurred only during the last year of the war, not over an extended period of time.
[86]On this, see also Langer's comments on Grimmelshausen's works in *ZfG* 26 (1978): 510ff.

torians, stressing the European nature of the war, deny that the treaty ended the war, because its Franco-Spanish phase continued for another decade. One East German historian concludes that although the war left its mark on some individual countries, from a European view it was not an essential milestone in the transition from feudalism to capitalism, as were the simultaneous bourgeois revolution in England and its forerunner, the revolutionary war of independence of the Dutch people against the reactionary absolutism of Spain. In regard to its German aspects, however, Marxists agree with non-Marxists that the treaty's main significance lay in its confirmation of Germany's political and religious divisions, blocking the creation of a nation-state and delaying the development of a dynamic expanding economy. This condition was aggravated, of course, by large population losses, physical destruction (even if not as immense as assumed earlier), and severe territorial losses, including important harbors on which an increase in trade was dependent.[87]

Such facts, touching on the ever-important realm of production, overshadow any possible positive aspects the Westphalian Peace may have had. If Western historians acknowledge that it provided the basis for a new legal order, extending into vast areas of church, state, and international law, DDR scholars find no constructive achievement in this. As they see it, the treaties, in establishing the equality of the confessions and the sovereignty of the imperial princes, merely strengthened the old feudal powers. These were the same "antinational" forces that were ultimately responsible for Germany's political weakness and economic stagnation. Unlike West German historians, East German historians thus place the chief blame for Germany's misfortune on emperor and princes rather than on the intrusions of foreign powers.[88]

Germany succeeded nonetheless in rising again from this catastrophe, a fact that the East Germans attribute to the hard work of the masses. Germany, Schmiedt points out, owed its material and cultural resurrection after 1648 to the "creative powers of its working people in town and country, who attained this tremendous achievement under the most difficult conditions—in spite of feudal restraints and impediments, in spite of the self-centered an-

[87]See Polisensky, 500 Jahren, p. 99; Langer, "Neue Forschungen," pp. 931, 950; Mottek, Wirtschaftsgeschichte Deutschlands, vol. 1, pp. 253ff.; Schmiedt, in Steinmetz, Deutschland, pp. 379ff. On the other hand, Hroch ("Dreissigjährige Krieg, pp. 542–43) points out that the production of war-essential goods did increase significantly, as did the trade in foodstuffs, textiles, and lumber. This point is also made by the West German economic historian Wilhelm Treue, in Gebhardt, vol. 2, p. 503.
[88]See Schmiedt, in Steinmetz, Deutschland, p. 382; Grundriss, p. 173; compare those works to Fritz Dickmann, Der Westfälische Frieden (Münster, 1959), pp. 494–95; Holborn, vol. 1, p. 374.

tinational policies of the dominant feudal class and its princely spokesmen, in spite of the intervention of foreign countries that had a stake in the preservation of the economic and political divisions for the sake of their own position as a great power." Schilfert, too, praises the German people, especially the peasants and artisans, for the role they played in building up the country again, but then adds, with disarming candor, "so far no detailed research has been undertaken to provide concrete information."[89] Such research would doubtless reveal that although the long-neglected masses fully deserved the tribute rendered to them, other forces were also at work to promote the process of reconstruction.

[89]See Schmiedt, in Steinmetz, *Deutschland*, pp. 382–83; Schilfert, *Deutschland*, p. 17. Also see *Grundriss* (p. 177), which sweepingly states that "artisans and peasants rebuilt many of the badly destroyed towns, villages, and production sites."

4

From Feudalism to Capitalism

The Age of Absolutism

The Genesis of Absolutism

THE CENTURY AND A HALF after the Thirty Years War seemed to offer little support to the thesis of history as essentially a record of social progress. From the Marxist perspective, that period looked at first sight like one of the saddest chapters of German history. Princely particularism and aggressiveness held sway and were reinforced by the establishment of absolutist regimes in most German states. The Bürgertum remained powerless, and peasant exploitation continued unchanged, if it did not actually increase.

To uncover for this period of time the operation of historical laws aiming at progress was no easy task. To fail, however, would have been "tantamount in a sense to extrapolating German developments from all lawful world-historical evolution," as Gerhard Schilfert observed in a similar context. East German historians therefore take special pride in being able to show that even this period of princely profligacy and parochial divisiveness, of bürgerlich weakness and new peasant enserfment, was not one of complete stagnation, but did contain elements of progression in keeping with historical Gesetzmässigkeit.[1]

The task of tracing such progress was made more difficult by the special manner in which, according to the Marxist view, absolutist regimes were established in most of the German states. As part of the political superstructure, absolutism was conditioned by the socioeconomic foundation on which it rested. Generally speaking, that foundation was slowly being transformed by the advance of capitalism and a corresponding decline of the feudal order. Marx had defined absolutism as that transitory situation in which "the old feudal states decay and the medieval burgher estate evolves

---

[1]See Schilfert, "Zur Problematik von Staat, Bürgertum und Nation in Deutschland . . . ,: ZfG 11 (1963): 518; also Herbert Langer et al., in ibid. 18 (1970): suppl., p. 351. This is now acknowledged by West German historians; see Rudolf Vierhaus, "Deutschland im 18. Jahrhundert," in Aufklärung, Absolutismus und Bürgertum in Deutschland, ed. Franklin Kopitzsch (Munich, 1976), pp. 177–78.

into the modern bourgeois class without either one being strong enough to defeat the other."[2] The evolving conflict between the nascent bourgeois-capitalist class, already sufficiently strong to insist on concessions, and the declining feudal system was, in this view, resolved by the absolute monarchy: its objective function was to contain the new bourgeois class within the old feudal order. "In the last analysis," Erich Donnert and Peter Hoffmann write, "absolutism [was] the product of certain forms of class conflicts within feudal society."[3]

It was this confrontation that enabled rulers, anxious to shake off restraints on their government, to play the new urban forces against the feudal nobility, which was weakened by its own inefficiency. In France, Louis XIII used the deadlock between clergy, nobles, and the third estate in the Estates-General to emasculate the nobility; at the same time, it is noted, he shored up the declining feudal order by no longer summoning the Estates General, thereby eliminating what influence bourgeois elements had exercised by way of that body. Marxist historians do not ignore factors, such as the religious wars and the threats emanating from Spain, that can be seen as causes leading up to the assumption of absolutist powers by the French kings. What is considered historically more important, however, is the social setting that enabled the kings to acquire these powers. That environment set France on a course that brought it national unity and allowed it, some time later, to sweep away its feudal system in a mass revolution.[4]

Marxists view the French road to absolutism as the "classic" one. Most German states, they note with regret, lacked a socially mature, self-confident capitalist bourgeoisie that could have served as a counterweight against the nobility. Thus, when the German rulers established their absolutist regimes in order to improve their

---

[2]Marx, in MEW, vol. 4, p. 346.

[3]Schilfert, *Deutschland*, pp. 54–55; Erich Donnert and Peter Hoffman, "Zur Frage . . . des Absolutismus in Russland," *ZfG* 14 (1966): 760; Hannelore Lehmann and Helga Eichler, review, ibid. 18 (1970): 1616; "Absolutismus," *Swb*, vol. 1, pp. 9ff.

[4]See Heinz Köller and Bernhard Töpfer, *Frankreich: Ein historischer Abriss* (Berlin [East], 1969), vol. 1, pp. 242–44, 255; vol. 2, pp. 7ff. However, their overall discussion of the circumstances surrounding the rise of French absolutism, with its detailed account of political developments, seems difficult to reconcile with the thesis of the primacy of social developments that are reported only sketchily (vol. 1, pp. 231ff.). Although non-Marxists give far more weight to political factors in their discussions of absolutism than do Marxists, their analyses of its social causes do not differ greatly from Marxist ones. See Roland Mousnier, "The Development of Monarchical Institutions and Society in France," in *Louis XIV and Absolutism*, ed. Ragnhild Hatton (Columbus, 1976), pp. 37ff.. Also, see Georges Durand, "What is Absolutism?" in ibid., p. 25; Rudolf Vierhaus, "Absolutismus," *SDG*, vol. 1, pp. 33–34.

countries' military and diplomatic posture, they did so by working out compromises with the nobility over the head of the Bürgertum—a phenomenon that Marx called a "stunted" development. Here, too, the social conditions under which absolutist regimes were set up receive far more attention than the political causes that brought them about. In Austria's case, these political causes were the multinational character of the empire, the Thirty Years War, and the wars with Turkey; in that of Brandenburg-Prussia, they were the wide dispersal of its territories and again the experiences of the Thirty Years War. As always, the social situation is considered more significant than the political one in regard to later developments.[5]

Under the circumstances prevailing in the German states, the connection between absolutist government and capitalist ascendance—an axiom since that correlation was postulated by Marx and Engels[6]—has been much harder to ascertain. In fact, at first no effort was made to determine the specific connection between German absolutism and capitalism.[7] More recently, however, when some Soviet historians sought to establish such a link between Tsarist absolutism and capitalism in even more backward Russia, DDR scholars undertook the same task for Germany. The Soviet authors distinguished between two types of absolutist regimes—those, like France's, that derived their strength from capitalist growth within their own country and those, like Russia's, that owed their existence to external impulses. On this basis, Ingrid Mittenzwei argued that the emergence of absolutist monarchies in countries with weakly developed capitalist elements was necessitated by the challenge posed by regimes founded on a more advanced capitalist system. The pressures thus generated made imperative the restructuring of the antiquated ruling apparatus in the more backward countries and their adjustment to the new, historically inevitable trends that were spreading across the continent.[8]

Absolutist regimes established in this way differed greatly from the French model because of the lack of an advanced capitalist economy and a sizable bourgeoisie. Without the counterweight of a strong bourgeoisie, centralization of power on the state level could be achieved only by means of major financial and other con-

---

[5]Schilfert, *Deutschland*, p. 51; Donnert and Hoffmann, p. 760; Marx, in MEW, vol. 4, p. 346.

[6]Ingrid Mittenzwei, "Über das Problem des aufgeklärten Absolutismus," *ZfG* 18 (1970): 1164.

[7]See, for example, Meusel, cited in *ZfG* 4 (1956): 777–79; Schilfert, *Deutschland* (1962 ed.), pp. 39ff.

[8]See Mittenzwei, "Über das Problem," p. 1165; also see Lehmann, "Zum Wandel des Absolutismusbegriffs in der Historiographie der BRD," *ZfG* 22 (1974): 7. Surprisingly, this new analysis of German absolutism is ignored in the 1975 edition of Schilfert's textbook.

cessions to the landowning nobility on the local plane. The socioeconomic position of the nobility thus grew stronger while the
Bürgertum lost what little influence it had formerly had as an
estate. If government in cooperation with the estates had been a
"concealed dictatorship of the nobility," Klaus Vetter notes, absolutist government constituted the "open dictatorship of the princes
in the service of the basic interests of the entire noble class."[9]
Absolutism, which shored up the rule of the feudal nobility vis-
à-vis peasants and burghers, was "the highest and last phase in the
development of the feudal state" according to the *Great Soviet
Encyclopedia,* which DDR authors like to quote.

This assessment, which will be examined in greater detail in
the next section, is further confirmed in a study by Gerhard Heitz,
the leading specialist on the agricultural history of the period. Heitz
sees a direct connection between the growth of peasant resistance
during and after the Thirty Years War and the rise at that time of
absolutist monarchies. If the landowning nobility acquiesced in the
creation of absolute governments, he points out, it did so because it
saw in such government bulwarks against a recalcitrant peasantry.
Yet the reluctance of the nobility to accept such regimes suggests
that this aspect of the rise of absolutism, accepted also by some
non-Marxists, has probably been given undue weight.[10]

If the absolutist regimes in the German states were established while capitalist enterprises in these lands were still in their
infancy, these regimes, it is noted, could not have maintained
themselves, let alone have grown stronger, had capitalism not
also grown in their territories. Capitalist productivity provided
the rulers with the material resources, both civilian and military,
that enabled them to consolidate their absolute power—thus bearing out once again the connection between absolutism and
capitalism.

Unlike in France, it was the rulers, who promoted the
growth of capitalism. There is general agreement that these regimes therefore had at first a progressive effect and furthered capitalist enterprise directly or indirectly. Later, Marxist historians
claim (unjustifiably), the governments failed to respond to the
need for an enlarged mobile labor force and wider entrepreneurial
scope by preserving serfdom and the restrictive guild system.
Above all, the governments are taken to task for their obstruction
of national unity, without which there could be no full-scale de-

[9]Günter Vogler and Klaus Vetter, *Preussen: Von den Anfängen bis zur Reichsgründung* (Berlin [East], 1970), p. 44; Schilfert, *Deutschland,* p. 51.
[10]See Gerhard Heitz, "Der Zusammenhang zwischen den Bauernbewegungen und
der Entwicklung des Absolutismus in Mitteleuropa," *ZfG* 13 (1965): suppl., 71ff.;
Lehmann, "Zum Wandel," p. 6.; Schilfert, *Deutschland,* pp. 10, 26. On the non-
Marxist side, see Vierhaus, "Absolutismus," *SDG,* vol. 1, p. 35.

velopment of capitalist potentialities. Gerhard Schilfert derives some solace, however, from the knowledge that historical necessity could not be blocked forever. National unity eventually was achieved, not with the help of absolutism as in France, but in spite of it.[11]

With their focus on socioeconomic developments, the analyses of the absolutist era deemphasize the role of the individual rulers. Such rulers are considered historically relevant only as protagonists of the feudal nobility—the class with which they are always identified. Accordingly, the personal impact of absolute rulers receives relatively little attention.[12] Whereas non-Marxists attribute the strength of the Brandenburg-Prussian and Bavarian regimes to the personal qualities of their rulers and explain the weakness or nonexistence of absolutist regimes in Austria, Saxony, Wuerttemberg, and Mecklenburg by the lack of capable monarchs in these states, DDR historians trace the specific character of these regimes to the respective strength or weakness of Bürgertum and nobility, with the status of the Bürgertum invariably tipping the scales. In the Marxist view, a relatively strong Bürgertum could either help prevent the establishment of absolutism, as in Wuerttemberg, where the estates continued to hold their own, or keep it within bounds, as in Saxony. A less well developed Bürgertum, on the other hand—one that lacked political strength but was economically proficient—could provide the material basis for a strong absolutist regime, as in Brandenburg-Prussia. In a state without any Bürgertum to speak of, and hence no adequate material foundation, no absolutist government could be imposed, as was the case in Mecklenburg. All in all, it could thus be shown that even in those German states in which the Bürgertum was still weak and submissive, the correlation of absolutism and bourgeois ascendance was not entirely absent.[13]

---

[11]Mottek, *Wirtschaftsgeschichte Deutschlands*, vol. 1, pp. 256–57; Schilfert, *Deutschland*, pp. 51–52, 54–55; Horst Krüger *Zur Geschichte der Manufaktur und der Manufakturarbeiter in Preussen* (Berlin [East], 1958), pp. 52–53, 55–56.

[12]Even so, one reviewer reproved Joachim Streisand for paying too much attention to the German rulers in his *Deutsche Geschichte*, while presenting the masses as the "heroes of history" only when they took part in major actions (Schmiedt, in *ZfG* 8 [1960]: 826–27). Similarly, Mottek is criticized for his "subjectivist" treatment of Frederick II in his *Wirtschaftsgeschichte Deutschlands* (Uwe-Jens Heuer, *Allgemeines Landrecht und Klassenkampf* [Berlin (East), 1960], p. 53 n. 8).

[13]See Schilfert, *Deutschland*, pp. 53ff.; Vogler and Donnert and Hoffmann, cited in *ZfG* 18 (1970): suppl., p. 364; Peter Wick, *Versuche zur Errichtung des Absolutismus in Mecklenburg in der ersten Hälfte des 18. Jahrhunderts* (Berlin [East], 1964). The fact that absolutism depended in large part on a productive Bürgertum is now also recognized by many non-Marxist scholars (Max Braubach, "Vom Westfälischen Frieden bis zur französischen Revolution," in Gebhardt, vol. 2, p. 255; Holborn, vol. 2, pp. 203, 265; Vierhaus, "Absolutismus," pp. 31, 34).

Absolutism and Nobility

Because they view the rulers as members and protagonists of the feudal nobility, East German scholars consider absolutism not so much as a way of strengthening the monarchy against that class but as an attempt to shore up the feudal system for the benefit, at least in effect, of the nobility. "The nobility," Schilfert writes,

> rules no longer together with the monarch, the first nobleman of the state, but rather as the *only* authority, as the unimpeded administrator of the nobility's interests. The nobility no longer enjoyed any *independent* freedom of action, but the government apparatus served to preserve the power of the feudal class. Even if that apparatus grew comparatively independent of the dominant feudal class, it remained essentially an instrument—in fact, a stronger one than before—designed to preserve the feudal social and economic order in which the nobility enjoyed a privileged position.[14]

This privileged position was hedged in with considerable restrictions. For example, the nobles were subjected to increasing economic controls by Frederick William I and Frederick II (the Great), controls such as export embargoes, price controls, forced food deliveries in emergencies, and forced plantings of unprofitable crops such as flax and tobacco to ensure sufficient supplies. They were also subjected to farreaching personal restraints—no longer could they abandon their military careers to manage their estates, no longer could they serve in another state, no longer could they travel in foreign lands without royal permission. Finally, having lost the power of the purse, they no longer had any impact on foreign, financial, and economic policies and in fact were excluded from policy decisions, because the rulers relied on commoners as their immediate counselors. These limitations are dismissed by DDR historians, however, as largely irrelevant.[15]

What matters is that the social and economic privileges of the Junkers were little affected by these restraints: the nobles remained the unchallenged masters on their estates and in fact were

[14]Schilfert, *Deutschland*, p. 52 (italics in original); also Krüger, *Geschichte der Manufakturen*, p. 444.

[15]See Wilhelm Naudé and August Skalweit, *Acta Borussica (A.B.): Die Getreidehandelspolitik und Kriegsmagazinverwaltung Brandenburg-Preussens* (Berlin, 1901–1931), vol. 2, pp. 57ff., 97–98, 100, 244–46, 251, 468 (doc. no. 87); Carl Hinrichs, *A.B.: Die Wollindustrie in Preussen unter Friedrich Wilhelm I.* (Berlin, 1933), pp. 30–33, 40–44, 58ff.; Otto Hintze, *Die Hohenzollern und ihr Werk* (Berlin, 1915), pp. 516–17; Hans Rosenberg, *Bureacracy, Aristocracy and Autocracy: The Prussian Experience: 1660–1815* (Cambridge, 1958), especially chapters 3, 7, and 8. A contemporary observer also noted the restraining effect on Junker approaches to the king that resulted from Frederick II's reliance on commoners as his closest advisers (Christian Wilhelm von Dohm, *Denkwürdigkeiten meiner Zeit* [Lemgo and Hanover, 1814–1819], vol. 4, pp. 114–15, 117–18).

given more power over their peasants than they had held before. Thus Olaf Groehler concludes that "while on the one hand the political power of the Brandenburg-Prussian feudal nobility was reduced, on the other it acquired so much economic power that the rulers in the last analysis became dependent again on its good will." In the same vein, Schilfert notes that the personal and political restraints imposed on the nobles were measures taken to sustain governments that catered to the class interests of the nobles and thus redounded to their benefit, too. That such measures were justified by reasons of state goes to show, he concludes, that the doctrine of *Staatsräson*, then current, merely served as an ideological underpinning for the priority of feudal interests as perceived by the rulers.[16]

Whatever the policies of the Prussian kings, a basic community of interests did indeed exist between these rulers and the Junkers. As fellow landowners, the monarchs took measures to protect and promote agriculture, and these measures also benefited the landowning nobles. Similarly, a close connection existed between the organizational structure of the Brandenburg-Prussian army and the Gutswirtschaft. The re-enserfment of the peasants not only provided the Gutsherren with adequate manpower to work their estates, it also provided an ever-available manpower reservoir for the army. A detailed study by the West Berlin historian Otto Büsch, *Militärsystem und Sozialleben im alten Preussen*, has again confirmed this close correlation with a wealth of material, extending from the coordination of annual leaves with the sowing and harvesting seasons to the retention of serfdom on the grounds, among other reasons, that emancipation would endanger the food supply of the army and disrupt its recruitment system. Again, the officer corps provided a living for large numbers of noblemen, and the rulers, for their part, could not afford to see impoverished noble families driven from their estates because these same families provided the officers on which the army depended. Indeed, this realization accounts for the ineffectiveness of all attempts to limit the local omnipotence of the Junkers as much as did the latter's resistance to these endeavors.[17] Correspondingly, measures taken by Frederick II against the expulsion of peasants from their lands by the Gutsherr were not meant to protect the individual peasant; in reality, the peasant could still be deprived of his land as long as another was settled in his place and food pro-

[16]Olaf Groehler, *Die Kriege Friedrichs II* (Berlin [East], 1968), pp. 12–13; Schilfert, *Deutschland*, pp. 53–54, 185–86. Vetter ("Die Stände im absolutistischen Preussen," *ZfG* 24 [1976]: 1290ff.) has also shown that the nobility continued to exercise some influence on state policies by way of the surviving diets of the estates.

[17]Otto Büsch, *Militärsystem und Sozialleben im alten Preussen* (Berlin [West], 1962).

duction assured in this manner.[18] The Bavarian nobles enjoyed many similar privileges, as did the nobility of other German states.[19]

The entrenchment of the nobility in its rural domains set obvious limits to the power of the "absolute" rulers.[20] These limits were reinforced by the additional concessions accorded landowners by Frederick II. Here again, however, DDR authors do not consider the primary significance of this new accretion to noble strength to be the further limitation of royal power. Whatever shift of power occurred was in the Marxist view an intraclass one within the dominant feudal class and as such was not decisive. These authors are far more concerned about the effect that the increased powers of the Junkers had on the socioeconomic plane, for they retarded the further advance of the capitalist mode of production, keeping the peasants attached to the soil and impeding the free development of capitalist enterprise. Social progress, however, was bound up with the removal of all such obstacles, and this required the abridgment and eventual elimination of noble privileges.

For the same reason, little importance is attached to the signs of independence the bureaucracy displayed vis-à-vis some of the absolutist rulers. Although some Western scholars—Hans Rosenberg and Hubert C. Johnson in particular—argue that the Prussian bureaucracy was able to ignore, delay, or counteract orders of Frederick II,[21] Ingrid Mittenzwei, the major DDR specialist on the period, has shown that most Prussian officials had no views of their own and were too ambitious, obsequious, or intimidated to oppose the king on matters of policy. The few men who had new ideas found themselves obstructed by both king and fellow officials in their efforts to implement their proposals. Mittenzwei also notes that when these men did have an opportunity to pursue their plans under Frederick's weak-minded successor, Frederick William II,

[18]See ibid., p. 56; Naudé and Skalweit, *A.B.: Getreidehandelspolitik*, vol. 3, p. 241; also, G. Schmoller and O. Hintze, *A. B.: Behördenorganisation* (Berlin, 1892ff.), vol. 7, pp. 562–63 (doc. no. 401); Reinhold Koser, *Geschichte Friedrichs des Grossen* (Stuttgart and Berlin, 1913), vol. 2, p. 89. Significantly, although Frederick II went out of his way to subsidize noble landowners who had run into economic difficulties without any fault of their own, he refused help to those who were poor managers of their estates. Schmoller and Hintze, *A. B.: Behördenorganisation*, vol. 13, pp. 49, 85–88, 731; Naudé and Skalweit, *A.B.: Getreidehandelspolitik*, vol. 3, pp. 240–41.

[19]Siegmund von Riezler, *Geschichte Bayerns* (Aalen, 1964), vol. 7, pp. 137ff.; Michael Doeberl, *Entwicklungsgeschichte Bayerns* (Munich, 1928), vol. 2, pp. 91ff., 244ff.

[20]One Western scholar even describes the system of government that existed in eighteenth-century Prussia as government by consent of the ruled, including, he claims, not only the nobility but also parts of the Bürgertum (Hubert C. Johnson, *Frederick the Great and His Officials* [New Haven, 1975], pp. 9ff.).

[21]Rosenberg, *Bureaucracy*, pp. 175ff.; Johnson, *Frederick the Great*, pp. 42ff. and *passim*.

they made no effort to do so. At that, she concludes, these plans envisaged at best some liberalizing adjustments; they proposed no comprehensive reforms that would have brought about the changes that were needed.[22]

These conclusions are not incompatible with the findings of Johnson's and Rosenberg's studies. Both authors make clear that effective bureaucratic opposition was limited largely to technical and organizational questions. The one major exception was the sabotage of Frederick's efforts to reform agrarian conditions and improve the lot of the peasantry. In this case, however, the obstruction of the king's policies was successful only because the king himself did not insist on these reforms and readily gave up his plans.[23]

Ever ready to detect political implications, DDR authors view the studies of the two Western scholars as part of an effort to illustrate the essential adaptability of nonsocialist social systems, for the purpose of showing that such systems can be adjusted to changing needs without revolution. They grant, on the other hand, that Rosenberg and, to a lesser extent, Johnson are critical of absolute rulers, nobles, and bureaucrats, unlike those West German historians who have stressed the limits rather than the dangers of absolute power in order to prove that the absolutism of the Brandenburg-Prussian rulers was not an eighteenth-century type of totalitarianism and that Frederick the Great ought not to be lumped with Hitler. The latter authors, moreover, praise the absolute rulers for their willingness to leave the estates a measure of power and consider this union of rulers and estates a positive feature of absolutism. Marxists, of course, consider such a coalition a "reactionary" effort to shore up the feudal order. In the same vein, they dismiss as misleading West German attempts to see germinal forms of bourgeois parliamentarianism in the activities of the estate diets.[24]

DDR historians find further confirmation for their view of the ability of the nobles to regain a dominant role in the conduct of government under the weak successors of Frederick II—Frederick

---

[22]See Mittenzwei, "Die preussischen Beamten und ihre Auseinandersetzungen um wirtschaftliche Probleme der Zeit (1763 bis 1789)," *Jahrb. f. Gesch. d. Feudalismus* 1 (1977): 349ff., especially pp. 397–99. Some of Mittenzwei's points were also brought up by Rosenberg (*Bureaucracy*, pp. 65, 142, 148ff., 192).

[23]See Rosenberg, *Bureaucracy*, pp. 175ff., 195–96; Johnson, *Frederick the Great*, pp. 194–95, 210ff., 241, 243ff., 248. The fact that the noble-led bureaucracy invariably sided with the landowning nobility in matters touching on noble rights suggests that Western objections to the Marxist treatment of the nobility as a unified group are not tenable in the case of eighteenth-century Prussia. See, for example, Karl Bosl and Hans Mommsen, "Adel," *SDG*, vol. 1, p. 68.

[24]Heitz, review, *ZfG* 20 (1972): 1169ff.; Lehmann, "Zum Wandel," pp. 12ff., 17–18, 21; Mittenzwei, "Die preussischen Beamten," p. 354.

William II and Frederick William III. To them, this reassertion of the nobility illustrates, once again, the relative insignificance of individual rulers: they may for a time obscure the actual power relationships, but they cannot basically change them.[25]

Absolutism and Capitalism

Although the socioeconomic status of the landowning nobility did not suffer from the establishment of absolutist regimes and in fact improved as a result of the additional privileges the nobles managed to extract from the rulers, East German historians nonetheless see absolutism as contributing to the long-range decline of that class. To increase their revenues and equip their armies (or maintain their courts), many of the rulers became sponsors of capitalist enterprises and, as such, helped to erode the feudal system. In a sense, Ernst Engelberg has suggested, the nobility also furthered its own demise: by insisting on its tax-exempt status, it forced the rulers to search for other sources of revenue and thus aided in the rise of the very class that would eventually supersede it.[26]

These interrelationships are of special importance to Marxist scholars because they provide proof, once again, of the irresistible force of developments that follow the pattern set by historical laws. On the basis of its class interests, the German Bürgertum should have been the one to promote the growth of capitalism, the socioeconomic system then on the "agenda of history" to provide full scope to the expanding productive forces. Yet, because the burghers lacked the strength and initiative to engage in capitalist manufacture, it was the rulers who became the initiators of capitalist undertakings and as such the agents of progress. In tracing this connection between absolutism and the growth of capitalism, East German historians see themselves as fulfilling the cardinal assignment, incumbent upon them as Marxist scholars, "of demon-

---

[25]Schilfert, *Deutschland*, pp. 184ff.; Vogler and Vetter, *Preussen*, pp. 75–76.
[26]See Engelberg, *Probleme*, pp. 150–51. One East German historian has wondered whether the Junker seizures of peasant lands (*Bauernlegen*) ought not to be viewed as capitalist accumulations. The answer has been that no genuine capitalist developments could occur in agriculture as long as the peasants remained tied to the soil. Capitalism, by Marxist definition, presupposes the existence of a mobile labor force and the separation of labor from all means of production—a definition that centers on the objective relationship of man—that is, both worker and capitalist—to the means of production rather than on the capitalist and his purposes. See the debate between Johannes Nichtweiss and Jürgen Kuczynski in *ZfG* 1 (1953): 701–8, 716–17 and *ZfG* 2 (1954): 467–71, 473; Nichtweiss, *Das Bauernlegen in Mecklenburg* (Berlin [East], 1954), pp. 30ff. See also the summary of the debate in Heuer, *Allgemeines Landrecht*, p. 41 n. 54; also Schilfert, *Deutschland*, p. 86.

strating that in Prussia, too, the historical inevitability of the transition from feudalism to capitalism asserted itself during the era of
manufacture even though it was greatly impeded by the existing
feudal production relations.[27] This satisfaction is mingled, however, with sorrow over the fact that capitalism gained ground in
Prussia neither through bourgeois initiative and on behalf of the
bourgeoisie, as in England and in the Netherlands, nor within a
disintegrating feudal framework that could be swept away by a
mass revolution, as in France; instead, capitalism gained ground as
the result of governmental measures that had their "deforming"
effect on the subsequent development of German society.[28]

These ill effects are analyzed at great length in the case of
Brandenburg-Prussia. Although the Hohenzollerns are given credit
for having launched capitalist enterprises in their state and in fact
established most manufactures in Brandenburg-Prussia in the latter
half of the seventeenth and the first half of the eighteenth centuries, they are reprimanded for having hedged in the rise of capitalism with excessive restrictions. Elector Frederick William (the
Great Elector) (1640–1688) is taken to task for having sponsored
capitalist undertakings only for fiscal and military purposes and, at
that, only insofar as these enterprises did not intrude on the interests of the *Junkertum*. What is held against Frederick William is
his failure to further capitalist entrepreneurs for their own sake in
order to create a class of self-reliant bourgeois manufacturers as a
counterweight against the nobility—an expectation that is hardly
compatible with the view of the Elector as himself essentially a
feudal aristocrat.[29]

Fault is also found with the Elector because he tolerated the
re-enserfment of peasants—a development that withheld manpower from the urban labor market. Here again, however, Frederick
William was not a free agent. Because of the weakness of the
Bürgertum and its inability to offset the pressures of the nobility,
even Schilfert allows that "Elector Frederick William, on coming
to terms with Brandenburg's landed nobility, *had* to grant it more
far-reaching rights over the peasantry than was done in many other
German states."[30] At that, a mobile peasantry could have relieved
the existing manpower shortage only partly. What was needed
most was skilled labor, and this could not be supplied by the peasants. Moreover, ways were found by Frederick William and his

---

[27]Krüger, *Geschichte der Manufakturen*, p. 17.
[28]Ibid., pp. 53, 101, 152; Schilfert, *Deutschland*, pp. 192–93.
[29]Neither, for that matter, did the French monarchs or any others make such efforts
(Fritz Wagner, in *Handbuch der europäischen Geschichte*, ed. Theodor Schieder
[Stuttgart, 1968], vol. 4, pp. 107, 109); on Austria, see Schilfert, *Deutschland*, p. 57.
[30]Schilfert, *Deutschland*, p. 63 (italics added); but see also the critique by Heinz
Heitzer, in *BzG* 1 (1959): 871.

successors to relieve these difficulties—by the large-scale settlement of foreign craftsmen in Brandenburg, by military leaves granted to soldiers and the encouragement of their outside employment (which made it possible also to keep their service pay at a minimum), and by the drafting of vagrants, beggars, and convicts into factory work. Similarly, guild restrictions were set aside to attract skilled workers and to allow for increased production, especially of military supplies. East German historians do not ignore the Elector's contribution to Brandenburg's economic development—his building of roads, bridges, and canals and his institution of a regular mail service. They complain, however, that all these efforts served ultimately only to consolidate the "terrorist class rule of the Junkers" rather than to allow the unhampered spread of capitalist enterprise.[31]

The policies of Frederick William I (1713–1740), the Soldier King, are viewed with similar skepticism. Because the monarch is perceived as but another protagonist of the feudal class, Schilfert tries to attribute the king's policies either to the Prussian state or to the indefinite "one" (man)—an incongruous approach in the case of this autocrat and one that Schilfert is unable to maintain consistently. The analysis of the king's policies is not novel: the need for a permanent army is not denied; criticism is directed rather against the army's disproportionate size, which is not justified by any security needs, because Prussia's two major neighbors, Poland and Austria, were poorly equipped to threaten Prussia militarily. (If later, in the Seven Years War, Prussia did have to fight for its very existence, Schilfert blames this necessity on Frederick II, who had placed Prussia in that position by his earlier acts of aggression.) Of course, criticisms are also directed at the role of the army, which laid the foundation for Prussia's ruinous militarism by promoting the primacy of all military concerns, the privileged position of the officer corps, and the militarization of civil relations.[32]

Of special interest in this context is the connection that has been established between militarism and capitalism. Although militarist regimes are found in all ages, eighteenth-century Prussian militarism is perceived as closely related to the emergence of capitalism. Given the vast gap between military requirements and available resources, it is noted, the feudal-agrarian system by itself could not make up the country's deficiency in fertile soil and mineral wealth. The large military apparatus could be maintained only

[31]Schilfert, *Deutschland*, pp. 63, 65–66, 69; see also Vogler and Vetter, *Preussen*, p. 41; Mittenzwei, "Über das Problem," 1167, 1172.

[32]Schilfert, *Deutschland*, pp. 121ff., 180–81; Vogler and Vetter, pp. 71ff., 93–94; see also Mottek, *Wirtschaftsgeschichte Deutschlands*, vol. 1, pp. 260–61; Krüger, *Geschichte der Manufakturen*, pp. 222, 438; Streisand, pp. 90–91 (Streisand devotes less than half a page to Frederick William I).

because capitalist developments were raising urban productivity to the point that the urban economy could provide much of the money and equipment the army required (with foreign subsidies covering the remaining needs). In view of the dependence of the military build-up on the bürgerlich economy and its capitalist undertakings, DDR historians insist that modern militarism was an outgrowth of capitalism rather than feudalism and that to argue, as non-Marxists do, that militarism was a product of feudalism or, in the nineteenth and twentieth centuries, of feudal relicts that survived into the capitalist age, was to confuse cause and effect. The great concern of DDR historians is that such misapprehensions might encourge the equally misleading conclusion that fascism was the creation of feudal and other pre-bourgeois elements rather than of monopoly capitalists.[33]

With militarism becoming institutionalized under Frederick William I, the negative effects of the subordination of the entire economy to the needs of the army are stressed with new emphasis. The point is made in particular that because of the military priorities the country did not derive the full benefit from the growth of capitalist productivity. The supervision and regulation of civilian pursuits, economic and otherwise; the continued drain on the state's meager resources; and the disproportionate promotion of enterprises considered important for military or fiscal reasons obstructed and deformed all progressive developments. Eventually, under Frederick II, these factors encouraged a policy of military solutions and conquests.[34]

This critical stance enables East German authors to view certain aspects of Frederick William I's regime with greater discernment than their West German counterparts. Schilfert objects rightly to the tendency of many West German historians to regard Frederick William as a sort of citizen-king like France's Louis Philippe. To be sure, Frederick William displayed some of the burgher's virtues—frugality, industry, sense of duty—but essentially this irascible autocrat had nothing in common with the downcast, pliable burgher whom, in fact, he despised and distrusted. DDR historians have rejected with equal justification the claim, most stridently promoted by the philosopher Oswald Spengler (in his famous essay *Preussentum und Sozialismus*) that Frederick William I was the creator of an equitable system of state socialism in

---

[33]"Militarismus," *Swb*, vol. 2, pp. 92ff.; Albrecht Charisius, "Zur Genesis und Entwicklung des deutschen Militarismus," *Militärgeschichte* 13 (1974): 310; Horst Giertz and Wolfgang Küttler, "Zur Inhaltsbestimmung und historischen Dimension des Militarismusbegriffs," ibid. 15 (1976): 412–14.

[34]See Krüger, *Geschichte der Manufakturen*, pp. 53, 101–2, 152. The self-defeating results of economic policies geared only to fiscal and military needs have more recently been pointed out also by non-Marxist historians (Holborn, vol. 2, p. 193).

which all people, high and low, served the state equally. To Marxists this thesis seems but another attempt to mislead the workers and keep them from pursuing their fight for their true class interests.[35]

Frederick the Great (1740–1786), too, receives credit for his fostering of capitalist undertakings. Under him, moreover, private entrepreneurs grew in numbers and importance, because the king found it more economical to have them establish their own businesses, generally with a helping hand from him, rather than to have the state own and administer such enterprises. Yet, as Horst Krüger points out, the helping hand often consisted in granting a manufacturer a monopoly in his field—a privilege that eliminated the incentives of competition and also allowed the entrepreneur to exploit his workers without fear of losing them to a more humane competitor. As for the subsidies that the king granted, these were often necessitated by the heavy taxes that such enterprises had to pay to the state. Moreover, compared to the huge sums that were poured into the army, Krüger and others point out, Frederick spent only a fraction of the state's revenues on economic developments. Thus, heavy financial burdens and bureaucratic restrictions continued to impede capitalist expansion and the emancipation of the Bürgertum from the tutelage of the state. There were some indications of bürgerlich ascendance, both economic and social, at that time—marriages between nobles and well-to-do commoners became more frequent—but as a class the Bürgertum remained ineffective and without ambition to improve its status. Merchants adjusted to the feudal-absolutist policies of the state to do business with it rather than attempting to have the state adjust its policies to their needs in order to facilitate business expansion. Krüger found only a few cases of more independent entrepreneurship during that time, and of these enterprises none survived for more than a few decades. He concludes that there was no more than a "limited possibility" in eighteenth-century Prussia for a somewhat more independent bürgerlich stance.[36]

[35]On Frederick William I as *Bürgerkönig*, see Ernst Klein, in *Preussen: Epochen und Probleme seiner Geschichte*, ed. Richard Dietrich (Berlin [West], 1964), p. 83; see also Richard Dietrich, *Kleine Geschichte Preussens* (Berlin [West], 1966), p. 77. Another West German historian, Carl Hinrichs, found it deplorable, an injustice of history, that the "honorable Puritan" policy of Frederick William I, trying to establish Prussia as a Great Power on his own, resulted in the militarization of the entire domestic life of the state while Sweden was saved from such a militarization of everyday life by its morally highly questionable policy of maintaining an army at other people's expense (Hinrichs, *Preussen als historisches Problem* [Berlin [West], 1964], p. 36).

[36]See Vogler and Vetter, *Preussen*, pp. 59ff.; Krüger, *Geschichte der Manufakturen*, pp. 105, 120ff., 233ff., 245ff., 276ff.; see also Kurt Hinze, *Die Arbeiterfrage zu Beginn des modernen Kapitalismus in Brandenburg-Preussen* (Berlin [West],

Nonetheless, most DDR scholars blame the Bürgertum for not having fought more determinedly for its emancipation. Given their dependence on the state's orders and help, the argument runs, merchants and manufacturers never grasped the communality of their interests, nor did they perceive the fundamental antagonism that existed between their interests and the late-feudal system. Thus, despite its occasional opposition to specific measures of the absolute state, this nascent bourgeoisie continued to support the state throughout most of the century. Although this collaboration would seem to prove that there was no serious collision of interests between the emerging bourgeoisie and the feudal forces, Marxists insist that that conflict was an objective one and existed whether or not it was understood: it grew out of the many restrictions by which an agrarian-dominated government, serfdom, and guild system impeded the growth of capitalism.[37] These conclusions can draw substantial support from the findings of Hubert Johnson, who has illustrated how greatly serfdom, the guild system, and the self-centered parochialism of the landowning nobility interfered with the creation of an adequate labor force. Johnson also found that although a small entrepreneurial elite prospered in eighteenth-century Prussia, it became so closely intertwined with the state that its economic and bureaucratic power increased the dependence of less favored entrepreneurs on their good will and that of the state.[38]

The never-ending search for capitalism's progress according to historical laws thus finds evidence of some quantitative growth, but no corresponding political ascendance of the nascent capitalist bourgeoisie. Writing about Prussian conditions, all that Vogler and Mittenzwei can say is that, unlike the medieval burghers, the capitalist merchants and manufacturers no longer aided the development of the feudal system; instead, along with the increasingly restive peasantry, they slowly eroded that order. On the whole, the conclusion remains that the "most reactionary elements of the German feudal class," the East Elbian Junkers and their main rep-

---

1963); Skalweit, "Die Berliner Wirtschaftskrise von 1763 und ihre Hintergründe," *VSWG*, suppl., no. 34 (1937): 15. Mittenzwei ("Über das Problem," p. 1167) states that an unpublished dissertation found evidence of bourgeois opposition to the economic policies of Frederick William I, but provides no specifics. For a non-Marxist analysis that reaches somewhat similar conclusions concerning the adjustment of entrepreneurs to government tutelage, see Krieger, *The German Idea of Freedom* (Boston, 1957), pp. 39–40.

[37]Hoffmann and Mittenzwei, "Die Stellung des Bürgertums in der deutschen Feudalgesellschaft von der Mitte des 16. Jahrhunderts bis 1789," *ZfG* 22 (1974): 205–6; Mittenzwei, review, ibid. 25 (1977): 479, as compared to Kopitzsch, "Einleitung," in Kopitzsch, *Aufklärung*, p. 36.

[38]Johnson, *Frederick the Great*, pp. 79–80, 82ff., 90ff., 103ff., 271–72.

resentatives the Hohenzollerns, continued to maintain their retarding hold on the country.[39]

In Saxony, on the other hand, bourgeois progress was greater, because many of the Saxon electors let manufacturers shift for themselves. When rulers did intervene, as did Augustus the Strong (1694–1733), such interventions were on the whole restrained. Yet capitalist growth, it is noted, encountered hurdles in Saxony, too. The rulers took few steps to aid the economy as a whole; in particular, no governmental effort was made to attract foreign craftsmen. Court luxury and military ventures, moreover, dissipated substantial parts of the country's resources. Only the acquisition of the Polish crown by Augustus the Strong proved a boon to Saxon entrepreneurs, who found Poland a receptive market for their products and a source of low-priced raw materials.

Although the Saxon rulers made few efforts to improve overall conditions in their electorate, they, rather than the Bürgertum, are nonetheless found to have been—at least at first—the main agents of capitalist progress. Rudolf Forberger and others point out that they became supporters of capitalism by founding, for personal profit, various manufacturing enterprises. Although contemporary critics condemned these undertakings as intrusions into the bourgeois domain that hindered the expansion of private entrepreneurial activities, Marxist scholars welcome them as signposts of progress, because these enterprises were financially sounder and more productive than those that were privately owned. Backed by governmental authority, the princely enterprises could adopt new techniques over guild objections and prepare the way for an eventual mechanization on the basis of a coordinated division of labor. Once again, Forberger writes, the ruler became the unwitting agent of lawful progress: "He reinforced the feudal system by utilizing the new lawful processes; thus he could be the executive agent of the new capitalist industrial bourgeoisie without neglecting his role as the agent of feudal class interests." Wearing their two hats, the Saxon electors functioned as symbols of the transition from feudalism to capitalism.

After the Seven Years War a significant change occurred. Under pressure from the estates, Saxony abandoned its military ambitions, reduced its army, and concentrated on its economic rehabilitation. Most important, bourgeois elements played a significant role in developing the policies that helped the country

---

[39]See Vogler, "Probleme der Klassenentwicklung in der Feudalgesellschaft," *ZfG* 21 (1973): 1207–8; Mittenzwei, "Zur Klassenentwicklung des Handels- und Manufakturbürgertums in den deutschen Territorialstaaten," ibid. 23 (1975): 185–86. On Junkers, see Schilfert, *Deutschland*, p. 193.

overcome the effects of the war. "For the first time," Forberger comments, "the primacy of princely revenues ... gave way to the demands of the rising capitalist economy and the merchants and manufacturers as the agents of the emerging bourgeois society; others were soon to follow." As a result, Saxony expanded its manufactures and began industrializing at a more rapid pace than any other German state. Saxony also became one of the first German states to move toward free trade. This development, it is noted, appeared to be a much more promising course toward genuine national strength than was the Prussian road of military conquests.[40]

East German researchers have explored the growth of capitalism extensively only for Prussia and Saxony, the two states for which they have had most ready access to archival materials. For developments in some of the South German states, a brief survey has been provided by Heinrich Scheel in a study on south German Jacobin movements in the wake of the French Revolution. While it stagnated in Bavaria, Scheel notes, capitalist growth derived its erratic momentum in Wuerttemberg alternately from the ruling dukes anxious to augment their revenues and from Wuerttemberg's Bürgertum, which was somewhat more enterprising than that of other German states and which was also aided by Swiss investors and manufacturers. Similarly, Swiss entrepreneurs played a role in furthering capitalist enterprises in Baden. In Austria, on the other hand, where both government and private initiative did little to promote capitalist expansion until the latter part of the eighteenth century, developments trailed behind those of both Baden and Wuerttemberg. Only in Wuerttemberg, Scheel concludes, did the growth of capitalism erode the feudal order to any noticeable degree and help to develop a Bürgertum of some economic strength and self-confidence.[41]

As DDR scholars trace the tortuous paths by which capital-

[40]See Schilfert, *Deutschland*, pp. 69–70, 133–34, 209–10; Rudolf Forberger, *Die Manufaktur in Sachsen vom Ende des 16. bis zum Anfang des 19. Jahrhunderts* (Berlin [East], 1958), pp. 209–11, 227ff., 260–61, 281–82, 286ff.; Blaschke, *Bevölkerungsgeschichte von Sachsen bis zur Industriellen Revolution* (Weimar, 1967), p. 117; Hans Baumgärtel, *Bergbau und Absolutismus: Der sächsische Bergbau in der zweiten Hälfte des 18. Jahrhunderts und Massnahmen zu seiner Verbesserung nach dem Siebenjährigen Kriege* (Leipzig, 1963), pp. 59–60; Horst Schlechte, *Die Staatsreform in Kursachsen: 1762–63* (Berlin [East], 1958). It seems, however, that bourgeois participation in the determination of economic policy occurred not on its own, but on the government's initiative (Schlechte, *Staatsreform*, pp. 25–26). See also the somewhat skeptical review of Schlechte's book by Hausherr, in *VSWG* 67 (1960): 131–32.

[41]Scheel, *Süddeutsche Jakobiner: Klassenkämpfe und republikanische Bestrebungen im deutschen Süden am Ende des 18. Jahrhunderts* (Berlin, [East], (1962), chapter 1; for Bavaria, see also Schilfert, *Deutschland*, pp. 72–73, 134; for Austria, see ibid., pp. 131–33.

ism gradually eroded the feudal system, they also explore the corresponding formation of an urban proletariat, or "preproletariat," as it is called because the workers frequently still were subject to restrictions in their mobility and thus were not the "free" laborers postulated by the Marxist concept of the proletariat. The picture of working conditions these authors paint is obviously a grim one, but little time is spent on the contemporary rationale that the lower classes were by nature idlers and wastrels and could be compelled to work only by economic necessity, that is, by wages that barely provided for their subsistence needs. Because exploitation of labor is viewed as a constitutive feature of capitalism in the Marxist conception, all rationalizations of such exploitation, however captious, are considered irrelevant.[42]

The East German accounts find the emerging working class outwardly passive and cowed by feudal traditions. Thus, to the regret of the present-day chroniclers, the workers found no fault with the system as such and tended to look on their rulers as father figures. Because they lacked class consciousness, they carried on the class struggle only in its lower forms—working slowly and badly, cheating and stealing materials to make ends meet. Rarely did they resort to strikes and violent action until the Seven Years War, after which the number of strikes increased with the expansion of manufactures. Sometimes such actions did secure better pay and improved working conditions, but on the whole these acts of resistance were badly led, poorly organized, and quickly suppressed. Workers' petitions for relief and law suits produced no better results: in most cases, the government sided with the manufacturers against the workers. Nonetheless, these manifestations of the class struggle, while admittedly sporadic and limited in extent and duration, are viewed as first harbingers of a new era.[43]

Because the feudal system rested on control of the land and agrarian production, DDR scholars pay special attention to the impact the advance of capitalism had on agrarian conditions. They note that after the Seven Years War, bürgerlich elements began to penetrate into agriculture. Unlike in manufacture, it is found, it was the Bürgertum that set off this trend. It did so partly because landed property enhanced social status, but also partly because less capital was required for land purchases than for manufacturing enterprises. Landed estates, weighted down by debts, were leased or sold to non-nobles either surreptitiously or by special permission. Hans-Heinrich Müller, an agrarian historian, estimates that

---

[42]Schilfert, *Deutschland*, pp. 98ff.; Mottek, *Wirtschaftsgeschichte Deutschlands*, vol. 1, pp. 291ff.; Vogler and Vetter, *Preussen*, pp. 99ff.
[43]Schilfert, *Deutschland*, pp. 102ff., 140; Krüger, *Geschichte der Manufakturen*, pp. 405–7, 413–15, 420; Forberger, *Manufaktur in Sachsen*, p. 263.

by 1776 between two-thirds and three-fourths of all nonpeasant lands in Brandenburg (including royal domains) were run by bürgerlich owners or lessees—a figure somewhat reduced in significance by the fact that lands worked by peasants amounted to between 60 and 70 percent in that province.

In this context, the determination of the new bürgerlich proprietors to treat their land as an investment is considered especially significant. Unlike most noble landowners, they worked hard at improving the quality and quantity of their crops. So did those tenants who held their land beyond the usual six-year lease. At the same time, landowners also became manufacturing entrepreneurs, establishing sawmills, distilleries, textile plants, and other nonagricultural enterprises on their properties.[44]

By Marxist tenets, however, these changes still took place within a feudalist framework, because labor was based primarily on servitude rather than on contract. Nonetheless, such changes are viewed as heralding a new phase in the transition from feudalism to capitalism. At one point, Müller speaks of a capitalist infiltration (Unterwanderung) into feudal modes of production by large-scale lessees (Generalpächter); in another place, he notes that the lessees' way of thinking and acting was "to a large extent capitalistic," especially in the second half of the eighteenth century. Heitz, too, quoting Marx, finds that the serf-based production of the landed estates contained features that signaled the approach of the capitalist age. The dialectic of these developments generated the specific form that was assumed by the transition from feudalism to capitalism in the agriculture of Prussia, and as such has been and will continue to be a major topic of East German research.[45]

One development frequently cited as bearing out these analyses is the tendency of the new agricultural entrepreneurs to hire laborers (Tagelöhner) to work their fields—a procedure they found more efficient and profitable than forced services. Many landlords even let their peasants pay off their servitudes or sometimes set

---

[44]See Hans-Heinz Müller, *Märkische Landwirtschaft vor den Agrarreformen von 1807* (Potsdam, 1967), pp. 117ff., 131ff., 145ff., 165; concerning the lack of corresponding developments in Saxony, see Berthold, "Einige Bemerkungen über den Entwicklungsstand des bäuerlichen Ackerbaus vor den Agrarreformen des 19. Jahrhunders," *Beiträge zur deutschen Wirtschafts- und Sozialgeschichte des 18. und 19. Jahrhunderts* (Berlin [East], 1962), pp. 81ff. For the much less developed situation in Mecklenburg, see Peter Wick, "Versuche zur Erbverpachtung und Aufhebung der Leibeigenschaft in Mecklenburg zu Beginn des 18. Jahrhunderts" (*JWG* 1 [1961]: 46ff.), which indirectly confirms Müller's conclusions for Brandenburg. DDR historians have little to say about nobles who were equally progressive in their activities, but few apparently were (Fritz Martiny, *Die Adelsfrage in Preussen vor 1806 als politisches und soziales Problem* [Stuttgart, 1938], pp. 11ff.; Wilhelm Abel, "Landwirtschaft 1648–1800," *HbDtWSG*, vol. 1, pp. 521, 522).

[45]Müller, "Domänen und Domänenpächter in Brandenburg-Preussen im 18. Jahrhundert," *JWG* 4 (1965): 154, 183; Heitz, "Zum Charakter der 'zweiten Leibeigenschaft,'" *ZfG* 20 (1972): 36ff.

them free without payments, which also freed the landowners of what protective obligations they owed these peasants. Müller hastens to add, however, that such changes were not important enough to change either the feudal basis of the existing system or its political superstructure. The Generalpächter,

> though of bürgerlich descent and using capitalistic productive forces, could not be compared to capitalistic entrepreneurs. They were not bourgeois in the real meaning of the word, for in addition to their activities as lessees and agrarians, they also exercised governmental and other superstructural functions of the feudal state. In this respect they were, apart from a few exceptions, essentially faithful servants of their state. At best, the Generalpächter were semi-feudal entrepreneurs, although clearly more entrepreneurs than officials.

The conclusion, then, is that although the lessees affected the character and composition of the ruling class, these bürgerlich elements, as a part of that class, were not likely to challenge the existing order and call for an unfettered bourgeois capitalism. As these painstaking investigations of the shift from feudalism to capitalism point out, the changeover occurred in such a way as to leave intact the dominant position of the nobility and give it time to adjust to the emerging capitalist techniques. Here again avenues opened up that enabled Prussia's Junker nobility to preserve the core of its feudalist privileges far into the capitalist era.[46]

Recent East German researches into the status of the East Elbian peasantry, however, have uncovered data that suggest the existence of possible alternative developments. Contrary to traditional assumptions, the status of Prussia's peasantry did not remain rigidly fixed throughout the absolutist era. Müller has found, for example, that peasants, too, leased land either singly or in groups; such transactions not only promised higher returns but also freed the lessees of the traditional servitudes and permitted their children to move wherever they wished to. Peasants were also able to raise their yields; Müller provides interesting examples of their resourcefulness and efficiency. In effect, however, improvements were less extensive than his presentation suggests, because peasant leases were generally confined to *Vorwerke*, peripheral offshoots of the actual Gutswirtschaften. Nonetheless, Müller does successfully refute the traditional view of the complete stagnation of peasant life during that period.[47]

---

[46]Müller, "Domänen," pp. 183–85, 192; Müller, *Märkische Landwirtschaft*, pp. 79–81; Mottek, *Wirtschaftgeschichte Deutschlands*, vol. 1, pp. 358–59; Heitz, "Bauernwirtschaft und Junkerwirtschaft," *JWG* 2/3 (1964): 88.

[47]Müller, *Märkische Landwirtschaft*, pp. 79–81, 145ff., 162; Müller, "Der agrarische Fortschritt und die Bauern in Brandenburg vor den Reformen von 1807," *ZfG* 12 (1964): 636ff.; Mittenzwei and Lehmann, "Die marxistische Forschung in der DDR zum brandenburg-preussischen Territorialstaat," *JfG* 3 (1969): 340ff., with additional references.

In the West, in the Rhineland and Hanover, developments ran more directly according to the expected historical pattern. Servitudes were converted into money rents at an early date, which allowed a free peasantry to participate in the adoption of capitalist operations. Little work has been done by Marxist historians on these developments, but note is taken of the social differentiations that evolved among peasants as capitalist trends gained momentum. Ranging from those engaged in large-scale operations (*Grossbauern*) to small peasants and day laborers, this diversification is welcomed as evidence of the disintegration of the feudal order. In another sense, however, the East German accounts deplore this stratification. They regard it as an impediment to further improvements of the peasantry's status, on the grounds that these disparate interests precluded the formation of a united peasant front against the feudal nobility.[48]

The inhibiting effects of these conflicts on the peasants' class struggle were not hard to detect. That struggle gathered momentum in the latter part of the eighteenth century as, in Marxist parlance, intensified agricultural operations collided with outdated feudal production methods. (On the other hand, where developments were lagging behind, as in Mecklenburg, no social necessity existed as yet, in this view, for any large-scale resistance on the part of the peasants. In consequence, the class struggle there continued to manifest itself in its lowest forms—occasional single-handed acts of resistance, low-quality work, and apathetic performance.) A great deal of material, much of which has long been known, has been compiled for Prussia, Saxony, Austria, and the South German states on peasant resistance in the form of escapes from bondage, demands for the reduction of servitudes, withholding of payments and services, and widespread poaching. What is noted as particularly significant is that peasants after the mid-eighteenth century resorted more often to risings, that higher form of the class struggle, indicating an increasing discrepancy between the evolving productive forces and production conditions. If the rebels gained only limited concessions from their landlords or were altogether defeated, these setbacks are once again blamed on the Bürgertum, which was unable to provide the necessary leaders and a coherent program of action. Yet the comparative ineffectiveness of the rural class struggles is also attributed to the peasants' own internal divisions—the result of their developing social stratification—and to their failure to understand that no gains within the existing system, but only the complete elimination of the feudal order, could improve their lot permanently. In making this point, Gerhard Heitz notes that among

[48]Schilfert, *Deutschland*, pp. 141–43.

the settlers on Prussia's newly colonized lands were large numbers of peasants escaping intolerable conditions in other states. Thus, these people had fled from the abuses of one feudal lord only to put themselves at the mercy of another, the king of Prussia. Their class struggle, aiming merely at personal relief rather than basic change, served in effect to reinforce the absolutist regime of the Prussian rulers.[49]

Enlightened Absolutism

Absolutist regimes in Prussia and other German states drew further strength, in the Marxist view, from modifications they underwent under the influence of the Enlightenment. The term *modification* is used here advisedly, because all authors stress that enlightened absolutism (or despotism) remained absolutist, tempered only peripherally by Enlightenment goals. Enlightened absolutism thus is described as an effort of absolutist monarchs to adjust to the rise of the Bürgertum and to fend off the antifeudal attacks of peasants and urban masses. "Because the declining feudal class," Schilfert writes,

> could no longer think of checking bourgeois ascendance by force and expected the worst from a united opposition of burghers and peasants, it sought to make the feudal-political superstructure at least in some way acceptable to the Bürgertum. The absolutist state thought it advisable to meet the Bürgertum part of the way—among other reasons, in order to keep it from joining forces with the peasants. It sought to appear as "enlightened" as possible, but essentially remained what it had always been. Its main task was the same as before: as always, it strove to protect the basic interests of the feudal class.

The reforms of the so-called enlightened rulers, then, originated not in philosophical ideals, but in the "objective" needs of their governments.[50]

Here, once again, theory outpaces reality. The weak and passive Bürgertum was not likely to pose any threat to its rulers, and

---

[49]Schilfert, *Deutschland*, pp. 86ff., 142ff.; also Müller, *Märkische Landwirtschaft*, pp. 144–45; Heitz, "Zum Charakter," pp. 34–35, 39.

[50]See Schilfert, *Deutschland*, pp. 167–68; also Baumgärtel, *Bergbau und Absolutismus*, pp. 58–59; Mittenzwei, "Über das Problem," pp. 1164. Whereas earlier non-Marxist historians viewed enlightened absolutism as merely retaining the form of absolutism, but transforming its substance (Fritz Hartung, quoted by Mittenzwei in "Theorie und Praxis des aufgeklärten Absolutismus in Brandenburg-Preussen," *JfG* 6 [1972]: 66; Kurt von Raumer, quoted by Lehmann in "Zum Wandel," p. 26), more recently they have come to share the view of its essential absolutism (Vierhaus, "Deutschland," pp. 185–86; Krieger, *Kings and Philosophers* [New York, 1970], pp. 253ff.).

the thought of an oppositional coalition of burghers and peasants seems just as contrived. The reforms were introduced because they were useful, not because they were forced on the rulers. Accordingly, Mittenzwei has modified Schilfert's thesis and has shown that the reforms of Frederick II were inspired, not by any immediate threat, but by a life-long concern that unbridled absolutism might *eventually* lead to upheavals. She quotes a number of the king's statements to the effect that the stability of the regime depended on the contentment of its people. In the same vein, she finds it indicative of the decline of the feudal system that in order to maintain his absolutist rule Frederick had to resort to an ideology alien to his own class (*klassenfremd*)—an ideology that in fact challenged the feudal order and ultimately aimed at superseding it.[51]

The reference here is to the ideas of the Enlightenment as anticipations of and, later, reflections of the Bürgertum's dissatisfaction with its inferior status.[52] Thus, it is thought to be significant that the German Enlightenment flourished particularly in such centers of bürgerlich activity as Hamburg, Frankfurt, and Leipzig. Although the German spokesmen of the Enlightenment are found to confine themselves largely to the moralizing-idealist plane, misguided by a naive confidence in the receptivity to their views on the part of the rulers, it is acknowledged that they had nonetheless a strong impact on bürgerlich thought and on the Bürgertum's sense of identity. In pursuit of this theme, DDR scholarship has paid a great deal of attention to the literature and philosophy of the period, as it centered on bürgerlich values and interests and gave the burgher his social due. If this flowering of a specifically bürgerlich culture, nurtured by such illustrious minds as Kant and Lessing, Klopstock and Wieland, and later Goethe and Schiller, did not generate any political demands by the Bürgertum, this inaction is attributed to the reforms of the enlightened rulers. However limited, these reforms created the illusion that they would soon be followed by political concessions and thus kept the

[51]See Mittenzwei, "Über das Problem," pp. 1167–68; additional materials can be found in Mittenzwei, "Theorie und Praxis," pp. 58ff. Mittenzwei also cites two unpublished studies (in "Über das Problem," p. 1167 n. 21, and in "Die preussischen Beamten," pp. 352 n. 12, 353, 355, and 363) that indicate the Prussian manufacturers were beginning to show signs of self-assertiveness, but she also shows that Frederick easily put an end to such assertions (ibid., p. 353). She weakens her thesis further by attributing the cancellation of some of the reforms of Joseph II and Frederick II by Joseph himself and by Frederick's successor, respectively, to the growth of oppositional forces in Austria and Prussia ("Theorie und Praxis," pp. 105–6). See also Schlechte, *Staatsreform*, pp. 8–9. Putting it somewhat differently from a non-Marxist perspective, Fritz Valjavec notes that rulers welcomed the Enlightenment as a means of increasing their powers (*Die Entstehung der politischen Strömungen in Deutschland: 1770–1815* [Munich, 1951], pp. 22, 36–38). See also Krieger, *German Idea*, pp. 23ff.

[52]Stiehler, *Gesellschaft und Geschichte* (Berlin [East], 1974), p. 152.

burghers contented. Another reason for the Bürgertum's quietism is found, however, in the backwardness of bourgeois-capitalist developments; without an adequate material basis, the ideas of the Enlightenment lacked the thrust that could have put an end to the obsolete feudal order.[53]

As an outstanding example of enlightened despotism, the rule of Frederick II has received special attention. As in the economic domain, the pros and cons of other major policies are also carefully weighed. Of course, Frederick's aggressions are condemned, especially because his territorial acquisitions created the Prusso-Austrian dualism and with it another barrier to national unity, on which the optimal growth of the capitalist forces depended. On the other hand, all authors acknowledge Frederick's special abilities and accomplishments. They value his contributions to progress—his judicial and educational reforms, as far as they went, as well as the economic improvements he made.[54] At the same time, they note that religious toleration may have seemed a rational stance to the king because he was indifferent toward religion; tolerance was also expedient because it allowed him to recruit immigrants from any denomination—Lutherans and Catholics, Hussites and Calvinists, Quakers and Mennonites. That Frederick found tolerance simply an opportune stance is also deduced from his refusal to apply it to Jews. The latter were granted a few new commercial privileges, from which the king expected to derive some financial benefits, but they remained otherwise subject to severe discrimination that was even increased in the course of his reign. Nor, one might add, did Frederick ever appoint Catholics as ministers or councilors, and he even hesitated to appoint them to municipal posts in the Catholic parts of Silesia.[55]

Similarly, Frederick's judicial reforms are explained as responses to the need of commercial and industrial enterprise for legal security. The reforms aimed at a well-trained, respected judiciary, speedy trials, and judicial independence. The crowning

---

[53]"Aufklärung," *Swb.*, vol. 1, pp. 205–6; Schilfert, *Deutschland*, pp. 108ff., 150ff.; *Grundriss*, pp. 189, 196ff.; Streisand, pp. 99ff.

[54]Here again, however, it is pointed out that Frederick's land-reclamation projects and other agricultural improvements could not have been accomplished without the peasantry. The " 'quiet labor' [Marx] of the masses . . . was the precondition of the farreaching melioration endeavors that led to the considerable increase of the arable soil in Bavaria, northwestern Germany and Brandenburg-Prussia" (Heitz, "Volksmassen und Fortschritt," pp. 1172–73).

[55]See Krüger, *Geschichte der Manufakturen*, pp. 393–94, 253ff.; Schilfert, *Deutschland*, pp. 170–73, 176–79; Vogler and Vetter, *Preussen*, p. 116; Mottek, *Wirtschaftsgeschichte Deutschlands*, vol. 1, pp. 260, 277–80, 303–6, 359. On Frederick's attitude toward Catholics, see Hintze, (*Hohenzollern*, p. 399), who nonetheless writes that the king was tolerant, "not only because of his denominational indifference, but from a strong deeply ethical need that grew out of his philosophical world view."

achievement was to be a new legal code, which, however, was completed only after Frederick's death. All accounts emphasize that the *Allgemeine Preussische Landrecht* embodied all the ambiguities of enlightened absolutism. Although the codifiers drew on bourgeois (though mostly non-Prussian) experts to accomplish their task, they were careful not to infringe on the privileged status of the nobility. The code thus serves as another example of the endeavor to reconcile the privileged rights of the Junkers with the demands of merchants and manufacturers, officials and intellectuals, and even of parts of the nobility and non-noble landowners for uniform laws and lawful procedures, in order to head off a potentially revolutionary situation.[56]

On balance, all accounts find the reforms inadequate, because they left unresolved the deep gap between the state's claim to power and its insufficient material resources. Agricultural output never attained its full potential, because no basic change in the landlord-peasant relationship was permitted. Any loosening of the peasants' bondage might have interfered with military recruitment, which rested on the serf-based agrarian system. Similarly, there could be no departure from mercantilist principles, giving merchants and manufacturers more scope, because the king used import and export duties as weapons in his continuing confrontations with Austria and in his attempts to subjugate Saxony. Thus, the final verdict is negative: Frederick kept the economy from realizing its full potentialities and continued to rely on militarization and repression in pursuit of his policies.[57]

Unlike Western historians, East German authors have no difficulty reconciling Frederick's governmental practice and his philosophical views; the genuineness of these beliefs, which shared the Enlightenment's faith in human rationality, was never questioned by East German authors. These "contradictions" are seen as the inevitable results of feudal attempts to block the advent of the bourgeois-capitalist order. As Ingrid Mittenzwei puts it, Frederick, as the protagonist of the feudal order, always interpreted the tenets of the Enlightenment in a feudal sense—that is, he accepted them only to the extent that they proved useful within the feudalist framework. In consequence, despite his professed belief in the power of reason, birth always counted for more with him than did

[56]See Heuer, *Allgemeines Landrecht, passim.* Although Heuer speaks of the ever more insistent demands for legal rules (p. 69), he provides no evidence of such demands, but contents himself with a few quotations from Marx and Engels to the effect that the bourgeoisie always demand legal equality and security.
[57]Schilfert, *Deutschland,* pp. 175, 184–86, 188, 192–93; Mittenzwei, "Theorie und Praxis," pp. 101–3; *Grundriss,* p. 188. On Frederick's use of tariffs and tolls as foreign policy tools, see also W. O. Henderson, *Studies in the Economic Policy of Frederick the Great* (Liverpool and London, 1963), pp. 96, 98ff., 112ff., 118ff.

intellectual qualities. In addition, although he prided himself on his intellectual tolerance, he could just as easily forbid any criticism of his policies. Summing up the Marxist attitude on Frederick as a representative enlightened despot, Schilfert concludes:

> As an analysis based on the class situation shows, the Prussian state promoted the interests of the nobility in new ways and was forced, because of the growing weakness of the declining feudal class, to defend its existence before the ascending bourgeoisie in a language that the latter could understand. This is also the basic social explanation (*der gesellschaftliche Hauptgrund*) for the contrast between the philosopher Frederick, who liked so much to meet with the finest bürgerlich minds of Europe, and the politician Frederick, who ruthlessly dismissed deserving bürgerlich civil servants and officers. The dualism between theory and practice that we notice in Frederick II derives from objective causes and not from a penchant for hypocrisy or other subjective traits of the king. Fundamentally, Frederick's personal "enlightenment" is the subjective expression of the objective situation of the feudal class, which could no longer hope, in its declining phase, to maintain its power without some limited concessions to the Bürgertum.[58]

The assessment of Austria follows the same pattern. Like Prussia, Austria remained a feudal-absolutist state, the reforms of Maria Theresa (1740–1780) and Joseph II (1780–1790) notwithstanding. Maria Theresa is credited with having expanded her powers at the expense of the Estates and, by increasing the state's revenues, having given some new impulses to capitalist developments. By singling out feudal elements for favored treatment, however, she not only set narrow limits to the growth of capitalist enterprise but also allowed the exploitation of the peasantry to continue. Under the impact of a major peasant revolt in 1775, however, the empress' son and successor, Joseph II, abolished serfdom (a measure hailed also as aiding the growth of capitalism, because it created a free labor force). In addition, the emperor ended some noble privileges, after his mother had already rescinded the nobility's tax exemption. Joseph also proclaimed religious tolerance, soon extended it to the Jewish community, curbed the powers of the Catholic Church, eased censorship regulations, and pursued economic policies aimed at aiding the Bürgertum.

[58]See Schilfert, *Deutschland*, pp. 176ff. (quotation on pp. 178–79); Mittenzwei, "Über das Problem," p. 1169. On the ambivalent attitude of non-Marxist historians, see Hans Rothfels, "Friedrich der Grosse and der Staat," *GWU* 13 (1962): 628, 634–35; Holborn, vol. 2, pp. 242, 262ff.; Gerhard Ritter, *Das deutsche Problem* (Munich, 1962), pp. 30ff. However, in recent years some West German scholars have pointed out Frederick's essential utilitarianism; Kopitzsch, "Einleitung," in Kopitzsch, *Aufklärung*, p. 52; Eberhard Weis, "Absolute Monarchie und Reform im Deutschland des späten 18. und frühen 19. Jahrhunderts," in ibid., p. 197; but see also Gerhard Oestreich, ("Verfassungsgeschichte . . . bis zum Ende des alten Reiches," in Gebhardt, vol. 2, p. 423), who still maintains that Frederick "acted as an enlightened monarch throughout his entire reign."

Schilfert concludes that Joseph was more consistent in adapting his regime to enlightened standards than most other German rulers, but again finds the emperor's subjective intentions of secondary importance: as in the case of the Hohenzollerns, the advance of productive forces and the rural class struggle are considered the primary impulses from which these measures derived. "[The emperor] had no intention of placing nobility, burghers, and peasants on the same footing," Schilfert adds, "but wished only to neutralize the class enemies of the nobles rather than let their opposition gain enough strength to sweep away the feudal-absolutist order." Despite its progressive features, which brought the Austrian empire under Joseph II "as close to a bourgeois state as was possible for a pre-bourgeois regime," the Austrian state remained "objectively" a feudal state. For evidence, Schilfert points to the Bürgertum's failure to exert any political influence and to its adjustment to a territorially oriented antinational policy—antinational in the sense that it failed to launch capitalist undertakings large enough to erode tariff barriers and legal and monetary divisions in search of new markets and raw materials.[59]

All in all, given the narrow scope of the reforms introduced by the enlightened rulers, DDR scholars find these changes far from revolutionary. They stress this point because a number of West German and Austrian authors have argued in recent years that the reforms of Frederick II, Joseph II, and other German monarchs anticipated many of the changes brought about in France forcibly by the French Revolution and thus made revolutions unnecessary in the German states. In reply, East German authors point out that the reforms, initiated in the interest of the feudal class state rather than that of their alleged beneficiaries, raised the status of the Bürgertum only in very limited ways and did even less for the peasants and urban masses. Thus, they were no "substitute for revolution" (Mittenzwei), because the fundamental changes needed to free production, both rural and urban, from its social and political fetters still remained to be made. The efforts of Western historians to focus on the positive nature of the reforms are rejected as politically inspired manipulations. As Ingrid Mittenzwei puts it:

It is surely not wrong to see a connection between the extraordinary interest in the reform policies of absolutist rulers in the late phase of the feudal state and the historical experiences that these ideologues

[59]See Schilfert, *Deutschland*, pp. 194ff. (quotations on pp. 198, 201); Groehler (*Die Kriege Friedrichs II*, p. 35) treats this subject similarly, though in a different context. The limits that Joseph set to his reforms so as not to jeopardize the existing order are also stressed by Valjavec, *Der Josephinismus* (Munich, 1945), pp. 15–16. See also Klaus Epstein (*The Genesis of German Conservatism* [Princeton, 1966], p. 43) on the limits of the reforms of Grand Duke Charles Frederick of Baden.

of imperialism were forced to make in the present age. The fear of revolutionary upheavals in our time has led them to devote special attention to historical periods that seem to prove that revolutions can be avoided [because] the ruling class allegedly showed moderation and preserved "social peace" by a "prudent" policy of reforms.

She warns that just as the commercial and manufacturing burghers of the eighteenth century were lulled into a false faith in the good will and reforming zeal of the rulers, today's monopoly bourgeoisie is trying to mislead the working class by making some adaptive changes, with Western historians lending a helping hand in these endeavors. The task of illustrating the true nature of enlightened absolutism thus becomes one that has present-day relevance.[60]

Foreign Affairs

To East German scholars, absolutism has been of interest primarily as a domestic phenomenon. Foreign developments, on the other hand, have been given only perfunctory coverage in textbooks and surveys.[61] This treatment of foreign policy is surprisingly nonideological: diplomatic shifts and maneuvers of individual rulers are viewed as plain quests for power; the analyses of the War of Spanish Succession, of the Nordic War, and the Seven Years War differ little from non-Marxist interpretations. This impression is reinforced by what Marxists dismiss otherwise as an unscientific individualizing approach—the discussion of diplomatic activities and martial developments in terms of personal ventures of ambitious monarchs rather than as outgrowths of feudal conditions.[62] Occasionally these analyses touch on familiar topics of the domestic scene. Brandenburg-Prussia's rulers are taken to task for launching their wars from a wholly inadequate material foundation, forcing them to rely on foreign intervention in German affairs on their behalf. Other princes are similarly chided for resorting to alliances with outside powers, weakening further the empire's structure and

[60]Mittenzwei, "Theorie und Praxis," pp. 55–56 (quotation on p. 55), 58, 104–6; Lehmann, "Zum Wandel," pp. 25–27; Schilfert, *Deutschland,* pp. 168, 193–94; *Grundriss,* pp. 198–99.

[61]Not a single essay or monograph on foreign developments during the absolutist era is listed in "Historische Forschungen in der DDR: 1960–1970," *ZfG* 18 (1970): suppl., 351ff.

[62]See Schilfert, *Deutschland,* pp. 67–69, 173–74, 179–83; Streisand, pp. 91–93; Vogler and Vetter, *Preussen,* pp. 41–44, 79, 82ff. Exceptions are *Grundriss* (pp. 187–88, 190), which explains the Prusso-Austrian wars as products of Prussian militarism, and Groehler (*Die Kriege Friedrichs II,* pp. 18–20), who attributes the War of the Spanish Succession to dynastic and bourgeois-commercial rivalries and the Anglo-French conflicts to bourgeois competitive clashes.

contributing to its loss of more territory. Princely particularism is blamed in particular for the inability of the empire to resist the attacks of Louis XIV and his annexations of German lands; thus "antinational" selfishness is contrasted with the popular protests against the French inroads that swept across Germany and with the resistance the population of the affected territories put up on its own. That the empire did not disintegrate altogether is explained by the intervention of foreign states, which wished to preserve it as a counterweight against France and Turkey.[63]

This strategy was based on the principle that the establishment of a power equilibrium offered the best protection against the hegemonial aspirations of other rulers. To Marxist scholars, the significance of this doctrine lies in the fact that it justified a pragmatic policy on rational grounds rather than on religious pretensions. (A domestic parallel is seen in the concept of "reason of state," which explained the pursuit of feudal-absolutist policies in practical terms instead of invoking "God's will."[64])

Only on rare occasions is this dark picture of cynicism and greed relieved by some more hopeful development. Thus, Schilfert accords great national significance to the wars against the Turks (who in 1683 besieged Vienna), because these campaigns united "all German states and the Slavic and Hungarian peoples under Habsburg rule in the fulfillment of a task of all-European import, . . . the only case of this kind that we find in this period of political division and impotence of the Empire between the Peace of Westphalia and the Wars of Liberation. At the same time, it was the one war that was popular among the suppressed classes throughout Germany. (This is attested, for example, by many popular songs [Volkslieder].)"[65]

Schilfert modifies his conclusion, however, by his complaint that the courageous stance of the Hungarian and Slavic peasants aroused fears among the nobility lest the struggle for national liberation lead to demands for social emancipation. The nobles therefore moved closer to the Habsburgs, who used these fears to tighten their own absolutist rule. This development DDR scholars find just as deplorable. Grundriss points out that the attempt to unite the German, Hungarian, and Slavic lands in a centralized

[63]See Schilfert, Deutschland, pp. 49–51, also 174, 181–82; Grundriss, pp. 177, 180. In their bitterness about the particularism of the German princes and their praise of the popular attitude, the East German accounts present a striking contrast to the detached discussion of these events by West German historians, such as Braubach, "Vom Westfälischen Frieden," pp. 257–74, 278–84.

[64]Streisand, pp. 100–101; Schilfert, Deutschland, pp. 53–54.

[65]See Schilfert, Deutschland, pp. 59–60, 130–31. Actually, Brandenburg joined the campaign against the Turks only three years after the Turks had been driven from Vienna and had been pushed back deep into Hungary (ibid., p. 68).

multinational state ran counter to the "objective tendency" toward the formation of independent bürgerlich nations, for which the emergence of capitalism was calling.[66]

The constraining impact that the princely and noble "class egoism" had on material and cultural progress remains an ever-recurring theme of the East German approach to history, which considers the growth of production to be the mainspring of progress. This theme derives fresh impulses from the Prusso-Austrian rivalry that emerged in the eighteenth century and that raised new obstacles to German national unity.[67] As is pointed out again and again, delays in national unification meant delays in productive growth, for bourgeois capitalism, so obviously on the economic "agenda" by then, was not getting the national market, law code, currency, and other instrumentalities that it needed for its full unimpeded development.

[66]Schilfert, *Deutschland*, pp. 131–32; *Grundriss*, p. 185.
[67]In this vein, *Grundriss* notes as the most significant long-range result of the "German" phase of the Seven Years War that it reinforced the Prusso-Austrian dualism (p. 191).

5

The Rise of
Bourgeois Capitalism

The Road to Unification

From the French Revolution of 1789
to the German Upheavals of 1830

THE FRENCH REVOLUTION of 1789–1794 gave new momentum
to the transition from the feudal to the capitalist order in
Germany as well as France. As the mainspring of this quickened
pace, the revolution has received much attention in East German
research. What impresses DDR authors above all is the finality of
its results: the revolution solved with one stroke, as it were, the
conflict between feudalism and capitalism in France. The feudal
system was completely destroyed and the rule of the bourgeoisie
securely established, without compromises with the nobility. DDR
scholars attribute this victory to the willingness of the French
bourgeoisie to assume the leadership of the revolution: once the
revolution got under way, its determination in turn unleashed the
revolutionary energies and the creative powers of the popular
masses, which assured the victory of the revolution. No matter
how tragic subsequent developments were, it is pointed out, they
could not affect the triumph of the bourgeois-capitalist order in
France.[1]

Germany, it is regretfully noted, was less fortunate: what the
French achieved in five years, the Germans attained only after eight
decades; not until the German empire was founded in 1871 did
capitalism win out fully over the feudal system. Even then, the
bourgeoisie did not obtain political dominance, and many feudal
and particularist relics survived. The nobility managed to control
the changes and adjust to and profit by the advance of capitalism;
thus they retained political power.[2] DDR scholars do not regard this

---

[1]Walter Schmidt, "Sieg und Festigung des Kapitalismus . . . und die Rolle der Arbeiterklasse . . . ," *ZfG* 20 (1972): 1246–47; Schmidt, "Zu einigen Problemen der
bürgerlichen Umwälzung in der deutschen Geschichte," in *Bourgeoisie und
bürgerliche Umwälzung in Deutschland: 1789–1871*, ed. Bleiber et al. (Berlin
[East], 1977), p. 6.
[2]See Schmidt, "Zu einigen Problemen," pp. 3–5, 9, 33; Schmidt, "Sieg und Festigung," p. 1250; Mottek, *Wirtschaftsgeschichte Deutschlands*, vol. 2, p. 4; Wolfgang Kütler, "Zum Begriff der bürgerlichen und bürgerlich-demokratischen Revo-

course of events as inevitable; they are convinced that a more courageous and farsighted Bürgertum could have taken the lead, as did its
French counterpart, and could have effected the victory of the capitalist order on a bürgerlich-democratic foundation. The accounts of
the period from 1789 to 1871 are concerned therefore not only with
developments as they unfolded but also with the several revolutionary crises that could have been used, it is claimed, to overthrow the
old ruling class. As Walter Schmidt notes, "Marxist-Leninist historiography . . . considers as the essence of German history between
1789 and 1871 the confrontation between the reactionary-counter-
revolutionary and progressive-revolutionary forces that represented
and fought for one or the other alternative of a bourgeois transformation of [German society]."[3]

As part of this theme, the dialectic of evolutionary and revolutionary progress ranks as a major topic of the East German analyses.
The issue has its political dimension as well, for the question of
whether, and to what extent, the rise of capitalism in nineteenth-
century Germany was a revolutionary process derives its special
significance from the fact that West German historians have
stressed the reformist nature of Germany's shift from the feudal-
absolutist states of the eighteenth century to the unified constitu-
tional-parliamentarian capitalist German empire of 1871. DDR
scholars take it for granted that this stance, like those mentioned
earlier, is designed to suggest the feasibility of avoiding revolutionary changes by reforms at the proper time. This conclusion is unacceptable to Marxists-Leninists, who are ever mindful of the role of
the reformist Social Democratic party, which in their view was and
is but the handmaiden of monopoly capitalism and imperialism.
Therefore, DDR historians have striven hard to prove the revolutionary nature of Germany's transformation into a bourgeois-capitalist society. Denying all the revolutionary attributes of this transformation, Ernst Engelberg warned in a related context, opens all
doors to evolutionist reformism.[4]

This task has not been an easy one, and the scope of the
ensuing discussion, extending now over many years, is indicative

---

lution bei Lenin," in *Studien zur vergleichenden Revolutionsgeschichte: 1500–
1917,* ed. Manfred Kossok (Berlin [East], 1974), p. 186. For corresponding views of
a West German historian, see Wolfram Fischer, *Wirtschaft und Gesellschaft im
Zeitalter der Industrialisierung* (Göttingen, 1972), pp. 61–62.
[3]Schmidt, "Zu einigen Problemen," pp. 15–17; also Kossok, "Vergleichende Revolutionsgeschichte der Neuzeit: Forschungsprobleme und Kontroversen," *ZfG*
26 (1978): 11; Siegfried Schmidt, "Liberale Parteibewegung und Volksmassen während der bürgerlichen Umwälzung in Deutschland: 1789–1871," ibid., p. 404.
[4]Bleiber, "Vorwort," in Bleiber, *Bourgeoisie,* p. vii; W. Schmidt, "Zu einigen
Problemen," p. 14; Engelberg, "Über die Revolution von oben: Wirklichkeit und
Begriff," *ZfG* 22 (1974): 1211.

of the difficulty of finding a satisfactory answer. Various theses have been advanced to show that a revolution did indeed take place or that the changeover contained at least some revolutionary elements. One theory has it that although the various changes that occurred were carried out by way of reforms, the transformation to the bourgeois-capitalist order was revolutionary in its cumulative effect, because one socioeconomic formation replaced another. Yet whether such a shift was revolutionary by Marxist criteria was arguable. It was not accompanied by the transfer of political power from one class (the nobility) to another (the bourgeoisie), and such a transfer, to cite Lenin again, is one of the constituent features of a revolution. The resolution to this dilemma was found in the increasing *embourgeoisement* of the old noble ruling class and in the conclusion of a noble-bourgeois "class compromise." These trends were considered adequate, though not ideal, substitutes for a full-scale transfer of power.[5]

Proof of the revolutionary nature of the transformation has also been found in the fact that that process was completed between 1866 and 1871 by a "revolution from above" launched by the Prussian government and army. Above all, however, most changes were forced upon the ruling feudal-aristocratic class by the sustained pressures and revolutionary activities of the popular masses.[6] More will be said later about these efforts to verify the presence of revolutionary elements in this transformation and about the problems that these endeavors have raised.

Forever mindful of possible present-day implications, the East German analyses hasten to add that this kind of reformist-revolutionary changeover was and is possible only when one system of exploitation gives way to another: the new bourgeois class was able to develop its system of exploitation within the old order, and the old nobility managed to adjust economically to the new system. The shift from capitalism to socialism, on the other hand, could never occur in this manner; nonexploitative socialism could not develop within the exploitative capitalist system, nor could the bourgeoisie flourish in the classless socialist order. A suspension of the class struggle by means of reforms would thus be impossible, and only a complete break with the old system—that is, a revolution from below—could initiate the needed changes. Non-Marxist suggestions that reforms can accomplish as much as revolutions

---

[5]W. Schmidt, "Zu einigen Problemen," pp. 8–9, 12; Streisand, p. 112; "Revolution," *Swb*, vol. 2, p. 382; Bleiber (*Bourgeoisie*, p. vii) speaks of a revolution because the reforms of the period added up to a qualitative transformation rather than mere quantitative changes; see also Mottek, *Wirtschaftsgeschichte Deutschlands*, vol. 2, pp. 1ff.

[6]*Grundriss*, pp. 205–6; W. Schmidt, "Zu einigen Problemen," pp. 8, 32–33; Küttler, "Zum Begriff," p. 188.

are dismissed as misleading and historical parallels that are inapplicable and are used only to divert the working class from its revolutionary mission.[7]

To reinforce the point of the presence of revolutionary activity even in periods of apparent reforms, the tracing of revolutionary movements and risings and their impact on those in power constitutes a major assignment of East German research. This becomes evident at once in the countless studies that have explored the democratic-revolutionary forces in late eighteenth-century Germany. These forces had earlier manifested themselves in occasional localized actions, but they burst forth under the impact of the French Revolution in a plethora of demands and petitions, minor disturbances, and full-scale risings. DDR scholars have collected considerable materials on such activities that can be related directly or indirectly to the French events.[8]

This connection was easiest to establish in regions that are geographically close to France—especially in southwestern Germany, where German Jacobin leaders collaborated with their French counterparts in efforts to overthrow the existing monarchist-feudal order. On the whole, the accounts are careful not to claim more than is warranted by the evidence; in their endeavor to picture the vigor of revolutionary activities inspired by the French Revolution, however, the authors have not fully escaped the temptation of reading into the available data a greater extent and impact of revolutionary radicalism than their sources permit. Thus, the accounts of the short-lived Republic of Mainz depict the creation of that ill-fated bourgeois parliamentary republic as the outgrowth of a strong popular movement; actually, it was the work of a small minority protected by French bayonets from assaults by enraged fellow citizens. (French protection is acknowledged, but only as a safeguard against attacks by the old feudal regimes.)

The Mainz Republic has aroused the special admiration of DDR authors because it rose above a narrow nationalism: to guard

---

[7]Mottek, *Wirtschaftsgeschichte Deutschlands*, vol. 2, p. 2; Bleiber, *Bourgeoisie*, p. viii; Herwig Förder, *Marx und Engels am Vorabend der Revolution* (Berlin [East], 1968), p. 11.

[8]See Percy Stulz and Alfred Opitz, *Volksbewegungen in Kursachsen zur Zeit der Französischen Revolution* (Berlin [East], 1956), pp. 44ff., 120ff., 149ff., 228–29; Scheel, *Süddeutsche Jakobiner: Klassenkämpfe und republikanische Bestrebungen im deutschen Süden Ende des 18. Jahrhunderts* (Berlin [East], 1962), pp. 49ff., 149ff., 190–91; Johannes Schildhauer, "Gesellen- und Tagelöhnererhebungen in den mecklenburgischen Städten von 1790 bis 1800," *ZfG* 7 (1959): 1256ff.; Krüger, *Geschichte der Manufakturen*, pp. 427ff.; Streisand, *Deutschland von 1789 bis 1815* (Berlin [East], 1961), pp. 12ff., 35ff., 41ff. Of Streisand's book, one reviewer wrote that it considered all events and developments "under the basic world-historical aspect of the capitalist order superseding the feudal system"—an approach that "outgrows the nationalist limitations of bourgeois historiography," Heitzer, in *ZfG* 8 (1960): suppl., p. 198.

against recapture by the old powers, Mainz's new government decided to seek a union with France. The step is acclaimed as a truly national move, because it was meant to serve the interest of the nation. By insuring the survival of Mainz's democratic forces, such a union with France was to enable these forces to work more effectively for the destruction of the German feudal and particularist order.[9] Again, however, more is involved here than mere historical interest: East German historiography prides itself on having recovered what it considers a significant milestone of the German democratic-revolutionary tradition by thus salvaging from oblivion this first attempt to launch a bürgerlich revolution on German soil.[10]

In other areas—Silesia, Saxony, Hamburg—the French Revolution also had an impact; it helped touch off or injected added momentum into strikes, risings, and other manifestations of discontent. Yet, unlike in the western part of the Empire, it is noted, these movements had no political goals, but rather aimed at remedying specific hardships. With the exception of the Saxon rising of 1790, which did have an antifeudalist thrust, peasant risings thus remained poorly organized and localized, and urban revolts were equally uncoordinated. Nor was there any cooperation between town and country.[11]

The cause of this disarray was easily found: what these movements lacked, and what western and southwestern Germany had too little of, was bürgerlich leadership. The Bürgertum once again was unable to fulfill its "historical task" of assuming that leadership as the protagonist and main beneficiary of the emerging capitalist mode of production; though receptive to the ideas of the French Revolution, the Bürgertum shied away from translating

[9]See Streisand, pp. 117–18; Grundriss, p. 207; Scheel, Die Mainzer Republik: Protokolle des Jakobinerklubs (Berlin [East], 1975). In a review of Scheel's work, Walter Grab now agrees with the East German evaluation of the Mainz Republic (Archiv für Sozialgeschichte 17 [1977]: 494ff.), abandoning his earlier noncommittal position ("Eroberung oder Befreiung: Deutsche Jakobiner und die Franzosenherrschaft: 1792–99," ibid. 10 [1970], 16ff.). Most non-Marxists still view the Mainz Republic as a minor episode.

[10]Scheel, "Das Verhältnis der Klassiker des Marxismus zu den Anfängen der bürgerlichen revolutionären Demokratie in Deutschland," in Scheel, Bourgeoisie, pp. 35, 38–39; see also Holzapfel and Walter Markov, review, ZfG 11 (1963): 1373; Grundriss, p. 207

[11]See Streisand, Deutschland, p. 14; Scheel, Süddeutsche Jakobiner, pp. 34–35, 93–95, and passim. On the non-Marxist side, see also Klaus Epstein, The Genesis of German Conservatism (Princeton, 1966), pp. 441ff. That there existed a strong revolutionary potential in these various popular movements and that the urban and rural unrest of those years, had it occurred everywhere at the same time, would have overwhelmed the Prussian government is, however, acknowledged by some non-Marxist historians (Grab, "Eroberung," p. 38ff.; Henri Brunswig, La Crise de l'État prussien à la fin du XVIIIe siècle et la genèse de la mentalité romantique [Paris, 1947], p. 141).

them into political action. Many burghers saw no need for such action, still confident that the rulers would eventually grant them political rights; others feared that rebellious mass movements might endanger their own position—fears heightened by the growing radicalism of the French petty bourgeoisie and the role of the Jacobins. As Heinrich Scheel concludes, the "purely metaphysical reception of French ideas" kept the German Bürgertum from "transforming the revolutionary energies of the masses into an active and irresistible power directed at the destruction of the feudal order." Similarly, Streisand complains that the intelligentsia did not comprehend the requirements of the fight for democracy:

> When France's Third Estate split up into different factions and the internal contradictions of the anti-feudal movements became apparent, when the radical *petite bourgeoisie* seized power and under the democratic dictatorship of the Jacobins defeated the internal counterrevolution that had allied itself with the country's external enemies, most observers in Germany, economically and politically torn and backward as it was, thought this a betrayal of the Revolution and its idea of freedom. This sympathy turned into indignation or indifference toward political developments. . . . Few of them understood that only the "despotism of freedom" (Marat) could safeguard the results of the Revolution.

With the Bürgertum unprepared to seize the leadership in the fight against the old order, most insurgent activities could be suppressed without much difficulty. Only in a few cases, as during the Saxon peasant revolt of 1790, were large numbers of troops required to defeat the risings. For the same reason, governments made only minor, if any, concessions to restore order.[12]

Unlike on other occasions, DDR authors explain rather than attack the Bürgertum's failure to act. Many accounts point out that it lacked the economic strength and independence that inspired the French bourgeoisie and gave it a social status that made its lack of political rights and influence particularly incongruous. Similarly, it is recognized that there was no "German" Bürgertum, let alone a broadly based capitalist bourgeoisie, and that the multitude of states that existed—some 300 of them—also helps to account for the local limitations of the various revolts. As Scheel notes, France had a center in Paris, on which French political and economic concerns converged and control of which facilitated the task of the revolutionaries to take control of the rest of the country. Scheel also concedes that "second serfdom" and territorial divisions rendered the task of the Bürgertum difficult. Bold initiatives, he acknowledges, presuppose strength: "Where in Germany could the

[12]Scheel, *Süddeutsche Jakobiner*, p. xi; Stulz and Opitz, *Volksbewegungen*, pp. 83–84 and *passim*; Streisand, *Deutschland*, pp. 19–20; see also Epstein, pp. 446–47.

Bürgertum acquire such strength?" On a more positive note, Streisand hails the original enthusiasm with which the French Revolution was greeted in Germany as an expression of the hope for a better future and hence as part of the liberating and progressive traditions of the German nation. He also finds that although the Bürgertum turned its back on the French Revolution, the original impact of the Revolution was not entirely lost. Its ideals of freedom, equality, and self-government lived on in German minds and reinforced the conviction that society, like nature, was shaped by a process of continued, though not uninterrupted, progressive development. Through Hegel, moreover, who conceived his philosophy of dialectical idealism under the impact of the French upheavals, this view of the world was transmitted to Marx and Engels, who translated it into their system of dialectical materialism.[13]

The wars between Europe's old absolute monarchies and the young French republic in the 1790s are viewed as a confrontation on the international level between the old feudal system and the new bourgeois-capitalist order. If the armies of the anti-French coalition—though superior in resources, manpower, and experience—failed to defeat the French forces, the success of the French, Streisand concludes, was due to the moral superiority of their cause, their close relationship to the people whose revolutionary gains they were defending, and above all to their struggle for social progress, which required the replacement of the feudal by the capitalist order. On the other hand, their opponents were doomed to defeat because they sought to defend a moribund system. Other moves to uphold that system—such as Prussia's withdrawal from the war against France (Peace of Basel, 1795) in order to help suppress peasant unrest in Silesia and a Polish rising against Prussia and Russia—could but contribute to this defeat.[14]

Prussia's role in concluding the Peace of Basel, long a subject of controversy among German historians, has also aroused considerable controversy among DDR scholars. Like most non-Marxist historians, some of them condemn Prussia's conclusion of that peace as a betrayal of German national interests inasmuch as Prussia submitted to France's continued occupation of German left-Rhenish territories. Others deny that Prussia had any "national" mission and that to argue along those lines simply helps to perpetuate the legend of such a mandate. Ultimately, it is, as always, the objective effects that are considered decisive. Thus, the main

---

[13]Scheel, *Süddeutsche Jakobiner*, p. 699; Schmidt, "Zu einigen Problemen," p. 10; Streisand, pp. 121–23; Streisand, *Geschichtliches Denken von der deutschen Frühaufklärung bis zur Klassik* (Berlin [East], 1964), pp. 93ff., especially pp. 105ff.
[14]Streisand, *Deutschland*, p. 30; *Grundriss*, p. 211; Vogler and Vetter, *Preussen*, pp. 137ff.

criterion, as Streisand points out, was the effect of the Peace of Basel on the relative strength of feudalism and capitalism in this phase of transition. Streisand's answer is not conclusive: Prussia's role at Basel was "objectively" progressive, because in coming to terms with the French republic Prussia enabled the latter to consolidate its bourgeois-progressive order and extend it into the German territories left of the Rhine. The fact that Prussia could assert itself more effectively in the Third Partition of Poland was seen as offsetting this progressive result. In consequence, Prussia could shore up its weakening feudal nobility by substantial new land grants and improve its own strained financial position. Moreover, as a more recent East German study points out, the annexation of a hostile Polish population forced Prussia into continued close collaboration with reactionary Russia and Austria. Thus Prussia's domination of part of Poland blocked Prussia's own road to freedom, as Marx and Engels already had shown. Indeed, because no nation that suppressed other peoples could be truly free, Germany's freedom depended on the liberation of Poland. On the other hand, one of the younger historians, Kurt Holzapfel, summarily views the Peace of Basel as a triumph of historical progress, because it strengthened the French bourgeoisie—the decisive result, he points out, from a worldwide historical perspective. All in all, Marxism's scientific approach has produced no more clearcut answers than has the traditional approach.[15]

If the feudalist powers suffered a serious setback with Prussia's withdrawal from the war against France, it is regretfully noted that France did not exploit its victory in order to advance the Revolution's goals and support the democratic, reform-minded movements across the Rhine. By this time, the Jacobin rule of Robespierre and Marat had given way to that of the Directory dominated by the *grande bourgeoisie*. As the organ of the latter, the Directory was not concerned with any progressive political or social reforms. Neither was its successor, Napoleon Bonaparte, who to most Marxists was also an agent of the *haute bourgeoisie*.[16]

[15]See Streisand, *Deutschland*, pp. 59–61, and the discussion reported by Scheel, in *ZfG* 4 (1956): 562–64; Erhard Moritz, *Preussen und der Kosciuszko-Aufstand* (Berlin [East], 1968), pp. 184–86, 192ff. (Marx and Engels quotations on p. 198); Holzapfel, "Robespierre und Preussen," *ZfG* 26 (1978): 886. See also Braubach, "Von der Französischen Revolution bis zum Wiener Kongress," in Gebhardt, vol. 3, pp. 16–18; Holborn, vol. 2, p. 363; Grab, "Eroberung," pp. 38–40, 42.

[16]On the question of Napoleon's relationship to the *grande bourgeoisie*, so like that of Hitler to Germany's great bourgeoisie, see Andreas Dorpalen, "The German Struggle against Napoleon: The East German View," *Journal of Modern History* 41 (1969): 488 n. 7, 504. That Napoleon, while not unmindful of bourgeois concerns, subordinated them to his own ambitions is seen by at least two East German historians—Köller and Töpfer, *Frankreich*, vol. 2, pp. 140–41. See also Marx and Engels, in MEW, vol. 2, p. 130.

Both the Directory and Napoleon were anxious to consolidate their position by conservative policies at home and abroad. Rather than carry the Revolution across the Rhine, they tried to play off the old feudal-absolutist monarchies against one another. In this manner the revolutionary potential that East German scholars detect in the German masses was not utilized, and the destruction of the feudal system was delayed.[17]

Of course these authors do not ignore the reforms that were imposed or encouraged by the French in western Germany,[18] and they acknowledge that the changes, including the abolition of serfdom in the French-dominated Confederation of the Rhine (Rheinbund), provided new opportunities for capitalist expansion. Their complaint is that no reforms were demanded beyond those needed to improve the economic and military efficiency of any potential allies. At that, these measures were not allowed to jeopardize the economic supremacy of the French bourgeoisie, and the Continental System, which cut off Britain from trade with the Continent, brought textile, timber, and grain exports virtually to an end.[19]

The French, the East German critics complain, thus became allies of the old feudal forces, who continued to block all reforms that they were not forced to make by the French government or by pressing domestic need. Because Germany still divided into some fifty separate territories, even after it had been reorgainzed in 1803, it continued to be much farther removed from a national economy than France was in 1789. In addition, in Germany, unlike in France, there existed no social forces strong enough to challenge this trend.[20]

Yet DDR scholars find once again that historically inevitable progress cannot be delayed forever, and Prussian developments

[17]Scheel, Süddeutsche Jakobiner, pp. 233ff., 250ff., 704–5; Streisand, Deutschland, pp. 79–80, 84, 87, 90.

[18]Grundriss, in describing this process for the German lands left of the Rhine that were annexed by France, speaks of French troops coming to the aid of popular mass movements, suggesting a role similar to that claimed for the Red Army in the transformation of East Germany into a socialist state (see chapter 9); Grundriss, p. 208. Unlike most of the reforms imposed by the Soviets, however, the French-inspired reforms appear to have been genuinely popular in the affected territories (Holborn, vol. 2, p. 386; also Braubach, "Französischen Revolution," p. 51).

[19]See Streisand, Deutschland, pp. 120, 127, 133, 138; Mottek, Wirtschaftsgeschichte Deutschlands, vol. 2, pp. 79ff.; Stulz, Fremdherrschaft und Befreiungskampf: Die preussische Kabinettspolitik und die Rolle der Volksmassen in den Jahren 1811 bis 1813 (Berlin [East], 1960), pp. 17, 20; Heitzer, Insurrectionen zwischen Weser und Elbe: Volksbewegungen gegen die französische Fremdherrschaft im Königreich Westfalen (1806–1813) (Berlin [East], 1959), pp. 16–17, 23–24. On the East German view of France's Continental System, see Dorpalen, "German Struggle," pp. 491–92.

[20]Streisand, Deutschland, p. 146; Scheel, "Zur Problematik des deutschen Befreiungskrieges 1813," ZfG 11 (1963): 1287.

serve as a test case. Prussia's reform movement received its main impetus from the country's defeat by Napoleon in 1806–1807. Because of the reforms it generated, that defeat, although a humiliating experience, is not regarded as a catastrophe. (Conversely, there is also general agreement that the defeat of France by Austria and/or Prussia would have meant a grave setback to social progress; not only would there have been no Prussian reforms, but France's newly established bourgeois-capitalist order would have been seriously weakened or destroyed altogether.) As for the reforms, the emancipation of the peasants and the extension of the right of land ownership to all classes weakened the feudal system, while the abolition of guild monopolies and the introduction of freedom of trade aided the growth of capitalist enterprise. However, although these measures are welcomed as genuine progress, it is also noted that they were introduced not by a bourgeoisie determined to free itself from all feudal fetters, but by somewhat more liberal-minded aristocrats whose social parochialism set narrow limits to the reforms. In the absence of a strong bourgeoisie, the resistance of the feudal nobility to any changes and King Frederick William III's fears of a mass upheaval also blocked any more far-reaching changes.[21]

Thus, while acclaiming the progressive nature of the Prussian reforms, the East German accounts do not minimize the price at which the improvements were bought. As a consequence of the "class attitude" of the reformers, king, and nobility, the agrarian reforms, while granting the peasants their personal freedom, placed new economic burdens upon them. To become freeholders, most of them had to give up part of their land, and their release from servitude attached to the land required payment of substantial redemption dues. Later the number of peasants who could establish secure and unencumbered land tenure was further reduced. As a result, it is noted, the nobles not only increased their holdings but could also draw upon a cheap labor force, because most peasants could not support themselves on the lots they retained. The Junkers thus became the main beneficiaries of the breakthrough of capitalism that was touched off by the abolition of serfdom, the creation of a "free" labor force, and the legalized mobility of real property. With credit readily available to them, the Junkers transformed themselves from feudal estate owners into agrarian capitalists who retained, however, many of their seigniorial prerogatives.

[21]For details, see Dorpalen, "German Struggle," pp. 488–89. The East German viewpoint of the beneficial results of the Prussian defeat is not novel; Max Lehmann wrote in his *Scharnhorst* ([Leipzig, 1886–1887], vol. 2, p. 83): "The Prussia of the early 19th century was saved through misfortune and misery." On the willingness of a substantial part of the nobility to accept some narrowly circumscribed reforms, see Vetter, "Der kurmärkische Adel und das Oktoberedikt," *ZfG* 27 (1979): 439ff.

This process is defined, in Lenin's words, as the "Prussian way" of capitalist development in agriculture. Lenin contrasted it with the more democratic "American way," in which feudal land ownership either never existed—as in North America—or was swept away without compensation by a bourgeois-democratic revolution—as in France—and in which capitalist methods were adopted by a multitude of entrepreneurial farmers or peasants (Grossbauern).

According to Marxists, these differing modes of agrarian capitalist developments had decisive impact on subsequent sociopolitical developments. They claim that the Prussian way, which in more or less stringent form applied to all of Germany,[22] not only retarded productivity but also prevented the formation of a large class of prosperous farmers and kept the peasants subjected to continued seigniorial abuses. Most serious, however, from the perspective of "lawful" historical progress, the Prussian way enabled the nobles to preserve their political power at the expense of the bourgeoisie. At the same time, the conversion of feudal landowners into agrarian capitalists created some communality of interests between Junkers and bourgeoisie, which blunted the conflict between the two classes and served further to buttress the nobles' position. The most important consequence of the Prussian way, however, is that as a result of the Junkers' continued predominance, Germany was ultimately unified by a revolution from above rather than by a broadly based bourgeois-led mass movement.[23]

Limitations that curbed other Prussian reforms are attributed to the same social obstacles. Here again, ideological "partisanship" simplifies complex dilemmas. In part, these limitations did derive from the refusal of king and nobility to yield much ground to middle and lower classes, but they cannot be explained simply as a function of the class struggle. The effectiveness of the municipal reforms, for example, was greatly impaired by the reluctance of many burghers to assume the responsibilities that local self-government demanded of them. Yet the explanation that municipal self-government presupposed an independent, political-minded citizenry that the reforms were meant to create, is dismissed as a pretentious attempt to credit the Prussian government with having

[22]Georg Moll, "Zum 'preussischen Weg' der Entwicklung des Kapitalismus in der deutschen Landwirtschaft," ZfG 26 (1978): 57ff.
[23]See Streisand, Deutschland, pp. 149ff.; Vogler and Vetter, Preussen, pp. 161ff.; Bleiber, "Zur Problematik des preussischen Weges der Entwicklung des Kapitalismus in der Landwirtschaft," ZfG 13 (1965): 64–65, 69–71; Reinhard Gross, Die bürgerliche Agrarreform in Sachsen in der ersten Hälfte des 19. Jahrhunderts (Weimar, 1968); Moll, " 'Preussischer Weg' und 'Revolution von oben,' " WZ Rostock 21 (1972): 88. On the non-Marxist side, see the less pointed, but in many respects similar, analysis by Reinhard Koselleck, "Staat und Gesellschaft in Preussen," in Moderne deutsche Sozialgeschichte, ed. Hans-Ulrich Wehler (Cologne, 1966), pp. 69ff; also Treue, "Die Bauernbefreiung," p. 92.

forced self-government on an unwilling Bürgertum and being the actual creator of the bourgeoisie of the nineteenth century; in reality, internal conditions and needs on which the reformers could build must have existed, and further research would have to test and refute this misleading thesis.[24]

In the case of the military reforms, East German scholars welcome as progressive achievements the elimination of the worst physical abuses, the admission of non-nobles to the officer corps, and the modernization of military training and organization; at the same time, King Frederick William III's rejection of the reformers' proposal to organize a mass militia for a war of liberation against the French is condemned as another instance of crass class egoism. It is true that in rejecting the plan the king responded to his ingrained conservatism and readily listened to pleas of the Pomeranian nobility, who abhorred universal military service as an outgrowth of the "French fraud of liberty and equality." What his East German critics do not mention, however, are the king's serious concern about the military effectiveness of a hastily trained militia and his fear of precipitating a crisis by premature actions.[25]

The negative reaction of the king and his entourage to the militia proposal is also criticized on the grounds that a militia would have had considerable popular support. Austria's war against France in 1809 touched off stirrings in Prussia, and attempts by some of the military leaders who tried to organize anti-French insurrections on their own aroused considerable enthusiasm. Once again, Heinz Heitzer and others assert, it was the masses who tried to make history, and once again their efforts were blocked by the class egoism of the king and his counsellors. However, the rebelling military leaders are also taken to task for turning down most of the volunteers who wished to join them. Yet these officers did so not because of their distrust of the lower classes, as Heitzer maintains (against his own evidence), but because they wished to enlist only armed and experienced men. The wisdom of this decision was demonstrated when the Hessian Colonel Wilhelm von Dörnberg was forced by events to lead some 1,500 peasants armed with lances fashioned from scythes against 500 Westphalian cavalrymen. The encounter ended with the instant rout of the peasants.[26]

[24]Bleiber, "Bourgeoisie und bürgerliche Umwälzung in Deutschland," *ZfG* 25 (1977): 311, as compared to Koselleck, *Preussen zwischen Reform und Revolution* (Stuttgart, 1967), pp. 169–70, 320ff.
[25]Lehmann, *Scharnhorst*, vol. 2, pp. 188–89, 295–96; also Hintze, *Hohenzollern*, pp. 455, 459; Holborn, vol. 2, p. 417; Schnabel, *Deutsche Geschichte*, vol. 1, p. 393.
[26]See Heitzer, *Insurrectionen*, pp. 183–85, 161ff.; Stulz, *Fremdherrschaft und Befreiungskampf*, pp. 52–53, 144; Scherer,"Zur Geschichte des Dörnbergischen Aufstandes im Jahre 1809," *HZ* 84 (1900): 259–62. Vogler and Vetter (*Preussen*, pp. 172–74) are less sanguine about the extent of popular unrest.

Their class-centered approach leads DDR authors to discount all nonsocial motives. They admit that the prospect of winning a war against France was uncertain, yet they do not regard this uncertainty as a relevant reason for the king's reluctance to act. As Klaus Vetter concludes, "It does not matter in judging the Prussian government and the ruling circles in Prussia whether they considered a war in 1809 as promising or not, but rather that they rejected altogether a war of liberation that could be carried out only with the help of the masses, and tried to prevent it."[27] Similarly, the king's personal diffidence, his lack of initiative, and his dull-wittedness are dismissed as irrelevant. If non-Marxists consider it important that, at a time when decisiveness and flexibility were required, a hapless indecisive monarch occupied the Prussian throne, such "psychologizing" is condemned as ignoring the realities of class antagonisms and giving undue weight to accidental circumstances, such as the king's character. By thus blunting the issues, it is charged, bourgeois historians distort historical reality and open the door to an unhistorical conciliatory approach that encourages acquiescence in the world as it was (and is)—a stance that is incompatible with the didactic function of history.[28] This, of course, is a warning that ought not to be taken lightly; the attempt to understand motivations requires perspective lest it explain those motivations away. The old adage of *tout comprendre—c'est tout pardonner* is not one to guide the historian, but neither is an approach that discounts all individual traits.

What power the masses could wield, DDR scholars note, was demonstrated during Napoleon's Russian campaign in 1812. Their conclusions are based on the findings of the Soviet historian Eugene Tarlé, who has shown that severe cold set in that winter only long after Napoleon had withdrawn from Moscow. Most East German authors therefore attribute the French rout to supply shortages rather than to weather conditions or military defeats. It was partisan raids, they stress, that destroyed French stores or caused them to be abandoned, and noncooperation and sabotage by the peasants prevented the French from replenishing their supplies. "Napoleon's strategy," Tarlé summed up this view, "took into account troops and [Tsar] Alexander's troops, but he had to fight the

---

[27]See Streisand, *Deutschland*, pp. 174–75; Heitzer, *Insurrectionen*, pp. 172–73; Vogler and Vetter, *Preussen*, p. 174. Austria's inept conduct of the war also contributed to Frederick William's reluctance to join that country in its campaign against France. Yet he seems to have been ready to come to Austria's aid had it not been defeated in the battle of Wagram (Lehmann, *Scharnhorst*, vol. 2, pp. 280 ff.). On this, see also Dennis E. Showalter, "The Prussian *Landwehr* and Its Critics," *CEH* 4 (1971): pp. 7–8.
[28]S. B. Kahn, "Der Befreiungskrieg von 1813 in der deutschen historischen Literatur," *ZfG* 3 (1955): 259–60.

Russian people, whom he had not taken into account. It was the hand of the Russian people that inflicted the irreparable, mortal blow."[29] Yet the desire to point up the history-making power of the masses may have led Tarlé and his followers to give undue weight to peasant activities. Some East German scholars consider that the share of the regular Russian army in Napoleon's defeat was at least as important, as that of the peasants, if not decisive.[30] It would be difficult in any event to measure precisely the respective contributions of army and partisans.

The tendency to overstress mass activities becomes especially marked in the endeavor to view the fight of the Russian people as the main inspiration of anti-French activities among the peoples of Europe. Yet, at least in Germany's case, all contemporary sources indicate that the population was unaware of the role of the Russian people and attributed the French collapse to weather conditions, the vastness of the country, and military defeats. Many sources saw in the debacle the manifestations of a divine judgment.[31]

If any specific act aroused Germans to rise up against the French, it was the decision of the commander of the Prussian contingent attached to the French forces in Russia, General Hans David York von Wartenburg, to abandon the French and proclaim his neutrality late in December 1812, contrary to the orders of Frederick William III. York's move has traditionally been described as the courageous deed of an individual patriot. He was praised for his willingness to risk execution for disobedience because he was convinced he was serving the true interests of his country. The East German historian Percy Stulz has shown, however, that York's decision was forced on him by attempts of his junior officers to take their men over to the Russians and by large-scale desertions among the rank and file. Thus, "mass" pressure is found to have played a key role in this episode, and it was the rebellious elements in the Prussian corps rather than York who should receive credit for his decision and for the anti-French actions that were inspired by that decision.[32]

[29]See Eugene Tarlé, *Napoleon's Invasion of Russia 1812* (New York, 1942), pp. 266–70, 342–55, 390; Streisand, *Deutschland*, pp. 200–201; Stulz, *Fremdherrschaft und Befreiungskampf*, pp. 146–47; Heitzer, *Insurrectionen*, p. 231. On the fact that severe cold weather set in unusually late that year, see also, on the non-Marxist side, *A German Conscript with Napoleon: Jakob Walter's Recollections*, ed., Otto Springer (Humanistic Studies of the University of Kansas, 1940) vol. 6, no. 3, p. 50 n. 119. For specific meteorological data that appeared long before Tarlé's work, see August Fournier, *Napoleon I* (New York, 1912) vol. 2, pp. 217 n. 1, 219 n. 1.
[30]Fritz Straube, review, *ZfG* 3 (1965): 1459–60; "Vaterländischer Krieg," *Swb*, vol. 2, p. 679.
[31]For details, see Dorpalen, "German Struggle," pp. 505–6.
[32]Stulz, *Fremdherrschaft und Befreiungskampf*, pp. 176ff.; also Vogler and Vetter, *Preussen*, pp. 179ff.

In this sense, the subsequent months are considered of even greater significance, because "the role of the masses as the decisive propelling power of history manifested itself [at that time] so clearly."[33] East German combings of archives and published sources have produced a considerable array of materials in support of this claim. Anti-French sentiment, on the increase throughout the Russian campaign, burst forth in clashes between Prussians—both civilians and soldiers—and French forces. In some areas, French soldiers were forcibly disarmed and their arms stores seized by peasants and artisans; elsewhere, they were denied food and lodgings. Conversely, wherever Russian soldiers appeared they were warmly welcomed. Considerable attention is paid to the ensuing Russo-German "comradeship-in-arms," which, it is claimed, laid the foundation for a tradition of friendship between the German and Russian peoples.

It is recognized, on the other hand, that the anti-French sentiments of urban workers and peasantry were on the whole apolitical, directed against French abuses of power, heavy taxation, and military conscription or against the "Anti-Christ" whom Napoleon seemed to embody. However, the substantive distinction between bürgerlich circles, which prepared for liberation activities on a national scale, and localized peasant/worker activities is considered irrelevant: what mattered was the objective cumulative effect of all these actions, which forced Frederick William III to issue decrees calling for volunteer detachments and universal conscription. Yet, this popular movement, it is regretfully noted, proved short-lived. Once the king had been compelled to assume the command of the liberation movement, all restive elements, irrespective of class, submitted again to the leadership of the established authorities.[34] The war against the French became one of liberation from external French domination, but not from domestic repression. For this reason, DDR historiography refers to the war as Befreiungskrieg rather than Freiheitskrieg, as non-Marxists have traditionally done, and Grundriss even speaks of the Unabhängigkeitskrieg (War of Independence) to make it still clearer that the war brought liberation only from foreign domination.[35]

Actually, according to historical laws, the Bürgertrum should

[33]Scheel et al., ZfG 18 (1970): suppl., p. 388.
[34]See Stulz, Fremdherrschaft und Befreiungskampf, pp. 106ff., 166ff., 195ff.; Heitzer, Insurrectionen, pp. 227–28; Streisand, Deutschland, pp. 208–9, 213–14; Vogler and Vetter, Preussen, p. 183; "Thesen zum 150. Jahrestag des Befreiungskrieges von 1813," ZfG 11 (1963): 1303; also see Lehmann, Scharnhorst, vol. 2, pp. 477, 488–89, 508ff.; Hintze, Hohenzollern, pp. 470ff. On the initial reluctance of the East Prussian estates to act without royal authorization, see Dorpalen, "German Struggle," p. 508.
[35]See Bock, "1789 und 1813," ZfG 12 (1964): 1365 n. 38; Grundriss, pp. 216–17. Many West German historians, too, now use the term Befreiungskrieg, but there are still occasional references to the Freiheitskriege. That Befreiungskrieg is the

have played the leading role in the struggle against Napoleon. France's defeat at the hands of the Bürgertum, the argument runs, would have secured political power for the Bürgertum, and that group would have opened the door as widely as possible to the emerging capitalist system, by which the Bürgertum itself stood most to gain. As it was, the old feudal elements were allowed to retain their power, and the Bürgertum missed the opportunity to destroy altogether the feudal order. The commercial bourgeoisie, it is pointed out, even tolerated continued French domination where it provided prosperity, as in Saxony and other *Rheinbund* states. Feudalism thus was not always seen as a barrier to capitalist enterprise. Only in Prussia, where the negative effects of the Continental System were strongly felt, did grain-exporting nobles and bourgeois businessmen align themselves with the anti-French forces. As Marx already had claimed, lack of sugar and coffee was "the real basis of the glorious Wars of Liberation of 1813."[36] Non-Marxists, in turn, have shown that even Prussia's Bürgertum, insofar as it was engaged in business, was less inclined to do battle against the French than were academic and professional groups. In several cities, merchants and manufacturers tried to obtain exemptions from service in the militia.[37]

The subsequent role of the masses, too, seems to have been less significant than the doctrine of their creative function has led its advocates to assume. As one of them has justified their analyses, "The problem is . . . less a question of source interpretations than of the conception of history: Is history made by individuals or by the masses?"—an approach that all but preordains its conclusions.[38]

---

more accurate term is attested by Frederick William III, who insisted that this designation rather than *Freiheitskriege* be used in textbooks so as to discourage any hopes for greater domestic freedoms (Helmut Berding, "Freiheitskriege," *SDG*, vol. 2, p. 685).

[36] See Streisand, *Deutschland*, pp. 127, 221; Vogler and Vetter, *Preussen*, p. 159; Marx in MEW, vol. 3, p. 46; also Schnabel, *Deutsche Geschichte*, vol. 1, p. 489. Much has been made of the seeming discrepancy between Marx's statement and that of Engels to the effect that for once the nation took matters into its own hands and, without waiting for all-highest permission, rose on its own against the French (MEW, suppl., vol. 2, p. 121. The respective contexts make it clear that Marx referred to the East Prussian upper classes, whose insurrectional actions were prompted by the effects of the Continental System, whereas Engels wrote about the attitude of middle and lower classes. See also Engels in MEW (vol. 2, p. 569), where he, too, speaks contemptuously of the attitude of the upper classes. Engels also took the nation to task for returning so quickly to its earlier political somnolence after its initial spontaneous efforts (ibid., p. 579; suppl. vol. 2, p. 121).

[37] Lehmann, *Scharnhorst*, vol. 2, pp. 537–38; Walter M. Simon, *The Failure of the Prussian Reform Movement, 1807–1819* (Ithaca, 1955), pp. 165–66.

[38] See Reinhard Röder, quoted in Berding, "Freiheitskriege," p. 691; also Stulz, *Fremdherrschaft und Befreiungskampf*, p. 1; Heitzer, *ZfG* 8 (1960): suppl., p. 189. Conversely, distrust of the masses often inspired a negative evaluation of their role, as in the case of Ritter (Berding, "Freiheitskriege," p. 686).

The number of volunteers was comparatively small, and as Franz Schnabel has noted, only in the case of the non-Prussians can we be certain that they enlisted entirely voluntarily. Prussians, on the other hand, may well have decided to volunteer because they were otherwise subject to the draft and moreover forfeited the substantial advantages in promotions, military assignments, and postwar government employment that voluntary enlistment entailed. At that, few Prussians enlisted.[39]

What war enthusiasm did exist was largely confined to Prussia, the kingdom of Westphalia, and some of the smaller north German states. Some East German authors have pointed to anti-French demonstrations in Saxony and Bavaria as evidence of widespread unrest in central and southern Germany, but as another, Jürgen Kuczynski, has shown, the available evidence does not bear out this claim. Most Germans outside the north considered Napoleon their benefactor, because they credited him with whatever improvements in their lot they had gained. Similarly, the readiness with which Saxons, Wuerttembergers, and Hessians fought side by side with the French against the Prussians in the spring of 1813 also suggests that they were willing allies of the French. In addition, as the mutiny of Saxon forces under Prussian command shortly before the battle of Waterloo indicates, at least in this case, Francophile feelings were strong enough to survive the changeover of Saxony from the French to the anti-French camp.[40]

Whereas the East German accounts paint an overly rosy picture of the patriotism of the middle and lower classes, they find that the established authorities hampered the war against France. Military decisions, the critics complain, were affected by the policy-makers' determination to maintain at all costs the political status quo. They point out that the Prussian *Landsturm*, a last-ditch home guard, was hedged in with severe restrictions and, a few months later, was dissolved altogether. The plan had been to activate the Landsturm in case the French should penetrate deep into Prussia; in such an emergency the Landsturm was to engage in

---

[39]See Schnabel, *Deutsche Geschichte*, vol. 1, pp. 492–93; Lehmann, *Scharnhorst*, vol. 2, pp. 526–29; Hintze, *Hohenzollern*, p. 472. On the limited number of volunteers, see Showalter, "Prussian Landwehr," p. 9.

[40]See Streisand, *Deutschland*, pp. 226–27 and Lange, *Die Lützower* (East Berlin, 1953), pp. 55ff. as compared to Kuczynski, *Geschichte*, vol. 1, pp. 50–51 (with numerous illustrations); see also Steiger, *Aufbruch: Urburschenschaft und Wartburgfest* (Leipzig, 1967), pp. 48–49; letter from Field Marshal von Blücher to King Frederick August of Saxony, May 6, 1815, in Heinrich von Treitschke, *Deutsche Geschichte im neunzehnten Jahrhundert* (Leipzig, 1927), vol. 2, p. 622. Despite its title, Kurt Uebe's "Der Stimmungsumschwung in der bayerischen Armee gegenüber den Franzosen: 1806–1812" (*Münchener Historische Abhandlungen* [Munich, 1939], vol. 12) fails to refute the view of a Francophile stance of the Bavarian army, let alone of Bavaria as a whole.

guerrilla warfare, sabotage, and scorched-earth devastation, and for this reason it was suspect of revolutionary potential. Yet here again the East German analyses simplify. Although such suspicions were a major cause of the early demise of the *Landsturm*, the effectiveness of such an ill-trained, ill-equipped force was also a serious concern. There were also equally legitimate warnings concerning the grave economic effects of scorched-earth tactics.[41]

Complaints that the famous volunteer free corps of Major Adolf von Lützow, too, fell victim to political conservatism and narrow class prejudice are similarly simplistic. It is true that the corps aroused the suspicions of the Prussian king and his government; they saw it as a threat to the dynastic and feudal-aristocratic order, because many non-Prussians joined it and because members took an oath of allegiance not to the king of Prussia but to the "Vaterland," stressing the corps' role as a symbol of national unity. If the corps got little support from the Prussian authorities and, like the Landsturm, was soon dissolved, one reason was that the government thought its fears of the corps were confirmed by the *Lützower*'s reckless bravado and their widespread looting and pillaging—facts that DDR critics either play down or pass over in silence.[42]

These authors are on firmer ground in their analysis of the overall conduct of the war. For the reasons just noted, King Frederick William III wished to pursue the war with as little dependence as possible on any irregular forces. His main concern therefore was to draw Austria into the war—partly in order to reduce his dependence on Landsturm and free corps and partly as a counterweight against Russia, which seemed bent on further territorial annexations during its advance into central Europe. The king thus delayed the all-out attack on the French that in the East German view would have led to their speedy defeat. (To DDR scholars, the suspicions affecting Prusso-Russian relations reflect the ambitions, fears, and cabals that are typical of the propertied classes and that are tempered only by their common interest in the preservation of the old order. The masses—shopkeepers, peasants, and artisans—on the other hand, are commended for welcoming the Russian soldiers, their social peers, as liberators and allies.[43])

---

[41]See Lehmann, *Scharnhorst*, vol. 2, pp. 544ff.; Simon, pp. 168ff.; as compared to Streisand, *Deutschland*, p. 220.

[42]See Streisand, *Deutschland*, pp. 220–21; Vogler and Vetter, *Preussen*, pp. 184–85; and Lange, *Die Lützower*, which, while basically a eulogy of the corps, does present materials suggesting some of its shadier activities (pp. 99–100). On these, see Dorpalen, "German Struggle," p. 511 n. 71.

[43]East German research has shown that the delaying strategy in the spring of 1813 was not due to the indecision of the Russian commander-in-chief, Field Marshal Kutusov, as has generally been assumed, and that in fact Scharnhorst and Kutosov had made plans for an offensive, to which the Prussian king, however, refused to commit his troops (Dorpalen, "German Struggle," pp. 511–12).

Further confirmation of this assessment is found in the fact that Austria joined the war only after Napoleon had rejected a negotiated settlement—a solution that Prince Metternich would have preferred in order to avoid a mass mobilization and any further westward advance by the Russians. With Austria's entry into the war, the Prussian government felt strong enough to dispense with all irregular forces, and these were dissolved one after another. The war thus changed from a people's war to a cabinet war. Accordingly, when the *Rheinbund* states that had sided with France switched to the anti-French coalition, they were welcomed with their sovereignty and, in most cases, their territory vouchsafed; these commitments, it is stressed, served to safeguard the old order and prolong the political fragmentation of Germany.[44]

In the same vein, East German scholars rightly place great emphasis on the fact that the shifting nature of the war was welcomed by large parts of the Bürgertum. Fearful of the lower classes, the Bürgertum helped to suppress popular movements and at times even collaborated with the French for that purpose. Nor did laborers and artisans object to the changing weight of the social forces that were propelling the conflict. Nonpolitical by nature, they were content to retain their old rulers or see them restored, in the expectation that those rulers would now help them improve their lot. This the old feudal-dynastic powers were reluctant to do, and the war against France, at first "just" in Marxist terms because its original goals, aimed at Germany's liberation, turned into an "imperialist" one. In this latter phase, Prussia and Austria seized non-German lands, failed to pursue the social and political emancipation of the German people, and reimposed upon France the old Bourbon regime.[45]

The peace settlement drawn up by the Congress of Vienna, Karl Obermann notes, marked the extent of the victory of the feudal-reactionary forces. Their intrigues and deceptions, he points out, doomed all efforts of German patriots to attain the unification of Germany and political influence for the Bürgertum. Here again developments are measured against a model "agenda of history"

---

[44]Streisand, *Deutschland*, pp. 231–32; *Grundriss*, p. 217.

[45]See Heitzer, *Insurrectionen*, pp. 256, 281, 283ff.; Stulz, *Fremdherrschaft und Befreiungskampf*, pp. 253–54; Scheel, "Zur Problematik," pp. 1295–96. For somewhat different views, see also Streisand, *Deutschland*, p. 242–43; Kuczynski, *Geschichte*, vol. 1, pp. 51ff. It was about this outcome of the war that Engels made his oft-quoted statement that "the 'glorious War of Liberation' of 1813–14 and 1815 . . . was an attack of madness at the thought of which the face of every honest and intelligent German will turn red for many a year still" (*Deutsche Zustände*, MEW, vol. 2, pp. 569–70; see also Marx, ibid., vol. 5, pp. 294–96). Engels later changed his mind (ibid., vol. 2, p. 669 n. 156), but in early DDR historiography his original negative view was widely accepted (see Abusch, *Der Irrweg einer Nation*, p. 85; Kuczynski, *Geschichte*, vol. 32, pp. 127–28).

that called for the creation of a bourgeois capitalist system and for a unified Germany as the prerequisite of the rapid development of all productive forces and social progress. However, the necessary material and psychological conditions for the achievement of these goals simply did not exist. On the East Germans' own showing (Heitzer, Scheel, Obermann), the desire for unity was confined to a relatively small circle of government officials, academics, and students, whereas mass support for the war against France had flowed from anti-French feelings and economic frustrations. Obermann, while complaining about the abortion of all unification plans by princely maneuvers,[46] presents considerable material that points up the weakness and self-isolation of the Bürgertum. Nor has any East German scholar examined the practicality of the proposed unification plans, none of which resolved the problem of Prusso-Austrian dualism and the middle states' refusal to accept the hegemony of the two main German powers. Instead, most of the plans envisaged a loose association of states resting on common national feelings but also clearly delineated social ranks characteristic of the hierarchical feudal order.[47]

The DDR critics derive some solace, however, from the inability of Europe's rulers to set the clock back to pre-1789 days; they could do this least of all in the economic domain. The socioeconomic forces released by the French Revolution and the Napoleonic Wars would not long be contained. This meant that "the struggle of the German people for a united and progressive nation-state could now be pursued on a new higher level of social development."[48]

Until the mid-1970s, the year 1815 thus was considered a milestone in the period between the French Revolution of 1789–1794 and the Revolution of 1848–1849, in keeping with the traditional view. On reexamination, however, this periodization has been found unsatisfactory, on the grounds that the end of the Napoleonic era did not usher in any *qualitatively* new social changes.

---

[46]Obermann even goes so far as to claim, without any substantiation, that the territorial assignments were made for the express purpose of weakening the progressive national movements ("Der Wiener Kongress 1814–1815," *ZfG* 13 (1965): 476). In another passage in the same essay he himself notes, however, that territorial bargaining ("Länderschacher") revolved around foreign political considerations, pointing to Prussia, whose main concern was to receive an equitable share of the booty in terms of square kilometers (ibid., p. 480).

[47]See Obermann, *Deutschland von 1815 bis 1849* (Berlin [East], 1967), pp. 9, 21ff.; Hietzer, *Insurrectionen*, pp. 291, 296ff., 305; Scheel, "Die nationale Befreiungsbewegung," in *Das Jahr 1813*, ed. Straube (Berlin [East], 1963), pp. 9–10. On the unification and liberalization plans of Baron vom Stein, Alexander von Humboldt, et al., see Schnabel, *Deutsche Geschichte*, vol. 1, pp. 546ff.; Krieger, *German Idea*, pp. 204ff.; Holborn, vol. 2, pp. 442–43. The impracticality of Stein's proposals is seen by Streisand, *Deutschland*, p. 216.

[48]Streisand, *Deutschland*, pp. 239, 244.

The German states still remained firmly under the control of the feudal nobility (which began to adjust, however, to capitalist conditions), and although the forces of progress were gaining ground, the shift was slow and merely a continuation of earlier processes. As the starting point of qualitatively new developments, the year 1830 is considered far more significant: the 1830s were a decade of revolutionary initiatives on the part of some bürgerlich elements, and they were also the years of the "take-off" of the Industrial Revolution in Germany and of the genesis of an industrial working class.[49]

After Vienna, then, the advance toward the bourgeois-capitalist order continued with no noticeable increase in momentum. After a careful analysis, Hans Mottek finds, as non-Marxists also have noted, that the Napoleonic era set back rather than furthered capitalist developments in Germany. Wartime destruction, contributions to France, and the restrictions of the Continental System caused serious harm to the German economy. After the wars, territorial divisions, remaining feudal prerogatives, lack of capital, and the influx of English industrial products continued to interfere with the development of industrial capitalism.[50] Yet, once again, the emphasis is on the few auguries of future progress that the post-Vienna period produced—mostly moves by which the commercial bourgeoisie sought to improve its economic position. Thus calls by businessmen for the removal of internal trade barriers are hailed as significant challenges to the existing absolutist-feudal system.

In the first edition of his textbook, *Deutschland von 1815 bis 1849*, Obermann, having listed a few such pleas, concluded that "Even these few examples are evidence of a great movement of the German bourgeoisie on behalf of the economic unification of Germany."[51] He eliminated this statement from later editions, but still insists, as do other East German authors, that post-Vienna economic reforms—such as the Prussian customs laws of 1816 and 1818, which eliminated internal tariffs within and between all Prussian provinces—were forced upon the German governments by an energetic, purposeful bourgeoisie.[52]

[49]See Schmidt, "Zu einigen Problemen," pp. 18ff.; *Grundriss*, pp. 205–6; "Vormärz," *Swb*, vol. 2, p. 760. See also the arrangement of materials in *Grundriss* (p. 8) as opposed to Streisand, *Deutschland*, and Obermann, *Deutschland*; also compare the 1974 edition of Streisand, *Deutsche Geschichte*, p. 5, with the 1970 edition, p. 5.

[50]See Mottek, *Wirtschaftsgeschichte Deutschlands*, vol. 2, pp. 79ff.; on the non-Marxist side, see Frank B. Tipton, "The National Consensus in German Economic History," *CEH* 7 (1974): 199, with extensive bibliographical data.

[51]Obermann, *Deutschland*, 1961 ed., p. 21.

[52]See Obermann, *Deutschland*, pp. 20, 27, 99; see also Vogler and Vetter, *Preussen*, p. 204; Kuczynski, *Geschichte*, vol. 1, p. 129. For an attempt to explain the apparent discrepancy between the denial of a bourgeois class consciousness and the alleged successful pursuit of bourgeois economic objectives, see Kuczynski, *Geschichte*, vol. 1, pp. 116ff., especially pp. 123ff.

Actually, bourgeois efforts to exert any influence either nationally or locally were ineffective. As an American economic historian has noted after a thorough examination of the available evidence,

> people tried to improve conditions by sending petitions to the government. Although bitter necessity compelled many to resort to this action, no attempt was made to put organized pressure on the governments, nor was more than a special interest, either local or regional, represented. The governments were only too often expected to develop the overall policy as well as to determine the administrative details which were to remedy the petitioner's grievances. There was a certain enthusiasm for Germany's economic welfare, but not enough persistence to carry out plans. . . . Furthermore public opinion on the problem also lacked force and unity.[53]

Moreover, almost all such efforts were aimed at protection against English competition, not at economic unification, with which measures such as the Prussian customs laws were concerned.[54]

In fact, there was little need for any special efforts aimed at economic unification. The creation of a large domestic market was as much in the interest of the grain-producing nobility as it was in that of middle-class businessmen. The Prussian government, too, favored large markets as the basis of economic prosperity: forward-looking officials recognized that a flourishing economy was the main source of political strength, social stability, and, of course, fiscal revenues. Yet, where bourgeois concerns and those of government and landowning nobility parted ways, as in the matter of external tariffs, the impotence of the small bourgeoisie became evident. The latter's need for protection against foreign competition was disregarded, and tariffs were kept low. As disciples of Adam Smith, the governmental policymakers believed in the salutary effects of free trade and conceded tariffs only to meet fiscal needs. Agrarians, for their part, opposed any restrictions on their exports of grain, wool, and lumber and their imports of cheap machinery.[55]

In their quest for evidence of a bourgeois awakening, East German historians point in particular to the formation of the Ger-

[53]Arnold H. Price, *The Evolution of the Zollverein* (Ann Arbor, 1949), p. 31.

[54]There is some confusion on this point in the East German analyses. Obermann (*Deutschland*, p. 26) lists as an appeal for internal unification a project actually aiming at anti-English protection. For details, see Kuczynski, *Geschichte*, vol. 1, pp. 126–27. On business attitudes toward tariffs, see also *Vorgeschichte und Begründung des deutschen Zollvereins: 1815–1834*, ed. W. von Eisenhart Rothe and A. Ritthaler (Berlin, 1934), vol. 1, pp. 3–4, 6, 69ff.

[55]On the preservation of the agrarians' economic predominance, see Schnabel, *Deutsche Geschichte*, vol. 2, p. 299–301; Holborn, vol. 2, p. 461. Surprisingly, this point receives much less attention among Marxist historians (see Mottek, *Wirtschaftsgeschichte Deutschlands*, vol. 2, pp. 50ff.; Bock, *Ludwig Börne* [Berlin (East), 1962], pp. 233–35). Obermann (*Deutschland*, p. 31) touches on it only indirectly.

man Commercial and Manufacturing League (Allgemeiner Deutscher Handels- und Gewerbeverein) by the economist Friedrich List in 1819. They hail it as the "earliest bourgeois organization based on all-German political-economic interests . . . in which the unification of Germany was viewed from the sober perspective of bourgeois economic considerations."[56] This it was, and it called for a nationwide customs union and protective external tariffs. Yet, although it was supported by businessmen in all parts of Germany and engaged in a variety of activities, the league accomplished nothing and was dissolved after little more than a year.

The propelling forces of the period's socioeconomic changes were to be found, then, not among the Bürgertum, but among the governmental bureaucracies. Though predominantly of middle-class background, DDR authors note, members of such bureaucracies initiated reforms, not on behalf of the bourgeoisie, but on behalf of the feudal-absolute state. For this reason, they could and would act only within the limits that state needs required and feudal-agrarian concerns tolerated. Within these limits, however, the bureaucracies are recognized as instruments of entrepreneurial progress and are seen by Marxist historians as implementing the inevitable process toward unification and the capitalist system. Even in the absence of a strong bourgeoisie, they point out, progress could not be blocked.[57]

In the political arena, too, the Bürgertum displayed little activity during the post-Vienna years. Earlier attempts to picture it as engaged in a sustained struggle for constitutional rights are not borne out by the evidence and have since been abandoned.[58] The only bürgerlich element that would not stay quiet was centered in the universities. DDR historians praise the student movement as the one public voice for German unity and bürgerlich liberties. Yet they are not uncritical of the movement, taking it to task for its naive call for unification as a matter of pride and moral justice rather than of socioeconomic necessity. This lack of realism and the concomitant failure to recognize the sociomaterial needs that made unification "historically necessary" are explained as reflections of the as yet insufficiently developed capitalist mode of production. It is also noted that with few exceptions the student movement was reformist rather than revolutionary, expecting the German rulers to acquiesce in the demands of the *Burschenschaf-*

[56]Steiger, *Aufbruch*, p. 53.
[57]See Wolfgang Jonas, "Zum Problem Ideologie und Produktivkräfte zur Zeit der industriellen Revolution," *JWG* 2/3 (1964): 99; Bleiber, review, *ZfG* 19 (1971): 114. Bleiber criticizes a non-Marxist author for depicting the Prussian bureaucracy as an autonomous force rather than as the agent of historical inevitability. See also note 82.
[58]Obermann, *Deutschland*, pp. 31ff., as compared to *Grundriss*, p. 220.

ten. The movement as a whole thus remained wholly bürgerlich and refrained from arousing the masses—a "vanguard of the German bourgeois intelligentsia" without an army. However, though ineffectual, the movement is not dismissed as insignificant. If it did not launch a bourgeois-democratic revolution, it did help prepare it. Its enthusiasm, its speeches and songs, and the nationwide student meeting at the Wartburg Castle in 1817 (the "first bürgerlich national festival") are credited with nurturing those progressive thrusts that culminated in the revolution of 1848.[59]

Of special interest to Marxist historians are the Burschenschaften at the universities of Giessen and Jena. Known as the "Unconditionals," they called for a Germany united in a unitarian republic and for social equality, a people's militia, and other democratic institutions. To achieve these goals, they also were ready to launch a revolution and sought to organize a mass movement. As one East German scholar suggests, they may have helped to stir up the unrest in Hesse-Darmstadt that led the grandduke to grant that state a constitution in 1820.[60]

Although the Unconditionals' "alliance with the popular masses" is applauded as "wise and politically correct," resort to terror is not. The distinction is made because Karl Follen, the Unconditionals' leader, approved of terror if applied in pursuit of an ethically valid goal. The objection is that such a strategy substitutes subjective judgments for objective assessments of socioeconomic conditions and political power relationships as the basis for political action. Accordingly, the assassination by an Unconditional in 1819 of a Tsarist agent, the playwright August von Kotzebue, is denounced as a puerile gesture. [61]

The resulting repressive measures, codified in the Carlsbad Decrees, put an end to political activities outside authorized channels. The Burschenschaften were dissolved; secret student associations that were organized in their place remained weak. Being ever ready to find indications of continuing progress toward bourgeois-democratic institutions, however, East German accounts stress that these underground societies were more revolutionary minded than their legal predecessors. There is, however, no evidence that the new groups aroused any interest beyond their immediate membership.[62]

[59]Steiger, *Aufbruch*, pp. 20, 28ff., 52–53; Obermann, *Deutschland*, pp. 38ff.

[60]Steiger, *Aufbruch*, pp. 162–63; also Maria Wawrykowa, "Die studentisch Bewegung in Deutschland im ersten Jahrzehnt nach dem Wiener Kongress," in Streisand, *Bourgeoisie*, pp. 57ff.

[61]See Steiger, *Aufbruch*, pp. 163–64, 188–89; Bock, *Ludwig Börne*, pp. 146–47. This issue is also discussed, less explicitly, by Streisand (*Deutsche Geschichte*, p. 154, and Obermann, *Deutschland*, p. 39).

[62]See Obermann, *Deutschland*, pp. 45ff.; Vogler and Vetter, *Preussen*, p. 198; Wawrykowa, "Studentische Bewegung," pp. 61–63. See, however, Holborn (vol. 2, p. 468), who denies the revolutionary character of the secret societies.

What is considered important in terms of immediate progress is the accelerated expansion of capitalism that occurred in the 1820s. This expansion aided the growth of industry, preparing the way for a full-scale Industrial Revolution. (This view of the preparatory character of the 1810s and 1820s is the accepted view now; earlier, some DDR historians, among them Kuczynski and Obermann, had dated Germany's Industrial Revolution from the beginning phase of industrialization in the post-Vienna period.[63]) Equally significant, but viewed as more ominous because of the form it took, was the penetration of capitalism into agriculture—a trend furthered by the aborted agrarian reforms that forced many peasants to sell their lands to their former lords. These lords thus came to own an even larger part of the land, and the landless peasants, now rural laborers, were from then on subjected to capitalist exploitation without even that modicum of security that serfdom provided. By retaining their economic power and adjusting to capitalism, it is pointed out, the large landowners, mainly members of the nobility, also managed to preserve their social and political power and to delay the political ascendance of the Bürgertum, with grave consequences for German developments. Yet, even though the "Prussian way" of capitalism's advance into agriculture impeded progress, Grundriss finds the situation not wholly discouraging: "The resulting struggles and changes aroused the social consciousness of [many] people who showed a growing concern for the social and political questions of the times."[64] Lately, moreover, the tendency has been to stress also the progressive aspects of the role of the capitalist nobility, which, as Walter Schmidt puts it, became in a sense the caretaker of the basic economic and political interests of the bourgeoisie and as such furthered that revolutionary process by which Germany moved from feudalism to capitalism. More will be said later about this.[65]

The Bourgeoisie between Semifeudal Nobility and Industrial Proletariat

The emerging social and political consciousness of both Bürgertum and toiling masses and the translation of this awareness into prac-

[63]See Kuczynski, Geschichte, vol. 1, p. 87; Obermann, Deutschland, p. 52, as compared to Mottek, 76; Streisand, p. 158; Vogler and Vetter, Preussen, p. 201; Grundriss, p. 227. For a new flare-up of the discussion, see Karl Lärmer, cited in JWG 3 (1974): 317–18; also Berthold, ibid. 1 (1972): 261, as compared to ibid. 2 (1974): 13.
[64]Mottek, Wirtschaftsgeschichte Deutschlands, vol. 2, pp. 36ff.; Grundriss, pp. 219, 221.
[65]Schmidt, "Zu Problemen der europäischen Revolutionen von 1848–49," ZfG 27 (1979): 647.

tical action are main themes of the analyses probing the years 1830 to 1848. Specifically, these investigations seek to trace the rise of an industrial bourgeoisie chafing at feudal and bureaucratic restrictions and the corresponding formation of an industrial working class (or proletariat), which gradually also took up the fight against the existing restrictive practices. Yet, although these two classes were linked in their common opposition to feudal constraints, they faced each other, it is pointed out, as class enemies in the capitalist system.[66] Their common antifeudal objectives and their conflicting interests in the capitalist order, as well as the corresponding dialectics of bourgeois confrontation and collaboration with the nobility, are also major topics of research for this period.

Because of their revolutionary upheavals and notable economic advances, sparked by *Zollverein* and Industrial Revolution, and because of their new class alignments and a democratic movement evolving apart from the liberal one, the 1830s and 1840s are considered years of preparation for a bourgeois-democratic revolution. During these years the required forces for the "assault on the bastions of the still extant semi-feudalism" were readied; because of the bourgeois fears of the working class, however, they were shaped in a manner that greatly limited the success of that assault.[67] The key term here is *bourgeois-democratic.* In the Marxist view, which denies the class-neutral nature of democracy and regards it as a distinctly class-oriented form of asserting power, this term refers to a type of formal democracy that the bourgeoisie, essentially antidemocratic as an exploiting class, is supposedly willing to tolerate to further its own class interests. Bourgeois democracy, by this definition, includes the parliamentary system and such civil liberties as freedom of speech, press, and assembly, which, however, the bourgeoisie can manipulate and control because of its economic and political power. Even though bourgeois democracy does not give the masses political power, it is progressive compared to an absolutist or semiabsolutist monarchy, because it gives the workers a better chance to fight for their rights.[68] Genuine democracy, on the other hand, furthers the specific class

---

[66]On the interchangeable use of both terms in Marxist terminology, see *Swb*, vol. 2, p. 304 and *Wörterbuch*, p. 373. *Bourgeoisie* and *Bürgertum*, too, are often used interchangeably by Marxist historians; see, for example, Küttler, "Zum Begriff," p. 186. The term *bourgeoisie* will replace that of *Bürgertum* here in correlation with the spread of capitalism, with the various strata of the bourgeoisie referred to as great, middle, or petty (see Zwahr, in *Die grosspreussisch-militaristische Reichsgründung 1871*, ed. Bartel and Engelberg [Berlin (East), 1871], p. 501).

[67]W. Schmidt, "Zu einigen Problemen," pp. 19ff.; S. Schmidt, "Liberale Parteibewegung," pp. 401ff.; Kossok, "Vergleichende Revolutionsgeschichte," p. 23; Zwahr, "Bourgeoisie und Proletariat am Beginn der bürgerlichen Umwälzung in Sachsen," *ZfG* 25 (1977): 669ff.

[68]"Bürgerliche Demokratie," *Swb*, vol. 1, pp. 340–41.

interests of the popular masses—of workers, peasants, and petty bourgeoisie. It is not equated with universal suffrage and a parliamentary form of government, but with the dictatorship of the proletariat and ultimately with the classless socialist order. As Bleiber sums up this distinction, "The popular masses as a means or an end—this is what distinguishes bourgeois liberals from democrats." The distinction, needless to say, also has obvious present-day implications.[69]

The first indications of these developments are found in the upheavals that the French Revolution of 1830 touched off in some of the German states. In its wake, popular unrest forced the rulers of Saxony, Braunschweig, Hanover, and Hesse-Cassel to grant their states constitutions. In several states, remaining servitudes were abolished, censorship liberalized, and tax relief granted. What DDR historians find highly significant is the predominance of urban risings. For the first time, moreover, the industrial working class raised demands of its own, foreshadowing its subsequent central role in the class struggle. On the other hand, the less extensive rural upheavals are seen as indicative of the declining role of the peasantry and its relegation from primary to secondary class status.

The attitude of the bourgeoisie is considered just as revealing: having secured political and other concessions thanks to the risings launched by workers and petty bourgeois, the bourgeoisie immediately turned around and sided with government and nobility to restore quiet. Discussing this turnabout, Hartmut Zwahr sees here the first visible evidence of the "historically new class conflict between bourgeoisie and proletariat." For the first time, he notes, "backed by the force of arms, the great-bourgeois opposition in Saxony chose, during the initial phase of the bourgeois transformation for which it had not fought itself, the road of a negotiated accommodation with monarchy and nobility." Zwahr finds the bourgeoisie pursuing from then on the strategy of extracting further concessions from rulers and governments by utilizing the driving force (Triebkraft) of the working class, but repressing that force as soon as a compromise had been worked out with the ruling powers.[70] Earlier DDR analysts of this strategy denounced it as a betrayal of nation, masses, and/or the bourgeoisie's own interests, but more recent accounts refrain from such condemnations. Evidently it is realized now, as Lenin already had noted, that the "objective" interests of the bourgeoisie called for reforms rather

[69]Bleiber, "Bourgeoisie," p. 320ff. (quotation on p. 330); "Demokratie," Swb, vol. 1, p. 372; Unb. Verg., p. 271.
[70]Obermann, Deutschland, pp. 59ff; W. Schmidt, "Zu einigen Problemen," pp. 19–20; "Volkserhebungen 1830–31," Swb, vol. 2, p. 748; Zwahr, "Bourgeoisie," pp. 656ff.; Bleiber, "Die Unruhen in Wien im August 1830," ZfG 22 (1974): 722ff.

than revolutions, because the latter might give the masses more rights than the bourgeoisie would find compatible with its own class interests. In the context of their class-struggle perspective, Marxists can hardly blame the bourgeoisie for acting in accordance with these interests.[71]

One issue that the upheavals bypassed entirely, as all accounts point out with regret, was the national one: the demands for change called for concessions only on the local and state level. This lack of concern with national issues is explained by the fact that socioeconomic conditions had not yet matured sufficiently to make national unification imperative. The lack of a national revolutionary movement that could have lent the local revolts greater force also contributed to the limited effectiveness of the risings.[72]

In the events of a year later, however, DDR scholars detect evidence of renewed nationwide stirrings. The Polish rising against Tsarist Russia in 1831 was greeted by liberals throughout Germany as a fight for freedom akin to their own. Efforts to assist Polish refugees, some authors find, attained a slight measure of coordination on a national basis. More important, because initiated by design rather than circumstance, a Patriotic Press Association was founded in the Bavarian Palatinate on February 1832; it called on all Germans to work for the rebirth of Germany and the organization of Europe "within the limits of the law and along democratic lines." Obermann and others are critical of the association's faith in legality, which assumed that an aroused public opinion could compel governments to make reforms, but they note with some satisfaction that the association enjoyed popular support throughout South and West Germany and aroused some interest also in the northern and central parts.[73]

These efforts culminated in the Hambach Festival in May 1832, the "first national mass festival of the Germans." It was attended by at least 20,000 people, mostly from southern Germany, but also by French and Polish delegations, emphasizing the European dimensions of the struggle for national sovereignty and politi-

[71]Obermann, *Deutschland*, p. 2; Kuczynski, *Geschichte*, vol. 1, p. 84, as compared to Zwahr, "Bourgeoisie," pp. 659, 668–69; *Grundriss*, p. 225. See also Dorpalen, "Die Revolution von 1848 in der Geschichtsschreibung der DDR," *HZ* 210 (1970): 329–31.

[72]See Obermann, *Deutschland*, pp. 59ff.; Bock, *Ludwig Börne*, pp. 239ff., 249ff.; Zwahr, "Bourgeoisie," p. 662. In making the point of the comparative backwardness of the "German" economy, the authors follow Engels, who concluded that the bourgeois demands for political rights, constitutional safeguards, and trial by jury were dictated not by material needs but by considerations of prestige and civic pride and could therefore be satisfied by a few concessions (Engels, "Deutsche Zustände," in MEW, vol. 2, p. 581).

[73]Obermann, *Deutschland*, pp. 78ff.; Bock, *Ludwig Börne*, pp. 275ff.; Streisand, p. 165.

cal freedom. Except for great bourgeoisie and industrial proletariat, it is noted in *Sachwörterbuch*, all social strata were represented. The two exceptions are seen as indicative of Germany's lagging socioeconomic development, and the otherwise broad social representation is seen as proof of the growing political awareness of the nation as a whole. (At the Wartburg Festival in 1817, barely 500 academics had gathered.) On the positive side, the presence of democrats for the first time is stressed. Outnumbering the more restrained liberals, they left their imprint on the gathering with their call for a German federal republic and for armed resistance against forcible repression. The latter demand is deemed realistic; the call for a federal rather than a unitarian republic, on the other hand, is criticized as a particularist aberration. "Nonetheless," Helmut Bock concludes, "the republicans at Hambach constituted a democratic left whose merits have been acknowledged by Engels and are part of the prehistory of the later German workers' party."[74] On the other hand, the attempt of a handful of professional men, students, and artisans to set off a nationwide revolution by a raid on the main guardhouse in Frankfurt in April 1833 is dismissed as "adventurous putschism." It was based on the "unscientific" assumption that a revolution could be launched by a few determined men, regardless of the state of social conditions and without proper ideological preparation.[75]

The founding of the Zollverein a few months later is hailed as a decisive step towards the twin goals of unification and a bourgeois-capitalist system. As in the case of the Prussian customs union, most DDR scholars attribute the formation of the Zollverein to bourgeois pressures, presumably because they consider the bourgeoisie the main beneficiary of economic unification. How this conclusion is to be reconciled with the finding that only a short time earlier, during the upheavals of 1830, socioeconomic conditions had not yet matured to the point that the bourgeoisie would raise the issue of national unification, political or economic, is not explained. In fact, as the thoroughly documented research of non-Marxist historians has revealed, the bourgeoisie did little to support governmental efforts on behalf of a customs union. The little bourgeois activity that did exist was directed *against* any such union—partly from fear of competition from other states' industries and partly because a Prussian-led customs union would maintain low external tariffs or, conversely, would not permit free

[74]Bock, *Ludwig Börne*, pp. 293ff.; Obermann, *Deutschland*, pp. 86ff.; "Hambacher Fest," *Swb*, vol. 1, p. 764.
[75]See Bock, *Ludwig Börne*, pp. 325ff.; Obermann, *Deutschland*, pp. 92ff. Though conceding its folly, Steiger (*Aufbrach*, p. 28) acclaims the foray as the first revolutionary storm signal.

trade with nonmembers.[76] If the regional customs unions and ultimately the German Zollverein were meant to appease any part of the population, it was the restive artisans, peasants, and workers, the moving forces of the risings of 1830 and the main participants in the Hambach Festival and other mass gatherings.[77] Whereas such mass pressures may have had some effect on the South German governments, in Prussia the initiative came from farsighted bureaucrats who saw in intra-German free trade a stimulus to business activities and who, as officials, welcomed a nationwide customs union for political, fiscal, or administrative reasons (it would end widespread smuggling). Obviously, the Zollverein was of great benefit to the bourgeoisie, but in permitting the free exportation of grain, wool, and lumber and the unimpeded import of English machinery it also reinforced the position of Prussia's landowning nobility and granted it far more than minor advantages, contrary to what Obermann, following Engels, claims in a curious misjudgment of the true situation.[78]

This misapprehension of the Junkers' position sets Obermann apart from those of his colleagues who have noted that the Prussian landowning nobility also benefited in other ways from the Zollverein. For example, it learned to reap profits from the industrialization touched off by the customs union and thus fended off a decline of its economic position. The Junkers' adjustment to industrialization also deepened the communality of interests between them and the bourgeoisie, a communality that the "Prussian way" of introducing capitalism into agriculture had initiated.[79]

One of the most informative studies on this subject was published by an economic historian, Dietrich Eichholtz, who traced

[76]See Obermann, *Deutschland*, pp. 99–101; Vogler and Vetter, *Preussen*, p. 205; Streisand, p. 159; *Grundriss*, p. 227; *Geschichte der deutschen Arbeiterbewegung (GdA)*, ed. Institute of Marxism-Leninism at the Central Committee of the Socialist Unity party (Berlin [East], 1966), vol. 1, p. 20; compare these works to Price, *Zollverein*, pp. 179ff.; William O. Henderson, *The Zollverein* (Chicago, 1969), pp. 70ff.; Schnabel, *Deutsche Geschichte*, vol. 3, pp. 333ff.

[77]See Price, *Zollverein*, pp. 175ff., 185ff. Henderson (*The Zollverein*, p. 81) indicates that mass unrest rather than some tentative bourgeois pressures may have had an impact on the Zollverein negotiations. The passage is misinterpreted by Mottek (Wirtschaftsgeschichte Deutschlands, vol. 2, p. 63 n. 34), who is altogether vague on the role of the bourgeoisie. Bleiber ("Zur Problematik," pp. 69–70) is even more noncommittal. *Swb*, vol. 1, p. 450, credits "broad strata" of the people, along with the bourgeoisie, with having forced through the foundation of the Zollverein.

[78]See Obermann, *Deutschland*, p. 101; Engels, in MEW, vol. 4, p. 46. The motivations of the bureaucracy are correctly seen by Jonas, "Zum Problem Ideologie," p. 99. Concerning the Junkers, see Schnabel, *Deutsche Geschichte*, vol. 3, pp. 334–36.

[79]See Moll, "Bürgerliche Umwälzung und kapitalistische Agrarentwicklung," *ZfG* 27 (1979): 143. That the nobility, too, benefited from the industrialization, and in fact gained new strength from it, has been seen also by some non-Marxist scholars (Carl Brinkmann, in *Grundriss der Sozialökonomik* [Tübingen, 1926], vol. 9, pp. 19–20; Koselleck, *Preussen*, p. 437).

the convergence of bourgeois and noble interests in the area of railroad construction, which had beneficial results for both camps. When large landowners, members of princely families, high government officials, and other mainstays of the old order began to invest in railroads, they in turn used their governmental connections to secure for the railroads concessions, suspensions of rules, and other favors that facilitated railroad construction. Accommodations made by the state on its own also narrowed the gap between monarchical-feudal and bourgeois-capitalist interests. Additional evidence of this trend is found in the fact that some nobles even joined the liberal bourgeoisie in its demands for a constitutional government. Eichholtz sees here the first seed of the collaboration between the old feudal elements and the representatives of the new bourgeois order that was to culminate in their close partnership in later years.[80]

The "class compromise" that East German historians have here detected was reinforced, Eichholtz points out, by another common concern of Junkers and bourgeoisie. As joint partners in railroad enterprises, both classes were anxious to suppress the demands of dissatisfied railroad construction workers, who were, next to Silesia's weavers and Berlin's cotton printers, the most restive element of the working class. Here the primacy of the feudal-capitalist confrontation is found to be giving way to the capitalist-proletarian class struggle.[81] DDR historians insist, however, that the main "class contradiction" remained that between semifeudal nobility and capitalist bourgeoisie. It would remain so, in their judgment, until the capitalist order had superseded the feudal one in the 1860s. In consequence, most authors continued to attribute difficulties arising between state and nobility on the one hand and the bourgeoisie on the other to the "reactionary class egoism" of Junkers and bureaucrats, and they discounted the validity of any governmental objections to entrepreneurial plans based on fiscal or safety considerations. Only Bleiber conceded that the nobility was not the "wholly parasitical" class its French counterpart had been in 1789.[82] Similarly, little jus-

---

[80]Eichholtz, Junker; also Manfred Kliem, "Die Rolle der feudaljunkerlichen Reaktion in der Revolution von 1848–49 in Deutschland," ZfG 17 (1969): 313.

[81]See Eichholtz, Junker, pp. 193ff., 199–200. See also his essay, "Bewegungen unter den preussischen Eisenbahnbauarbeitern im Vormärz," in Beiträge zur deutschen Wirtschafts- und Sozialgeschichte des 18. und 19. Jahrhunderts (Berlin [East], 1962), pp. 252–53, 283. On the non-Marxist side, these interrelations are seen by Koselleck, Preussen, pp. 635–37.

[82]See Eichholtz, Junker, passim, especially pp. 197ff.; Mottek, in Mottek et al., Studien zur Geschichte der industriellen Revolution in Deutschland (Berlin [East], 1960), pp. 34ff.; Kuczynski, Geschichte, vol. 10, pp. 62ff.; Berthold, ZWG 1 (1972): 13; Bleiber, "Zur Problematik," p. 71. For a more detailed analysis of some of Eichholtz's arguments, see Dorpalen, "Revolution von 1848," pp. 327–29. On the generally helpful attitude of the bureaucracy toward bourgeois economic endeavors, see also Koselleck, Preussen, pp. 611ff., 635–37, and the literature cited there.

tice was done to those Prussian officials who successfully furthered entrepreneurial activities, because DDR scholars see such officials, not as a relatively autonomous force that transcends feudal class interests, but as representatives of these interests; as such these officials were merely making some unavoidable concessions.[83]

Yet here again, in keeping with their general reevaluation of the "objective" role of the nobility, DDR authors have more recently stressed the contributions of that nobility, however limited, to the advance of capitalism; thus, according to Siegfried Schmidt, "the identification of conservatism and 'feudal restoration' and the characterization of conservatism prior to 1871 as 'feudal' are wrong. We agree with H[elga] Grebing [a West German historian], who considers conservatism an 'integral component of the genesis of bourgeois society.' " What matters, Walter Schmidt adds, is the basic thrust of a social transformation and the totality of all participating social forces, so that a transformation tending toward bourgeois capitalism may properly be described as bourgeois even if the bourgeoisie did not lead it. This argument is in accord with the train of thought that explains the Reformation as an early bourgeois revolution and with the Marxist view of history as forever moving, on balance, in a progressive direction. All in all, if earlier it was regretfully noted that the nobility was able to preserve its privileged position by making some adjustments to changing economic conditions, Marxist studies now emphasize that the nobility was willing to make such adjustments and thus further the emerging capitalist order.[84]

Still, the agrarian nobility was interested only in a "minimal version" of a bourgeois transformation, and the struggle against the declining, yet still dominant, feudal order thus remains a subject of major import. What DDR authors find particularly significant in

[83]See Mottek, *Wirtschaftsgeschichte Deutschlands*, vol. 2, pp. 43ff.; *Grundriss*, pp. 227–28; Streisand, pp. 158–59. The liberalizing economic policies of the Prussian bureaucracy are not as hard to reconcile with the East German scenario of the feudal-absolutist Prussian state as a West German critic, Jürgen Kocka, has claimed. The ruling Junker class may not have supported many of these policies—some of them, such as the creation of the Zollverein, it did support—but neither did it actively oppose these policies in the 1830s and 1840s. Thus, DDR scholars can argue that historical progress asserted itself through the activities of the bureaucracy, which were intended to benefit the nobility and objectively did so by preserving its political power. Consistent with this position, East German historians also maintain that this evolutionary transformation of Prussia (and Germany) from a feudal to a capitalist society made a revolutionary completion of this changeover imperative in order to remove the Junkers from political power—a demand that Kocka, misunderstanding its meaning, finds incomprehensible (Kocka, "Preussischer Staat und Modernisierung im Vormärz: Marxistisch-leninistische Interpretationen und ihre Probleme," in *Sozialgeschichte heute*, ed. Hans-Ulrich Wehler [Göttingen, 1974], pp. 216ff., 226 n. 38).
[84]Siegfried Schmidt, "Junkertum und . . . Konservativismus [*sic*] im 19. Jahrhundert," *ZfG* 27 (1979): 1060; W. Schmidt, "Zu Problemen," 645, 647; also Dieter Fricke, "Zur Erforschung konservativer Politik und Ideologie," *ZfG* 27 (1979): 1140ff.

probing this confrontation is the shift of the oppositional leadership from the bürgerlich intelligentsia to the banking and industrial bourgeoisie. Reflecting the increased economic importance of the bourgeoisie, the change is considered a milestone in the larger context of the transition from feudalism to capitalism. At the same time, it is welcomed for injecting a practical, political element into the liberal movement, superseding the somewhat abstract academic and parochial demands that had previously guided the bürgerlich liberals. The new leaders, hampered in their entrepreneurial activities by territorial divisions and ubiquitous government supervision, called for a united nation-state—a historically inevitable necessity as a result of the growth of capitalism—and for liberal constitutions that would give them access to political power. At the United Prussian Diet, which was convoked by King Frederick William IV in 1847, the crucial demand on which the Diet foundered was the liberals' insistence on some say in policy matters and especially in financial ones. To give their demands greater thrust, it is noted, the bourgeois liberals even worked at first with the more radical democratic forces that had broken away from the liberal movement. The liberals moved away from the democrats, however, as strikes and other protest activities, culminating in some violent rising, alerted the bourgeoisie to the potential threat to its own position inherent in the demands of the working class.[85] The bourgeoisie's failure to see that, at the time, that threat was still minor compared to the restrictions imposed by the semiabsolutist monarchy and the nobility was in the East German judgment the most grievous mistake the bourgeoisie made; the mistake was all the more grievous, all analyses stress, because the liberal goals of the bourgeoisie could not be achieved without the driving force of the masses.[86]

The emergence of an industrial working class in the 1830s and 1840s also receives close attention. Given the pivotal role assigned to the working class in the eventual creation of the socialist order, and through it in the social emancipation of mankind, a major Marxist concern has been to trace the rise of the working class and its role in the class struggle. A voluminous literature has recorded the history of the German labor movement from its beginnings in the 1830s in exiled workingmen's associations in

[85]*Grundriss*, pp. 205, 231–32; W. Schmidt, "Zu einigen Problemen," pp. 4–5; S. Schmidt, "Liberale Parteibewegung," pp. 403ff.; Helmut Asmus, "Die 'Rheinische Zeitung' und die Genesis des rheinpreussischen Bourgeoisliberalismus," in Bleiber et al., *Bourgeoisie*, pp. 135ff.; Helmut Kubitschek, in *JWG* 3 (1963): 281.

[86]See S. Schmidt, pp. 402, 407; Bleiber, "Bourgeoisie," p. 330. Kocka ("Preussischer Staat," p. 217–18) points out, however, that petty bourgeois groups, an important part of the "masses," frequently called for retrogressive economic and social changes that were totally incompatible with the expanding capitalist system that the bourgeoisie sought to create (also see p. 225 n. 33).

France and Switzerland, associations that lost "utopian" reform programs based on the illusion of class harmony, through the "League of the Just" (Bund der Gerechten), which is condemned for indulging in moral pleas rather than scientific analyses but which is praised for first realizing the need for revolutionary action.[87]

The "utopianism" of these groups is attributed to the backwardness of German capitalist developments, which in turn held up the industrialization of Germany and the formation of a class-conscious proletariat. Marx and Engels, on the other hand, developed their scientific approach to the workers' problems at a time when the proletariat began to grow under the impact of the Industrial Revolution—when, as *Grundriss* puts it, the creation of a scientific theory of the working class became both possible and necessary. Among the new industries, railroad construction in particular required large numbers of laborers; in the strikes and other protest activities of railroad workers, involving often several hundred and in a few cases between 1,000 and 2,000 men, Marxist authors see evidence of an "upward-directed" process of the political and intellectual emancipation of the proletariat according to the laws of history. Though concerned almost wholly with matters of wages and working conditions, these actions are viewed as "germinal formations" of a proletarian class consciousness. As such, Eichholtz concludes, they created a receptive audience among railroad workers for the ideas of scientific socialism. "This process," he states, "came to predominate in the pre-March era and shaped the historical development of the working class, the gravedigger of the capitalist system."[88]

The most important rising of the period was that of some 3,000 Silesian weavers in June 1844—to Marxists the "first class battle of the German proletariat." DDR accounts state that the revolt was marred by the misconception that mechanization was a root cause of the weavers' troubles; the workers had not yet learned to distinguish between the machine's value as a material productive force and its use on behalf of private capitalists. Nonetheless, East German authors regard the rising as further evidence of the beginning class struggle between proletariat and bourgeoisie. Its special significance is found in the wide reverberations it called forth: it touched off unrest in many parts of Germany and evoked a strong literary echo in the poetry of Heinrich Heine, Georg Herwegh, and Ferdinand Freiligrath. Streisand sees the rising as proof

---

[87]Obermann, *Deutschland*, pp. 106ff., especially pp. 17ff.; Streisand, pp. 160–61; *GdA* 1, pp. 28ff.

[88]See *Grundriss*, p. 234; Eichholtz, "Bewegungen," pp. 274, 280ff. (quotation on p. 283); Gerhard Puchta and Eberhard Wolfgramm, "Spontaneität und Keimformen der Bewusstheit in der Frühzeit der deutschen Arbeiterbewegung," *WZ Leipzig* 6 (1956–1957): 673ff. The term *pre-March (Vormärz)* refers to the 1840s—the period prior to March 1848, when the German revolution broke out.

that Germany had become the center of revolutionary unrest. Although that was not true—Marx and Engels rightly called France the "heart of the revolution"—revolutionary forces were gathering momentum in Germany, and, as *Grundriss* points out, the fate of other revolutionary movements in Poland, Bohemia, Hungary and Italy also depended on German developments.[89]

Discussions of the evolution of the ideas of Marx and Engels during those years take up, of course, a vast amount of space in the research and the analyses of that period. The transformation of the two men from philosophical idealists to materialists, their shift from bürgerlich democrats to proletarian revolutionaries, their formulation of scientific socialism based on the dialectical method, and their conclusion that theories can become historically relevant only through action—and only through action of the popular masses, at that—these matters are discussed with meticulous care in countless studies. Because of their conviction that theory and practice are interdependent, DDR historians have explored with equal thoroughness the efforts of Marx, Engels, and their associates to rouse the workers to action. This meant instilling in workers the class consciousness and the reality of the class struggle that alone could forge them into a self-reliant, purposeful fighting force. All activities that were aimed at this goal—from the establishment of correspondence committees to the transformation of the moralizing League of the Just into the hardhitting League of Communists, as well as the drafting of the *Communist Manifesto*—are traced step by step and examined at length. Most DDR scholars acknowledge that these endeavors had no immediate impact on developments. What is nonetheless considered important is that for the first time German workers learned about Marxist ideology, which, in Walter Schmidt's words, was "unmatched in its clarity and scientific precision." However slight this first contact was, Schmidt adds, it helped lift the dissociation of the working class from bourgeois influences to a "qualitatively new level." It contributed to the transformation of the impotent proletariat into a class aware of its rights, its strength, and its mission. To Schmidt, then, as to other DDR authors, a determining characteristic of the period from the 1830s to the 1870s is the growth of the working class into a class-conscious, anticapitalist force ready to take up the class struggle.[90]

---

[89] *GdA*, vol. 1, pp. 35ff.; Obermann, *Deutschland*, pp. 150ff.; Streisand, pp. 161–62; *Grundriss*, p. 234; Marx and Engels, quoted in *ZfG* 18 (1970): suppl., p. 415.

[90] See Obermann, *Deutschland*, pp. 194ff.; *GdA*, vol. 1, pp. 53ff., 66; W. Schmidt, "Zu einigen Fragen der sozialen Struktur . . . in . . . Vormärz und Revolution 1848–1849," *BzG* 7, 655; W. Schmidt, "Zur Rolle des Proletariats in der Revolution von 1848–1849," *ZfG* 17 (1969): 271–72. An exaggerated importance is attributed to Communist activities by Obermann, in *ZfG* 16 (1968): 1031–33; also by Vogler and Vetter, *Preussen*, pp. 224–25.

The effects of this growth, however, served to refute the confident prediction of the *Communist Manifesto*, drawn up during the winter of 1847–1848, that the bourgeoisie would be forced to call on the proletariat for help in the impending bourgeois revolution. Instead, the bourgeoisie became frightened by the recurrent self-assertion of the workers and sought to achieve freedom of speech, power of the purse, and parliamentary government by non-violent means. For Marxist historians, this development has presented interpretive problems that to date they have not solved.[91]

The Revolution of 1848–1849

The revolution that broke out in 1848 is singled out by DDR historiography as a milestone in the transition from feudalism to capitalism. "The German bourgeois-democratic revolution of 1848–1849," *Grundriss* declares,"was the climax in the overall process of the bourgeois transformation (*Umwälzung*). In the era from 1789 to 1871, this revolution was the decisive confrontation between princes, aristocracy, and Junkers, on the one hand, and the popular masses, on the other; it created new conditions for the total victory of capitalism. The revolution put the final breakthrough of the bourgeois social order on the agenda."[92]

That final breakthrough, however, led not to a "pure" bourgeois-capitalist order, with the bourgeoisie in both political and economic control, but to a system in which the old "feudal" nobility still retained the lion's share of political power. The nobles could retain this power, it is explained, because the final phase in the transition from feudalism to capitalism was completed not by a democratic revolution from below, which would have swept the nobles from power (as happened in France), but by limited reforms and an antidemocratic revolution from above. Nonetheless, the revolution remains an "unrenounceable element of the revolutionary tradition in the history of the German people; [that tradition] attained victory for the first time in the DDR and so far has reached its culmination in the creation of the socialist order."[93] Because of this significance, the

[91]Oscar J. Hammen, "The Spectre of Communism in the 1840's," *Journal of the History of Ideas* 14 (1953): 404ff.; Werner Conze, "Vom Pöbel zum Proletariat," in Wehler, *Moderne deutsche Sozialgeschichte*, pp. 118–19; Kuczynski, *Geschichte*, vol. 1, pp. 177–78; Bleiber, *Zwischen Reform und Revolution* (Berlin [East], 1966), pp. 181, 214.
[92]*Grundriss*, p. 241; also W. Schmidt, "Zu einigen Problemen," p. 21; Bleiber, "Bourgeoisie," p. 306.
[93]See W. Schmidt, "Zu einigen Problemen," p. 33; W. Schmidt, "Zur historischen Stellung der deutschen Revolution von 1848–1849," in Bartel and Engelberg,

revolution ranges before the creation of the German nation-state in 1871 in the order of priorities of East German historiography; Federal Chancellor Willy Brandt was severely reproved when he called Bismarck's unification of Germany a "highlight of [German] national history." In the East German view, the *Reichsgründung* of 1871 "embodies that reactionary class line of German history to which Bonn's present-day imperialist state feels beholden."[94]

If in the context of successive socioeconomic formations the Revolution of 1848 is perceived as an advance that accelerated the final victory of the capitalist order and the creation of an industrial proletariat whose mission would be to lead the nation to socialism and communism, in the narrower context of immediate developments, as mentioned earlier, the revolution is viewed as a setback on Germany's road to democracy. The responsibility for this defeat is placed largely on the shoulders of the bourgeoisie. As the protagonist of the capitalist order, the bourgeoisie is considered the preordained leader of the antifeudalist forces in their struggle against the feudal-reactionary camp—hardly a cogent conclusion because, as Lenin already had noted, the "objective" concerns of the bourgeoisie—that is, the replacement of the feudal system by the capitalist one—could also be realized without a democratic revolution.[95] (The leadership role that the bourgeoisie is expected to play in the struggle against feudalism does suggest, however, the secondary role to be played once again by the masses, the much-vaunted makers of history, in this struggle.) In any case, frightened by the self-assertion of the popular masses and what it considered to be a threat to its status and property, the bourgeoisie abandoned the masses, to whose revolutionary activities it owed its access to power in March 1848. In return for various social and economic concessions, the bourgeoisie accepted the continued rule of monarchs and nobles, forfeiting the chance of assuming full political power and completing the transition to the capitalist order by means of a bourgeois-democratic revolution.[96]

Grosspreussisch, vol. 1, p. 1. On the other hand, West German efforts to establish a connection between the *Paulskirche* and the Federal Republic are dismissed as misleading (Bleiber, "Die bürgerlich-demokratische Revolution 1848–1849 in Deutschland," in *Unb. Verg.*, p. 266).

[94]W. Schmidt, "Zur historischen Stellung," pp. 10–11; Bleiber, "Bürgerlich-demokratische Revolution," pp. 267–68, 277.

[95]Stiehler, *Gesellschaft und Geschichte*, pp. 233–34, with Lenin quotation.

[96]See Streisand, pp. 176ff.; *Grundriss*, pp. 242, 244; W. Schmidt, "Zu einigen Problemen," pp. 24ff.; Gerhard Becker, "Zur Rolle der preussischen Bourgeoisie nach der Märzrevolution 1848," *ZfG* 24 (1976): 172–73, 176ff. That an alternative outcome of the revolution was a realistic possibility is now also suggested by some non-Marxist historians (Werner Boldt, "Konstitutionelle Monarchie oder parlamentarische Demokratie . . . 1848," *HZ* 216 [1973]: 558–59, 607ff.; Christoph Klessmann, "Zur Sozialgeschichte der Reichsverfassungskampagne von 1849," ibid. 218 [1974]: 334–35).

DDR scholars have elaborated on this theme in countless studies. They have shown above all that the antigovernmental forces parted ways not as the result of excessive demands of radical democrats or the June Days rising of the Parisian masses, as non-Marxists have long argued, but because of the liberal bourgeoisie's determination from the very beginning to achieve its goals without mass upheavals and to arrange itself with rulers and aristocracy to contain the forces of revolution. There is some disagreement, however, as to whether the bourgeois stance caused the collapse of the revolution at its outset or at a later stage; some recent studies have also acknowledged that the bourgeoisie did introduce some progressive reforms while in a position to do so.[97]

The assessments of the bourgeoisie have also given rise to a number of more basic controversies. In the spirit of *Parteilichkeit*, the bourgeois shift from the progressive to the conservative camp has been branded as a betrayal, but opinions differ as to who or what was being betrayed.[98] Some authors charge that bourgeois treachery had let down the masses, whose revolutionary actions had forced the old regimes to appoint members of the bourgeoisie to their governments. This argument is hard to maintain, however, in view of the fact that the masses had not risen to further the advance of the bourgeois-capitalist order, as Walter Schmidt, for example, maintains;[99] the artisans were opposed to that order and wished to return to the preindustrial guild system, and large numbers of workers, underpaid and abused by capitalist entrepreneurs, were equally opposed to capitalist enterprise and joined with the

[97]See *GdA*, vol. 1, pp. 99, 163; Obermann, *Deutschland*, pp. 277–78; Kuczynski, *Geschichte*, vol. 1, p. 199; Joachim Strey, "Zu Karl Marx' Verallgemeinerung der revolutionären Erfahrungen... 1848–1849," *BzG* 10 (1968): 249; W. Schmidt, "Zu einigen Problemen," pp. 26ff. Obermann, "Zur politischen Haltung der gemässigten Liberalen am Vorabend und in der deutschen Märzrevolution 1848," *ZfG* 27 (1977): 209ff. For a more detailed discussion, see Dorpalen, "Revolution von 1848," pp. 329ff. On progressive reforms, see Becker, "Zur Rolle," pp. 187f.

[98]This view has been challenged by a West German historian Thomas Nipperdey, on the grounds that the liberals actually assumed an independent middle position between the conservative right and the radical left; according to him, they were as opposed to the one as they were to the other, anxious to secure a liberal constitutional government protecting them against an arbitrary absolutism on the right and to obtain guarantees of individual freedom that could not be suppressed by majority rule on the left (Nipperdey, "Kritik oder Objektivität? Zur Beurteilung der Revolution von 1848," in Nipperdey, *Gesellschaft, Kultur, Theorie* [Göttingen, 1976], pp. 266ff.). Whether or not Nipperdey describes the liberal position correctly, the fact is that the liberals' stance aided the conservative camp. On the other hand, Nipperdey warns rightly against reducing liberal interests to bourgeois commercial interests (ibid., p. 268), but here again, in dissociating themselves from the masses, commmercial bourgeoisie and academic intelligentsia, however different their motives may have been, played into the hands of both the rulers and the nobles.

[99]W. Schmidt, "Bourgeoisie, Arbeiterklasse, Volksmassen in den Kämpfen um die Wege der bürgerlichen Umgestaltung," *ZfG* 14 (1977): 1189.

artisans to vent that opposition in the destruction of factories and machines.[100]

Some authors therefore perceive the strategy of the bourgeoisie as a betrayal of its own interests, which called for the removal of all obstacles hampering the further development of capitalism.[101] It has already been noted that a mass revolution in which petty bourgeois elements—tradesmen, artisans, small storekeepers with strong anticapitalist prejudices—played an important role would not necessarily have benefited capitalist enterprise. It is not certain either that the creation of a nationwide legal system, a national currency, and uniform weights and measures in the 1840s rather than in the 1870s would have sparked a greater expansion of capitalistic activities than did occur; a recent study has shown that the unification of Germany in 1866–1871 did not accelerate its economic growth.[102] In effect, DDR historians admit as much. Bleiber concludes that the bourgeoisie could renounce its claim to political power without jeopardizing its fundamental class interests, because its arrangements with the nobility were predicated on the latter's acceptance of basic bourgeois class interests. Kuczynski goes even further and claims that the bourgeoisie attained such strength in the 1850s and 1860s that the state, which until 1848 had served primarily the interests of the Junkers, came to serve primarily the interests of the bourgeoisie by the end of the 1860s.[103]

A deep incongruity runs through these Marxist critiques of the bourgeoisie. Whereas non-Marxists encounter no logical difficulties in reproving the bourgeoisie for being unduly fearful of the restive masses and forfeiting its chance to seize political power with their support, a Marxist who "knows" that the bourgeoisie is doomed to be overthrown by the working class can hardly expect it to ally itself with its own "gravediggers." One West German critic has indeed pointed out that what the betrayal thesis really holds against the bourgeoisie is its failure to do away with itself by entrusting its fate to the masses.[104] Bleiber's reply—that there was no *immediate* danger of the overthrow of the bourgeoisie had the

---

[100]Dorpalen, "Revolution von 1848," p. 330 n. 14; Kocka, "Preussischer Staat," p. 225 n. 33; James J. Sheehan, *German Liberalism in the Nineteenth Century* (Chicago, 1978), pp. 67–68.

[101]W. Schmidt, "Zu einigen Problemen," pp. 26, 28.

[102]See Tipton, "National Consensus," pp. 203ff. There were many other ways in which remaining feudal or bureaucratic obstacles could have been removed or evaded (Dorpalen, "Revolution von 1848," p. 339).

[103]See Bleiber, "Bourgeoisie," pp. 318–19; Kuczynski, *Geschichte,* vol. 2, pp. i, v, 104n. My own conclusions to this effect, with due stress on its dangerous political consequences (Dorpalen, "Revolution von 1848," pp. 335–39) have been assailed as cynical in a barrage that does not seem to abate (W. Schmidt, in *ZfG* 21 [1973]: 302; Bleiber, "Bourgeoisie," p. 313; *Unb Verg.,* p. 274).

[104]Michael Stürmer, "1848 in der deutschen Geschichte," in Wehler, *Sozialgeschichte heute,* p. 229.

revolution succeeded—although doubtless correct, would have offered small comfort to that class; the bourgeoisie would hardly have found it reassuring to learn that their overthrow would occur not right away, but somewhat later. At the time, moreover, the *Communist Manifesto* predicted that the bourgeois revolution in Germany would be merely the prelude to a proletarian revolution that would follow immediately. Many DDR authors are aware of the inconsistency of their position, without, however, abandoning it as untenable, but one at least—Walter Schmidt, the leading expert on 1848—concedes that the launching of a revolutionary mass movement by the bourgeoisie would not have been without risks for the latter.[105]

The fact is that the bourgeoisie cannot be justifiably attacked on the grounds that in submitting to the feudal powers the bourgeoisie acted against its own interests and impeded the growth of the capitalist system. As DDR authors are aware, economic developments in the 1850s and 1860s disprove this charge. To deal with this problem, Walter Schmidt has argued that the quality of a social system cannot be measured simply in terms of its material and technical productivity, but is also determined by the status of its major productive force—the immediate producers, the workers. Their working, living, and fighting (!) conditions, too, must be considered in assessing the scope and reality of historical progress, for the popular masses and the working class in particular are the revolutionary social forces that are the carriers of further progress.[106]

This last statement provides the key to the Marxist position on the role of the bourgeoisie. The issue that concerns DDR historians when they assail bourgeois conduct in 1848 is not the fate of the bourgeoisie or of capitalism, but rather the impact of that stance on the working class, which can grow, organize, and prepare for revolutionary action with less difficulty in the more benign climate of a bourgeois regime. As two authors have written, "the Marxist position on capitalist progress is not concerned with the

---

[105]See Bleiber, "Bourgeoisie," pp. 317–19; W. Schmidt, "Zu einigen Problemen," pp. 8, 10–11. See also Dorpalen, "Revolution von 1848," pp. 335–37, with a list of Marxist authors who are aware of the inconsistency of the "betrayal" thesis. On risks, see W. Schmidt, "Zur Rolle der Bourgeoisie in den bürgerlichen Revolutionen von 1789 and 1848," *ZfG* 21 (1973): 308, 310, 317; this work also contains a tortured explanation of the logic of the betrayal thesis (p. 315). It might also be pointed out that the conduct of the German bourgeoisie was by no means unusual and that its English and French counterparts were just as unwilling to ally themselves with the masses in pursuit of their interests (Michael Gugel, *Industrieller Aufstieg und bürgerliche Herrschaft* [Cologne, 1975], pp. 244ff.; George Rude, "Why Was There No Revolution in England in 1830 and 1848?" in *Studien über die Revolution*, ed. Kossok [Berlin (East), 1969], pp. 231ff.).

[106]W. Schmidt, "Zur Rolle," pp. 312ff.; but see also Bleiber ("Bourgeoisie," p. 320), who points out that the bourgeoisie as an exploiting class could not be expected to concern itself with the interests of the working class.

greatest possible gain for the bourgeoisie or the best use of capital, but with the most favorable turn of events for the popular masses, the proletariat, and the other toiling classes and strata." Schmidt maintains nonetheless that the bourgeoisie should have kept up the fight for political power in its own interest, but this argument is refuted by his own reasoning.[107]

Wolfgang Küttler is more candid in presenting the thesis that it was the working class rather than the bourgeoisie that was harmed by the latter's abandonment of the revolution. Unlike his colleagues, Küttler admits that the bourgeoisie did not betray its own interests when it abandoned the revolution. The particular significance of the revolution, he points out, lay not just in the acceleration of capitalist developments but also in the opportunities it could have opened up to the working class. Whereas the bourgeoisie was interested mainly in achieving its socioeconomic supremacy, the workers were concerned chiefly with the realization of the democratic aims of the revolution—freedom of speech, freedom of assembly, and free elections—which would have enabled them to pursue their own cause more effectively. In fact, Küttler quotes Lenin, "in a certain sense the bourgeois revolution is more advantageous for the proletariat than for the bourgeoisie." A bourgeois-democratic revolution, then, transcends its immediate capitalist objective and aims at the quickened attainment of those conditions under which the proletarian revolution matures. Therefore, Küttler concludes, what the bourgeoisie betrayed was social progress in its widest sense (which, concretely, is identified with the progress of the working class, the class enemy of the bourgeoisie). Yet, Küttler is evidently not entirely comfortable with this conclusion; he concedes that this betrayal ought not to be judged as a moral failure. This concession apparently means that although he does not blame the bourgeoisie for its unwillingness to sacrifice itself for the greater good of society, he nonetheless regrets its failure to do so.[108]

Although the bourgeoisie is assigned the key role in the Marxist scenario of a bourgeois revolution, DDR historians actually have paid greater attention to the role of the popular masses, particularly to that of the working class. In the view of these scholars, the class struggles of the revolution of 1848 were fought on two levels— between the bourgeoisie and the rulers and nobles in the crucial feudalist-capitalist confrontation and between the bourgeoisie and

[107]W. Schmidt, "Zur Rolle," pp. 317–19; Wolfgang Küttler and Gustav Seeber, ed., *Theorie, Empirie und Methode in der Geschichtswissenschaft* (Vaduz, Liechtenstein, 1980), pp. 207–8 (quotation on p. 208).

[108]Küttler, "Zum Begriffe," pp. 180–81, 186–87 (italics in orginal); Küttler, cited in *ZfG* 26 (1978): 540; also W. Schmidt, "Zu einigen Problemen," pp. 8, 28 n. 66; Stiehler, *Gesellschaft und Geschichte*, pp. 233–34.

the working class in a preliminary skirmish of the approaching capitalist-socialist conflict. As Marx already had written, "the German bourgeoisie finds itself facing the proletariat before it has established itself politically as a class. The fight between the 'subjects' has broken out before princes and nobles have been chased out of the country." Even if the confrontation between the still extant semifeudalism and the rising capitalism constituted the "main contradiction" of the existing social order, the struggle between the bourgeoisie and the working class is found to have been "relatively strongly developed" already (Bleiber)—sufficiently strongly, in any event, to enable the working class to make its first appearance on the world's historical stage in 1848 as something of an embryonic class ("Klasse in Ansätzen").[109]

This interest in the role of the working class does not imply, however, an overestimation of that role in the revolution. Rather, it derives from a basic concern with the revolutionary tradition of the working class from its earliest, very modest beginnings. The need for such a tradition, which would establish the historical legitimacy of the German Democratic Republic, overrode all other priorities. As a result, DDR researchers dealing with the events of 1848–1849 focused their attention first, not on the bourgeoisie as the pivotal class of the upheaval, but on the working class as that class which would ultimately play the key role in the creation of the socialist order and the emancipation of mankind. (Of the twenty pages that the 1970 survey of DDR research devotes to work done on the Revolution of 1848, studies concerned with the bourgeoisie take up less than half a page as compared to twelve pages that list studies on Marx and Engels, the League of Communists, and the workers' movement. On the other hand, the corresponding figures in the 1980 survey are five and ten pages, respectively.[110])

In addition to purposes related to ideology and political strategy, the emphasis on the role of the workers has also served tactical political purposes. In 1948, on the centenary of the revolution, the party directorate (*Parteivorstand*) of the Socialist Unity party passed a resolution assessing the revolution; it concluded that the German people did not make use of its initial victory in 1848 because there was no class "ready to assume the determined and purposeful leadership of the revolution." With the destruction of fascism the nation had a new opportunity to complete the "democratic transformation initiated in 1848." Because this could be done only under the leadership of the working class, in conjunction

---

[109]Marx, in MEW, vol. 4, p. 351; Bleiber, *Zwischen Reform*, p. 73; W. Schmidt, "Zur historischen Stellung," pp. 14–15.

[110]W. Schmidt, "Zur historischen Stellung," pp. 6–7; *Grundriss*, p. 244. Surveys in *ZfG* 18 (1970): suppl., pp. 408ff.; 28 (1980): suppl., pp. 143ff.

with petty bourgeois and peasants, much was to be learned from the earlier event concerning the tasks of the working class and its political vanguard. Though it is hard to see what specific lessons could be taught by events that occurred one hundred years earlier, East German historians nonetheless hailed the resolution for the guidance that it provided. What concrete impact it had on their work is, however, not clear.[111]

The working class, consisting of factory workers, journeymen, and apprentices in the East German accounts, is considered important, then, not because of its size—the number of factory workers in particular was still rather small—but because of the qualitative significance of its role. Although the working class acted only rarely as an independent political force, it is nonetheless credited with having injected into the struggles the elemental revolutionary thrust that induced the feudal powers to grant the initial far-reaching concessions. Walter Schmidt concludes that these concessions were not the doing of the bourgeoisie, which has traditionally been acclaimed as the hero of the revolution, but that of the workers, who (according to Schmidt) outdistanced all other revolutionary strata—peasantry, petty bourgeoisie, revolutionary intelligentsia—in their fervor and dedication. Yet they acted at best as history's unwitting agents, for the concessions that were obtained with their help furthered capitalist enterprise and industrialization, not the goals for which they had been fighting.[112]

In this connection, the activities of Marx and Engels, the policies and impact of their *Neue Rheinische Zeitung*, the number and influence of their followers, and the significance of workers' organizations in general have been explored in exhaustive detail. Much attention is paid to the Communist program, "Demands of the Communist Party in Germany," an adaptation of the *Communist Manifesto* to German conditions, which provided for a "united indivisible republic"; universal suffrage; the abolition of all feudal privileges; the expropriation without compensation of all large landed estates, banks, mines, and means of transportation; comprehensive financial and educational reforms; and a people's militia. This program is hailed as the "revolutionary-democratic alternative" to the counter-revolutionary schemes of the Junkers and the incomplete "antirevolutionary" plans of the bourgeoisie.[113]

East German researchers do not ignore the small number of actual Communists, the inexperience and disagreements weakening the working class, or the limits set to the efforts of Marx and

[111]*ZfG* 8 (1960): suppl., pp. 217, 430.
[112]W. Schmidt, "Zur historischen Stellung," pp. 14–15.
[113]"Forderungen der Kommunistischen Partei in Deutschland," *Swb*, vol. 1, pp. 595–96; *Grundriss*, p. 245.

Engels, but to them this incipient attempt to apply Marxist tenets to political practice is important as the initiation of a new historical phase. "What is decisive for the historical evaluation of the League of Communists," Walter Schmidt and Rolf Dlubek point out, "is the fact that here for the first time a workers' organization broke completely with bourgeois ideology, politics, and organization. . . . In the League of Communists, Marxism, for the first time, appeared on the historical stage as an *organized* force, even though it was small at the time, having only a few hundred members." The revolution thus became "a necessary milestone of social transit" ("ein notwendiger gesellschaftlicher Durchgangspunkt"); in its course, Marx, Engels, and their associates nurtured the first weak seeds of a separate class consciousness among German workers. As East German historians see it, whatever the outward failures of the revolution, it was a progressive event as the incubator of proletarian class consciousness and proletarian self-help, for without these attributes the workers could not fulfill their historical mission. In turn, these accomplishments allowed Marx and his followers to continue on a "higher level" their efforts to prepare labor for the tasks that awaited it.[114]

The ultimate task, of course, was the destruction of the bourgeois-capitalist order. As Marx argued, the workers would have to carry it out because they had no stake at all in that system. Any attempt to create such a stake therefore impeded the accomplishment of that mission. For this reason, efforts of reformist workers organizations—such as the *Arbeiterverbrüderung*, established by a one-time disciple of Marx, Stefan Born—were condemned as opportunistic: by seeking mainly to ease the workers' material lot they deceived the workers about the irreconcilable nature of the existing class conflicts. More recently, however, DDR historians have conceded that most workers were not yet receptive to the radical Marxist approach. In consequence, they have come to view Born's endeavors more favorably. His activities are now assessed as a helpful, though dangerous, means of impressing upon the workers the need for independent collective action in pursuit of their rights.[115] These

---

[114]See Schmidt and Dlubek,, "Die Herausbildung der marxistischen Partei der deutschen Arbeiterklasse," *ZfG* 14 (1966): 1311 (italics in original); W. Schmidt, "Zur Rolle des Proletariats in der deutschen Revolution von 1848–49," ibid., 17 (1960): pp. 270ff., especially pp. 275–76; Bartel, "Um die Durchsetzung des Marxismus in der deutschen Arbeiterbewegung," *BzG* 6 (1964): 860–61. For an interesting documentation of the growing self-awareness of the workers, see *GdA* vol. 1, pp. 139–41 and document nos. 28, 34–36.

[115]*GdA*, vol. 1, pp. 139–41; W. Schmidt, "Zur Rolle des Proletariats," pp. 283–84; for a slightly different view, see Bartel, "Um die Durchsetzung," pp. 862–63; *Grundriss*, pp. 251–52; Rolf Weber, "Die 'Verbrüderung'—ihre Rolle in der elementaren Arbeiterbewegung," in *Evolution und Revolution in der Weltgeschichte*, ed. Bartel et al. (Berlin [East], 1976), vol. 2, pp. 435ff.

authors still reject, however, the view that the *Arbeiterverbrüder-ung*, with its considerable membership, was historically more significant than the infinitely smaller League of Communists. As they see it, the implementation of scientific socialism, however limited, constituted true historical progress and therefore was more important in the long-range perspective than the "petty bourgeois illusions" of the *Verbrüderung*. Accordingly, West German historians who pay more attention to Stefan Born than to Marx are accused of ulterior political motives: under the guise of "objective" research, which claims to deal impartially with all classes, they are trying to create a pseudo-scholarly underpinning for the claim that the integration of the working class into bourgeois society is an inevitable historical process. One of the lessons to be learned from the events of 1848, DDR scholars insist, is the falsity of this assertion.[116]

Underscoring this argument, they also point out that when conservative forces recovered lost ground, workers played an important role in the risings (in Frankfurt, Berlin, and Vienna) that attempted to stem that tide. Similarly, Marxist research has shown that workers participated more actively in the final uprisings in 1849 in the Rhineland, Westphalia, and Saxony than most non-Marxist scholars have so far assumed. Not only did the revolution generate the first signs of a genuine class consciousness on the part of the workers, DDR historians contend, but the young German working class also gave evidence of its political awareness. All in all, labor's stance in the events of 1848–1849 is considered new proof of its historical right to the leadership of the nation on the grounds that more than any other class it acted in the nation's true interest.[117]

Strong revolutionary potential is also found among peasants and rural laborers. East German historians have shown that peasant unrest was widespread in Germany in 1848, affecting not only Baden and Wuerttemberg, as has generally been held, but also Prussia, Saxony, and the two Mecklenburgs. They have further shown that although peasant demands were aimed mainly at social and economic improvements, the rural population of Saxony and Silesia was also active in some political associations. Moreover, Bleiber claims that some peasant demands, such as the recovery of

---

[116]*Kritik der bürgerlichen Geschichtswissenschaft*, ed. Werner Berthold et al. (Cologne, 1970), pp. 314, 321ff.

[117]See Förder and W. Schmidt, *ZfG* 8 (1960): suppl., p. 258; *Grundriss*, pp. 248, 253, 256; *GdA*, vol. 1, pp. 163, 167–68. Some of the East German findings have been confirmed by Klessmann, "Zur Sozialgeschichte," pp. 290ff., 297ff. Differences between Marxist and non-Marxist assessments of the workers' role result in large part from differing definitions of the term *worker*. Whereas Marxists are guided by the status of the individual within the production process, non-Marxists consider the individual's subjective self-classification as decisive (Klessmann, "Zur Sozialgeschichte," pp. 288–89).

redemption payments and lands lost in return for their emancipation, had they been met, would have bankrupted the estate owners and eliminated them as a class. "Aimed at the economic foundations of the estate owner class," he concludes, "the movement of peasants and rural workers served the interests of the nation more effectively than did the bourgeoisie, which, contrary to many pompous national orations, protected the Junkers after March 18, 1848, and allowed this outdated class to play its pernicious role for another hundred years."[118]

The ultimate failure of the rural movement is ascribed to its lack of organization and coordination, which made its suppression easier. In addition, peasant credulity led many insurgents to content themselves with vague promises of reforms. The main reason for the defeat, however, is found in the lack of collaboration between town and country. In the case of the peasants and workers, this failure is blamed on ineptness and ignorance; in the case of the bourgeoisie, it is blamed on timidity and class egoism. The fact was that the bourgeoisie, insofar as it did concern itself with rural developments, viewed the peasant risings as a threat to personal property rather than as potentially beneficial to its own cause. Because landed property was largely capitalist and to a considerable extent bourgeois-owned, the bourgeoisie could hardly be expected to side with the peasants.[119]

The class that has so far received the least attention in East German research on the year 1848 is the nobility. In sharp contrast to many non-Marxists, DDR scholars are convinced that it was not so much the skilled and purposeful strategy of "Junker-militarist reaction" that enabled the latter to crush the revolution as it was the determination of the bourgeoisie to put a stop to that revolution. Given this lesser impact of the nobility on the course of events, the more systematic probe of its role must therefore wait until the activities of workers and bourgeoisie have been fully examined. Doubtless that role will be more closely explored in the years to come.[120]

---

[118]The prevalent East German position on the role of the peasantry in 1848 is conveniently summarized in Bleiber, "Bauern und Landarbeiter in der bürgerlich-demokratischen Revolution von 1848–49 in Deutschland," *ZfG* 17 (1969): 289ff. (quotation on p. 297). On rural activities in 1848, see also Obermann, *Deutschland*, pp. 297ff.

[119]In the Rhineland, where the Communists had some influence on the workers, Marx and Engels achieved a measure of cooperation between workers and peasants (Becker, *Karl Marx und Friedrich Engels in Köln* [Berlin (East), 1963], pp. 114ff., 157ff., 169).

[120]Bleiber and W. Schmidt, "Forschungen zur Geschichte der Revolution von 1848–49," *ZfG* 18 (1970): suppl., pp. 426–27; Kliem, "Rolle der feudaljunkerlichen Reaktion," pp. 310ff.; Konrad Canis, "Ideologie und politische Taktik der junkerlichmilitaristischen Reaktion ... im Herbst 1848," *JfG* 7 (1972): 459ff.

Another characteristic that distinguishes DDR studies of the revolution from non-Marxist ones is that DDR studies assign a subordinate place to the Frankfurt Assembly.[121] Marxist authors do not find the assembly noteworthy as the first nationwide parliament of modern Germany, because, in their view, the dominance of the liberal bourgeoisie rendered the assembly undemocratic— that is, unrepresentative of the interest of workers, peasants, and petty bourgeois. By abandoning the popular masses, *Grundriss* charges, the bourgeoisie turned the assembly into an "instrument of the counter-revolution." Thus, it did not create a unitarian nation-state but contented itself with a federal state based on an agreement with the old particularist German states. As a provisional head of state it selected an Austrian archduke, and the government it set up consisted of representatives of the aristocracy and the great bourgeoisie; only the foreign minister, a lawyer, belonged to the democratic left.[122] Without an army and administrative apparatus, the assembly remained dependent on the cooperation of the various state governments to enforce its decisions. It was this self-emasculation, Streisand concludes, that accounts for the impotence of the assembly; this conclusion differs from that of non-Marxist historians, who have seen the verbose idealism of doctrinaire individuals as a root cause of the Assembly's ineffectiveness. No matter how strongly these "personalities" disagreed on political questions, DDR historians state, the great majority shared what mattered most in the Marxist view—the social perspective of the liberal bourgeoisie.[123]

That perspective, the East German accounts maintain, shaped the policies of the assembly throughout its existence. In its stand on nationality issues, it is claimed, the assembly invariably allowed narrow class interests to prevail over national rights. Thus, DDR scholars are convinced that the assembly supported the Prussian government in its suppression of the Polish independence movement because the latter was a democratic mass movement

[121]In their 1970 survey of the pertinent literature, Bleiber and W. Schmidt (Forschungen," pp. 408ff.), do not list a single book or article on the Frankfurt Assembly. See also Bleiber's criticism of the West German concern with the assembly, in "Bürgerlich-demokratische Revolution," pp. 266–67, 273, 277.

[122]*Unb. Verg.*, pp. 271–72; *Grundriss*, pp. 247, 253; Streisand, p. 177.

[123]See Streisand, p. 177; Obermann, *Deutschland*, pp. 338–39. The emphasis here is once again on the antidemocratic consensus of the liberals; compared to that consensus, the differing positive concerns of officials, businessmen, academics, and other bourgeois groups seem of lesser importance to Marxists. That it was not the stubbornness of doctrinaire individuals that accounted for the weakness of the assembly but rather purposeful political decisions is now accepted also by a non-Marxist scholar (Boldt, "Konstitutionelle Monarchie," pp. 607ff.). Characteristically, Obermann (*Deutschland*) sees in the earlier non-Marxist stress on individualistic strong personalities an attempt to belittle the history-making powers of the masses.

whose victory might have injected further momentum into the democratic movement in Germany. Although not entirely without merit, the argument overlooks the fact that the Polish issue was perceived above all as a question of power, which explains why German democrats, too, supported the suppression of the Polish insurgents.[124]

The wavering attitude of the Frankfurt Assembly vis-à-vis the problem of the Schleswig-Holstein duchies is also attributed to the prevalence of narrow class interests over the existential rights (*Lebensrechte*) of the nation. Again, this assertion rests on an unjustifiable dismissal of the assembly's real dilemma. Originally an enthusiastic supporter of Prussia's military intervention on behalf of the duchies when their German inhabitants rose against Danish rule, the assembly at first rejected as a betrayal of German national rights the armistice that Prussia concluded with Denmark a few months later. In the end the assembly relented because it could not continue the war without Prussia's help, especially because Russia and Britain could be expected to come to Denmark's aid should the war be resumed. All this is ignored in the East German analyses: what is stressed is Frankfurt's determination not to mobilize the revolutionary-democratic forces that could have provided the manpower for a war against Denmark. This determination doubtless did play some role in the assembly's change of mind, at least partly as a military problem, given the poor training of these forces; it was, however, only one of several factors that entered into the final decision. The most important aspect of the situation that the East German critics ignore, however, is the decline of the revolutionary élan that had inspired the March days. The protest actions that were touched off in Frankfurt and other cities by the assembly's approval of the Prussian armistice with Denmark, and in which DDR historians see the potential nucleus of another revolutionary upheaval, were isolated outbursts that lacked the support of the nation.[125]

Finally, the controversy as to whether the new German state should include and be led by Austria or whether Prussia should head it at the exclusion of Austria is also considered to be the product of economic rivalries and bourgeois class interests as much as it is a collision of conflicting power-political drives. From this perspective, the plan that proposed a greater Germany within a reorganized German Confederation reflected the interests of those in Austrian business circles, who hoped to outdistance their Prussian competitors in a confederation extending from the North Sea to the Black Sea and the Mediterranean and controlled largely by a

[124]For details, see Dorpalen, "Revolution von 1848," pp. 354ff.
[125]Ibid., pp. 354, 356ff.

centralized Austrian state. In turn, a German nation-state excluding Austria and based on a liberal constitution is viewed as more in keeping with the interests of Prussian entrepreneurs, for whom such a state would have provided a more favorable climate for capitalist expansion. These plans are contrasted with the solution proposed in the "Demands of the Communist Party," which envisaged the establishment of a unitarian, indivisible German republic including the German-speaking parts of Austria but providing for the independence of all non-German parts. Such a unified state could have been established only after the abolition of monarchical absolutism and aristocratic feudalism, that is, on a genuinely democratic basis. Only the Communists, it is stressed, perceived this connection, neither liberals nor democrats saw the one way by which they could have disposed of "feudal absolutism," unified Germany democratically, and set up an unfettered capitalist order. That the few who realized the full promise of the Marxist program were mainly workers serves as proof once again of the leadership role that the working class was destined to play.[126]

The constitution that was drawn up by the Frankfurt Assembly and promulgated in 1849 also is readily fitted into the framework of bourgeois class egoism. Most analyses, it is true, grant that in the fundamental rights accorded each citizen the document contained some democratic features, and the creation of a united German nation-state on a constitutional basis is welcomed as another progressive step. At the same time, however, it is noted that the new German nation-state was set up as a hereditary monarchy rather than as a republic and as a federal rather than a unitarian polity; in addition, in matters of social and economic policy, the constitution reflected the outlook of the great bourgeoisie. Accordingly, the constitution does not have the paradigmatic significance for DDR historiography which it is accorded in non-Marxist analyses.[127]

On the other hand, the uprisings that broke out after Prussia rejected the constitution, which most non-Marxist historians have treated as a peripheral epilogue of the revolution,[128] are events of major concern to DDR scholars. These authors are convinced that the upheavals, which in the grandduchy of Baden escalated into a

---

[126]See Obermann, *Deutschland*, pp. 305–6, 374–78; *GdA*, vol. 1, pp. 103–4, 163. See also Helmut Böhme, *Deutschlands Weg zur Grossmacht* (Cologne, 1972), pp. 14–16.

[127]"Reichsverfassung," *Swb*, vol. 2, pp. 363–65; Streisand, p. 181; *Grundriss*, p. 255; Obermann, *Deutschland*, pp. 380–81.

[128]See the perfunctory accounts in Holborn, vol. 2, pp. 88–89; Schieder, in Gebhardt, vol. 2, p. 152; Sheehan, *German Liberalism*, p. 76. Exceptions are Veit Valentin, *Geschichte der Deutschen Revolution 1848–1849* (Berlin, 1931), vol. 2, pp. 473ff.; Klessmann, "Zur Sozialgeschichte," pp. 283ff.

major campaign—"one of the most important armed struggles of the German people against the forces of reaction," according to *Grundriss*—provided another chance to complete the revolution and to establish the bourgeois-capitalist order. This was a goal that Marx and Engels had set, and in reality it went far beyond the goals of most of the insurgents, who merely wished to secure the acceptance and implementation of the new Reich constitution. The risings that occurred in the spring and summer of 1849 thus are considered an integral part of the revolutionary upheavals that began in March 1848, and DDR historians therefore make it a point to speak of the Revolution of 1848–1849 (rather than of the Revolution of 1848).

The defeat of these uprisings is blamed on the opposition of the great bourgeoisie, the timidity and illusionism of the petty bourgeoisie, and the Frankfurt Assembly, which would not assume the leadership of the insurrectional movement and provide a rallying point for the democratic forces of the nation. Here again, positions are taken for which there existed no realistic basis. Moreover, the conservative forces were not caught by surprise this time; self-confident once again in their newly restored power, they were prepared to strike back. Faced with the professionalism of the Prussian army, which had remained immune from all revolutionary influence, the uncoordinated, ill-trained, and poorly armed rebel forces were quickly routed.[129]

The East German conclusions of the significance of the revolution are summed up concisely by *Grundriss:*

> Despite its defeat, the Revolution of 1848–1849 is one of the greatest progressive events of German history. It was the climax of the class struggle in the period of the rise and consolidation of capitalism and the most important revolutionary event since the German Peasants' War of 1525–1526. The Revolution of 1848–1849 was the time of the greatest unfolding of the strength of the revolutionary masses in the progressing bourgeois transformation. . . . This had permanent positive consequences. Though defeated, the revolution rendered the final verdict on the reactionary feudal order. The revolutionary actions of the masses forced Junkers and aristocracy to complete the bourgeois transformation, although in counter-revolutionary ways . . . and [to make] room for the free development of capitalism. The revolution thus helped to speed up considerably the formation of the working class.

Above all, *Grundriss* notes, the revolution provided the first proving ground for Marxism and led to its spread in the German

---

[129]See Obermann, *Deutschland*, pp. 387ff.; *GdA*, vol. 1, pp. 155ff.; "Reichsverfassungskampagne," *Swb*, vol. 2, pp. 365–66; *Grundriss*, p. 265. On the causes of the defeat, see also Klessmann, "Zur Sozialgeschichte," pp. 329ff.

workers' movement and thus to the formation of the "most conse-
quent revolutionary force in the history of the German people."[130]

The Revolution from Above

The Revolution of 1848 thus is seen as hastening Germany's transformation into a capitalist society. Under the impact of the revolution, governments liberalized economic policies, spurring the
growth of capitalism and industrialization. Capitalism also pene-
trated deeper into agriculture, allowing growing numbers of bourgeois non-nobles to become landowners and turning nobles into
capitalists, which made them more responsive to bourgeois needs.

The dynamics of this expanding capitalism, DDR scholars
point out, created a common economy within the Zollverein—a
trend accentuated by a growing network of railroads. These same
dynamics, it is agreed, made unification inevitable: as Marx already had said, unification was not a matter of opinion, but grew
out of the "course of history." The crucial question thus was not
whether but *how* Germany was to be unified—by a nationwide,
bourgeois-led democratic movement or by a Prussian-led antidemocratic revolution from above. This question, it is constantly
stressed, was not decided by the Revolution of 1848. (The problem
of Austria's inclusion, so prominent in non-Marxist discussions,
receives little attention in the East German literature. The modus
of unification would also resolve this question: as a national movement unification from below would automatically include German
Austria in a unified Germany; a Prussian-led unification from
above, on the other hand, would exclude Austria.) The manner of
unification was the central issue, the argument runs, because unification from below would have carried the bourgeoisie into power
and enabled it to remove all remaining particularist, feudal, and
bureaucratic obstacles to capitalist production. It would also have
kept militarist elements from playing a key role in politics, as they
did subsequently because of their part in the process of unification.
Above all, the inauguration of a liberal bourgeois-capitalist regime
would have spurred the growth and influence of the working class,
the ultimate carrier of social progress.[131]

Once again, it is noted, everything turned on the stance of the

[130]*Grundriss*, pp. 257–58; W. Schmidt, "Zu Problemen," pp. 657–59.
[131]See *Grundriss*, pp. 263ff.; Engelberg, *Deutschland*, (Berlin [East], 1965), pp. xi
(with Marx quotation), 39–40, 59, 71; Dlubek and Weber, in *ZfG* 18 (1970): suppl.,
pp. 428–29. On East German views on possible foreign political repercussions of a
Greater German unification, see Dorpalen, "The Unification of Germany in East
German Perspective," *AHR* 73 (1968): 1071 n. 3.

bourgeoisie, and once again that class did not fulfill its "historical task," which was to convert Germany's semiabsolute, semifeudal, particularist old order into a unitarian bourgeois-capitalist society when growing discontent with existing conditions in the late 1850s and early 1860s made such a transformation possible with the help of the masses. Instead, various studies point out, the bulk of the industrial, banking, and commercial bourgeoisie dissociated itself from the liberal movement and its parties. It pursued its interests through its direct contacts with court and government and through its chambers of commerce and trade associations. It was clearly content to achieve its objectives—national unification and liberal economic reforms—through cooperation with the existing powers. Above all, it was satisfied with the economic policies of the Prussian government, in which it was represented and which catered to its concerns.

The Prussian bourgeoisie had little sense of involvement in the conflict that arose between the government and the lower house of the parliament over the reorganization of the army and the budgetary rights of the parliament. It displayed a similar lack of involvement regarding Bismarck, who was appointed minister-president in 1862 to resolve the resulting deadlock. When he, defying the House of Delegates, collected taxes without its approval, bankers and industrialists had some misgivings about his personal qualifications and methods, but they soon accommodated themselves to his government, especially after his victorious war against Denmark. Because stability and prosperity were the major concerns of the bourgeoisie, it is noted, members of that class did not object to the continued rule of the nobility. Again, many great bourgeois opposed the war against Austria, but as Roland Zeise shows, they did so more because of fear lest Prussia be defeated than because they opposed the war on principle. Zeise also finds that although leading bankers did not approve of the aims of the war, they nonetheless helped Bismarck to finance it.[132] Once again, it is pointed out, these were not unilateral moves. Bismarck, for his part, knew that he could not preserve the monarchical-conservative Prussian regime unless he adjusted his economic policies to

[132]See Roland Zeise, "Gemeinsamkeiten und Unterschiede in der politischen Konzeption der deutschen Handels-, Industrie- und Bankbourgeoisie in der politischen Krise von 1859 bis 1866," *JfG* 10 (1974): 175ff.; Zeise, "Zur Rolle der kapitalistischen Interessenverbände beim Abschluss der bürgerlichen Umwälzung in den deutschen Staaten," ibid. 14 (1976): 125ff.; Gerd Fesser, "Zur Struktur und politischen Konzeption der Deutschen Fortschrittspartei in der Konfliktszeit," in Bleiber et al., in *Bourgeoisie*, pp. 468–69. These findings are supported by recent Western studies (Friedrich Zunkel, *Der Rheinisch-Westfälische Unternehmer: 1834–1879* [Cologne, 1962], pp. 214ff.; Theodore S. Hamerow, *The Social Foundations of German Unification: 1858–1871* [Princeton, 1969–1972], vol. 1, pp. 90ff., 349ff., vol. 2, pp. 67ff., 135–36, and *passim*; Gugel, *Industrieller Aufstieg*, pp. 154ff.).

bourgeois concerns, and his pursuit of a united nation-state also met a long-standing bourgeois demand.[133]

The middle bourgeoisie, largely the *Bildungsbürgertum* and medium-sized entrepreneurs, fares little better in these accounts. It is given scant credit for its opposition to the conservative and high-handed policies of the Prussian government, the formation of the Progressive party, and its active pursuit of national unification, because, again from fear of the masses, it would not ally itself with the latter in a revolutionary movement.[134]

Under these circumstances, it comes as something of a surprise to find that some accounts describe the Prussian constitutional conflict as a struggle for power between bourgeoisie and nobility.[135] According to the East Germans' own evidence it was not such a contest. Far from seeking to take over the government, DDR authors complain, the opposition contented itself with calling for a modicum of influence on political decisions and the extension of some parliamentary prerogatives, with the right-liberals even suggesting that such claims might be yielded, should they impede progress toward national unification.[136] (Going further and reinforcing the East German position, one West German author, Michael Gugel, has concluded that even the aims of the less conciliatory left-liberals differed in method rather than principle from those of the great bourgeoisie.) Many a democrat, too, was unwilling to challenge the existing government system directly.[137]

The bourgeoisie, then, did not turn the constitutional conflict into a struggle for power. Such a struggle, it is pointed out, could have been won only with the help of the masses. However, rather than assume the leadership in a nationwide movement in order to

[133]See Engelberg, *Deutschland*, pp. 118ff.; Engelberg, "Die politische Strategie und Taktik Bismarcks von 1851 bis 1866," in Bartel and Engelberg, *Grosspreussisch*, vol. 1, pp. 73ff. See also, on the non-Marxist side, Fritz Stern, *Gold and Iron: Bismarck, Bleichröder, and the Building of the German Empire* (New York, 1977), pp. 25–26.

[134]*Grundriss*, p. 265; Zeise, "Gemeinsamkeiten," p. 204; Karl-Heinz Börner, "Bourgeoisie und Neue Ära in Preussen," in Bleiber et al., *Bourgeoisie*, pp. 422, 426, 430ff.; Fesser, "Zur Struktur," pp. 467–68.

[135]See *Grundriss*, p. 265; Zeise, "Gemeinsamkeiten," p. 200, but also, contradicting this position, p. 205. Similarly, see Fesser, "Zur Struktur," p. 473. W. Schmidt sees the bourgeoisie trying to share power with the nobility ("Zu Problemen," p. 647).

[136]Zeise, "Gemeinsamkeiten," pp. 203ff.; Fesser, "Zur Struktur," p. 466; Schulze, "Zur linksliberalen Ideologie und Politik," in Bartel and Engelberg, *Grosspreussisch* (n. 66), I, 289.

[137]See Gugel, *Industrieller Aufstieg*. See also the following, although they are not quite as specific: Sheehan, *German Liberalism*, pp. 113, 116; Heinrich August Winkler, *Preussischer Liberalismus und Deutscher Nationalstaat* (Tübingen, 1964), pp 5–6, 14 n. 52, 23–24 n. 34; Adalbert Hess, *Das Parlament, das Bismarck widerstrebte* (Cologne, 1964), pp. 48–49; Hamerow *Social Foundations*, 34ff., 155–56, 162ff., 170ff.

democratically unify Germany and transform it into a full-scale bourgeois-capitalist society, the cowardly bourgeoisie, ever afraid of the masses, let Bismarck and the Prussian Junkers and generals fulfill this task in an undemocratic manner.[138] Occasionally bourgeois inaction is also blamed on an excessive concern with immediate profits; rather than wait for the greater profits that a bourgeois government would supposedly yield them, bankers and industrialists preferred to arrange themselves with the Bismarck regime.[139]

DDR authors maintain that a determined fight of the bourgeoisie would have had mass support and that such support would have been much greater than non-Marxists conclude from the available data. *Sachwörterbuch der Geschichte Deutschlands* claims that the liberals in the House of Delegates enjoyed the "almost unanimous" support of the "bourgeois and laboring masses" in all of Germany. Engelberg, too, asserts that a successful revolutionary movement could have been organized and points to a number of clashes between the authorities and the urban and rural masses as evidence of the revolutionary temper of the country. Some authors finally find proof of the bourgeoisie's influence in the fact that liberal papers had a far wider circulation (250,000) than conservative ones (40,000).[140]

The claim that there was "almost unanimous" support of the liberal position by the "bourgeois and laboring masses" is refuted by the widespread indifference that large parts of the population displayed toward the constitutional conflict and that was reflected in the low participation of all classes and strata in the elections of those years. Similarly, whatever else the figures on newspaper circulation suggest, they make clear that relatively few people read newspapers. In addition, although Engelberg's data establish that there was some localized unrest in Prussia, they do not show that "the entire country was restive [and that] only strong and purposeful leadership was required to arouse [it] to political awareness and militant action." (Elsewhere he himself points out that the democratic forces were weak and disorganized.) Neither the working

---

[138]See *Grundriss*, p. 265; Engelberg, *Deutschland*, pp. 135ff.; Börner, "Bourgeoisie," p. 422. The role of the army leaders has been the subject of relatively few East German studies, but one author notes that Bismarck found cooperation easiest with generals such as Roon, the Prussian minister of war who engineered Bismarck's appointment as minister-president, and Moltke, the chief of the general staff, because both were more flexible in their attitude towards the bourgeoisie (Canis, "Die politische Taktik der führenden preussischen Militärs 1858 bis 1866," in Bartel and Engelberg, *Grosspreussisch*, vol. 1, pp. 128–29, 133–34, 135–36).

[139]Fesser, "Zur Struktur," p. 469; Zeise, "Gemeinsamkeiten," pp. 205–6, 208ff.

[140]See "Heeres-und Verfassungskonflikt," *Swb*, vol. 1, p. 781; Engelberg, *Deutschland*, pp. 123, 135–36. However, the clashes mentioned by Engelberg had no connection with the conflict over army reform and constitutional authority and are indicative only of some general discontent. On the press, see Engelberg, "Über die Revolution," p. 1197; Fesser, "Zur Struktur," pp. 472–73.

class nor the peasantry were prepared, psychologically or organiza-tionally, to provide the mass basis for a revolutionary movement. Nor has any author explained how mass discontent, whatever its scope, could have been translated into forcible action against a government supported by a loyal army and police force.[141]

Apart from these considerations, the question again arises whether with capitalism spreading readily even under a semifeu-dal, semiabsolutist regime, the bourgeoisie could have been ex-pected to attain the completion of the capitalist transformation by a democratic mass movement. It is the same question that Marxist critiques of bourgeois conduct in 1848 have raised, and from the Marxist perspective an affirmative answer seems this time even more difficult, given the socioeconomic conditions that prevailed in the 1860s. Engelberg, for example, so sharply critical of bour-geois inaction, nonetheless grants that the "objective" interests of the bourgeoisie did not require the unification of Germany under liberal-democratic auspices. Other East German scholars agree with him. Gerd Fesser grants that the revolutionary road involved grave risks for the bourgeoisie. Rolf Weber carries this realization to its logical conclusion: "As the economic basis of the Junkers became fully capitalist, [their] resistance against the national con-sequences of the emergence of the bourgeoisie was bound to weaken. As a result, the objective conditions for a firm alliance of the two became favorable. For the German bourgeoisie, the revolu-tionary-democratic, uncompromising road to national unification thus was out of the question." It was all the more unlikely, Weber adds, because the rapid growth of the working class suggested the possibility of major class struggles in future political crises.[142]

The insistence that the bourgeoisie should nonetheless have sought to obtain political power thus postulates a departure from the basic axiom that the political superstructure is conditioned by the material basis. Such an idea injects a voluntarist element into

[141]Engelberg (Deutschland, pp. 125–26) denies any widespread indifference toward the elections and interprets poor participation in some cases as a protest against improper pressures by officials and industrialists in an uncorroborated generaliza-tion of a cautious statement by Eugene N. Anderson (Anderson, The Social and Political Conflict in Prussia: 1858 to 1864 [Lincoln, NE, 1954], p. 439). On this, see also Hamerow, Social Foundations, vol. 1, pp. 269–70, 273ff., 286ff., 304ff., 379–80. Elsewhere, Engelberg himself concedes the weakness of the democratic forces (Deutschland, p. 186).

[142]See Engelberg, Deutschland, pp. 73–74, 151–52; S. Schmidt, "Zur Frühgeschichte der bürgerlichen Parteien in Deutschland," ZfG 13 (1965): 990; Kuczynski, Ge-schichte, vol. 2, p. 72; Fesser, "Zur Struktur," p. 471; Weber, Kleinbürgerliche Demokraten in der deutschen Einheitsbewegung: 1863–1866 (Berlin [East], 1962), p. 23. See also Walter Nimtz, "Über den Charakter der Novemberrolution von 1918–19 in Deutschland," ZfG 6 (1958): 697. What was said earlier about the corresponding conduct, mutatis mutandis, of the English and French bourgeoisies applies here too; cf. note 105.

the historical process that runs counter to Marxist tenets. In the words of one West German critic, the attacks on the bourgeoisie imply a "pluralistic coexistence" of political and economic forces that reduces the economic ones to merely one factor among a variety of separate components. Although a non-Marxists cannot quarrel with such an approach, a Marxist should find it hard to defend.[143]

The fact is that the conduct of the bourgeoisie cannot be faulted on bourgeois-capitalist grounds. Engelberg implies as much when he distinguishes between the objective interests of the bourgeoisie, which did not require the unification of Germany by means of a bourgeois-led mass revolution from below, and its subjective interests, which did require this kind of a revolution. His and his colleagues' position is informed, however, not merely by the contemporary scenario but also by subsequent German developments whose disastrous course is partly attributed to the unwillingness of the bourgeoisie to assume political leadership either in 1848 or in the 1860s. Although this linkage is undeniable, such causation can hardly be made the basis for judgments of historical responsibility.[144]

Yet the inconsistency of the East German position has other roots, too. As DDR authors point out, the working class, too, was deeply affected by developments in the 1860s. The attainment of German unification by a revolution from above, as it subsequently occurred, was the most disadvantageous form any revolutionary change could take, from the workers' viewpoint. That type of revolution, according to Lenin, retained "the monarchy, aristocratic privileges, legal defenselessness in the rural areas, and other medieval relics" and thus set even narrower limits to social and political progress than does a bourgeois society. By Marxist criteria, however, this again was not a bourgeois concern.[145]

Because of the renewed failure of the bourgeoisie to live up to its "historical task," East German historians have also explored other alternatives to a Prussian-led unification from above. Viewing unification as a social much more than a political problem, these efforts are focused, not on initiatives that might have been undertaken by other German states, but on moves that could have been made by classes other than the bourgeoisie. Reviewing the attitude of petty bourgeois elements in the unification movement—storekeepers, artisans, teachers, and employees—DDR au-

---

[143]Gugel, *Industrieller Aufstieg,* p. 226 n. 28.
[144]Engelberg, *Deutschland,* p. 249; Streisand, p. 211.
[145]W. Schmidt, "Zu einigen Problemen," pp. 8, 33; Engelberg, "Revolution von oben," p. 1204; Seeber, "Preussisch-deutscher Bonapartismus und Bourgeoisie," *JfG* 16 (1977): 90.

thors find that they are divided politically; wavering between unitarian and federalist solutions, some of them follow the liberal lead and others assume a more militant democratic stance. However, only a small minority was ready to resort to revolution. Nor could this have been otherwise, Rolf Weber points out, because petty bourgeois modes of production were antiquated, uncoordinated, and hence economically reactionary; inevitably, this impeded whatever political progressivism the Kleinbürgertum may have displayed. Wedged in between the two main classes of the capitalist order and torn by the multifaceted nature of its constituent elements, the petty bourgeoisie is found lacking in political purposefulness and economically dependent on both the old noble strata and the great bourgeoisie. Moreover, liberal elements, ever fearful of any mass movements, kept control of the gymnastic, shooting, and singing Vereine, the mainstays of petty bourgeois organization. No East German author, however, gives adequate weight to the fact that the bulk of these societies called for unification not because of an urgent material need—in fact, unification might hurt many small manufacturers, merchants, and artisans by furthering large-scale capitalist enterprise—but for reasons of national prestige and political status. The means of unification were not as important as the end result to men whose motivations were mainly emotional.[146]

In their quest for a democratic alternative to the "revolution from above," some DDR historians have also examined the possibility of a worker-led unification movement. At the height of the constitutional conflict, Engels already had pointed out that the workers would have to compel the bourgeoisie to fight for its principles. Yet an analysis of the class situation in the 1860s has led most DDR historians to conclude that the working class was not yet strong enough to assume the leadership of the national movement and force other classes to follow its lead.[147]

[146]See Engelberg, Deutschland, pp. 102–4; GdA, vol. 1, pp. 203–4; Weber, Kleinbürgerliche Demokraten, pp. 31ff., 277ff. For a more detailed discussion of petty bourgeois attitudes toward unification, see Dorpalen, Heinrich von Treitschke (New Haven, 1957), pp. 57ff.; Otto Pflanze, Bismarck and the Development of Germany (Princeton, 1963), pp. 36ff.
[147]See Engels, "Die preussische Militärfrage und die deutsche Arbeiterpartei," in MEW, vol. 16, p. 58; GdA, vol. 1, p. 204; Kuczynski, Geschichte, vol. 2, p. 78; Engelberg, Deutschland, p. 179. Why such a mass movement, if strong enough, would have forced the bourgeoisie to join forces with it rather than drive the bourgeoisie even closer into the arms of government and aristocracy, as it did in 1848, remains unexplained. Evidently the French Revolution of 1789 serves as a model. If the French bourgeoisie associated itself with the urban and rural masses on that occasion, however, it did so because French government and nobility were not responsive to its economic needs, as were the Prussian authorities to bourgeois interests in the 1850s and 1860s. For other differences, see W. Schmidt, "Zur Rolle," pp. 309–10.

Nonetheless, because in the East German view the future of German democracy rested with the working class, DDR authors have traced with painstaking thoroughness the development and political emancipation of that class during the 1850s and 1860s.[148] However limited its immediate impact on events may have been, this facet of the unification period is considered historically more significant than such aspects as the Austro-Prussian dualism, the problem of Schleswig-Holstein, or the subtleties of Bismarck's diplomacy. Indeed, Marxist historians deplore the preoccupation of non-Marxists with Bismarck on the grounds that this approach, in the words of Joachim Streisand, "made the German people the mere object of Bismarckian politics and did not point out the positive countercurrents. Instead of the class struggle, Bismarck's personal intrigue appeared as the motor of history." The class-struggle approach, on the other hand, serves to refute attempts to use the history of the labor movement in order to integrate the working class into the bourgeois state and society; such attempts are "dictated by the immediate political needs of the imperialist West German bourgeoisie."[149]

The main task of Marxist historians, then, lies in tracing the political emancipation of the working class from the bourgeoisie during the 1850s and 1860s. This complex process, with its advances and setbacks, is viewed as historically lawful on the grounds that it corresponded to the objective social and economic conditions of this period, in which the capitalist mode of production was gaining ascendancy and bourgeoisie and proletariat were emerging as the two leading classes. Only Marxism recognized this objective inevitability and could provide the working class with the political ideology that it needed to attain its independence. "In fact," Schmidt and Dlubek conclude, "the complete separation of the working class from the bourgeoisie coincided with the spread and acceptance of Marxism." Similarly, Dlubek and Weber hail the formation of a Marxist-oriented working class party at the end of the period as the "highest expression of historical inevitability.[150]

---

[148]See materials in *ZfG* 8 (1960): suppl., p. 273; ibid. 18 (1970): suppl., pp. 428ff. There were also political reasons for these endeavors. As Engelberg explained at the time, "Today [1965] when for the sake of the nation we have to develop the socialist perspective for all of Germany, the study of the struggle that led to the creation of a socialist workers party in the [eighteen-]sixties constitutes a great history-making force" (*Deutschland*, pp. xxii–xxiii).

[149]Streisand, "Bismarck und die deutsche Einigungsbewegung," *ZfG* 2 (1954): 350; Engelberg, "Unser Arbeiter- und Bauernstaat—Erbe und Krönung der demokratischen Traditionen des deutschen Volkes," *Einheit* 15 (1960): 85ff.; "IV. Historiker-kongress der DDR to Walter Ulbricht," Oct. 11, 1968, *ZfG* 17 (1969): 8; *Unb. Verg.*, pp. 515ff.

[150]Schmidt and Dlubek, "Die Herausbildung der marxistischen Partei der deutschen Arbeiterklasse," *ZfG* 14 (1966): 1282–84; Dlubek and Weber, ibid. 18 (1970): suppl., p. 430; Martin Hundt, "Zur Kontinuität der deutschen Arbeiterbewegung," *BzG* 11 (1969): 605.

Actually, when the workers proceeded to set up a new political organization after the quietism of the 1850s, they turned for guidance to Ferdinand Lassalle rather than to Marx and Engels—whose names, Engelberg notes, were all but forgotten.[151] Unlike his former mentors, Lassalle wanted to move toward socialism within the framework of the national state. Having secured universal suffrage, the workers would have the state finance producers' cooperatives; because the program was directed against the bourgeoisie, the common foe of both state and workers, Lassalle was confident that he could enlist the help of the Prussian monarchy. Once the workers controlled a substantial part of the economy, however, the monarchy would be overthrown by the workers, just as Marx and Engels proposed to discard the bourgeoisie after it had fulfilled *its* historical mission. Although Lassalle's plan to utilize the Prussian monarchy in the proposed sense was utterly unrealistic, he perceived earlier than did Marx and Engels that the liberal bourgeoisie would not play the activist role assigned to it by the Marxist program. He also foresaw correctly that the Prussian state could not be destroyed by an attack from without.[152]

Marxists concede that Lassalle made some positive contributions to historical progress: by creating a separate workers' organization, the *Allgemeine Deutsche Arbeiterverein* (ADAV), he strengthened the workers' class consciousness, and he also called for universal, direct, and secret suffrage. Yet these same critics insist that Lassalle betrayed the interests of the working class by aligning himself with the semifeudal Prussian monarchy. He ought to have gathered all democratic forces, including the peasants, into one oppositional movement that might have forced the hesitant bourgeoisie into a showdown fight for political power. Worse, DDR authors charge, Lassalle's program, resting on idealist speculations rather than material reality, encouraged the dangerous illusion that the existing state could be transformed into a socialist one without a revolutionary class struggle and the establishment of a proletarian dictatorship. It is not clear that Lassalle entertained such hopes, although his speeches and writings, vaguely worded so as not to arouse the government's wrath, could be and were thus interpreted.[153]

---

[151]Engelberg, *Deutschland*, pp. 140–41.

[152]For a thorough and balanced analysis of Lassalle's views, see the essay on him by Mommsen, *SDG*, vol. 3, pp. 1332ff., especially pp. 1356ff. See also Thilo Ramm, *Ferdinand Lassalle als Rechts- und Sozialphilosoph* (Meisenheim and Vienna, 1953), especially pp. 168–70, 180ff.; Arthur Rosenberg, *Democracy and Socialism* (New York, 1939), pp. 156ff. The romanticizing, fuzzy discussion in Hermann Oncken, *Lassalle: Eine politische Biographie* (Stuttgart, 1923), especially pp. 480–81, is not helpful.

[153]See *GdA*, vol.1, p. 211; Engelberg, *Deutschland*, pp. 143–44; Mommsen, in *SDG*, vol. 3, pp. 1348–50. Engelberg (*Deutschland*, p. 147) objects rightly to non-Marxist efforts contrasting the "national-minded," state-supporting Lassalle with the

The pitfalls of Lassalle's strategy, DDR authors stress, were revealed in the stand he took on the problem of Schleswig-Holstein. This issue flared up again in November 1863 when Denmark prepared to annex outright the duchy of Schleswig. The plan injected new life into the German national movement. Although the liberals called for the liberation of both duchies from Denmark and their establishment as a separate state within the German Confederation, Lassalle, in keeping with his strategy of collaboration with Bismarck, proposed to support the annexation of the duchies by Prussia (in the expectation of some concession on Bismarck's part in the suffrage question).

East German scholars point out that this plan, pursued by Lassalle's successors after his death in a duel, isolated the Lassallean workers from the democratic elements in the national movement. These circles wished to combine the fight for the liberation of Schleswig-Holstein with their own domestic emancipation. In this manner they hoped to utilize the momentum created by the deliverance of the duchies to unify all of Germany under democratic rather than authoritarian auspices, thus securing political freedom along with national unity.[154] The national movement, DDR authors stress, was not a self-contained political phenomenon with which the various classes somehow had to come to terms. Instead, its character and goals were determined by the contending social forces whose concepts of national unity and whose strategies were defined in accordance with their respective class interests. In Horst Bartel's words, "The issue was never just national unity, but always the question of which class elements would determine the fate of the nation." As it was, the war against Denmark was fought as a dynastic rather than a people's war, thus driving Germany further toward unification by governmental rather than popular action.[155]

---

internationalist and hence destructive and unpatriotic Marx and denying that an internationalist may be at the same time a national patriot. On this point, see also Dlubek and Günter Wisotzki, "Arbeiterklasse, Demokratie und Nation," in Bartel and Engelberg, *Grosspreussisch*, vol. 1, p. 27; on the non-Marxist side, see Golo Mann, *Deutsche Geschichte im 19. und 20. Jahrhundert* (Frankfurt, 1963), p. 424.

[154]Engelberg, *Deutschland*, pp. 156ff.; Weber, *Kleinbürgerliche Demokraten*, pp. 84ff., 98ff., 103–5.

[155]See Engelberg, *Deutschland*, p. 160; Engelberg, "Der preussische Militarismus und die Reichsgründung 1870–71," *ZfMilitärgesch.* 10 (1971): 19; Streisand, pp. 199–200; Weber, *Kleinbürgerliche Demokraten*, pp. 105–6; Bartel, "Die Reichseinigung 1871 in Deutschland," *ZfG* 17 (1969): 170. The danger of equating class and national interests during the unification period is also seen by the West German historian Hans-Josef Steinberg in his essay "Sozialismus, Internationalismus und Reichsgründung," in *Reichsgründung 1870–71: Tatsachen, Kontroversen, Interpretation*, ed. Theodor Schieder et al. (Stuttgart, 1970), p. 342. See also Dorpalen, "Marxism and National Unity: The Case of Germany," *Review of Politics* 38 (1977): 505ff., especially p. 509.

In 1865–1866, it is claimed, new opportunities presented themselves—opportunities that, under proper leadership, might have guided the national movement into democratic channels. The workers showed signs of an increasing militancy, striking frequently and becoming more active politically in the quest for a democratic nation-state. Efforts were made in several South German states to form closer links between the working-class movement and the democratic Kleinbügertum. As Prussia's war with Austria was approaching, political protests touched off clashes with the police, and there were fights between workers and military and a number of cases in which draftees refused to obey induction orders. August Bebel, subsequently the leader of the German Social Democratic party, summed it up: "Almost everyone in Germany, except for East Elbia, believed that a victorious revolution was possible." Many DDR historians agree; Engelberg speaks of the "great revolutionary potential that became manifest among the German people in the 1860s. Unfortunately, the leading elements representing the democratic revolution from below (the bourgeois-democratic revolution)—that is, the petty bourgeois democracy and the various workers organizations—did not fulfill this potential." In this same vein, Roland Zeise finds in this period a "national-revolutionary situation" in which "the outcome of the class struggle would determine by which of the two possible alternatives the task of unification, historically necessary, would be accomplished."[156]

Again Rolf Weber proves more sober-minded than his colleagues. "As conditions were at that time," he notes, "any attempt at a popular rising would have been a hopeless *Putsch* that would have been crushed within a few hours." Not only was there no leadership to fuse the oppositional elements into a coordinated movement, but no attempt was made to arouse the peasantry—a precondition of a successful popular rising, as Marx and Engels already had stipulated. (At that, it was highly unlikely that the peasantry could have been stirred up into any oppositional activity.) In fact, virtually all contemporary observers who considered a

---

[156]See Engelberg, *Deutschland*, pp. 145, 166–70, 177–79; quotation of Engelberg in *Beiträge zum neuen Geschichtsbild*, ed. Klein and Streisand (Berlin [East], 1956), p. 246; Karl-Heinz Leidigkeit, *Wilhelm Liebknecht und August Bebel in der deutschen Arbeiterbewegung: 1862–1869* (Berlin [East], 1958), pp. 67–70, 74–82 (Bebel's statement is on p. 81), 94–105; Herbert Schwab, "Von Düppel bis Königgrätz," *ZfG* 14 (1966): 601; Zeise, "Zur Rolle der sächsischen Bourgeoisie . . . in den fünfziger und sechziger Jahren des 19. Jahrhunderts," in Bartel and Engelberg, *Grosspreussisch*, vol. 1, pp. 250, 268. An informative non-Marxist survey can be found in Hamerow, *Social Foundations*, vol. 2, pp. 269ff.; Hamerow notes the oppositional attitude of some bourgeois circles. On the other hand, Hamerow considers the militancy of the workers less pronounced than do Marxist authors. See also Karl Heinrich Höfele, "Königgrätz und die Deutschen," *GWU* 16 (1966): 400ff.

revolution possible expected it to break out only if Prussia suffered a major military defeat. As Weber puts it, "The atmosphere was only potentially explosive; it could become a serious political factor only after a defeat of the [Prussian] army."[157]

Even this is speculative, and it is therefore not surprising that the non-Marxist literature has rarely explored the question of whether Bismarck, in addition to risking military defeat in attacking Austria, also endangered the Prussian social and political order in case of such a defeat. Moreover, DDR authors are mistaken when they assert that the laboring classes drove Bismarck into his "revolution from above," or conversely, that Bismarck could not have launched the war against Austria without his appeal to the people (promising them universal manhood suffrage for a national parliament). On the East Germans' own evidence, opposition to the war was strongest among those who, according to the East German analyses, were supposed to be among its immediate beneficiaries— that is, both business and labor.[158] All in all, whatever alternatives may have existed to Bismarck's method of unification, DDR historians have failed to establish a "democratic" one that would have been realistic.

The Prussian victory over Austria, DDR scholars never tire of pointing out, led to the creation of the German state and the completion of Germany's transformation into a bourgeois-capitalist society by a "revolution from above." At the time, this term referred to one of two scenarios: the forcible unification of northern and central Germany into the North German Confederation and the exclusion of Austria from "Germany," which was hailed as historical progress by liberals, or the violation of the principle of dynastic legitimacy by the removal from their thrones of the rulers of Hanover, Hesse, and Nassau and the incorporation of their states— along with the free city of Frankfurt—into the kingdom of Prussia, which was deplored by conservatives. In either case, the "revolution" was viewed as a political event, affecting the structure and organization of states.[159]

To Marxists, the violation of dynastic legitimacy is, of course, a matter of utter indifference. Similarly, they find the resort to force objectionable only because it was used by antidemocratic

---

[157]See Weber, *Kleinbürgerliche Demokraten*, pp. 237ff. (quotations on pp. 269, 256); also *Grundriss*, pp. 268–69. For details, especially on the peasantry, see Dorpalen, "Unification of Germany," pp. 1075ff.

[158]Dlubek and Wisotzki, *Arbeiterklasse*, vol. 1, p. 71; Engelberg, *Deutschland*, p. 175; Joachim Schuchardt, "Die Wirtschaftskrise vom Jahre 1866 in Deutschland," *JWG* 2 (1962): 129–30.

[159]Engelberg, "Revolution von oben," pp. 1184ff.; Schieder, in Gebhardt, vol. 3, p. 149; Heinrich Heffter, *Die deutsche Selbstverwaltung im 19. Jahrhundert* (Stuttgart, 1950), p. 453.

rather than democratic agents. The "revolution from above," as noted before, is important to them as a socioeconomic rather than a political change—it is to be the gateway to the completion of Germany's capitalist transformation, with both its progressive and its regressive aspects. For DDR scholars of German history, through nationwide institutions and through the prestige and power resources of a unified nation-state, the unification of Germany provided the potential for the further unfolding of bourgeois-capitalist society. For this reason, DDR authors reject the contention of their non-Marxist critics that the wars of unification refute the validity of the Marxist approach, because to the critics the wars were not fought for economic reasons. As they insist, the laws of dialectical and historical materialism do apply to these campaigns, because these wars, whatever their immediate causes, were part of that process by which Germany was transformed into a bourgeois-capitalist society.[160]

At the same time, it is noted, Bismarck's revolution, controlled from above, preserved the political power of the old ruling class—a class, however, that was itself becoming increasingly capitalist and was gradually turning into a "bourgeois" nobility. Thus, whereas to non-Marxists, subsequent developments are characterized by the social feudalization of the bourgeoisie, Marxists find it decisive that the nobility was becoming increasingly *embourgeoisé*. Bismarck is seen as implementing this historical trend, striking a careful balance between the political conservatism of the king and the nobility and the material interests of the bourgeoisie and at the same time trying to neutralize the masses by introducing universal, direct, and secret male suffrage. The minister-president thus brought about what DDR historians call a "class compromise" between the bourgeoisie and the nobility. The arrangement was fittingly symbolized by the Indemnity Bill.[161]

The bulk of the Prussian liberals supported this bill, by which they retroactively sanctioned all governmental expenditures incurred without an approved budget; this support is not considered an opportunist turnabout, however. DDR authors do not see the

---

[160]There is some disagreement, however, as to what was specifically revolutionary about the revolution from above. Engelberg and Schmidt insist that the political measure—that is, the forcible creation of a nation-state by war—was revolutionary whereas the ensuing social measures were mere reforms, because they did not curtail the power of the old ruling class, even though the latter had to adopt capitalist ways. Seeber, "in turn, sees the revolutionary element in the social effects of the political moves (Engelberg, "Revolution von oben," pp. 1205–6; W. Schmidt, "Zu einigen Problemen," pp. 9–10, 29ff.; Seeber, "Preussisch-deutscher Bonapartismus," p. 89).

[161]*Grundriss*, pp. 265–66; Engelberg, "Revolution von oben," pp. 1183ff.; Engelberg, "Politische Strategie," vol. 1, pp. 73ff.; Seeber, "Preussisch-deutscher Bonapartismus," p. 89.

liberals as abandoning basic principles, but rather look on their conduct as a logical consequence of their essentially antidemocratic attitude. Concerned with the defense of their class interests, which called for a unified nation-state and an unfettered capitalist social order, most liberals, the argument runs, opposed Bismarck only as long as he did not seem willing or able to fulfill these demands, going over to him when he did fulfill them.[162]

On the basis of this accommodation between bourgeoisie and nobility and with the support of the military, Bismarck established what Marxists, following Engels, describe as a Bonapartist dictatorship. They see it not only as balancing and safeguarding the interests of these three groups, but also as uniting them in a common front against the rising—though still relatively weak—working class (which was, because of its weakness, unable to block such a system). Because the power of the Bonapartist dictatorship was exercised by a military and bureaucratic caste that was recruited largely from the ranks of the Junkers, the bourgeoisie exerted no direct power in this regime. Because the government catered to capitalist concerns, however, this regime is described as an essentially bourgeois dictatorship with some feudal ingredients. If that description is accurate, however, it seems that, by Marxist criteria, the bourgeoisie had come close to achieving what it wished to attain.[163]

The question is raised nowhere, because this analysis of the Bismarck regime, like other such analyses, is tested less against contemporary conditions than against the subsequent course of events. DDR authors maintain that their analysis of the Bismarck regime, with its emphasis on the class content, is the only one to explain correctly Germany's later troubles. Western theories of modernization, which attribute these difficulties to a gap between a modern economy and antiquated political institutions, are found defective because they simplistically blame agrarian-conservative

---

[162]See Engelberg, *Deutschland*, p. 185; Engelberg, "Politische Strategie," vol. 1, pp. 110–11; Fesser, "Zur Struktur," pp. 468–69, 474; Nadja Süssmilch, "Die deutsche Fortschrittspartei im preussisch-österreichischen Krieg 1866," in Bleiber et al. *Bourgeoisie*, pp. 494ff. This thesis has been confirmed by Gugel's well-documented study (*Industrieller Aufstieg*, especially pp. 139–40). See also Sheehan, *German Liberalism*, pp. 123ff.; Sheehan, however, does not explore the socioeconomic implications of the liberal attitude. On the liberals who opposed the Indemnity Bill and, for that matter, the Bismarck regime, see Seeber, "Preussisch-deutscher Bonapartismus," p. 93.

[163]"Bonapartismus," *Swb*, vol. 1, p. 281; Engelberg, "Zur Entstehung und historischen Stellung des preussisch-deutschen Bonapartismus," in Klein and Streisand, *Beiträge*, pp. 236ff.; Engelberg, "Revolution von oben," pp. 1203–4; Seeber, "Preussisch-deutscher Bonapartismus," pp. 88ff. Winkler's argument that Bismarck's regime was not a dictatorship (Winkler, *Revolution, Staat, Faschismus* [Göttingen, 1978], pp. 54–55) would be rejected by Marxist historians on the grounds that a dictatorship is the rule of one class (or a coalition of classes) over other classes with the help of the state ("Diktatur," *Swb*, vol. 1, p. 482)—criteria that the Bismarck regime met by Marxist standards and that it came close to by non-Marxist ones.

groups for blocking Germany's democratization and all but acquit the bourgeoisie. Similarly, West German historians who have borrowed the concept of Bonapartism from DDR historiography are taken to task for perceiving that concept as merely a political technique used by Bismarck, thus once again releasing the bourgeoisie from all responsibility for the establishment of the Bismarck regime. Other West German analyses of Bismarck's regime (government by "negative integration") are similarly dismissed as blurring the role of the bourgeoisie and paving the way for explanations of Nazism that present it as the product of an allegedly precapitalist and preindustrial conservatism rather than of monopolist-capitalist and imperialist schemes.[164]

Even if the Bonapartist dictatorship sought to hold the masses at bay, the masses still turn out to be the ultimate makers of history: all progressive achievements of the period are ultimately attributed to the pressures of the "revolution from below"; as Engelberg puts it, "there can be no *revolution from above* without the threat of a *revolution from below*. As the driving force of revolutions, the popular masses always make themselves felt, even though their power may be only latently present." He and Walter Schmidt content themselves with invoking Marx and Lenin in support of this thesis; Gustav Seeber, however, admits that further studies are needed to determine the dialectical relationship between the revolution from above, and the revolutionary activities of the popular masses and the working class in particular.[165]

In the same vein, the plebiscitary element of Bismarck's Bonapartist regime—universal, direct, and secret male suffrage bestowed on the nation—becomes a token of historical progress. It made possible the utilization of the Reichstag elections in order to publicize the demands of the masses and facilitate their nationwide organization. These opportunities are considered all the more important because the growth of capitalist production also speeded up the growth of the working class. As a result, the main class conflict is shifting further from that between aristocracy and bourgeoisie to that between exploiting capitalists and exploited working class. "In trying to master history," Engelberg observes, "Bismarck was at the same time its servant."[166]

[164]See Seeber, "Preussisch-deutscher Bonapartismus," pp. 82ff. However, on p. 80 he quotes approvingly Wehler's preference for the term *Bonapartist dictatorship* over *chancellor dictatorship* on the grounds that the latter is too "personalist" and, with its focus on the chancellor, conceals the class content of the regime.

[165]W. Schmidt, "Zu einigen Problemen," pp. 13–14, 30, 32–33; Engelberg, "Revolution von oben," p. 1190 (italics in original); Seeber, "Preussisch-deutscher Bonapartismus," pp. 89–90.

[166]See Engelberg, *Deutschland*, pp. 184ff., 198; his quoted statement in "Politische Strategie," vol. 1, p. 83; *GdA*, vol. 1, pp. 239–41; Streisand, pp. 203–4, 206–7.

On the other hand, Bismarck also followed the laws of history when he completed Germany's unification in 1870–1871: he accomplished what was "historically necessary"—the establishment of a powerful unified nation-state in which bourgeois capitalism could fully unfold. That the chancellor baited France into a war with Prussia in order to do so is regarded as immaterial—East German historians have no use for the voluminous West German literature that has explored the problem of Bismarck's "war guilt." They are agreed that the war was at first fought "objectively" in defense of the country's national interest, because it was to prevent France from interfering with German unification. Only when the war was continued after France's defeat at Sedan, when France could no longer block German unity, did it become a war of conquest.[167]

This argument ignores the fact that the anti-Prussian attitude of Bavaria and Wuerttemberg was a more immediate obstacle to unification and that France was trapped into the war against Prussia in order to help arouse the national passions that would sweep away the anti-Prussian, anti-militarist mood of South Germany.[168] Moreover, unification remained an important objective when the war was continued after Sedan, because the union of North German Confederation and South German states was not yet assured at that time. Thus, if Bismarck prolonged the war by his demand for Alsace-Lorraine, which France's new republican government refused to surrender, he did so not merely from territorial ambitions or strategic concerns but also because unification might have been further jeopardized had he abandoned the claim to the two provinces. The south, after all, had been the first to call for the seizure of these provinces as a safeguard against any future French threat. DDR authors reject this argument, however, on the grounds that, as Marx had shown, unity with the north would be a far greater safeguard of south German security than control of Alsace-Lorraine and the Vosges Mountains would be and that their con-

---

However, Engelberg's claim (*Deutschland*, pp. 194–95) that the introduction of the secret ballot attests to the strength of popular pressures is erroneous: the secret ballot was introduced at the insistence of the bourgeois National Liberals, who wanted to forestall any abuses of open voting, especially in the rural areas (see Becker, *Bismarcks Ringen um Deutschlands Gestaltung* [Heidelberg, 1958], p. 437).
[167]Engelberg, *Deutschland*, pp. 227, 233–34; Streisand, pp. 208–9, 211; *GdA*, vol. 1, pp. 291, 295; Vogler and Vetter, *Preussen*, pp. 305–7; *Grundriss*, p. 272.
[168]Erich Eyck, *Bismarck: Leben and Werk* (Erlenbach-Zurich, 1941–1944), vol. 2, pp. 479ff.; Becker, "Zum Problem der Bismarckschen Politik in der spanischen Thronfolge 1870," *HZ* 212 (1971): 591ff.; Holborn, vol. 3, p. 215; Pflanze, *Bismarck*, pp. 437–38; Hamerow, *Social Foundations*, vol. 2, pp. 384ff.; Marx, in *MEW*, vol. 17, p. 3.

quest would merely lead to a new war in which France would seek to recover those provinces.[169]

As part of the revolution from above, the completion of national unification in 1871 again failed to attain many of the goals postulated in the Marxist design. State particularism and aristocratic prerogatives survived in some measure, self-government remained hedged in on all levels by bureaucratic authority, and militarism weighed as an even heavier mortgage on the entire nation. The working class, in particular, continued to suffer from many disabilities and soon was to suffer more. What Bismarck achieved, it is concluded, was the creation of a common nationality within a united state rather than a united nation; national unity in this sense meant that identification with the German state superseded Prussian, Bavarian, and other attachments. Marxists insist that genuine national unity, on the other hand, was predicated on a basic social cohesion that Bismarck's unification did not and could not attain in a class-divided society. Despite these limitations, the founding of the empire did constitute progress in the Marxist view: it completed the transition from feudalism to capitalism, thus opening up new opportunities for capitalistic growth, and it allowed the working class to obtain an agitational basis on a national scale.[170]

The Social Democratic Workers Party

In view of the "historical task" assigned to the workers, their obtaining a national base is considered of special significance. The workers' struggle against their exploiters was entering a new phase just then by Marxist criteria. In 1869, the Social Democratic Workers party (SDAP) was founded, which incorporated some of Marx's tenets into its program. Though hailed as "revolutionary" by DDR authors, the party was revolutionary only in the sense that

[169]Hamerow, Social Foundations, vol. 2, pp. 403–5; Lothar Gall, "Das Problem Elsass-Lothringen," in Schieder et al., Reichsgründung 1870–71, pp. 372ff., as compared to Engelberg, Deutschland, pp. 234–35; Marx, in MEW, vol. 17, p. 273.
[170]See Engelberg, Deutschland, pp. 240, 242–44; Engelberg, "Fragen der Demokratie, des Sozialismus und der Partei in der deutschen Arbeiterbewegung 1868–69," in Bartel and Engelberg, Grosspreussisch, vol. 1, p. 627; Vogler and Vetter, Preussen, pp. 309ff.; Streisand, p. 211; Grundriss, pp. 272–73. The fragmentary character of Bismarck's unification is also recognized by some West German historians (Wolfgang Sauer, "Das Problem des deutschen Nationalstaates," in Wehler, Moderne deutsche Sozialgeschichte, p. 419; Hans-Jürgen Puhle, "Parlament, Parteien und Interessenverbände 1890–1914," in Das kaiserliche Deutschland, ed. Michael Stürmer [Düsseldorf, 1970], p. 363; Steinberg, "Sozialismus," p. 342).

it called for radical social and political changes and did not rule out revolution as an ultimate means of attaining its goals.[171]

Like Lassalle's ADAV, the SDAP called for the establishment of a democratic republic (cautiously described in Lassallean terms as a free people's state), a people's militia, and other traditional democratic reforms. Unlike, the ADAV, however, it embraced the principle of the international solidarity of all proletarians and associated itself with the First International. It also differed from the ADAV in its firm rejection of the Prussian-led North German Confederation (on this point it was at odds with Marx and Engels as well, for the latter had accepted the confederation as a step toward national unity even though they did not approve of the way in which it was brought about). Beyond its immediate goals, the party pledged itself to the abolition of class rule and all private property in the means of production. However, to the dismay of Marx and Engels, who pointedly refused to attend the SDAP's founding congress, the party also adopted such Lassallean demands as the creation of producers' cooperatives with state help, and, like the ADAV, it viewed the democratic republic not as a transition to the dictatorship of the proletariat, but as the appropriate framework of a socialist society.[172]

Nonetheless, in East German assessments the SDAP is regarded as essentially Marxist on the grounds that it was moving in accord with historical necessity and hence was bound to become increasingly Marxist. Moreover, its adoption of some of the tenets of scientific socialism is viewed as proof of the growing confrontation between workers and bourgeoisie. This trend would gather momentum as these two classes became the main antagonists in the class struggle. The new party thus was welcomed as the "highest expression of historical inevitability." [173]

The effort to establish Marx's and Engels' intellectual paternity of the SDAP and to depict it as the heir to the ideological heritage of the League of Communists also has political implica-

[171]Kurt Brandis, *Die deutsche Sozialdemokratie bis zum Fall des Sozialistengesetzes* (Leipzig, 1931), pp. 31ff.; Guenther Roth, *The Social Democrats in Imperial Germany* (Totowa, NJ, 1963), pp. 85ff., 163ff.; Vernon L. Lidtke, *The Outlawed Party: Social Democracy in Germany, 1878–1890* (Princeton, 1966), pp. 30ff.

[172]Engelberg, "Fragen der Demokratie," vol. 1, pp. 654ff.

[173]See *GdA*, vol. 1, pp. 276ff.; Engelberg, *Deutschland*, pp. 212ff.; Leidigkeit, *Liebknecht*, pp. 192ff.; Dlubek and Weber, in *ZfG* 18 (1970): suppl., p. 435; Marx and Engels, in *MEW*, vol. 21, p. 241. To call the party Marxist, as Engelberg (*Deutschland*, p. 229) and Schwab (in Bartel and Engelberg, *Grosspreussisch*, vol. 1, p. 331) do is obviously incorrect. On this point, see Brandis, *Deutsche Sozialdemokratie*, pp. 34ff.; Roth, *Social Democrats*, p. 52; Roger Morgan, *The German Social Democrats and the First International* (Cambridge, 1965), pp. 173–75; Steinberg, *Sozialismus und deutsche Sozialdemokratie* (Hanover, 1967), p. 13ff. *Grundriss* (pp. 271–72) describes the new party as "revolutionary," "proletarian" and formed on a "Marxist basis."

tions. It is intended to help discount the fact that the workers had first tried to become active politically within bourgeois political organizations and had established a party of their own, the ADAV, only because of the exclusionist attitude of the bourgeoisie. Non-Marxists who have pointed this out have concluded that the working class might have been integrated right away into state and society, which would have avoided much social tension, had the bourgeoisie been more responsive to the needs and aspirations of the workers. To Marxists this "theory of integration," which denies the inevitability of class struggles, is not only unscientific but also pernicious because it provides justification for the reformist attitude of the present-day West German Social Democratic party and its "opportunist" collaboration with West Germany's "imperialist" elements. Conversely, the demonstration of the Marxist revolutionary thrust of the Social Democratic Workers party, compared to which the ADAV is disparaged as a sectarian digression, legitimizes East German's Socialist Unity party as the workers' true spokesman.[174]

The Social Democratic Workers party met its first test a year later, during the war against France. Faced with the question of whether to support the war effort, thus endorsing the hated Bismarck regime, or to oppose it, in effect siding with the equally objectionable Napoleon, the party directorate came out in support of the war as one being fought in defense of German national interests. Yet August Bebel and Wilhelm Liebknecht, the party's representatives in the Reichstag, were still firmly opposed to Bismarck and abstained from a vote on the war loan. After Sedan, however, when the party no longer saw any national interests at stake, it opposed the continuation of the war and the annexation of Alsace-Lorraine. Faithful to the party's internationalist attitude, its leaders proclaimed their solidarity with the French people. In this, the leadership also followed the counsel of Marx, who warned with remarkable foresight that the annexation of Alsace-Lorraine not only would preclude a reconciliation of Frenchmen and Germans but also would strengthen the hands of the military in preparation for another war to which annexation would lead but in which France would be allied with Russia.[175]

[174]A representative non-Marxist analysis of labor's secession can be found in Ernst Schraepler, "Linksliberalismus und Arbeiterschaft in der preussischen Konflikts-zeit," in Forschungen zu Staat und Verfassung: Festgabe für Fritz Hartung, ed. Richard Dietrich and Gerhard Oestreich (Berlin [West], 1958), pp. 358ff.; also Conze and Dieter Groh, Die Arbeiterbewegung in der nationalen Bewegung (Stuttgart, 1966); Pflanze, Bismarck, pp. 12, 323–25. Opportunism is defined by Sachwörterbuch as the "political-ideological commitment of parts of the working class to the capitalist system," Swb, vol. 2, p. 223.

[175]Engelberg, Deutschland, pp. 234–35; Marx, in MEW, vol. 17, p. 273.

As a result of their antiwar stance, most of the Socialist leaders, including Bebel and Liebknecht, were in prison on charges of high treason when the empire was proclaimed in January 1871. Under the circumstances, DDR authors find it fitting that the proclamation ceremony was attended only by princes, courtiers, and military: the exclusion of the "real" German people attested to the antidemocratic character of the unification process. It bore out the thesis that the German nation, unlike the German state, had not yet been unified.[176]

The socialists' self-restrained stance toward Alsace-Lorraine was to prove more realistic in determining what constituted the true national interest than were the ambitions of government and upper and middle classes. Similarly, East German historians point to the party's antiannexationist position as being the only one in accord with the concept of the nation as a community held together, in the "bourgeois" view as well, by a conscious communality—something the two French-tending provinces lacked.[177]

Assessing the *Reichsgründung*, Engelberg dismisses as misleading contemporary cartoons that depicted Bismarck, the gigantic Iron Chancellor, towering over Bebel, the frail powerless man of the people. "Considering the actual historical situation, this was not unjustified," he grants; as he adds, however, the dialectical approach tells a different story: "The appearances of historical life, especially their shortcomings, are fully determined and understood only if they are also viewed through their negation." From that perspective, Engelberg concludes, Bebel emerges as the wiser of the two men and the one who was oriented toward the future.[178]

---

[176]See Engelberg, *Deutschland*, p. 241; Vogler and Vetter, *Preussen*, p. 309; Schleier, in Bartel and Engelberg, *Grosspreussisch*, vol. 2, p. 553. That in fact only a minority of the nation approved of the establishment of the empire or of the manner in which it was founded was also demonstrated by the Reichstag elections of March 1871: only 46.1 percent of the vote went to the parties supporting the unification without reservation (Hamerow, *Social Foundations*, vol. 2, pp. 424–26).

[177]See, on the other hand, the difficulties this fact poses for West German historians. Gall ("Das Problem Elsass-Lothringen," pp. 372, 373ff.) can only argue that any other state, too, would have called for annexations under the circumstances.

[178]Engelberg, *Deutschland*, pp. 249–50.

6

From Competitive to Monopoly Capitalism

The Empire

Bismarck, Junkers, and Bourgeoisie

I N THE MARXIST VIEW, the foundation of the empire—that is, the creation of the united nation-state, brought to an end the transition from feudalism to capitalism. Yet, although it is emphasized that the new state, because of its size and strength, provided new opportunities for capitalistic expansion, as an institution the *Kaiserreich* receives relatively little attention in the East German accounts. Constitutional problems, the relationship between the Reich and its member states, the roles of emperor, chancellor, federal council, and Reichstag, which are of major concern to non-Marxist scholars, hold little interest for those who view the state as an instrument of the ruling classes. DDR historians find it more useful to focus their research on the activities of those ruling classes—bourgeoisie and nobility—and their rising new challenger, the working class.[1]

The point of departure for the East German analyses is the fact that the *Reichsgründung* achieved German unity only in a territorial and organizational sense; it failed to attain the political and social cohesion that could have generated true national unity. On this point many West German historians now agree with their East German counterparts. Their views differ, however, on the means by which this deficiency might have been remedied. Non-Marxists see the major cause of this weakness in the empire's failure to integrate the working class into the public life of the nation and in the lack of an effective parliamentary sytem that could have translated social needs into social policy. Marxists, for their part, attribute the inadequacies of the Reich to the inherent flaws of the exploitative, class-divided capitalist system, which neither social integration nor any parliament could have remedied, because both of these proposals were but euphemisms for subjecting the workers to bourgeois rule.

[1]Seeber, "Preussisch-deutscher Bonapartismus," pp. 75–76, 81.

Marxist historians are all the more certain that the bourgeois-capitalist order could not effect decisive social improvements because its "progressive" phase was approaching its end. If non-Marxists view the Imperial period as an era of economic and technical triumphs, Marxists insist that behind this facade of prosperity the capitalist system began to decline, throwing its main beneficiary, the bourgeoisie, on the defensive. As they see it, after 1871, German capitalism deteriorated from its progressive competitive form to the restrictive phase of monopoly capitalism, in which the growing concentration of capital led to the replacement of a multitude of separate enterprises by a few large-scale concerns or other types of market-controlling organizations. Although production kept expanding as the result of continued technological progress, profits went to a relatively small number of beneficiaries. These beneficiaries, in turn, were confronted with a growing proletariat that was more exploited than ever before because of the overwhelming power of the monopolist enterprises. With class contradictions deepening, the way was being prepared for the collapse of the capitalist order and the demise of the bourgeoisie. Anticipating this outcome, however remote, Kuczynski, following Lenin, speaks of the "dying German capitalism" in regard to that period.[2]

From this perspective, the rising of the Paris Commune did not constitute an isolated event, but formed part of those worldwide "class battles" that grew out of the increasing tension between bourgeoisie and proletariat. In addition, because, in the Marxist view, the historical role of the *Reichsgründung* is determined by its place in the struggle between these two classes, the relationship of the new empire to the Paris Commune assumes a special significance. In fact, that relationship is considered a constituent element of the new state: the fear that the working-class rising in Paris aroused among Germany's upper classes facilitated the preservation, by means of a Bonapartist dictatorship, of the backward social and political structure of the new Reich as a bulwark against the "forces of revolution."[3]

This fear, it is noted, also allowed the Prusso-German nobility to retain its preeminent political position. It explains why court, army, and bureaucracy, those strongholds of the nobility, became mainstays of Bismarck's Bonapartist regime even though the bourgeoisie occupied the center of economic power. There is general

---

[2]Streisand, p. 212. Engelberg, *Deutschland*, pp. 12, 29ff., 49; *GdA*, vol. 1, pp. 306, 316–17; Kuczynski, *Geschichte*, vol. 3, p. 6.

[3]See Bartel, "Zur historischen Stellung der Reichsgründung von 1871," in *Die grosspreussisch-militaristische Reichsgründung 1871*, ed. Bartel and Engelberg (Berlin [East], 1971), vol. 2, pp. 4, 9ff.; *GdA*, vol. 1, p. 315; Seeber, in *ZfG* 18 (1970): suppl., p. 468. See also, on the non-Marxist side, Steinberg, "Sozialismus," p. 320; Conze and Groh, *Arbeiterbewegung*, pp. 106ff.

agreement among East German authors that if the bourgeoisie did not have the political strength to which it was preordained by its role in the capitalist system, this was the result not of any bourgeois awe of the nobility and a concomitant social feudalization of the bourgeoisie, as Western historians have claimed, but of the bourgeoisie's antidemocratism and its unwillingness to press for its rights with the help of the masses. In fact, DDR authors object to the very concept of the bourgeoisie's feudalization on the grounds that it accentuates a surface phenomenon and ignores the essential basis of the Junker-bourgeois rapprochement—the two classes' common hostility toward the working class. It is stressed that the bourgeoisie, propelled by its expanding economic power, was in the ascendance, while the Junkers, hemmed in in East Elbian Prussia, Mecklenburg, and parts of Saxony and dependent on the bourgeoisie's capital, were clearly on the defensive. In fact, rather than feudalizing the bourgeoisie, the Junkers were adopting bourgeois traits as a result of their transformation into capitalists. Of a West German author's claims that "throne and altar, barracks and manor house were the foundations of political rule in the German Empire," Gustav Seeber argues that this was true only in a technical sense.[4]

Thus, although government, nobility, and military have traditionally been considered the forces dominating the German Empire in its early years, with the bourgeoisie trying not very successfully to change conditions, DDR authors consider the bourgeoisie even at that time a determining factor in the fate of the empire. The bourgeoisie's impact is traced to its very inaction; its responsibility is seen in its abdication of its leadership function in the capitalist order. What is held against it specifically is its willingness to leave the conduct of foreign affairs wholly to Bismarck and its tolerance of reactionary domestic conditions in return for economic concessions (whose "progressive character" is, however, acknowledged). Paralyzed by its fear of the masses, the argument runs, the bourgeoisie shied away from all confrontations with monarch and government lest such conflicts weaken the authoritarian-militarist regime and lead to what was thought of as mob rule and anarchy. Because of this "self-emasculation," bourgeois circles would not make use of their economic superiority to obtain political conces-

[4]See Walter Steglich, "Beitrag zur Problematik des Bündnisses zwischen Junkern und Bourgeoisie . . . 1870–1880," WZ Berlin 9 (1959–1960): 324ff., 336; Engelberg, Deutschland, pp. 12, 18; GdA, vol. 1, pp. 319–20; Seeber, "Die Bourgeoisie und das Reich," in Bartel and Engelberg, Grosspreussisch, vol. 2, pp. 166–68; Wolfgang Schröder, "Junkertum und preussisch-deutsches Reich," ibid., vol. 2., pp. 170ff.; Seeber and Heinz Wolter, "[Zum] bürgerlichen Geschichtsbild der BRD über . . . 1871," ZfG 20 (1972): 1088; Seeber, "Preussisch-deutscher Bonapartismus," pp. 81–82. Seeber quotes the West German historian Michael Stürmer. On the non-Marxist viewpoint, see Helmut Böhme, Deutschlands Weg zur Grossmacht (Cologne, 1966), pp. 580–82; Holborn, vol. 3, p. 389.

sions from government and nobility. Similarly, the bourgeoisie failed to take advantage of its strong representation in both the Reichstag and the Prussian House of Delegates to curb the power of Junkers and military. In the bourgeois view, this power was needed to control the workers—a strategy that is found to be similar to that used by the bourgeoisie in the Weimar Republic when it fostered the army and Nazis as instruments of repression against the workers' ascendance. Any attempt, then, to deny the bourgeoisie's key role in the empire is condemned as an attempt to efface its historical responsibility.[5]

Further support for this view is found in the outcome of the *Kulturkampf*, Bismarck's confrontation with the Catholic Church. DDR authors appreciate the concern of the liberals who judged the Catholic position a threat to the newly united German state. They also point out that Catholic federalist inclinations posed threats to the progress of capitalism. So, they maintain, did Church declarations against the materialist spirit of the capitalist order. They also find, however, that liberal support of Bismarck's repressive and discriminatory strategy violated basic liberal principles. The liberals, these critics point out, neither called for the separation of state and church (which would have weakened the monarchy) nor considered the enactment of civil liberties (which would have aided the masses); yet, such measures would have more effectively curbed the spiritual authority and political influence of the Catholic Church than did the punitive legislation to which Bismarck resorted. Even worse, liberal approval of such tactics weakened the liberals' own oppositional stand on later occasions. In the end, it is noted, the Kulturkampf was settled on terms that reconciled both clerical and capitalist concerns (anti-Socialist legislation, protective tariffs) but also reinforced the predominance of the state and curbed the competitive structure of capitalism.[6]

Viewed as a collision between capitalist unitary and anticapitalist-particularist elements, the Kulturkampf, to East German authors, is overshadowed by the confrontation between liberal-capitalist and antiliberal-restrictive forces touched off by the panic of

[5]See *Grundriss*, p. 288; Seeber, "Bourgeoisie," pp. 82–83, 100, 135ff., 158–59, 166ff.; Schröder, "Junkertum," pp. 208 nn. 128–29, 210–11, 288. The same criticisms have been voiced by some non-Marxist historians, too, in recent years; see in particular Sheehan (*German Liberalism*, pp. 131ff., 145ff.), who, however, discusses these issues almost entirely as ideological ones, with little reference to their social moorings.

[6]See "Kulturkampf," *Swb*, vol. 1, pp. 1052–53; Engelberg, *Deutschland*, pp. 66, 70–71; *Grundriss*, pp. 287–88; Seeber, *Zwischen Bebel und Bismarck* (Berlin [East], 1965), pp. 4–5, 12, 47; Seeber, "Bourgeoisie," pp. 159–60. That the liberal position in the Kulturkampf was self-defeating has also been seen by some non-Marxist scholars (Eyck, *Bismarck*, vol. 3, pp. 92–93; Sheehan, *German Liberalism*, pp. 135–37).

1873, a product of fraudulent stock-market manipulations, poor business management, and overproduction. What Marxists consider of special significance here is the elimination, as a result of the ensuing depression, of a substantial number of small enterprises and a corresponding concentration of industrial production, especially in the mining and steel industries, and in banking. At the same time, the Prussian state expanded the state-controlled sector of the economy by taking over the railroads within its jurisdiction. Like the Kulturkampf, DDR authors note, the economic crisis ended with a weakening of the liberal forces, the strengthening of the authoritarian government, and the acceleration of the trend toward monopoly capitalism at the expense of capitalism's competitive features.[7]

The picture of the liberals' timidity is rounded out by studies of their failure to subject the army to parliamentary checks. Rather than insist on effective controls when that issue had to be settled in the new state, they allowed the size and budget of the armed forces to be fixed for a seven-year period, which rendered future retrenchment all but impossible. The price seemed worth paying, DDR critics note, because the army was regarded not only as a shield against foreign threats but also as a protecting force against domestic upheavals. Above all, it was regarded as a school of the nation in which the lower classes were taught patriotism, discipline, and obedience. In aligning themselves with the antidemocratic forces, the liberals thus were accelerating the social and spiritual militarization of the country, placing the main burden of the antimilitarist struggle on the working class. Efforts of the left-liberal Progressives to fight the predominance of the military are not ignored but are dismissed as too half-hearted to be effective. DDR historians insist, moreover, that such endeavors were also foredoomed, because the antidemocratic stance of the Progressives precluded any mass action or other joint moves with the Socialists.[8]

[7]See Mottek et al., *Studien zur Geschichte der industriellen Revolution in Deutschland* (Berlin [East], 1960), pp. 61–62; Elisabeth Giersiepen, in *ZfG* 8 (1960): suppl., p. 237–38; Engelberg, *Deutschland*, pp. 54ff. The term "monopoly capitalism" should, of course, be taken with a grain of salt. As Maurice Dobb, the English Marxist economist, writes, "Although the original meaning of the word monopoly is sole seller of something, monopoly has come to mean in economic writing the power of appreciably influencing the supply and hence the price of a commodity. This is of course a matter of degree and need not be absolute to be economically important." See his *Capitalism Yesterday and Today* (New York, 1962), p. 44; see also "Monopol," *Swb*, vol. 2, pp. 106–7, which speaks of an economic and political power position "on the basis of a high degree of production and capital."

[8]See Engelberg, *Deutschland*, pp. 79ff; Streisand, pp. 216–17; Seeber, "Bourgeoisie," pp. 164ff; Seeber, *Zwischen Bebel*, pp. 15–16. For non-Marxist analyses, see Eyck, *Bismarck*, vol. 3, pp. 65ff; Stürmer, "Konservatismus und Revolution in Bismarcks Politik," in Michael Stürmer, *Das kaiserliche Deutschland: Politik und Gesellschaft 1870–1918* (Düsseldorf, 1970), p. 150.

The bourgeois attitude toward foreign political issues is found to reflect the same antidemocratic spirit. Confined by its class compromise with the Junkers, the argument runs, the bourgeoisie neither could nor would develop its own foreign policy, but rather submitted to Bismarck. If earlier, the bourgeoisie had been strongly opposed to the reactionary Tsarist regime, after 1871 it approved of the chancellor's collaboration with Russia (and Austria). A rapprochement with Russia was clearly needed, Gustav Seeber grants, in order to keep Russia from allying itself with revenge-bent France, but as Seeber points out, that rapprochement was also hailed by the bourgeois press as a check on the Polish and other national movements and on the international labor movement. To Marxists this strategy had direct domestic implications, for in their eyes, repression of freedom abroad was a function of repressive measures at home, and foreign repression should be fought as determinedly as that at home. All this shows, Seeber notes, that domestic politics was not dominated by an alleged primacy of foreign policy, as had long been claimed—a conclusion with which increasing numbers of West German historians, too, have recently come to agree.[9]

Bismarck's own foreign political stance is evaluated in the same terms. To be sure, non-Marxists have also seen the domestic facets of the chancellor's diplomacy. To them, however, his collaboration with the Tsarist and Habsburg regimes, apart from isolating France, was merely a none-too-successful device to protect the old monarchical governments against all internal challenges.[10] East German historians do not quarrel with this assessment, but they find that the endeavor to present the new German Empire as a bulwark against the forces of revolution achieved more than a fictitious sense of community among the three monarchies. It lent credence to Bismarck's professions of Germany's territorial saturation and eased Russian and Austrian apprehensions concerning German expansionist aspirations. Nor was this policy without effect on Western Europe. It facilitated peace negotiations with France in 1871 and relieved existing tensions with Britain. There is considerable evidence to support Heinz Wolter's conclusion that

[9]See Seeber, "Bourgeoisie," pp. 148–50; Engelberg, in Bartel and Engelberg, *Grosspreussisch*, vol. 1, p. 106. West German repudiations of the alleged primacy of foreign policy can be found most conveniently in the essays of Böhme, "Politik und Ökonomie in der . . . Bismarckzeit," and Wehler, "Bismarcks Imperialismus und . . . Russlandpolitik," in Stürmer, *Das kaiserliche Deutschland*, pp. 26ff., 235ff. See also Böhme's *Deutschlands Weg zur Grossmacht*; Wehler's *Bismarck und der Imperialismus* (Cologne, 1969); and among earlier challenges, Eckart Kehr, *Der Primat der Innenpolitik* (Berlin [West], 1965).

[10]See Eyck, *Bismarck*, vol. 3, pp. 31–33; Holborn, vol. 3, pp. 236–37; Gustav Adolf Rein, *Die Revolution in der Politik Bismarcks* (Göttingen, 1957), pp. 178ff. Rosenberg (*Grosse Depression und Bismarckzeit* [Berlin (West), 1967], pp. 260ff.) is one non-Marxist scholar who sees the full significance of Bismarck's diplomacy.

Bismarck's concept of the new German state as an antirevolutionary factor of stabilization helped to determine the constellation of
political power in the 1870s and to consolidate the international
standing of the new Reich.[11]

Some new findings also emerge from the East German analyses as they explore Bismarck's diplomacy as an instrument of domestic policy. They note that his unchallenged control of foreign
policy enabled him to reinforce his Bonapartist regime by assigning
to foreign economic and trade relations a strictly subordinate role
in his scale of diplomatic priorities, thus setting some limits to
bourgeois-capitalist expansionism. Similarly, with foreign affairs
his uncontested preserve, the chancellor enjoyed considerable leverage in military matters as well. His insistence that the success of
his foreign policy depended on a strong army, exempt from the
vagaries of parliamentary control, helped him fend off the demands
of the liberals for annual military budgets.[12]

All this adds up to a rather negative verdict on Bismarck's
foreign policy. Not only was it meant to isolate and repress the
working class and any other democratic forces, it also sought to
hamper the bourgeoisie and strengthen the Junker and militarist
elements of the chancellor's Bonapartist regime. Whereas traditionally a distinction is made between Bismarck's imaginative foreign
policy and his domestic parochialism, East German historians find
his domestic policy, thanks to its economic reforms, a bit more
progressive than his diplomacy. Both policies were essentially reactionary, however, for which they blame the bourgeoisie more than
the Junkers or the chancellor; the chancellor, they note, could act
only within the existing class context.[13]

The Social Democratic Movement

Non-Marxist accounts of the Bismarck era see the nation as politically divided, the conservative Bismarck camp being separated
from the liberals and the Social Democrats being relegated to a
peripheral role. Marxist historians, however, find conservative

[11]See Engelberg, *Deutschland*, pp. 89ff.; Wolter, "Die Anfänge des Dreikaiserver-
hältnisses," in Bartel and Engelberg, *Grosspreussisch*, vol. 2, pp. 235ff.; Walter
Wittwer, "Zur Politik des preussisch-deutschen Staates gegen die revolutionäre
Arbeiterbewegung . . . 1871–1878," in ibid., vol. 2, pp. 318ff. On the concept of
the Bismarck Empire as a bulwark of order, see also the essay by the West German scholar Eberhard Kolb, "Der Pariser Kommune-Aufstand und die Beendigung
des deutschfranzösischen Krieges," *HZ* 215 (1972): 292ff.
[12]Wolter, "Zum Verhältnis von Aussenpolitik und Bismarckschem Bonapartismus," *JfG* 16 (1977): 129ff.; Seeber, "Bourgeoisie," p. 166.
[13]Wolter, "Zum Verhältnis," pp. 135–37.

Junker agrarians and liberal bourgeois sharing so many basic concerns that the differences that set them apart from each other are regarded as minor compared to the issues that separated both from the workers. In the Marxist view, the deep division that split Imperial Germany was that between the Bismarck-Junker-bourgeois camp and the working class; the history of the empire is written in these terms by East German authors.

The bourgeoisie is assigned to the conservative camp by DDR analysts, because of its failure to fulfill its "class mandate" to establish a bourgeois regime. The working class, on the other hand, is credited with living up to its historical mission. In lieu of the bourgeoisie, Bartel and Seeber note, the revolutionary German labor movement, impelled by its class needs, became the standard-bearer of bourgeois democracy, the next goal to be attained in the nation's development. The Social Democratic Workers party (SDAP), the labor movement's only legitimate spokesman, is praised as an uncompromising protagonist of democracy; as such it alone presented a consistent alternative program that met the true needs of the nation. A heightened class consciousness on the part of the workers, which DDR authors attribute to worsening living and working conditions, gave added impetus to this struggle. It manifested itself most directly in the growing numbers of strikes, many involving thousands of workers; in recurrent mass protests against rising prices and rents; and in organized demands for reduced working hours and higher wages.[14]

On the whole, the attempt to connect such increased activities with the growing impact of Marxist ideas and the agitational work of the SDAP is pursued with proper caution. DDR researchers are aware that the party was not "Marxist"; in Engelberg's words, it merely "absorbed, piece by piece, as it were, segments of scientific socialism, in accordance with its practical fighting needs and experiences." Similarly, Engelberg grants that this was an "extraordinarily complex" process, but he also points out: "In this endeavor the SDAP could count on the steady assistance of Marx and Engels, just as, conversely, the German revolutionary workers' party provided important support for the propagation and defense of Marxism in the First International." Yet, the receptivity of Bebel and Liebknecht to Marx's advice had its limits. Engelberg attributes difficulties to the fact that the "leading forces of the SDAP [were] still far from having a firm grasp of scientific socialism." He was right, of course,

---

[14]See Engelberg, *Deutschland*, pp. 108ff.; *GdA*, vol. 1, pp. 324, 326ff.; Kuczynski, *Geschichte*, vol. 3, pp. 39ff.; Bartel and Seeber, "Pariser Kommune, Reichsgründung und revolutionäres Proletariat," in Bartel and Engelmann, *Grosspreussisch*, vol. 2, pp. 25, 66ff. Of non-Marxists, Barraclough sees the working class as the only force striving consistently for democracy (*Origins*, pp. 426, 429; also Wehler, *Das Deutsche Kaiserreich: 1871–1918* [Göttingen, 1973], p. 87).

but the fact was also that the German leaders, pursued by repressive governments, found the counsel of Marx and Engels rather unrealistic at times.[15]

The attitude of German leaders was also affected by their realization that a merger with the Lassallean General Workers Union (ADAV) became a possibility after 1871. A major divisive issue—whether Germany ought to be unified by Prussia (acceptable to the ADAV but not to the SDAP)—had been settled meanwhile by events; government persecution, deepening social inequities, and a growing activism on the part of both groups were drawing them closer together. In 1875, they merged into the Socialist Workers Party of Germany (SAPD).

The program of the new party contained Lassallean, Marxist, and traditional democratic features. Because of this "unscientific" approach, it aroused the sharp opposition of Marx and Engels. Both men expressed their objections—Marx in his *Critique of the Gotha Program* and Engels in a letter to Bebel. Although these statements had no immediate effect on the program of the new party (lest they endanger the merger, they were not made public), they are discussed at some length in the East German literature. DDR authors find the critiques important not only as "classic" analyses of basic tenets but also as perceptive warnings against illusions that are thought to have laid the foundation for later "revisionist" tendencies.

In this context, East German historians object to the program's goal of a "free people's state" (a censor-proof circumlocution for a democratic republic that had already been adopted in the SDAP program of 1869 and that was derived from Lassalle), calling it misleading. As Marx warned in his *Critique*, this formula encouraged the belief that the transformation of the existing authoritarian state into a parliamentary democratic republic would assure the socialization of all means of production. Here, form and substance were being confused, because a formally democratic republic could have a "capitalist" as well as a socialist class content. Only a socialist democratic republic that was predicated on the seizure of power by the proletariat could effect the transition from a capitalist to a socialist society.

The danger that the program fostered "opportunist" illusions seemed all the more serious because the program also called for producers' cooperatives financed by the state. This again, it is

[15]Engelberg, *Deutschland*, pp. 112ff., 123, 136; *GdA*, vol. 1, pp. 329–30; as compared to the contrived argumentation of Bartel, "Um die Durchsetzung des Marxismus in der deutschen Arbeiterbewegung," *BzG* 6 (1964): 863ff.; but see also Bebel, *Aus meinem Leben* (Berlin [East], 1961), pp. 520ff., especially p. 524, and the non-Marxist accounts of Morgan, *The German Social Democrats and the First International: 1864–1872* (Cambridge, 1965), pp. 224ff.; Lidtke, *The Outlawed Party: Social Democracy in Germany 1878–1890* (Princeton, 1966), pp. 29ff., 43ff.

stressed, was a Lassallean inheritance that, had it been implemented, would have perpetuated the workers' financial dependence upon the government and thus would have kept them subject to that government.

Another weakness of the program, DDR critics note, was that it dismissed all those who were not part of the urban proletariat as "one reactionary mass." In doing so, as Marx and Engels already had noted, the Social Democrats deprived themselves of potential allies, especially among rural workers. Engels, in fact, tried repeatedly to arouse the Socialists to the need for an alliance with agricultural laborers, but efforts in that direction remained halfhearted, partly for ideological reasons but mainly because of the apparent hopelessness of making converts in rural areas.[16]

Ultimately, the flaws in the program are attributed to a lack of theoretical training on the part of its drafters. The East German critics are aware of the predicament of the Socialist leaders, hounded by a powerful state. They also acknowledge the stability of conditions and grant that no revolution was possible during this "relatively peaceful period of capitalism." Their complaint is that too little was done to provide the party with a proper sense of direction, impress on it the need for an eventual revolution, squelch any illusions concerning the spontaneous outbreak of such a revolution, and move gradually toward the active preparation of that ultimate upheaval. Such guidance was all the more necessary, it is argued, because the main class struggle was now being fought between workers and capitalists; as the workers' only authentic spokesman, the SAPD assumed a role of increasing importance on the social and political stage.[17]

Subsequent developments are discussed in terms of this shift of fronts in the class struggle. Thus, the series of policy changes that Bismarck introduced in 1878–1879 are seen as efforts aimed primarily at subduing the growing strength of the Socialist party and the workers' movement. Whereas non-Marxists believe that the Socialist Law of 1878, which all but outlawed the SAPD, was as much a maneuver designed to disorient the liberals and pave the way for a protectionist tariff policy as it was a means of repressing the Socialists,[18] DDR authors consider the law as simply part of a

---

[16]*GdA*, vol. 1, pp. 334ff., 346–47, 379–80, 17*–18*, (quotation on p. 338; italics in original); Engelberg, *Deutschland*, pp. 138ff.; Marx and Engels, in MEW, vol. 19, pp. 3ff. 15ff.; Hans Hübner, in Bartmuss et al., *Volksmassen*, pp. 217–18; Erich Kundel, "Der Weg der Arbeiterklasse zur politischen Macht," *ZfG* 10 (1962): suppl., p. 273ff.

[17]*GdA*, vol. 1, pp. 306, 324–25; Engelberg, *Deutschland*, pp. 32–33, 124, 149–50; also Lidtke, *Outlawed Party*, pp. 32, 46–48.

[18]See Eyck, *Bismarck*, vol. 3, pp. 222ff.; Böhme, *Deutschlands*, pp. 489–90, 499ff.; Stürmer, "Konservatismus," pp. 150ff.; Rosenberg, *Grosse Depression*, pp. 205ff.

strategy of open repression by which the ruling classes sought to protect themselves against the rise of the working class. (The recourse to force is regarded as evidence of Bismarck's helplessness, and there are hints in at least one account that the attempts on the life of Emperor William I, which provided the occasion for the enactment of the Socialist Law, may have been staged by the government.[19])

Supplementing this strategy, it is further explained, the class compromise between Junkers and bourgeoisie was transformed into a class alliance between heavy industrialists and agrarians. *Grundriss* adds, in an astonishing misjudgment of the actual situation, that it was the "chaining" of the working class by the Socialist Law that enabled big industrialists and large estate-owners to secure industrial and agricultural tariffs, raise domestic prices, and engage in an aggressive export policy. The Socialist Law and tariffs thus led to increased exploitation, monopolist concentrations, and more armaments to deal with the tensions provoked by the intensified export campaigns. *Grundriss* concludes: "Protective tariffs, forced expansion of militarism, and Socialist Law were all interconnected." Such interconnection is also recognized by non-Marxist historians, but the latter, as noted before, see the connecting link as having an antiliberal rather than an antisocialist thrust.[20]

Marxists also part ways with non-Marxists in their evaluation of the social insurance program that Bismarck initiated during the 1880s. What non-Marxists welcome as a constructive step, Marxists dismiss as a move to bribe workers into accepting their exploitation. In the same vein, Western scholars' approval of the reforms

---

That Bismarck himself did not consider the SAPD as grave and immediate a threat as he claimed has been shown on the basis of many of his statements (Rein, *Revolution*, pp. 289–90). See also Bismarck's statements quoted in *GdA*, vol. 1, p. 370, and by Stürmer, "Konservatismus," p. 150; also the incident reported by Eyck, *Bismarck*, vol. 3, p. 228.

[19]See *Grundriss*, pp. 292-93; Streisand, pp. 219–21; "Sozialistengesetz," *Swb*, vol. 2, p. 519; Kuczynski, *Geschichte*, vol. 3, pp. 47ff.; Seeber, "Bonapartismus," pp. 104ff. On the other hand, Engelberg (*Deutschland*, pp. 151 ff.) presents a surprisingly traditional account, centered on Bismarck's personal ambitions and political needs. *Grundriss'* claim of the key role of the working class is supported by Lothar Rathmann, "Bismarck und der Übergang Deutschlands zur Schutzzollpolitik," *ZfG* 4 (1956): 899ff., especially 924–26, 943–44; Rothmann claims that the "revolutionary workers' movement" was the "most dangerous enemy" in the eyes of the protectionists. Actually the Socialists had no clearcut position on tariffs, and their few votes were repeatedly cast in opposing ways (Franz Mehring, *Geschichte der Deutschen Sozialdemokratie* [Stuttgart, 1913], vol. 4, pp. 116–17; letter from Bebel to Engels, Oct. 23, 1879 [Bebel, *Aus meinem Leben*, p. 660]).

[20]Ibid. Also see Engelberg, *Deutschland*, pp. 183–84; Streisand, p. 223; *GdA*, vol. 1, pp. 369–70. On the non-Marxist position, see Eyck, *Bismarck*, vol. 3, pp. 222ff.; Böhme, *Deutschlands*, pp. 489–90, 499ff.; Sheehan, *German Liberalism*, pp. 181ff. On the interrelationships of antisocialist and tariff policies, see also the perceptive observations of Rosenberg, *Grosse Depression*, pp. 206 with 187.

is assailed as another instance of the pernicious "theory of integration" by which the working class is to be subjected forever to bourgeois rule.[21]

On the ideological plane, DDR analysis of the period has probed the impact of the Socialist Law and social reforms on the progress of Marxism.[22] The impact of social reforms, in particular, has received increasing attention in recent years, in accordance with SED directives that have stressed the need for studies of the theory and inevitability of the historical process.[23] As a result, there has been a marked shift of emphasis. Earlier studies approached the years of persecution as the "heroic epoch" of German Social Democracy and focused on the organizational and oppositional activities of the party, its defiance of courts and police, and the hardships its members endured.[24] More recent accounts still pay tribute to the resourcefulness of the party's underground work and the fortitude of the masses, but the rank and file's main contribution to the struggle is now seen as its ability to perceive, more clearly than most of the leaders, the correct "revolutionary" path to be followed. (That this "revolutionism" may have been an emotional reaction to the repression of the Socialist Law rather than a thought-out, principled position is nowhere considered, however.[25])

Indeed, in varying degrees, the leaders all are found wanting. Although the workers could force the leaders to assume a more militant stand on specific occasions, only the leaders, as the critics point out, could provide the theoretical underpinning for a consistent, purposeful policy. Such a policy had to be predicated on the irreconcilable conflict between the aims of the working class and those of Bismarck's regime, which was supported by the Junkers, the bourgeoisie, and the army; the ultimate solution to this conflict would be the establishment of the dictatorship of the proletariat. There were, to be sure, a few leaders who were guided by Marxist principles, who insisted on a sharp demarcation of the party from all bourgeois parties, and who considered revolution a necessary and rapidly approaching objective, but throughout this period the Marxist segment was hampered by deviationist elements. A small "anarchist" wing that opposed all parliamentary activity and urged resort to violent action could quickly be dealt with by the expulsion of its leaders from the SADP. An "opportun-

[21]Engelberg, *Deutschland*, pp. 192ff.; Streisand, p. 223; *Grundriss*, p. 294; Mottek et al., *Studien zur Geschichte*, vol. 3, p. 109.

[22]Seeber, in *ZfG* 18 (1970): suppl., pp. 455–56.

[23]Bartel et al., in ibid., p. 22.

[24]On this, see Lidtke, *Outlawed Party*, pp. 358ff.

[25]On the "revolutionary" attitude of the rank and file, see Steinberg, *Sozialismus*, pp. 30–31; Horst Lademacher, "Sozialdemokratie," *SDG*, vol. 5, p. 931; both of these authors stress the emotional nature of that revolutionism.

ist" faction, on the other hand, caused continuous difficulties. This faction considered revolution a distant goal, if a goal at all, and sought to take full advantage of the existing parliamentary opportunities in order to improve the lot of the workers. Unmindful of the consequences of their strategy, it is charged, the opportunists were splitting the workers' movement and, according to the *Sachwörterbuch*, were committing parts of the working class to the capitalist system politically and ideologically." The "Marxists" emerged victorious at all party congresses and secured resolutions supporting their more militant stance, but the "opportunists" were in the majority in the Reichstag delegation, which was the acting directorate of the party in the era of the Socialist Law, and they did not feel bound by such resolutions.[26] Thus, they reacted more positively than the radicals to Bismarck's social reforms. On another occasion, anxious to secure jobs for unemployed shipyard workers, the "opportunists" urged support of a bill proposing state subsidies to overseas steamship lines, provided the lines did not service any German colonial ports. (This conscience-salving proviso was to protect them against the charge of having furthered Bismarck's colonial policies.) In the end, however, they voted against the bill, because it did not exclude shipping lines sailing to German colonies.[27]

While stressing the errant ways of the "opportunists," East German accounts gloss over the fact that the "Marxists," too, had their "opportunist" moments. No accounts mention that the "Marxists," with Engels' approval, supported the building of the Kiel Canal, connecting the Baltic and North seas, as an employment-providing project, despite its freely avowed military connotations. Socialist cooperation with the left-liberal *Freisinnige Partei* against a renewal of the seven-year army budget in 1886–1887 also remains unmentioned. Such collaboration per se was, of course, no violation of Marxist tenets, but it assumed a different character when the Social Democrats decided not to dissociate themselves from the Freisinnig delegation when the latter proposed a three-year budget without insisting on basic military reforms and when

---

[26]Ibid., pp. 129ff. The above is a somewhat simplified summary. Actually there existed factions also within the two factions. For a perceptive analysis of the moderates' background and motivations see Heinrich Gemkow, *Friedrich Engels' Hilfe beim Sieg der deutschen Sozialdemokratie über das Sozialistengesetz* (Berlin [East], 1957), pp. 68–69; Seeber, "Wahlkämpfe, Parlamentsarbeit und revolutionäre Politik," in *Marxismus und deutsche Arbeiterbewegung*, ed. Bartel et al. (Berlin [East], 1970), pp. 260–62, 263–64; "Opportunismus," *Swb*, vol. 2, p. 223.

[27]See Lidtke, *Outlawed Party*, pp. 193ff.; also the somewhat differing accounts of Mehring, *Geschichte*, vol. 4, pp. 266–67; Brandis, *Deutsche Sozialdemokratie*, pp. 89ff.; as compared to *GdA*, vol. 1, p. 392; Engelberg, *Deutschland*, pp. 225–26; Engelberg, *Revolutionäre Politik und Rote Feldpost: 1878–90* (Berlin [East], 1959), pp. 95ff.; Streisand, p. 224; Seeber, "Wahlkämpfe," pp. 260–62.

they chose to abstain from voting rather than vote against the amendment when it was passed by the Reichstag.[28] Convinced that compromises with an iniquitous system were self-defeating, DDR critics show little appreciation of the problems facing a movement that had to offer some positive benefits to its hard-pressed constituency and that, despite its basic opposition to bourgeois parliamentarism, could not look on the Reichstag as merely an agitational platform.[29]

What made this issue so difficult to resolve in the Marxist perception was the danger that social reforms might reconcile the workers to their condition, foster illusions of further and more comprehensive improvements, and deceive them concerning the continuing need for revolutionary action as the sole route to their complete and permanent emancipation. Any social progress, moreover, delayed the full exploitation of the productive forces, thus delaying the advance toward socialism. For this reason, the East German accounts see the danger of Bismarck's social reforms in the delaying effects they had on the supposedly self-destructive processes of capitalism, and Engels specified expressly how far socialists ought to go in fighting for the workers' social improvement lest they strengthen the capitalist order unduly. Wilhelm Bracke, one of Bebel's and Liebknecht's associates, even wondered whether his party did right in opposing monopolies (nationalization of railroads, the state's tobacco monopoly), which it did on the grounds that monopolies exploited workers even more ruthlessly than did competitive capitalists. Yet, as Lenin was to point out subsequently, monopolies also constituted a higher stage of capitalism, inasmuch as they called for the planning of production and in this sense accelerated the advance towards socialization (*Vergesell-schaftung*). If such socialization was of immediate benefit only to the monopolists, at the expense of the workers, the latter's increased misery in turn served to intensify the class struggle and thus hastened the collapse of the capitalist order. The problems that resulted from this dialectical dichotomy between productive and social progress—the need to work for the destruction of the capitalist order as a barrier to permanent social progress and yet to fight for immediate social alleviations that not only would delay

---

[28]Compare Lidtke (pp. 221ff., 254ff.) with *GdA*, vol. 1, pp. 402–4; Engelberg, *Deutschland*, pp. 234ff.; "Budgetabstimmung," *Swb*, vol. 1, p. 300.

[29]Engels was aware of this need (see his letter to Bebel, Nov. 24, 1879, [Bebel, *Aus meinem Leben*, p. 674]), but perhaps he took comfort from the realization that bourgeois concessions to the workers, such as higher pay or shorter working hours, placed greater burdens on small businessmen than on large enterprises, thus tending to eliminate the former, promote capital concentration, and in this way hasten the ultimate collapse of capitalism. See the statement quoted by Kuczynski, *Geschichte*, vol. 3, p. 307; also Seeber, *Zwischen Bebel*, pp. 31–32.

that destruction but also would weaken, if not dissipate altogether, the workers' determination to abolish that system—was for a brief time a major internal issue of the workers' movement.[30]

All in all, however, East German historians are satisfied that Marxism kept gaining ground despite all obstructions. Great weight is placed on the electoral success of the SAPD in the Reichstag elections of February 1887, in which the party obtained 10.1 percent of the vote (against 9.7 in 1884) despite stepped-up expulsions, prosecutions, and other repressive measures. In the same vein, the party congress at St. Gall, Switzerland, later that year is given credit for enabling the Bebel-led "Marxists" to win out over "Lassallean" and other "opportunist" elements. In addition, although the congress is chided for leaving unanswered questions of strategy, both immediate and long-range—in particular, the problem of revolution—it is praised for making arrangements for the drafting of a new program, with specific instructions to replace the Lassallean demand for producers' cooperatives with the Marxist call for the expropriation of the land and other means of production. "The St. Gall party congress," *Geschichte der deutschen Arbeiterbewegung* concludes, "showed that Marxism was permeating the German workers' movement ever more decisively." Further proof of the workers' growing class consciousness is derived from the increasing number of demonstrations and strikes, culminating in a miners' strike in 1889 in the Ruhr area—a strike that involved 100,000 men. In the face of such progress, it is noted, the bourgeoisie turned against the Socialist Law; it was not renewed in 1890, and Bismarck's Bonapartist regime collapsed.[31]

The Politics of Capitalism

The shift in policy between 1878 and 1879, as reflected in the Socialist Law, the assault on the liberal parties, and the tariff legislation, has traditionally been considered a deep incision in the Bismarck era, ending its liberal phase and inaugurating a conservative one. More recently, Western scholars have even spoken of the

[30]Lidtke, *Outlawed Party*, pp. 152–54, 157–58; Brandis, *Deutsche Sozialdemokratie*, p. 87; Helga Nussbaum, *Unternehmer gegen Monopole* (Berlin [East], 1966), pp. 3–4. See also Seeber ("Wahlkämpfe," pp. 255ff.), who points out that a physically and mentally debilitated working class could not take up the class struggle and that reforms assuring it the strength and the time to take up the fight were clearly imperative.
[31]Engelberg, *Deutschland*, pp. 251–52; GdA, vol. 1, pp. 404ff.

"reorganization of the Prusso-German state—a reorganization that could be compared to a new founding of the Reich."[32] DDR authors deny that so fundamental a change took place; their position is that there was no liberal phase in the 1870s, because, except for the economic legislation, the tenor of that decade was essentially conservative. They note that this basic conservatism corresponded to the dominant political role of the Junker-militarist class and that, in this respect, nothing changed as the result of the policy shifts of 1878–1879.[33]

On the governmental level, East German scholars see the significance of these shifts in the changing basis of Bismarck's Bonapartist regime, which from then on rested on, apart from the army, the class *alliance* of bourgeois industrialists and Junker agrarians and was reinforced by the continuing class *compromise* between these groups and those segments of great and middle bourgeoisie that were opposed to protective tariffs but that, once again from fear of the working class, did not dare to turn against Bismarck's Bonapartist dictatorship.[34] Thus, agrarians and the industrial bourgeoisie moved closer together as fellow capitalists, while the capitalist concerns of the banking and commercial bourgeoisie kept these latter strata from fighting for their particular interests with the help of the workers. Without the support of the workers, however, the bourgeoisie could not hope to defeat Bismarck's authoritarian government, and the road to a bourgeois-democratic regime remained blocked.[35]

Whether such a regime was a realistic alternative is nowhere examined; there is sharp criticism, on the other hand, of West German arguments to the effect that all social strata were subject to an ineluctable economic thrust that reduced the failures of the bourgeoisie to objective factors and relieved that class of all responsibility for the consequences of its passivity.[36] DDR scholars insist that the changing balance of the class forces was the pivotal factor of the policy shift of 1878–1879, but there is some disagreement as to which class imposed its will on the state. Whereas some see the industrial bourgeoisie as mobilizing the resources of the state to protect its interests by obtaining protective tariffs, others maintain that it was the Junker agrarians who did so, because only their call for tariffs made possible the decisive turn in

[32]Böhme, *Deutschlands*, p. 419 (with quotation); Wehler, *Bismarck*, p. 492; Sheehan, *German Liberalism*, pp. 181ff.

[33]Seeber and Wolter, "Bürgerlichen Geschichtsbild," pp. 1079–81.

[34]Seeber, "Preussisch-deutscher Bonapartismus," pp. 106–7.

[35]*Grundriss*, pp. 293–94; Engelberg, *Deutschland*, pp. 180ff.; "Deutsche Fortschrittspartei," *Swb*, vol. 1, pp. 407–8; Seeber, *Zwischen Bebel, passim*.

[36]Seeber and Wolter, "Bürgerlichen Geschichtsbild," pp. 1093–94.

economic policy.[37] On the other hand, all are agreed that it was not Bismarck who cast the deciding vote for his own financial and political reasons, as non-Marxist historians have claimed. This view, it is argued, glosses over the crucial significance of the new Junker-bourgeois alliance, without which the chancellor could not have carried through the policy shifts of these years.[38] Yet this conclusion, in turn, ignores the chancellor's role in bringing about this alliance and his strong involvement on behalf of tariffs, without which the policy shifts would not have been enacted at that time.[39] All in all, this attempt to rank the respective contributions of the participating forces, which depended on one another in the pursuit of their various goals, demonstrates the futility of such ratings. In this case, of course, the purpose is to point out once again the "class content" of all individual actions.

If East German historians have some question as to the weight of the bourgeoisie's impact on the policy shift in 1878–1879, no such doubts exist concerning its subsequent role. The new alliance between great agrarians and bourgeois industrialists is considered proof of the ascendance of the great bourgeoisie to a political role more commensurate with its economic strength. DDR authors find this new status reflected in a significant change of attitude on the part of the agrarians toward their bourgeois fellow capitalists. As victims of the recent financial panic, many landowners had become disenchanted with financial and industrial capitalism and had given vent to their disillusionment in a vociferous anticapitalism and anti-Semitism. United now with the industrialists over the tariff issue, they dropped their anticapitalist tirades, and their anti-Semitism receded into a quiet social exclusionism.[40]

[37] See Kuczynski, *Geschichte*, vol. 3, pp. 53ff.; Steglich, "Beitrag," pp. 323ff.; as compared to Mottek et al., vol. 3, p. 109. Although Kuczynski finds the bourgeoisie strong enough to compel the state to do its bidding in the matter of tariffs, he also finds evidence of the beginning decline of capitalism on the grounds that the bourgeoisie required state help to fight off its foreign competitors (Kuczynski, *Geschichte*, vol. 3, p. 63).

[38] See Rosenberg, *Grosse Depression*, pp. 182ff.; Wehler, *Bismarck*, pp. 105ff.; Wolfgang Zorn, "Wirtschafts- und sozialgeschichtliche Zusammenhänge der deutschen Reichsgründungszeit 1850–1879," in *Moderne deutsche Sozialgeschichte*, ed. Wehler (Cologne, 1966), pp. 265–66. Compare those works to Seeber and Wolter, "Bürgerlichen Geschichtsbild," pp. 1088ff.; Konrad Canis, "Wirtschafts- und handelspolitische Aspekte der deutschen Aussenpolitik zu Beginn der 80er Jahre des 19. Jahrhunderts," *JfG* 16 (1977): 147ff. How difficult DDR authors find it to describe Bismarck's role, Steglich's cautious wording makes clear (Steglich, "Beitrag," pp. 332, 335, 336–37). Böhme's and Rosenberg's accounts of the sequence of events (Böhme, *Deutschlands*, pp. 378ff., especially 446ff.; Rosenberg, *Grosse Depression*, pp. 164ff.) support the East German position. Also close to it is Gugel, *Industrieller Aufstieg*, pp. 214, 216.

[39] Böhme, *Deutschlands*, pp. 470, 489–90, 530ff., and *passim*.

[40] See Mottek et al., vol. 3, p. 107. DDR authors have paid little attention to the anti-Semitic wave that swept across Germany in the 1870s. Earlier studies dealing with this phenomenon traced it to aristocratic-agrarian origins; at the same time,

Evidence of the growing political influence of the bourgeoisie is also found in the campaign for colonies, which got under way in the 1880s.[41] The first proponents of this campaign were merchants and shipowners; bankers and industrialists soon joined in the clamor, partly in the expectation of new markets, investment opportunities, and raw materials and partly in the hope of shipping off socialist malcontents to remote overseas territories. Spurred by a propaganda campaign promoted by these groups, large-scale support of the colonial movement came from academic, professional, and small-business circles, which demanded colonies as symbols of national prestige and world power. In the end, Bismarck, for political and economic reasons of his own, yielded to these pressures. In the mid-1880s he acquired a number of colonies for Germany in Africa and Australasia.[42]

If the colonial ventures proved unrewarding, East German analysts find part of the explanation in the unwillingness of bankers and industrialists to engage in colonial activities when their active participation was needed. This aloofness, they claim, bears out Lenin's thesis that the greatest need for imperialist expansion develops during the monopolist stage of capitalism, when the capitalist system supposedly seeks to avert its collapse by expansionist ventures. Because Germany's imperialist undertakings were launched before the nation had reached this stage, those most closely involved in colonial activities were shipping and trading concerns. Banking and industrial interests, on the other hand, had no pressing need yet for colonial supplies or investments.[43] Here, however, cause and effect are confused. If bankers and industrial-

they ruled out any roots among the lower middle class, even though rural anti-Semitism also carried strong anti-Junker overtones. More recent East German analyses consider even the anti-Semitism of the Bismarck era a diversionary bourgeois tactic by which the masses were to be kept in the dark about the real causes of their misery. These assertions are based on highly contrived arguments—not surprisingly so, given the very nonbourgeois aim of the anti-Jewish atttacks, which was to restore the noncompetitive, estate-oriented order of preindustrial times. See Schleier and Seeber, "Zur Entwicklung und Rolle des Antisemitismus in Deutschland von 1871–1914," *ZfG* 9 (1961): 1592–93; Streisand, pp. 367–68; also see the letter from Engels to Isidor Ehrenfreund, Apr. 19, 1890 (MEW, vol. 22, pp. 49–50). Compare these works to "Antisemitismus," *Swb,* vol. 1, pp. 94–95; Walter Mohrmann, *Antisemitismus* Berlin [East], 1972), pp. 15–16. Mohrmann is, however, refuted by his own data (ibid., pp. 45ff.).

[41]"Kolonialismus," *Swb,* vol. 1, p. 945; Mottek et al., vol. 3, p. 146 with p. 178. The ability of the banking and shipping interests to mobilize the resources of the state on their behalf is well described by Wehler, *Bismarck,* pp. 158ff., 168ff.

[42]On Bismarck's reasons, see Wehler, *Bismarck, passim;* Eyck, *Bismarck,* vol. 3, p. 401.

[43]"Kolonialismus," *Swb,* vol. 1, p. 946; Nussbaum, *Vom "Kolonialenthusiasmus" zur Kolonialpolitik der Monopole* (Berlin [East], 1962), pp. 52ff., 132ff.; Helmuth Stoecker, ed., *Kamerun unter deutscher Herrschaft* (Berlin [East], 1960), pp. 17ff.; Kuczynski, *Geschichte,* vol. 3, pp. 110ff.

ists showed little interest in colonial exploitation (after a strong initial involvement in the colonial movement), the reason was that they saw few profitable opportunities in the specific territories that the Reich acquired.[44]

To Marxist researchers, then, German colonialism during the Bismarck era presents no special problems. The pertinent East German literature views it primarily as an illustration of the Leninist analysis of imperialism. Some attention has also been paid to the hardships and cruelties of which capitalist exploitation and militarist ruthlessness were capable. In keeping with this approach, non-Marxist analyses of German colonialism, which have long centered on Bismarck's personal shift from opposition to support of colonial enterprises and have explained it as dictated by economic or diplomatic considerations, are dismissed as irrelevant.

In the early 1970s, however, a novel approach by the West German historian Hans-Ulrich Wehler touched off some bitter rebuttals. Wehler's views explicitly challenged basic Marxist-Leninist axioms. He maintained that German colonial expansion was propelled not so much by economic impulses—although the chancellor was not insensitive to them—as by Bismarck's realization that an expansionist policy would help divert the nation from its internal problems and tensions, hold out new goals to it that would arouse its national fervor, and thus reinforce the weakening political and social hierarchical order and the authoritarian power structure of the greater Prussian state.[45]

In Marxist terms, this analysis treated imperialism not as a phase of capitalist development but as a special type of political maneuver. Bismarck, in this view, emerged as a "manipulator of history" instead of being its agent. For this reason, East German historians rejected Wehler's interpretation as an "arrogant" repudiation of Lenin's theory of imperialism. Wehler's approach also clashed with the claim that the expansionist policy of the 1880s reflected the bourgeoisie's power to have the state serve its purposes. Far from uncovering these bourgeois manipulations, some

[44]See, for example, Wehler, Bismarck, pp. 284–85; Stern, Gold and Iron, pp. 394ff. As a prime example of the premonopolist stage of German finance capital, the reluctance of German bankers to underwrite the German East Africa Company, modeled on the British East India Company, is sometimes cited. Yet the reason for this reluctance was not the lack of interest in such investments, but distrust of the operations of the company and its manager, the vainglorious adventurer Carl Peters. Once Bismarck had persuaded Emperor William I to invest 500,000 marks in the company, many banks followed the latter's lead, confident that some way would be found to reimburse them should the company fail. See Nussbaum, "Kolonialenthusiasmus," p. 55, as compared to Wehler, Bismarck, pp. 336ff., 344, 351–52, 359ff.

[45]See Wehler, Bismarck. His basic arguments are conveniently summed up in the essay "Bismarcks Imperialismus: 1862–1890," reprinted in his Krisenherde des Kaiserreichs: 1871–1918 (Göttingen, 1970), pp. 135ff.

DDR critics warned, Wehler in effect acquitted the bourgeoisie of being the driving force in the imperialist ventures and pictured that class as a "quite respectable, historically untainted" element. He blandly ignored the fact, it was charged, that Bismarck could play whatever role he did play only because of the Junker-bourgeois alliance. The conclusion was that Wehler was making a deliberate attempt to divert attention from the imperialist goals of the present-day West German bourgeoisie.[46]

The question of the ultimate driving forces also dominates the analyses of foreign policy for that period. Because foreign policy is viewed as primarily a function of internal developments, it received little attention at first in East German historiography. Perhaps for lack of such spadework, the standard account, in Ernst Engelberg's *Deutschland von 1871 bis 1897*, reads much like a traditional non-Marxist one. Focused on Bismarck, it explores the chancellor's decisions and actions; even one or two general references to his Bonapartist regime and to unspecified economic conflicts do not modify the impression that Bismarck's policies were his own, albeit influenced by diplomatic and military considerations. A few years later, however, Streisand, in his survey of German history, pictured Bismarck's foreign policy as being shaped in this manner only as long as it was compatible with the dominant economic interests. Once the capitalist system of free competition turned into monopoly capitalism and imperialism, Streisand points out, the "relatively restrained" diplomacy of the chancellor came into conflict with the expansionist designs of German "finance capital." In the end, the artful network of Bismarck's foreign relations broke down altogether when the two leading capitalist countries of Europe—Britain and Germany—began to collide. Streisand concludes that the status-quo–oriented diplomacy of the chancellor was suitable only for the transition period between the competitive and monopolist stages of capitalism.[47]

The major monographic studies dealing with the foreign political issues of the 1880s seek to bear out this thesis. Whereas Heinz Wolter showed, in an article cited before, that Bismarck's anti-revolutionary stance enabled him in the 1870s to pursue a politics-oriented conservative foreign policy, Sigrid Kumpf-Korfes concludes in a carefully researched study that economic interests began interfering with this diplomacy during the last decades of Bismarck's administration. Kumpf-Korfes finds that agrarians who

[46]Walter Wimmer, review, *ZfG* 20 (1972): 223–25; Seeber and Wolter, "Bürgerlichen Geschichtsbild," pp. 1082–83, 1088ff., 1097; Schleier, "Explizite Theorie, Imperialismus, Bismarck und Herr Wehler," *JfG* 6 (1972): 477ff.

[47]Engelberg, *Deutschland*, pp. 89ff., 203ff., 231ff., 240ff.; Streisand, pp. 214–15; also Canis, "Aspekte," pp. 140–41, 150, 175ff.

suffered from Russian agricultural competition and banking and industrial interests that had important stakes in the Russian market and that clashed with Russian thrusts in the Balkan Peninsula, called on the chancellor for remedial action. In the end, those pressures proved stronger than any other and prevented Bismarck from maintaining the friendly relations with Russia on which his diplomacy rested.

A study by Konrad Canis, which examines Bismarck's foreign policy from a military and diplomatic perspective, reaches similar conclusions. Dealing with the crisis of 1887, in which the military advocated a preventive attack on Russia and possibly France, this study shows that Bismarck was not averse to an armed showdown, though only with France and only provided Russia were at the time involved in a war with Britain. Canis shows that Bismarck gave up that plan only when he grew fearful (mistakenly) of the likelihood of a war between Russia and Austria, into which Germany would be drawn. Nonetheless, Canis notes, Bismarck, who was deeply afraid of a two-front war against both France and Russia, was forced by agrarian-industrial pressures to adopt an economic policy against Russia (agricultural tariffs, prohibition of accepting Russian securities as collateral) that was bound to drive that nation over to France's side. Similarly, he argues (in accord with Kumpf-Korfes), Austrian and German economic interests kept clashing with Russian activities in the Balkan Peninsula and the Near and Middle East, depriving the government increasingly of its freedom of action and causing the very alignments that made inevitable the two-front war Bismarck was working to avoid.[48]

As Marxists, both Kumpf-Korfes and Canis maintain that whatever other factors helped shape German foreign policy, the socioeconomic ones were decisive. Some West German studies, on the other hand, show Bismarck explicitly not as yielding to interest-group pressures but rather as initiating a campaign of economic warfare for his own reasons and urging bankers and industrialists to pursue their foreign objectives more aggressively. Again, the East German objection is that Bismarck's foreign policy is misrepresented as a Bonapartist technique, whereas in reality it was an inevitable outgrowth of capitalist expansionism.[49]

DDR scholars, then, would not deny that in most cases Bismarck's diplomatic maneuvers resulted from political and military

[48]Wolter, "Anfänge"; Wolter, "Zum Verhältnis," pp. 134ff.; Sigrid Kumpf-Korfes, Bismarcks "Draht nach Russland," (Berlin [East], 1968); Canis, "Bismarck, Waldersee und die Kriegsgefahr 1887," in Bartel and Engelberg, Grosspreussisch, vol. 2, pp. 397ff.; Canis, "Aspekte," pp. 176ff.
[49]Böhme, "Politik," pp. 42–43, 46; Wehler, "Bismarcks Imperialismus," pp. 244–45, 248ff.; Wehler, Bismarck, pp. 217, 235, 237, 239ff., 441; Seeber and Wolter, "Bürgerlichen Geschichtsbild," p. 1083.

considerations, but these immediate causes in turn are considered to be responses to conflict situations that ultimately were created by the same agrarian, industrial, and financial interests that the chancellor and his political and military advisers thought they could easily subordinate to their political and military goals. In fact, DDR authors consider it one of their major tasks to show how Bismarck's diplomacy was thwarted by economic forces he thought he could contain by his policies.[50] They also point out that during the last years of his administration, the chancellor tried to pursue a policy that ran counter to the dominant trend of economic developments and favored agrarian over industrial interests. In his failure to appreciate the growing importance of the industrial bourgeoisie, they see another cause of his downfall, for by disregarding major industrial interests he alienated a key social force, on whose support the Bonapartist regime depended.[51]

However much Marxist and non-Marxist historians may disagree about the respective impact of the government, the military, agrarians, and the commercial and industrial bourgeoisie on German colonial and foreign policies, they do agree that these forces combined were the shapers of these policies. East German historians have, however, rightly complained that their West German counterparts still tend to cling to the traditional historiographical approach "from above," even though they no longer view history as the exclusive domain of rulers, prime ministers, military leaders, and diplomats. In consequence, they all but ignore the views of socialist spokesmen such as Bebel and Liebknecht on Germany's colonial and foreign policies. These men kept pointing out that economic problems could be solved only internally, not by colonial expansionism, and that stepped-up armaments only provoked retaliatory actions on the part of Germany's neighbors, thus endangering rather than strengthening the country's security. As Engelberg puts it in a similar context, the Socialists illustrated "the deep gap between the existential interests of the peoples and the drive toward conquest of the ruling classes."

On the positive side, Socialist spokesmen called for the democratization of foreign policy—that is, for the right of the Reichstag to declare war and make peace, for disarmament and peaceful international cooperation, national self-determination, an independent Poland, and a self-governing Alsace-Lorraine under "European" control. Hardly any of these demands could have been ful-

[50]See Canis, "Waldersee," pp. 347ff., 404ff., 433; Wolter, "Zum Verhältnis," pp. 126ff., 135ff. Although not directly concerned with this issue, Stern, *Gold and Iron*, pp. 440ff., contains some interesting data bearing out the East German thesis.
[51]Wolter, "Zum Verhältnis," pp. 135ff.; Canis, "Aspekte," pp. 175–76, 180; Canis, "Waldersee," pp. 406–7; Kumpf-Korfes, *Bismarcks*, pp. 189–90 and *passim*.

filled under existing conditions; essentially their realization was predicated on a radical restructuring of the social order in Germany and beyond. Still, some of them, and especially those concerned with the armament issue, might have been taken up, if only in modified form, by non-Socialists. (In this context, several DDR studies that deal with the ambiguous attitude of the left-liberal Progressives on the armament question deserve attention.) Yet, whether or not the socialist views were adopted, they had the support of a growing segment of the electorate and thus are part of the historical record if history is not to be written solely from the rulers' perspective.[52]

If the Social Democrats had no impact on foreign policy, their growing strength, all accounts happily note, did make itself felt in domestic developments. Among the causes that brought about Bismarck's downfall in 1890, the growth of the "revolutionary workers' movement," so clearly reflected in the election returns, is considered the most significant.[53] (Whether that movement *was* really revolutionary, as noble and bourgeois contemporaries thought at the time and as DDR historians maintain today, will be examined in the next section.) By Marxist definition, the chancellor's Bonapartist dictatorship rested on the confidence of the propertied classes that his regime offered the best protection against the demands of the workers. Yet the growing strength of the SAPD and the increasing restiveness of the workers, culminating in the months-long strike of the Ruhr miners in 1889, raised doubts about the efficacy of the Socialist Law and the ability of the Bismarck regime to safeguard the established order. Disagreements between industrialists and agrarians about the appropriateness of tariffs to further the German economy and between the chancellor and the bourgeoisie about overseas expansion, as well as rifts between the chancellor and the military on matters of strategy, also weakened the cohesion of the class alliance and compromise that held Bismarck's system together. In the end, it is noted, the system collapsed under the existing pressures and cleavages, the critical issue being the question of how to deal with the working class. Whatever the personal differences be-

---

[52]Schleier, "Explizite Theorie," p. 489; Wolter, "Die Alternativkonzeption der revolutionären deutschen Sozialdemokratie zum aussenpolitischen Kurs des preussisch-deutschen Reiches unter Bismarck," *BzG* 10 (1968): 12ff.; Wolter, *Alternative zu Bismarck: Die deutsche Sozialdemokratie und die Aussenpolitik des preussisch-deutschen Reiches 1878–1890* (Berlin [East], 1970); Engelberg, *Deutschland*, pp. 91, 232–33; Seeber, *Zwischen Bebel*, pp. 160ff. See also Wehler, *Bismarck*, p. 175.

[53]Streisand, p. 225; Engelberg, *Deutschland*, pp. 265–67; *GdA*, vol. 1, pp. 415–16. That Bismarck's fall was due to the strength of the radical labor movement is also argued by Barraclough, *Origins*, p. 428. See, on the other hand, Wolfgang Pack, *Das parlamentarische Ringen um das Sozialistengesetz Bismarcks* (Düsseldorf, 1961), pp. 204ff.; Stürmer, "Konservatismus," pp. 162–63.

tween Bismarck and William II, DDR scholars see the chancellor's dismissal as rooted in those class conflicts rather than in a clash between two incompatible individuals.[54]

Because the collapse of Bismarck's regime grew out of class confrontations, East German historians regret that no essential changes occurred in class alignments. The bourgeoisie is once again chided for not having used the opportunity to transform, with the help of the working class, the semiabsolutist empire into a bourgeois-democratic, parliamentary state that would have curbed the power of the Junkers and given the bourgeoisie political influence commensurate with its economic importance. Even though events had shown that its support of reactionary forces only spurred the growth of revolutionary social democracy, the bourgeoisie remained on the side of these forces. Interestingly, DDR authors regret the passivity of the bourgeoisie although they know, judging from developments in western Europe and the United States, that such a bourgeois-parliamentary regime would have been better able to integrate the workers into its system and could thus have impeded the growth of a revolutionary movement. Given the alternatives, however, these authors apparently find this a price it would have been worthwhile to pay—doubtless because of their certainty that the inequities of the capitalist order would, in any event, eventually call forth the inevitable socialist revolution.[55]

The "personal regime" of William II thus offered no genuine alternative to Bismarck's Bonapartism in the East German view; apart from dealing somewhat less repressively with the workers, it differed little from Bismarck's regime. Fear of the working class continued to haunt the upper and middle bourgeoisie. New proposals to tighten and/or expand existing curbs—the Subversion Bill (*Umsturzvorlage*) (1895) and the Penitentiary Bill (*Zuchthausvorlage*) (1899)—touched off bitter debates between the advocates of forcible measures and those calling for social reforms. Whereas non-Marxists stress the significance of this rift, Marxists emphasize the class-related aspects of the reformers' stance. The reformers' support of the right to form unions, shorter workdays, and better accident and health protection, East German analyses stress, was dictated solely by their desire to safeguard industrial peace, improve workers' productivity, or increase labor's purchasing power.[56] In consequence, when their class interests demanded a

[54]*Bismarcks Sturz: Zur Rolle der Klassen in der Endphase des preussisch-deutschen Bonapartismus: 1884/85 bis 1890,* ed. Seeber (Berlin [East], 1977).

[55]Schröder, in ibid., pp. 358ff.; Seeber, "Preussisch-deutscher Bonapartismus," p. 98; Bleiber, "Bourgeoisie," pp. 319–20.

[56]Engelberg, *Deutschland,* pp. 300ff., 370–71; Streisand, p. 227; Seeber, *Zwischen Bebel,* pp. 175ff., 202ff.; Ludwig Elm, *Zwischen Fortschritt und Reaktion* (Berlin [East], 1968), pp. 28ff., 97ff.

different posture, the liberals would be found in the opposite camp. In the same vein, many left-liberals, though opposed to the growth and autonomy of the army, supported military bills of which they did not approve, either for tactical reasons—to keep Bismarck's successor, Chancellor Leo von Caprivi, in office because of his awareness of the needs of commerce and industry—or because they were anxious to demonstrate their patriotism and "sense of responsibility." All in all, liberals of all persuasions are found to have been vacillating and unprogressive and hence unable to offer the country democratic alternatives to the extant policies. Nor is this considered surprising: as Lenin already had pointed out, their differences with the conservative hardliners were basically only tactical.[57]

Although the confrontation between the Junker-bourgeois camp and the workers remains the major "class contradiction" in this judgment, the fact that divergent interests were once more weakening the coalition of Junker agrarians and industrial bourgeoisie receives due attention. Once again, the disagreements concerned tariffs and other aspects of foreign trade; on a later occasion, a bitter controversy erupted over the construction of a canal linking the Elbe and Rhine rivers (Mittellandkanal)—a canal that was to expedite the transportation of West German industrial products to the east but that was viewed by the agrarians as another gateway for inexpensive food products from abroad. In the face of the continued growth of the workers' movement, these differences were patched up in a new bourgeois-agrarian coalition (Sammlungspolitik). Once again, however, DDR authors find the bourgeoisie taking second place to the Junkers; although industrial interests made substantial gains economically, the bourgeoisie failed again to transform its advances into political power. Thus, Prussia's large estate owners were able to beat off attempts to strip them of their police and administrative powers in their rural preserves and were able to secure substantial tax reductions at the expense of the urban population. In addition, closer relations with heavy industry were reestablished only at the price of the restoration of the pre-Caprivi agricultural tariffs.[58]

Fear of the workers' movement, all studies stress, thus overshadowed all disagreements and inevitably brought the Junkers and the bourgeoisie together again. Engelberg notes that "all power struggles and confrontations among the ruling classes were ulti-

[57]Engelberg, Deutschland, pp. 297ff.; Seeber, Zwischen Bebel, pp. 191ff.; Kurt Gossweiler, Grossbanken, Industriemonopole, Staat: Ökonomie und Politik des staatsmonopolistischen Kapitalismus in Deutschland, 1914–1932 (Berlin [East], 1971), pp. 21ff.
[58]Engelberg, Deutschland, pp. 325ff.; Klein, Deutschland von 1897/98 bis 1917 (Berlin [East], 1969), pp. 36ff.

mately determined by their attitude toward the revolutionary workers' movement; this was the decisive issue—it was of primary importance in all strategic and tactical considerations." Whatever their differences, large landowners and banking and industrial capitalists were agreed on the necessity of stemming the rising tide of worker rebellion. Compared to this issue, the vagaries of William II, long a major concern of non-Marxist historians, are dismissed as peripheral reflections of the basic class conflict. Whereas if a recent non-Marxist study views the year 1897 as a milestone because William II rid himself then of the remaining cautionary counselors in his entourage, DDR scholars regard that year as significant because it led to the renewed collaboration of agrarian and business interests on the parliamentary plane. With large parts of the bourgeoisie once more tied firmly to the reactionary monarchist-Junker camp, the conclusion is that the bourgeoisie would never be able to fulfill its historical task, and the drive toward bourgeois democracy would have to come from the working class. To quote Engelberg again, "the socialist workers' movement that represented the nation's democratic and socialist alternative to the militarist and exploiter state remained the only hope for an organized resistance against the policy of imperialist recklessness that the ruling classes pursued." How that movement would discharge its own historical mission of eliminating exploitation and militarism was therefore of crucial importance in the Marxist view.[59]

The Social Democratic Party:
From Erfurt Program to Revisionism

Surface indications seemed reassuring. As industrialization expanded, the working class grew and so did the Socialist party and the labor unions. The party scored impressive electoral victories, and after the economic crisis of the early 1890s strikes became more effective as a means of securing better pay and working conditions. The continued fight of the Social Democrats against militarism and armaments, it is claimed, not only was supported by

[59]See Engelberg, *Deutschland*, pp. 342ff., 385ff. (quotation on p. 387); *GdA*, vol. 1, pp. 471–72; Bartel and Seeber, "Pariser Kommune," p. 25; Klein, *Deutschland*, pp. 48ff., 95ff. Klein stresses the fact that William's vainglorious and erratic behavior ought not to be blamed on his physical handicap (a withered left arm) or on any character flaws; it reflected the instability of the Junker-bourgeois regime and in its assertiveness appealed to large parts of the German bourgeoisie, white-collar employees, and the worker aristocracy (ibid., pp. 44–45). On the consolidation of the emperor's personal regime in 1897 as a turning point in the non-Marxist view, see John C. G. Röhl, *Germany without Bismarck*, (Berkeley, 1967).

workers but also spurred the growth of antimilitarist sentiments among left-liberal Progressives and Catholic Centrists. Yet there were also signs of ideological confusion.

In 1891, at its congress in Erfurt, the party adopted a new program and a new name, the Social Democratic Party of Germany (SPD). The general part of the new program, pointing out the evils of private ownership of the means of production and calling for socialization of these means and the abolition of class rule, was, according to Engelberg, "essentially Marxist." Nor could there be an objection to the immediate social and political reforms that the program proposed—among them were a democratic suffrage system, self-government on all levels, the replacement of the standing army by a militia, a progressive income tax, free medical care, and better and safer working conditions. What DDR critics find alarming is the absence of any indication that such objectives as democratic suffrage and self-government were viewed only as means to attain the interim goal of a bourgeois-democratic republic. In pursuit of the final goal, this republic would subsequently have to be transformed into the dictatorship of the proletariat. Obviously the basic alternatives to the existing inequities could never be realized within an order in which the working class was not in full control.

In part, the reticence of the program was admittedly due to legal and political concerns that made it impossible to call openly for such revolutionary measures as a democratic republic and beyond it the dictatorship of the proletariat. Yet, as all DDR authors stress, caution was not the main reason for these omissions. The leaders were convinced of the inevitability of the collapse of the capitalist system and thus felt no need to work out a long-range revolutionary strategy to speed its breakdown—the less so because its implementation was clearly not imminent.[60]

East German historians find this inaction all the more dangerous because "opportunism" was once more threatening to divert the party from its "lawful," proper historical course. A few months before the adoption of the Erfurt Program, Georg von Vollmar, a Bavarian deputy, publicly stated that Bismarck's removal was opening the way for reforms by which the capitalist order could gradually be transformed into a socialist one. The danger of Vollmar's position, Engelberg notes, lay in its systematization of the reforming approach. Tactical moves for social improvements and political gains ceased to be temporary digressions from a principled class policy and became ends in themselves; in turn, the socialist

[60]See Engelberg, *Deutschland*, pp. 314ff.; *GdA*, vol. 1, pp. 430ff.; "Erfurter Parteitag der Sozialdemokratie," *Swb*, vol. 1, pp. 547ff.; Bartel and Seeber, "Pariser Kommune," p. 72. Non-Marxists sometimes have erroneously attributed this viewpoint also to Engels.

class struggle receded into a distant and uncertain future. Indeed, soon SPD delegations in the Bavarian and Wuerttembergian *Landtage* defied the official party directive of "not a man, not a dime to this system" and began to approve state budgets, including military appropriations, to obtain some political leverage. Whatever the mental reservations of the South German deputies, they seemed to accept the existing system. Similarly, labor unions are found to have been indifferent to ideological issues and mainly concerned with improving the material lot of their members—a parochialism that party leaders encouraged.

With the fundamental issues clouded, the East German accounts see the working class in danger of losing sight of its historical mission. Bebel is given credit for recognizing this danger, but other party leaders are taken to task for negotiating with the "opportunists" of Vollmar's persuasion. The risk to party unity of a more uncompromising stand is discounted. What mattered was that Vollmar's views weakened the fighting spirit of the party, created dissension, and made the membership receptive to an even more systematic challenge of its revolutionary objectives in the form of "Revisionism." That the decline of the revolutionary spirit may have been due to the expiration of the Socialist Law rather than to Vollmar's proposals is not considered.[61]

Revisionism transcended the conciliatory posture of Vollmar and his followers. It sought to provide a theoretical underpinning to their views and thus to revise Marxist theory. Its intellectual father, Eduard Bernstein, claimed that experience had refuted many of Marx's and Engels' predictions: capitalist concentration was not as rapid and all-embracing as expected, the middle class had not been driven into the ranks of the proletariat but was growing in numbers and property, and the working class had not been plunged into greater misery—it was in fact improving its lot. There was also no indication of deepening economic crises and the impending collapse of the capitalist order; instead, crises were occurring less frequently and were less severe.

From these facts Bernstein concluded that social progress was not the product of dialectical processes operating through class struggles and revolutions; rather, it sprang from a unilinear evolution that did not rule out class conflicts but depended essentially on cooperation across class lines. He called specifically for cooperation between the working class and some middle-class segments, within the framework of a democratic parliamentary system. At the same time, Bernstein rejected the materialist determinism of the orthodox doctrine that precluded all ethical motivations and

[61]Engelberg, *Deutschland*, pp. 311ff., 354ff., 361ff.; *GdA*, vol. 1, pp. 426–27, 433ff., 459ff.

that, as he charged, had degenerated into a developmental automatism that discarded even the voluntarist elements on which Marx's and Engels' prognoses were predicated. There was no proof, Bernstein warned, that the advent of socialism was inevitable as a result of the concentration of the means of production—that is, the increasingly social organization of those means; only determined efforts, spurred by both ethical and material motives, could bring about socialism.

Subsequent developments have borne out some of Bernstein's conclusions and refuted others. As he predicted, capitalist concentration continued but did not eliminate small or medium-sized enterprises. The middle class kept expanding, and parts of it prospered; the working class met with a varied fate but over the long run benefited from increased productivity, although benefits kept lagging behind the growth of production.[62] On the other hand, Bernstein's prediction of milder crises was not borne out by developments. He also overestimated the chances of converting the Wilhelmine system into a parliamentary democracy and the willingness of bourgeois elements, petty or other, to cooperate with workers and Social Democrats.

DDR critics direct the main thrust of their attack against the Revisionists' dissection of Marxist theory—their rejection of dialectical materialism as the propelling force of historical progress, their deemphasis of the class struggle, and their renunciation of revolution, and their reliance, in part, on ethical impulses in their efforts. As orthodox Marxists, East German historians perceive that the Revisionist changes struck at the heart of the Marxist doctrine. From a practical political viewpoint, moreover, Revisionism hampered the workers' movement by ignoring the bourgeois-oriented class content of bourgeois democracy and bourgeois legality, indulging in parliamentary illusions, and spreading the myth of a peaceful evolution into socialism. Nor did it matter in the face of such deviations that Bernstein and his circle agreed with Marx on important points, that they too noted the increasingly social character of production, the inequitable distribution of the expanding wealth, the need for collective action on the part of the workers, and the leading role of the working class as the only true progressive force. Neither

---

[62]On this, see Kuczynski (*Geschichte*, vol. 3, pp. 319ff.), who grants that the bulk of workers were improving their lot inasmuch as their real wages were rising, their food became more nutritious, and clothing more varied. At the same time, educational opportunities were expanded and leisure time extended. On the other hand, his data suggest that workers suffered setbacks because of their greater exhaustion from work, increasing accidents, and deteriorating health and living conditions. On balance, Kuczynski finds Marx's law of the growing immiseration of the working class borne out by these latter facts, which in his view outweigh the more positive aspects of the workers' position (ibid., pp. 414–16).

these agreements nor Bernstein's insistence that he was still a
Marxist could make Revisionism a system of modified Marxism.
Bernstein merely added to the existing ideological confusion by
claiming a Marxist pedigree while laying claim at the same time to
the liberal heritage.[63]

Since Rosa Luxemburg and Lenin first took issue with Revisionism, orthodox Marxists have regarded it as a scientifically inevitable outgrowth of imperialism, designed to inject bourgeois
values into the labor movement and split it. East German historians, too, have adopted this view. "The objective task of Revisionism," states *Geschichte der deutschen Arbeiterbewegung*, "was to
keep the working class from fulfilling its historical mission in the
imperialist era." The rationale behind this thesis is summed up by
Ludwig Elm: "The objective function of Revisionism is not determined by the individual intentions of its spokesmen, but primarily
by its inner connection with the ideology of the liberal bourgeoisie
and by the role assigned to it by the bourgeoisie." By the testimony
not only of Marxists but also of non-Marxists, of whom Elm quotes
a fair number, liberalism could not survive except by making inroads into the ranks of the Social Democrats; as self-avowed heirs
of the liberal heritage, the Revisionists thus "objectively" had to be
viewed as protagonists of the liberal bourgeoisie.[64]

That this bourgeois infiltration of the Social Democratic party
was highly effective is attributed to the sustained bribery by promotions and better pay of the so-called labor aristocracy. DDR
historians follow Lenin in explaining that capitalist entrepreneurs
forewent part of the "surplus value" extracted from labor to raise
wages for highly skilled workers—no great sacrifice in view of the
huge profits they reaped from their monopolist and imperialist undertakings. As the argument continues, rounding out the link to
imperialism, capitalists did this to assure industrial peace while
they ventured abroad. To quote *Geschichte* once more, "[Revision-
ism] . . . was an international phenomenon that evolved lawfully

[63]"Revisionismus," *Swb*, vol. 2, pp. 379ff.; Klein, *Deutschland*, pp. 86ff.; also Peter
Gay, *The Dilemma of Democratic Socialism: Eduard Bernstein's Challenge to
Marx* (New York, 1952), p. 241; Lidtke, "Revisionismus," in *SDG*, vol. 5, p. 679.
[64]See "Revisionismus," *Swb*, vol. 2, pp. 379–80; *GdA*, vol. 2, p. 57; *Grundriss*,
p. 320; Elm, *Zwischen Fortschritt*, pp. 37ff. (quotation on p. 50). Elm points out
that left-liberals such as Friedrich Naumann and Theodor Barth, who supported
the government's armament and imperialist policies, took an active interest in
Revisionism. But he also notes that liberals with petty bourgeois and middle and
small-peasant affiliations, such as Eugen Richter, were as suspicious of the Revisionists as they were of the orthodox Social Democrats. Elm's analysis of these
differences within the liberal ranks is characteristic of the dichotomy of his anti-
bourgeois approach: whereas Barth and his circle are taken to task for trying to
split the Social Democratic party by offering to work with the Revisionists,
Richter and his followers are reprimanded for failing to see that the interests of
the Bürgertum demanded cooperation with the Revisionists.

with the advent of imperialism." That Bernstein and many of his fellow Revisionists were not opposed to colonial acquisitions only confirmed this correlation between Revisionism and imperialism. So did the fact that, apart from the labor aristocracy, Revisionism drew its support from the worker bureaucracy and proletarianized petty bourgeoisie—all elements with a penchant for bourgeois values who were hence thought especially vulnerable to bourgeois bribes. Higher pay for special skills, simply a function of the law of supply and demand, thus became part of the Machiavellian capitalist strategy to break up the working class.[65]

What these observations also discount is the receptivity of workers in general—not just the "aristocracy" of the working class—to the Revisionist-reformist approach. There is an abundance of contemporary testimony to the effect that once the Socialist Law expired, the bulk of the workers preferred a gradual to a revolutionary approach. At least two East German historians do not rule out this explanation when they admit that "the causes of the relatively wide impact of Opportunism, Revisionism, and Reformism on German Social Democracy, which had developed into a revolutionary mass party [!], still need to be examined more thoroughly." Most accounts, however, insist that the workers were the victims of deceit or corruption. Whatever the reason, the claim of *Geschichte der deutschen Arbeiterbewegung* that the Social Democratic party was, at the turn of the century, a party "in which the ideas of Marxism were deeply rooted" is not borne out by the facts.[66]

The dominance of reform over revolution was also ensured by the inclination of many party leaders, under the influence of Darwin and a misunderstood Engels, to rely on an ineluctable evolution as the proper avenue to the socialist order—another fact ig-

[65]See *GdA*, vol. 2, pp. 52ff.; Klein, *Deutschland*, pp. 85ff.; Bartel, "Zur historischen Stellung," p. 15. Both *GdA* and Klein admit that the increasingly complex organization of industrial production required supervisors, foremen, store managers, and highly skilled workers, yet they denounce nonetheless the granting of supervisory powers or the payment of higher wages for special skills as attempts to bribe the beneficiaries into submissiveness. Because Marxists maintain that utility is not a value-determinant of labor in capitalism (only the costs of reproducing labor and labor's ability to fight for higher wages are effective in this area), the need to reward scarce special skills and experience is simply ignored ("Arbeitslohn," *Swb*, vol. 1, p. 187). See also the contradictory statements of Streisand, p. 245, and Kuczynski, *Der Ausbruch des ersten Weltkrieges und die deutsche Sozialdemokratie* (Berlin [East], 1957), pp. 135–36. Actually, wages of unskilled workers tended to rise faster than those of skilled ones during the period 1887–1913 in some industries (Gerhard Bry, *Wages in Germany: 1871–1945* [Princeton, 1960], pp. 81–83).

[66]Horst Lademacher, "Sozialdemokratie," *SDG*, vol. 5, pp. 931–32; Steinberg, *Sozialismus*, pp. 29ff.; Gutsche and Seeber, "Bourgeoisie, Arbeiterklasse, Volksmassen von der Pariser Kommune bis zur Grossen Sozialistischen Oktoberrevolution," *ZfG* 25 (1977): 1206; *GdA*, vol. 2, p. 19.

nored or discounted by DDR authors. Darwin's evolutionist theory exerted a strong impact on the leaders; for example, by comparing the course of history to the evolution of nature, Engels—in his *Anti-Dühring* and elsewhere—unwittingly helped to lead the party away from the activist revolutionary approach that was and is the essence of Marxist strategy.[67]

The German failure to adhere to an unadulterated revolutionary Marxism is contrasted with the attitude of Lenin's Bolshevik faction, which allowed the Russian Social Democratic Workers' party to break up over a controversy of similar import in order to safeguard the revolutionary nature of Marxism. The Bolsheviks thus are seen as setting the example for carrying on the struggle against the capitalist order in its last, imperialist stage, when the working class could no longer content itself with scoring a few economic and political points. As a result,

> the center of the international revolutionary workers movement was shifting to Russia, the country with the sharpest internal contradictions. Lenin created the foundations for the new phase in the development of Marxism and the international workers movement by his relentless struggle against opportunism and the purity of scientific Communism, by the revolutionary training of the proletariat, by the creative application of Marxism to Russian conditions, and by the political and theoretical generalization of the new experiences of the Russian and international workers movement. The party of Lenin gave the correct, needed answer to the imperialist challenge, not only for Russia, but for the entire international workers movement.[68]

From this perspective, the subsequent history of the SPD was saddening. The impressive electoral victories of the party are duly recorded, but it is also noted that along with the increase of members and voters, Revisionism kept gaining ground. The German Social Democrats are chided for not having understood that the tactics that had furthered the cause of the working class in the period of competitive capitalism were no longer adequate in the monopolist-imperialist era. What was required now was the "creative adaptation" of Marxist theory to the new situation. Only a transformation of the party into the kind of tightly disciplined, centralized "new-type party" (*Partei neuen Typus*) that Lenin had created in the Bolshevik party could enable it to fulfill its historical—that is, revolutionary—mission; *revolutionary* in this context is always understood in the general sense of the "quickest possible transformation of the existing bourgeois order into the socialist one," not a headlong plunge into a violent revolution for

---

[67]Steinberg, *Sozialismus*, pp. 41ff.; George Lichtheim, *Marxism: An Historical and Critical Study* (New York, 1968), pp. 237ff.; Lademacher, "Sozialdemokratie," pp. 928–29.
[68]Klein, *Deutschland*, p. 14. See also *GdA*, vol. 2, pp. 13–14.

which the time had not yet come. A victory of Revisionism, on the other hand, was bound to deliver party and working class into the hands of the bourgeoisie, which, it is relentlessly pointed out, was the "objective function" of Revisionism.[69]

Social Democratic and general worker reaction to the Russian Revolution of 1905 seemed to hold out hope that the party might live up to its responsibilities. There was a notable increase in strikes, many of them with political overtones, in the years 1905–1906, an increase that is attributed to the Russian developments. There were also innumerable party meetings in support of the Russian fighters, and collections among workers in support of victims of the revolution netted respectable sums of money. In addition, renewed efforts were made to democratize Prussia's three-class suffrage and similarly inequitable voting systems in Hamburg and Saxony. Finally, in pursuit of these and other democratic rights, there were now increasing demands that, following the Russian example, strikes ought to be called for political purposes. Responding to these demands, the Social Democratic party congress of 1905 passed a resolution approving of the political mass strike as a class-struggle weapon, if only against attacks on the democratic suffrage system and the right of association. But "revolutionary" Social Democracy gained ground only temporarily, and Revisionism soon made new inroads upon it.

In support of this interpretation, DDR authors have collected what evidence they could find.[70] There can be no doubt that events in Russia helped to raise the political temperature, as an English historian, J. P. Nettl, has put it. Yet, contrary to East German claims, there is no proof that the rapid increase in strikes in 1905–1906 can be attributed to the Russian uprising. Measured against the slump years of 1900–1903, 1905 was a prosperous year, and prosperous years are always times of increased strike activity; when the economy declined once more in 1907, the number of strikes also decreased. A study by the East German historian Dieter Fricke, examining the influence of the revolution on German workers, has produced little evidence of any strong impact. And if the issue of political strikes did remain on the agenda of the SPD, it did so in spite of rather than because of the mass strikes of Russian workers in 1905. These Russian strikes were effective only

[69] *GdA*, vol. 2, p. 57; Streisand, pp. 246–47; Annelies Laschitza and Horst Schumacher, "Thesen über die Herausbildung ... der deutschen Linken," *BzG* 7 (1965): 24ff. On the term *revolutionary*, see Klein, *Deutschland*, p. 111, and Laschitza and Schumacher, "Thesen," p. 26.

[70] The most useful East German collection of materials on the impact of the Russian revolution of 1905 is to be found in *Archivalische Forschungen zur Geschichte der Deutschen Arbeiterbewegung* (Berlin [East], 1955–1961), vol. 2, especially parts i and ii.

while the tsar's armies were committed in the Far East, fighting Japan; when the troops returned to European Russia at the end of the war, the strikes were quickly and bloodily suppressed—a fact that is barely mentioned in the DDR literature but that was not lost on the SPD leaders and was a major reason for their unwillingness to press for such strikes. In the Marxist-Leninist view, however, the inaction of the workers meant they had failed to understand that they were witnessing the transition from the "relatively peaceful" period of capitalism to the eve of the socialist revolution, with all this entailed.[71]

The Imperialist Era

In the Marxist scenario, Germany had by this time entered the stage of imperialism. By Lenin's definition, which has become an integral part of Marxist dogma, imperialism constituted the final phase of the decaying capitalist order, paving the way for its overthrow by a socialist revolution. Imperialism had been brought on by increasing capital concentration; by the absorption of smaller enterprises into even larger and fewer ones; and by the formation of cartels, syndicates, and concerns that, since the 1890s, had come to dominate the production and/or distribution of such vital resources as coal, iron, and steel, and subsequently chemicals and electricity. By a similar process of mergers, a few banks dominated the capital market. Eventually, as Fritz Klein and others point out, following in the footsteps of the Socialist Rudolf Hilferding, these industrial and banking monopolies joined forces and by their mutual interpenetration developed a new type of "finance capitalism" that further encouraged monopolistic combinations.[72]

As this concentration of industry and banking progressed, the "basic contradiction" of the capitalist system is found to have deepened: production became an increasingly social concern, in-

---

[71]Klein, *Deutschland*, pp. 144ff.; Dieter Fricke, "Die deutsche Arbeiterklasse und die russische Revolution 1905," *ZfG* 5 (1957): 770ff; Günter Griep, "Über das Verhältnis zwischen der Sozialdemokratie und den freien Gewerkschaften während der Massenstreikdebatte 1905/06 in Deutschland," ibid. 11 (1963): 915ff., especially pp. 917, 931. Griep's work is highly critical of the inaction of the SPD leaders, but he is unable to show what they ought to have done (on this, see pp. 929–30) (*GdA*, vol. 2, pp. 84–85). See also Carl E. Schorske, *German Social Democracy: 1905–1917* (Cambridge, MA, 1955), pp. 36ff.; J. P. Nettl, *Rosa Luxemburg* (New York, 1966), vol. 1, pp. 296–98; Rosenberg, *Die Entstehung der deutschen Republik* (Berlin, 1930), pp. 47–48.

[72]Klein, *Deutschland*, pp. 19ff.; *GdA*, vol. 2, pp. 20ff.; Kuczynski, *Geschichte*, vol. 4, pp. 52ff., 66ff.; vol. 14, pp. 8ff., 135ff., and *passim*. See also, by way of illustration, Dirk Stegmann, "Hugenberg contra Stresemann," *VfZ* 24 (1976): 331ff.

volving enterprises controlling ever-larger segments of the economy and ever-larger numbers of workers, while the number of those controlling the profits kept growing smaller. Moreover, it is claimed that the nature of capitalism made it more profitable to reinvest excess capital in less highly developed countries that could be more profitably exploited than to permit its use for the raising of living standards at home. Thus, imperialism, the inevitable corollary of monopolist growth, kept the bulk of the working class mired in poverty despite increased productivity and national wealth. In consequence, the class struggle sharpened, with strikes and lockouts increasing and entrepreneurs banding together in special organizations (*Hauptstelle Deutscher Arbeitgeberverbände, Verein Deutscher Arbeitgeberverbände*) to fight off labor's demands more effectively. At the same time, industrialists and agrarians are found to have been moving ever closer together. Although the divergence of the interests of agrarians and those of industrial and banking "monopoly capitalists" is not ignored, whatever conflicts arose from such differences are considered subordinate to the common concern of members of these classes to preserve the status quo against labor. In the last analysis, they all were fellow capitalists.[73]

Developments that point in a different direction are discounted as diverging only apparently. Thus, the defeat of the Subversion and Penitentiary Bills, aimed at curbing Social Democratic and labor union activities; the introduction of a series of social reforms during Chancellor Bülow's administration; and the various abortive attempts to modify the Prussian three-class suffrage are dismissed as clever maneuvers to defuse the class struggle and gradually integrate the workers' movement, with the help of the SPD's "opportunists," into the existing bourgeois-monopolist state.[74] Similarly, East German historians find little to cheer about in the fact that efforts to do away with the Reichstag's universal male suffrage and to enact antilabor exceptional laws came to nothing. Not only were such liberalizing trends offset by numerous incidents of open repression—brutal state intervention against demonstrations and strikes and the continued prejudicial attitude of courts and police toward workers, especially Social Democratic

[73]See Klein, *Deutschland*, pp. 43–44, 48ff., 181ff.; *Grundriss*, pp. 313–14, 324ff. On the growing "capitalization" of the East Elbian estates, see also Ilona Ballwanz, "Zu den Veränderungen in der sozialökonomischen Basis der Junker zwischen 1895 und 1907," *ZfG* 27 (1979): 759ff.; on the class relationships between Junker agrarians and bourgeoisie, see the rather intricate exegesis of Küttler, "Zu den Kriterien einer sozialen Typologie des Junkertums im System des deutschen Imperialismus vor 1917," ibid., pp. 721ff.

[74]Klein, *Deutschland*, pp. 103ff.; Gutsche, "Einleitung," in *Herrschaftsmethoden des deutschen Imperialismus 1897/98 bis 1907*, ed. Gutsche and Baldur Kaulisch (Berlin [East], 1977), pp. 29–30.

ones—but the more flexible strategy of some segments of the "monopoly bourgeoisie" also strengthened the influence of the opportunists in the Social Democratic party. Willibald Gutsche notes to his horror that Chancellor von Bethmann Hollweg, the protagonist of a more liberal stance, even predicted that some day he might govern along with the bourgeois parties, for the "preservation of the existing order."[75] Greater flexibility on the part of the ruling class thus would merely lull the working class into a false sense of security; the workers could attain full release from their oppressed state only through the replacement of the capitalist order by a socialist one.[76]

DDR authors find these conclusions borne out also by the outcome of the crises touched off by William II's *Daily Telegraph* interview in 1908, an alarming demonstration of his lack of sound judgment that offended almost all major world powers, and by the Zabern affair, a case of the military's lawless arrogation of police power over civilians. Both incidents aroused strong enough discontent to threaten the very foundations of the political order, but in the end they remained episodes without consequence, because the initiation of parliamentary controls would have given the Social Democrats direct access to political power, and this step the nonsocialist parties were not prepared to take.[77]

Although the "monopolist bourgeoisie" is considered the dominant social force as the protagonist of the extant socioeconomic formation, it is not considered all-powerful. Given the clout of large landowners and the military establishment and given the growth and increasing unrest of the working class, DDR authors have modified their earlier view and no longer see the state as simply a tool of the monopolists: although the state on the whole had to follow the course of production, Gutsche explains, it did not simply take orders from the financial oligarchy (meaning banking and industrial capital, which, moreover, did not always present a united front) but also had to consider the interests of other groups. East German analyses thus admit that the state enjoyed a measure of independence vis-à-vis the monopolies, but they also insist that it nevertheless served above all the monopoly bourgeoisie, because all segments of the ruling class acted within a capitalist framework, and within this framework the great bourgeoisie was the economi-

[75]Gutsche, "Probleme des Verhältnisses zwischen Monopolkapital und Staat in Deutschland vom Ende des 19. Jahrhunderts bis zum Vorabend des ersten Weltkrieges," in *Studien über den deutschen Imperialismus vor 1914*, ed. Klein (Berlin [East], 1976), p. 52.

[76]Klein, *Deutschland*, pp. 249ff.; *Grundriss*, pp. 337ff.; Gutsche, "Einleitung," pp. 10ff.

[77]Klein, *Deutschland*, pp. 219–20, 261–62; Streisand, pp. 250–51.

cally dominant group.[78] Moreover, the great bourgeoisie reinforced its influence by its financial support of the nonsocialist parties and of propaganda organizations such as the Pan-German League, the Army and Navy Leagues, and the Reich Association Against Social Democracy, which articulated the longings and fears of bourgeois and petty bourgeois circles and harnessed them to the antilabor, militarist, and expansionist goals of the monopolies. The result was an emotional climate that compelled the government to adapt its policies to their concerns.[79]

Nonetheless, it has not been easy to reconcile this interpretation, which meets all ideological postulates, with a reality in which the East-Elbian agrarians played hardly a lesser role than the industrialists and the bankers. The agrarians dominated the governmental machinery in both Reich and Prussia and showed great effectiveness in protecting their legal prerogatives and their material interests, as in matters of taxes and tariffs. Indeed, the tortuous arguments by which Gutsche seeks to explain the predominance of the "monopoly bourgeoisie" over the Junker agrarians suggest that the predominance was not as clearcut as his premises claim.[80]

Whatever steps the ruling class took to ensure its political and economic domination at home, DDR authors find such steps closely connected with expansionist foreign ventures. With the banking and industrial monopolies in the vanguard of all imperialist moves, monopoly capitalism is identified with imperialism, in

[78]See Gutsche, "Zur Erforschung des Verhältnisses von Ökonomie und Politik im deutschen Imperialismus vor 1917," ZfG 25 (1977): 719–20; Gutsche, "Probleme," pp. 51–52; Dieter Baudis, "Wirtschaft und Kriegsführung im imperialistischen Deutschland 1914 bis 1918," JWG 3 (1974): 249. Baudis on the one hand rejects as "unrealistic" the concept of a bloc of monopolies subordinating the state to its interests, but he also insists that the state rested on and was dominated by the monopoly bourgeoisie as the economically strongest group. For the earlier view of the omnipotence of the monopolies see "Imperialismus," Swb, vol. 1, p. 807; Gutsche, "Zum Funktionsmechanismus zwischen Staat und Monopolkapital . . . (1914–1915)," JWG 1 (1973): 63.

[79]See Klein, in Deutschland im ersten Weltkrieg, ed. Klein (Berlin [East], 1968), vol. 1, p. 74; Klein, Deutschland, pp. 55–56; Fritz-Ferdinand Müller, Deutschland-Zanzibar-Ostafrika (Berlin [East], 1959), pp. 97ff. On the relations between big business and the nonsocialist parties during this period, see WZ Jena 14 (1965): no. 2; on those between big business and Pan-German League and other nationalist propaganda associations, see Kuczynski, Studien zur Geschichte des deutschen Imperialismus (Berlin [East], 1950), vol. 2. Kuczynski points out rightly that the role of business in these organizations cannot be determined on the basis of the relatively few directorships businessmen held in them, but on the other hand he goes too far in sweepingly calling these associations "propaganda organizations of monopoly capitalism."

[80]Gutsche, "Zur Erforschung," pp. 715ff.; also Küttler, "Zu den Kriterien," pp. 733–35. On the impact of the agrarians, see, too, the informative West German study by Groh, Negative Integration and revolutionärer Attentismus (Frankfurt, 1973), pp. 88ff.; also see Hans-Jürgen Puhle, Agrarische Interessenpolitik und preussischer Konservatismus im wilhelminischen Reich (1893–1914) (Hanover, 1967).

keeping with Lenin's contention. In his words, it was the last phase of the capitalist order in which its main beneficiaries—the monopolies—in their unending search for new profits were investing their capital abroad rather than in less profitable domestic ventures. At the same time, capitalism in the monopolist stage is claimed to have grown increasingly parasitical: it exploited underdeveloped countries, blocked technical progress or failed to use fully, for profit's sake, the available productive resources; it also created a large stratum of nonproductive, coupon-clipping *rentiers*, thus causing decay and stagnation everywhere. Finally, rival imperialist drives for markets and raw materials must lead to war once the world was divided up, plunging the masses into still greater misery. On the other hand, as Lenin also argued, the sharpening of the "contradictions" of the capitalist system on a worldwide plane made the conquest of power by the working class and the establishment of the socialist order a historical necessity. "Monopoly," he concluded, "is the transition from capitalism to a higher socioeconomic system." In this dialectical sense, imperialism, the "monopoly stage of capitalism," is viewed as progressive.[81]

The association of imperialism with monopoly capitalism creates some historiographical difficulties. It means that colonial acquisitions and economic dominions prior to the monopolist phase cannot be labeled as imperialist manifestations. Lenin, it is true, acknowledged that imperialism existed long before the era of monopoly capitalism, even in the slave-holding society of ancient Rome, and he made it clear in his analysis of imperialism that for the purposes of his argument he was concerned only with that type that was the corollary of monopoly capitalism.[82] His East German followers, however, speak of imperialism as if it existed only in the monopolist era. They have studiously refrained from calling Bismarck's colonial acquisitions in the 1800s imperialist or have termed them *proto-imperialist*, as products of the country's transition toward monopoly capitalism.[83] The exclusive identification of imperialism with monopoly capitalism obviously also implies that socialist expansion, such as that of the Soviet Union, is not imperialist.[84]

If the post-Leninist definition of imperialism raises serious questions, the interdependence of monopoly capitalism and imperialism, as postulated by Lenin, is equally hard to accept. Britain,

---

[81]Lenin, *Imperialism, the Highest State of Capitalism*, in *The Lenin Anthology*, ed. Robert C. Tucker (New York, 1975), pp. 204ff. (quotations on pp. 243, 270).
[82]Ibid., pp. 238–39.
[83]Engelberg, *Deutschland*, pp. 214ff., 297, as compared to pp. 374ff.; Streisand, pp. 223, as compared to p. 231; Klein, "Einleitung," in Klein, *Studien*, pp. 8, 10; "Imperialismus," *Swb*, vol. 1, p. 808; "Kolonialismus," ibid., vol. 1, p. 945.
[84]Klein, "Einleitung, in Klein, *Studien*, p. 5.

for one, though condemned as a leading imperialist power by Lenin and his disciples, had reached only a modest stage of monopolization by the turn of the century.[85] Germany, in turn, had arrived at a high degree of monopolization only in a few areas, and in some of its most flourishing export industries—pig iron, machines, textiles—there had been no monopolization at all or such monopolization was still in an early stage.[86]

On the other hand, in Germany's case, subsequent studies have borne out Lenin's thesis of the intimate connection of imperialism and capital exports at that time; it was the abundance of British and French foreign investments and the lack of sufficient exportable capital on Germany's part that so greatly concerned German political and financial circles during the pre-1914 period and that played into the hands of the warmongering forces.[87] In addition, whereas the lot of the masses did not grow worse, as Lenin had claimed, neither did it improve overall in this period of growing national wealth; thus, it declined, at least relatively.[88] This decline undoubtedly has made it easier to accept Lenin's definition of imperialism despite its various lapses from historical reality.[89] For, as Lenin argued, the fact that a theory cannot be applied "in its *pure* form" in practice does not invalidate it.[90]

The Marxist concept of imperialism differs from the non-Marxist one not only in regard to the time span it covers or in its definition of the driving forces and manifestations of imperialism; what is equally crucial for an understanding of the Marxist approach

[85]For a contrived East German answer to this problem, see the summary account in Peter Hampe, *Die 'ökonomische Imperialismustheorie'* (Munich, 1976), pp. 68ff.

[86]Hampe, *Die 'ökonomische Imperialismustheorie,'* pp. 72-73; also Mottek et al., *Studien zur Geschichte*, vol. 3, p. 190.

[87]Fritz Fischer, *Krieg der Illusionen: Die deutsche Politik von 1911 bis 1914* (Düsseldorf, 1969), pp. 413ff., 516ff.; George W. F. Hallgarten, *Imperialismus vor 1914* (Munich, 1963), vol. 2, pp. 464ff. and *passim;* also see additional data, though from a French perspective, in Raymond Poidevin, "Weltpolitik allemande et capitaux français (1898–1914)," in *Deutschland in der Weltpolitik des 19. und 20. Jahrhunderts*, ed. Immanuel Geiss and Bernd Jügen Wendt (Düsseldorf, 1973), pp. 237ff.

[88]See note 62 and Hampe (*Die 'ökonomische Imperialismustheorie,'* p. 308), who, however, considers the increase in real wages rather noteworthy, as unlike Groh (*Negative Integration*, pp. 40 n. 49, 85 n. 13), who finds it minimal. See also Knut Borchardt (in *HbDtWSG*, vol. 2, pp. 225ff.) and Conze (in ibid., pp. 619ff.), who essentially bear out Kuczynski's conclusions.

[89]That the lot of the worker has greatly improved in recent years in West Germany once again is dismissed as a clever monopolist tactic by DDR analysts (*Unb. Verg.*, pp. 399–401); "Formierte Herrschaft," *Swb*, vol. 1, pp. 596ff.

[90]See Klein, "Einleitung," in Klein, *Studien*, pp. 8–9, with Lenin quotation. On the other hand, to argue, as a West German author has done (Schröder, *Sozialistische Imperialismusdeutung* [Göttingen, 1973], p. 49), that Lenin's pamphlet on *Imperialism* analyzed a specific world situation rather than codified a scientific theory and should therefore not be treated as a theoretical treatise is not convincing. Rightly or wrongly, Marxists have made the study the *theoretical* foundation of their concept of imperialism.

is the axiom that imperialism was and is not a policy that can, or could, be changed at will or called off altogether. As mentioned before, it is considered instead an inevitable developmental phase of the capitalist system, and as such, it is subject to the laws of that system. Lenin put it succinctly in his pamphlet on *Imperialism:*

> If capitalism *could* raise the living standards of the masses, who, in spite of the amazing technical progress, are everywhere still half-starved and poverty-stricken, there could be no question of a surplus of capital. . . . But if capitalism did these things it would not be capitalism. . . . As long as capitalism remains what it is, surplus capital will be utilized not for the purpose of raising the standard of living of the masses in a given country, for this would mean a decline in profits for the capitalists, but for the purpose of increasing profits by exporting capital abroad to the backward countries.

Similarly, the quest for profits was bound to lead to war, for once the world had been divided up, an imperialist power could secure further profits only by the forced redivision of the world. With the profit motive a constituent element of imperialism, imperialism thus could not be ended except by the overthrow of that order.[91] To this, DDR authors now add that since Lenin's day imperialism has had to accept many constraints: it is barred from the growing number of socialist countries while, at the same time, the Soviet Union holds its protecting hand over large parts of the underdeveloped world and by its very existence puts a check on the ambitions of the imperialist powers. As Wolfgang Ruge has put it, imperialist monopoly capital must now worry first of all about its political survival and only secondarily can concern itself with increasing its profits. Thus, even if Western imperialism is considered far from dead and its nefarious activities are found to be causing trouble in the Middle and Far East, Latin America, and Africa, its demise is seen to be drawing closer.[92]

Because the nature of imperialism poses no conceptual problem for East German historians, they view with considerable distrust the extensive West German discussions on the origins and impulses of the imperialist era. According to Helmut Böhme, they are convinced that these discussions are merely attempts to obfuscate the key role of the monopoly bourgeoisie by blaming imperialist expansionism on pre-industrial elites—army, agrarians, churches, bureaucracy—that are anxious to buttress their faltering power; Hans-Ulrich Wehler also blames such expansionism on the government's trying to divert domestic discontent by expansionist ventures, and Wolfgang J. Mommsen blames it on a general aggressive nationalism. Nationalism, militarist aggressiveness, and domestic political considerations

[91]Lenin, *Imperialism*, pp. 209–10, 225–26, 255, 267.
[92]"Imperialismus," *Swb*, vol. 1, pp. 813–15; Ruge, review, *ZfG* 23 (1973): 85.

are not ignored but are viewed as mere contributing factors to developments rooted in the existing mode of production. As Helmut Stoecker puts it,

> Was not the economic basis of capitalist production relations (and with it the capitalist profit motive) the decisive foundation of the 'established social and political structure' of the imperialist powers prior to 1918 (and into the present)? For this simple reason every manifestation of imperialist policy, however little it may have had (and may have) to do with immediate and tangible profit concerns could (and can) be traced back ultimately to capitalist profit considerations that may be specific individual interests or basic interests of a general nature.[93]

The danger of the differing West German explanations, however, is seen not only in an exoneration of the industrial and banking monopolists; the unscientific nature of these explanations also makes it possible to deny the need for revolutionary changes, because they suggest that a bad imperialist policy can be replaced by a "better" one.[94]

That all these considerations have obvious present-day implications need hardly be mentioned. Because monopolist organizations of various types exist in West Germany, that state is by definition imperialist and, again by definition, the monopoly bourgeoisie is the dominant force in it. Blaming the imperialist expansion of Wilhelmine Germany on the East Elbian Junkers—"a stratum, in other words, which, unlike the German monopoly bourgeoisie, no longer exists," as one author puts it—is thus suspect as an attempt to protect the monopolists of today and must be fought. The avalanche of studies doing just that is indicative of the importance assigned to this task.[95]

Little needs to be said about the substantive aspects of the East German work on imperialism. Because the generic connection of monopolism and imperialism is an unquestioned axiom and because relatively little attention is paid to military and noneconomic aspects, East German research has focused on the mechanics by which the collaboration between state and monopoly bourgeoisie was effected. A great deal of material on this topic has been compiled, but the East German findings have added little qualitatively to the publications of Fritz Fischer, George W. F. Hallgarten,

[93]See Helmut Stoecker, "Bürgerliche Auslegungen des Imperialismusbegriffes in der Gegenwart," in Klein, *Studien*, p. 25. Stoecker, of course, paraphrases here Engels' famous letter to Joseph Bloch, in MEW, vol. 37, p. 463. See also Gutsche, "Grundtendenzen im Funktionsmechanismus zwischen Monopolkapital und Staat in der Aussenpolitik des deutschen Imperialismus vor 1914," *ZfG* 27 (1979): 1042ff.
[94]Eichholtz, review, *ZfG* 25 (1977): 1483; *Unb. Verg.*, pp. 298–99, 302–303.
[95]Stoecker, "Bürgerliche Auslegungen," p. 26; Klein, "Einleitung," in Klein, *Studien*, pp. 5–6; Gutsche, "Probleme," pp. 33–34; Gutsche, *Zur Imperialismus-Apologie in der BRD* (Berlin [East], 1975). See also note 109.

Dirk Stegmann, Klaus Wernecke, and other non-Marxist scholars. It can be argued, in fact, that non-Marxists have traced more convincingly Germany's drive toward war than have their DDR counterparts. Because the latter saw their main task in corroborating an accepted thesis, their assignment called for less exacting evidential requirements than that of the West German authors, who had to document a highly controversial thesis. For Marxist authors, Lenin summed it up well: "War is no accident, no 'sin.' . . . it is rather an inevitable phase of capitalism, as law-determined a form of capitalist life as is peace."[96]

The Struggle against Imperialism and Militarism

One group in Germany saw developments in this light of the connection between monopolism and imperialism—the radical left wing of the SPD, in Marxist parlance the German Left. Confident that imperialism was moving Germany closer to the socialist revolution, the German Left hailed the Russian Revolution of 1905 as the opening phase of an era of social crises and wars that would culminate in the overthrow of the capitalist order. DDR authors devote special attention to this group because of its "creative development of Marxism" in the imperialist age and its efforts to keep alive the revolutionary German workers' movement: in these endeavors the German Left maintained the best Social Democratic traditions and would eventually carry them into the German Communist party. The Left's greatest immediate contribution to the cause of the working class is seen, however, in its valiant struggle against German imperialism and militarism and the attending internal and external war preparations. The Left would not content itself with organizational and parliamentary action, but called for mass strikes, street demonstrations, antiwar propaganda among the young (the army's future recruits), and other protest activities on a mass scale.

Yet the Left does not win unstinted praise. Its leaders, Rosa Luxemburg, Karl Liebknecht (Wilhelm's son), and Franz Mehring among them, are taken to task for not understanding the true nature of Revisionism and for overestimating the effectiveness of spontaneous mass action. As a result, they did not establish a separate revolutionary party modeled on Lenin's "new-type" Bolshevik party, "without which the working class of no country can win."

---

[96]Fischer, *Krieg der Illusionen*; Hallgarten, *Imperialismus vor 1914*; Dirk Stegmann, *Die Erben Bismarcks* (Cologne, 1970); Klaus Wernecke, *Der Wille zur Weltgeltung* (Düsseldorf, 1970). Lenin, quoted by Klein, in *ZfG* 23 (1975): 491–92.

Nor did they create a separate faction within the party in preparation for an eventual secession and as an organizational focus for their views and activities. Instead, they expended themselves in the hopeless task of fighting the Revisionists and other reformists on their home ground.[97]

Thus viewed, the last prewar decade became a duel between reformists and the German Left, a duel in which the latter was increasingly outmaneuvered. In this view, moreover, the Revisionist faction was reinforced by the so-called Centrists, who occupied the middle ground between the two camps and dominated the party directorate; essentially reformist, the Centrists envisaged, however, an eventual political revolution as possibly the only way to establish a genuine democracy and give the workers access to political power. East German authors find Centrism more dangerous than Revisionism on the grounds that its opportunism was less overt. They also note that at times it took positions close to those of the Left, thus causing further confusion.[98]

Centrism constitutes a puzzling analytical problem for DDR scholars. Actually, the reasons for its strong impact are not hard to detect. The emphasis on reforms corresponded to the basic attitude of most workers, and the vague calls for an eventual revolution appealed to their hatred of the existing political system without requiring a militant activism. The East German analyses fail to see that the party consisted mainly of the very "labor aristocrats" and bureaucrats who, according to the Leninist charges, had been bribed into passivity and therefore were satisfied with the cautious strategy of their leaders.[99]

DDR authors find this hard to accept. Because they consider the socialist revolution the inevitable outcome of monopolism/imperialism, they tend to take seriously all calls for revolutionary action and detect evidence of revolutionary Marxism in almost any mass action. The difficulties such misconceptions create for them

[97]Klein, *Deutschland*, pp. 178, 228; *GdA*, vol. 2, pp. 74, 110–12; W. Gutsche and A. Laschitza, "Forschungen zur deutschen Geschichte von der Jahrhundertwende bis 1917," *ZfG* 18 (1970): suppl., p. 481; "Deutsche Linke," *Swb*, vol. 1, p. 422. See also Nettl, *Rosa Luxemburg*, vol. 1, pp. 285ff.; Ritter, *Die Arbeiterbewegung im Wilhelminischen Reich* (Berlin [West], 1959), pp. 207–8. Another deviation from Leninist strategy held against the German left-wing radicals is their failure to mobilize rural workers; *GdA*, vol. 2, pp. 89, 112. The quotation is found in Laschitza and Schumacher, "Thesen," p. 25.

[98]See *GdA*, vol. 2, pp. 109, 155–56; Klein, *Deutschland*, pp. 176–77; "Zentrismus," *Swb*, vol. 2., p. 859. For an interesting analysis of the impact of Centrism on internal party politics, see Laschitza, "Zur Rolle des Zentrismus 1911–12," in Klein, *Studien*, pp. 143ff.

[99]Robert Michels, "Die deutsche Sozialdemokratie: I. Parteimitgliedschaft und soziale Zusammensetzung," *Archiv für Sozialwissenschaft* 23 (1906): 513–14, 517, 539 n. 102; Paul Kampffmeyer, "Historisches und Theoretisches zur sozialdemokratischen Revisionsbewegung," *Sozialistische Monatshefte* 8 no. 1 (1902): 345ff.; Rosenberg, *Entstehung*, pp. 48–50; see also *GdA*, vol. 2, p. 57, and Kuczynski, *Ausbruch*.

are reflected in their treatment of August Bebel, the SPD party leader. Although Bebel is not considered part of the German Left, claims that he was a Centrist are vehemently denied. Whatever his position in the East German spectrum, DDR authors treat Bebel with great reverence, forever stressing his unswerving loyalty to revolutionary Marxism—contrary to the basic historiographic principle, on which they are otherwise so insistent, that men be judged by their actions rather than by their words. Yet when Bebel is occasionally found at fault—for taking the wrong side in the escalating debate between radicals and reformists, for maintaining a party unity that became increasingly artificial, or for ignoring the revolutionary potentialities of mass activism as reflected in the numerous rank-and-file protests, strikes, meetings, and street demonstrations—the reprimands are usually gentle.[100]

Bebel's stand on foreign policy issues, his responses to the militaristic and imperialistic tendencies of the period—not always satisfactory ones in the East German view—are treated with similar leniency, while other leaders who shared his views are dealt with more roughly. Militarism and imperialism were problems on which the SPD parted ways with all other parties, but both issues also created deep frictions within the party itself: radicals and reformists disagreed sharply as to how far the struggle against militarism and imperialism should be pursued. For this and other reasons, these issues have received considerable attention in the East German literature. Their domestic dimension in particular has been the subject of extensive research. Not only did the insistence on increased armaments place ever heavier financial and service burdens upon the working class, militarism was also aimed directly against that class: the larger the army, the greater its effectiveness in suppressing strikes, street demonstrations, and other working-class efforts to improve labor's lot.[101] Beyond this, as the surveys on DDR historiography stress, the special attention de-

---

[100]See Gutsche and Laschitza, "Forschungen," pp. 488–89; see also Gerd Irrlitz, "Bemerkungen über . . . de[n] Zentrismus" (*BzG* 8 [1966]: 43ff.) and Laschitza, "Karl Kautsky und der Zentrismus" (ibid. 10 [1968]: 798ff.), both of which deal with the ideological and political problems that Centrism presents to Marxist historians. On Bebel, see Gutsche and Laschitza, "Forschungen," p. 488; Fricke, "Das Vermächtnis von August Bebel erfüllt," *ZfG* 8 (1960): 279; Laschitza and Schumacher, "Thesen," pp. 30–31. See also the literature cited in *ZfG* 18 (1970): suppl., pp. 484–85, but also Laschitza, "Zur Rolle," which contains a number of instances of Bebel's Centrist position, although the author does not admit this (pp. 152–53, 158). Concerning Bebel's Centrism, see also Roth, *The Social Democrats in Imperial Germany* (Totowa, NJ, 1963), pp. 185ff.; Steinberg, *Sozialismus*, p. 76 n. 208. If anything, Bebel was farther removed from the radical left than was Kautsky (ibid., p. 81; Nettl, *Rosa Luxemburg*, vol. 1, pp. 409–10). Bebel's "objective" Centrism was earlier acknowledged by the DDR historian Leo Stern, in *Archivalische Forschungen*, vols. 2, 59.

[101]Klein, *Deutschland*, vol. 1, pp. 60ff.; also Fricke, "Zur Rolle des Militarismus nach innen in Deutschland vor dem ersten Weltkrieg," *ZfG* 6 (1958): 1298ff.

voted to these topics is to help find answers in history to present-day threats of imperialism and militarism.[102]

Viewing war as simply a tool of imperialism abroad and re-pression at home, East German historians assail all war prepara-tions of the time. They insist that there were no longer any justifi-able wars.[103] If Marx and Engels had been willing to go to war against Russia, they had felt justified because nineteenth-century Russia had been a bulwark of reaction, strong enough to block progressive movements even beyond its borders. After 1905, how-ever, Russia was weakened by military defeat and internal unrest and was merely one imperialist power among many others. A Ger-man war against Russia thus would constitute imperialist aggres-sion, which the German working class must not support. Nor could Germany fight any longer any justifiable wars of defense in the age of imperialism, as not only the Revisionists but even as "revolutionary" a Marxist as Bebel claimed. If there was danger of war, Fritz Klein notes, "that threatening war was not the surprise attack of an aggressor on a peace-minded Germany, but an unjust imperialist war over the redistribution of the world, toward which German imperialism more than any other was driving." What dan-gerous ramifications a distinction between wars of aggression and wars of defense would lead to could be gathered from Revisionist statements that approved armaments as being needed for the al-leged defense of the nation. Klein finds equally reprehensible the sanction of armament bills on the grounds that because wars would not be abolished in the foreseeable future, it would be irre-sponsible to withhold such support and send workers into battle without proper equipment.

DDR authors also reject the view that wars were permissible ways of settling international disputes. They maintain that wars enjoyed such a reputation only among the ruling classes, which resorted to wars to increase their profits. Even if these groups man-aged to persuade parts of the working class that wars could be fought for legitimate reasons, such manipulations could not end the irreconcilable clash of interests that divided the nation on the question of war and peace.[104]

The one group credited with never forgetting that wars were rooted in the existing social order is the German Left. Only the Luxemburg-Liebknecht group adhered steadfastly to the conviction

[102]ZfG 8 (1960): suppl., p. 311, and 18 (1970): suppl., p. 477.
[103]However, they agree with Liebknecht, who, like Lenin, allowed that wars might contribute to historical progress if they were used by the proletariat to launch revolutions (Bartel, *Die Linken in der deutschen Sozialdemokratie im Kampf gegen Militarismus und Krieg* [Berlin (East), 1958], pp. 71–72).
[104]Klein, *Deutschland*, pp. 186ff. (quotation on p. 188), 305; Klein, *Deutschland*, vol. 1, pp. 146ff.; especially pp. 146, 159–60, 194–95.

that as tools of the exploiting classes imperialism and militarism were international phenomena and had to be fought on an international scale, by enlightening the proletariat of all imperialist powers about the true nature of war. Wars, then, could be prevented only by concerted working-class action across national boundaries, and ultimately only by a socialist revolution. Thus, East German researchers trace with meticulous care the antiwar activities of the German Left, the corresponding work of the Second International, and the struggle in Germany between the radical Left and reformists over mass strikes, street demonstrations, and other mass actions. Yet, if the Left was unable to overcome the resistance of the reformists, once again it is found not entirely guiltless. Klein concludes that it indulged in abstract internationalism and did not sufficiently stress the specific relevance of the international struggle to the true interests of the nation.

Despite this extensive research, contradictory statements, based on inadequate data, make the determination of the Left's actual influence a matter of speculation. As on other such occasions, the "knowledge" that the Luxemburg-Liebknecht group embodied history's proper, inevitable development has led DDR analysts to attribute an impact to its activities that is not borne out by the available evidence. East German researchers admit as much when they grant that the influence of the German Left made itself felt not on the upper levels of the party but in the local organizations. Even on the local level, however, that impact varied from district to district.[105]

Thus, the Left was unable to change conditions. Such changes would have required nationwide action, and proposals in that direction—such as calls for mass strikes to attain political goals—were either watered down to the point of irrelevance by the party or rejected outright. Indeed, as DDR authors note ruefully, the readiness of the SPD leadership to follow a conciliatory strategy increased during these years: not only did Social Democrats cooperate with bourgeois parties and governments in the more liberal South German states, they did so also on the national level. In 1913 they ignored the party's antimilitarist position and voted for the enactment by the Reichstag of a direct property tax that was to finance another army expansion. That this was done to prevent the levy of indirect taxes that would have weighed more heavily on the poor than a direct tax does not seem an adequate justification to the East German critics. "There

[105]See Klein, *Deutschland*, pp. 169ff., 184ff.; Klein, *Deutschland*, vol. 1, pp. 146, 170, 199; Laschitza and Schumacher, "Thesen," p. 33. Some studies on the local activities of the German Left have been published in recent years, but they cover too little territory to establish the Left as a group with a nationwide following.

existed no longer in Germany a revolutionary Marxist party to provide leadership to the working class, which was ready to fight in defense of its class interests and Germany's national interests, fulfilling its historical mission in accordance with Karl Liebknecht's anti-imperialist concepts," *Geschichte der deutschen Arbeiterbewegung* concludes mournfully.[106]

That the workers were ready for such a fight East German historiography still must prove. The activism of mass demonstrations and strikes that was practiced by part of the working class ought not to be mistaken for revolutionism.[107]

The Outbreak of World War I

Because the German working class, and for that matter the working class of any of the imperialist powers, was unable to stop the rivaling imperialist drives of their ruling classes, a collision of these drives, culminating in war, was inevitable in the Leninist view. DDR scholars, unlike Western historians, thus do not view the outbreak of World War I as a historical turning point, marking off one historical era from another, but rather as merely a part of an ongoing inevitable process. In this view, the incision between eras occurred only in 1917, the year of the Bolshevik Revolution, which brought to an end the age of capitalism and ushered in the worldwide transition from capitalism to socialism.[108]

In discussing the critical weeks between the assassination of the heir to the Austro-Hungarian throne, Archduke Francis Ferdinand, on June 28, 1914, and Germany's entry into the war on August 1 of that year, the East German accounts start from the premise that all European powers were propelled into the war by

---

[106]*GdA*, vol. 2, p. 202; *Grundriss*, pp. 337–39; Klein, *Deutschland*, pp. 250–52.

[107]See the careful investigations of Groh, *Negative Integration*, pp. 125ff., 249–50, 557ff.; and Rosenberg, *Entstehung*, pp. 48ff.; Holborn, vol. 3, pp. 354ff., especially p. 363; also Kuczynski, *Ausbruch*. One reason for the emphasis on the revolutionary nature of the activities of the masses is the determination of DDR historians to repudiate what they term a deliberate strategy on the part of their non-Marxist counterparts to deny the history-making role of the masses and to attribute all social progress not to the class struggles of the masses but to an advancing industrialization, structural crises in the empire, or to a general process of democratization (see Gutsche and Seeber, "Zu einigen Problemen des Verhältnisses zwischen Bourgeoisie, Arbeiterklasse und anderen Teilen der Volksmassen beim Übergang zum Imperialismus," *ZfG* 27 [1979]: 635ff.).

[108]See the periodicization of the material in Streisand, Klein (*Deutschland*), and *Grundriss*; also see Klein, *Deutschland*, p. 327; Baudis, "Wirtschaft und Kriegsführung im imperialistischen Deutschland 1914 bis 1918," *JWG* 3(1974): 247. For some non-Marxist observations along similar lines, see Hans Rothfels, "Zeitgeschichte als Aufgabe," *VfZ*, I (1953): 6–7.

their respective imperialist goals.[109] They see no fundamental difference between Germany's conduct and that of the other states, merely one of degree. Germany's imperialism is found especially virulent because as a latecomer to the imperialist race it had acquired only a small share of the world's riches and thus was especially anxious to see the world redivided. Moreover, Germany's deep-rooted militarist tradition and its semiabsolute Junker-bourgeois regime served to reinforce the aggressiveness of its imperialist drive.[110] However, although it is recognized that Germany's leaders were readier than most others to plunge Europe into war in pursuit of their goals and therefore bore the main responsibility for its outbreak, DDR accounts emphasize that all powers considered war as a proper and adequate way of settling conflicting claims—not a last desperate resort to be avoided if at all possible. Thus Britain, too, is included among the deliberate warmongers: London's reluctance to side unequivocally with France and Russia during the post-Sarajevo crisis is interpreted as a precautionary measure designed so as not to deter Germany from going to war—a war that Britain is alleged to have wanted in order to rid itself of its German competitor.[111] If, nonetheless, Russia, France, and Britain are shown on the whole as reacting to German and Austrian moves rather than acting on their own "imperialistic" initiative,[112] the reason is (as Fritz Klein, the leading East German specialist on the causes of World War I, points out) that the origins of the war cannot be determined on the basis of the events of a few weeks or months, but must be seen as the result of long-range developments.[113]

This approach also makes it unnecessary for Marxist historians to show that "monopolist" interests played a determinant role

[109]One of the East German criticisms of Fischer's work has been that it tends to present Germany's imperialist opponents in too favorable a light (*Unb. Verg.*, p. 309; Klein, "Zu einem neuen Buch von Fritz Fischer," *ZfG* 26 [1978]: 114–15).
[110]See Klein, *Deutschland*, vol. 1, pp. 64ff., 104ff.; "Weltkrieg, erster," *Swb*, vol. 2, pp. 804ff. Helmut Bleiber has warned, however, against overstressing the impact of militarist traditions or of the Prussian Junkers on German imperialism: "The effectiveness of historical traditions is ultimately determined not by these traditions themselves, but in each case by specific class forces which use them to realize concrete present interests. What determined the special aggressiveness of German imperialism was not primarily the pact between bourgeoisie and nobility in the nineteenth century and the tradition attached to it, but the fact of Germany's belated participation in the division of the world. To view a negative historical tradition as the determinant factor of the especially aggressive character of German imperialism results logically in an exoneration of the monopoly bourgeoisie" (Bleiber, "Bourgeoisie," p. 319).
[111]Streisand, pp. 251–53; *Grundriss*, p. 344; Klein, *Deutschland*, pp. 273, 275–76; Klein, in Klein, *Deutschland*, vol. 1, pp. 244–46 (this is the only passage in which some corroborating, but far from conclusive, evidence is cited).
[112]Klein, *Deutschland*, vol. 1, pp. 240ff.
[113]Klein, "Neue Veröffentlichungen in der BRD zu Geschichte und Vorgeschichte des ersten Weltkrieges," *ZfG* 20 (1972): 212; see also *GdA*, vol. 2, p. 213.

during the critical weeks in July 1914 (of which there is, in fact, no indication). Similarly, unlike non-Marxist historians, DDR authors have almost nothing to say about any domestic factors that may have precipitated the crisis. Streisand notes briefly that the war was welcomed by Germany's "ruling class" as an opportunity to consolidate its position vis-à-vis the working class, and *Grundriss*, too, alludes to this point.[114] From this long-range perspective, the war could not have been brought closer by the action or inaction of any individual. The question of whether Chancellor von Bethmann Hollweg exerted a moderating or an aggressive influence on the course of events, which has aroused a spirited debate among non-Marxist historians, seems wholly irrelevant to Marxists.[115] For them the responsibility lay with the ruling class as a whole; its greed and aggressiveness rather than any genuinely national concerns pushed the country into the war.[116]

Yet, it is noted, there were other culprits as well. Bitter charges are leveled against the Social Democratic leaders for having assured the government of their party's cooperation during the critical days after Austria had declared war on Serbia and for their willingness to support and help finance the war, when Germany launched it, as a war fought in defense of the country.[117] In doing

[114]Streisand, p. 254; *Grundriss*, p. 344.

[115]See Klein, in Klein, *Deutschland*, vol. 1, pp. 255–56; Gutsche, "Probleme," pp. 65ff., 71–72. The inconclusive West German debate on this issue is summed up by Wolfgang Schieder in *SDG*, vol. 6, pp. 855–57. Schieder's own position is contradictory: although he rejects the view that Bethmann's role was not decisive, he admits that the chancellor had little freedom of action within the existing government system. Klein also notes that if Hungarian Prime Minister Tisza opposed a war against Serbia, he did so as the spokesman of the Hungarian nobility, which feared it might lose its privileged position if further Slav-settled territories were added to the Austro-Hungarian empire (Klein, *Deutschland*, vol. 1, pp. 225, 230–31). This had been noted already by the Italian historian Luigi Albertini, who, however, had pointed out that Tisza's opposition derived as much from a genuine abhorrence of war—a fact that Klein does not consider worth mentioning. Cf. Albertini, *The Origins of the War of 1914* (Oxford, 1965), vol. 2, p. 127.

[116]Much is made of the fact that Krupp, the arms manufacturer, Karl Helfferich, one of the directors of the Deutsche Bank, and the heads of the Hamburg-America Line and the North German Lloyd were forewarned of the likelihood of war, and no one else was. These precautionary measures are claimed to illustrate again the close ties between the government and certain monopolies (Klein, *Deutschland*, p. 270; Streisand, p. 252; Kuczynski, *Ausbruch*, pp. 13–14, 16–18; Kuczynski, *Geschichte*, vol. 14, pp. 183–85).

[117]Both Marxist and non-Marxist historians have mistakenly claimed that the Social Democratic assurances of cooperation strengthened the government's determination to go to war. Actually, the decision to risk going to war had been made before Bethmann and other government members sounded out the Socialist leaders as to their attitude. The soundings were made only in order to reassure the civil authorities that they were right in opposing the repressive measures the military wanted to impose on the Social Democrats in the crisis. See Groh, *Negative Integration*, pp. 625ff.; Fischer, *Krieg der Illusionen*, pp. 698–99.

so, DDR authors maintain, the leaders sabotaged the impressive antiwar demonstrations that were sweeping the country. Thus, whereas the workers had been able to fulfill their historical task of defending the true interests of the nation and had prevented the ruling class from going to war during the first Morocco Crisis in 1905 and during the Balkan crisis of 1912, the treachery of the workers' leaders in 1914 kept them from carrying out their national mission. Worse, it misled them into succumbing to a chauvinistic propaganda campaign that gave German aggression the appearance of a war of defense against tsarist Russia. Without proper guidance from their leaders, the masses, rather than fight for peace, came to support the war.[118]

A bitter controversy arose over this issue among DDR historians in the late 1950s. Jürgen Kuczynski challenged the view that it was solely or even primarily the fault of the party leadership that the working class did not try more determinedly to prevent the outbreak of war and that the workers, once war had been declared, readily took up arms. Kuczynski acknowledged the guilt of the SPD leaders (sparing no invective to show his contempt for them), but he insisted that the primary responsibility for the workers' inaction rested with the workers themselves—as it must, he stressed, according to Marxist-Leninist tenets. His argument was that the workers had been corrupted economically by the ruling class into an opportunist posture; they had been misled by a relentless propaganda campaign of press, churches, and schools into viewing the war as one of defense—a campaign whose success, he admitted, was helped, but not caused, by the passivity of the party leadership. Thus, when war broke out, "everyone enthusiastically [got] into the act—everyone, that is, Junker and proletarian, great bourgeois and petty bourgeois: one people, besotted, and the masters of the slaughterhouse, fixed up as a saloon, happily joined in the fun. . . . One comes to understand what Marx means when

[118]See Klein, *Deutschland*, pp. 276ff.; Klein, in Klein, *Deutschland*, vol. 1, pp. 259ff. Whether antiwar demonstrations helped to avert war during the Morocco and Balkan crises is questionable. For 1905 this assertion is based on one general remark of William II (Klein, *Deutschland*, vol. 1, p. 168; also Streisand, pp. 247–48), but it is not confirmed by the more thorough investigations of Hedwig Wachenheim, *Die deutsche Arbeiterbewegung 1844–1914* (Cologne, 1967), pp. 502–3; Georges Haupt, *Socialism and the Great War* (Oxford, 1972), pp. 18, 32, 33–34. In the case of the Balkan crisis of 1912, the claim that Socialist agitation averted the war (Klein, *Deutschland*, pp. 246–47) has some support in uncorroborated statements of Haupt (pp. 83–85, 91–92, 224) to the effect that the antiwar demonstrations and the Second International's Basel Congress of November 1912 made a deep impression on governments and public opinion. It seems refuted, however, by Fritz Fischer's detailed discussion of the German government's attitude in December 1912, according to which Berlin's policies were not at all affected by these events (Fischer, *Krieg der Illusionen*, pp. 226ff.).

he speaks of the "moral degredation" that the rule of capitalism entails for the working class—for the working class, the greatest creative force in history."[119]

This reassignment of responsibilities met at once with strong opposition. Beginning with an acrimonious critique in *Neues Deutschland*, the main newspaper of the Socialist Unity party (SED), the attacks quickly gathered momentum. In the *Zeitschrift für Geschichtswissenschaft* they were taken up in no less than five lengthy articles, all but one written by members of research institutes affiliated with the central committee of the SED.[120] There is no need here to go into the details of these verbose broadsides;[121] the criticisms centered on Kuczynski's conclusion that the working class was directly responsible for not having launched the powerful antiwar activities that might have created enough insecurity among the ruling class to let its hesitant faction prevail and prevent the outbreak of war. In rebuttal, the critics point to the sizable peace meetings and demonstrations that swept the country after the Austrians sent their ultimatum to Serbia. If no more was done, this was the fault of the leaders: without proper leadership and organization the masses could not assert themselves. Neither could the masses be said to have supported the war when Germany did enter it, because they were never consulted and thus had no chance to express their views. However, what is found particularly objectionable in Kuczynski's analysis—and here history merges into politics, as it must in Marxist-Leninist practice—is his alleged claim that the masses are virtually incapable of preventing a war of aggression that is dressed up as a war of defense by the imperialist ruling class. With the Western powers believed at the time (1957–1958) to be preparing for war against the socialist camp, this meant that the working classes of the Western countries were being written off as barriers to such a war—a conclusion that was considered "revisionist" because it believed the masses incapable of fighting imperialism.[122]

The controversy revolved around two basic issues—the rela-

[119]Kuczynski, *Ausbruch*, especially pp. 39, 49–50, 89–90, 140ff.; quotation on pp. 89–90.
[120]See the bibliography in *ZfG* 8 (1960): suppl., p. 311 n. 51.
[121]From a methodological viewpoint, however, the arguments are not without interest, with their painstaking exegeses on statements of Marx, Engels, and Lenin, their obvious contradictions, their misquotations and misinterpretations of what Kuczynski actually said, and their vituperative tenor.
[122]On this last point in particular see Meusel, in *ZfG* 6 (1958): 1054, 1059–60, 1067; Heinz Fliegner, ibid., p. 315; Hans-Joachim Bernhard and Fricke, ibid. 8 (1960): suppl., p. 310. Both Meusel and Fliegner also make the point that in 1914 the masses were not able to prevent the war because imperialism dominated the entire world, whereas in 1958 the proletarian movement in capitalist countries could count on the help of the socialist countries. Actually, Kuczynski had implicitly said this too (*Ausbruch*, p. 39).

tionship between leaders and led in a working-class party and the evaluation of the events in late July and early August of 1914. As for the respective roles assigned to leaders and led in the Marxist-Leninist view, Kucyznski's position accords with Marx's and Lenin's views. *Foundations of Marxist Philosophy* defines these roles as follows: "No class in history has seized power, according to Lenin, unless it assigned as its leaders its progressive spokesmen, who could organize and guide the struggle of their class. This applies also to the working class. Without farsighted, wise, and experienced leaders who are appointed and taught by the party, the working class cannot achieve its emancipation." It then adds: "The power of the leaders of the working class rests on their ties with the masses, in the power of the mass movement. If the leaders . . . become supercilious or bureaucratic, *party and masses will correct them.* But if the leaders betray the trust of the masses, *party and masses will no longer support them, will remove them from the posts to which they were appointed, and replace them with leaders loyally devoted to the people.*[123]

Thus, although the masses cannot effectively act without leadership and organization, the ultimate decision over the type of leadership and organization they should have rests with them, as it must if the Marxist concept of the history-making role of the masses is to be more than an empty phrase.[124] Yet, as Kucyznski shows, the workers did not insist that their leaders continue, let alone intensify, their pro-peace activities in July 1914. Rather, once they had done their demonstrating, the workers went back to their gardening or planned dances and hikes for the following Sunday.[125]

As for the workers' alleged lack of opportunity to voice their opposition to the war, they could have expressed such opposition,

---

[123]*Grundlagen*, pp. 686–87. Italics mine.

[124]I am pursuing here the Marxist approach to its logical conclusion. A non-Marxist might of course argue that the distinction is pointless and that leaders and masses are mutually dependent on each other. That Marxists, too, have some misgivings about the validity of their theoretical stance may be concluded from the ambiguous way in which another basic work, *Grundlagen* (pp. 205–6, 209–12) deals with this question. It should also be noted that one critique, in support of its view, quotes Marx's observation in his "Inaugural Address" that the working class "meets one precondition of success—numbers. But numbers count only if they are organized and guided by knowledge." Yet Marx said also at that time that "the emancipation of the working class must be the work of the working class itself." In the same vein he warned, when unification was about to provide the workers with a nationwide basis of operations: "If the German working class is not going to play the role assigned to it, this will be its own fault," thus placing the ultimate responsibility squarely upon the workers. See Günter Benser, Xaver Streb, and Winkler, in *ZfG* 6 (1958): 175; Marx, in MEW, vol. 16, pp. 12, 14; vol. 17, pp. 269–70. See also "Volksmassen," *Swb*, vol. 2, p. 753: "The popular masses are the main impetus and the pace-setting actors of social progress."

[125]Kucyznski, *Ausbruch*, pp. 56ff.; also letter from Clara Zetkin to Fritz Westmeyer, August 5, 1914 (ibid., p. 98). See also Haupt, *Socialism*, pp. 189, 224ff.

without organized action and leadership, by staying away from the jubilant crowds. Yet large numbers joined the rejoicing crowds at the news of the war. Nor is there any evidence that workers did not flock as readily to the colors as did other segments of the population. As Fritz Klein has noted in unwitting support of Kuczynski, the state of emergency and the ceaseless propaganda concerning the "Russian threat" had their paralyzing effect on the Social Democratic masses.[126] Not surprisingly, Kuczynski has not abandoned his thesis.[127]

The War and State-Monopolist Capitalism

The war, according to the Marxist assessment, touched off the general crisis of the capitalist system that will eventually end with that system's collapse. As the product of clashing imperialist drives, the war demonstrated the inability of the capitalist order to evolve peacefully; because of its self-destructive nature, Lenin called imperialism the highest—that is, the final—stage of capitalism. All the elements of crisis were present: the war, accelerating the concentration of capital, increasing the misery of the proletariat, and deepening the contradiction between the progressing socialization of production and the disposal of the profits of that production by a dwindling minority of private monopoly lords (*Monopolherren*), was preparing the way for the revolution that would overthrow the parasitical capitalist order and replace it with a socialist one. This conceptual framework has determined all research on World War I (just as research on the postwar period has focused on the question of how capitalism managed to survive in Germany after the defeat and collapse of the imperial state even though conditions were "objectively ripe" for a socialist revolution).[128]

[126]See Wachenheim, *Arbeiterbewegung*, pp. 594–95; Rosenberg, *Entstehung*, p. 71; Klein, "Sonst kriege ich die Sozialdemokraten nicht mit, *BzG* 9 (1967): 852; Kuczynski, *Geschichte*, vol. 4, p. 241; also Schorske, *German Social Democracy*, p. 290. Ernst Gläser's *Jahrgang 1902* (Berlin, 1931) is a novel that depicts with great sensitivity the mood of that time. Heinz Fliegner, one of Kuczynski's critics, notes in a characteristically Marxist a priori approach: "The Soviet historian R. J. Jevserov writes, most likely correctly, that the growing revolutionary mood was reflected but weakly in the official documents and the press of the parties of the Second International, that such a mood did, however, exist, and that it is the task of the historian to make it as clearly visible as possible (cf. *Sowjetwissenschaft*, Gesellschwiss. Beiträge, 1957, no. 3, p 351)," *ZfG* 6 (1958): 317 n. 10. In his detailed account of the workers' attitude in July 1914 in *Deutschland*, vol. 1, pp. 259ff., Klein cites Kuczynski repeatedly as a source of factual information, but does not mention Kuczynski's differing evaluation of that attitude—evidently something to be ignored.
[127]See Wolfgang Ruge, review, *ZfG* 21 (1973): 85.
[128]*ZfG* 8 (1960): suppl., p. 317; Streisand, p. 255; *GdA*, vol. 2, p. 214; see also Helmut Dan Schmidt, "Imperialismus," *SDG*, vol. 3, pp. 34–35.

Militarily, the war raises no special problems for East German historiography. Because of the vast gap between Germany's military and economic potential and her far-ranging war aims, Germany's plans are dismissed as "adventurous" and her defeat seen as inevitable. "The attempt of German imperialism to conquer the 'place in the sun,'" as *Geschichte der deutschen Arbeiterbewegung* sums up the general view, "inevitably had to end with its defeat, regardless of the varying fortunes of war." Military events thus take up relatively little space in most accounts, and the military coverage differs from non-Marxist ones primarily in its emphasis on the futility of the various campaigns and on the senselessness of the losses, which were incurred not on behalf of the nation but on behalf of its small ruling class.[129]

On the other hand, considerable attention is paid to Germany's war aims. DDR scholars probe these aims not as a controversial problem (which to them it is not) but as a corroboration of their analysis of imperialism. As they see it, these aims had long been determined by the very nature of imperialism: the war was to provide monopoly capitalism with the elbow room for profit expansion that the homeland, under capitalist conditions, could no longer supply. (That agrarian and petty bourgeois organizations proclaimed similar goals is considered merely an echo of monopolist aspirations, encouraged by the monopolies to disguise their own quest for profits.) The territorial range of the German aims, from the Atlantic to the Ukraine, to Africa, and beyond, has never been questioned by East German analysts; they are agreed that monopoly capitalism made Germany fight the war, not in order to secure the country's position as one world power among others, but in order to attain eventual world domination. They note differences in the formulation of these war aims; the call for annexations is attributed to a monopolist group centering around the coal, iron, and steel industries and the banks affiliated with them, whereas another bloc, led by the petrochemical, electrical, machine, and shipbuilding industries and their banking connections, is found to have favored few outright annexations, preferring indirect domination through customs unions and puppet regimes. Nor do DDR analysts overlook disagreements as to the geographical direction expansion should take or the attitude to be adopted toward Britain (compromise peace versus military defeat). Yet they maintain that these were tactical rather than substantive divergences and that both monopolist blocs aimed at Germany's rule over and beyond Europe. (The establishment of an indirect hegemony, it is pointed out, also had the advantage of being less likely to be opposed by Social Democratic "opportunists.") With the war

---

[129]Streisand, pp. 238–40; Mottek et al., *Studien der Geschichte*, vol. 3, p. 199; *Grundriss*, pp. 346–47; *GdA*, vol. 2, p. 233.

thus seen as having been fought on behalf of monopoly capitalism, the main Marxist concern is to show how the demands of the monopolists were translated into official policy—an assignment that East German researchers, by their own admission, have not yet solved satisfactorily.

At the same time, it is taken as a matter of course that the war aims of the Allied powers were just as imperialistic as Germany's. Nonetheless, it is recognized that the Allied aims did not enable any one power to dominate the Continent. Klein also notes that although the Allies were fighting the war in pursuit of their own interests, their aims in case of victory were to enable the subject nationalities of Germany and the Habsburg Empire to achieve their independence—"doubtless a forward move, even though—as things turned out in 1918—the new nation-states remained part of the capitalist social order."[130]

DDR analysts also minimize the differences in policy that the two industrial groups pursued in the domestic arena. Here again the repressive policies advocated by the heavy-industrial bloc and the more flexible posture of the electrochemical group are viewed merely as different tactical approaches to the class struggle, designed to control the working class by either ignoring or blurring the existing class contradictions. Thus, Willibald Gutsche notes, the political truce—the *Burgfrieden* proclaimed by the government—in effect upheld the military dictatorship, because it left intact the unlimited emergency powers of the military authorities. Similarly, the reforms that Chancellor Bethmann Hollweg proposed were to be granted only within the framework of the "monarchist-imperialist-militarist system," or, as the war wore on, in order to salvage as much of that system as was possible. Thus, whereas non-Marxists hail Bethmann's proposals as steps on the road to democracy, even if not intended as such, Marxists dismiss them as evident efforts to obstruct democracy without overt repression.[131]

[130]See Werner Basler, *Deutschlands Annexionspolitik in Polen und im Baltikum 1914–1918* (Berlin [East], 1962), pp. 20–21; Gutsche and Johanna Schellenberg, in Klein, *Deutschland*, vol. 1, pp. 352ff.; Klein, *Deutschland*, pp. 298–300; Weber, *Ludendorff und die Monopole* (Berlin [East], 1966), p. 46; also Fischer, *Krieg der Illusionen*, pp. 761, 765, 783. On the irrelevance of the war aims of peasants and middle class, see Joachim Petzold, "Zu den Kriegszielen der deutschen Monopolkapitalisten im ersten Weltkrieg," *ZfG* 8 (1960): 1401–2; Gutsche, "Grundtendenzen," pp. 1046–47. On the inadequacy of DDR research, see Gutsche, in Klein, *Deutschland*, vol. 2, p. 61; Klein, "Stand und Probleme der Erforschung der Geschichte des deutschen Imperialismus bis 1945," *ZfG* 23 (1975): 488. On the convergence of extremist and more moderate war aims, see also (on the non-Marxist side) Konrad H. Jarausch, "Die Alldeutschen und die Regierung Bethmann Hollweg," *VfZ* 21 (1973): 449–50; Dorpalen, "Will the Real Bethmann Hollweg Stand Up?" *Reviews in European History* 1 (1974): 110ff.
[131]*GdA*, vol. 2, p. 213; Gossweiler, *Grossbanken*, pp. 58–59; Gutsche, "Bethmann Hollweg und die Politik der Neuorientierung," *ZfG* 13 (1965): 209ff., especially

What East German historians find far more significant in the long-range perspective of socioeconomic developments is the accelerated emergence of what they call *state-monopolist capitalism*. *Sachwörterbuch* defines state-monopolist capitalism as "characterized by the union (*Verschmelzung*) of the economic power of the monopolies with the political power of the imperialist state into an all-encompassing mechanism (*Gesamtmechanismus*) for the domination of the entire society by monopoly capital." Thus, although, by this definition, a coordination of state and monopolies (rather than a subordination of one to the other) takes place, the monopolies nevertheless emerge as the dominant element. This inconsistency, reflecting the difficulty of fitting the concept into the reality of existing conditions, reappears more clearly even in a subsequent passage: "State-monopolist capitalism does not mean simply subordination of the state to the dominance of the monopolies, but a union with them into one political and economic instrument of domination. Its main economic characteristic is the process of concentration and centralization in the hands of the financial oligarchy, reinforced and expanded by this pooling of power. The monopolies inject the state directly into the process of profit appropriation (*Profitaneignung*), direct and organize this process with its help, and charge it with specific tasks in the economy." This definition has been adopted by most DDR authors. Some, however, who are more consistent, define state-monopolist capitalism as a collaboration of both camps on the basis of their pooled resources; others, like Kuczynski, do acknowledge the subordination of the state apparatus to the rule of the monopolies.

Some disagreement also exists about the material status of capitalism in this phase. To at least two East German authors, Kuczynski and Alfred Schröter, state-monopolist capitalism is evidence of the further decline of capitalism, because it could hold its own only by falling back on the machinery of the state. There is full agreement, however, on the role of state-monopolist capitalism in the historical process: it deepened the inherent contradictions of the capitalist system by further socializing production through the state's apparatus while profits continued to accrue to the private owners of the monopolies. With the misery of the working class supposedly mounting as these profits increased, state-monopolist capitalism resulted in an immense redistribution of the national income to the advantage of a small group of monopolists. For this reason, it is noted, Lenin spoke of this type of capitalism as the "most complete *material* preparation

---

212, 216, 221–22, 230, 234; Schellenberg, in Klein, *Deutschland*, vol. 1, pp. 412ff.; vol. 2, pp. 355ff. See, among non-Marxist authors, Stegmann, *Die Erben Bismarcks*, pp. 450–51, 458ff.; Gerald D. Feldman, *Army, Industry, and Labor in Germany: 1914–1918* (Princeton, 1966), p. 136.

of socialism." *Sachwörterbuch* even calls it socialism's "immediate prelude." The close cooperation between government and business that was brought forth by the exigencies of the war thus is viewed not as a temporary emergency arrangement but as a "lawful," scientifically inevitable stage of capitalist development, which the war accelerated but did not create.[132]

East German researchers have traced the trend toward state-monopolist capitalism most easily in the conversion of the economy from peacetime pursuits to its wartime functions. That this transformation was initiated by a "monopoly capitalist" (Walther Rathenau, head of the [German] General Electric Company) is considered only natural. So is Rathenau's policy of appointing leading figures of other large-scale concerns to the top posts in the Raw Materials Control Office that he set up. Although allowance is made for Rathenau's philosophical penchant for a state-run economy, the possibility that he made his appointments because of the special skills and expertise of the appointees is ignored by most authors.[133] The consensus, implied or explicit, is that these assignments were made to enrich and strengthen the monopolist enterprises and to reinforce their position at the expense of small and medium-sized firms. That the government provided loans, subsidies, and guarantees (which it did in order to speed the conversion to war production) serves as a further confirmation of such conclusions. Here again, intentions are dismissed as irrelevant: granted even that the war economy was set up, not in order to open up new sources of profits to some groups of monopoly capitalists, but to lay the economic basis for a military victory, "the assurance of profits to the ruling class is nonetheless implied in such a system under imperialist conditions. Neither the war nor the war economy change[d] the basic aspects of the capitalist mode of production." In the light of such determinism, even a more differentiated approach fails to modify the overall picture. Thus, Gutsche claims that the more flexible chemical and electrical concerns readily accepted the restrictions of a wartime economy, whereas heavy industry reluctantly submitted to it as a highly objectionable wartime emergency measure. However, he, too, insists that disputes that arose between business and government over economic policies were not the results of an adversary relationship but differences of opinion between partners who were in basic agreement, with the government representing overall monopolist interests

---

[132]"Staatsmonopolistischer Kapitalismus," *Swb*, vol. 2, pp. 602ff.; Klein, *Deutschland*, pp. 326–28; *GdA*, vol. 2, pp. 231–32; Gossweiler, *Grossbanken*, pp. 66ff.; Kuczynski, *Geschichte*, vol. 14, pp. 203, 206; Alfred Schröter, *Krieg, Staat, Monopol: 1914–1918* (Berlin [East], 1965), pp. 113ff., 119; also Gutsche, "Grundtendenzen," pp. 1042ff.
[133]Mottek et al. (vol. 3, p. 207) do acknowledge this consideration.

while the individual monopolies pursued their particular goals. In consequence, Alfred Schröter concludes, the growing interpenetration of business and government made capitalist production especially profitable, thus bearing out the thesis of state-monopolist capitalism as consolidating monopolist dominance.[134]

That the war industries derived huge profits from their government contracts is an established fact. As DDR authors note, business and government shared a basic communality of interests and goals that allowed industry to take advantage of the state's need for quick and ever greater production. Governmental efforts to fend off excessive profits by negotiations thus were not very successful, nor was any attempt ever made to limit profits by legislative action. Whatever success the authorities scored in wresting concessions from manufacturers, the East German critics maintain, these successes were due not so much to the forcefulness of the authorities as to disagreements within the monopolist camp that gave the army and government some leverage in their negotiations. Moreover, ultimate credit for any concessions is accorded to the workers and to their only authentic spokesman, the radical Left, on the grounds that their sustained pressures aroused the fears of both government and monopolies.[135]

DDR analyses also point out that the monopolies could make a few domestic concessions the more easily because they were able to reimburse themselves by highly remunerative exports. Depriving the German war machine of needed materiel, it is noted, they sent abroad substantial amounts of war-essential raw materials and finished goods because these products commanded higher prices abroad than in the domestic market. Some of these exports even went to enemy countries. Admittedly, such shipments did help improve Germany's balance of payments, and they secured for Germany in return strategic materials that would not have been obtainable otherwise. Walter Bartel, who does acknowledge this fact, admits that such transactions might have been defensible on these grounds; what was indefensible, however, he stresses, was the fact that the bourgeoisie derived exorbitant profits from these dealings. To which it might be added that, equally indefensibly, these profits remained all but untaxed.[136]

[134]Schröter, *Krieg*, pp. 78, 91ff. (quotation on p. 93); Gutsche, "Zum Funktionsmechanismus," pp. 66, 85; Gutsche, review, *ZfG* 24 (1976): 1195–96.

[135]Gutsche and Laschitza, "Forschungen," *ZfG* 18 (1970): suppl., pp. 498–99; Klein, *Deutschland*, pp. 292–93, 366–67; Kuczynski, *Geschichte*, vol. 4, pp. 191–93; Gossweiler, *Grossbanken*, pp. 10–11, 51–52, 85ff. See also Feldman, *Army*, pp. 47–48, 60ff., 77–79, 156–58, 385–87, 392–94.

[136]See Bartel, "Die Linken," pp. 335ff.; see also Feldman, *Army*, p. 157; Feldman, *Iron and Steel in the German Inflation* (Princeton, 1977), pp. 59–61; in this book, however, he speaks of exports reaching enemy countries "inadvertently."

Despite these and other accommodations, most German entrepreneurs were not happy in their partnership with the government. They were anxious to rid themselves of the controls and restraints to which they were subject, and there were continuous complaints, not only from heavy industry but also from the more "flexible" electrical, chemical, and finished-goods industries, about the bureaucratization of the economy and about "state socialism" and even "communism." What was important to the entrepreneur was not only his independence—his "master of his own house" status, on which the government directives kept impinging—but also efficiency, consistency, and firmness of purpose, which often were lacking in the state-business relationship as the result of bureaucratic entanglements or strategic reconsiderations. For these reasons, which again are reduced to profit concerns, the entrepreneur wished to hold government intervention down to a minimum.[137]

This demand drew considerable encouragement from the appointment in mid-1916 of the Hindenburg/Ludendorff team to the supreme command of the armed forces. The two generals were known to be sympathetic to the industrial grievances, hopeful that greater entrepreneurial freedom and stricter labor controls would result in increased arms production. Fritz Klein's suggestion that the promotion of the two generals was decided upon ultimately in response to demands of mining and steel-producing monopolists is not, however, borne out by the few fragmentary data that have been submitted in evidence.[138] According to all accounts, Bethmann Hollweg and his circle played a crucial role in obtaining the appointment, and they called for it for reasons that were totally unacceptable to the Pan-German and heavy-industrial camp: not certain that the two national heroes could win the war, they hoped that if victory should prove unobtainable, the legendary Hindenburg as commander-in-chief could make a negotiated peace palatable to the nation and thus guard the country against internal upheavals. DDR authors, however, reject this interpretation of Bethmann's conduct and see in his support of the Hindenburg/Ludendorff appointment further proof of their thesis that the poli-

[137]Kocka, *Klassengesellschaft im Krieg 1914–1918* (Göttingen, 1973), pp. 114ff., 198ff.; also Feldman, *Army*, pp. 154ff., 161ff., 379ff. and *passim*. Gutsche's claim (Klein, *Deutschland*, vol. 2, p. 131, and Gutsche, "Zum Funktionsmechanismus," p. 66) that the "more flexible" industries welcomed the state-monopolist partnership and viewed it as a prelude to a new economic system is not supported by any evidence and is apparently based on the false assumption that the ideas of Walter Rathenau, who envisaged such a system, were widely shared (Kocka, *Klassengesellschaft*, p. 201 n. 109). On Marx, see MEW, vol. 23, p. 647.

[138]See Klein, *Deutschland*, pp. 324–25. The only industrialist named specifically as having had a hand in the appointment is Carl Duisberg, who was not a heavy industrialist but headed a chemical concern (Klein, *Deutschland*, vol. 2, p. 408).

cies of the chancellor and those of Ludendorff differed in method rather than in substance.[139]

Once Hindenburg and Ludendorff had taken over the supreme command, collaboration between industry and military leadership became close and continuous, and the industrialists, with the help of the generals, were able to exert greater influence on government policies. The Hindenburg Program, providing for increased production of arms and ammunition, was based on demands of these same industrial circles and was worked out in close contact with them.

Directly related to that program was an Auxiliary Service Law that was passed by the Reichstag in December 1916. In the non-Marxist literature, that law, which drafted civilians into war-essential jobs, has been considered a noteworthy step toward parliamentarism, because Social Democratic and trade-union insistence secured the inclusion of certain provisions that protected the workers against managerial abuses, allowing them to move on to better paying jobs and giving the Reichstag the right to supervise the implementation of the law.

That implementation, however, was widely sabotaged by entrepreneurs and local government officials, and labor derived only limited benefits from the law. For this reason, if the protective provisions are mentioned at all in the East German literature, they are dismissed as "formal concessions that merely disguised the true character of this dictatorial law." Similarly, there is hardly any mention of the fact that these concessions resulted from trade-union pressures and the firm stand of the Social Democrats in the Reichstag. In fact, unions and the SPD are taken to task for having participated in the enactment of a law that could only mislead the workers and perpetuate their enslavement. Thus, while the entrepreneurs are chided for their selfish pursuit of their class interests, the labor leaders are berated for "betraying" the class interests of the workers. There is no sense of inconsistency here: whereas the class interests of the bourgeoisie kept the nation engaged in a war that could not be won, the interests of the working class, aspiring to social justice and peace, coincided with the true interests of the nation.[140]

[139]Gutsche, in Klein, *Deutschland*, vol. 2, pp. 401ff.; Gutsche, "Einleitung," in Klein, *Studien*, pp. 6–7; Schröter, *Krieg*, pp. 95, 99–100. On the non-Marxist side, see Feldman, *Army*, pp. 137ff., 155ff.; Karl-Heinz Janssen, "Der Wechsel in der Obersten Heeresleitung 1916," *VfZ* 7 (1959): 337ff.

[140]Schröter and Weber, in Klein, *Deutschland*, vol. 2, pp. 472f.; "Gesetz über den vaterländischen Hilfsdienst," *Swb*, vol. 1, p. 696; Klein, *Deutschland*, p. 365–66. See also Kocka (*Klassengesellschaft*, p. 200 n. 103), who notes the misleading use of a statement by a labor union official to corroborate the East German position.

The War and the Radical Left

If the military-industrial complex was able to impose its will on the nation, DDR scholars point out, it could do so because no effective counterforce existed as yet to block its activities. From the dialectics of the class struggle, it followed, however, that such a force existed potentially in the working class. "Never will the proletariat let the flag of progress be wrested from its hands," Kuczynski exclaims, "even if the leadership betrays it or millions become confused: there will always be a nucleus that will continue the fight until the traitors have been unmasked and the confused have clarified their thinking."[141] In Germany's case, that nucleus is found in the Liebknecht-Luxemburg group. East German assessments of the wartime role of the German working class are therefore focused on that group's views and activities. The regular Social Democrats, on the other hand, are dismissed as deviationists from the revolutionary Marxist path and receive attention only as opportunists or Social chauvinists, whose subservient posture delayed the attainment of peace and democracy. Much of this deserves serious attention from non-Marxists. Fritz Klein makes the point, for example, that it was wrong for the Social Democrats to hope for the democratization of Germany as the result of a Russian defeat. A victory over Russia could only strengthen the ruling class under whose leadership that victory had been won. The chances of peace and democracy rose in inverse proportion to those of German imperialism. "The Weimar Republic was the result of defeat and revolution, not of the victory of German imperialism and its Burgfrieden politics.[142]

The antiwar efforts of the radical Left are carefully traced from the first oppositional moves of Rosa Luxemburg and Karl Liebknecht (after the latter had voted for the first war credits for the sake of party discipline). The emergence of oppositional groups on the local level, Liebknecht's first vote in the Reichstag against further credits, agitational work in factories and among housewives, and propagandist and press activities are analyzed with the meticulous care that Marxist historians devote to any developing movement that is still weak and of little immediate effect but that from the Marxist perspective initiates long-range historical progress. With Lenin's views as the measuring rod, Liebknecht is acclaimed for perceiving the war as an opportunity to hasten the overthrow of the capitalist system—by the conversion of the conflict from an imperialist war into a civil one. Rosa Luxemburg, on the other hand, is taken to task for not yet arriving at this conclu-

[141]Kuczynski, *Ausbruch*, p. 99.
[142]Klein, *Deutschland*, pp. 304–5.

sion in her famous analysis of the German situation, *Die Krise der Sozialdemokratie*, better known as the *Junius-Broschüre* from the pseudonym with which she signed as the pamphlet's author. Yet Liebknecht's more advanced position is not regarded as wholly Leninist either: he did not yet see the need for a complete break with the opportunists and for the creation of a separate revolutionary party. Neither did he perceive the necessity of drafting a concrete plan for the destruction of the imperialist power structure and the creation of a socialist order in Germany. Instead, he, like Rosa Luxemburg, sought to reform the SPD from within. Both, moreover, relied on the spontaneous energies of the masses, which, once fully aroused, would sweep away the old order—an assumption much at variance with the fundamental tenets of Leninism.

However, historical progress cannot be stopped; "objectively," DDR authors note, Liebknecht and his associates were paving the way, by their publicist and agitational work, for the eventual organization of a Marxist revolutionary party. Once again, stress is laid on the fact that the German Left, still branded as "antinational" by many bourgeois and right-wing Social Democratic historians, was the only organization that was genuinely nationally-minded: while those who boasted of their nationalism were abusing that concept as a cover for their imperialist class interests, Liebknecht and his associates fought against these imperialist and militarist concerns, which in reality were the enemies of the nation's interests and the people's rights.[143]

According to East German findings, the activities of the radical Left began to have some effect in 1915. The Left is credited with initiating the first antiwar demonstrations, primarily in Berlin, where the Liebknecht-Luxemburg group had its strongest organized support. Yet, DDR analysts are aware of the limits of the Left's impact, and they know that most strikes and other manifestations of mass discontent were sparked by food shortages, excessive overtime work, and related hardships rather than the Left's agitation. What they find significant is the concern the emerging unrest caused among other Social Democratic leaders. Evidently worried about losing the workers' support, deputies of left-centrist persuasion joined Liebknecht and cast their vote against the granting of further war credits when the government requested such credits from the Reichstag in December 1915. The East German accounts stress, however, that the new converts cast these votes

---

[143]See Klein, *Deutschland*, pp. 308ff., 340ff., 354ff.; *GdA*, vol. 2, pp. 234ff., 251ff., 258, 278–80, 311–13; Helmut Kral, in Klein, *Deutschland*, vol. 2, pp. 284ff. The traditional concept of nationalism is defined representatively in the analysis of the socialist schism in 1916–1917 in Conze and Groh, *Die Arbeiterbewegung in der nationalen Bewegung* (Stuttgart, 1966), pp. 123–24.

only half-heartedly and without repudiating their prowar posture of August 1914. The fact is that these leaders still viewed the war as originally one of defense, but they felt that with Germany's security assured, the conflict was deteriorating into one of conquest, which they opposed. Contrary to Marxist assessments, dictates of conscience and ideology guided these men and women at least as much as the fear of losing their following.

Some attention is paid to bourgeois pacifist organizations that called for an early settlement of the war and opposed all annexationist plans. They remained ineffective, DDR authors conclude, because they shunned contact with the revolutionary working-class movement and hence were backed only by a small group of bourgeois democrats and intellectuals. Efforts to promote the antiwar movement on an international scale—at an international socialist women's conference in Berne in March 1915, at a similar youth meeting in Berne the following month, and at a conference of antiwar socialists of twelve European countries at Zimmerwald, Switzerland, in September 1915—are recognized as well-meant endeavors but are criticized for their failure to adopt Lenin's call for the transformation of the war into civil wars in the various belligerent countries.[144]

Early in 1916, the radical Left launched a frontal attack on the twin evils of imperialism and militarism. The group, that "band of intrepid revolutionaries, small at first but rapidly growing, who were the true heroes of our people in World War I," according to Klein, adopted the name of Spartacus, after the leader of a Roman slave rising. With hardships mounting as the war continued, the group's antiwar agitation met with a growing response. As a result of that work, Berlin and other major cities witnessed political mass strikes of considerable proportions. As DDR historians regretfully note, however, the Spartacus group still limited itself to fighting the war and the capitalist class regime solely as an international phenomenon of which the German struggle was but one part. Thus, it did nothing to prepare for a socialist revolution in its own country.

Nor would the Spartacus group break with the left-center faction when the latter continued to maintain its antirevolutionary stance. In fact, when these dissidents, upon their expulsion from the SPD, established an Independent Social Democratic party (USPD) in April 1917, the Spartacists joined the new party, although the USPD confined its opposition to the parliamentary arena and opposed all illegal oppositional activities outside the Reichstag. Yet, East German authors complain, by giving the im-

[144]Bartel, *Linken*, pp. 234ff.; Kral, in Klein, *Deutschland*, pp. 307ff.

pression of an unreserved antiwar stance, these "Social Pacifists" created confusion among the workers and rendered more difficult their mobilization for the revolutionary struggle.

To the treachery of the right-wing Social Democrats and the ambiguities of the left-centrists the East German accounts attribute the continued ability of civil and military authorities to preserve their power and check all efforts to attain peace and democracy. Moreover, right-wing betrayal and left-centrist timidity also caused the Spartacus group to misjudge its own opportunities. As a result, the argument runs, the group did not establish itself as a separate revolutionary party that might have hastened the overthrow of the imperialist-militarist regime, but joined the USPD, albeit as a separate ideological and organizational unit within the new party. DDR critics consider the move a backward step, because the USPD was formed in part to block the formation of a left-wing radical party—a plan some local Spartacus organizations were then considering. Actually, the Spartacists joined the USPD because they felt they could carry on their agitational work more effectively under cover of a legal party, because a separate party of their own, suspected of revolutionary goals, would have been suppressed immediately. This reasoning is dismissed by Walter Bartel, expressing the views generally held in the East German literature, as ignoring the

> undoubtedly favorable conditions for founding a party of Karl Liebknecht and Rosa Luxemburg. The war had become senseless to broad strata of the masses. The great sacrifices of blood at the fronts and starvation at home made everyone wonder how much longer the war must go on. The Russian revolution suggested to workers and soldiers that there was a way out of the desperate situation on the part of the people. To show the way to the people, to forge the party that would come to the aid of the masses, was the most urgent national task and the most serious duty of proletarian internationalism. The Spartacus group missed the historical opportunity to break with centrism.[145]

With Lenin ever the pace-setting model, there seems to be no awareness of the immense differences between German and Russian conditions. Whereas the Bolsheviks built up their party in a disintegrating, demoralized state, run by a corrupt and inefficient bureaucracy, an equally incompetent police force, and a lethargic, indifferent army, the Spartacists were confronted by a highly efficient bureaucracy, a tightly organized, well-trained police, and an army equipped with full powers and every determination to squash ruthlessly any sign of activity considered detrimental to the state

---

[145]Klein, *Deutschland*, pp. 352ff.; Karl Köstler and Gutsche, in Klein, *Deutschland*, vol. 2, pp. 413ff., 435ff.; *GdA*, vol. 2, pp. 265ff., 306ff.; Bartel, *Linken*, pp. 402ff. (quotation on pp. 417–18); Streisand, pp. 262–63.

and war effort. Under the circumstances, the Spartacists showed greater realism in their reluctance to follow Lenin's example and set up a separate party than do their East German critics.

The Turning Point

During the latter part of 1916, class tensions sharpened. Food shortages, rising prices, and worsening working conditions weighed ever more heavily on the bulk of the people. Widening disparities in living conditions and growing casualty lists deepened popular discontent. Rather than deal with these frustrations and avoid defeat, Streisand points out, the ruling Junkers and bourgeois monopolists pursued their mirage of annexationist victory. They failed to take advantage of Russia's mounting difficulties and to seek a peace settlement with her; such an agreement in turn might have led to a settlement with the Western powers if coupled with a renunciation of all territorial designs. As Fritz Klein puts it, "the historical laws that ruled the actions of German imperialism, noted for its exceptional aggressiveness and militarism, . . . made it impossible to utilize the objectively existing opportunity of avoiding the total defeat of German imperialism."[146]

The decision to resort to unrestricted submarine warfare fits readily into this assessment. Ultimate responsibility for this step is assigned to the extremist segments of the ruling class—the most reactionary and aggressive monopolists, along with the supreme army command and the naval leaders. When victory could no longer be won on land, these groups, rather than end the war, gambled on winning it at sea. The decision thus was not a carefully designed move to protect the true interests of the nation but a hazardous venture (as Ludendorff himself is claimed to have known), again designed to help realize the exorbitant war aims of the ruling class and to forestall any democratic reforms in the wake of a negotiated peace settlement. The decision is found to have satisfied only one sector of the monopolists, however. Those with business ties to the United States opposed it either because they anticipated adverse economic repercussions after the war or because, aware of America's war-making potential, they thought it militarily reckless.

In turn, viewed from the American side, America's entry into the war is regarded as the inevitable outgrowth of American imperialism. Whereas American monopoly capitalists had found neu-

---

[146]Streisand, p. 270; Klein, *Deutschland*, pp. 360–61.

trality, or the formal adherence to it, profitable at first, their attitude changed when German land victories and submarine warfare
threatened their exports and investments in Britain and France.
Unrestricted submarine warfare, coupled with Russia's impending
collapse, brought the prospect of Allied defeat closer, which would
mean the loss not only of lucrative markets but of huge loans and
investments as well. Moreover, by opening the door to Germany's
domination of the European continent, an Allied defeat was bound
to jeopardize the plans of U.S. imperialism to play its own dominant role in world politics. (This at least is the interpretation read
into the balance-of-power concerns of Colonel House and some of
President Wilson's other advisers.) For all these reasons, Baldur
Kaulisch concludes,

> America's entry into the war not only had been prepared by the
> preceding economic and political developments but had become vir-
> tually inevitable, especially in order to safeguard the economic inter-
> ests of American monopoly capital in Europe, in view of the Allies'
> troubled economic position, the fears—ultimately unjustified—of a
> German victory, and the threatening revolutionary developments.
> American imperialism carried on, with different means and under
> changed conditions, its policy of consolidating and expanding its
> economic and political power, a policy initiated during the preceding
> years and particularly during the period of its formal neutrality. With
> its direct participation in the war, it took the first step toward open
> interference in Europe and at the same time started its fight for
> world domination.[147]

Shortly before America's entry into the war, the tsarist regime
was overthrown and replaced by an aristocratic-agrarian, bourgeois-
capitalist coalition government. This upheaval, too, fits easily into
the Marxist scenario, which had placed on Russia's "agenda" the
very bourgeois-democratic revolution that had now occurred.
Again, in conformity with historical inevitability, the revolution,
though bourgeois in character, had been launched not by the reluctant bourgeoisie but by the masses who had forced the bourgeoisie's hand. Nonetheless, Marxist historians have had some difficulty reconciling these objectively predictable developments with
the fact that the masses had risen spontaneously, without leadership or organization, contrary to the Marxist-Leninist denial of the
efficacy of such spontaneity. Inevitably, the East German literature
on the February (March) revolution has encountered the same problems with which Soviet historiography has long had to wrestle;

---

[147]Klein, *Deutschland*, pp. 368ff.; Weber, *Ludendorff*, p. 67; Kaulisch, in Klein,
Deutschland, vol. 2, pp. 555, 569ff. (quotation on p. 581); Otto, in ibid., pp. 584ff.;
Mommsen, "Bethmann Hollweg und die öffentlich Meinung 1914–1917," *VfZ* 17
(1969): 141, 148–49; Erich Ludendorff, *Meine Kriegserinnerungen 1914–1918* (Berlin, 1919), p. 249.

they are reflected in the divergent analyses of the upheaval. Interpretations range from outright claims that the Bolsheviks launched
the revolution (*Deutschland im ersten Weltkrieg*) or suggestions
that the Bolsheviks had prepared it at least indirectly (*Geschichte
der deutschen Arbeiterbewegung; Sachwörterbuch*) to efforts to
minimize the significance of the uprising (Streisand believed that
the most important result of the revolution was that it enabled the
Bolshevik party to shed its illegality, rally the masses, and carry
the revolution into its socialist phase; *Grundriss* expresses similar
views). Finally, some accounts, such as that of Kuczynski, ignore
the revolution altogether.[148]

The impact of the revolution on German developments is, of
course, of special importance to DDR authors. Viewing the revolution as the accomplishment of the Russian working class and the
Bolsheviks, Horst Schumacher rejects all suggestions that the defeats inflicted by Germany were the primary cause of the revolution. Several authors note with some gratification that the overthrow of the tsarist regime demolished the "propaganda lie"
("Zwecklüge") that the war was being waged to fight off tsarist
despotism. The revolution thus served to discredit further the German bourgeoisie and the "social chauvinists" who still supported
the war. Conversely, it strengthened the determination of the left-
centrist Social Democrats to press for a negotiated peace and lent
added momentum to the founding of the USPD in April 1917.

The Spartacists are credited with having been the one group
that perceived the full significance of the February Revolution. They
realized that the upheaval was more than merely a Russian event
and that it provided a model for the Marxist vanguard of the working
class everywhere. In accordance with Lenin's injunction, moreover,
the program of Russia's newly created workers' and soldiers' councils (*soviets*) linked the revolution with the call for a peace without
annexations and indemnities—a connection that confirmed the
Spartacists in the correctness of their own strategy. Thus equipped
with a "scientific program for a revolutionary liquidation of the
war . . . the Spartacist group was objectively the leading force of the
process from which the revolutionary party in Germany evolved."

Even without a separate revolutionary party, it is pointed out,
the class struggle grew more intense in Germany. A wave of strikes
shook the country in mid-April 1917, and although these strikes
were called to protest the desperate food situation and intolerable

---

[148]See Schumacher, in Klein, *Deutschland*, vol. 2, pp. 652–53; *GdA*, vol. 2, p. 304;
"Februarrevolution 1917," *Swb*, vol. 1, p. 581; Streisand, p. 268; *Grundriss*, p.
354; Kuczynski, *Geschichte*, vol. 4, p. 268. On the Marxist dilemma see also
Dietrich Geyer, "Oktoberrevolution," *SDG*, vol. 4, pp. 940–41; Nettl, *Rosa Luxemburg*, vol. 2, p. 684.

working conditions, they are found to have carried political overtones in their demands for peace and democracy. At the same time,
the deteriorating morale in the army and the navy is carefully
traced and it is emphasized that discipline was especially poor
among sailors marooned in home ports where the crews had ready
access to newspapers and were in touch with the USPD.[149]

The growing longing for peace among middle and petty bourgeoisie also seemed to bear out this assessment of the decline of
the ruling class's hold on the country. Yet when the desire for
peace brought forth a peace resolution of a Reichstag majority of
SPD, Centrists, and Progressives, DDR authors complain, the supporters of the resolution did not insist on the abandonment of all
annexationist and financial war aims. Rather, they contented
themselves with rejecting forced annexations and indemnities,
thus implicitly approving territorial acquisitions or financial im-
posts that were "negotiated" at a peace conference (as indeed was
intended by the Centrist deputy Matthias Erzberger, the spiritual
father of the resolution; this decision was also tolerated by Philipp
Scheidemann, the Social Democratic spokesman). In this limited
sense, the peace resolution was also accepted by Chancellor Georg
Michaelis, Bethmann's successor. Not without reason, Klein calls
the resolution an "imperialist minimum program."

In the Marxist-Leninist perspective, the events of July 1917
thus did not mark a major change. If Western scholars view this
first self-assertion of the wartime Reichstag, however ineffectual,
as the initial step toward the future parliamentary system, their
East German counterparts regard it as a weak and hypocritical
attempt to appease the masses while at the same time catering to
those in power. These apparent moves toward peace and parliamentarism, they maintain, could only confuse the masses. Accordingly, the real victors in this confrontation were the generals and
the monopolist circles allied with them: the supreme command
could now consolidate its dictatorship and render the civil government even more subservient to the Hindenburg/Ludendorff team
and, through them, to the monopolist bourgeoisie.[150]

---

[149]*GdA*, vol. 2, pp. 305ff., 313–15 (quotation on p. 313); Schumacher, Kaulisch, and
Baudis, in Klein, *Deutschland*, vol. 2, pp. 623, 657–58, 676ff., 695ff.; Scheel, "Der
Aprilstreik in Berlin," in *Revolutionäre Ereignisse und Probleme in Deutschland
während der Periode der Grossen Sozialistischen Oktoberrevolution 1917/18*, ed.
Schreiner (Berlin [East], 1957), pp. 1ff.; Bernhard, "Die Entstehung einer revolutionären Friedensbewegung in der deutschen Hochseeflotte im Jahre 1917," ibid.,
pp. 89ff.

[150]See Klein, *Deutschland*, pp. 381–83; Gutsche, in Klein, *Deutschland*, vol. 2,
pp. 744ff.; *GdA*, vol. 2, pp. 318–19; Weber, *Ludendorff*, pp. 94ff.; cf. Rosenberg,
Entstehung, pp. 163–64; Holborn, vol. 3, pp. 475–76. On Erzberger, see also Klaus
Epstein, *Matthias Erzberger and the Dilemma of German Democracy* (Princeton,
1959), pp. 185ff., 202ff.

Because the militarist-imperialist forces were more firmly entrenched than ever before, DDR authors are convinced that a revolution, as the only way to end this regime and obtain peace, had become more imperative, too. They find, however, that the dissident Independent Socialists were just as firmly opposed to a revolution as their one-time brethren, the Majority Socialists. When approached by embittered sailors, some accounts note, the USPD refused to support any mutinous actions, just as it dissociated itself from such risings when they did occur in August 1917. The fact was that the USPD, like the SPD, regarded any revolutionary activities as senseless, even though, unlike the latter, it did not consider them necessarily unpatriotic. It preferred therefore to focus its efforts on attaining peace: it refused to support the Reichstag Peace Resolution because of its ambiguities—a fact ignored in the DDR literature—and consistently voted against granting the government any more war credits. Outside the parliament, too, going into the streets, the party called for peace rather than the overthrow of the regime.

East German historians find this an inadequate strategy; in their judgment, only the Spartacus group offered a genuine alternative to the destructive policies of the military-monopolist coalition: by feeding the fires of revolutionary unrest, the Spartacists showed the true path to peace. Although DDR authors do not give the Spartacists sole credit for the mass strikes, demonstrations, food riots, and other disturbances of the last two years of the war, the Spartacists are the only people specifically mentioned as having helped spark the unrest. The role of the non-Leninist—that is, non-revolutionary—USPD, on the other hand, is ignored and its name is brought up only when that party is charged with having obstructed the revolutionary process.[151]

Actually, by centering its activities on achieving peace rather than calling for revolution, the USPD was able to attract a much wider following, extending from revisionists to left-center radical elements. The demands voiced in demonstrations and strikes, focusing on an immediate end to the war and better living and working conditions, indicate that these were the issues to which the workers responded. That Spartacist calls for revolution and socialization had little effect is also suggested by the fact that East German documentary collections, which in their introductions explic-

[151]See Klein, *Deutschland*, pp. 371ff.; Kaulisch, in Klein, *Deutschland*, vol. 2, pp. 646ff.; Bernhard, "Entstehung," pp. 111ff. Compare also Rosenberg, *Entstehung*, pp. 158–159, 171ff.; Feldman, *Army*, pp. 520, 523ff. DDR scholars might also have argued, which surprisingly they never seem to have done, that if the Spartacists invited defeat, history showed that this was not unpatriotic: military defeat had proved beneficial to Prussia when that state had reached a similar social and political impasse in 1806–1807.

itly emphasize the role of the Spartacists, include only a few governmental and police reports on worker unrest that mention any Spartacist influence. Some DDR authors have tried to explain away the Spartacists' limited impact by arguing that the USPD absorbed a substantial part of that influence when the Spartacus group remained in the USPD; the Spartacist influence on the masses, the result of the group's persistent struggle against the war and Burgfrieden politics, thus was transferred to the USPD as a whole. This argument affords scant consolation, however, for by staying in the USPD, it is also noted, the Spartacists stayed in a party that failed to see that only the destruction of the imperialist Junker-bourgeois regime could secure lasting peace.[152]

The ultimate proof of the historical role of the Spartacists, however, is found in the Bolshevik revolution of October/November 1917. That event, it is stressed, not only gave further impetus to the revolutionary movement in Germany but also—most importantly according to the Marxist "agenda"—ushered in the world-historical era of the transition from capitalism to socialism, that socioeconomic phase preceding the communist order, of which the Spartacists were the heralds in Germany.[153]

---

[152]Rosenberg, *Entstehung*, pp. 193ff.; Müller, *Vom Kaiserreich zur Republik* (Vienna, 1924), vol. 1, pp. 125ff. and *passim*. Müller stresses the agitational and organizational role of the Revolutionary Shop Stewards (*Revolutionäre Obleute*) in the factories and criticizes the Spartacus leaders as too dogmatic and unsuited to deal with the necessities of the day-to-day struggle; compare this work with *Dokumente und Materialien zur Geschichte der deutschen Arbeiterbewegung* (Berlin [East], 1957–1958), vols. 1–2, especially vol. 1, pp. 5*–6*; Laschitza and Schumacher, "Thesen," p. 37.

[153]Bartel, *Linken*, pp. 464ff.; Klein, *Deutschland*, pp. 390ff.; *GdA*, vol. 3, pp. 14ff., 22ff.

7

The Era of
State-Monopolist Capitalism

The Weimar Republic

The October Revolution and German Defeat

O N ONE SIXTH of the globe," *Geschichte der deutschen Arbeiterbewegung* exults in its analysis of the Bolshevik Revolution,

> the working class assisted in the breakthrough of the objective laws
> of social development and set out to fulfill its historical mission. . . .
>   The contradictions that were resolved by the Great Socialist October
> Revolution were not only national contradictions of the old Russia.
> They were also contradictions characteristic of the imperialist era in
> general. This applied above all to the contradictions between the ex-
> ploiting and conquering interests of rapacious finance capitalists and
> the peaceful and democratic life interests of the people. The overthrow
> of the exploiters' rule and the establishment of the dictatorship of the
> proletariat by Russia's working class thus showed the way to the
> solution of the basic contradictions of imperialism everywhere. Thus,
> the fundamental questions of the Great Socialist October Revolution
> were not, as imperialist ideologues have claimed and still claim, a
> "purely Russian affair" but were and are fundamental questions of the
> socialist revolution in every country. Because the basic features of the
> October Revolution inevitably recur, its fundamental lessons and ex-
> periences were and are of universally valid significance.

The particular lessons to be learned from the Russian experience, *Geschichte* adds, are the world-historical importance of Leninist strategy and tactics of revolution and the need for a new
party on the Bolshevik model, tightly organized and disciplined
and impervious to opportunism and all bourgeois ideologies. Only
such a party could apply revolutionary theory creatively to the
practice of class struggle and socialist reconstruction and could
gather all democratic forces, the toiling masses of town and country, under its leadership and that of the working class. Thus the
breakthrough to socialism anywhere depended on the existence of
a Marxist-Leninist new type of party.[1]

---

[1] *GdA*, vol, 3, pp. 16–17; also "Grosse Sozialistische Oktoberrevolution," *Swb*, vol.
1, p. 730; Ruge, *Deutschland*, pp. 16–18; *Abriss*, pp. 27–28.

This assessment implies that Russia's socioeconomic development in 1917 differed from that of the more highly industrialized
Western countries in degree rather than in fundamentals. Marxist-
Leninist views are indeed based on that assumption. In the Marxist
perception, the Russia that entered the First World War was but
another imperialist power with all the attributes such status entails:
it had its banking and industrial monopolies, though few in number,
with clear state-monopolist tendencies, and it had a proletariat that,
according to some Soviet computations, together with the so-called
half-proletarians amounted to more than half (53.2 percent) of the
population (the half-proletarian earned his livelihood in part by the
sale of his labor power). If Russia was economically backward in
other respects, especially in the management of agriculture, this did
not impair its "ripeness" for a socialist revolution; on the contrary,
the resulting weaknesses rendered Russia more susceptible to such
an upheaval. According to the Leninist "Law of Differing Economic
and Political Developments of Capitalist Countries in the Imperialist Era," Russia was in fact the first such country to embrace socialism, because the internal contradictions evolving out of this combination of progress and backwardness made it the most vulnerable
member of the world capitalist system.[2] Given this vulnerability,
Lenin argued, Russia did not follow the route prescribed by the
Communist Manifesto on the basis of the more advanced Western
European conditions. Instead, it created the missing socioeconomic
prerequisites for the socialist order by removing the country's landlords and capitalists. "Has that," Lenin asked, "altered the general
line of development of world history?" The answer was no, because
the process did not violate the proper sequence of socioeconomic
formations culminating in the socialist-communist order.[3] It could
even be said, although the argument apparently has never been used,
that Russia's transition to socialism was more "conventional" than
the evolution of other societies that had bypassed entire socioeconomic formations.

Like their Soviet colleagues, East German historians accept
the Bolshevik Revolution as entirely within the perimeter of Marxist theory, and no question has ever been raised on this point.[4]
Convinced of its model character, DDR authors are mainly inter-

---

[2]Dietrich Geyer, "Oktoberrevolution," in *SDG*, vol. 4, pp. 935ff.; *GdA*, vol. 2,
p. 302; Schmidt, in Klein, *Deutschland*, vol. 3, pp. 62–63; Fritz Straube, "Die
Leninsche Theorie der sozialistischen Revolution und ihre Verfälschung durch die
westdeutsche bürgerliche Geschichtsschreibung," *JfG* 2 (1967); 204.
[3]Lenin, "About Our Revolution," in Tucker, *Lenin Anthology*, pp. 703ff.
[4]Straube ("Leninsche Theorie," pp. 193ff.) touches on some of the questions raised
by non-Marxists, but not on the one discussed here. Undoubtedly Straube would
argue with Lenin ("About Our Revolution") that the manner of Russia's advance
toward socialism is *wholly* compatible with Marxist theory.

ested in its effect on the nonsocialist world and on Germany in particular. Its worldwide significance is found in the fact that it put an end to the global dominance of the capitalist order. "The world was now split into two camps, into the camp of the dying capitalist system and that of the unfolding socialist order. The struggle between them, the decisive characteristic of the general crisis of capitalism, has ever since been the main content of world history." As for Germany, geography, strategy, and politics as well as the exceptional greed and aggressiveness of German imperialists and militarists made that country the focal point in this struggle between imperialism and socialism. It is within this framework that DDR scholars have analyzed German developments during the last year of the war.[5]

Two familiar themes dominate these investigations—the fight of the working class for peace and democracy and the antinational selfishness and rapacity of the imperialist ruling class. The latter passed up its chance of securing peace as proposed by the Bolsheviks and instead, with the help of the treacherous SPD and the wavering USPD, plunged Germany into defeat and disaster. Once more, however, the Spartacists, too, must accept their share of the blame on the grounds that they failed again to form a separate party and create their own mass movement with the help of the peasantry. Lacking such organized power, they could not exploit the existing revolutionary potential that manifested itself in the mass strikes and demonstrations of early 1918.

On the other hand, East German analysts argue, had the Soviet offer of a peace without annexations and indemnities been accepted, the Allies would have been forced by their own peoples to participate in the general peace conference proposed by Lenin. This not only would have put an end to the expansionist policy of German imperialism and done away with the privileged position of the ruling class but also would have spared Germany the kind of peace that it had to accept at Versailles. As it was, the German imperialists imposed on the Soviet state the brutal peace treaty of Brest-Litovsk and fought against Soviet forces in the Ukraine, the Baltic states, and Byelorussia. The successes they scored were problematic, however. Contact with the new Soviet spirit had its effect on the morale of the German forces and contributed to the failure of the German spring offensives on the western front. As Kuczynski puts it, "Once German imperialism continued the war against

---

[5]See *GdA*, vol. 3, pp. 17–18; Schmidt, in Klein, *Deutschland*, pp. 63ff.; Nimtz, "Zur Rolle des deutschen Imperialismus im Kampf zwischen Kapitalismus und Sozialismus in der Zeit der Grossen Sozialistischen Oktoberrevolution," *JfG* 2 (1967): 224. See also the more fanciful interpretation of Gossweiler, *Grossbanken*, pp. 96–98.

the workers and peasants of Soviet Russia after the Great Socialist October Revolution, it had lost it." Or in Walter Nimtz's words, "whoever tries to block social progress, as Imperial-imperialist Germany did, is doomed to defeat."[6]

Whereas DDR authors give considerable weight to the impact of Soviet developments on both the German home front and on troops in the field, they regard as ultimately decisive Germany's military defeat at the hands of the Western powers. In the dialectics of the historical process, however, those Western powers served as the instruments of social progress: though imperialist and anti-Soviet themselves, they, by defeating Germany, removed the most immediate threat to the new Soviet state and opened the door to political changes in Germany. In addition, because DDR scholars see the German defeat as primarily military, they also reject the "stab-in-the-back legend," which alleged that the German army was not defeated in open battle, but "stabbed in the back" by home-front agitators and traitors. Their rejection of that myth is obviously regretful rather than scornful, because it concedes the essential ineffectiveness of Spartacist and other left-radical endeavors.[7]

To Marxist scholars, this admission is all the more painful because in their view conditions in Germany had revolutionary potential: as Lenin said, "the working class and the other toiling classes no longer were willing to live in the old ways, and the ruling class, too, was aware that it could not rule any longer in the old ways." As it was, the "ruling class" managed to retain essential control of developments. It granted the country some democratizing reforms and ended the fighting.[8]

As in the case of the outbreak of the war, the "mononpoly bourgeoisie" is accorded a disproportionate role in these moves. Two inconclusive interviews of the shipping magnate Albert Ballin with William II and Foreign Secretary von Hintze, in which Ballin pleaded for talks with President Wilson and for the "modernization" of the empire, serve as evidence of "monopolist" manipulations. Actually, as Joachim Petzold is forced to admit, the implementation of Ballin's proposals can no longer be proven for lack of documentation, and Ballin himself later complained that he had been prevented by the emperor's entourage from speaking his mind

---

[6]Nimtz, "Zur Rolle," pp. 226ff. (quotation on p. 231); Ruge, *Deutschland*, pp. 18ff.; *GdA*, vol. 3, pp. 20ff.; Schmidt, in Klein, *Deutschland*, pp. 65ff.; Bartel, "Der Januarstreik 1918 in Berlin," in *Revolutionäre Ereignisse und Probleme in Deutschland während der Periode der Grossen Sozialistischen Oktoberrevolution 1917/18*, ed. Schreiner (Berlin [East], 1957), pp. 141ff.; Kuczynski, *Geschichte*, vol. 4, p. 185; Weber, *Ludendorff*, pp. 127–28.

[7]Ruge, *Deutschland*, pp. 36–38, 54; *GdA*, vol. 3, p. 69; Joachim Petzold, *Die Dolchstosslegende* (Berlin [East], 1963), pp. 19ff., 42.

[8]*GdA*, vol. 3, pp. 40, 70 (with Lenin quotation).

openly. The extant evidence suggests instead that the military, on its own, was instrumental in securing an armistice and parliamentary reforms (with interesting new details supplied by Petzold about the pressures to which the hesitant Ludendorff was subjected by some of his aides).

In the accepted DDR version, nevertheless, militarists and monopolists, acting jointly, decided to appease the masses and preserve their power by promises of peace and reforms. Accordingly, Prince Max von Baden, another "imperialist," invited the Social Democrats to join his new government. Their participation conveyed the impression of greater democracy, but also deepened the divisions within the working class and successfully hampered the revolutionary movement. To be sure, armistice negotiations were set into motion and reforms giving the Reichstag more power were introduced. However, these reforms were made, it is stressed, not in order to pave the way for a full-fledged democratization, but rather in order to avert any major curbs on the political and economic power of the monopoly bourgeoisie and its allies.[9]

The Spartacists are acclaimed as the only ones who recognized the deception perpetrated on the working class. They demanded the establishment of a unitarian republic; restoration of all civil liberties; the expropriation of banks, mines, and all large and medium-sized landed property; and a thorough democratization of the army. In other ways, too, DDR authors note, the relentless endeavors of the Spartacus group—allied with a militant group of workers' representatives in the factories, the Revolutionary Shop Stewards—strove to offset the treachery of the SPD and the inertia of the USPD. (Of the two groups, the Revolutionary Shop Stewards actually were the more important in terms of numbers and organized strength.) Both Spartacists and Shop Stewards helped to launch new demonstrations, mass rallies, and strikes for peace and more fundamental political and economic changes, thus paving the way for the revolution. In mid-October, these activities gathered further momentum when the armistice negotiations kept dragging on inconclusively; they also received increasing support from the left wing of the USPD. At the same time, it is noted, preparations were made for an armed insurrection, and arms and ammunition

[9]See Petzold, "Die Rolle führender Vertreter des Monopolkapitals bei der Einleitung der Waffenstillstandsverhandlungen," in *Monopole und Staat in Deutschland: 1917–1945* (Berlin [East], 1966), pp. 79ff.; Petzold, in Klein, *Deutschland,* vol. 3, pp. 417ff.; Weber (*Ludendorff,* p. 141) is wholly misleading. See also Bernhard, *Der "Hugenberg-Konzern"* (Berlin, 1928), p. 25—a source that seems to have escaped the attention of East German researchers despite its provocative statement that the Krupp industrialist Alfred Hugenberg and his circle "withdrew from the war" (*trat . . . aus dem Kriege heraus*) on learning of the hopeless military situation in July 1918.

were collected in Berlin. These plans, however, were overtaken by events before they could be carried out.[10]

The November Revolution

The revolution that broke out in November 1918 is viewed by Marxist historians, not as the concluding chapter of the war and the melancholy symbol of defeat, but as the expected climax, albeit aborted, of developments long in the making. Indeed, the revolution is welcomed as accelerating the historical process and raising it to a higher plane. In consequence, East German authors condemn the efforts of the Social Democrats to suppress the upheavals that grew out of the mutinies of the German high-seas fleet in late October 1918. When the workers at the Kiel naval base joined the revolt, DDR accounts complain, the Social Democrats helped to restrain the uprising. However, the revolutionary wave could not be contained, and it spread inland. Thus, on November 9, it is noted, the workers and soldiers of Berlin, led by the Spartacus group, the Revolutionary Shop Stewards, and the revolutionary wing of the USPD, forced the removal of the emperor and the government of Prince Max. Yet, as these accounts regretfully add, the new government formed by the right-wing Social Democrat Friedrich Ebert was not a revolutionary one, despite its deceptive designation as Council of People's Commissars, consisting instead of men willing to preserve the old system. What replaced the monarchy was not the anti-imperialist, democratic republic that history called for in this era of transition from capitalism to socialism and that Karl Liebknecht proclaimed that day, but the bourgeois-democratic republic that the Social Democrat Philipp Scheidemann had announced a few hours earlier.

What the East German analyses ignore, however, is the lack of concern most soldiers and workers evinced for such differences. Up to the time of the revolution, the demands voiced in demonstrations, strikes, and naval revolts called mainly for immediate peace and bread-and-butter issues, only secondarily for political changes and much more rarely for socialization. When the monarchy did become an issue in late October, it did so not so much as a matter of principle but because it was viewed as an obstacle to an early armistice. Similarly, the USPD leader Kurt Eisner could

---

[10]*GdA*, vol. 3, pp. 70ff., 87ff.; Ruge, *Deutschland*, pp. 44ff., 56ff.; Petzold, in Klein, *Deutschland*, vol. 3, pp. 449ff., 493, 501ff., 524ff., 534ff.; Streisand, pp. 216–17, 275ff. Cf. D. K. Buse, "Ebert and the German Crisis, 1917–20," *CEH* 5 (1972): 239–40.

topple the Bavarian monarchy despite the minimal support his party had in Bavaria because that party stood unequivocally for peace—the overriding concern of panic-stricken Bavarians who feared, after Austria's collapse, that their state might become a battleground in the war. Petzold admits how much the risings of November 1918 were triggered by war weariness rather than by revolutionary aspirations when he states that the conclusion of the armistice, two days after the founding of the republic, "deprived the revolution of much of its original élan." Rosa Luxemburg summed up the prevailing mood in one of her first editorials in the Spartacists' new daily newspaper, *Die Rote Fahne:* "The image of the German government corresponds to the inner ripeness of German conditions. Scheidemann-Ebert are the proper government of the German revolution in its present stage."[11]

Still, East German historians dismiss the new government's program as unjustifiably bourgeois-reformist when, in conformity with its character, it confined itself to promulgating some political rights and minor social reforms. Similarly, it is denounced for indulging in socialist phraseology, because it called for the socialization of the major means of production by parliamentary vote. As East German critics see it, Ebert and his associates willfully disregarded the Spartacist warning that "the struggle for real democracy does not revolve around parliament, suffrage, or parliamentary ministers and other such frauds, but aims at the real bases of all enemies of the people—landed property and capital, control of the armed forces and the judiciary." Any compromise on these measures, which alone could eradicate imperialism and militarism, was bound to doom even the establishment of a genuine bourgeois democracy.[12]

The immediate policies of the Ebert government, it is noted, drove the new state further along this dangerous road. To anyone viewing revolutions as engines of social progress, Ebert's concern with restoring order carried little conviction. It seemed a maneuver to salvage the old power apparatus in open betrayal of the revolution and the government's own supporters. In its blind struggle against the revolution, East German authors point out, the new regime did not purge the bureaucracy of its nondemocratic elements, but retained the old imperial officials right up to the ministerial level. In the same vein, Ebert entered an alliance with the old

---

[11]Rosenberg, *Entstehung*, pp. 238ff., 251–53; Müller, *Vom Kaiserreich zur Republik* (Vienna, 1924), vol. 1, p. 132; Hans Beyer, *Von der Novemberrevolution zur Räterepublik in München* (Berlin [East], 1957), pp. 4ff.; Nimtz, "Über den Charakter der Novemberrevolution von 1918/1919," *ZfG* 6 (1958): 705; Petzold, "Rolle," p. 83; Petzold, in Klein, *Deutschland*, vol. 3, pp. 409–10; Luxemburg, quoted in Nettl, *Rosa Luxemburg*, vol. 2, p. 714.
[12]GdA, vol. 3, pp. 112–13, 468; Nimtz, pp. 705–6.

militarist forces—those "mortal enemies of the nation"—thus shielding the officer corps from all revolutionary aspirations inside and outside the army. Similarly, the government sanctioned a pact between labor unions and private "monopolists," the *Zentralarbeitsgemeinschaft*. The pact, it is noted, had been carefully prepared by the monopolists since mid-October in order to contain the social changes that had become inescapable. It secured for labor the right to join unions, collective bargaining, arbitration, and improved social insurance benefits, but at the same time protected the entrepreneurs against attacks on the capitalist system. In this manner, Streisand comments, the working masses were diverted from one of the main goals of the revolution—the elimination of the economic bases of German imperialism. A newly created Office of Demobilization is found to have been misused from the very beginning for monopolist manipulations, at the expense of the labor and small and medium-sized enterprises, and an equally new Commission of Socialization was packed with reformists willfully playing for time; these facts could but confirm this picture of bourgeois sabotage and Social Democratic betrayal of the revolution. In fact, dependent as it was on the monarchist-Junker officer corps, buraucracy, and judiciary and collaborating as it did with the monopoly bourgeoisie and Junker agrarians, the Ebert government, in the words of *Geschichte der deutschen Arbeiterbewegung*, was "essentially a bourgeois regime."[13] More recent publications have even spoken of the new republic as a mere temporary device in which "finance capital," the real power, reconciled itself to the establishment, for the time being, of a bourgeois-parliamentary state and entrusted the Social Democrats with some governmental functions in it.[14]

The armistice signed on November 11, two days after the proclamation of the republic, provided further proof of the new

[13]See Streisand, pp. 277, 285–86; Ruge, *Deutschland*, pp. 51–52, 65ff., 74ff.; Ruge, "Friedrich Ebert am 10. November 1918," *ZfG* 26 (1978): 955ff.; Habedank, "Die 'Zusammenarbeit' der Rüstungsmagnaten mit dem Rat der Volksbeauftragten bei der Verhinderung der Nationalisierung der Grundstoffindustrie während der Novemberrevolution," in *Monopole und Staat*, pp. 85ff.; Schmidt, "Zur Staats- und Machtfrage in der Novemberrevolution," *JfG* 2 (1967): 257ff.; *GdA*, vol. 3, p. 156. That the Council of People's Commissars was actually a bourgeois regime had already been concluded by Rosenberg, *Geschichte*, p. 9. See also Gerald D. Feldman, who points out that Social Democrats and trade union leaders entrusted themselves from the beginning to the economic ideas and expertise of businessmen such as Hugo Stinnes, while the latter in turn used the unions as tools to promote their entrepreneurial interests (Feldman, "German Business between War and Revolution: The Origins of the Stinnes-Legien Agreement," in Ritter, *Entstehung*, pp. 314, 330, 336, 338).

[14]*Grundriss*, pp. 372–73; *Abriss*, pp. 44–45; Ruge, "Die Weltwirkung der Grossen Sozialistischen Oktoberrevolution und die deutsche Geschichte . . . , " *ZfG* 20 (1972): 1267.

government's determination to present itself as a bulwark against the hopes and aspirations of the revolutionary working class. The armistice tolerated, by tacit consent, the preservation of the army and its old command; left it equipped with more machine guns than originally intended, for the "maintenance of internal order"; and allowed German troops to remain in the occupied eastern territories. "The imperialists of the West proceeded from the assumption," Ruge concludes, "that the only way they could control the German economy and turn Germany into a battering ram against Russian Soviet power was by preserving the imperialist rule in Germany." To prevent the revolutionary breakthrough of socialism, he further charges, the new government was even willing to infringe on Germany's sovereignty and proposed to the United States that it send troops into Germany should Germany not be able to control the revolution. Similarly, it pleaded for American food shipments rather than accept help from the Soviet government. (How the latter could have provided such help beyond a few token car loads is not explained.)[15]

The only ones to take up the cause of the working class, DDR authors stress, were again the Spartacists and their allies, the Revolutionary Shop Stewards and some left-wing elements of the USPD. These groups sought to convince the workers that their trust in the leaders of the SPD and USPD was misplaced and that they must maintain the momentum of the revolution in order to destroy the foundations of the imperialist-militarist forces. To do this, the Spartacists reorganized their loose Spartacus group into the more centralized Spartacus League. But again the Spartacists would not part ways with the USPD, still hopeful they could convert that party into the revolutionary mass party that was needed in order to completely uproot German imperialism and militarism.

Even then, DDR authors claim, avenues to revolutionary action did exist. The workers' and soldiers' councils that sprang up throughout Germany in early November 1918 could have provided the institutional basis for a government willing to destroy permanently German militarism and imperialism. East German historians have paid considerable attention to these councils as offshoots of Russian developments. Consequently, just as the Bolsheviks gained the ascendancy in the Petrograd and other key soviets, the argument runs, the Spartacists might have asserted themselves in the German councils. From that vantage point they could have

[15]See *GdA*, vol. 3, pp. 138–40; Petzold, in Klein, *Deutschland*, vol. 3, pp. 544–46; Ruge, *Deutschlands*, pp. 71–72. Much supporting material can be found in Arno J. Mayer, *Politics and Diplomacy of Peacemaking: Containment and Counterrevolution at Versailles, 1918–1919* (New York, 1967), chs. 2 and 3; also see Müller, *Vom Kaiserreich*, vol. 2, pp. 114ff.

mobilized the masses for the overthrow of the bourgeois order. Given the political immaturity of the working class, however, this strategy required time. The fate of the revolution therefore depended on whether the ultimate political power would devolve onto the councils or onto a bourgeois-democratic parliament such as a national constituent assembly.

The decision in favor of a national assembly was made by a Reich congress of workers and soldiers that met in December 1918. Unlike the Russian soviets, whose impact on German developments DDR analysts tend to exaggerate, the majority of the German councils, dominated by members of the SPD and the moderate wing of the USPD, never aspired to exclusive governmental authority. Their option accorded with this self-limitation. As all accounts note, the decision to form a national assembly was crucial for the fate of the revolution because it returned full political freedom to the bourgeoisie and thus served to reinforce the bourgeois order. The councils, on the other hand, in the words of *Geschichte der deutschen Arbeiterbewegung*, "imposed their own death sentence upon themselves."[16]

With SPD, USPD, and councils abdicating their power, the Spartacus League decided to transform itself into the indispensable revolutionary mass party. On December 30, 1918, the Communist party of Germany (KPD) was founded. In the Marxist view, the event was the culmination of an inevitable historical process. According to *Geschichte der deutschen Arbeiterbewegung*, "it confirmed the teachings of V. I. Lenin that in the transitional era from capitalism to socialism, the formation of Marxist-Leninist parties, parties of the new type, is a universally valid, objective inevitability in all countries."

Yet the KPD was not the new type of party envisaged by Lenin, in which a tightly organized leadership corps would provide firm guidance to its membership and to the masses. Although no formal decision was made concerning the party's internal structure, the official reporter on organizational matters at the first congress proposed full autonomy for the local units—a suggestion that went unchallenged in the ensuing discussion. It was subsequently incorporated in somewhat modified form in the organizational charter enacted by the KPD's second congress in October 1919.

However, East German analysts are mainly concerned with the strategic mistakes the first congress committed. The bulk of

[16]GdA, vol. 3, pp. 143ff. (quotations on pp. 160, 162); Streisand, pp. 286–88; Ruge, *Deutschland*, pp. 73–74, 83ff. Cf. Walter Tormin, *Zwischen Rätediktatur und Sozialer Demokratie* (Düsseldorf, 1954), pp. 94ff., 117ff.; Kolb, *Arbeiterräte in der deutschen Innenpolitik* (Düsseldorf, 1962), pp. 244ff.; Oskar Anweiler, "Rätebewegung," *SDG*, vol. 5, pp. 432–33.

the delegates, *Geschichte* complains, misjudged the temper of the majority of the workers and failed to see that the dictatorship of the proletariat was not imminent. Consequently, they would not concentrate on such immediate tasks as the consolidation of the results of the revolution and the implementation of a limited anti-imperialist program. Instead, they called for the all-out socialization of the economy, the creation of a workers' militia in lieu of the army, the replacement of all parliamentary bodies by newly elected workers and soldiers' councils, and other equally sweeping changes. Overruling their leaders, the delegates also decided to boycott the elections to the national assembly. In the same vein, they dissociated themselves from the labor unions. All in all, election and union activities were regarded as opportunistic diversions from the revolutionary struggle. The congress thus failed to exploit the existing legal opportunities to win the working class over to its side.

The party is found to have been equally unrealistic in its treatment of the peasants, who were needed as allies in the revolutionary struggle. While correctly calling for the expropriation of the large estates, it proposed transferring the land thus obtained to socialist rural cooperatives rather than breaking them up into small peasant farms. Similarly, the proposed expropriation of medium-sized holdings is judged premature and likely to have kept middle-class peasants from joining the workers in the struggle against the exploiters.[17]

DDR authors are less critical of the KPD's participation in an equally premature workers rising in Berlin in January 1919. Convinced that the rising was doomed to defeat, the party had at first been opposed to it; it was nonetheless drawn into it by a precipitate commitment on the part of Liebknecht and Wilhelm Pieck, the later president of the DDR, and out of a mistaken sense of loyalty to the insurgents, a fact that is recorded with unusual equanimity—presumably because of the stature of the chief culprits. No attempt, however, is made to disguise the magnitude of the defeat when the rising was suppressed by the military and when Liebknecht and Luxemburg were brutally murdered by government soldiers.[18]

According to all accounts, the fate of the revolution was sealed with the assembly elections on January 19, 1919. The bourgeois parties won 49 more seats than the two socialist parties, confirming Spartacus's worst expectations. Concomitant with this consolidation of the bourgeois-monopolist position, the revolution-

---

[17]*GdA*, vol. 3, pp. 163ff. (quotations on pp. 169–70); Streisand, pp. 289ff.; Ruge, *Deutschland*, pp. 91ff.

[18]*GdA*, vol. 3, pp. 182ff.; Streisand, pp. 291–92; Ruge, *Deutschland*, pp. 98ff. Cf. Rosenberg, *Geschichte*, pp. 66ff.; Nettl, *Rosa Luxemburg*, vol. 2, p. 733.

ary initiatives are found to have subsided after the collapse of the
November Revolution. Mass strikes and other protest actions
against the restoration of the old militarist forces and against delays in socialization or the terrorism of government troops were
quickly suppressed. Special attention is paid to Communist policies and activities. Although the KPD's small size is not ignored,
its actions are nonetheless carefully scanned as a measuring rod of
the progress of revolutionary Marxism. Thus, the party is praised
when it proved adept at implementing Marxist-Leninist precepts
but is reprimanded when it did not. Accordingly, it is commended
for having opposed as pointless isolated "putschist" actions, yet it
is taken to task for its expectation of an early collapse of capitalism. This misconception, it is regretfully noted, led the party to
prepare for a revival of the revolution that could not succeed rather
than concentrating on the immediate social needs and rights of the
masses.

Despite this sharp refutation of an unrealistic strategy, East
German historians acclaim a group of Bavarian Communists who
came to the aid of a utopian Soviet republic that was established in
Munich in April 1919 by a group of Independent Socialists, left-
wing Social Democrats, and anarchists. Even though the last-
minute intervention of the Communists merely aggravated the defeat of the proletariat, DDR accounts do not condemn that decision
as the result of a mistaken sense of loyalty toward the masses but
hail it as a notable example of self-sacrifice, boldness, and courage.
They also pass over in silence the Communists' mistaken assumption, so clearly at variance with "objective" conditions, that the
defense of the Bavarian Soviet regime might rekindle the revolution throughout Germany.[19]

With this setback, the declining phase of the revolution came
to an end, according to the now prevailing periodization.[20] Yet the
outcome is not seen as entirely negative. *Geschichte* points out that
although "the election results enabled the imperialist German bourgeoisie to reestablish its class rule in bourgeois-parliamentary form
with the help of the right-wing Social Democrats, the counterrevolution could not liquidate all accomplishments of the revolution or
destroy the young KPD." The revolutionary working class attained
some important successes despite its defeat: it replaced the Junker-
monarchist regimes in Germany and its member states with bourgeois-democratic republics; it secured some political rights and

---

[19]Ruge, *Deutschland*, pp. 109ff; *GdA*, vol. 3, pp. 212ff.; Beyer, *Novemberrevolution*,
pp. 89ff.
[20]*Grundriss*, p. 388; Ruge, review, *ZfG* 27 (1979): 677; also see the arrangement of
materials in Ruge, *Deutschland*, 1967 edition, p. 5, as compared to 1978 edition,
p. 5.

liberties for the masses, including women; it secured such social rights as the eight-hour day for urban workers and the abolition of near-feudal restrictions on rural labor. On balance, however, all East German analysts are agreed, the working class suffered a grave defeat. As Ruge puts it, not only did it fail to destroy the imperialist class rule, its very achievements also had their inherent drawbacks: although these accomplishments created a fairly favorable terrain for the further unfolding of the proletarian class struggle, they also encouraged reformist illusions and opportunist positions. Under the circumstances, he concludes, "the most important result was the foundation of the Communist party of Germany." In the activities of the party, historical inevitability was asserting itself. The party provided the instrument by which the cause of the working class could really be advanced and the foundation created for the eventual reunification of the working class by the Socialist Unity party (SED), "the leading force in the socialist development of the German Democratic Republic." Through its work, the KPD also furthered the cause of world revolution beyond Germany's borders and helped to inflict further setbacks on international imperialism.[21]

As the "first revolution of the German working class against imperialism and militarism and the most extensive movement, since the Peasants' War, of the popular masses in Germany,"[22] the revolution of November 1918 thus is considered a milestone, despite its shortcomings, in the transitional era from capitalism to socialism. Given its special significance, the determination of its exact place within that transition has been a major concern of Marxist historians. On one occasion this question even touched off a spirited controversy. In 1957–1958, several East German historians defined the upheaval as an aborted socialist revolution—a view widely held by German and other Marxists in Weimar days.[23] History, they reasoned, had placed a socialist revolution on the German agenda; objectively conditions were ripe, with capitalism having reached its last, state-monopolist, stage and with the ruling class and its tools of power, police and army, badly demoralized.

[21]*GdA*, vol. 3, pp. 194ff.; Ruge, *Deutschland*, pp. 118ff.; Diehl, "Die Bedeutung der Novemberrevolution 1918," *ZfG* 17 (1969): 32.

[22]Ruge, *Deutschland*, p. 118.

[23]The immediate occasion was the political and ideological dethronement of Stalin by the 20th party congress of the Soviet Communist party in 1956, which encouraged historians to reexamine Stalinist interpretations of history. In this context, the view of the November revolution as a bourgeois upheaval—prevalent in the Stalin era—was subjected to such a reexamination (Nimtz, "Über den Charakter," p. 688). Nimtz noted, however, that the interpretation of the 1918 revolution as a bourgeois one predated Stalin's rise to power; yet his data make clear that its classification as a bourgeois-democratic upheaval became generally accepted only in Stalin's day, though not necessarily as a specifically Stalinist proposition (ibid., pp. 691–92). See also Walter Ulbricht, "Über den Charakter der Novemberrevolution," *ZfG* 6 (1958): 718, 723–24.

The masses, for their part, were rising against the existing capitalist system, and the emerging workers' and soldiers' councils pointed the way to the dictatorship of the proletariat. If the revolution failed despite such auspicious beginnings, this was due to the cleverness of the bourgeoisie, the treachery of the Social Democrats, and the absence of an organized, purposeful Leninist party. It was also argued that if the revolution had been bourgeois in nature, it would be illogical to charge the Social Democrats with having betrayed the cause of the workers, for in that case the party had acted in accord with the mandate of history. However, the state-monopolist stage of socioeconomic developments (according to Lenin the "most complete *material* preparation of socialism") and the "class content" of the revolution (proletariat versus bourgeoisie) left no doubt that history had meant this to be a socialist revolution.[24]

This interpretation touched on basic questions of Marxist-Leninist theory and practical politics. For these reasons it ran at once into sharp opposition, and in the end the Central Committee of the SED intervened to settle the controversy. There was no quarrel with the analysis of the "objective" criteria of the upheaval—"class content" and socioeconomic conditions—but the critics noted that if these alone determined the nature of a revolution, "subjective" factors, such as the work of the Leninist party and the revolutionary will of the working class, were unimportant. Such a conclusion would run counter to a basic tenet of historical materialism: that, in Nimtz's words, "the solution of the lawfully evolved tasks requires the conscious activity of the revolutionary classes." A socialist revolution can therefore be carried out only, in the words of Walter Ulbricht, "when through persistent struggles and under the leadership of the Marxist-Leninist party, class consciousness and organization of working class and toiling masses have grown to such an extent that the working class can establish its hegemony and by the build-up of its own power lay the foundation for a proletarian revolution."

Because of the weakness of the revolutionary working class in 1918 and the lack of a revolutionary party, the Central Committee's *Theses on the November Revolution of 1918* pointed out, the revolution could not advance beyond the bourgeois-democratic stage. Its immediate objectives were limited to the destruction of militarism, the purging of the bureaucracy, and the expropriation of Junkers and war criminals, that is, imperialist monopoly capital-

[24]Schreiner, "Auswirkungen der Grossen Sozialistischen Oktoberrevolution auf Deutschland vor und während der Novemberrevolution," *ZfG* 6 (1958): 29ff.; Roland Bauer, "Zur Einschätzung des Charakters der deutschen Novemberrevolution 1918–1919," ibid., pp. 136ff., esp. 151ff.; Fricke, in ibid. 5 (1957): 1253–54.

ists. The workers still had to form a Communist party, enter an alliance with the peasantry, and gain revolutionary experience. Only after these goals had been attained could there be the social-ist revolution for which the historical agenda indeed was calling.

To classify the November Revolution as a socialist revolution was viewed not only as historically wrong but also as politically dangerous, and here again the close interrelationship of Marxist theory and practice asserted itself. As Ulbricht warned, anyone who belittled the role of the revolutionary party and paid attention only to the objective factors actually believed in the "bourgeois-objectivist" falsehood of spontaneity. "To call the November Revo-lution a socialist one negates consciously or unconsciously the role of the party." As it was, without guidance by a revolutionary party, the bulk of the working class contented itself with some parlia-mentary-democratic reforms and put its faith in the Constituent National Assembly and a socialization commission to bring about socialism. The revolution of 1918, therefore, was not a socialist one but, in the official wording, "a bourgeois-democratic revolu-tion that was carried out to a certain extent with proletarian means and methods." At the same time, the tenor of Ulbricht's remarks also reveals the concern that any other interpretation might raise doubts about the indispensability of a Marxist-Leninist party.[25]

The nonsocialist nature of the revolution was not an unex-pected discovery. Earlier discussions of the character of the revolu-tion, which the KDP leadership had carried on during its exile in Moscow in 1938–1939, had led to the conclusion, in keeping with Lenin's teachings, that socialism could be attained only *after* the working class was in full control of political power. Such a concen-tration of power in the hands of the workers was in turn predicated on the stripping of monopolists, agrarians, and militarists of their power resources and on the destruction of the old governmental apparatus. The primary task of the revolutionary forces in 1918 therefore should have been the establishment of a united demo-cratic and anti-imperialist front, including progressive bourgeois elements and the peasantry as a prelude to a dictatorship of the proletariat. Only after such a dictatorship had been established— with the reactionary bureaucracy replaced by a genuinely demo-cratic one, a land reform carried out, and all monopolies brought under state control—would the time have come for the introduc-tion of socialism.[26] This was the strategy that the KPD and the

---

[25]Nimtz, "Über den Charakter," pp. 688ff.; Nimtz, *Die Novemberrevolution 1918 in Deutschland* (Berlin [East], 1962), pp. 32ff. (Ulbricht quotation on p. 33); Ul-bricht, "Über den Charakter," pp. 717ff.

[26]See Berthold, *"Marxistisches Geschichtsbild,"* pp. 86ff., especially pp. 92–93; An-ton Ackermann, at meeting of SED directorate, October 1946, quoted in *BzG* 10

SED had followed in East Germany (with Soviet backing) after the Second World War. At the time of the debate the hope was that this strategy could be applied in West Germany, too.

Here the controversy also touched on practical politics. For, as both Ulbricht and Nimtz indicate, it was feared at the time that the reunification of Germany—in the manner envisaged by the DDR—would be rendered even more difficult if it were thought that a reunification on East German terms would be predicated on a socialist revolution in the West. The interpretation mentioned above was to make clear that collective action by the working class and anti-imperialist and antimilitarist bourgeois groups would suffice and, given the existing distribution of forces, was the only route that promised success.[27]

All in all, then, East German historians deal soberly with the events of that period. From the class-struggle perspective of Marxism-Leninism, DDR analyses cannot but be highly critical of the policies of Ebert and his associates, and seeing revolutions as the motor power of progress, they must condemn the Social Democrats' striving for order at almost any price. (The preoccupation in 1918 with the restoration of order rather than the enactment of changes has lately been criticized also by non-Marxist scholars.[28]) If East German researchers pay special attention to the activities of the Spartacists, they do so not because they consider the Spartacus League the key factor in the upheaval but because the League was the one group, in their view, that came at least close to assuming the "correct" position during the revolution.

In their assessment of Spartacist and left-Independent weakness, DDR scholars have proved better historians than their non-Marxist colleagues, who until recently greatly overrated the strength of the Spartacists during that revolutionary winter of 1918–1919. West German analysts have now revised this view and in fact have suggested that given the essentially moderate character of the workers' and soldiers' councils, the Ebert government might well have utilized the councils in its quest for stability, acceding at the same time to their demands for reforms, rather than ally itself with the monarchist officer corps, bureaucracy, and big business, thus launching the Weimar Republic on its sad course. Marxists, of course, would deny that such a coali-

---

(1968): suppl. 2, p. 110; *Grundriss*, pp. 374ff., 388ff.; Ruge, *Deutschland*, pp. 121ff. On Lenin's views, see his "Two Tactics of Social Democracy in the Democratic Revolution," in Tucker, *Lenin Anthology*, pp. 120ff.; also Allan K. Wildman, "Lenin," in *SDG*, vol. 4, pp. 5–7.

[27]Ulbricht, "Über den Charakter," pp. 717ff.; Nimtz, "Über den Charakter," pp. 688ff.

[28]See, for example, Ralf Dahrendorf, *Gesellschaft und Demokratie in Deutschland* (Munich, 1968), pp. 217–18.

tion of Ebert's government and the SPD-dominated councils could have changed the actual course of events.[29]

The Revolutionary Postwar Crisis

Whatever the achievements of the November Revolution, most of them were minor in the East German view, because monopolists, agrarians, and militarists retained the foundations of their power and looked upon the republic as a temporary accommodation to be abandoned at the first possible moment. To DDR authors, then, the revolution's most significant attainment was the formation of the Communist party; a truly revolutionary working class party, it was willing to take up the fight for peace and democracy and against imperialism and militarism by attacking the socioeconomic foundations on which these two forces rested. In this context, the civil liberties and electoral and plebiscitary arrangements provided by the Weimar Constitution assume significance for Marxist historians, for they facilitated the Communist struggle.[30]

On the whole, however, East German historians find that the Weimar Constitution served as a stepping stone toward the consolidation of bourgeois power. It kept intact the institution of capitalist property, leaving the democratic rights it established without the material guarantees that the liquidation of the monopolies and the breakup of the large landed estates would have provided. The powers of the Reichstag were checked by the continued retention of the bulk of the old bureaucracy and by the continuing exemption of the judiciary from control by the parliament. By endowing the Reich president with the special emergency powers of Article 48, the constitution placed him above the Reichstag, thus further curbing the latter's authority prior to eliminating it altogether. The new state, *Grundriss* concludes, was a "dictatorship of the monopoly bourgeoisie in bourgeois-parliamentary guise." In the same vein, Ruge sums up, "Junker-bourgeois German imperialism changed into bourgeois-Junker imperialism." In thus reestablishing its class rule behind a parliamentary facade, it is charged, the bourgeoisie had, moreover, the support of the rightist leadership of the Social Democrats, who once again became the allies of the imperialist and militarist forces. If some social and political concessions

---

[29]Erich Matthias, *Zwischen Räten und Geheimräten: Die deutsche Revolutionsregierung 1918/19* (Düsseldorf, 1970), pp. 15ff.; Tormin, *Zwischen Rätediktatur,* pp. 130ff.; Kolb, *Arbeiterräte,* pp. 405ff.
[30]Streisand, pp. 294–95; *GdA,* vol. 3, p. 241.

could be secured from the ruling class, such reforms resulted from the impact of the Bolshevik Revolution and from the efforts of the popular masses.[31] These critiques badly misrepresent the motivations of Social Democratic inaction, but they picture correctly the effects of this inactivity.[32]

The peace treaty of Versailles between the Allies and Germany fits readily into this scenario of a carefully planned bourgeois comeback. In this case, the manipulations of Allied imperialists allowed German imperialism to survive as a bulwark against both Soviet Russia and the democratic forces at home. Evidence for this contention is found in the fact that the socioeconomic foundations of German militarism were not dismantled and in the Allies' failure to try German war criminals as provided for in the peace treaty. As for the domestic aspects of the military arrangements, the point is made that the army was left strong enough to defend the regime against any revolutionary risings.

However, DDR authors also note that the Allies' own imperialist interests did not allow Germany to escape unharmed from the war: the final settlement imposed on it heavy territorial, financial, and other economic penalties that would have been even heavier except for the conflicting aims of the imperialist rivals. The working class was the ultimate victim of these penalties, because industrialists and landowners rid themselves of their share of this burden by unscrupulous inflationary manipulations. Moreover, by blaming the ensuing misery, unemployment, and other hardships solely on the Versailles treaty and by calling for the recovery of lost territories and additional living space, thus nurturing a spirit of chauvinism and revanchism, the German monopolists diverted the attention of the masses from their own culpability. Only the Communist party, it is stressed, perceived that the peace treaty was part of the class struggle and that as such it aggravated, though it did not cause, the misery of the masses. The ruthless machinations of both German and Allied imperialists were responsible for this result. In Streisand's words, all that the Versailles Treaty achieved was to arrange the transition from an imperialist war to an imperi-

[31]See *Grundriss*, p. 392; Ruge, *Deutschland*, pp. 119–20; Streisand, pp. 304–6. Ruge's thesis of a shift from Junker-bourgeois to bourgeois-Junker imperialism runs counter to the generally accepted East German view that the bourgeoisie had played the dominant role in its partnership with the Junker agrarians ever since capitalism entered its imperialist phase. *Grundriss* (p. 393) is more consistent in this regard when it says of the bourgeois-Junker alliance in the early days of the new republic: "Within the ruling class the distribution of power had shifted further toward monopoly capitalism, compared to the Empire."

[32]Richard Löwenthal, "Einführung," in George Eliasberg, *Der Ruhrkrieg von 1920* (Bonn–Bad Godesberg, 1974), pp. xiff.; Charles S. Maier, *Recasting Bourgeois Europe* (Princeton, 1975), pp. 53ff.

alist peace. An imperialist peace, however, intensifying class conflicts and imperialist rivalries, could only prepare the ground for
new wars.[33]

In support of these claims, DDR analysts also maintain that
the government's decision to side with the Western powers rather
than with the new Soviet state served the German national interest poorly. By trying to ingratiate itself with the imperialist West,
the government merely encouraged the latter to impose its extor-
tionist peace dictate on Germany. Soviet Russia, for its part, would
never have exacted as high a price for any aid to Berlin. Again the
argument bypasses the question of how Germany would have fared
had it in fact collaborated with the Soviet regime. Apart from all
international consequences, what could Germany, in desperate
need of foodstuffs and raw materials, have gained from collaborating with a state in the throes of a civil war, impoverished, exhausted, unable to feed its own people, and cut off by Poland from
direct contact with Germany?

A year later the Kapp Putsch provided further proof of the
determination of militarist and imperialist forces to recover their
one-time power. The insurrection was launched in March 1920 by
parts of the army, free corps, and agrarian-conservative elements
under a one-time Prussian official, Wolfgang Kapp. East German
accounts also claim that it was quietly backed by some coal and
steel interests and by most major banks, but these claims are not
corroborated by adequate evidence and have been refuted in large
part by Western scholars. If business did not support the insurgents, however, it did not support the legal government either. Its
opposition to the putsch, moreover, was a result of its feeling that
the timing was inopportune, not that the objectives of the putschists were wrong.

The putschists seized power for a few days from the republican government. In the East German views, credit for the defeat of
Kapp's semimilitary dictatorship belonged to the working class,
whose determined resistance, by means of a general strike, defeated the rebels. Once again, the working class proved itself as the
only dependable defender of democracy. (There is no mention anywhere of the noncooperation of the upper echelons of the government bureaucracy, which also prevented the Kapp regime from
consolidating itself.)

Always concerned with illustrating the history-making powers of the masses and with the role of the working class as the
motive force of the class struggle, DDR authors have paid special
attention to the reaction of the workers to the revolt. They have

[33]Streisand, pp. 295ff.; *GdA*, vol. 3, pp. 228ff.; Ruge, *Deutschland*, pp. 127ff.; also
Mayer, *Politics*, pp. 234–36.

explored at some length the resort to force against the insurgents by workers' units that seized arms from local militias, found secret caches of the free corps, or raided arms factories. Detailed investigations have also been made of the takeover of local governments by a number of these units. Thus, DDR researchers have uncovered numerous cases of resistance activities even in predominantly rural areas, such as Mecklenburg and Pomerania, where agricultural laborers came to the aid of the urban workers.[34]

Because class struggles, like all struggles, are decided by preponderant power, East German research has also explored the widespread efforts at concerted working-class action against the putschists and their various backers. Because the disunity of the working class is considered the root cause of the workers' weakness in the class struggles of those years, this brief moment of working-class unity has received much attention in the East German literature. A multitude of articles and dissertations pictures the KPD, advised and supported by the newly founded Third (Communist) International (Comintern), as a chief promoter of such a united front, after an initial moment of opposition blamed on "ultra-leftist" elements. The workers' defeat of the Kappists demonstrated the potential of united action: for once, Communists, Independent Socialists, Social Democrats, and labor unions had worked together—loosely in the general strike on the national plane, more closely in armed action or administrative activity on the local and regional level.[35]

Yet, as is also regretfully noted, collaboration did not survive the collapse of the Kapp regime. The old divisions reasserted themselves. The traitorous Social Democrats were anxious to return as quickly as possible to pre-Putsch conditions, while the left-wing Independents and Communists wanted to put an end once and for all to all counterrevolutionary endeavors. Thus, the Social Democrats broke off the general strike before the government's promises

[34]See Ruge, *Deutschland*, pp. 148ff.; *GdA*, vol. 3, pp. 264ff.; Gossweiler, *Grossbanken*, p. 141; Erwin Könnemann and Hans-Joachim Krusch, *Aktionseinheit contra Kapp-Putsch* (Berlin [East], 1972), p. 143; Martin Polzin, *Kapp-Putsch in Mecklenburg* (Rostock, 1966). One DDR historian has tried to picture the Kapp Putsch as part of an international anti-Soviet conspiracy, but his evidence does not make a convincing case for his claim that Britain was backing the Putschists in order to use them against Soviet Russia (Edmund Jauering, "Der Kapp-Putsch—eine internationale Verschwörung gegen Sowjetrussland," *BzG* 10 [1968]: 876ff.). In the 1967 edition of his *Deutschland*, Ruge, too, alludes to some "inadequate" support of the Kappists by the "Entente states" (p. 156), but he does so no longer in the 1978 edition (p. 153). For a non-Marxist analysis of the role of business during the Kapp Putsch, see Feldman, "Big Business and the Kapp Putsch," *CEH* 4 (1971): 99ff. See also Johannes Erger (*Der Kapp-Lüttwitz-Putsch* [Düsseldorf, 1967]), who found no evidence of any support of the putsch by banks (pp. 97, 230) and also refutes some of the other unsubstantiated claims of support in the East German literature (pp. 95ff.).

[35]Karl and Ruge, in *ZfG* 18 suppl., pp. 523–25; Diehl, "Zum Kampf der KPD um die Einheitsfront der Arbeiterklasse," *BzG* 7 (1965): 3ff.

of reforms had been implemented. Conversely, an attempt to establish a workers' government composed of representatives of SPD,
USPD, and labor unions failed because the left-wing Independents
did not wish to share governmental power with Social Democrats,
the "mass murderers of workers." Inevitably, as soon as parties and
unions went their separate ways, the workers lost what striking
power they had.[36]

As a result, the East German accounts complain, a new Social
Democratic-bourgeois coalition government was formed that dispatched the army and volunteer free corps to crush all further
attempts of the workers to prevent any bourgeois comeback. In the
Ruhr valley, the workers renewed the general strike, drove out the
government forces with the help of a hastily assembled "Red Ruhr
Army," and took over the local government. Contrary to the traditional version of a rampant "red terror," DDR accounts maintain
that the take-over was disciplined and that no atrocities were committed. They also insist that the bulk of the workers was ready to
lay down their arms after a settlement had been negotiated with
the government, promising the disbandment of all forces involved
in the Kapp Putsch and granting a series of democratizing social
and political reforms (*Bielefelder Abkommen*). Yet, in violation of
this agreement, army and free corps—among the latter some of
those very units that should have been liquidated—moved into the
Ruhr district and unleashed a "white terror," in which large numbers of workers were massacred. Although the brutalities of the
government forces had long been known, the DDR accounts of the
workers' restrained conduct have thrown a different light on the
course of the "Ruhr War." These accounts are not well enough
documented to be wholly convincing, but their essential accuracy
has more recently been confirmed by a carefully documented West
German study that found that although there were some spontaneous killings (and some looting) on the part of the Red Ruhr Army,
there were none of the systematic mass massacres and executions
of which the government forces were guilty.

What also appalls East German authors is the fact that the
workers suffered this new defeat once again at the hands of a
government in which the Social Democrats held key posts. Not
only, it is bitterly noted, did this latest treachery of the SPD
leaders deepen the divisions within the working class—which the
Social Democrats indeed intended to do, hoping to isolate the
more radical workers—but Junkers and great bourgeoisie emerged
virtually intact from a debacle that ought to have led to their
downfall. These circles did, however, learn from the putsch's failure, the East German critics conclude, that the Weimar Republic

[36]Ruge, *Deutschland,* pp. 155–56; *Grundriss,* p. 400.

would have to be subverted by a more gradual strategy and that they would need a mass movement in order to implement this strategy of subversion.[37]

For the period following the Kapp Putsch, attention shifts to various efforts of labor and "monopoly bourgeoisie" to gird for new struggles. The outcome of the Reichstag elections in June 1920 encouraged such polarization. Both the monarchist right and the radical left, in particular the USPD, scored substantial gains at the expense of the moderate parties, including the SPD. Sensing the disillusionment of many workers with any reformist approach, the KPD urged the militant elements of the USPD to join forces with it. The rift within the USPD was deepened when the Comintern, at its Second World Congress in August 1920, tightened its admission standards. It imposed on its member parties the duty to submit to all Comintern resolutions, disavow all reformist and centrist views, and adopt the principle of democratic centralism as its organizational basis. The USPD broke up over these issues, with a majority of its members joining the KPD—now briefly known as the United Communist party (VKPD)—while the remainder eventually returned to the SPD.

To DDR historians, this accretion of Communist power is of decisive importance, because it turned the minuscule KPD into a "mass party." *Geschichte* dramatizes this development into an event of long-range significance: "For the first time in the history of the international labor movement, the common struggle of two workers' parties in a highly industrialized country had led to their merger on a revolutionary basis"—the term *revolutionary* again understood as a call for the most expeditious transformation of the bourgeois-capitalist order into a socialist one, not as a call for an immediate violent uprising.[38]

As opponents of Rosa Luxemburg's advocacy of party democracy, the East German authors also welcome the introduction of the procedural principle of democratic centralism in the enlarged party, in accordance with the Comintern directives. (Democratic centralism combines—in theory—the election of all party organs with the demand for strict discipline and unquestioning acceptance of decisions of the higher party organs by the lower ones, with party policy thus fully controlled by the party's top echelon.) The step was considered all the more important because the party was constantly torn by factional disputes. New efforts to create a united working-class front served to sharpen these differences. In Marxist terms, an "opportunist" faction on the right attacked the

[37]See "Rote Ruhrarmee," *Swb*, vol. 2, pp. 421–22; Ruge, *Deutschland*, pp. 157–58. The West German study is Eliasberg, *Ruhrkrieg*, pp. 116–17, 124–25, 143, 194–95, 239–40; also 226, 228–29 (see above n. 32).

[38]*GdA*, vol. 3, p. 311; Ruge, *Deutschland*, p. 167.

Comintern strictures on all Social Democratic parties; calling them self-defeating; on the other hand, an "adventurist, petty bourgeois, ultra-left" wing, pointing to the restiveness of German labor, thought that revolution was imminent. Embracing a "theory of revolutionary offensive," it opposed all cooperation with Social Democrats and wished to prepare for that revolution.[39]

The controversy assumed immediate significance when Prussian police forces moved into the province of Saxony in March 1921 to put an end to the growing unrest in that region. According to the East German accounts, the move was touched off by "monopolist" circles that wanted to crush all worker resistance to further onslaughts on labor's livelihood. As *Geschichte der deutschen Arbeiterbewegung* puts it, a long-planned provocation was to provide the pretext for such suppression.

> [It] was worked out in detail in agreements between the managements of the [leading chemical, copper, and lignite mining] concerns and the Prussian government led by rightist Social Democrats. It was carried out by the Social Democratic Prussian Minister of the Interior, Carl Severing, and the Social Democratic *Oberpräsident* of the province of Saxony, Otto Hörsing. The plan was to goad the revolutionary workers into an armed struggle by moving heavily armed police detachments into the central German working-class centers, smash them in a bloody encounter after having isolated them from the working class elsewhere in Germany, disarm them, and break the strong influence of the VKPD.

Geschichte does, however, concede that by then the "adventurist" views of the VKPD's "ultra-left" had gained ground in the party. Under the influence of the ultra-left's "theory of revolutionary offensive," the party leadership had openly called for the overthrow of the government, in bland disregard of the actual distribution of "class power" and the attitude of those elements of the working class who supported the SPD and the USPD. At a leadership meeting that was held on the very day on which the Prussian authorities announced their proposed police intervention, it was decided, on the Comintern's prodding, to prepare actively for a revolution for which the time, it was thought, would soon come. Although it was not known to the Prussian government and although the Communists did not have time to make any preparations, the government's claim that it was acting to forestall an uprising was not entirely wrong.

However, the police action did not arouse the anticipated militant reaction among the workers. The call for a general strike issued by VKPD headquarters in Berlin met only with moderate

[39]*GdA*, vol. 3, pp. 320ff.; Ruge, *Deutschland*, pp. 168–70; "Offensivtheorie," *Swb*, vol. 2, p. 215.

success in Prussian Saxony and had little impact on most other parts of the country. The call to arms was equally ineffective. An armed insurrection in the province was stirred up primarily by an ex-party member, Max Hölz, who managed to organize bands of strikers and unemployed miners and who fought his own private war. Risings in Hamburg, the Rhineland, and a few other areas remained isolated local events that were quickly squashed. On April 1, 1921, twelve days after the police had moved into Saxony, the party called off both the strike and the uprising. This calamitous outcome—rendered even more disastrous by more than 100 deaths and large numbers of jail sentences—the East German analyses note, demonstrated the lack of realism of all those who thought the time for a revolution was near.[40]

This conclusion conforms to the changed views of Lenin and the Comintern, who raised the question of Communist tactics at the Comintern's Third Congress in July 1921. In the light of a succession of serious setbacks, not only in Germany, the Congress denounced the "theory of revolutionary offensive." Instead, it called for a united proletarian front, because the working class could seize power only if it overcame its internal divisions. This strategy was also adopted by the VKDP's party congress, which met a month later.

Because these decisions settled a critical issue of party policy, the DDR accounts discuss them in detail. What they do not mention is that in helping the strife-torn KPD (as it again called itself from then on) reach this decision, the Comintern also strengthened its permanent hold on the German party.[41] Obviously there is no need, from the Marxist perception, to point out this consequence, because it is considered constructive and natural, reflecting that worldwide commonality of working-class interests on which the Marxist movement is based. Indeed, if the Comintern's influence grew, it was largely because various factions within the KPD leadership called on the Moscow authorities to settle their intraparty disputes.[42]

[40]See GdA, vol. 3, pp. 322ff.; "Märzkämpfe 1921," Swb, vol. 2, pp. 82–83; Ruge, Deutschland, pp. 170ff.; Reisberg, An den Quellen der Einheitsfront (Berlin [East], 1971), vol. 1, p. 89ff. None of these works delineates clearly the actual role of the VKPD; instead, they allude to it in varying degrees of specificity. The frankest account can be found in Swb. For a careful and balanced investigation of this entire episode, see Werner T. Angress, Stillborn Revolution: The Communist Bid for Power in Germany (Princeton, 1963), pp. 105ff.

[41]See GdA, vol. 3, pp. 329ff.; "Kommunistische Internationale," Swb, vol. 1, pp. 968–69; Reisberg, An den Quellen, vol. 1, pp. 117ff. For the Comintern's growing influence on the VKPD, see Angress, Stillborn Revolution, pp. 193ff.

[42]See GdA, vol. 3, p. 349. See also Ossip K. Flechtheim, Die Kommunistische Partei Deutschlands in der Weimar Republik (Offenbach, 1948), p. 80; E. H. Carr, The Bolshevik Revolution (New York, 1950ff.), vol. 3, pp. 394ff.

The implementation of the united-front policy created serious tactical and ideological problems for the KPD. How far was it to go in its collaboration with SPD, USPD, and labor unions? Its left wing assailed some of the central committee's proposals as bordering on Revisionism, while the right wing did not hesitate to shelve ideological reservations for the sake of working-class unity. At that, whatever agreement there was with non-Communist parties and groups—on such issues as a capital levy, expropriation of princely properties, and state participation in all major enterprises—joint action foundered on the insistence of non-Communist groups that they proceed within the democratic-parliamentary framework. The Communists, on the other hand, wished to transfer the struggle from the capitalist-dominated Reichstag to streets and factories. The question of the Communist attitude toward a workers' government (the "inevitable consequence of a united-front policy," according to *Geschichte*), specifically the question of KPD toleration of or participation in such a government, and on what terms, heightened intra-party dissension. So did the conclusion in April 1922 of the Rapallo Pact, which provided for German-Soviet collaboration. Although such a rapprochement had long been advocated by the KPD, it raised the question as to how to pursue the goal of overthrowing a bourgeois-capitalist government that was now an ally of Moscow.[43]

Geschichte attributes these difficulties to a lack of ideological maturity and the failure to absorb fully the principles of Leninism—that is, the failure to maintain tactical flexibility, as Lenin had just a year earlier demanded it in his guidebook on revolutionary tactics, *Left-Wing Communism—An Infantile Disorder*. In this regard, as East German research has shown, the Comintern proved of notable help. In contrast to previous occasions, the advice it offered was realistic; at the same time its liaison men with the German party exercised a restraining influence on the KPD's hotheads. Specifically, the Comintern urged a less rigid attitude toward the SPD and the labor unions (including Catholic ones) in order to draw these forces away from the bourgeois camp. It also counseled participation in a workers' government even if such a government could operate only within the framework of bourgeois democracy. What mattered was that such participation would enable the Communist party to help shape developments until, eventually, it could pursue its "revolutionary-democratic alternative." The issue was of immediate significance, because some German

[43]The pact is praised by DDR authors as an important contribution to peace inasmuch as it prevented the formation of an anti-Soviet coalition and opened the path to peaceful coexistence between Soviet Russia and the "imperialist" powers, apart from its economic advantages (Ruge, *Deutschland*, pp. 185ff.; *GdA*, vol. 3, pp. 356–57).

states—Saxony, Thuringia, and a few others—offered possibilities for the formation of such workers' governments; in Saxony and Thuringia, two were actually formed in 1923. Still, the unending debates among the KPD leadership suggest something of the difficulties of implementing Moscow's advice without getting mired in "opportunism" and "reformism."[44]

DDR analyses find the bourgeois camp, on the other hand, much more united. Divisions among the great bourgeoisie never proved irreconcilable. In fact, they are viewed as mere tactical variations on the common monopolist and imperialist themes. The contending factions are the familiar ones. Although an "adventurist-militarist" group (supported chiefly, but not exclusively, by the coal, iron, and steel industries) was determined to return to an authoritarian state and deprive labor of most of its recent social and political gains, it did adjust to the necessities of the moment and at times joined forces with a "flexible, parliamentary" group (identified, but again not exclusively, with electrical, chemical, and other light industries) that was prepared to pursue its objectives within the parliamentary-democratic system. It is charged, however, that within that framework, the "flexible, parliamentary" group also sought to emasculate labor's position. The two camps thus derived much of their strength from a measure of cooperation that the working class never could muster.[45]

As always, DDR authors place the responsibility for this continued disunity on the SPD leadership. In this assessment they are correct inasmuch as the SPD leaders and the workers for whom they spoke were not prepared to give up the livelihood, however lean, that the bourgeois state provided for them, at least not for the uncertainties of the dictatorship of the proletariat. As a result, Ruge notes, the monopolist bourgeoisie could quickly reestablish its dominant position after the debacle of the Kapp Putsch. "Ten

[44]*GdA*, vol. 3, pp. 334, 349ff., 370ff.; Reisberg, *An den Quellen*, vol. 2, pp. 257ff., 293ff.; Reisberg, "Zur Losung der Arbeiterregierung in Jahre 1922," *BzG* 9 (1967): 1043ff. (quotation on p. 1045); Angress, *Stillborn Revolution*, pp. 202–3, 248.

[45]Because equating the first group with heavy industry and the second with electro-chemical industries, first called for by Kuczynski (*Geschichte*, vol. 5, pp. 77ff.), turned out to be incorrect for the period under discussion, it has now been modified by most DDR authors and in this less categorical form is useful. On the other hand, there is no point in examining here Gossweiler's thesis—as propounded in his (unpublished) dissertation, *Die Rolle des Monopolkapitals bei der Herbeiführung der Röhm-Affäre* (Humboldt-Universität, 1963), and subsequently in his book, *Grossbanken*—that the decisive dividing line within the monopolist camp ran, not between two industrial camps, but between two banking groups—one calling for the attainment of its antidemocratic and anti-Soviet objectives at the side of and in temporary subordination to the United States, the other aiming at the formation of a European bloc directed as much against the United States as against the Soviet Union. This thesis, based on inadequate data, assumptions, and various non sequiturs, has been ignored by other DDR historians, although most of them list Gossweiler's writings in their bibliographies.

weeks after the magnificent defense action of the working class against the militarists, the first purely bourgeois government stood at the head of the republic."[46]

The issues on which East German attention is focused in its analysis of the "monopolists" ' role are reparations and inflation. Both are treated as class problems rather than national ones, with the state once again serving as the handmaiden of the monopolies. On this perspective, reparations became a means by which the "monopolists" sought to reinforce their position at labor's expense. Accordingly, DDR authors discount the differences between those who advocated a policy of nonpayment and those who proposed fulfillment. The former were willing to risk a French occupation of Germany because they were confident that, backed by Britain and the United States, they would emerge stronger from such an occupation than would the French. That such tactics would impose immense hardships on the nation did not concern them. Moreover, such adversities would arouse the fighting spirit of the country, discredit the parliamentary-democratic regime, and pave the way for the establishment of an authoritarian-militarist government. The advocates of fulfillment, on the other hand, merely pretended to be willing to meet Germany's reparations debts; in reality, they expected to demonstrate their senselessness (a correct assessment of their motives, except that there was nothing secret about this strategy). In the meantime, both groups would try to reap as much profit as possible from these obligations by converting reparations payments into deliveries of industrial products through commercial arrangements between German and French concerns.

The charge doubtless applied to an agreement concluded in 1922 between the German industrialist Hugo Stinnes and a French industrial spokesman, Marquis de Lubersac. It is borne out also by the negative reaction of both German and French businessmen to an earlier, less profitable, pact signed by the German Minister of Reconstruction, Walther Rathenau, and his French counterpart, Louis Loucheur. In further confirmation of their analysis, East German historians can also point to Stinnes' later proposal, which called for a German-French mining consortium combining Ruhr coal and French minette (with the Germans controlling a majority of the stock) in conjunction with the reconstruction of the devastated French territories. The proposal was to be underwritten partly by German labor that would have had to work an additional

---

[46]see Ruge, *Deutschland*, pp. 159ff. (quotation on p. 160); Kuczynski, *Geschichte*, vol. 5, pp. 92ff., vol. 16, pp. 22ff.; Gossweiler, *Grossbanken*, pp. 103ff. Gossweiler criticizes Kuczynski for overstressing the disagreements between the "monopolist" camps. Ruge (p. 175) even goes so far as to attribute the murder of Erzberger and Rathenau, both identified as spokesmen for the flexible, parliamentary camp, to assassins hired by rival monopolists, with assumptions substituting for evidence.

two hours each day without additional pay for the next ten to fifteen years and would have had to forgo its right to strike for five years. The government, for its part, was expected to remove all restrictions on entrepreneurial activities, including "excessive" taxes, and the Allies would end their occupation of the Rhineland and rescind all limitations on German armaments. This brazen scheme, DDR authors note, foundered on the opposition of the French "imperialists," who in turn proposed an arrangement that would have assured their hegemony in Europe.[47]

Just as DDR analysts find reparations being used as a class-struggle weapon, the inflation that engulfed Germany at the time is attributed to monopolist manipulations. Little, if any, attention is paid to the fact that the inflation dated back to the war; the fact that it could have been stopped in 1919–1921 by appropriate measures, but was not, makes its origins in war and defeat irrelevant in this view.[48] A possible inflationary effect of reparations is likewise discounted on the grounds that few reparations payments were made at that time.[49] Similarly, the perception of inflation as a class-struggle tool used by the bourgeoisie to enrich itself at the expense of the working class all but precludes the acknowledgment of any possible positive results inflation may have produced in the form of a reconstructed industrial plant and capital base, greater production than would otherwise have been possible, and above all full employment.[50]

DDR authors see the inflation as being nurtured by entrepreneurs who took advantage of it to pay off their debts in devalued

[47]See Ruge, *Deutschland*, pp. 175ff.; Kuczynski, *Geschichte*, vol. 5, pp. 93ff., vol. 16, pp. 68ff.; Gossweiler, *Grossbanken*, pp. 103ff., 114ff., 190–92. On the non-Marxist side, see David Felix, *Walther Rathenau and the Weimar Republic* (Baltimore, 1971): pp. 75ff., 83ff. Felix, too, considers the differences between the advocates of fulfillment and nonfulfillment matters of form rather than substance (p. 63). On the continued unwillingness of German business to bear a share of taxes and reparations proportionate to its resources and its relative immunity to the effects of inflation, see also the material presented by the West German historian Lothar Albertin, "Die Verantwortung der liberalen Parteien für das Scheitern der Grossen Koalition im Herbst 1921," *HZ* 205 (1967): 578ff. and *Das Kabinett Cuno: 22. November 1922 bis 12. August 1923*, in *Akten der Reichskanzlei: Weimarer Republik* (Boppard, 1968), doc. 31. On Stinnes' plans, cf. Hallgarten, *Hitler, Reichswehr und Industrie* (Frankfurt, 1955), pp. 13ff.

[48]Mottek et al., vol. 3, pp. 233–34; Ruge, *Deutschland*, pp. 191ff.; Gossweiler, *Grossbanken*, pp. 145–46. Similarly, on the non-Marxist side, see Peter Czada, "Ursachen und Folgen der grossen Inflation," in *Finanz- und wirtschaftspolitische Fragen der Zwischenkriegszeit*, ed. Winkel (Schriften des Vereins für Sozialpolitik, n.s. vol. 73) (Berlin [West], 1973), pp. 22–23.

[49]This is now also accepted by many Western historians (Holborn, vol. 3, pp. 595–96; Czada, "Ursachen," pp. 27–28; Sally Marks, "The Myths of Reparations," *CEH* 11 [1978]: 238–39).

[50]An exception is Mottek et al, vol. 3, pp. 240–41. On the positive by-products of the German inflation, see Czada, "Ursachen," p. 34; Feldman, *Iron and Steel in the German Inflation: 1916–1923* (Princeton, 1977), pp. 4ff., 346ff.

marks, pay disproportionately low taxes because of delayed assessments, and above all reap additional profits at the expense of the workers, whose wages never kept pace with the declining purchasing power of the mark. Monopoly capitalists also are charged with promoting the depreciation of the mark: through their representatives in the directorate of the Reichsbank, they supported the disastrous credit and currency policies of the bank in order to buy out weak entrepreneurs and thus strengthen further their stranglehold on the economy. Finally, their hope supposedly was that the chaotic currency situation could also be utilized to force the Allies to revise or cancel the onerous reparations settlement.[51]

Beyond these objectives, however, entrepreneurial interests are found to diverge. Export industries—coal, minerals, chemicals—derived huge profits from greatly expanded foreign sales, because the declining real wages enabled them, as Kuczynski puts it, to "leap over" the eight-hour day and outproduce and underbid their competitors in the world market. Similarly, they netted additional profits from using their foreign currency holdings to purchase domestic goods and services. According to Ruge, they thus were the main beneficiaries of that vast redistribution of the national income which the inflation effected in favor of the great bourgeoisie. Yet other industries, dependent on the import of raw materials or on domestic sales—textiles, machines, electrotechnics—found the advantages of the inflation offset by higher-priced imports and a shrinking internal market. They therefore wished to slow down the inflation, and some of them called for a new stabilized currency. This group of industries, more sensitive to the growing misery of workers and petty bourgeoisie and to their increasing political radicalization, is also found to be worrying about the survival, for the time being at least, of the republic. The heavy industrial-chemical faction, on the other hand, as "adventurist-militarist" as ever, was anxious to destroy the republic, do away with its social achievements—especially the eight-hour day—and establish a military dictatorship. The government helped the intransigents by its willingness to let the inflation continue in order to rid the state of its debts.[52]

[51]See *GdA*, vol. 3, pp. 313–16; Kuczynski, *Geschichte*, vol, 16, pp. 50–51; Ruge, *Deutschland*, pp. 191ff.; Gossweiler, *Grossbanken*, p. 154; Mottek et al., vol. 3, p. 245; Manfred Nussbaum, *Wirtschaft und Staat in Deutschland während der Weimar Republik* (Vaduz, 1978), pp. 23ff., especially on the inflationary price policies of many entrepreneurs. Kuczynski (*Geschichte*, vol. 16, pp. 50–51) also claims that German monopolists encouraged foreign capitalists to buy up German businesses in the hope that such investors, with a special stake in German stability, would prove useful as further safeguards against revolutionary upheavals. Gossweiler, however, finds German industrialists strongly opposed to such foreign penetration of the German economy (*Grossbanken*, pp. 190–92).

[52]See Gossweiler, *Grossbanken*, pp. 143ff.; Ruge, *Deutschland*, pp. 177, 192; Mottek et al., vol. 3, pp. 224ff. Concerning governmental mistakes and the ruinous

Beyond their domestic uses, inflation and reparations are claimed to have lent themselves also to "imperialist" manipulations in the foreign arena. Here, once again, confirmation is found of the interrelationship of monopoly capitalism and imperialism. Accordingly, the monopolists exploited the economic ills of the country in order to pave the way for the resurgence of German power and the resumption of their imperialist schemes. They played off American and British concern about the German economy against French intransigence, which viewed reparations primarily as a political weapon, designed to keep Germany weak. The German "imperialists" knew that their British and American counterparts were anxious to do business with them but would move only when Germany had regained her economic stability. Such stability presupposed a reduction or, better still, the cancellation of all reparations. On the strength of this knowledge, East German authors conclude, the "adventurist-militarist" faction of the German monopolists risked the French occupation of the Ruhr Basin. They were confident that Anglo-American pressures would soon drive the French out of the Ruhr and force them to relent on the reparations issue. These same interests also pointed out to the Western powers that an unstable poverty-stricken Germany might easily fall prey to the Communists. The Rapallo Pact thus served as a warning as to where Western intransigence was driving Germany—a warning addressed in particular to the United States, which wished to build up Germany as a bulwark against Soviet Russia.

East German research has assembled a considerable number of statements attesting the readiness of German industrialists and financiers to risk a Ruhr occupation—too many of them and too frequently voiced to dismiss all of them as mere bluster. Doubtless the expectation that the Ruhr invasion would prove self-defeating for the French inspired some of these pronouncements. Yet other statements quoted in the East German literature do not seem to have been the products of shrewdly laid plans and in fact suggest a high degree of irrationalism. They rather resemble the embittered outcries of men who simply wished to escape from the uncertainties of the times. Marxist historians show a curious reluctance to

policy of the Reichsbank, see Constantino Bresciani-Turroni, *The Economics of Inflation* (London, 1937), pp. 75ff., 398ff.; Gustav Stolper et al., *Deutsche Wirtschaft seit 1870* (Tübingen, 1964), pp. 101–2; Feldman, *Iron and Steel*, pp. 315ff., 360ff.; on the abuses of industrialists, see Bresciani-Turroni, *Economics*, pp. 103ff., 399. Kuczynski's account of an intervention in April 1923 by Stinnes, allegedly in order to sabotage governmental support of the currency, is inaccurate on some crucial points and rests also on various non sequiturs (*Geschichte*, vol. 16, pp. 58ff.). On this incident, compare the report of a Reichstag investigation committee that clears Stinnes of any sabotage intent but leaves some questions unanswered (*Verhandlungen des Reichstags* 380 [1924]: 7924–26). The report also throws some revealing light on the inept policies of the Reichsbank (pp. 7903ff.). For a rejection of Kuczynski's views, see also Gossweiler, *Grossbanken*, p. 145.

grant that capitalists, too, might be susceptible to such emotional impulses. Although workers, peasants, and petty bourgeois are frequently reprimanded for being confused or misled, the upper bourgeoisie, in Marxist analyses, is always assumed to act rationally, shrewdly pursuing its drive to increase its profits. Bourgeois elements thus would never succumb to the proposition that a "horrible end" was preferable to "unending horror."[53]

In any event, there is no proof that the government acted on such "monopolist" suggestions. Although the various governments were dependent on industry's cooperation in pursuit of their reparations policies, there is also clear evidence of the limits set to industrial influence. No government was prepared in its efforts to settle the reparations problem to abandon its more conciliatory stance in favor of the aggressive alternatives urged on it by various industrialists.[54]

The Ruhr Occupation and the Climax of the Revolutionary Crisis

In the Marxist perspective, the Ruhr occupation brought to a climax the struggle between German and French "imperialists" over the hegemonial control of the European continent. When the French "imperialists" failed to attain that hegemony through the control of the proposed Franco-German mining consortium, they decided, according to this interpretation, to forcibly take over the Ruhr industries. For this move they found a convenient justification in the German default on reparation deliveries.

Their German counterparts, in turn, are claimed to have welcomed the showdown, for they hoped to emerge from it as the victors, with the help of the Anglo-American "monopolists." In this expectation they were mistaken, Günter Hortzschansky and Wolfgang Ruge maintain, because British and American "imperialists" were just as anxious to establish their own domination over the continent. For this reason, the two authors argue, London and Washington welcomed the Franco-German collision in order to dictate on their own terms the eventual settlement between Berlin and Paris. In the same vein, both Britain and the United States are

---

[53]Joachim Petzold is one author who allows for irrational attitudes of "monopolists" ("Zur Funktion des Nationalismus," *ZfG* 21 [1973]: 1298).

[54]Gossweiler, *Grossbanken,* ch. 4; Günter Hortzschansky, *Der nationale Verrat der deutschen Monopolbourgeoisie während des Ruhrkampfes 1923* (Berlin [East], 1961), p. 53, as compared to *Kabinett Cuno* docs. 20 n. 6–8, and 24 n. 3; also Ernst Laubach, *Die Politik der Kabinette Wirth 1921/22* (Lübeck, 1968), pp. 295, 312, as compared to the incorrect account of Kuczynski, *Geschichte,* vol. 16, p. 71.

also charged with delaying negotiations about reparations in order to further weaken their French and German fellow imperialists.

None of this is entirely wrong, but in its onesidedness leaves no room for other facets of a highly complex situation. London's inability to restrain the French and the need it felt, as did Washington, to allow for a cooling-off period are turned into Machiavellian maneuvers. By a similar tergiversation, American inaction is dissociated from all isolationist strictures, a powerful brake on any imperialist ambitions: in fact, in a sense the East German interpretation turns isolationism into the very mainspring of imperialist aspirations. French considerations of national security, it might be added, are wholly ignored in these analyses.[55]

However, the Ruhr struggle is viewed not only as a clash of imperialist rivalries but also as another phase of the class struggle, fought on both the national and international level. Internationally, that struggle manifested itself as workers' resistance against the French and Belgian occupation forces, who were serving as tools of their imperialist masters, and in this struggle French and Belgian Communists readily joined. On the national plane, it aimed in turn at the domestic monopolists. For this reason, it is explained, the KPD would not join the German national unity front against the French: it was convinced that this new political Burgfrieden, like that of 1914, was intended to prolong the subordination of the working class to the bourgeois state.[56]

Similarly, the call for passive resistance to the occupation forces is dismissed as a deceptive nationalist slogan designed to shield the monopolists. Ever hungry for profits, the monopolists had first tried to do business as usual, offering to *sell* coal to the French and Belgians (as distinct from delivering it on reparations account); they had to be stopped by the government, which, it is noted, acted on behalf of all German imperialists at the expense of the mineowners. When the mineowners could no longer sell coal to anyone because of French restrictions or lack of transportation facilities, they kept mining it merely to keep their men off the streets, where they might have come under Communist influence. Because the entrepreneurs were reimbursed by the government for any losses they suffered, not only did they not sacrifice anything,

[55]See GdA, vol. 3, p. 376; Ruge, *Deutschland*, pp. 194–96, 200–201, 213; Hortzschansky, *Verrat*, pp. 89, 91–93. For English efforts to revive reparations negotiations, see *Kabinett Cuno*, docs. 123 n. 1, 135 n. 2. See also W. M. Jordan, *Great Britain, France, and the German Problem: 1918–1939* (London, 1971), pp. 52, 179ff.; U.S. Department of State, *Papers Relating to the Foreign Relations of the United States* 2 (1923): 53, 56; Werner Link, "Ruhrbesetzung und amerikanische Wirtschaftsinteressen," *VfZ* 17 (1969): 372ff.

[56]See especially Heinz Köller, *Kampfbündnis an der Seine, Ruhr und Spree: Der gemeinsame Kampf der KPF und der KPD gegen die Ruhrbesetzung 1923* (Berlin [East], 1963); Hortzschansky, *Verrat, passim*; Ruge, *Deutschland*, pp. 201, 204–5.

but they managed to garner profits, too, as before. For all these reasons, the great bourgeoisie opposed the proclamation of a general strike in the Ruhr territory—only passive resistance would allow it to go on making its profits and keep the workers under control. This strategy is also condemned, however, because of its self-defeating approach to impeding French efforts: it saved the French the trouble of mining the coal themselves; they merely had to make their own arrangements for carting it off. Temporarily, French and Belgian coal transports were, however, effectively hampered by the noncooperation of the (state-owned) railroads until the occupation authorities brought in their own personnel.[57]

Thus, it is argued, there could be no genuine resistance under bourgeois auspices. As Hortzschansky concludes, "The sine qua non of a fully effective national resistance struggle was the overthrow of monopoly capitalism in Germany." This, all DDR authors keep pointing out, only the KPD understood. Proceeding from its conviction that the Ruhr occupation was the work of both German and French monopoly capitalists, the KPD made it clear from the outset that the struggle would have to be carried on not only against the French in the Ruhr but also against the Cuno government in Berlin. Accordingly, it called for a general strike at the news of the forthcoming occupation; the strike was to fend off the French move and at the same time secure the replacement of the Cuno government by a workers' government. The appeal failed because the Social Democratic leaders rejected it, preferring to collaborate with the bourgeois parties. Such "divisive" policies, it is claimed, deprived the working class of its chance to prevent the Ruhr occupation. There is no evidence that such a chance did exist, nor do East German researchers make any attempt to substantiate these charges. Moreover, the appeal was published on January 11, 1923—the very day on which French and Belgian troops started moving into the Ruhr territory—and hence was in any event much too late to prevent their entry. Nor do East German authors attempt to disprove the Socialists' claim at the time that a general strike was likely to force the unemployed starved German workers to their knees long before the French would be seriously weakened. As it was, not even passive resistance could be maintained for long without catastrophic injury to the German economy.[58]

[57]See Hortzschansky, *Verrat*, pp. 92ff,; Ruge, *Deutschland*, pp. 205–6. The charges against the mineowners are apparently based on the pro-entrepreneurial account by Hans Spethmann, *Zwölf Jahre Ruhrbergbau* (Berlin, 1928–1930), vol. 3, pp. 63ff., vol. 4, pp. 13ff; Spethmann, however, indicates that production continued only on a limited scale.

[58]See Hortzschansky, *Verrat*, pp. 107ff. (quotation on p. 108), 122; Ruge, *Deutschland*, pp. 206ff. Concerning the domestic aspects of passive resistance, see also *Kabinett Cuno*, docs. 95 n. 3, 112, 134, 170. About the Communists' unrealistic assessment of a general strike, cf. Friedrich Stampfer, *Die vierzehn Jahre der ersten deutschen Republik* (Hamburg, 1952), p. 318.

DDR accounts of the Ruhr occupation stress rightly, however, the uneven nature of the sacrifices made by the big-business community, sustained by continued government grants, and the bulk of the population, which saw its earnings and savings wiped out by the accelerating inflation. These disparities, DDR historians conclude, made growing numbers of workers aware of the class character of the Ruhr struggle. Increasingly they became dissatisfied with the Burgfrieden strategy of the SPD and turned to the Communists. Strikes kept breaking out in all parts of the country, among them some major ones even in rural areas. Whether as many of the strikes were Communist-inspired as these authors suggest is a matter of debate that may never be settled. Doubtless, however, the Communists were gaining ground, as is also attested by their successes in various local elections.[59]

Yet, it is noted, the KPD could not take full advantage of the rising revolutionary mood of the country. Once again, it was torn by serious internal dissension concerning the course to be followed. A large element, headed by Heinrich Brandler, the party chairman, dismissed as premature all thought of revolution. This faction adopted too cautious an attitude, unmindful that, as Hortzschansky puts it, the fighting spirit of the party could be steeled only by continued mass actions. (That some spokesmen, following Karl Radek, even tried to woo rightist extremists, appealing to them as misguided revolutionaries whose real home was among the masses, is rarely mentioned in the East German literature—presumably because no useful purpose would be served by keeping alive the memory of a regrettable aberration.) An "ultra-left" faction, on the other hand, precipitately called for revolutionary action without proper preparation. In Hortzschansky's words, the party thus was not yet the closely integrated new-type Marxist-Leninist party that had outgrown all residues of Social Democratic and other erroneous views.[60]

Still, whatever its shortcomings, the KPD is found to have remained essentially a militant party. To this militancy East German authors attribute the removal of the Cuno government in mid-August 1923. Ultimately that government collapsed, they maintain, because it could not cope with a wave of strikes for which they give the KPD major credit. Whether they are justified

---

[59]Hortzschansky, *Verrat*, pp. 175ff.; cf. Holborn, vol. 3, pp. 496–98; *Kabinett Cuno*, docs. 25, 101 n. 6, 128–29, 138, 222, also ns. 4–5, 7; Feldman, *Iron and Steel*, pp. 360ff.

[60]See Ruge, *Deutschland*, pp. 208ff.; Hortzschansky, *Verrat*, pp. 145ff. Concerning Radek and his famous "Schlageter" speech, which initiated the soundings of right-wing radicals, see the conflicting analyses of Hortzschansky, (*Verrat*, p. 146) and *GdA* (vol. 3, pp. 401–2). Neither Ruge (*Deutschland*) nor *Swb* mentions this incident or its repercussions. For details on this interlude, see also E. H. Carr, *The Interregnum* (New York, 1954), pp. 159–60, 179ff.; Angress, *Stillborn Revolution*, pp. 335, 338ff.

in assigning such a key role to the Communists is a matter of argument, but unlike some non-Marxist historians, they rightly view the strikes as a major factor in causing the Social Democrats to withdraw their support from Cuno—a step that made Cuno's position untenable. Moreover, as DDR authors see it in their search for progress in accordance with historical laws, even if the Cuno government was not succeeded by a workers' government, but by a bourgeois-Social Democratic coalition headed by a spokesman of industry, Gustav Stresemann, Cuno's fall demonstrated to the class-conscious workers that they now had the strength to overthrow bourgeois governments. Similarly, it is claimed, events of those days aroused rank-and-file Social Democrats, union members, and unaffiliated workers to the need for concentrated action with the Communists. Thus seen, the militant actions of those August days, whatever their immediate effect, are credited with having raised the class struggle to a new, higher level.[61]

Accordingly, Stresemann's decision to call off passive resistance is explained as the dialectical response of the bourgeoisie to the growth of the revolutionary movement. In East German parlance, the step was taken primarily to allow the government to marshal its forces against the revolutionary forces at home. This interpretation corresponds to the East German view of passive resistance as a weapon not of the nation but of the monopoly bourgeoisie in the latter's struggle against French imperialism. Again, the decision to break off resistance could be made more easily, according to these analyses, because it was assumed that the surrender would not subject the German monopolists to the mercy of their French rivals. The British had meanwhile made clear (or so some East German authors believe) that they would not tolerate such French domination.

Actually, as these same authors note, the Ruhr industrialists had no such assurance, and they were in fact bitterly opposed to the break-off of passive resistance. They now tried catering to the French by negotiating trade agreements with them (MICUM Agreements)—in what the DDR accounts castigate as a brazen arrogation of government functions. To reassure Paris, a number of Rhenish and Ruhr bankers, industrialists, and politicians also

[61]See Hortzschansky, Verrat, pp. 213ff.; Ruge, Deutschland, pp. 207ff., 220–21; as compared to Angress, Stillborn Revolution, pp. 371–72, 374; Carr, Interregnum, pp. 188–89. That Communist activities were instrumental in Cuno's fall was also the view at the time of the rightist German National People's party (Lewis Hertzman, DNVP: Right-Wing Opposition in the Weimar Republic, 1918–1924 [Lincoln, NE, 1963], p. 199). East German authors rightly do not attribute the removal of the Cuno government to the general strike proclaimed by the KPD on August 11, because news of that decision did not reach the lower echelons of that party until August 12, the day of Cuno's resignation; cf. Rosenberg, Geschichte, p. 161, who erroneously does attribute Cuno's resignation in this way.

considered creating a Rhenish state that would be independent of Prussia but that preferably would be a constituent part of the German federal state. In DDR accounts, this "legal" separatism, pursued with the knowledge and tacit consent of the German government, as distinct from the French-supported "street" or "putschist" separatism, was merely the cynical product of antilabor and profit considerations, foreshadowing the establishment of the "separatist" West German state after the Second World War by some of these same leaders. At the same time, East German analyses fail to face up to the question of whether the formation of a workers' government, as proposed by the Communists, would not merely have stiffened France's stance, given what DDR authors call her counterrevolutionary attitude.[62]

East German accounts find further confirmation for these class-struggle interpretations in the use the government made of the emergency powers it obtained when it ended passive resistance. On the strength of this crisis authority, DDR authors note, Berlin had the army remove constitutionally established Social Democratic–Communist governments in Saxony and Thuringia. Stresemann did nothing, however, when an illegal dictatorial regime in Bavaria openly defied the Berlin authorities. In this latter case, the East German critics are clearly on firmer ground. The chancellor did remain passive in the face of Bavaria's rebellion, being unsure of army support had he ordered an intervention. He was aware, too, of the widespread sympathies the Munich regime enjoyed among heavy industrialists and agrarians and other conservative groups in the north. Dependent on them, he also stood by while these circles were drawing up plans for a dictatorship on the national level. If nothing came of these plans, this was because of rightist dissension and Hitler's precipitate Beer Cellar Putsch. These conditions enabled the chancellor to outmaneuver the plotters.

Stresemann faced no similar difficulties in dealing with Saxony and Thuringia. Yet, contrary to East German claims, his intervention against the "workers' governments" of these two states was legally justified. Although both governments were formally constitutional, they, too, on the East Germans' own showing, presented a threat to Berlin. As DDR analysts themselves have made clear, the Communists entered these two governments merely in order to secure weapons needed for the nationwide rising on which

[62]Ruge, *Deutschland*, pp. 217ff.; Hortzschansky, *Verrat*, pp. 236ff., 260ff. (Hortzschansky is, however, careless in the use of his sources); Gossweiler, *Grossbanken*, pp. 266ff.; *GdA*, vol. 3, pp. 409–10. Cf. Maier, *Recasting Bourgeois Europe*, pp. 390ff. On the ambiguity of the English position, see Eyck, *Geschichte*, vol. 1, pp. 341–43; also, for a different angle, see Gossweiler, *Grossbanken*, pp. 193ff. On "legal" separatism, cf. Karl Dietrich Erdmann, *Adenauer in der Rheinlandpolitik* (Stuttgart, 1966).

the party leaders, prodded by the Comintern, had meanwhile decided.[63]

Actions and attitudes of the KPD and the workers during those turbulent autumn months of 1923 are traced with great care. In the party's judgment, German capitalism was on the verge of collapse and the country thus close to a revolution. As Streisand puts it, "The revolutionary crisis sharpened into a revolutionary situation, as indicated by the general strike against Reich Chancellor Cuno, the formation of workers' governments in Saxony and Thuringia, and [a] rising in Hamburg." This revolutionary potential is deemed significant also as a manifestation of a much wider crisis (of which repercussions are found in growing unrest in Bulgaria and Poland). As always, however, Germany was the focus of the worldwide struggle between imperialism and socialism.

Having established this revolutionary potential, Marxist historians are faced with the question as to why the revolution did not occur. Part of the answer is found in the resourcefulness of the bourgeoisie, which discovered ever new ways to cope with the crisis. The major share of the blame, however, is placed on "right-wing" SPD and labor union leaders, who joined the Stresemann government rather than form a common front with the KPD in its struggle on behalf of the workers. However, the KPD is also found wanting—torn as it was by internal disputes, neglecting Leninist teachings, and unmindful of its political tasks. Between the "opportunist" leadership under Party Chairman Heinrich Brandler and a "sectarian" left wing that overrated the revolutionary momentum, the realistic element in the party was still too weak to assert itself (Ernst Thälmann, the party's future leader, and Walter Ulbricht, the later head of the DDR, are singled out as two of its members). When the Brandler faction finally did accept the imminence of a revolutionary situation, it confined itself largely to military preparations. Accordingly, Communists who entered the Saxon and Thuringian governments in October did so merely in order to gather arms (which they failed to do). On the other hand, they undertook nothing to ease the hardships of the popular

---

[63]See Ruge, *Deutschland*, pp. 226ff., 236ff., Gossweiler, *Grossbanken*, pp. 241ff.; *GdA*, vol. 3, pp. 423ff.; also Klara Zetkin, quoted in Flechtheim, *Kommunistische Partei*, p. 250. Cf. Eyck, *Geschichte*, vol. 1, pp. 358–60; Holborn, vol. 3, pp. 609–10. Gossweiler's claim (p. 214) that Stinnes backed Hitler as the coming dictator is not conclusively proven by the Stinnes statement on which the assertion is based. The statement is reprinted is full in Hallgarten, *Hitler*, p. 67, and *GdA*, vol. 3, pp. 662–63. It may well have referred to Gustav von Kahr, the dictatorial head of the Bavarian government at the time, as the man envisaged by Stinnes as the future dictator. Cf. Harold J. Gordon, *Hitler and the Beer Hall Putsch* (Princeton, 1972), pp. 218–23. Gossweiler's further claim (pp. 252–53) that Stinnes touched off the Hitler Putsch through his middleman Ludendorff is not borne out either by the circumstantial evidence that he cites.

masses, let alone purge the bureaucracy or dissolve any of the innumerable conterrevolutionary organizations—charges that disregard the short-lived existence of these governments (eighteen and twelve days, respectively). The failure to prepare the masses politically for revolutionary action, it is further noted, also accounted for the impossibility of organizing a general strike that was to precede the armed uprising. The workers' governments in Saxony and Thuringia could thus be removed without difficulty by Berlin, with the masses meekly submitting. When a few days later a rising did break out in Hamburg, there was again no large-scale response, either in Hamburg or elsewhere, because of the masses' lack of training for the revolutionary tasks that awaited them. (Quickly suppressed, the rising thus was hardly the harbinger of an approaching revolution that Streisand detects in it.)[64]

These defeats of the working class brought to an end what DDR accounts describe as the "revolutionary postwar crisis" of capitalism. The immediate victor, according to these analyses, was the more flexible section of the monopoly bourgeoisie, which considered the bourgeois-parliamentary system indispensable for the time being and which relied on American imperialism to provide it with new capital and help it fend off French imperialist designs on Germany. A tenuous economic and political stabilization of capitalism followed, which allowed German imperialist and militarist forces to gain new strength and which eventually led to a fascist dictatorship and the Second World War.

In the context of historical dialectics, however, DDR historians view the events of 1923 as merely temporary setbacks of an ultimately progressive development. From this vantage point, they also find some positive aspects in the occurrences of that year. The missed opportunities, caused partly by the inability of the KPD to develop ideological firmness, demonstrated the need for a closely integrated Soviet-style Marxist-Leninist party. Only such a party, united ideologically and headed by leaders able to apply Leninist principles "creatively" to German conditions, could perform the tasks that the situation demanded. Foremost among these tasks was the formation of a united front of the working class and subsequently an alliance of such a front with the broad masses of the peasants—an indispensable precondition for the seizure of power.

[64]See Streisand, p. 319; Hortzschansky, *Verrat,* pp. 223ff.; Raimund Wagner, "Zur Frage der Massenkämpfe in Sachsen vom Frühjahr bis zum Sommer 1923," *ZfG* 4 (1956): 246ff.; Ruge, *Deutschland,* pp. 221ff., 229ff.; *GdA,* vol. 3, pp. 415ff.; Erhard Wörfel, "Die Arbeiterregierung in Thüringen im Jahre 1923," *WZ Jena* 20 (1971): 257ff. The lack of a widespread response to the Hamburg rising is evident even in the account of Habedank, *Zur Geschichte des Hamburger Aufstandes 1923* (Berlin [East], 1958), especially pp. 92ff.; Habedank tries to present that action as a mass rising.

As it was, *Geschichte der deutschen Arbeiterbewegung* concludes, the struggles and controversies of those days nurtured the very forces that produced soon afterwards the needed Leninist leadership under Ernst Thälmann. In long-range perspective, therefore, the events of 1923 constituted an advance toward the socialist revolution.[65]

The "Relative Stabilization of Capitalism"

The bourgeoisie, then, in the Marxist view, had fended off the advance of the working class. Conversely, the workers had shaken the declining capitalist order to its foundations but had not been strong enough to overthrow it. Demoralized and in disarray, they could even be enlisted in the rehabilitation of that system. The capitalist recovery thus was achieved by the increased exploitation of the working class, its political emasculation by the tactics of bourgeois parliamentarism, and the large-scale injection of American capital, of which German monopoly capitalism was the main beneficiary. In particular, growing worker productivity, resulting from improved techniques and increased efficiency, was not matched by corresponding increases in wages.

As always, German developments are also viewed in the context of worldwide developments: the United States, Britain, and other capitalist countries, too, had experienced postwar crises; some, it is noted, had already turned to fascist or semifascist regimes in order to preserve the bourgeois-capitalist order. Such common interests, moreover, produced new international alignments, to the advantage of Germany, because the recovery of German capitalism was a strategic imperative in the relentless battle of the imperialist powers against the socialist USSR.

At the same time, all DDR authors are agreed that the capitalist recovery could only be temporary. Given the way in which it took place, it was bound to intensify the "contradictions" between bourgeoisie and working class, between the major capitalist powers and colonial and other economically dependent countries, and among the imperialist powers themselves. Inevitably, new class struggles, national revolutionary independence movements, economic difficulties, and imperialist confrontations would touch off

---

[65]See Karl and Ruge, in *ZfG* 18 (1970): suppl., p. 525; *GdA*, vol. 3, pp. 436–37; Ruge, *Deutschland*, pp. 221–22, 234-35, 239–41. See also Hortzschansky (*Verrat*, pp. 279–80), who also feels that the "Hamburg rising strengthened the confidence of the workers in their own power, because they had seen the bourgeoisie hovering on the brink of the abyss for three days."

new crises, leading to the depression of 1929, the Second World War, and the victory of socialism over capitalism in one third of Germany, most of eastern Europe, and other parts of the world.[66]

German domestic developments are readily fitted into this scenario of a "relative stabilization." In December 1923, the Reichstag passed an Enabling Act, which was used by the government, in keeping with its state-monopolist structure, to speed economic recovery at the expense of workers, peasants, and petty bourgeoisie. Decrees issued on the strength of this act all but eliminated the eight-hour day, sharply reduced social benefits, provided for the compulsory settlement of wage and other disputes, and greatly increased consumer and other indirect taxes that weighed more heavily on the poor than on the well-to-do. Wages rose but never kept pace with productive growth. In addition, it is noted, the monopoly bourgeoisie strengthened its position by forming new groups, such as the chemical trust, I. G. Farben, and the steel trust, Vereinigte Stahlwerke, as well as by national and international price and market-controlling cartels. By 1928, Ruge states, over 95 percent of German mining, chemical, and alkali production and 85 percent of all electro-technical and metallurgical output were controlled by monopolies. Such concentrations of economic power enabled the monopolists to subject the state to more sustained pressures and force it to do their bidding. Not satisfied with this accelerated development of state-monopolist capitalism, however, these same banking and industrial circles sought to reinforce their position by discrediting the parliamentary republic in the hope of replacing it with an authoritarian regime. Their sponsorship of various paramilitary organizations, the election of Field Marshal von Hindenburg as Reich president in 1925, and continued attempts to amend the constitution along authoritarian lines were milestones on the road toward such a government. Correspondingly, expressions of support for the parliamentary republic on the part of some business leaders are dismissed as mere tactical gestures.[67]

The election of Hindenburg is also viewed as a confirmation of the close ties between imperialism and militarism. Accordingly, the *Reichswehr* is considered the major armed force (*bewaffnete Hauptmacht*) of the ruling class. The army in turn shared the goals of the imperialist bourgeoisie as part of the bour-

[66]See "Relative Stabiliserung des Kapitalismum," *Swb*, vol. 2, pp. 369–70; Ruge, *Deutschland*, pp. 245–47. For the rationale of seeing the Communization of East Germany and other countries as part of an inevitable historical process see chapter 9.

[67]Ruge, *Deutschland*, pp. 247–48, 271–72, 285ff., 299ff.; Gossweiler, *Grossbanken*, pp. 308–9, 312–13; Nussbaum, *Wirtschaft*, pp. 122ff.; Fritz Klein, "Zur Vorbereitung der faschistischen Diktatur durch die deutsche Grossbourgeoisie (1929–1932)," *ZfG* 1 (1953): 881ff.

geois state apparatus. It could hope to recover external power for Germany only if the country's economy regained its earlier strength. For this reason, the argument runs, the army's political mastermind, Colonel von Schleicher, pursued a political strategy similar to that of the great bourgeoisie; in addition, he worked for the gradual dismantling of the parliamentary system. The Reichswehr, Streisand concludes,

> was not, as a slogan has it, a "state within a state." For that its ties with the ruling circles of finance capitalism and Junkers and its basic concurrence with their interests were far too close. However, unlike other institutions of the ruling classes, which did their planning mostly from day to day, the Reichswehr was an instrument of the ruling class as a whole and as such pursued long-range policies.

At the same time, it is claimed, the armament orders of the Reichswehr and government subsidies for arms research provided welcome sources of income for industry. Yet, whereas DDR authors make much of the ties between army and industry and the secret rearmament carried on in Sweden and Spain, they pass over in silence the important assistance rendered the Reichswehr by Soviet Russia.[68]

This picture of conditions during the years 1924–1928 does not differ greatly from that presented in more recent non-Marxist accounts. Such non-Marxist accounts place great emphasis on the fact that even in the seeming heydays of the republic many of the important decisions were made, not in the Reichstag, but in agreements between industry, agriculture, and organized labor, with labor generally in the weaker bargaining position; agreements were also made between the various governments and these "estates." East German analysts, on the other hand, make less of this decline of parliamentary authority, because it merely bears out their conviction of the spuriousness of bourgeois democracy. The Western interpretations of differences within the industrial camp do not differ greatly from the East German analyses; although West German historians see the acceptance of the republic and labor unions by the spokesmen of the more flexible finishing industries as more than mere lip service, they also recognize that the cooperation of these industries with labor was predicated on the latter's subordination and that the acceptance of the new state and of Social

---

[68]See "Reichswehr," *Swb*, vol. 2, p. 367; Streisand, pp. 309–11; *GdA*, vol. 4, p. 155; *Anatomie des Krieges*, ed. Eichholtz et al. (Berlin [East], 1969), pp. 82ff. Actually, industry at the time had little interest in armament orders, because armament production was politically risky and also unprofitable: the unsystematic army orders did not allow for adequate use of the special arms production facilities (Georg Thomas, *Geschichte der deutschen Wehr- und Rüstungswirtschaft (1918– 1943/45)* [Boppard, 1966], pp. 53, 56, 60–61; Bernice A. Carroll, *Design for Total War* [The Hague, 1968], pp. 69–71).

Democratic participation in the government was not upheld when it came under bitter attack from other branches of industry.[69]

The real difference between the Marxist and non-Marxist analyses lies in the underlying assumptions. Where Western historians see a deplorable development that could have been avoided by a more open-minded business leadership and a more resourceful political one, DDR authors see an ineluctable process rooted in the capitalist system and foreseen by the *Communist Manifesto*. In this perception, it does not matter whether the business community was plagued by economic difficulties that might help to explain its anti-Weimar position[70] or whether small and medium-sized enterprises helped fuel the oppositional fires,[71] because the secondary role of such enterprises in the production process precluded any significant impact on their part on the course of developments. Marxists, pointing to the commanding heights the monopolies occupied in the production process, see the banking and industrial giants as the ones who put their imprint on governmental policies, through spokesmen who assumed ministerial posts, through a bureaucracy sympathetic to them because of family ties or social outlook, and above all through political or economic pressures.[72] (Here again, the commitment to history's "lawful" process substitutes for empirical evidence,[73] and once again it was Western research that was the first to provide the substantiating documentation.[74]) DDR authors thus are convinced that only the abolition of the capitalist system can usher in an equitable social order. Despite the apparent functioning of the parliamentary systems, the "golden years" of the mid-1920s are to Marxists an integral part of that sustained antidemocratic

[69]Holborn, vol. 3, pp. 636ff.; Maier, *Recasting Bourgeois Europe*, pp. 442ff.; Karl Dietrich Bracher, *Die Auflösung der Weimarer Republik* (Stuttgart, 1955), pp. 199ff.; Stegmann, "Die Silverberg-Kontroverse 1926; Unternehmerpolitik zwischen Reform und Restauration," in Wehler, *Sozialgeschichte Heute*, pp. 594ff.; Albertin, "Faktoren eines Arrangements zwischen industriellem und politischem System in der Weimarer Republik 1918–1928," in *Industrielles System und politische Entwicklung in der Weimarer Republik*, ed. Mommsen et al. (Düsseldorf, 1974), pp. 658ff., Feldman, "The Social and Economic Policies of German Big Business, 1918–1929," *AHR*, 75 (1969): 47ff. See also Ruge, *Deutschland*, pp. 299ff.

[70]Thus, the serious plight of heavy industry even in the prosperous mid-1920s is nowhere mentioned as a possible cause (among others) of that industry's unrelenting opposition to the Weimar Republic. On heavy industry's problems, see David Abraham, "Constituting Hegemony: The Bourgeois Crisis of Weimar Germany," *JMH* 51 (1979): 422–23; also Feldman, "Big Business," pp. 52–53.

[71]Stegmann, "Silverberg-Kontroverse," p. 605.

[72]Ruge, *Deutschland*, pp. 286–87; Gossweiler, *Grossbanken*, pp. 311–12.

[73]The inadequacy of the evidence is admitted by Klein in *ZfG* 23 (1975): 490.

[74]See especially Klaus-Dieter Krohn, *Stabilisierung und ökonomische Interessen: Die Finanzpolitik des Deutschen Reiches, 1923–1927* (Düsseldorf, 1974); Albertin, "Faktoren," pp. 670–71. Cf. now, however, Nussbaum (*Wirtschaft*, pp. 129ff.), who relies to a large extent on Krohn.

campaign of the "monopoly bourgeoisie" that culminated in the establishment of the Nazi dictatorship.

East German analyses of the foreign policies of the period are based on a corresponding class-struggle orientation that finds these policies determined by the confrontation of German imperialism with the challenge of Soviet socialism. In the context of a capitalist-socialist confrontation, the Dawes Plan, adopted in August 1924, not only emerges as an arrangement to place German reparations payments on a new basis and thus speed Germany's recovery but is also claimed to have been an attempt to manipulate Germany into sabotaging the socialist reconstruction of the USSR. As the argument runs, the Western powers did not want Germany to compete with them in their own markets when it set out to export the additional goods by which German reparations payments would have to be financed. They therefore sought to deflect the German export campaign toward Soviet Russia. Their hope was, in the East German view, that agrarian Russia could thus be made to depend on the West for industrial products and be kept from developing her own industries and her military potential.[75]

If there is any evidence to support this assessment of the Dawes Plan, it is nowhere presented. Actually, American businessmen were unwilling to forgo the great potential of the Russian market and wished to do business with the Soviets themselves. (During the years 1924–1932, American exports to the USSR were the second largest of any industrial nation, surpassed only by those of Germany, and during two of these years—1924–1925 and 1930—U.S. exports were larger than Germany's.) Yet, if there is no evidence of any specific anti-Soviet thrust in the Dawes Plan, it is true, however, that the West looked upon trade as a means to undermine the socialized economy of the Soviets. Stresemann was not merely trying to reassure the Western powers concerning German-Soviet relations but was voicing a widely held view when he stated in 1927 that it was "necessary to link Russia's economy so closely with the capitalist system of the West European Powers that we are thus paving the way for an evolution in Russia. . . . "[76]

---

[75]Ruge, *Deutschland*, pp. 254ff.; *GdA*, vol. 4, pp. 131ff.; "Dawes-Plan," *Swb*, vol. 1, pp. 367–68.

[76]See Jürgen Kuczynski and Grete Wittkowski, *Die deutsch-russischen Handelsbeziehungen in den letzten 150 Jahren* (Berlin [East], 1947), pp. 49ff., especially p. 59; on American export figures, see Alfred Anderle, *Die deutsche Rapallo-Politik* (Berlin [East], 1962), p. 170. Cf., on the non-Marxist side, Werner Link, *Die amerikanische Stabilisierungspolitik in Deutschland: 1921–32* (Düsseldorf, 1970), pp. 117–18, 355 n. 66, 371, 376, 426–27, 478, 611–12; Carr, *A History of Soviet Russia* (New York, 1950–1969), vol. 3, pp. 477ff.; Hans W. Gatzke, "Von Rapallo nach Berlin: Stresemann und die deutsche Russlandpolitik," *VfZ* 4, (1956): 25–28 (with Stresemann quotation on p. 28); also Stresemann, quoted in Anderle, *Rapallo-Politik*, p. 194.

The Dawes Plan is also assessed as an agreement between imperialist powers that are essentially antagonistic toward one another. As such, it is noted, the plan not only enabled the United States to replace France as the leading imperialist force on the Continent but also assured German imperialism of greater freedom of action. Germany thus could work more effectively at removing the political and military restrictions of the Versailles Treaty. In the Marxist-Leninist judgment, this was further proof of the plan's anti-Soviet thrust.[77]

If the Dawes Plan helped put Germany back onto the road to economic expansion, the Locarno Pact, in this view, accelerated its imperialist comeback. It gave Germany further scope in evading the Versailles restrictions and re-embarking on its militarization. And although it reconfirmed Germany's western boundaries, it contained no such commitment concerning her eastern borders.

This omission in particular is cited as evidence of the anti-Soviet design of the pact. Moreover, this intent is confirmed, it is argued, by the Western insistence on Germany's entry into the anti-Soviet League of Nations as part of the Locarno arrangements. Germany's aspirations thus were to be harnessed to the Anglo-American offensive against the Soviet Union. Just as Germany's economic expansion was to be diverted eastward by the Dawes Plan, its territorial drive would be steered in the same direction. The nation was not to content itself with the recovery of formerly German lands lost to Poland (Polish Corridor, Poznan, Upper Silesia) but was to move across Poland into the Soviet Union, with France being forced to abandon her Polish ally. Correspondingly, Berlin's efforts to maintain its ties with the Kremlin are disparaged. The conclusion of a German-Soviet commercial treaty just prior to the Locarno conference is discounted as meaningless, as is Germany's insistence on her exemption, as a league member, from military and economic sanctions aimed at the Soviet Union. What makes Locarno especially ominous in East German eyes is the parallelism DDR analysts think they detect between Locarno and its presumed consequences and the resurgence of German imperialism and militarism as they see it reasserting itself within the framework of NATO.[78]

---

[77]*GdA*, vol. 4, pp. 33, 64; Ruge, *Deutschland*, pp. 256–57; Anderle, *Rapallo-Politik*, p. 92; Gossweiler, *Grossbanken*, pp. 266ff.; but see also *Locarno-Konferenz 1925*, ed. Ruge (Berlin [East], 1962), p. 36. Ruge rightly observes that the influx of American capital into Germany did not lead to the latter's subordination to the United States. Contrary to Marxist assumptions, subsequent developments were indeed to bear out Stresemann's contention that being a debtor country could prove an important asset in international relations.

[78]See Ruge, *Deutschland*, pp. 279ff.; Ruge, *Locarno-Konferenz*, pp. 5, 42–44; *GdA*, vol. 4, pp. 97, 105, 124; Karl Dichtl and Ruge, "Zu den Auseinandersetzungen

These analyses once again rest on the kind of ex-post-facto argumentation so tempting to the Marxist determinist. In reality, the Soviet government, unlike presentday DDR critics, was not concerned at the time with the failure of the Locarno Pact to uphold Germany's eastern boundaries, particularly the Polish one. In a note presented to Berlin in June 1925 and published by Wolfgang Ruge—who, however, ignores it in his analysis of the pact—the Kremlin stated expressly that in signing the treaty of Rapallo, "both parties proceeded from the tacit nonrecognition of the regime established in Europe after the war as the result of a series of peace treaties [concluded in] 1919. . . . [Rapallo] constituted the counterpart to the dictated treaties imposed forcibly by the Entente, among them the treaty of Versailles." The Soviet Union thus did not object to the ambiguities of Locarno's East European provisions; it too had lost territories to Poland—in the Russo-Polish War of 1920–1921—that it wished to recover. What did concern Moscow was Germany's entry into the League of Nations, on the grounds that it was, in the words of the above-quoted note, an "organization whose main purpose was the preservation of the conditions created by [the peace] treaties." For this reason, Moscow considered Germany's league membership and the "voluntary recognition of the regime established at Versailles an important step toward the actual destruction of the Rapallo treaty." Nor did Germany's exemption from any participation in anti-Soviet military or economic measures offset these dangers in Soviet eyes. The Kremlin feared that Berlin might be pressured into other anti-Soviet activities—concerns that were not unfounded.[79]

Still, the fact remains that both Britain and France insisted on Germany's league membership so as to restrain the country more effectively from attacking Poland or any other of her immediate

innerhalb der Reichsregierung über den Locarnopakt 1925," *ZfG* 22 (1974): 64–66. The documentation of Dichtl and Ruge's work, however, refutes their thesis of the pro-Western, anti-Soviet aims of the pact. See also Anderle (Rapallo-Politik, chs. 4–5), who, too, reads anti-Soviet designs into documents that do not contain any evidence of such intentions. According to *Grundriss* (p. 411), even France wished Germany to expand eastward—a statement not further explained despite its incompatibility with France's policy of supporting Poland as a counterweight against Germany.

[79]See the Soviet memorandum of June 7, 1925, in Ruge, *Locarno-Konferenz,* pp. 94ff.; quotation on p. 95. See also the implied Soviet approval of a new Polish partition, mentioned in Gatzke (*Rapallo,* pp. 14–16), and the statement of Foreign Commissar Chicherin, March 4, 1926, cited in Carr, *History,* vol. 3, pp. i, 432. On the rationale of Moscow's fears even if Germany were exempted from the obligations ensuing from articles 16 and 17 of the league covenant, see Stresemann's statements at Locarno, session of October 8, 1925, 4 P.M. in Ruge, *Locarno-Konferenz,* pp. 170–72; see also Stresemann's speech to the *Reichsrat,* October 21, 1925, quoted in Anderle, *Rapallo-Politik,* pp. 181–82.

neighbors.[80] Whereas this objective is ignored in the East German analyses, much is made of a supposedly anti-Soviet remark of the British Foreign Secretary, Sir Austen Chamberlain. If Germany were to participate in a military action of the league, Chamberlain promised during the Locarno negotiations, it could count on the help of all league members: "Those who have disarmed Germany would be the first to rearm Germany." No attention, however, is paid to another statement of Chamberlain, made "quite openly and categorically" at the same session, that the British government had "no thought of creating, through the pact, a bloc directed against Russia." The tenor of the negotiations, moreover, makes clear that if Britain and France wished to draw Germany away from the Soviet Union, they acted defensively, anxious to prevent the formation of what they viewed as a potentially dangerous Soviet-German power bloc.[81]

The double standard evident in these analyses has also left its imprint on other aspects of the East German accounts. Thus, the German government is taken to task for not seeking relations of genuine friendship with Soviet Russia, while the Comintern's activities directed against that same government are ignored. How "imperialist" Germany could develop a "genuinely friendly relationship" ("ein wirklich freundschaftliches Verhältnis") with socialist Russia, contrary to all the rules of the class struggle, also remains unexplained.[82]

In reality, the East German charges are not borne out by the Germans' intentions or actions. It is true, of course, that Germany's attitude toward Moscow was not beyond cavil, but if it was not wholly sincere toward Moscow, it was even less so toward the fellow capitalist Western powers. In April 1926, Berlin concluded a treaty of neutrality with the Soviet Union; it was to reassure the Kremlin that Germany's acceptance of the Locarno Pact and her proposed league membership were not directed against the USSR.

[80]West German research has since shown how Stresemann and his advisers planned to circumvent the Western precautions. The most promising chance for recovering the lands lost to Poland seemed to be a war between Soviet Russia and Poland; for this reason, Berlin welcomed such a war, and it assured Moscow that it would remain neutral vis-à-vis Russia even if Russia were the aggressor. See Jürgen Spenz, *Die diplomatische Vorgeschichte des Beitritts Deutschlands zum Völkerbund: 1924–1926* (Göttingen, 1966), pp. 103ff., 116–17, 118–19, 192 n. 40.

[81]Ruge, *Locarno-Konferenz*, pp. 25, 34, 74, 169, 172; see also Ludwig Zimmermann, *Deutsche Aussenpolitik in der Ära der Weimarer Republik* (Göttingen, 1958), pp. 263–64. Ruge denies the defensive character of the English and French moves despite his own documentary evidence to the contrary (cf. Ruge, *Locarno-Konferenz*, pp. 20, 34, 73–74). On Chamberlain's defensiveness vis-à-vis Soviet Russia, see also Jon Jacobson, *Locarno Diplomacy: Germany and the West, 1925–1929* (Princeton, 1972), pp. 21–22, 26, 130–31.

[82]Ruge, in Ruge, *Locarno-Konferenz*, pp. 27, 39.

As DDR authors have shown, the German position was not without ambiguities, but a careful analysis of the East Germans' own documentary materials makes clear that Berlin took its treaty with Moscow far more seriously than it took its pact with the Western powers.[83]

The dissection of monopolist abuses is supplemented by accounts of the struggle that the KPD was carrying on on behalf of the nation's true interests. The "relative stabilization of capitalism" confronted the party with the task of reassessing its strategy. The ensuing self-examination touched off a series of bitter factional disputes. East German analyses view these quarrels as the inherent dialectical form that the KPD's transformation into a Marxist-Leninist party assumed, for only a Marxist-Leninist party was equipped with a scientific concept of imperialism and could effectively fight its German manifestations.[84]

Until this transformation was achieved, lack of such a scientific approach is held to account for the inability of the German Communist party to deal correctly with the problems it faced. Taking an excessively leftist ("ultra-leftist") position after the "rightists" ' debacle in 1923, the party ruled out, against the Comintern's advice, the nomination of a joint candidate of both Communists and Social Democrats in the final presidential election in 1925. Regardless of whether such a candidate would have won, a promising chance thus was passed up to lay the foundation for a democratic, antimilitarist mass movement. (Of course, the Social Democrats, too, are rebuked for having made no attempt to work with the Communists.)[85]

[83]For a comparison of Germany's reservations about both pacts, see, for Locarno, the letter from Stresemann to Count Brockdorff-Rantzau, March 19, 1925, in ibid, pp. 70ff.; German cabinet protocols of June, July, and September 1925, in ZfG 22 (1974): 67ff. For the German-Soviet treaty, see the materials quoted in Anderle, Rapallo-Politik, pp. 180ff.; also Ruge, "Zur Problematik und Entstehungsgeschichte des Berliner Vertrages von 1926," ZfG 9 (1961): 828ff., 846–47.

[84]Karl and Ruge, in ZfG, 18 (1970): suppl., pp. 526–27. Despite their one-sided approach, East German accounts tell nonetheless more about the issues at stake between the various factions than does the detailed monograph by the West German political scientist Weber, Die Wandlung des deutschen Kommunismus (Frankfurt, 1969), vol. 1.

[85]See Ruge, Deutschland, pp. 273–75; GdA, vol. 4, pp. 75–76. Earlier, Marxist historians rejected all Communist responsibility for the election of Hindenburg on the grounds that the Catholic Bavarian People's Party was the real culprit, because it had withheld support from its fellow Catholic, ex-Chancellor Wilhelm Marx, and gone over to the Protestant Hindenburg. See Paul Merker, Deutschland—Sein oder Nicht Sein! (Mexico, 1944), pp. 118–19; Albert Norden, Lehren der deutschen Geschichte (Berlin [East], 1947), p. 81. This view has since been abandoned (Miriam Kölling, "Der Kampf der Kommunistischen Partei Deutschlands . . . für die Einheitsfront . . . (1924 bis 1927)," ZfG 2 (1954): 13–14; Hans-Joachim Fieber, "Die Bedeutung der Zentralausschusstagung von 9. und 10. Mai 1925 für die Herausbildung einer marxistisch-leninistischen Führung," ibid., 15 (1967): 1216–18. A purported Comintern proposal, which is mentioned by some Western writers (Flech-

The most harmful effect of the ultra-left's doctrinairism, however, is found in the increasing isolation of the KPD from the workers' movement. DDR authors carefully trace the party's growing awareness of this isolation and the inherently inevitable emergence of a realistic "Leninist" faction. In close collaboration with the Comintern, that faction endeavored to root the party more deeply in labor unions and factory cells. It also revived the call for a unity front with labor unions and Social Democrats as well as with all other parties and organizations willing to adopt a Communist minimum program of action (demanding the introduction of the eight-hour day, the abolition of all indirect taxes, the confiscation of princely properties, the purge of the civil service of all monarchist elements, the replacement of the monarchist *Reichswehr* with a people's militia, and the demilitarization of the police, some of whose units were stationed in barracks for antiriot duty).

In October 1925, the victory of the "Leninists" was sealed with the removal of all "ultra-leftists" from key positions and the appointment of Thälmann, a "leftist," as party chairman by the party's central committee. At the same time, the party organization was tightened on the Bolshevik model, with democratic centralism more vigorously enforced than had been the case before.[86] Surprisingly, these accounts have little or nothing to say on the shift of the basis of the party organization from street cells to factory cells (*Betriebszellen*). To make the place of work rather than the residence the nucleus of party activities was expected to render such activities more effective; cell members would have closer and more continuous contact among one another and could reach non-Communist workers more easily. Marxist teachings could also be understood and applied more readily in the factory cells than in the home-centered organizations, in which party members were apt to be distracted by other concerns.[87]

As all accounts emphasize, these actions were taken either at

---

theim, *Kommunistische Partei*, pp. 124–25; Carr, *History*, vol. 3, pp. i, 319 n. 4) and which suggested that the KPD support Marx (the nominee of the republican parties) to prevent the election of Hindenburg, is not mentioned in the DDR literature.

[86]See *GdA*, vol. 4, pp. 19–20, 28–29, 71, 90; Fieber, "Bedeutung," pp. 1212ff. Fieber provides interesting insights into the struggle between "Leninists" and "ultra-leftists." See also Stefan Weber ("Zur Herausbildung des marxistisch-leninistischen Zentralkomitees der KPD unter Ernst Thälmanns Führung," *BzG* 17 (1975): 616ff.), who is especially concerned with illustrating that this transformation was not imposed by the Comintern, but who does grant that the Executive Committee of the Comintern (EKKI) "considered it its absolute duty to intervene" in the KPD quarrels.

[87]See *GdA*, vol. 4, pp. 92–93, 412ff.; see also the report on a conference on the role of the KPD *Betriebszellen* in the Weimar Republic, (*ZfG* 27 [1979]: 767–68), which is possibly an indication of a beginning greater interest in this area.

the request of the Comintern or in close cooperation with it. Far from deploring the key role of the Comintern, East German historians note that involvement with evident satisfaction. The Comintern is given credit for providing guidance based on its ample experience and for coordinating German party activities with those of other Communist parties, especially those of the Soviet party. This last contribution is considered of special significance, for the USSR was the ultimate source of strength of all other Communist parties, just as their fate depended on that of the Soviet Union. In a struggle in which the battlefronts were drawn along class lines and developments were viewed on a worldwide scale, German national concerns could be of only secondary importance.[88] Yet, because the Soviet Union was at the time involved in a bitter debate between the Stalinist and Trotskyite camps as to what constituted the *Soviet* national interest, the policies of the KPD were in fact subordinated not to Soviet concerns, but to Stalin's factional ones. Thus, it was Stalin who insisted on the removal of the "ultra-leftists" from the German party, for when they attacked the policy of the unity front as opportunist, their criticisms paralleled Trotsky's attacks on the New Economic Policy. Of these implications there is, however, no word in the East German analyses.[89]

DDR authors are not, however, wholly uncritical of Comintern activities. They question the Comintern's tactic of branding the Social Democrats as a tool of the bourgeoisie, similar to fascism or even as a "wing" of fascism: such an equation misrepresented Social Democracy, which, after all, was a working-class movement, and hampered the chances of creating a unified front. The continued call for a dictatorship of the proletariat rather than for a worker-led government or one controlled by workers and peasants also is criticized; not only was this an unrealistic goal at that time, given the consolidation of the capitalist system, but it also put further obstacles in the path of a united democratic mass movement by frightening away such needed allies as peasants and petty bourgeoisie.[90]

Thus, DDR authors can report little progress on the road to the socialist revolution during those years. Full credit, however, is

---

[88]See Ruge, "Weltwirkung," pp. 1269ff. For a good illustration of the priority of Soviet over German concerns, see the statement of Wilhelm Pieck before the Central Committee of the KPD, February 21, 1932, in *ZfG* 23 (1975): 1435–37. The statement is discussed later in this chapter.

[89]Dietrich Geyer, "Sowjetrussland und die deutsche Arbeiterbewegung 1918–1932," *VfZ* 24 (1976): 26–27; Ruth Fischer, *Stalin and German Communism* (Cambridge, MA, 1948), pp. 432ff.

[90]*GdA*, vol. 4, pp. 47–49, 92; Ruge, *Deutschland*, p. 264; Streisand, pp. 317–18, "Kommunistische Internationale," *Swb*, vol. 1, p. 972.

given to the KPD for the one major leftist campaign that took place at that time—a popular referendum on the expropriation of formerly princely properties. Negotiations over the indemnification of the former German rulers for the loss of these properties—castles, estates, forests, and other possessions—had dragged on for years; the referendum, sponsored by KPD, SPD, labor unions, and some left-liberal organizations, called for an outright expropriation, without any indemnity. It had the support of 14.5 million voters, some 5.5 million less than the needed 20 million, but some 4 million more than Communists and Social Democrats had received in the last Reichstag elections. There is no evidence that this gain was due to any specific Communist efforts—in fact, it could well be argued that the referendum might have produced a majority in its favor had it allowed for the modest indemnifications that the Social Democrats had proposed and the Communists had vetoed. The outcome, however, as East German accounts rightly note, did point up the potentialities of united working-class action.[91]

The momentum generated by the referendum did not bring closer the hoped-for unified front despite repeated Communist efforts to capitalize on that momentum. For this failure the Social Democrats again are held chiefly responsible. They clung, it is charged, to their petty-bourgeois reformism and encouraged hopes that the workers' lot could be improved in a bourgeois state and a socialist order created step by step through reforms. These errors also reinforced those doctrinaire views, rife among Communists, that saw all Social Democrats as forever tied to the bourgeoisie.[92]

Such assumptions the East German critics find all the more harmful because the returns of the Reichstag elections in May 1928 showed the working class once more in the ascendance. Both SPD and KPD scored substantial gains, with the former getting 9.1 million votes (as compared to 7.9 million in December 1924) and the latter increasing from 2.7 million to 3.3 million votes. In an instant reaction, DDR authors claim, the "monopolist" German People's party offered to form a government with the Social Democrats in order to prevent an alliance between SPD and KPD. (In reality, the German People's party, because of its domination by big business, was reluctant to enter an SPD-led government and did so only for some short-range foreign-political and financial purposes.) Despite Communist pleas to reject a coalition with representatives of the monopoly bourgeoisie, the Social Democrats did

---

[91]"Fürstenabfindung," *Swb*, vol. 1, pp. 651–53; Ruge, *Deutschland*, pp. 295ff.; Streisand, pp. 318–20. On the Social Democratic proposal, see Stampfer, *Vierzehn Jahre*, p. 485.

[92]*GdA*, vol. 4, pp. 84ff., 141ff.; Ruge, *Deutschland*, pp. 312–13.

form a government with the latter, and the working class, it is bitterly noted, once again remained split.[93]

Toward a Monopolist-Bourgeois Dictatorship

To DDR historians, the new government, headed by the Social Democrat Hermann Müller-Franken, was merely a device of the more flexible wing of "finance capitalism" to pursue its reactionary policies behind the smoke screen of a coalition with the Social Democrats. Despite the latter's participation the government was a purely bourgeois one in this view. The East German fire is therefore trained on the Socialist members who, it is charged, yielded on all major issues to their bourgeois colleagues, at the expense of the workers and the true interests of the nation. They catered to imperialist aggressiveness by supporting the construction of a pocket-battleship (contrary to their election promises) and opposed a Communist-sponsored referendum against this project; they did not honor their promises for increased social benefits and in fact reduced these benefits; and they allowed the iron and steel industrialists of the Ruhr to defy a binding arbitration award in a major wage conflict. Outside the government, Social Democrats took part in antilabor and anti-Communist measures; the Social Democratic police commissioner of Berlin, Karl Zörgiebel, is charged with launching one of the bloodiest massacres of workers during May Day demonstrations in 1929. (The demonstrations were held in defiance of an official ban imposed in order to put an end to the recurring clashes between leftists and rightists—an even-handed treatment of the two camps on the part of a Social Democrat that Communists then found and DDR authors now find unforgivable. Zörgiebel, however, although not directly involved in the excesses of the police, did play a rather ambiguous role in this incident.) Nonetheless, East German critics complain, the Social Democratic party congress of 1929 still sanctioned the general course of developments, claiming contentedly, despite all signs to the contrary, that Germany was moving irresistibly toward a socialist order.[94]

[93]GdA, vol. 4, pp. 165ff.; Ruge, Deutschland, pp. 315–17. Cf. Eyck, Geschichte, vol. 2, pp. 205ff.; Holborn, vol. 3, pp. 633–34; Lothar Döhn, "Zur Verschränkung der Deutschen Volkspartei mit grosswirtschaftlich-industriellen Interessen . . . , " in Mommsen et al., Industrielles System, p. 905.
[94]See Klaus Mammach, "Der Sturz der grossen Koalition im März 1930," ZfG 16 (1968): 565; Ruge, Deutschland, pp. 321ff.; "Hermann-Müller-Regierung," Swb, vol. 1, p. 788; GdA, vol. 4, pp. 172–73, 198ff. Swb ("Blutmai 1929," vol. 1, p. 280) views the clashes on May Day 1929 as a direct attempt of the great bourgeoisie to crush the revolutionary vanguard of the working class and sees Zörgiebel, who

The Social Democrats faced a dilemma they could not solve. They were trying to keep the parliamentary system functioning, convinced that all social progress depended on it. On the other hand, the German People's party, at the other end of the government spectrum, was prepared to abandon that system in order to curb labor's influence, and it extracted increasing concessions in return for its cooperation with the Social Democrats. In effect, DDR analysts conclude, the SPD thus allowed the "monopoly bourgeoisie" to consolidate its position and steer the country towards a fascist dictatorship. Coupled with the restrictions imposed by Social Democratic ministers and officials on Communists and the workers movement in general, this added up to a pro-fascist posture on the part of the Social Democrats, too. In the Marxist view, this was in keeping with the petty bourgeois character of the party: a new corrupt workers' aristocracy, paid out of the monopolist profits, had gained the ascendancy among both leaders and followers. These elements kept large parts of the working class from pursuing the democratic alternative—that is, the creation of a unified front of the masses.[95]

At the same time, DDR authors concede that the formation of a unified front was precluded not only by the anti-Communist stance of the Social Democrats but also by the intransigent attitude of the Communists. In 1928, the Comintern had dropped its tactic of desultory cooperation with Social Democracy; foreseeing an impending economic depression and confident that that crisis would drive the masses into the Communist camp, it directed all Communist parties to turn on the Social Democrats and, because of their collaboration with the great bourgeoisie, brand them as "social fascists." The ensuing relentless campaign doomed all attempts to create a unified front from below by drawing into the Communist party local SPD units or individual workers and other "progressive" elements—as distinct from efforts to form such a front from above through a coalition of KPD and SPD as a whole. East German critics find equally unrealistic the KPD's continued demand for a dictatorship of the proletariat, again in line with Comintern directives; this goal was repugnant not only to the SPD leadership but also to the bulk of the German workers, who, DDR

---

imposed the original ban, as a mere tool of the bourgeoisie; see also Kurt Wrobel ("Zum Kampf Wilhelm Piecks . . . 1929–1932," *ZfG* 23 [1975]: 1424ff.), who feels similarly. See, on the other hand, the more restrained analysis in *GdA* vol. 4, p. 196.

[95]Katja Haferkorn, "Zum Wesen der Präsidialregierungen," in *Monopole und Staat*, p. 145; *GdA* vol. 4, p. 522; Weber, *Der deutsche Kommunismus: Dokumente* (Cologne, 1963), pp. 182ff.

authors grant, were not yet ready to engage in revolutionary activities.[96]

In this connection, DDR historians are also concerned with refuting charges that the KPD resembled the Nazis, the agents of finance capitalism, and in effect made common cause with them in its attacks on the Weimar Republic. Considerable effort has been devoted to showing that the KPD fought the Nazis from the moment they reemerged as a growing force on the political stage. From the fall of 1929, it is claimed, the party was in fact the "main force in the struggle for the liberation of the nation from imperialism and militarism." Only "leftist sectarians" continued making the SPD the primary target of their attacks—a claim that the Social Democrats would have found hard to accept, although it was perhaps technically true. As for the fight against fascism, the main task was to win its followers over to the cause of socialism and progress. This, however, could be done only on the ideological plane, because the petty bourgeois masses that supported the Nazis were the misguided victims of chauvinist demagoguery. As the KPD leadership emphasized, they could be disabused of their misconceptions only by reasoned arguments that would point out the speciousness of fascism's "socialist" promises.[97]

The Nazi movement, once more on the rise since 1929, has of course received much attention from East German scholars. The thrust of their investigations is circumscribed by the Marxist class analysis of the movement, which explains National Socialism, or rather fascism, as a by-product of the class struggle between monopoly capitalism and workers. In the face of a growing and increasingly self-assured workers' movement, the argument runs, the monopolies could no longer contain the sharpening contradictions—growing inequities in the distribution of the national income, escalating class struggles, a deepening economic crisis—that are the inevitable consequences of capitalist production. The most ruthless and uncompromising among the monopolists, primarily heavy industrialists—who were, according to Sachwörterbuch, the actual founders of the Nazi party—decided therefore to take advantage of the deepening economic Depression and use the Nazi terrorist organizations in order to crush the workers and subject them to a totalitarian

---

[96]See Ruge, Deutschland, pp. 330–31; GdA vol. 4, p. 239; Mammach, "Bemerkungen über die Wende der KPD zum Kampf gegen den Faschismus," BzG 5 (1963): 673. Once again, the parallelism of Soviet and German developments—the KPD struggle against Social Democrats and "rightist" deviationists in the party as a function of the Soviet campaign against kulaks and of the Stalin-Bukharin confrontation—is not discussed (cf. Geyer, "Sowjetrussland," pp. 33–35).

[97]Ruge, Deutschland, pp. 336–37; Mammach, "Bemerkungen," pp. 658ff.; GdA, vol. 4, pp. 234, 239–40. On the ambivalent tactics of the KPD at the time, see the materials assembled by Weber, Kommunismus.

dictatorship in which their rights could be readily curbed and monopolist profits expanded. (That heavy industry's economic difficulties kept increasing during these years is again nowhere mentioned as a possible partial explanation—although not a justification—of its call for an authoritarian regime.) To gain mass support in pursuit of this goal, the Nazis were to rouse middle and petty bourgeoisie against the workers, utilizing the growing hardships of these victims of the capitalist Depression to win them over by lies and false promises. "The German fascists," Manfred Weissbecker writes, "largely succeeded in paralyzing people's ability to think for themselves."[98]

As the tool of "monopoly capitalism" in its fight with the working class, "Hitler fascism" is viewed as the German phase of a widespread development. (In order to accentuate the speciousness of the allegedly socialist promises of Nazism and in refutation of its equally misleading national pretensions, Marxists insist on calling it fascism rather than National Socialism.) German fascism differed, however, from other such movements in the fiendishness and magnitude of the atrocities it committed. These, in turn, are attributed to the association of "Hitler fascism" with a defeated, but particularly aggressive, militarism and imperialism. These features, along with the existence of a supposedly more revolutionary-minded working class, also are claimed to explain why German monopoly capitalism turned to fascism to help it survive, unlike American and West European monopolism, which, though more highly developed, continued to control its working class by means of bourgeois-parliamentary dictatorships.[99]

From this perspective, the resort to fascism did not constitute an abrupt break with the past. What took place was rather the conversion of the "bourgeois-parliamentary dictatorship of German imperialism into a fascist one." Even in the parliamentary Weimar system, the great bourgeoisie, because of its superior material resources, had functioned as a "ruling class" and under a democratic

[98]See Streisand, pp. 325–27; "Faschismus," *Swb* vol. 1, pp. 571–72; Haferkorn, "Zum Wesen," p. 143; Weissbecker, "Die westdeutsche Presse zum 30. Jahrestag der Machtergreifung des deutschen Faschismus," *ZfG* 11 (1963): 1508–10; *GdA*, vol. 4, pp. 285, 328–29, 385–86. That the escalating dictatorial plans of industrialists and agrarians established an unbroken continuity from the Brüning government through the Papen-Schleicher regimes to the Nazi dictatorship is also recognized by non-Marxist historians (Bracher, *Anflösung*, p. 394; Gerhard Schulz, *Deutschland seit dem Ersten Weltkrieg: 1918–1945* [Göttingen, 1976], pp. 114–15).

[99]See "Faschismus," *Swb*, vol. 1, p. 571; Streisand, pp. 343ff.; Eichholtz, "Probleme einer Wirtschaftsgeschichte des Faschismus in Deutschland," *JWG* 3 (1963): 100; Eichholtz, *Geschichte der deutschen Kriegswirtschaft: 1939–1945* (Berlin [East], 1969, vol. 1, p. 12. On West European and American conditions, see Bleiber, "Bourgeoisie," pp. 319–20. On terror, see Weissbecker, "Extrem reaktionäre Organisationen des Imperialismus und werktätige Massen," *ZfG* 25 (1977): 288.

guise had imposed its terms; the difference, then, between the Weimar Republic and the Nazi regime was merely one of degree[100]—an adjustment of state-monopolist capitalism to the changing needs of the great bourgeoisie. For this reason, relatively little attention is paid to such aspects of Nazism as its totalitarianism, its leadership cult, or its racism—those features essential to the control and debasement of the individual citizen. Such degradation is considered intrinsic to the capitalist order; leader principle, racialism, and the mystique of the totalitarian state are viewed as merely new ways of controlling the masses and diverting the nation's attention from the misdeeds of those responsible for its plight. By the same token, Hitler, whose personality most non-Marxist historians consider crucial for the rise of Nazism, receives no special attention from Marxist scholars. Such preoccupation, they charge, again serves only to conceal the guilt of the real culprits, for it is classes, not individuals, that make history.[101]

As the outgrowth of intrinsic weaknesses in the capitalist order, Nazism, then, in the East German assessment, was not a product of the Depression, but had been nurtured by some monopolist circles long before the economic crisis of 1929. Analyses of the relationship between Nazis and monopolists, however, have undergone some careful refinements in the course of time. Originally, DDR researchers were mainly concerned with tracing monopolist support of the Nazis from the early 1920s and Hitler's Beer Cellar Putsch through the period of "relative stabilization," when, it is claimed, Rhenish industrialists kept the party alive as a "reserve force." In this context, attention was also called to parallel efforts to strengthen the power of the Reich president (Hinden-

---

[100]See Rolf Sonnemann and Rudolf Sauerzapf, "Monopole und Staat in Deutschland," in *Monopole und Staat*, pp. 17, 26; Eichholtz, "Probleme," pp. 100, 102. See also the corresponding contemporary assessments in Flechtheim, *Kommunistiche Partei*, pp. 164–65, and generally *Swb*, vol. 1, pp. 340–41, 372, 482. The main difference between the two types of dictatorship is found in the absence of open terror and in the ability of the working class to spread its views and organize openly, if within limits, in a bourgeois democracy, whereas no such opportunities exist any longer under fascism, and terror makes illegal activities extremely difficult ("Bürgerliche Demokratie," *Swb*, vol. 1, p. 340; *GdA*, vol. 4, p. 289; Kuczynski, *Geschichte*, vol. 6, p. 56).

[101]See Mohrmann, *Antisemitismus* (Berlin [East], 1972), pp. 19–20, 201–2; Weissbecker, "Zur Herausbildung des Führerkults in der NSDAP," in *Monopole und Staat*, p. 122; *Gda*, vol. 4, pp. 229–30. On Hitler, see Streisand (pp. 327ff.), the only who, somewhat apologetically, provides a biographical sketch. That the West German preoccupation with Hitler has served exculpatory purposes has also been noted by West German historians; Mommsen, "Betrachtungen zur Entwicklung der neuzeitlichen Historiographie in der Bundesrepublik," in *Probleme der Geschichtswissenschaft*, ed. Geza Alföldy et al. (Düsseldorf, 1973), pp. 132, 136; Hermann Graml, "Zur neuen Hitler-Biographie von Joachim C. Fest," *VfZ* 22 (1974): pp. 76ff., especially pp. 82ff.; F. Fischer, *Der Erste Weltkrieg und das Deutsche Geschichtsbild* (Düsseldorf, 1977), p. 358.

burg) at the expense of the parliament, while the bourgeois parties moved further toward the right with the election of their most conservative spokesmen as party chairmen (Alfred Hugenberg, the press magnate and one-time Krupp director, in the case of the German National People's party; Monsignor Ludwig Kaas, the papal prelate, in that of the Catholic Center party). Although it is granted that these moves were not in themselves fascist, they are seen as having lent further momentum to the trend toward fascism.[102]

These efforts to trace the links between "monopoly capitalism" and the Nazi party to the latter's beginnings were meant to establish the true "class content" of Nazism, for fascism, in the words of *Sachwörterbuch*, "expressed exclusively the class interests of the monopoly bourgeoisie."[103] Yet, in the face of the limited evidence indicating such links during the early years of the party's existence, it proved difficult to maintain that the party was systematically nurtured by monopolist cliques in order to further their authoritarian and imperialist interests. Similarly, it proved hard to explain why business leaders would foster a party that attracted much of its following by holding out visions of a more equitable "socialist" order—an objective that was anathema to the party's alleged sponsors and that, as the record shows, made it extremely difficult for a long time to obtain large-scale big-business support. DDR authors have therefore turned their attention from uncovering direct political and financial ties between big business and the Nazi party during those years to tracing the political and ideological affinities of the Nazis with demonstrably business-supported organizations, such as the Nationalklub, the Herren-Klub, and the Stahlhelm, which spread thoughts and values the Nazis picked up or prepared the ground psychologically for Nazi views and activities. As purveyors of the leader principle, of militarism and imperialism, of racism and the cult of violence, such neoconservative thinkers as Oswald Spengler, the philosopher, and the publicists Eduard Stadtler, Arthur Moeller van den Bruck, and Edgar J. Jung presented ideas, Joachim Petzold writes, that subsequently were implemented by the Nazis in the interest of the most reactionary and aggressive segments of the German monopoly bourgeoisie. In fact, as Petzold and other DDR authors see it, these neoconserva-

[102]See Ruge, *Deutschland*, pp. 224, 260, 321–22; "Nationalsozialistische Deutsche Arbeiterpartei," *Swb* vol. 2, p. 153; Mammach, "Bemerkungen," p. 663; Karl, "Zur Entwicklung der politischen Konzeption der KPD . . . 1925–1928," *BzG* 10 (1968): 989–90. For a more cautious evaluation of the Nazi-monopolies relationship, see Streisand (p. 331), who has maintained this position since the first edition of his book (1968 ed.; p. 240). Ulrich Roeske, in turn, is one DDR historian who does not consider the Nazi party a creation of monopoly capitalism ("Zur Verhältnis zwischen DNVP and NSDAP . . . 1931 bis 1933," *WZ Berlin* 22 [1973]: 27–28).
[103]"Faschismus," *Swb* vol. 1, p. 571; similarly, *Grundriss*, p. 394.

tives were no mere forerunners of fascism, but represented themselves a germinal type of fascism.[104]

Elaborating on this theme, Manfred Weissbecker and Herbert Gottwald submit that such supposedly fascist characteristics as the leader principle were "organically linked to the bourgeois social and economic order, to imperialism and the general crisis of capitalism," to judge from the call for a leader by virtually all bourgeois parties at that time. Leaders, they add, are of course needed by any state or organization, but the kind of omnipotent strong man for whom the call went out in Weimar Germany was the one required by a system of ruthless capitalist exploitation that was ready to resort to the utmost brutality. The Nazi party, then, was no "Hitler party" in the sense that it bore Hitler's personal imprint and was his instrument; what made it different from other bourgeois parties was that it had in Hitler the kind of leader for whom the "existential needs of the ruling class" called. "Just as the fascist dictatorship grew organically out of other forms of imperialist rule . . . , there exists a close organic correlation between the various forms of political leadership and the leaders of the monopoly bourgeoisie."

Rounding out this scenario, the East German analyses note that in the case of the Nazi party the authority of the leader was reinforced by the militarist structuring of the entire society. This militarization of all social relations was to cut off the toiling masses from the direction of state and society, assure the terrorist implementation of monopolist interests, and lend credibility to the demagogic equation of these interests with those of the oppressed and exploited toilers. All in all, the Nazi party, rigidly controlled by its leader, yet camouflaged as a popular movement, embodied the very features that were required of a movement needed to

[104]See Petzold, *Konservative Theoretiker des deutschen Faschismus: Jungkonservative Ideologen in der Weimarer Republik als geistige Wegbereiter der faschistischen Diktatur* (Berlin [East], 1978); Petzold, "Monopolkapital und faschistische Ideologie: Zur Rolle Der Jungkoservativen in der Weimarer Republik," *ZfG* 25 (1977): 295ff.; Weissbecker, "Extrem reaktionäre Organisationen," pp. 280ff., Weissbecker, "Konservative Politik und Ideologie in der Konterrevolution 1918–19," *ZfG* 27 (1979): 707ff.; Weissbecker and Gottwald, "Zur Rolle Der Führer bürgerlicher Parteien," ibid., p. 229ff. This rash of publications on the relationship between monopoly capitalism and masses—the above list is far from complete—was, it may be assumed, a response to the reminder of the Ninth Party Congress of the SED that "research into the history of the German exploiting classes, above all that of German imperialism, militarism, and fascism, remains directly relevant. It will long remain relevant in the struggle against present-day imperialism, which has not renounced its plans to maintain and expand its position and to undermine and destroy the socialist order, and will remain equally relevant in the confrontation with bourgeois-imperialist historiography over the defense, intensely pursued in the [Federal Republic], of German imperialism and militarism, over revanchism and neo-fascism" (Diehl, "Aufgaben der Geschichtswissenschaft der DDR nach dem IX. Parteitag der SED," *ZfG* 25 [1977]: 272). See also Weissbecker, "Konservative Politik," p. 709.

establish a monopoly-controlled dictatorship. Objections to the effect that most business leaders showed little interest in the party until it became a mass party are dismissed as confusing the class character of the party with the extent of its influence.[105]

In 1929, during a joint German National-Stahlhelm-Nazi campaign against the Young Plan (a new reparations schedule), financial support from big business began to flow more abundantly and, according to East German claims, remained at a respectable level ever after. The evidence in support of this assertion has been refuted conclusively by Western scholars,[106] but the lack of financial support on the part of big business does not necessarily absolve it of all responsibility in the rise of Nazism. What matters is the further East German contention that big-business support should not be assessed in financial terms only.[107] Here the data are incontestable: nonmonetary aid ranged from sympathetic reports on Nazi activities by the newspapers of Hugenberg's nationwide press concern to the continued nurturing of the antidemocratic, antilabor atmosphere on which Nazism thrived and the subsidization of other militant right-wing organizations.[108] Moreover, big-business opposition to the Nazis was based on pragmatic grounds rather than basic principles: it was the Nazis' "socialism" that was found objectionable, not their militarist authoritarianism or their terrorist tactics.[109] Above all, major industrialists played into the hands of the Nazis by

[105]See Weissbecker and Gottwald, "Zur Rolle," pp. 304–5, 307–9, 313–14; Weissbecker, "Konservative Politik," pp. 713–14; Weissbecker, "Extrem reaktionäre Organisationen," pp. 284–86, 292–94. Significantly, even though East German historians do not accord Hitler an all-dominant impact on developments, they nonetheless often refer to Nazism as "Hitler fascism."

[106]Concerning the unreliability of the financial data supplied by DDR authors (*GdA*, vol. 4, p. 232; Ruge, *Deutschland*, pp. 347–48), see Ernst Nolte, "Big Business and German Politics: A Comment," *AHR* 75 (1969): 73 74, Henry A. Turner, "Big Business and the Rise of Hitler," ibid., pp. 61ff.; Turner, "Fritz Thyssen und 'I Paid Hitler,' " *VfZ* 19 (1971): 233–34, 242.

[107]See Weissbecker, "Extrem reaktionäre Organisationen," p. 285 n. 25. This is also recognized by some West German scholars (for example, Dirk Stegmann, "Zum Verhältnis von Grossindustrie und Nationalsozialismus: 1930–1933," *Arch. f. Sozgesch.* 13 [1973]: 399, 401). On the other hand, see Alan S. Milward, "Fascism and the Economy," in *Fascism: A Reader's Guide,* ed. Walter Laqueur (Berkeley, 1976), p. 389: "[The] importance [of Big Business] for fascist parties has to be judged by counting neither heads nor votes, but cash."

[108]See also Kurt Koszyk, "Paul Reusch und die 'Münchener Neuesten Nachrichten': Zum Problem Industrie und Presse in der Endphase der Weimarer Republik," *VfZ* 20 (1972): 75ff. This documentation once again provides ample evidence of the independent course of the Nazis. The indirect responsibility of business for the rise of the Nazis is also recognized by non-Marxist historians (Turner, "Big Business," pp. 69–70; Nolte, "Big Business," p. 78; and especially Winkler, "Unternehmerverbände zwischen Ständeideologie und Nationalsozialismus," *VfZ* 17 [1969]: 341ff., especially pp. 369–71).

[109]There is no evidence, however, that business leaders saw in terrorism a necessary facet of the hoped-for authoritarian regime, as some East German authors have suggested (Petzold, "Monopolkapital," p. 303; Weissbecker, "Extrem reaktionäre Organisationen," p. 288; Weissbecker and Gottwald, "Zur Rolle," p. 307).

their self-centered business practices; in their determination to maintain prices at their highest possible level, they cut off demand and accelerated the decline in production, with the attendant economic and political consequences. Kuczynski has collected some signficant data on the correlation between monopoly-controlled prices and decreasing production in Germany during the years 1929–1932.[110]

Compared to the role assigned to the leaders of the industrial and banking concerns, the part played by agrarians and military in the rise of the Nazis appears of but secondary importance in the East German accounts—as it must within the framework of state-monopolist capitalism. In the same vein, the support of petty and middle bourgeoisie—and of substantial numbers of workers—is minimized on the grounds that these classes were but the hapless victims of fascist, that is, monopoly-inspired demagoguery.[111]

Although Nazism in the Marxist perception was the creation, direct or indirect, of the "monopoly bourgeoisie," it is granted, however, that the establishment of a fascist dictatorship was not planned systematically, step by step, in advance.[112] The breakup in March 1930 of the Social Democratic-bourgeois coalition government that had rested on a parliamentary majority is viewed as a first step toward the creation of the eventual terrorist fascist dictatorship. The breakup is presented therefore as a "monopolist" move, which to some extent, of course, it was. DDR authors do not admit, however, that this assessment ignores the significant role that agrarians and the army played in getting Reich President von Hindenburg to abandon parliamentary procedures. If a military man, General von Schleicher, took the lead in preparing the way for a new, more authoritarian government that was to derive its authority from the president's personal confidence rather than from the Reichstag, he acted, it is argued, as the spokesman of the monopoly-dominated state apparatus. Concomitantly, some East German authors imply that Schleicher owed his quick rise to the fact that his activities furthered the interests of the great bourgeoisie.[113]

---

[110]Kuczynski, Geschichte, vol. 5, pp. 20–22; also Nussbaum, Wirtschaft, pp. 299ff.

[111]The fact that significant numbers of workers joined the Nazi party and the storm troops is rarely mentioned in the East German literature. On this, see Timothy W. Mason, Sozialpolitik im Dritten Reich (Opladen, 1977), pp. 62ff.; also Max H. Kele, Nazis and Workers (Durham, 1972).

[112]Mammach, "Sturz," p. 569; Bertsch, "Die bürgerlichen Parteien in Deutschland und die Grosse Sozialistische Oktoberrevolution," in Die Grosse Sozialistische Oktoberrevolution und Deutschland (Berlin [East], 1967), p. 287.

[113]See Mammach, "Sturz," pp. 565, 579–80; Ruge, "Die 'Deutsche Allgemeine Zeitung' und die Brüning-Regierung: Zur Rolle der Grossbourgeoisie bei der Vorbereitung des Faschismus," ZfG 16 (1968): 24–25; Streisand, p. 215; "Schleicher-Programm 1930," Swb, vol. 2, p. 454. On the role of agrarians and army, see Dorpalen, Hindenburg, pp. 163ff.

The government collapsed over the question of adjusting the unemployment insurance system to the deepening economic crisis. The Social Democrats, as representatives of the workers and the business-dominated German People's party, could not agree on who was to bear the main burden of such an adjustment. In non-Marxist assessments, the breakup of the government is often blamed on the Socialists, who rejected a compromise providing for a temporary arrangement. Most non-Marxists condemn this opposition as short-sighted on the grounds that it led, predictably, to the formation of a government without Social Democrats, the only significant democratic-republican force. East German historians, on the other hand, deny that the Social Democrats had any real choice and maintain that actually the latter were dropped rather than withdrew from the government because the monopoly bourgeoisie no longer had any use for them.

Ever ready to credit the bourgeoisie with subtle cunning, these authors also maintain that the "monopolists" did not drive the Social Democrats from the government merely in order to establish a government more independent of the Reichstag so that they could pursue their particular economic, social, and constitutional goals with little interference from the parliament. According to this reasoning, business considered the SPD more useful as a "seeming" opposition party that would actually tolerate the new government. Specifically, the SPD would be in a better position, because of its formal opposition to that government, to block all Communist efforts to create an antifascist unity front. By expelling the Social Democrats from the government, the imperialists thus expected to move closer to a fascist dictatorship in more than one way.[114]

The Road to Fascism: The Brüning Government

Accordingly, the new government, headed by the center deputy Heinrich Brüning, is presented as the creation of the great chemical and electrical trusts, some Rhenish-Westphalian heavy industrial-

---

[114]See *Grundriss*, pp. 426–28; Ruge, *Deutschland*, pp. 356–57, 359–60; "Hermann-Müller-Regierung," *Swb*, vol. 1, p. 788; "Schleicher-Programm 1930," ibid., vol. 2, p. 454; Streisand, pp. 332–33; Hans Dress et al., "Zur Politik der Hermann-Müller-Regierung 1928–1930," *ZfG* 10 (1962): 1888–89. The claim of Turner that the heavy-industrial *Ruhrlade* was still willing to support a democratic-parliamentary government ignores the fact that the parties and publications its members supported called for a strong authoritarian government (Turner, "The *Ruhrlade*: Secret Cabinet of Heavy Industry in the Weimar Republic," *CEH* 3 [1970]: 199, 206ff., 209–10).

ists, a group of banks, Upper Silesian mining magnates, and Reichswehr commanders. (The strong representation of agrarian interests
in the new cabinet is mentioned only occasionally in the general
accounts, even though Hindenburg made himself the insistent
spokesman of these interests.) Special emphasis, of course, is placed
on the fact that the Brüning government derived its authority from
the president rather than from the Reichstag and that it was promised presidential emergency decrees to bypass the legislature should
the latter refuse to enact the government's bills. These arrangements, in Ruge's words, "inaugurated a new phase in the dismantling of bourgeois democracy, in the destruction of the political and
social rights of the German people, on the road that culminated in
the transfer of power to Hitler."[115] As Ruge sees it, "reactionary
finance capital"—that is, the coal-iron-steel industrialists—were using Brüning and the Center party as mere pawns. The party was
useful to these monopolists because it provided a petty bourgeois
mass basis, tended toward authoritarianism, and concealed its
monopoly-inspired imperialism behind a religious facade. It was to
be discarded, however, once the Nazis had proven themselves as
effective checks on the workers' movement.[116]

Here the wisdon of hindsight obviously transcends the
bounds of historical analysis. There is no evidence of any such
scheme. Except for an intransigent group that stayed with Hugenberg in the German National party and that opposed the Brüning
government from the beginning, business readily supported the
new chancellor. Nor did there seem any reason to do otherwise.
As several DDR authors have themselves pointed out, the budget
that Brüning submitted to the Reichstag provided for the very
steps that an economic program of the League of German Industrialists had demanded just a few months before. It proposed to
reduce social services, raise tariffs on foodstuffs and other essential imports, increase income and head taxes and introduce taxes
on the unmarried—all measures that would weigh most heavily
on the low-income groups. At the same time, the budget envisaged tax privileges for the affluent and their enterprises in order
to encourage the formation of capital. And when the proposals
were twice rejected by a majority of the Reichstag, the govern-

---

[115]See Ruge, *Deutschland*, pp. 347, 357ff.; *GdA*, vol. 4, pp. 241ff.; Streisand, pp. 315,
332ff.; "Brüning-Regierung," *Swb* vol. 1, p. 293; Sonnemann-Sauerzapf, "Monopole," p. 26. Agrarian pressures are mentioned, however, in specialized studies;
see Bruno Buchta, *Die Junker und die Weimarer Republic* (Berlin [East], 1958),
pp. 79ff.
[116]See Ruge, *Deutschland*, pp. 358, 360. Unlike Weimar Communists, DDR authors
do not view the Brüning regime as an outright fascist dictatorship (Ruge, *Deutschland*, p. 363).

ment, rather than strive for a compromise, dissolved the parliament and enacted the budget by Presidential decree.[117]

East German scholars attribute the chancellor's intransigence to industrial pressures and, in their preoccupation with the role of "monopoly capitalism," again ignore the obstructionist role of the agrarians. Only concessions by them as well could have assured parliamentary passage of the budget, but they were as much opposed to any accommodation with the Social Democrats as were the industrialists.[118] Once again, however, the evidence refutes the further assertion that Brüning's policies accorded with the alleged plan of the "monopoly bourgeoisie" to systematically move the country toward an openly terrorist dictatorship. In the subsequent elections, it is true, most entrepreneurs supported parties that called for a more authoritarian government; but when the elections produced the spectacular success of the Nazis, whose Reichstag delegation grew from 12 to 107 members, some banking and industrial circles, among them the directorate of the League of German Industrialists, suggested that Brüning strengthen his government by including some Social Democrats in it. It was Hindenburg who blocked all such changes at the urging of his military and agrarian friends and advisers. Obviously, the significance of these immediate reactions ought not to be overstressed—the advocates of a collaboration with the Social Democrats quickly dropped this idea. They do make clear, however, that the Nazis owed their electoral victory to their own efforts rather than to "monopolist" nurturing.[119]

Because, in the East German view, the differences between the Nazis and those supporting the Hindenburg-Brüning camp concerned tactics rather than strategy, DDR assessments regard the election campaign primarily as a confrontation between Communists on the one hand and fascists and profascist forces, including the Social Democrats, on the other. This struggle was fought on both the physical and ideological level. The KPD, it is claimed, became the main target of fascist terror, with raids directed at Communist election rallies and newspaper offices, assaults on party officials, and attacks on party offices, once even on party headquarters in Berlin. Protective formations were organized but

[117]On the similarity of Brüning's budget to a proposed financial program of the *Reichsverband der deutschen Industrie,* see ibid., p. 80; Streisand, p. 332; *Grundriss,* p. 428.

[118]Conze, in *Die Staats- und Wirtschaftskrise des Deutschen Reichs 1929–33,* ed. Conze and Hans Raupach (Stuttgart, 1967), pp. 213ff.; Bracher, *Auflösung,* pp. 336ff.; Dorpalen, *Hindenburg,* pp. 186ff.

[119]Turner, "Ruhrlade," pp. 209–11; Dorpalen, *Hindenburg,* p. 207; Udo Wengst, "Unternehmerverbände und Gewerkschaften . . . 1930," *VfZ* 25 (1977): 116–18; as compared to *GdA,* vol. 4, p. 256.

never attained adequate strength. Yet, although terror is considered the distinctive feature of all fascist movements, most accounts are focused on the ideological campaign the Communists launched. It alone is considered of long-range significance, because only ideological enlightenment could convert the misguided and misinformed Nazi masses.[120]

That campaign culminated in the KPD's "Program Declaration [*Programmerklärung*] Concerning the National and Social Liberation of the German People," worked out with the "assistance" (Streisand; *Grundriss*) of the Comintern. On the domestic front, the program called for the creation of a Soviet Germany, that is, a dictatorship of the proletariat, the nationalization of large enterprises, and the breakup of landed estates, as well as higher wages and increased social benefits for the working class. In the foreign domain, it promised the annulment of the Versailles treaty, the cancellation of all reparations and other international debts, and a close alliance with Soviet Russia. To attain these goals, the document declared all-out war on "finance capitalism," considered the backbone of the Nazi party. In the words of *Geschichte*, "The KPD fought the fight against the fascists as a class struggle against the monopolies." Yet, because the successes of Nazi propaganda "resulted from the twelve years of treacherous policies of Social Democracy," and because the Social Democrats served as the "accomplices" of the German bourgeoisie and the "willing agents" of French and Polish imperialism, they too would have to be crushed, along with the fascists.

East German commentators are not uncritical of the Program Declaration. Again they object to the call for the dictatorship of the proletariat as both premature and repugnant to potential petty bourgeois and other allies. Similarly, they are critical of the program's severe attacks on the Social Democrats, but they point out that the Declaration no longer referred to them as "social fascists"—an omission of little significance, because the party resumed use of that epithet a short time later.

Conversely, the program is praised for showing that, contrary to the claims of fascists and other rightists, only the Communists offered policies that were in the national interest. DDR analysts applaud the social goals for which the Communists fought and the truly national aims they stood for, their struggle against repara-

---

[120]See Ruge, *Deutschland*, pp. 372–73; *Grundriss*, p. 430. Neither *GdA* nor Streisand mentions the physical confrontations. *Sachwörterbuch* alludes only briefly to pre-1933 terrorist activities ("Faschistischer Terror," *Swb*, vol. 1, p. 578). The possibility that Nazis (or Stahlhelmers) may not always have been the attackers is nowhere considered.

tions and other international debts and against the Versailles Treaty—efforts that were to benefit the entire nation, not only a small upper stratum that identified its own narrow class interests with those of the nation. As the program insisted, the genuine liberation of the nation was predicated on the overthrow of the imperialist bourgeois regime.[121]

This was not "nationalist demagoguery," as West German critics have charged, but accorded with long-held beliefs. All along, the Communist party had denounced the Versailles Treaty, the Locarno Pact, and the reparations arrangements as capitalist stratagems, both foreign and German, that were designed to suppress and exploit the German working class and weaken the Soviet Union and that thus were contrary to the German national interest. In the same spirit, the program renounced all claims to lost territories that had not been German, as well as to overseas colonies, following here in the footsteps of Marx and Engels, who had warned that no nation that oppressed other nations could ever be free. Finally, the claim that a class society could act only in the interest of the ruling class and not that of the entire nation was (and is) one of the basic tenets of Marxism. Yet if the Communist appeal to national interests was not an opportunist maneuver, the resort at the same time to a Nazi-type leadership cult, with Thälmann pointedly hailed as "our *Führer*," clearly was. Of these tactics, however, the East German literature makes no mention.[122]

Despite its shortcomings, East German historians credit the program with a major share in the success the Communists scored in the Reichstag elections of September 1930. The KPD gained 1.3 million votes over the election of 1928 and, with 4.6 million voters, became the third largest party, after the Social Democrats and the Nazis. On the strength of this fact *Sachwörterbuch* concludes that the antifascist, anti-imperialist tenor of the program facilitated the approach to dissatisfied Social Democratic workers despite the program's attacks on the SPD. Other authors point out that the program gave guidance not just to the German workers but to all workers threatened by the "fascist offensive of monopoly

---

[121]"Programmerklärung . . . ," *Swb*, vol. 2, pp. 302ff. Text of the Declaration is found in Weber, pp. 58ff. See also Streisand, pp. 334–35; *GdA*, vol. 4, pp. 259ff.; *Grundriss*, pp. 431–32.

[122]Weber, *Kommunismus*, p. 58 n. 13; Weber, *Wandlung*, p. 278 and 278 n. 132; Flechtheim, *Kommunistische Partei*, pp. 173–74; Horst Duhnke, *Die KPD von 1933 bis 1945* (Cologne, 1972), pp. 20–21; Siegfried Bahne, "Die Kommunistische Partei Deutschlands," in *Das Ende der Parteien 1933*, ed. Erich Matthias and Rudolf Morsey (Düsseldorf, 1960), pp. 658–59. Significantly, the terms applied to Thälmann were adopted from Nazi nomenclature rather than from Stalin's "personality cult." On the Marxist concept of nationhood, see Dorpalen, "Marxism and National Unity: The Case of Germany," *Review of Politics* 39 (1977): 505ff.

capitalism," thus placing the German struggle in its world-historical context.[123]

Post-election accounts are focused on what is called the accelerating drift toward the fascist dictatorship. Efforts of some major
industrialists to reach an accommodation with the Nazis are carefully noted. This shift is attributed to Brüning's dependence on the
Social Democrats, whose votes he needed to preserve his Reichstag
majority. The chancellor thus was compelled to maintain wages
and social benefits at a higher level than business would tolerate.
For this the Social Democrats are given no credit, however, on the
grounds that Brüning merely delayed further wage cuts and other
infringements until a more opportune time. Correspondingly, the
difficulties that industry was facing are ignored—on the grounds
that because these problems were to be resolved by the political
and economic disenfranchisement of the workers, the real issue
was the exploitative nature of capitalism and the need to do away
with that system.

East German historians find their analyses borne out by the
growing discontent of big business. Given their particular objectives, DDR authors note, the entrepreneurs became convinced that
the Brüning government could only be the prelude to an outright
dictatorship. Only a dictatorial regime could curb, if not bar altogether, the workers' participation in determining wages and working conditions. The *Deutsche Allgemeine Zeitung*, the mouthpiece
of major banking and industrial interests, put it as follows in an
editorial quoted repeatedly in the East German literature; "Brüning's political activity can be summed up only as . . . constituting
the prelude to the national dictatorship, that is, he gets the nation
used to the dictatorship and enables his successors to maintain
themselves by referring to their predecessor."[124]

This assessment, DDR authors point out, was made despite
the government's willingness to protect the "finance capitalists"
from any losses, at the expense of the working class. Thus the
government came to the aid of two major banks, the Darmstädter
and Nationalbank and the Dresdner Bank, in July 1931 and some
months later bailed out some industrial and shipping concerns,

---

[123]Ruge, *Deutschland*, p. 376; Ruge, review, *ZfG* 20 (1972): 1440: *GdA*, vol. 4,
  pp. 262–63; "Programmerklärung," *Swb*, vol. 2, p. 304.
[124]The best account of the "monopolist" position can be found in Ruge, " 'Deutsche
  Allgemeine Zeitung' " (pp. 19ff.), which supplements and refines the earlier essay
  by Fritz Klein ("Zur Vorbereitung," pp. 884ff.). See also Ruge, *Deutschland*,
  pp. 401ff.; Sonnemann and Sauerzapf, "Monopole," pp. 17ff.; Eberhard Czichon,
  Wer verhalf Hitler zur Macht? (Cologne, 1967), pp. 18ff., a less careful report by an
  East German journalist. The accuracy of the picture that Ruge presents is largely
  confirmed by the West German economic historian Wilhelm Treue, "Der deutsche
  Unternehmer in der Weltwirtschaftskrise 1928–1933," in Conze and Raupach,
  Staats- und Wirtschaftskrise, pp. 107ff.

among them a near-bankrupt mining enterprise, *Gelsenkirchener Bergwerks-A.G.*, on terms excessively favorable to the latter. The agrarians proved just as insatiable despite the huge subsidies bestowed on them. At the same time, the demands for the dissolution of labor unions and workers' parties kept growing stronger. In Prussia these efforts led to a plebiscite (unsuccessful), calling for new state elections to remove the Social Democrats from the government and deprive them of control of the Prussian police.

Brüning, it is noted, responded with new financial restrictions and burdens, tailored to industry's explicit demands. Catering further to the monopolist-militarist interest bloc, he also gave his government a more authoritarian image, replacing members suspect of a liberal penchant with staunch monopolists and militarists. A director of I.G. Farben, Hermann Warmbold, became minister of economics, and the Reichswehr minister, General Wilhelm Groener, took charge of the ministry of the interior. An economic council, dominated by major industrialists, bankers, and great agrarians, was to give these groups additional leverage on government policies. Yet, the profascist forces, determined to obtain full control over state and government, would not relent. In October 1931 a gathering of Nazis, German Nationals, and other right-wing political and economic leaders and organizations, meeting at the little spa of Bad Harzburg, in the German National/Nazi–ruled state of Brunswick, demanded the removal of the Brüning government in the Reich and of the Social Democratic-Centrist coalition in Prussia. What Ruge considers especially noteworthy about the Harzburg meeting is the dominance of the Nazis over all other attending groups. Because he finds that by this time the Nazis were being supported more openly by "the [!] masters of the monopolies," the implication here is that "the" monopolists had cynically abandoned their less ruthless confederates in order to pursue their class struggle against the workers with the help of the Nazis.[125]

The picture that is thus presented is intentionally one-dimensional; its purpose is merely to show how those business leaders who had long planned to establish a Nazi dictatorship—Ruge and *Grundriss* call them the "decisive circles of finance capital"—proceeded to attain their objective.[126] On the other hand, those leaders who did not call for a Nazi regime are noticed only as they drew closer to the pro-Nazi elements; their reservations about the Nazis, however, are written off. "We must ask above all," writes Fritz Klein, "how these people conducted themselves when their original favorites—Hugenberg, for example—

[125]Ruge, *Deutschland*, pp. 409–11; Klein, *Deutschland*, pp. 893ff.; also "Brüning-Regierung," *Swb*, vol. 1, p. 293; Streisand, pp. 337–38.
[126]Ruge, p. 409; *Grundriss*, p. 439.

were dropped [from the Hitler government] with the active help of a part of the monopoly barons. . . . The Vöglers, Springorums, Krupps, Reuschs, etc. remained at their posts, which became ever more lucrative in the course of rearmament. They remained the main supporters and wire-pullers of German imperialism in its fascist phase, too, which renders irrelevant for historical judgments their earlier engagement for Hugenberg or Papen."[127] There is a point to Klein's argument: the ease with which the industrialists adjusted to the Nazi regime suggests that they did not have far to travel. Yet the historian, who does not want to be merely a chronicler of results, cannot simply ignore their earlier doubts but must distinguish between premeditation and ex-post-facto acceptance. The undifferentiated East German approach conveys an impression of consensus and purposefulness on the part of the business leaders that did not exist.[128]

For the time being, then, the economic policies of the Nazis continued to worry and mystify the bulk of the banking and industrial leaders. Even pledges to break the power of labor and prospects of large armament orders held out to industry by the Nazi leaders, who from 1931 on carefully cultivated major industrialists, could not allay such misgivings. They were finally swept away, as DDR authors see it, by a speech that Hitler made before a group of Rhenish industrialists in January 1932 and in which he pledged the preservation of private property and entrepreneurial freedom. As evidence, the testimony of Hitler's press secretary is invoked—hardly an unbiased source. Other contemporary accounts reported a less positive reaction to the address.[129]

The latter interpretations were borne out by the Presidential election that spring, on the expiration of Hindenburg's term. DDR accounts find the "monopoly bourgeoisie" still divided between those who supported Hitler's candidacy—a minority—and those who were not yet reassured about the Nazis' economic objectives and voted for Hindenburg. But they, too, it is noted, wished to see

[127]Klein, review, ZfG 21 (1973): 1524.
[128]On the lack of political acumen among the non-Nazi elements of the anti-Brüning forces, see Bracher, Auflösung, pp. 410–11; on the lack of political astuteness of business leaders in general, see Friedrich Glum, Zwischen Wissenschaft, Wirtschaft und Politik (Bonn, 1964), pp. 409–10; Jörg-Otto Spiller, "Reformismus nach rechts," in Mommsen et al., Industrielles System, p. 602. On the ineptness of Hugenberg, who was continuously outmaneuvered by Hitler, see Heinrich Brüning, Memoiren: 1918–1934 (Stuttgart, 1970), p. 257; Dorpalen, Hindenburg, pp. 156ff., 189, 228, 242, 256–57, 271ff.; on Reusch, see Koszyk, "Reusch," pp. 75ff.
[129]See Ruge, " 'Deutsche Allgemeine Zeitung,' " pp. 47, 52–53; Ruge, Deutschland, p. 417; Streisand, p. 338. Only Kuczynski (Geschichte, vol. 6, pp. 14–15) mistakenly claims that heavy industry was unconcerned about the Nazis' "socialism." On the corresponding concerns of agrarians, see Gossweiler and Alfred Schlicht, "Junker und NSDAP, 1931/32," ZfG 15 (1967): 644ff.

Brüning dismissed. In this they succeeded a few weeks later, aided by the agrarians, whose role is acknowledged, for once, by at least some accounts. By then, it is pointed out, Brüning had all but obtained the cancellation of all reparations and the right for Germany to rearm. His usefulness to the great bourgeoisie thus had come to an end, and a government not tied to the Social Democrats could now take over.[130]

In foreign affairs, Brüning is claimed to have been as much a monopolist mouthpiece as in the domestic arena. Accordingly, an attack he launched on the Young Plan late in 1931 is dismissed as merely voicing monopolist goals—a view that manages to reconcile the critique of the chancellor with the Communists' own rejection of the plan as the product of imperialist rivalries. (That Brüning in reality expressed views held by the entire nation is ignored—on the grounds that the nation, except for the Communists, had no views of its own but was misled by nationalist demagogues.)

On the other hand, the chancellor is not taken to task for preferring an American-sponsored moratorium that was unconditional to a French proposal that included the offer of a substantial loan but that asked in return that Germany drop for the next ten years all demands for a revision of the Versailles Treaty. Always opposed to that treaty, DDR commentators approve; one of them (Gossweiler) calls the rejection of the Paris offer "natural," even though the proffered French loan would have relieved unemployment and social misery.

DDR analysts, however, are highly critical of Brüning's insistence on Germany's right to rearm. They denounce as misleading the slogan of "equality of armaments" under which this right was demanded. Germany's economic superiority, they point out, was bound to make it in time militarily superior to all of its neighbors. In this perception, the reparations and disarmament policies of the Brüning government were imperialist also in a wider sense—as tactical moves in the unending battle between capitalism and socialism. Brüning, it is noted, obtained American backing for a moratorium on reparations by warning Washington that if rebuffed, Germany might turn to Communism; relief from the reparations burden, on the other hand, would preserve her as an anti-Communist bulwark both at home and abroad. (That the U.S. government, in assisting Germany on the reparations issue, was guided at least as much by its concern for American investments in Germany is mentioned only parenthetically or not at all—perhaps because in the Marxist-Leninist view "imperialist" efforts to impede the progress

---

[130]Ruge, *Deutschland*, pp. 408, 417–18, 424–25; Ruge, " 'Deutsche Allgemeine Zeitung,' " pp. 42–44; Streisand (pp. 338–39), who, however, belittles the role of the agrarians; Buchta, *Junker*, pp. 136ff.

of socialism outweigh any other motives. The Marxist historians' chief mandate, it will be recalled, is to determine how capitalism could survive in Germany although "objective" conditions called for its overthrow.)[131]

In the light of such implications, other foreign political moves also take on new significance. Economic expansionism becomes a prelude, thinly disguised, to political action: because Germany was unable to revise its boundaries forcibly, it attempted to "dissolve" them by customs unions and other economic arrangements, as one of Stinnes' sons put it in a letter to Hitler. The proposed Austro-German customs union of 1931, a Central European Economic Conference (*Mitteleuropäischer Wirtschaftstag*), and similar projects are seen as parts of this drive, which culminated in the subsequent fascist aggression.[132]

In the same vein, Wolfgang Ruge has found evidence in the late 1920s of a new approach to the "eastern" question. Originating among members of the Catholic nobility who had banking and industrial affiliations, it was taken up later by eastern agrarians and by industrial spokesmen as well. These circles, he notes, proposed to play up the class interests that linked them to the Western powers and Poland in order to establish a common front against Soviet Russia. In practice, this meant that they would no longer focus their aggressive designs on Poland, but would rather seek to destroy first the Soviet regime, joining with the imperialist powers in both east and west, which would allow Germany to rearm for such a campaign. Only after the Soviet regime had been destroyed would Germany, now militarily strong, turn against Poland. Ruge sees his findings confirmed in the marked aloofness the Brüning and Papen governments displayed toward Moscow and, even more unconvincingly, in the German-Polish nonaggression pact that Hitler concluded in 1934. Here confirmation is also found for the Marxist-Leninist thesis of the unbroken continuity of the Weimar and Nazi period, with the Nazis merely escalating Weimar developments.[133]

[131]See Ruge, *Deutschland*, pp. 398ff.; 422ff.; Streisand, pp. 336–37; *GdA*, vol. 4, pp. 303–4; Gossweiler, *Grossbanken*, pp. 369–70; "Hoover-Moratorium," *Swb*, vol. 1, p. 798; but see also Link, *Stabilisierungspolitik*, pp. 492, 495–96. Nussbaum (*Wirtschaft*, pp. 273, 285–86) points out that the average annual reparation payment amounted to less than 2 percent of the national income and thus hardly constituted the crushing burden that Germany claimed it to be.

[132]Ruge, *Deutschland*, pp. 384–85, and the well-documented essays by Ruge and Wolfgang Schumann, "Die Reaktion des deutschen Imperialismus auf Briands Paneuropaplan 1930," *ZfG* 20 (1972): 40ff. (Stinnes quotation on pp. 57–58); also Roswitha Berndt, "Wirtschaftliche Mitteleuropapläne des deutschen Imperialismus (1926–1931)," *WZ Halle* 14 (1965): 227ff.; Berndt, "Die Aussenpolitik der Regierung Brüning im Dienste der Monopole," in *Monopole und Staat*, pp. 127ff.

[133]Ruge, "Die Aussenpolitik der Weimarer Republik und das Problem der europäischen Sicherheit: 1925–1932," *ZfG* 22 (1974): 273ff.

In the face of such projects, the activities of the Communists, that sole counterforce actively fighting for social progress, assume special importance for East German researchers. A comprehensive public works program, proposed by the KPD and to be financed by taxes imposed on the well-to-do, is contrasted with Brüning's pro-monopolist policies of lower wages and reduced social benefits, which subjected the working class to ever new hardships. Similarly, attention is called to a Peasant Aid Program that provided relief for small-scale agriculture at the expense of large landowners and "finance capitalists." With its appeal to the small peasantry, that program was to lay the foundation for a united front of all toilers (*Werktätige*). It would thus pave the way for a broadly based "people's revolution," as distinct from a proletarian one for which the time had not yet come (although one wonders whether the difference was not lost on those for whose benefit it was introduced, because the latter type of revolution was just as remote as the former). Ruge concludes that "as a creative contribution of the German Communists to the coalition policy of the working class in a highly industrialized country [the Peasant Aid Program] has become a historical document." However that may be, the Communists clearly were more conscious of the potentialities of the peasantry as a political ally than were the Social Democrats at that time.[134]

East German researchers have gathered what evidence they could find to demonstrate the impact of these programs. They point to the formation of Communist units in rural areas, regional peasant meetings, and a nationwide peasant congress in January 1932 as proof of such effectiveness. Similarly, they have seized on any indications of a rapprochement between middle-class elements and the workers' movement. The case of Lieutenant Richard Scheringer, who joined the KPD while serving a sentence for pro-Nazi activities in the Reichswehr, is singled out as the most celebrated example. Naturally, the increase of registered party members, from 170,000 in March 1930 to 330,000 in March 1932, also is cited as proof of the growth of the revolutionary movement.[135]

Actually, Communism gained only limited ground during these years, as not only Western accounts but East German ones also make clear. The increase in registered party members loses

[134]See *GdA*, vol. 4, pp. 281–83, 290–93; Ruge, *Deutschland*, pp. 390ff. On Social Democrats, see Gordon A. Craig, *Germany: 1866–1945* (New York, 1978), pp. 500–501.

[135]See Ruge, *Deutschland*, pp. 389, 392; *GdA*, vol. 4, pp. 285–86, 310. The membership figures cited in the text refer to registered members. As *GdA* makes clear, the number of dues-paying members was considerably smaller—136,000 in March 1930, 287,000 in March 1932. See also Bahne, "Kommunistiche Partei" pp. 661–62; Bahne, however, does not distinguish between these two types of members.

much of its significance if viewed against the considerable turn-over of individual memberships. Few new members, moreover, came from middle-class circles, and the case of Lieutenant Sche-ringer remained an exception. Of more than 200 delegates at a national party conference in October 1932, only ten were peasants, vintners, or storekeepers. Nor did electoral gains necessarily sug-gest a notable growth in revolutionary sentiment—many voted for Communists from a spirit of protest without identifying them-selves with the party's basic objectives. Labor's earlier fighting spirit was moreover on the decline: as the economic crisis grew more severe, workers, fearful of losing their jobs, rarely responded to calls for strikes. At the same time, the bulk of the KPD's new recruits were unemployed workers who could not add to Commu-nist strength in the factories. Thus, from 1931 on, no large-scale strike could any longer be organized.[136]

In diagnosing the inadequacy of Communist progress, DDR authors always return to the Communists' inability to rally the working classs in a united front. Ultimately they trace this failure to ideological differences that led KPD and SPD to sharply divergent analyses of the fascist phenomenon. The SPD, it is noted, viewed Nazism as a product of the Depression, a movement of rabid petty bourgeois mobs that would disappear once the economic crisis had run its course. In the SPD's view, therefore, the proper policy was to keep Hitler out of the government until the Nazi wave would once more recede and meanwhile support the Brüning government as the lesser evil. This strategy also fitted in with the Socialists' expecta-tion that capitalism would gradually evolve into socialism by means of parliamentary majority votes and that the wisest policy was not to interefere with this process. Communist activism in this view would do just that and, with its radical goals, was as much a threat to social progress as was Nazism.

To the Communists, such inactivity was intolerable. They maintained that passivity merely abetted the monopolists on the road to fascism. DDR authors also point out that as a product of monopoly capitalism, fascism evolved independently of the De-pression and that the latter merely gave it added momentum. In existence prior to the Depression, it would consequently outlive the crisis, sustained by its sponsors. The Communists therefore insisted that, apart from counteracting Nazi demagoguery and fending off Nazi terror, the only way to keep the monopolists from

[136]See *GdA*, vol. 4, pp. 280, 310–11, 325; Ruge, *Deutschland*, p. 389. Cf. Bahne, "Kommunistische Partei," pp. 661–62; Flechtheim, *Kommunistische Partei*, pp. 171–72; Bracher, *Auflösung*, pp. 266, 478; Bauer, quoted in Leon Trotsky, *Schriften über Deutschland* (Frankfurt, 1971), vol. 4, p. 36. On the party confer-ence see *GdA*, vol. 4, p. 370, according to which the number of delegates exceeded 216; also *Die Antifaschistische Aktion*, ed. Karl (Berlin [East], 1965), p. 47*.

erecting a fascist dictatorship was to fight Brüning, their faithful proto-fascist spokesman, and his main supporters, the SPD and its labor unions; at the proper time, with the help of other repressed and exploited groups, a people's revolution would be launched that would establish a truly democratic order. That such a democratic order would give precedence to social necessities over political freedom, and that hence in this aspect, too, Communist goals differed sharply from Social Democratic expectations, is nowhere mentioned in the East German literature.[137]

The East German analyses help to explain the rationale of the Communist strategy, which has frequently been dismissed as senseless by non-Marxist critics. The KPD argued that the SPD and its unions were the "social mainstay" of the great bourgeoisie inasmuch as no industrial economy can function without the cooperation of labor. Moreover, in trying merely to reform the existing capitalist order, the Social Democrats implicitly upheld that order and blocked the path to a genuine socialist one in which the interests of the masses rather than those of an exploiting bourgeois minority would be paramount. Similarly, it seemed sensible to try to draw the rank and file away from the Nazi party by demonstrating the speciousness of the "socialism" in National Socialism that had attracted the bulk of that following. Yet logical arguments carried little weight with the emotionalized Nazi masses; moreover, the terror of the brawling storm troopers, as Ruge points out, made it all but impossible to reach them ideologically. Nor did sociological expostulations persuade many Social Democrats to risk their jobs and stand up for their rights. Thus the KPD strategy failed to weaken the Nazi party while at the same time deterring the Social Democrats from joining the Communists in a common working-class front.[138]

Yet, the impact of these blunders ought not to be overstressed. When West German critics charge the Communist leadership with "suicidal" folly in its attitude toward the SPD, they assume that the SPD strategy constituted a more effective defense of the Weimar Republic. Thus, Horst Duhnke argues that "for the strengthening of the republic, which in the last analysis was the lesser evil for the Communists, too, parliamentary toleration and an end to the bitter attacks on Social Democracy would have been sufficient." There is no evidence that Weimar democracy could have been saved in this manner. Given the "Marxist" phobia that was sweeping the country, the very existence of any Communist-Socialist cooperation, even on Social Democratic terms, would

---

[137]*GdA*, vol. 4, pp. 238, 277ff., 288–89, 312–14; Ruge, *Deutschland*, pp. 379, 387–88, 394ff.; *Grundriss*, pp. 434–35.

[138]Ruge, *Deutschland*, p. 389. Cf. Mason, *Sozialpolitik*, pp. 56ff., 79–80, 96–98.

have called forth a major political crisis and provided the pretext for a suspension of the Reichstag. From the entrepreneurial viewpoint, the SPD was as much or even more of a threat to entrepreneurial dominance as the KPD, because most unions were aligned with the SPD. Nor would Communist abstention from voting in the Reichstag have saved the Weimar system, as Duhnke suggests on the grounds that it would have given Brüning a solid majority in the Reichstag and thus have rendered him less dependent on Hindenburg and his camarilla. Upper- and middle-class opposition to the Social Democrats and to the parliamentary system was too strong to tolerate such independence, quite apart from Brüning's own incompatible concept of his government mandate. Morever, such inaction would have associated the KPD with Brüning's lopsided economic policies and might have driven its followers into the Nazi camp.

As two East German authors have put it, the Communists scored their gains, not because of the growing misery of the workers, but because they were fighting to relieve that misery. Convinced of the antidemocratic, that is, anti-toiler-oriented character of "bourgeois democracy," the Communists therefore warned that the workers' rights could be saved no longer by parliamentary votes but only by extraparliamentary action—mass protests and strikes against further wage cuts, evictions, and repossessments, by organized self-defense against Nazi terror, and by a concentrated ideological offensive counteracting Nazi and other distortions. Although one cannot be as certain as DDR authors are that such mass activities culminating in a general strike would have saved the republic, they might have provided the one chance to do so, if any such chance existed.[139]

As it was, the difficulties of uniting Communists and Social Democrats in a common front proved insurmountable. The hurdles blocking such cooperation have been explored all the more carefully by East German historians because they find conditions in an allegedly equally monopoly-dominated West Germany calling once again for a united front of all toilers. Intent on deriving lessons from the earlier failure, these probings are not uncritical of the conduct of the Weimar Communists—their sweeping attacks on the SPD as the bourgeoisie's "social mainstay," which in this unqualified form seemed to ignore the Nazis' role altogether, and their explicit insistence on a unified front from below. Such intran-

[139]Flechtheim, *Kommunistische Partei*, pp. 177–79; Bahne, "Kommunistische Partei," pp. 670–71; Duhnke (*KPD*, pp. 31, 38–39, 56–57, 59), whose bewildering accounts reflect his failure to perceive the rationale behind the Communist strategy; Karl and Kücklich, "Zum Kampf der KPD für die antifaschistische Einheitsfront . . . 1932," *BzG* 5 (1963): 871; Ruge, *Deutschland*, pp. 394–95; *Unb. Verg.*, p. 648; also Stampfer, *Vierzehn Jahre*, p. 601.

sigence could only confirm the anti-Communist stance of the SPD leadership and precluded any arrangements even with the SPD's local organizations.

These mistakes are blamed on "sectarian" elements that thwarted the correct strategy of the Marxist-Leninist forces, represented by Ernst Thälmann, Wilhelm Pieck, and Walter Ulbricht. The charges of sectarianism, scattered in various accounts, are vague and contradictory—on the grounds, no doubt, that doctrinal aberrations deserve no detailed attention. What apparently is being held against the deviationists—Heinz Neumann, one of the party's top leaders from 1928 to 1932, and some of his associates—is their failure to pursue proselytizing work among unions and Social Democrats on the grounds that a revolutionary situation was about to develop and would propel non-Communist workers into the Communist camp anyway.[140] Not only was the Neumann faction indulging in a mistaken faith in revolutionary spontaneity, a faith that was abhorrent to the true Leninist, but its call for revolutionary violence also deterred potential allies from joining the Communists. At the same time, the Neumann group also called for greater militancy against the fascists—"Beat the fascists wherever you find them"—all of which might well have provided the government with the hoped-for pretext to outlaw the party, bearing out once again Lenin's warning that individual terror is counterproductive.[141]

Yet, as always, the chief blame for the failure to create a unified front is placed on the Social Democrats—that is, on their leaders. Occasionally the rank and file, too, is blamed, but on the whole East German critics fail to see how closely the policies of the SPD leaders corresponded to the views of most of their followers. As Arthur Rosenberg, a perceptive contemporary observer, has pointed out, the SPD leaders were not forceful enough to simply impose their will on the masses. Moreover, as noted earlier (see chapter 6, pp. 51–52), Marxist-Leninist tenets also postulate that the working class bears the ultimate responsibility for the leaders

[140]There is an indirect confirmation of these charges in the memoirs of Jürgen Kuczynski. In 1931, Kuczynski suggested in two articles that the Depression might end in 1932 and was almost subjected to a party trial for "revisionist defeatism." He escaped being tried by promising that he would make no further predictions of an end to the Depression (Kuczynski, *Memoiren* [Berlin (East), 1975], pp. 224–26).

[141]On the charges against the Neumann group, see, for example, *GdA*, vol. 4, pp. 308, 312ff. Somewhat more specific information is found in Karl and Kücklich, "Zum Kampf," p. 866; "Neumann-Gruppe," *Swb*, vol. 2, pp. 181–82; also Resolution of the Central Committee on the KPD, in *Rundschau über Politik, Wirtschaft, Arbeiterbewegung* 2 (1933): 542. The memoirs of Neumann's life companion, Margarethe Buber-Neumann (*Von Potsdam nach Moskau* [Stuttgart, 1957], pp. 277–79, 286ff.) lack precision and leave many questions unanswered.

it follows. Yet there was never any attempt to dislodge the leaders, and the creation in 1931 of a more militant offshoot of the SPD, the Socialist Workers party, drew no large following away from the SPD.[142]

Whatever the reasons for the Communist failure to rally the working class around its banner, in February 1932 Pieck told the KPD's Central Committee that the party had failed to do so and had been unable to organize mass strikes in protest against Brüning's latest emergency decree. As Pieck pointed out, it was a question not of marshalling the masses for the seizure of power but merely of mobilizing them for a fight against the further reduction of wages. He concluded by warning that without sufficient influence over the masses the KPD might be unable to prevent a Nazi takeover. (Significantly, the speech considers even more important than the possible impact of the KPD's weakness on Germany the repercussions that weakness might have on the international position of the Soviet Union—at a time when Japan was threatening Soviet interests in the Far East, and the Western imperialists, claiming that the Soviet Union was the disturber of peace, might well align themselves with Japan.) Yet writing about that very time, *Geschichte der deutschen Arbeiterbewegung* claims, "The struggle between the working class and all democratic forces on the one hand and the fascist forces on the other was moving toward a climax in the spring of 1932." Ruge even asserts that the powerful impact of the antifascist mass actions in 1932 "brought imperialism in Germany close to the abyss," thus belatedly countenancing the myth spread by the Nazis that they saved Germany from a Communist takeover.[143]

In drawing such conclusions, these writers actually express the contemporary views of the "ultra-leftist" sectarians they are trying so hard to discredit. The Comintern and the "Leninist" fac-

[142]See Eichholtz, in *Monopole und Staat*, pp. 56–57; Haferkorn, "Zum Wesen," p. 139; Ruge, *Deutschland*, pp. 395–97, 413–14, 418–20; *GdA*, vol. 4, pp. 200–303, 312ff., 324, 325–26; Ulbricht, quoted in *ZfG* 8 (1960): 1021; Gossweiler, "Karl Dietrich Brachers 'Auflösung der Weimarer Republik,' " ibid. 6 (1958): 511. On East German views of the role of the SPD, see Berthold, "Zum Kampf der Führung der KPD gegen die faschistische Geschichtsideologie ... 1930 bis 1945," *ZfG* 17 (1969): 691; also *GdA*, vol. 5, p. 463; Kuczynski (*Geschichte*, vol. 5, p. 146), who, contrary to his earlier position (see chapt. 6), does not hold the party rank and file responsible for the SPD's inactivity in this case. For the opposite view, see Rosenberg, *Geschichte*, p. 229. On the DDR evaluation of the present-day situation in West Germany, see Werner Paff, "Zur Aktionseinheitspolitik der Deutschen Kommunistischen Partei 1968–1973," *ZfG* 22 (1974): 489ff., especially p. 492.

[143]See Pieck's statement in *ZfG* 23 (1975): 1435–37; *GdA*, vol. 4, p. 324; Ruge, *Deutschland*, p. 414. For what it is worth, it might also be pointed out as disproving Ruge's claim of the near-victory of the Communists that in the last elections prior to Hitler's appointment, in the state of Lippe in January 1933, the KPD lost 25 percent of the vote that had been cast for it in Lippe in the Reichstag elections of November 1932.

tion of the KPD (with the apparent exception of Thälmann) were much more skeptical about the prospects of an early revolution. The present-day East German stance is not as self-assured as it may seem, however. Something of the old doubts about the actual strength of the working-class movement in 1931–1932 reverberates in the continuing debate as to whether the monopolists' resort to fascism was a sign of their strength or their weakness—a question that is generally answered to the effect that it was both, a temporary reassertion of strength within the context of the general crisis of the capitalist order.[144]

Closer to Fascism:
The Papen and Schleicher Governments

For Marxist historians, the government that succeeded Brüning's constituted another logical step toward an overtly fascist regime. Headed by Franz von Papen, a one-time officer with close ties to heavy industry and the Reichswehr, it was composed of industrial spokesmen, agrarians, bureaucrats, and the army's policy maker, General von Schleicher. In keeping with its class purposes, the Papen cabinet sought to destroy the last remnants of Weimar democracy, deprive the working class of its remaining rights, and launch the country on its imperialist course of rearmament and aggression. Germany, then, was embarking on the decisive struggle over the choice it was facing in the Marxist perspective—fascist dictatorship or defeat of the fascist threat.

True to its mandate, DDR authors note, the Papen government readmitted the Nazi storm troops and elite guards, who had shortly before been disbanded by the Brüning regime under Social Democratic and Center pressure, and let them launch a campaign of terror against the working class. A new Presidential decree provided for a further reduction of unemployment relief payments and other social benefits and an increase in taxes on wages and salaries. The creation of a voluntary labor service was a first step toward Germany's remilitarization. In July the Social Democratic–Centrist government of Prussia was illegally removed from office, de-

---

[144]On the contemporary views of Comintern and KPD concerning the imminence of a revolutionary situation, see Thomas Weingartner, *Stalin und der Aufstieg Hitlers* (Berlin [West], 1970), pp. 49ff., 87ff. On fascism as a sign of capitalist weakness, see "Faschismus," *Swb*, vol. 1, p. 571; Mammach, "Bemerkungen," p. 664; Gossweiler, "Brachers," pp. 521–22; on fascism as a sign of strength, see Haferkorn, "Zum Wesen," pp. 142–43; on fascism as a sign of both strength and weakness, see D. S. Manuilski, quoted by Erwin Lewin, in *BzG* 12 (1970): 54–55; *GdA*, vol. 4, pp. 223, 226–28; Ruge, *Deutschland*, p. 361.

livering the Prussian police into the control of those who were propelling the country toward fascism. The results of new Reichstag elections, revealing the opposition of the bulk of the nation to the Papen regime, were ignored and the Reichstag was dissolved again. An economic decree allowing for the departure from collective wage contracts in return for the hiring of additional workers caused further bitterness. So did the continuing terrorism of the Nazis. Renewed Reichstag elections in early November again repudiated the Papen government, and it was forced to resign.[145]

By Marxist criteria, these developments did not differ basically from the course of events during Brüning's chancellorship. What did distinguish the Papen era in the Marxist perception was the "higher quality" of the fight of the working class against the process of *Faschisierung*. The KPD initiated a new counter-movement, the Antifaschistische Aktion (Antifa), which set out to create a "real" unified front of all democratic forces (Thälmann). It differed from other such attempts because of its professedly supraparty character that was to facilitate joint action by all individuals and organizations "genuinely" willing to fight fascist terrorism, the erosion of democratic rights and institutions, and the privation of the masses of their social gains.[146] The KPD, however, remained opposed to any cooperation with the SPD as a whole and from its first appeal on called for a unified front from below, for the enrollment of individual SPD members and unionists or at best local units of their organizations, willing to "really" fight "Hitler fascism." If through pressures from below the SPD could be forced to join the fight on a nationwide basis, so much the better, but this was not considered a likely prospect. "We leave no uncertainty whatsoever about our unrelenting, principled struggle against Social Democracy," Thälmann told a group of SPD functionaries at a meeting in July 1932. "We Communists do not want 'unity at any price.'" Any approaches made to the SPD outside Antifa, as in the Prussian diet and Reichstag, were made in the expectation of being rejected by the SPD—a fact ignored in the DDR literature.[147]

DDR authors credit Antifa with notable successes—the formation of a large number of local unity committees in which So-

---

[145]See Ruge, *Deutschland*, pp. 431ff.; *GdA*, vol. 4, pp. 334–35, 351, 363–65; Streisand, pp. 341ff. Ruge describes Papen's government as merely a transitory trailblazer for a fascist regime, to be replaced by a Nazi government once the Depression had bottomed out and the Nazi movement had correspondingly peaked and thus could be kept in its proper place by the monopoly bourgeoisie (pp. 432–33). Here again, the wisdom of hindsight outpaces historical analysis.

[146]"Antifaschistische Aktion," *Swb*, vol. 1, pp, 68ff.; Kücklich and Elfriede Liening, "Die Antifaschistitsche Aktion," *BzG* 4 (1962): 874ff.; Karl, *Die Antifaschistische Aktion*; *GdA*, vol. 4, pp. 338ff.

[147]Thälmann and Pieck, in Karl, *Antifasch. Aktion*, pp. 86–87, 213ff. (Thälmann quotation, p. 169); Dimitroff, in *GdA*, vol. 5, p. 463.

cial Democrats, Christian and Socialist trade uinionists, Reichs-
banner members, and nonaffiliated workers worked side by side
with the Communists. Similarly, Antifa organized local defense
units that fought off Nazi assaults and factory and landed-estate
committees that blocked further wage cuts and other infringements. On the national level, these analyses measure Antifa's effectiveness by the gains the Communists scored in the Reichstag
elections in July. Antifa has also been credited with Hitler's debar-
ment from the chancellorship at that time when the Nazis had
emerged as the largest party from the elections, but no attempt has
been made to provide even a modicum of evidence for this assertion, so completely at odds with the known facts.[148] On the other
hand, a wave of strikes, partly Antifa-inspired, did play some role
in emasculating Papen's second economic decree, which allowed
for further wage cuts and the suspension of collective agreements.
The best known of these strikes, into which also Nazi workers
were drawn, tied up Berlin's transportation system for nearly a
week. However, contrary to East German assertions, entrepreneurial objections to the decree—as an unwarranted intrusion in the
economic sphere—contributed at least as much to the nonapplica-
tion of this measure (which eventually was repcalcd by Papen's
successor, General Schleicher). The gain of anothcr 700,000 Communist votes in the Reichstag elections in November is also attributed to Antifa's efforts, as is the resignation of the Papen government shortly after the elections—a claim in keeping with the
thesis that fear of a Communist upsurge inspired all moves of the
ruling class.[149]

While underscoring Antifa's achievements, DDR historians
do not ignore the limits set to its impact. There was not, they
point out, the expected mass influx of the Social Democratic rank
and file that would have enabled Antifa to block the continuing
trend toward an all-out fascist dictatorship by strikes, mass demonstrations, and armed self-defense on a major scale. Nor was there
any chance of joint actions of KPD and SPD, initiated on the
leadership level. Because of their sharply differing analyses of Nazism, as is rightly noted, Communists and Social Democrats also
reacted very differently to a notable Nazi setback in the November
elections. That decline confirmed the Socialists in their conviction
that Nazism was a product of the Depression, was now receding as
the Depression was nearing its end, and thus was no longer a seri-

---

[148]GdA, vol. 4, p. 363; "Kabinett der nationalen Konzentration," *Swb*, vol. 1, p. 886.
[149]Kücklich, "Streik gegen Notverordnungen," *BzG* 13 (1971): 454ff.; Karl, *Antifasch. Aktion*, pp. 40˙ff., 237ff.; *GdA*, vol. 4, pp. 364ff.; Kücklich and Liening,
"Antifasch. Aktion, p. 884, as compared to Ludwig Preller, *Sozialpolitik in der
Weimarer Republik* (Stuttgart, 1949), pp. 416–17; Bracher, *Auflösung*, p. 625.

ous concern. The Communists, on the other hand, viewing Nazism as a monopolist tool, were convinced that the monopolists would continue to foster the Nazis in order to consolidate their dictatorship. The KPD thus saw no cause for rejoicing and kept up its struggle. East German historians find significant confirmation for this view in a petition submitted to President Hindenburg by a group of prominent businessmen and agrarians after the Nazis' electoral setback. The signers urged Hindenburg to appoint Hitler as chancellor—in an obvious effort, it is noted, to save the anti-working class Nazi party from disintegration and to keep labor from recovering its strength in an improving economy.[150]

Correspondingly, the new government, headed by Schleicher, constituted still another monopolist attempt in the Marxist assessment—this one supported mainly by the more flexible electro-chemical industries, as compared to heavy industry—to preserve and make use of the Nazis by taking them into the government, with or without Hitler. The Schleicher government, which was to be based on Nazis, labor unions, and army, in this view aimed at a "military fascism," with its land settlement and public works programs and the projected implementation of these programs by soldier-peasants (Wehrbauern) and a paramilitary Labor Service.[151]

The rapid decline of Schleicher's government was preordained according to the East German accounts by the determination of heavy industry to make Hitler chancellor. Grundriss, in fact, views it as merely another transitory government set up by "influential circles of the ruling class": "Its main task objectively was to give the imperialist forces that backed Hitler and the Nazi party a modicum of time to resolve the differences within Hitler's movement [caused by subleaders like the party's second-in-command, Gregor Strasser, who disagreed with Hitler's strategy of not entering the government except with him, Hitler, as its head] and to

---

[150]See Karl, Antifasch. Aktion, pp. 49*–50*; Ruge, Deutschland, pp. 456–57, 462–63, 466–67; GdA, vol. 4, pp. 380ff.; Gossweiler, "Der Übergang von der Weltwirtschaftskrise zur Rüstungskonjunktur in Deutschland 1933 bis 1934," JWG 2(1968):64; Schreiner, "Die Eingabe deutscher Finanzmagnaten, Monopolisten und Junker an Hindenburg für die Berufung Hitlers zum Reichskanzier," ZfG 4 (1956): 366ff. For DDR authors, the fact that only few major industrialists signed or at least approved the petition does not lessen the significance of the support the industrial leaders gave to the Nazi party, as it does for some Western historians (Turner, "Big Business," p. 66 n. 45; Turner, "Ruhrlade," p. 223; Turner, "Grossunternehmertum und Nationalsozialismus 1930–1933," HZ 221 [1975]: 58–60; Volker Hentschel, Weimars letzte Monate [Düsseldorf, 1978], pp. 69, 133–34). Grundriss (p. 441) reports incorrectly that the signers were above all Rhenish-Westphalian industrialists; Ruge (p. 457) and Streisand (pp. 344–45) list nonsigning sympathizers as signers.

[151]Streisand, p. 368; "Schleicher-Programm," Swb, vol. 2, p. 456; Kuczynski, Geschichte, vol. 5, pp. 129–30; Ruge, Deutschland, pp. 460–61; Nussbaum, Wirtschaft, pp. 381ff.; Haferkorn, "Zum Wesen," p. 140.

prepare the establishment of the fascist dictatorship." Opposed to Schleicher, whom they suspected of socialist leanings, and having no outlet for their production in the export market as the electro-chemical bloc did, the heavy industrialists saw in Hitler the man who would curb labor and provide them with lucrative government orders. As Streisand sees it, heavy industry obtained through its spokesman in the Nazi party, Hermann Göring, the removal (sic!) of Gregor Strasser, the alleged mouthpiece of the electro-chemical industries and an advocate of cooperation with Schleicher. As the agent of Rhenish-Westphalian heavy industrialists, Papen, in turn, resumed contact with Hitler and met with him in Cologne at the house of Baron von Schröder, a banker with close industrial links. A group of industrialists, for their part, saved the Nazi party from disintegration—and the loss of its members to the antifascist camp—by a gift of one million marks. Late in January 1933, when Schleicher too failed to obtain a Reichstag majority for his government, Hindenburg, on Papen's (that is, on heavy industry's) urging, appointed Hitler chancellor of a new government that included industrial and agrarian spokesmen.[152]

The East German accounts of these weeks prior to Hitler's appointment are vague and based on hypotheses designed to bear out the thesis of the key role in that appointment of the "most reactionary, the most chauvinist, the most imperialist elements of finance capitalism." To view the departure of Strasser in terms of a struggle between rival industrial camps—another undocumented assertion—pointedly minimizes Hitler's key role in the Nazi party, in accordance with Marxism's depersonalized concept of history. (As it was, Hitler sensed that he would be the captive of others if he or any associate would enter a government not headed by him, and for this reason he rejected Strasser's proposal to enter the Schleicher government.)[153] Streisand's and Ruge's claims of the approval of Hitler's appointment by specifically named industrialists are not borne out by the available evidence. (Streisand at least admits that he is making an assumption; Ruge did so in the first edition of his book, but no longer does so in the 1978 edition.) There is no evidentiary support either for the allegation of a financial contribution to the Nazi exchequer by these same circles or for

---

[152]See Streisand, pp. 345–46; *GdA*, vol. 4, pp. 381–82; Ruge, *Deutschland*, pp. 464–65, 468–69; *Grundriss*, p. 441; Czichon, *Hitler*, pp. 48–50, as compared to Turner, "Big Business," pp. 63–64; also see Erich Paterna et al., *Deutschland von 1933 bis 1939* (Berlin [East], 1969), pp. 11ff.; Gossweiler, "Brachers" p. 529. Gossweiler stresses, as by implication does Streisand (p. 345) that Papen's actions cannot be explained by irrelevant personal motives such as his resentment of Schleicher, but only by his function as spokesman of monopolist interests that gave him his leverage.

[153]See Dorpalen, *Hindenburg*, pp. 350, 374–75, 380.

the much farther reaching claims of Eberhard Czichon about un-
derstandings between these groups and the Nazis concerning specific tasks that the Nazis would have to accomplish should they
take over the government. Nonetheless, if only comparatively few
business leaders worked directly for a Nazi takeover, many did
help pave the way for it by their persistent call for an authoritarian
regime and by their willingness to concede to the Nazis some role
in such a regime.[154]

At the same time, few DDR authors pay any attention to the
concerted efforts of agrarian circles to replace Schleicher with Hitler (and no one else), and fewer still attribute to these endeavors
the considerable impact that they did have, given Hindenburg's
predisposition toward agrarian concerns. Even authors who do take
notice of the relentless agrarian pressures on the Reich president
ultimately give little, if any, weight to such efforts—in keeping
with both their certainty of the key role of the monopolists in the
era of state-monopolists capitalism and their denial of the import
of Hindenburg as an individual. Thus, after having reported the
frantic efforts of Junker agrarians to prevent, through Hitler's appointment, disclosures of their misuse of government subsidies,
Ruge in his final assessment still blames that appointment solely
on the "most reactionary elements of German finance capitalism."
Similarly, *Grundriss* finds that the "imperialist great bourgeoisie"
established the fascist dictatorship in order to pursue its expansionist policies and unleash a new war of conquest. Gossweiler,
finally, notes that the monopolists played a pivotal role not only in
the political superstructure of the Weimar state but in its socioeconomic basis as well: it was monopolist rigidity, he concludes, that
kept the economy from recovering from the Depression by its own
resilience, as it had after economic crises in premonopolist times.
This time state intervention was required—not as an abnormal,
temporary measure, as "bourgeois" economists would have it, but
as the scientifically inevitable, "lawful" consequence of the structural changes the capitalist system had undergone in the course of
its increasing monopolization.[155] Compared to the key role of the

---

[154]See Ruge, *Deutschland, 1967* ed., pp. 473–74, 1978 ed., pp. 464–65; Streisand,
    p. 346. Czichon's claim (*Hitler*, p. 51 n. 199) that Hitler met with Thyssen and
    Kirdorf after the Cologne meeting with Papen is not supported by the sources he
    cites. On the other hand, Fritz Klein quotes one of the directors of Vereinigte
    Stahlwerke, Ernst Brandi—writing on February 6, 1933, just a week after Hitler's
    appointment as chancellor—as saying that he had been calling for "Hitler's chan-
    cellorship as the only way out" since the previous summer (*ZfG* 21 [1973]: 1523).
    See also Winkler, "Standeideologie," pp. 367ff.; Joachim Radkau, "Industrie und
    Faschismus," *Neue Politische Literatur* 18 (1973): 260.
[155]On agrarian pressures, see Buchta, *Junker*, pp. 149ff.; Ruge, *Deutschland*, pp. 468–
    69; Gossweiler, "Junkertum und Faschismus," *WZ Berlin* 22 (1973): 21; Goss-

industrial and banking monopolies, any actions of the agrarians—
and army leaders—are considered of peripheral significance. At the
same time, this approach again absolves from responsibility all
those millions of Germans without whose support there could not
have been a Nazi takeover.[156]

That a Nazi government was established is explained, however, not only by monopolist manipulations, but once again, in
dialectical interaction, by the failings of the antifascist forces as
well. Again the familiar reasons that prevented the formation of a
unified front are cited, ranging from the illusions rife among peasants and petty bourgeois to "sectarian" influences within the Communist party. These lingered on, it is noted, even after Heinz Neumann's removal from the party directorate; by warning now that
an overt fascist dictatorship had become inevitable, the Neumann
faction impaired the effectiveness of the Antifaschistische Aktion.

The SPD, however, remains the chief culprit. It clung to its
legalist tactics even after the fight against fascism could clearly no
longer be won by legal means. Not only did the SPD leadership bar
all cooperation with Antifa—hardly a surprise in view of Antifa's
attitude toward the SPD—but in Prussia the Social Democratic
ministers and police commissioners also kept harassing the Communists, the defenders of democratic rights and institutions, restricting illegally their right of press freedom, assembly, and demonstration. Even when the Social Democrats had been stripped of
their only remaining power base, the Prussian government and
police, by the illegal military coup of the Papen government, they
still would not join the Communists in calling a general strike.
(The Communists could not organize a general strike on their own
because only a small percentage of their party members were employed at that time.) Instead, the Socialists sought redress through
a complaint to the bourgeois State Constitutional Court (*Staatsge-
richtshof*) and through an appeal to the voters, asking them only

---

weiler does acknowledge the key role of the agrarians because of their influence
on Hindenburg. For non-Marxist accounts, see Horst Gries, "NSDAP und Agrar-
verbände vor 1933," *VfZ* 15 (1967): 373–74; Otto Meissner, *Staatssekretär unter
Ebert-Hindenburg-Hitler* (Hamburg, 1950), pp. 264–66; Dorpalen, *Hindenburg*,
pp. 413–15, 431–32. Cf. Ruge, *Deutschland*, p. 469; *Grundriss*, p. 442; Gossweiler, "Übergang," pp. 59ff. In a curious volte-face, *Geschichte der deutschen
Arbeiterbewegung*, on the other hand, argues that the responsibility for the success of the Nazis rested with the "ruling class and its parties" on the grounds that
it could not show the masses a way out of the crisis and by its policies of
immiseration literally drove millions of desperate toilers into the arms of the
Nazis (which suggests that the great bourgeoisie did not intentionally build up
the Nazi movement) (*GdA*, vol. 4, pp. 328–29).
[156]Ruge, *Deutschland*, p. 472; *GdA*, vol. 4, pp. 385–86; Weissbecker, "Westdeutsche
Presse," pp. 1509–10.

to express their disapproval of Papen's unconstitutional conduct by supporting the Social Democrats in the forthcoming Reichstag elections.[157]

In blaming the SPD for rejecting all collaboration with Antifa, these accounts are less than candid. Antifa never expected such collaboration, convinced that the SPD leadership would not agree to the extraparliamentary mass actions—strikes, demonstrations, self-defense actions—in which the Communists saw the only means to defeat the Nazis.[158] On the other hand, DDR authors once again correctly insist that the Weimar state could no longer be saved by parliamentary means. The Papen government was determined to destroy the republican institutions no matter how peacefully labor would have conducted itself—as Schleicher later admitted, the claim that law and order were threatened in Prussia was merely a pretext to justify the takeover. By then, however, even united mass action could probably no longer have saved the republic; contrary to East German assertions, it is doubtful whether a general strike, as proposed by the KPD against Papen's Prussian coup, would have been effective. (One East German author grants that a general strike would not have been "easy" to endure for the workers, but insists cavalierly that it "cannot be disputed that most of the unemployed would not have acted as strikebreakers and that the unskilled and lazy stormtroopers would not have been able to keep the economy going.")[159]

Still, whatever action was undertaken in those months to counteract the encroachments of the forces on the right was organized by the Communists or with Communist help. DDR historians thus can claim with some justification that "objectively" the Communists, though no supporters of the republic, did more than any other group to defend it against the attacks from the antirepublican right.[160]

This claim loses some of its cogency, however, in the face of a Communist strategy that was based on the premise that no middle ground existed between the dictatorship of the proletariat and a fascist dictatorship and that a bourgeois-semiparliamentary govern-

[157]See Ruge, *Deutschland*, pp. 437–40; Streisand, pp. 341–42; *GdA*, vol. 4, pp. 352ff.; Kücklich, "Streik," p. 454. In late 1932, only 11 percent of all KPD members were employed factory workers; *WZ Berlin* 22 (1973): 129.

[158]See Kücklich and Liening, "Antifasch. Aktion," p. 883; *GdA*, vol. 4, p. 360. On KPD expectations, see the documentation in Karl, *Antifasch. Aktion;* also *GdA*, vol. 5, p. 463.

[159]Petzold, "Der Staatsstreich vom 20. Juli 1932 in Preussen," *ZfG* 4 (1956): 1179ff.; Petzold's retrospective evaluation of the prospects of a general strike can be found in ibid., p. 1175. See also Schleicher's admission, in Hermann Pünder, *Politik in der Reichskanzlei* (Stuttgart, 1961), p. 149.

[160]Kücklich, "Streik," p. 454; Karl, *Antifash. Aktion*, pp. 17*–18*; *GdA*, vol. 4, p. 360; also Paff, "Zur Aktionseinheitspolitik," p. 501.

ment à la Brüning was in effect a fascist dictatorship, too, if as yet not fully developed. Thus, Heinz Neumann and his associates were merely consistent when they made a full turnabout once they realized that a socialist revolution was not imminent and when they warned, as they are charged, that the advent of an overt fascist dictatorship was inevitable and that such a dictatorship was a necessary transitory phase on the road to the dictatorship of the proletariat.[161]

All accounts emphasize rightly, however, that when they warned of the inevitability of a full-fledged fascist dictatorship, Neumann and his circle no longer spoke for the party and that no authorized KPD spokesman ever called the advent of Nazism inevitable, let alone welcomed it as the final phase of monopoly capitalism prior to the Communist takeover. The few utterances to that effect attributed to KPD leaders outside the Neumann faction are either of doubtful authenticity or fail to bear out the claims made for them. There exist, on the other hand, a great many authentic statements made by official KPD and Comintern spokesmen, rejecting the inevitability thesis and warning also that a fascist dictatorship not only might be of long duration but would not necessarily be followed by the socialist order once Nazism had been defeated.[162]

If, then, Communist opposition to the Nazis was unsuccessful, it was not for lack of effort. The East German accounts have established that the KPD fought Nazism as best it knew, right up to Hitler's appointment as chancellor—and beyond. The ineffectiveness of these efforts, however, cannot be blamed only on "sectarian" deviations within the party's own ranks, on the "betrayal" of the Social Democratic leadership, or even on the fatuous Communist attacks on the Social Democrats. Ultimately it followed from the Communists' and, for that matter, the Social Democrats' inability to present to the masses a program that captured the latter's imagination. Thus, neither party was able to harness that powerful protest wave which was sweeping the country and of which the Nazis became the main beneficiaries. Although SPD and KPD betweem them retained their following, they, unlike the Nazis, failed to attract the uncommitted, including millions of

[161] Geyer, "Sowjetrussland," pp. 32–33.
[162] See Gossweiler, "Brachers," p. 516; Karl, *Antifasch. Aktion,* pp. 17*–18*. The most frequently quoted statements in support of the inevitability thesis, by Neumann's associate Hermann Remmele and by the Comintern spokesman Dimitri Manuilski, do not make this point (cf. Duhnke, *KPD,* pp. 27 n. 52, 35–36; statements of dubious authenticity, ibid., pp. 27–28). For statements rejecting the inevitability thesis and that of fascism as the trailblazer of Communism, see Knorin, quoted in Bahne, "Kommunistische Partei," p. 677 n. 6; Manuilski, quoted in *BzG* 12 (1970): 55; Thälmann, quoted by Flechtheim, *Kommunistische Partei,* p. 166; Thälmann, quoted in *GdA,* vol. 5, p. 447.

workers, who until then had stayed out of politics. But concomitantly the working class as a whole shares in the responsibility for the fate that befell it: in a time of crisis it allowed itself to be torn by disunity rather than close ranks and unite in defense of its rights. Of this failure, however, there is hardly a hint in the East German analyses, for it implies that once again the masses had failed to be makers of history.[163]

[163]On this point, see Rosenberg, *Geschichte*, p. 176; also Mason, *Sozialpolitik*, pp. 55ff., 63ff. Streisand (p. 346) hints at the responsibility of the workers by quoting a poem by Johannes R. Becher, which was published during those days and which warned that whoever remained inactive bore some responsibility ("trägt Schuld daran") for the continuing murders.

8

The Era of
State-Monopoly Capitalism

The Fascist Period

The Theoretical Basis

JANUARY 30, 1933, THE DAY OF Hitler's appointment as chancellor, does not mark a major break in Marxist accounts. The
event is viewed as the culmination of a process long in the making:
the concealed dictatorship of the monopoly bourgeoisie, ever less
thinly disguised until then, was now transformed into an overt
terrorist one, dominated by the "most reactionary, chauvinist, and
imperialist" elements of that same class. In this view, the question
of the legality of the appointment does not arise. If Western historians have challenged the constitutionality of the act by which Hitler, the sworn enemy of the Weimar constitution, was entrusted
with the task of upholding it, East German scholars maintain that
fascism was an organic outgrowth of bourgeois-parliamentary democracy; its advent, therefore, did not violate the spirit of the
Weimar constitution. What did change was the form in which finance capitalism—that is, the industrial and banking monopolies—asserted their power, not the substance of that monopolist
power. No accident, no demons or inscrutable destiny accounted
for these developments, all could be explained rationally.[1]

The conclusion that the Nazi ascendancy consitituted no
radical break with the past rests on the thesis that the advent of
the Nazis did not signal any change in the socioeconomic basis
on which the Weimar Republic had rested. In Eichholtz's words,
"Fascism represents no separate socioeconomic formation, no new
phase within the capitalist social order; its economic foundations
and trends are monopoly-capitalistic, imperialistic." Fascism thus
is seen as a phenomenon of the late phase of capitalism, by which
that historically obsolete and declining system seeks to preserve

[1]Kurt Gossweiler, "Karl Dietrich Brachers 'Auflösung der Weimarer Republik,' "
ZfG 6 (1958): 516 n. 26; Erich Paterna et al., *Deutschland von 1933 bis 1939*
(Berlin [East], 1969), pp. 90ff.; *Grundriss*, p. 443; Eichholtz, "Probleme," p. 103;
also *Anatomie des Krieges*, ed. Eichholtz and Schumann (Berlin [East], 1969),
pp. 9–10.

and strengthen its weakened rule and roll back the inevitable transition to the socialist order that began with the Bolshevik Revolution.[2]

In this view, then, the terror that descended on Germany was perpetrated by the "Hitler fascists," not on their own, but on behalf of the most ruthless among the monopolists. The latter had the fascists crush the revolutionary workers' movement and reduce labor to a helpless tool. At the same time, the fascists, now in control of the state apparatus, were to provide their sponsors with profitable government orders and prepare for and eventually go to war to obtain a redistribution of the world in favor of Germany's monopoly capitalists. DDR authors even insist that there was an obvious operation of historical law in the use of the Nazis by the monopolists. Confronted with the "really deadly danger" (in Ernstgert Kalbe's words) of the revolutionary working-class movement, the monopolists could protect their domestic power and profits only by the ruthless suppression of labor. In addition, once a monopoly held unchallenged sway at home, it had to rid itself also of its foreign competitors if it was to become a full-fledged monopoly and keep expanding its profits. Yet, whereas in the era of free competition, rivals had been eliminated by greater productivity, higher efficiency, and qualitative superiority, in the monopolist age domestic competitors were bought out, brought into the fold by government fiat, or forcibly closed. Foreign ones, in turn, were wrecked economically or forced out by war. The violence-prone, terrorist Nazis seemed best suited to help the most aggressive sector of the monopoly bourgeoisie attain these goals.

Among the victims of this process, then, were large parts of the bourgeoisie, too, especially its nonmonopolist strata. The beneficiaries of the fascist dictatorship, on the other hand, were reduced to an ever-narrowing circle. Fascism thus stood unmasked as the sharpest negation of any democracy. Given its thrust toward centrally planned production, however, it was also an inevitable milestone on the dialectical road toward socialism.[3]

As for the *form* that relations between the monopolist princi-

---

[2]Paterna et al., *Deutschland*, vol. 5, p. 11; Eichholtz, "Probleme," p. 103; Eichholtz, in *Monopole und Staat*, p. 34.

[3]See Streisand, pp. 349–50; Paterna et al., *Deutschland*, pp. 91ff., 110; *GdA*, vol.5, pp. 11–12, 55; Kuczynski, *Geschichte*, vol. 6, pp. 59–61; Eichholtz, "Probleme," pp. 108–9; Gerhard Förster et al., in *ZfG* 18 (1970): suppl., pp. 575–76; Ernstgert Kalbe, "Die Rolle der Reichstagsbrandprovokation bei der Konsolidierung der faschistischen Diktatur in Deutschland," ibid. 8 (1960): 1026. Attempts have been made to trace back the world-conquest plans ascribed to big business after Hitler's takeover to some statement made by a banker or industrialist in Weimar days, but these statements are much too vague to establish such a connection. See, for example, the remarks of Dr. Werner Kehl, a director of the Deutsche Bank, quoted by Gossweiler, "Bracher," p. 70; see also those of Albert Vögler, chairman of the board of Vereinigte Stahlwerke, ibid., p. 63.

pals and their Nazi agents assumed, analyses of that relationship take their departure from the postulate that the fascist system constitutes the extreme phase of state-monopolist capitalism. Here again (see chapter 6, pp. 273–74) the question arises as to the respective weight of the constituent elements of this partnership: it is described, respectively, as one between friends and accomplices, with the leaders of the monopolies playing the determining role as the ideological, political, and material sponsors and supporters of the Nazis (Drobisch); as one in which the supremacy of the monopolists was ensured by the inclusion of the Nazi leaders as fellow monopolists—Göring as the head of one of the world's largest iron and steel trusts, Hitler as the largest publisher (!), Himmler as the leading landowner—while the monopolists themselves took over key posts in the state (Kuczynski); or as one in which the state functioned as the "executive committee of the monopoly bourgeoisie" (Eichholtz).[4]

The two facets these definitions all share are basic to the Marxist-Leninist definition of the Nazi-business relationship: the preservation of the capitalist system and the dominance of the monopolies in this relationship—although some authors acknowledge that Nazi party and state enjoyed a measure of relative independence.[5] The preservation of the capitalist order is deduced from the apparent retention of all essential characteristics of capitalism—"private capitalist ownership of the means of production, private appropriation of the results of production, and the exploitation of the wage-earning workers by the owners of the means of production."[6] As a Trotskyite author has put it—and on this point Leninists would agree with him—

> It is pointless to find out whether Krupp or Thyssen faced Hitler with enthusiasm, reserve, or disgust at one point or another of his rule. What matters is to determine whether the Hitler dictatorship preserved or destroyed, consolidated or undermined the social institutions of private property of the means of production and the subordination of the toilers forced to sell their labor to the domination of capitalism. The historical balance sheet seems unequivocal to us in this respect.

The Nazi regime, he concludes, conformed to the "inherent laws of development of the capitalist mode of production."[7] Because that

[4]Drobisch, "Der Freundeskreis Himmler," *ZfG* 8 (1960): 327; Kuczynski, *Geschichte*, pp. 35–36, 38–39; but also see vol. 16, pp. 138ff., where Kuczynski concedes to Göring a quite independent role. On this aspect, see also Streisand, in *Monopole und Staat*, p. 163, and the text later in this chapter; Eichholtz, in ibid., p. 194; Eichholtz, "Probleme," pp. 108ff.
[5]Ruge, review, *ZfG* 21 (1973): 1521; *Unb. Verg.*, p. 342.
[6]"Kapitalismus," *Swb*, vol. 1, p. 898.
[7]Ernest Mandel, in his introduction to Leo Trotzky, *Schriften über Deutschland* (Frankfurt, 1971), vol. 1, pp. 14–15. Cf. Eichholtz, "Probleme," p. 124; Kuczynski, *Geschichte*, vol. 6, pp. 22ff.

mode of production was being preserved, it followed that capitalists must also be in political control. To grant the Nazis a status
separate from and above the monopoly-bourgeoisie, the argument
runs, would mean to separate politics from the economy, superstructure from foundation—a denial of the fundamental tenets of
dialectical materialism.[8]

But did the great bourgeoisie really play that dominant role?
Its power supposedly rested on its ownership and control of the key
segment of the means of production. That source of power, however, was steadily being reduced during the Nazi era. Property,
according to the definition of *Wörterbuch der marxistisch-leninistischen Soziologie*, connoted "unrestricted disposal and use of
things," yet under the Nazi regime entrepreneurs, both large and
small, gradually lost the power to make use of their property as
they wished.[9] Although the mechanics of production remained private and entrepreneurial, the scope and direction of that production were increasingly circumscribed by the government. In fact, as
DDR authors themselves admit, government orders became a constituent element of the state-monopolist economy, and the "command economy" that thus evolved, with its dependence on government orders, reinforced the leverage of the government.[10] Far from
being the master of either party or government, business resorted
to bribes and other types of manipulation to secure government
orders. It was also forced to make continued donations to the Nazi
party and its affiliated organizations and to groups such as the
Freundeskreis Himmler, not only in order to promote business but
also in order to avoid "trouble with the Gestapo" and other such
hazards.[11] As Arthur Schweitzer, an American economist, has

[8]Elfriede Lewerenz, *Die Analyse des Faschismus durch die Kommunistische Internationale* (Frankfurt, 1975), p. 44.
[9]See "Eigentum," *Wörterbuch*, p. 96. As one West German social scientist puts it,
"the relations between the [National Socialist] state and the subjects of the economy were determined by the comprehensive claim to dominance by the state. To
its goals all economic forces had to subordinate themselves." Dieter Swatek, *Un-
ternehmenskonzentration als Ergebnis und Mittel nationalsozialistischer Wirtschaftspolitik* (Berlin [West], 1972), p. 45. Also Winkler, *Revolution*, pp. 99–100.
[10]See Eichholtz, "Probleme," p. 111; also Gossweiler, "Der Übergang von der Weltwirtschaftskrise zur Rüstungskonjunktur in Deutschland 1933 bis 1934," *JWG* 2
(1968): 59ff.; Gossweiler attributes the permanence of government orders to the
inability of state-monopolist economies to overcome crises without continued
state intervention.
[11]See Franz Neumann, *Behemoth* (New York, 1966), pp. 293, 356–58, 360–61. On
bribes and other manipulations, see the essays on the Deutsche Bank, the
Deutsche Continental-Gas-Gesellschaft, and the Zeiss-Konzern in *Der deutsche
Imperialismus und der zweite Weltkreig* (Berlin [East], 1961), vol. 2. These facts
have, of course, also been noted by West German historians; see Bracher, Sauer,
and Schulz, *Die nationalsozialistische Machtergreifung* (Cologne, 1960), pp.
649–50, concerning the Hamburg-America Line. On the payment of protection
money, see the testimony of Otto Ohlendorff, in *TWC*, vol. 6, pp. 297–98; see

noted, "this financial backing was not a payment for services expected or received; rather, it was a form of protection money, voluntarily offered and readily paid for being exempted from the violence of the SA as well as from the spy system and concentration
camps of the Gestapo." Actually, these payments were not entirely
voluntary; when business tried to reduce them in 1939, it was
threatened with compulsory collections and had to keep paying the
full amount. Yet Klaus Drobisch, after having conceded that such
contributions were requested from rather than donated by businessmen and were considered by the latter as bribes and insurance
premiums against difficulties with the Gestapo, still concludes:
"No, the masters of the monopolies did not act under pressure. In
the Nazi state they saw their instrument with which they pursued
their world-conquering and repressive objectives."[12]

Thus, the insistence of East German authors that the "financial potentates" ("die Finanzgewaltigen") determined the policies
of the Hitler government cannot be based on their ownership or
control of the means of production. That control was threatened
from the early days of the Nazi regime, and the alleged power
brokers tried to preserve it by voluntarily reorganizing the sectors
of the economy under their jurisdiction in accordance with the
postulates of the Nazis. In turn, the government took a number of
measures that granted the major industrial concerns greater scope
in the sphere of production, thus assuring industry's whole-hearted
cooperation within the government's framework.[13]

The economy also failed to fully meet another criterion of
capitalism—the "private appropriation of the results of production"—because a law enacted in 1934 prohibited the distribution
of dividends over 8 percent. According to Kuczynski and Mottek,
this law strengthened the position of the monopolists: they could
now retain large sums of money that would otherwise have been
paid to stockholders, and they could reinvest these sums in their

---

also the revealing letter of Fritz Kranefuss to Heinrich Himmler, April 21, 1943,
ibid., pp. 266–68; Arthur Schweitzer, "Business Power in the Nazi Regime,"
Zeitschrift für Nationalökonomie 20 (1960): 438–39.

[12]Letter from Krupp to Schacht, May 29, 1933, in IMT, vol. 35, pp. 22–23;
Schweitzer, *Big Business in the Third Reich* (Bloomington, 1964), pp. 35–36;
Schweitzer, "Business Power," pp. 436ff.; Drobisch, "Der Freundeskreis Himm-
ler," pp. 316–18.

[13]See Krupp's letter to Hitler, April 25, 1933, in IMT, vol. 35, pp. 23ff.; Udo Wengst,
"Der Reichsverband der Deutschen Industrie in den ersten Monaten des Dritten
Reiches," *VfZ* 28 (1980): 94ff. For an interesting sidelight on Hitler's high-handed
treatment of such leading industrialists as Krupp and Siemens, see the scene
described in a letter from Ernest Jackh to Henry Goldman, May 3, 1933, in Ernest
Jackh, *The War for Man's Soul* (New York, 1943), pp. 94–95. On the government-
industry relationship during the Nazi era, see the perceptive account of Joachim
Radkau, in Hallgarten and Radkau, *Deutsche Industrie und Politik von Bismarck
bis heute* (Frankfurt, 1974), pp. 225ff.

concerns. At the same time, both authors point out, the monopoly leaders could reimburse themselves for their own diminished dividends by raising their salaries and granting themselves additional perquisites.[14] Yet because, here again, the reinvestment was subject to government plans and requirements, the "appropriation of the results of production" was hardly entirely private.

The fact is that economic power is not only derived from legal ownership or control of the means of production but can well rest on political power backed by physical force. This had been established already by Engels. "Why do we fight for the dictatorship of the proletariat if political power is economically impotent?" he once asked, and his answer was, "Force (that is, state power) is also an economic power!"[15] Hitler merely implemented that view when he wrote in his famed "Memorandum about the Tasks of a Four-Year Plan" in 1936: "The ministry of economics has only to establish the tasks of the nation's economy, and private enterprise has to fulfill them. But if private enterprise considers itself incapable of doing so, the National Socialist state will know how to solve these tasks on its own. . . . The German economy is not going to perish, but rather a few entrepreneurs."[16] This was the strategy he pursued; to show that that strategy was not his, but ultimately that of the economic leaders would have required proof of a cause-and-effect relationship between big-business goals and government policies. By their own admission, DDR authors have failed so far to furnish such proof.[17] One Soviet scholar, A. A. Galkin, has recognized the true nature of the Nazi-business relationship when he writes:

> In Nazi Germany the possibilities for the monopolies to influence state decisions were limited. The totalitarian state, created by Hitler, by its very essence excluded dualism at least in the political sphere. Having taken power into its hands, the fascist leadership sought to make it absolute, and therefore it liquidated any manifestation of independence. The regime established by the Nazis served the interests of the monopolies, but it was not a plaything in their hands. If it had only considered them, it would not have had its freedom for political and especially social maneuvering and would not have fulfilled its socio-political function.
>
> Therefore the transfer of power to the fascist regime brought with it the subordination of the monopolies to this regime in the name of the preservation and expansion of their position. Thus there could be

---

[14]Kuczynski, *Geschichte*, vol. 6, pp. 18, 22–23; Mottek et al., vol. 3, pp. 305–6.
[15]Letter from Engels to Joseph Bloch, September 21–22, 1890, in Robert Tucker, ed., *The Marx-Engels Reader*, 2d. ed. (New York, 1978), p. 765. Cf MEW, vol. 37, pp. 462–65.
[16]Hitler statement, in *VfZ* 3 (1955): 209.
[17]Eichholtz, "Zu einigen Fragen," pp. 72–73; Klein, in *ZfG* 23 (1975): 488–89. See also below in this chapter.

no question of their simply giving orders to the group in power whose representatives had themselves become great industrialists or at least well-to-do people. All that could be done was to meld further with the political and state apparatus and loyally cooperate with it. This tactic the German monopolists chose. A great many, of course, were not pleased.[18]

So far no East German author has advanced such views. The prevailing opinion instead clings to the tenet that, given the existing production relations, the Nazis were, whether they wished to be or not, the instruments of monopolist interests. It is within this conceptual framework that East German historiography analyzes the Nazi period.

The Nazi Party and the Monopolies: From Hitler's Appointment as Chancellor to the Blood Purge of June 1934

The Hitler government thus is assessed in terms of the mandate it allegedly got from its monopolist sponsors. By these standards it did the expected. The working class was suppressed by new curbs on the freedom of press and assembly and terrorist attacks on KPD and SPD members and offices. There followed mass roundups of the leaders of the two parties after the Reichstag fire, which DDR authors are convinced was laid by the Nazis themselves. At the same time, the last remnants of bourgeois democracy were eroded through terror, pseudo-legal decrees, and the Enabling Act of March 1933, passed by a newly elected Reichstag, from which all Communists had been excluded. This act deprived the Reichstag of what power it had had and allowed the regime to consolidate its position. Armed with the act, the government purged the bureaucracy of "unreliable" elements, subjected the states to its direct control, disbanded labor unions and political parties, and extended

[18]See A. A. Galkin, *Sotsiologiya neofashizma* (Moscow, 1971), p. 41. I am indebted to Dr. Myron W. Hedlin for the translation of this passage. Going much farther, Nikolai Bukharin, the Soviet theorist, argued in the 1920s that a "new ruling class," based not on private property, but on "monopolistic" authority and privilege, might arise in the Soviet Union. While Bukharin, and later Milovan Djilas (in *The New Class*), predicated the emergence of such a class on the abolition of private property in the means of production, a Soviet philosopher, Alexander Bogdanov, concluded that organizational control of the economy was the basis of political power and that such control could be attained by a ruling group even if property remained private (as it did in Nazi Germany). See Stephen A. Cohen, *Bukharin and the Bolshevik Revolution* (New York, 1973), pp. 143–44. Because Bogdanov's views are not incompatible with the fundamental tenets of Marxism and merely postulate a shift in the protagonists of the class struggle, it remains to be seen whether they may not some day be adopted by Marxist scholars as providing the basis for a more realistic analysis of Nazism.

its dominance to virtually all spheres of activity. It thus provided the most aggressive circles of the German great bourgeoisie with a tightly controlled domestic foundation for their imperialist foreign policy.[19]

In this context, DDR authors have devoted special attention to the relationship between the Nazi regime and its alleged principals. The facts of that relationship, however, did not bear out their thesis. Rather than back "its" government, the Reich League of German Industry treated it with notable reserve, announcing that "industry's attitude toward the new government would depend on the latter's economic policies." Kurt Pätzold seeks to explain this aloofness by attributing it to industry's uncertainty as to whether the Hitler regime would be able to stay in power—an odd way of dealing with a government that supposedly was industry's own creation.[20]

On the other hand, much is made of a meeting of Hitler and Göring with leading industrialists late in February 1933 that yielded the Nazis more than two million marks in funds for the forthcoming Reichstag elections. It is taken for granted that these lavish donations constituted an endorsement of Hitler and, beyond that, a payment for services rendered so far in the terrorizing of labor. The possibility is ignored that some of these contributions might have been meant as insurance premiums to keep friendly a government that, as Hitler made clear at that gathering, would stay in power no matter what the outcome of the elections; other donors, again, may well have been motivated by fear in the climate of terror that was pervading the country.

In a memorandum of Gustav Krupp, chairman of the Reich League of German Industry, in which he summed up his reply to Hitler on behalf of the attending industrialists, he expressed his general, though not unreserved, agreement with Hitler's views; the account does not convey the impression of Krupp talking to someone who could be expected as a matter of course to consider industry's interests, and a similar ambivalence is reflected in the account of another participant. The roles of principal and agent seemed even more clearly reversed when the presidium of the Reich League of German Industry promised after the passage of the Enabling Act that it would collaborate with the government "to the best of its ability." Again, Pätzold has no difficulty in reconciling this pledge with the "true" role of the monopolies: "To be sure, this wording turned the real situation around, for Hitler did not

---

[19]Streisand, pp. 352ff.; Paterna et al., *Deutschland*, pp. 212ff.; *GdA*, vol. 5, p. 25; Kalbe, "Rolle," p. 1042.
[20]Pätzold, in Paterna et al., *Deutschland*, pp. 32–33; as compared to Wengst, "Reichsverband," pp. 95–96.

take monopoly capitalism into his service; rather, the finance bourgeoisie had taken fascism into its service. The point was, here as in all similar statements, to reinforce the illusion of the supra-party character of the government and the commitment of the fascist state to the nation as a whole."[21] Similarly, when Krupp declared some six months later as chairman of Reichsstand Industrie, a newly created catchall organization of industrial entrepreneurs, that it was necessary to "fully align the new organization with the political goals of the Reich government," this again is interpreted as assisting the effort to "vigorously develop the state-monopolist system of dominance" (in which supposedly the monopolies rather than the government were to be the determinant force).[22]

The gradual subordination of business to government was less apparent at first because it was mitigated by a parallelism of interests between industry, armed forces, and Nazi leaders. Industry, especially the sector producing capital goods, needed government orders for its recovery and further growth; Nazi leaders and armed forces needed the cooperation of industry to carry out their rearmament plans. Their dependence on industry secured for the latter a relative autonomy that survived even the subordination of the economy as a whole to the Reich minister of economics (by the Law for the Preparation of the Organic Structure of the German Economy). Yet this relative freedom did not exempt industry from direct governmental controls and intervention, most notably in matters pertaining to Germany's autarky, such as the production of synthetic gasoline, textiles, and cellulose.[23]

Industrialists, in turn, were anxious to secure as many orders as possible and they did not hesitate to present plans of their own in order to generate such orders. Yet such endeavors did not make them shapers of policies. If, as technical experts, they had some influence on the implementation of the Nazis' and army's plans, it soon became evident that their advice would be heeded only as long as they could be expected to carry out these plans. Nonetheless, Erich Paterna maintains that when in December 1933 the government issued a law institutionalizing the ascendancy of the

---

[21]Pätzold, in Paterna et al., *Deutschland*, pp. 25–26; Streisand, pp. 356–57; Krupp memorandum of February 22, 1933, in IMT, vol. 35, p. 48; memorandum of Martin Blank, and Fritz Springorum to Paul Reusch, February 21, 1933, in *Archiv für Sozialgeschichte* 13 (1973): 477ff.; Wengst, "Reichsverband," pp. 98ff.

[22]*Deutschland im zweiten Weltkreig*, ed. by Gerhart Hass et al. (Berlin [East], 1974), vol. 1, p. 74.

[23]On the increasing subordination of business to Nazi objectives, see in particular Ingeborg Esenwein-Rothe, *Die Wirtschaftsverbände von 1933 bis 1945* (Berlin [West], 1965), pp. 10, 46, 49–50, 55, and *passim*, with good documentation; also Martin Broszat, *Der Staat Hitlers* (Munich, 1971), pp. 223ff.; Wolfram Fischer, *Deutsche Wirtschaftspolitik: 1918–1945* (Opladen, 1968), pp. 81–82.

Nazi party over the state, this was an "expression of zealous but lastly illusory efforts on the part of the Nazi leaders to rise above their role as agents of the dominant monopolist class into the position of irremovable members of the ruling class. . . . Actually, the recognition of the Nazi party as the one party on which the state rested merely stated in legal terms the need of monopoly capitalism for an effectively organized mass foundation of the fascist dictatorship and for its monopolization of political power."[24]

Although this view of the Nazi-business relationship reflects doctrine rather than reality, analyses of the position of big business vis-à-vis small and middle entrepreneurs and business's relations with labor are factual and perceptive. Here, as is noted, the large concerns indeed did hold sway. Immediate help had been promised to small and middle-sized businesses, from whose ranks the Nazis had drawn a large part of their following. Yet, many of these firms were forced into compulsory cartels under big business leadership if they were not compelled to close altogether. There was also discrimination against smaller businesses in the allocation of scarce materials and foreign exchange, which enhanced further the competitive strength of the major entrepreneurs. Similarly, banks and department stores, prime targets of Nazi attacks in pregovernment days, were left untouched. (In the case of Jewish-owned enterprises, there was merely a transfer of ownership, mostly to large concerns, but no structural change.) Nor was there a "breaking of interest slavery," as the Nazi program had promised. The one success small business scored—a "Law for the Protection of the Retail Trade"—prohibited the opening not only of new department stores but also of small retail shops. In August 1933 the Nazi organization catering to small tradesmen, the Kampfbund für den gewerblichen Mittelstand, was dissolved on Hitler's orders. "The Kampfbund," notes Manfred Ohlsen, "failed above all because . . . as a fascist organization it could never become an effective interest organization apart from large-scale capitalism. When the Kampfbund dared to go beyond its specific mandate [of converting the petty bourgeoisie to Nazism and keeping it in its place], it was made to feel the real distribution of power in the fascist order of things. . . . " Yet, notwithstanding complaints from large concerns about self-assertive small businessmen who in the early days of the Nazi regime seized control of chambers of commerce and trade organizations or tried to close dime and department stores, the decision to

[24]Paterna et al., *Deutschland*, pp. 48–50, 97 (quotation). Cf. on the non-Marxist side, Dieter Petzina, "Hitler und die deutsche Industrie," *GWU* 17 (1966): 487–88; Petzina, "Hauptprobleme der deutschen Wirtschaftspolitik 1932–33," *VfZ* 15 (1967): 40–41, 45–50, with much concrete information on the shaping of economic policy during that period; Schulz, in Bracher et al., *Machtergreifung*, pp. 630–32.

curb such actions was Hitler's. He intervened because his plans required a tightly organized, hierarchically structured economy not torn by conflicting interests. Large-scale concerns, moreover, were more useful to him than small enterprises in terms of efficiency and productive capacity. In the case of an output focused on capital goods and arms, as he needed it, large-scale production, in fact, was imperative.[25]

While within the bourgeois camp a small sector thus triumphed over the rest, in the class struggle against the workers DDR authors find all businesses, large and small, in a greatly strengthened position. The government's antilabor measures culminated in a law subjecting the workers to the orders of a "plant leader," either owner or manager, with sweeping powers. This "Law Regulating National Labor" also cancelled all wage contracts and allowed the plant leader, with the consent of a governmental "trustee of labor," to set new wages. The East German analyses conclude that this emasculation of the workers, along with the benefits derived from the improved economic conditions, reconciled the smaller entrepreneurs to their subordinate lot. Thus corrupted, Ohlsen explains, they let themsleves be misled by the Nazis into a sterile anti-Communist stance and submitted to the monopolists rather than ally themselves with the only consistently antimonopolist force—the working class. To the workers, in turn, their social and economic disenfranchisement was made more palatable by the rapid decrease in unemployment and the greater job security that they enjoyed.[26]

In most discussions, however, the point is made that the rise in employment was not a goal that was its own justification, but a political necessity that could conveniently be resolved by the pursuit of an objective much closer to the heart of the monopoly bourgeoisie—rearmament. As *Geschichte der deutschen Arbeiterbewegung* notes, "unemployment in Germany decreased above all in proportion to the extent to which fascist imperialism started up its preparations for war and built up its armies of aggression." Similarly, Kurt Gossweiler concludes that because of the rigidity of monopolist price and production policy the natural upswing of the economy remained limited and that only government orders could sustain its momentum. Such orders, moreover, did not spark a new self-propelling improvement; because of monopolist constraints,

[25]Paterna et al., *Deutschland*, pp. 49ff.; *GdA*, vol. 5, pp. 58–59; Manfred Ohlsen, " 'Ständischer Aufbau' und Monopole 1933–34," *ZfG* 22 (1974): 28ff. (quotation on p. 42). Cf. Bracher et al., *Machtergreifung*, pp. 639–40, 644; Holborn, vol. 3, pp. 758–59; Mason, "The Primacy of Politics: Politics and Economics in National Socialist Germany," in *The Nature of Fascism*, ed. S. J. Woolf (New York, 1968), p. 174; Neumann, *Behemoth*, pp. 264, 266, 274–75.

[26]Paterna et al., *Deutschland*, pp. 52, 98–99; Ohlsen, " 'Ständischer Aufbau,' " p. 46; *GdA*, vol. 5, pp. 75–76.

the economy could be kept functioning only by continued government orders. Rather than combat such restrictive practices, Gossweiler notes, the fascist regime took advantage of them; it did not
improve economic conditions as an end in itself, but in order to
launch its armament program which, as an added boon, ended unemployment as well.[27]

Agriculture, too, was to make its optimal contribution to war-
making purposes. The Junkers, Gossweiler points out, were as war-
minded as the monopoly bourgeoisie, quite apart from the fact that
they were beholden to the monopolists, who through their chemical, machine-building, food-processing, and banking concerns had a
firm hold on agriculture as well as other business. Because of their
shared martial goals and in keeping with the class nature of fascism, DDR analyses stress, estate owners and larger farmers were
accorded privileged treatment at the expense of small peasants and
rural laborers. As part of the country's preparation for war, all
agrarian producers were, moreover, supervised by the Reich Nutri-
tion Estate, whose officers, again in keeping with the class basis of
"Hitler fascism," were estate owners, large farmers, and representatives of major banks and industrial enterprises with agricultural
ties.

East German historians find it equally consistent with this
predominance of large-scale agrarian and monopolist interests that
Nazi promises of land reform and peasant resettlement were
quickly discarded in favor of the retention of larger holdings. The
fact that large landed properties were also the most efficient producers of food in a war-oriented economy rounded out fittingly the
reasons marshalled on behalf of their preservation.[28]

Increased food production became, in fact, a necessity almost
from the day of the Nazi takeover. The armament program required growing raw-material imports that soon exhausted Germany's meager foreign exchange reserves. To East German histori-

[27]*GdA*, vol. 5, pp. 74–75; Gossweiler, "Übergang," pp. 56ff.; Paterna et al., *Deutschland*, pp. 54ff.; also Mottek et al., vol. 3, p. 309, and Christine Böhm, "Zur Entwicklung der Arbeitslosigkeit und zur Lage der Notstandsarbeiter im faschistischen Deutschland 1933 bis 1934," *WZ Berlin* 22 (1973): 67ff. On the non-Marxist
side, see Petzina, "Hauptprobleme," pp. 38ff. Petzina, too, emphasizes that rearmament was Hitler's main goal, but he also stresses Hitler's awareness of the
political necessity to fight unemployment. Like his East German counterparts,
Petzina also attributes the inability of the private economy to achieve its recovery
by itself to the suspension of the price mechanism by the cartels so that prices
remained excessively high and blocked the expansion of sales (Petzina, *Autarkiepolitik im Dritten Reich* [Stuttgart, 1968], p. 20).
[28]Paterna, et al., *Deutschland*, pp. 63ff.; "Reichsnährstand," *Swb*, vol. 2, p. 346;
Klaus-Dieter Hoeft, "Die Agrarpolitik des deutschen Faschismus als Mittel zur
Vorbereitung des zweiten Weltkrieges," *ZfG* 7 (1959): 1221ff.; Wilhelm Herferth,
"Der faschistische 'Reichsnährstand' . . . ;" ibid. 10 (1962): 1046ff., 1067ff.; Gossweiler, "Junkertum und Faschismus," *WZ Berlin*, 22 (1973): 23–24.

ans, the effects of and reactions to the resulting price increases and growing scarcities are of significance as a test in the continuing class struggle between the rulers of the fascist dictatorship and the working class.

They find evidence of the class struggle in carefully collated cases of slowdowns and other forms of passive resistance to which workers resorted in protest against wage reductions and other privations. They also note escalations of these struggles into open strikes in some plants, and into mutinies in a few camps of the Labor Service in which intolerable living conditions existed. Similarly, they regard as a telling oppositional gesture the overwhelming rejection of the official candidates who ran in Factory Council elections held in the spring of 1934.[29]

Special attention is paid to signs of discontent among the stormtroopers (SA), because the dissatisfaction of the SA threatened the mass foundation of the fascist dictatorship. The stormtroopers, it is noted, resented the dropping of the anticapitalist goals of the Nazi program. They were also offended by the lack of the material benefits they had hoped to derive from the Nazi takeover; above all, they demanded the merger of stormtroopers and regular army in hopes of material security and military careers. Inevitably such demands alarmed not only the bourgeoisie, which saw its dictatorship threatened, but also the army, which felt itself challenged in its military supremacy.[30]

In the East German accounts, this confrontation transcended, however, the bounds of a class struggle. The bourgeois reaction to it, these analyses argue, turned it into a renewed contest between the competing monopolist camps. Heavy industry proposed to handle the crisis by expanding arms production and reducing imports for purposes of consumption on the alleged grounds that such a strategy would most effectively reduce unemployment. In reality, it is explained, industry hoped in this manner to make full use of its production facilities and to expand its profits. In its demands for a stepped-up armaments output, it had a natural ally in the leadership of the army. Chemical and electrical concerns, on the other hand, being less dependent on the domestic market, proposed a slowdown of arms production in favor of greater export production and a slight improvement in living standards to allay the existing discontent. (Again, it is stressed that these were merely tactical disagreements and that both camps were girding for war in their

---

[29]Paterna et al., *Deutschland*, pp. 104–5; *GdA*, vol. 5, pp. 59–60; Böhm, "Zur Entwicklung," pp. 72, 74; Böhm, however, finds resistance mainly passive and limited to workers employed on emergency public works projects, on whose ruthless treatment she has gathered a great deal of material.

[30]Paterna et al., *Deutschland*, pp. 108–9; Streisand, p. 362; "Röhm-Putsch," *Swb*, vol. 2, p. 406.

quest for world power.) The electro-chemical monopolists allegedly found allies in the restive stormtroops, with ex-Chancellor von Schleicher and Gregor Strasser, the one-time second-in-command of the Nazi party, coordinating the SA and the electro-chemical concerns into a common front.[31]

If these analyses could be corroborated, they would greatly change the traditional picture of the confrontation that culminated in the Blood Purge of June 30, 1934; this confrontation is traditionally seen as one between Hitler, backed by the army, and the high command of the SA, headed by ex-Captain Ernst Röhm. Obviously, both army and heavy industry were interested in maximal armament production, which lends some plausibility to their cooperation. No such demonstrable community of interests existed, however, between the electro-chemical industries and the stormtroopers. In fact, the "socialist" demands of the disgruntled stormtroopers and their call for a "second revolution" must have alarmed their alleged industrial allies. Moreover, the only evidence linking these two camps into a partnership has been the presence of an I. G. Farben official on Röhm's staff as an economic adviser (to which might be added, but rarely is, that Strasser, since his break with Hitler, had been a director of a major pharmaceutical concern in Berlin). These scanty proofs are the less convincing because I. G. Farben had far more significant contacts with Göring, the *Luftwaffe* chief (and, according to the East German accounts, heavy industry's chief spokesman in the Nazi party). The dye trust also worked closely with Göring's deputy, General Erhard Milch, in the development of synthetic gasoline.[32]

Hitler, it is claimed, after some delay sided with the heavy

[31]It has also been claimed that heavy and chemical industries clashed over the building of the *Autobahnen*, which assured I. G. Farben of a vast market, "already in peacetime" (!), for its synthetic gasoline (Gossweiler, "Übergang," pp. 88–89). Yet such a market was also predicated on the building of large numbers of motor vehicles, whether civilian or military, to the benefit of heavy industry—a fact that Gossweiler does not mention. His claim that the two industrial groupings were seriously divided on the question of autarky is equally unfounded in view of I. G. Farben's stake in synthetic developments.

[32]Paterna et al., *Deutschland*, pp. 108ff.; Streisand, pp. 362–64; "Röhm Putsch," *Swb*, vol. 2, pp. 406; Gossweiler, "Übergang," pp. 86ff. On the position of I. G. Farben, see Gossweiler, in *Monopole und Staat*, p. 165; *TWC*, vol. 7, pp. 571–73; Petzina, *Autarkiepolitik*, pp. 27–29; Kuczynski, *Geschichte*, vol. 16, pp. 185ff., with a statement of Heinrich Gattineau, a high-ranking I. G. Farben official during the period, who makes it clear that the concern maintained close contact not only with Röhm and the S.A. but with all sectors of the Nazi party and its affiliated organizations. No direct use has been made here of Gossweiler's dissertation, "Die Rolle der Monopolbourgeoisie bei der Herbeiführung der Röhm-Affäre" (Berlin [East], 1963). Most East German accounts rely on this work, although it is to a large extent an assemblage of unprovable assumptions and inferences and probably for that reason was never published. Parts of the material have been incorporated in Gossweiler, "Übergang."

industry–army coalition, not so much because the Röhm-Schlei-
cher-Strasser alliance threatened his position in both party and
government, but because the army insisted on the emasculation of
the SA and he required the army's support to ensure his succession
to Hindenburg as head of state after the president's impending
death. Equally important, the East German analyses claim, Hitler
was being subjected to strong heavy-industrial pressures.

To what extent the army pressed the demands ascribed to it
has never been clearly established, and the only evidence presented
in the East German literature is a number of third-hand accounts
reported by the English historian John W. Wheeler-Bennett. Still, its
active opposition to the SA can be deduced from the assistance it
rendered in the preparations of the Blood Purge. The claim of industrial pressures, on the other hand, can invoke only one proven
fact—a visit of Hitler to Krupp two days before the Blood Purge.
What was discussed between the two men is not known, but it is
probable, as has been suggested by a Western scholar (Wolfgang
Sauer), that Krupp did warn about the chaotic state of the economy,
thus adding weight to corresponding complaints and demands of
General von Blomberg, the Reichswehr minister, and Schacht, the
president of the Reichsbank. East German historians, however, ignore Sauer's work and rely instead on an account of the meeting
presented by Bernhard Menne, a journalist, in a book on the Krupps
(which, as Sauer's study makes clear, contains numerous inaccuracies). Menne, too, speculated on what was discussed between Hitler
and Krupp—his suggested topics included the concerns of German
industry in regard to political developments and Hitler's promise to
protect private enterprise against any "second revolution." According to Menne, the sequence of events indicated "compellingly" that
Hitler informed Krupp of his plan to quash that revolution and that
"he took with him [the] certainty that the Western industrial magnates would stand by him in his murderous blow against Röhm."
Menne concludes with a bland non sequitur: "This time there can
be no doubt as to who led the leader." (Actually, the decision to
proceed against Röhm and his circle had been made before Hitler
saw Krupp.)[33]

Gossweiler refers to Menne's account as reporting established
facts; Streisand, without citing Menne, states vaguely that the decision to move against Röhm and the SA "was made in consulta-
tion with leading monopolists"; and *Geschichte der deutschen Ar-*

---

[33]John W. Wheeler-Bennett, *The Nemesis of Power: The German Army in Politics,
1918–1945* (New York, 1964), pp. 319–20; Sauer, in Bracher et al., *Machtergreifung,* pp. 923–24, 955ff.; Bernhard Menne, *Blood and Steel: The Rise of the House
of Krupp* (New York, 1938), pp. 402–4. I am informed by the Krupp-Archiv in
Essen that it has no materials on the Hitler-Krupp meeting.

beiterbewegung asserts that "the carnage of June 30, 1934 . . . was carried out with the consent of the monopolist magnates around Friedrich Flick, Gustav Krupp von Bohlen und Halbach, Hjalmar Schacht, Fritz Thyssen, and others, as well as the Reichswehr generals around Werner von Blomberg and Walther von Reichenau [Blomberg's deputy]."[34]

In keeping with these interpretations, DDR authors maintain that the main result of the Blood Purge was not the settlement of the army-stormtroop relationship, let alone the establishment of Hitler's unchallenged position in the party and state. Above all, they claim, the purge reinforced the power of the monopolies vis-à-vis their mass foundation and enabled them to put an end permanently to the latter's "socialist" aspirations.

> The most important result of the murders [Gossweiler notes] was the elimination of the potential dangers that the conflict between the fascist dictatorship and its petty-bourgeois mass basis had brought on. . . . The 30th of June marked the end of a phase in the development of the fascist dictatorship that had begun with the destruction of the legal organizations of the working class by the National Socialist petty bourgeoisie and that now ended with the fascist dictatorship settling accounts with this very same Nazi following because of its opposition to the omnipotence of the monopolies. The 30th of June thus completed the establishment of the unlimited terrorist dictatorship of finance capitalism over the other classes and sections of the German people.

In doing so, Gossweiler concludes, the purge once again refuted the myth that fascism was a petty bourgeois upheaval.[35]

The identification of the real victor of the Blood Purge is most important from the Marxist perspective in order to refute the non-Marxist thesis that Hitler emerged as that victor, not only because he destroyed all oppositional elements in the Nazi party, but also because his emasculation of the SA assured him of the support of the army when in further consolidation of his position he made himself head of state after Hindenburg's death a few weeks later. East German historians disagree sharply, and Gossweiler speaks for all of them when he rejects the "bourgeois" thesis that on that day Hitler became the omnipotent and absolute dictator of Germany:

> The purpose of this thesis is to absolve the real masters of Germany—monopolists, Junkers, and militarists—of all responsibility for the crimes of Hitler Germany, especially the Second World War. Actually the policies that Hitler pursued were but the implementa-

[34] Gossweiler, in Paterna et al., *Deutschland*, pp. 116–17; Streisand, p. 364; *GdA*, vol. 5, p. 61.
[35] Gossweiler and Streisand, in *Monopole und Staat*, pp. 153–54, 163–65; Streisand, p. 365; Gossweiler, in Paterna et al., *Deutschland*, pp. 94, 119–20.

tion of their program, and as long as he was successful, they had no objection to him.[36]

The 30th of June, in this view, also settled the contest over economic policy in favor of the coalition of heavy industry and army, that is, stepped-up armaments and reduced living standards. Schacht, the leading advocate of this policy, became acting minister of economics. The provisional character of his appointment is attributed to the fact that he opposed the drive toward increased autarky regardless of the cost on which these policies were predicated. (Gossweiler claims, without evidence, that Schacht owed his appointment to American bankers, who hoped to do more business with Germany under his economic aegis than they would with a more rigidly autarky-oriented minister and who, as Germany's creditors, could exert sufficient pressure on Berlin to obtain his appointment.[37])

The need for autarky, it is noted, also benefited another group that had seemed threatened by the "socialist" wave of the pre-June 30th days—the Junker agrarians, especially those whose estates had survived only with the help of state subsidies. Now the manpower requirements of army and industry and the need of a war-oriented economy for intensified food production assured the preservation of all large estates, confirming once more the true nature of "Hitler fascism" as the rule of the most aggressive monopolies in conjunction with Junkers and militarists.[38]

The crushing of the "socialist" wing of the Nazi movement helped to reassure business about Hitler's "sense of responsibility." Yet that move safeguarded the entrepreneurs merely in their formal property rights and against interference in their technical operations—a matter of concern to Hitler who was anxious to put an end to the economic crisis and pursue his armament plans without any disruption. On the other hand, the harsh economic policies that Schacht now imposed on the country could be enforced without risk of domestic unrest only after the last legal organization harboring elements of discontent had been rendered harmless. To this extent, there indeed existed a direct connection between the execution of Röhm and his associates in and outside the SA and the belt-tightening rearmament measures that followed. To have brought out these links is a significant contribution of DDR scholars—no matter how mistaken some of their other conclusions concerning the effects of the purge may be.[39]

[36]Gossweiler, in Paterna et al., *Deutschland*, p. 121; also "Röhm-Putsch," *Swb*, vol. 2, p. 406.

[37]Gossweiler, "Übergang," pp. 105ff.

[38]Gossweiler, "Junkertum," pp. 21ff.

[39]One non-Marxist scholar who seems to have seen this connection is Schweitzer, *Big Business*, pp. 250ff.

Monopolist Preparations for War

Subsequent developments again are seen as governed by monopolist preparations for war. The driving force of these war-oriented
activities is traced to the relentless thrust of imperialism in its
state-monopolist phase. Because the market mechanism is largely
suspended in a monopoly-dominated economy, its proper functioning is predicated on production "on order," which supposedly only
the armament needs of the state can generate. Preparation for war
is, in Eichholtz's words, the "most important constituent element
of state-monopolist capitalism." The militarist fascist order thus
responded especially well to the needs of the monopolies. It also
proved useful, Kuczynski notes, in gearing the state apparatus to
the launching of imperialist wars. This again, he concludes, confirms the thesis that "fascism is but a specific form of rule of the
monopolies, which has highly militaristic traits because war is a
constant by-product of fascist dictatorships."[40]

In consequence, East German analysts regard the continued
tightening of the economy's organizational structure, the elimination of small enterprises, and the appointment of leading "monopolists" as heads of state and semi-state agencies not as steps designed
to make the economy more responsive to governmental directives
but as additional proof of the monopoly-dominated nature of the
fascist state. In this perspective, the personal union between public
agencies and major concerns also prepared the way for heightened
aggressiveness: "From that time on," Gertrud Markus concludes,
"the monopolist potentates could use the state for their war preparations to an extent unknown heretofore."

The war for which they prepared is perceived, in its all-
encompassing total nature, as an organic outgrowth of state-
monopolist capitalism. At the same time, DDR authors note, the
dialectics of the historical process assured that such a war, born of
concentrations and comprehensive planning, would move the
economy closer to the socialist order, in keeping with the predictions of Lenin. That these measures were taken because they
served Hitler's goals and that they proved beneficial to the monopolists only because and as long as they were prepared to cooperate with the Fuehrer is beyond the ken of such an approach. It also
ignores the extensive governmental controls to which business was
already subject in this early phase of Nazi rule.[41]

[40]Eichholtz, "Probleme," pp. 110–12; Kuczynski, *Geschichte*, vol. 6, pp. 21–23, 36
(quotation), vol. 16, pp. 124ff.
[41]See Markus, in Paterna et al., *Deutschland*, pp. 141–43; Kuczynski, *Geschichte*,
vol. 16, pp. 156ff.; Wulf Bleyer, in *Monopole und Staat*, p. 183. See also Jürgen
John, "Rüstungsindustrie und NSDAP-Organisation in Thüringen 1933–1939,"

The appointment of Schacht as acting minister of economics can be readily fitted into the Marxist analysis. For DDR historians, the basic significance of that appointment lies in Schacht's presumed role as the spokesman of heavy-industrial interests. Allegedly maneuvered by them into his new post, he helped them to avail themselves still more effectively of the state in the pursuit of their goals. Once more, the economy was reorganized—but now along lines that dissociated it from all Nazi corporate concepts. The application of the leader principle to management-stockholder relations in corporations was barred, and businessmen rather than veteran Nazis were placed in key posts of the organizational structure of the economy.[42]

To find in such measures proof of monopolist dominance is to mistake form for substance. These steps, to be sure, were taken to strengthen capitalism as a technical mechanism. As Schacht hastened to add, only a vigorous capitalist economy could produce the armaments that Germany needed. Thus, if he was able to carry out his reforms, he could do so only because they were undertaken in implementation of the government's plans.

To carry out such a policy, a "New Plan" was devised: business was subjected to still tighter import and export controls and raw material and foreign exchange allocations. Similarly, its organizational structure was overhauled at the request of the army in order to further increase the military usefulness of the economy. Arms manufacturers, moreover, were enrolled by the army as economic consultants (*Wehrwirtschaftsführer*), and as such were subject to military discipline. As a result, as Arthur Schweitzer has written, "orders received from procurement agencies not only involved contractual obligations, but were in effect military commands that had to be obeyed." Yet all that DDR authors will concede is that certain limits were set to the vast power ("*Machtfülle*") of the concerns—a power that, they insist, nonetheless remained greater than ever before.[43]

The East German explanation of Schacht's fall from grace in

ZfG 22 (1974): 412ff.; John tries to point out how large armament concerns managed to revamp Thuringia's economy, but he actually shows that the Nazis increasingly moved in on business, both big and small. On controls, cf. Bracher et al. *Machtergreifung*, pp. 663, 668ff.; Petzina, *Autarkiepolitik*, pp. 169ff.

[42] Paterna, et al., *Deutschland*, pp. 132ff., 138ff.; Streisand, pp. 365–66; *GdA*, vol. 5, p. 67.

[43] See Schweitzer, *Big Business*, pp. 234, 253–54, 259–61, 300–301, 533–34; Bracher et al., *Machtergreifung*, pp. 654–55, 663, 671; David Schoenbaum, *Hitler's Social Revolution* (Garden City, NY, 1967), pp. 149–50; Petzina, *Autarkiepolitik*, p. 96. The above data, some of them Schweitzer's own, refute his thesis (*Big Business*, p. 261 and *passim*) that big business shared control of overall economic policies with army and government at least until 1936. On the East German position on this question, see Wolfgang Schumann, in *ZfG* 27 (1979): 504.

1936 conforms to the concept of Nazism as a special type of monopolist rule, but again runs counter to the actual facts. According to this analysis, the German monopolists had to decide whether to pursue their war preparations in continued dependence on imports of raw materials from other imperialist nations—a procedure aggravated by the growing shortage of foreign exchange—or to strive for economic autarky, which would assure them of full freedom of action as to the time, place, and type of imperialist war they decided to launch. Schacht, in this view, was dismissed by Hitler as the victim of the aggressive I. G. Farben concern: the dye trust wished him removed because of his opposition to the autarky program, in which Farben, as the manufacturer of synthetic substitute products, was vitally interested. Schacht, for his part, opposed an all-out conversion to autarky as uneconomical. Instead, he called for a slowdown in arms production and an expansion of exports to redress the balance of payments. (Pursuing this theme, some East German analyses claim that Schacht was acting not only on behalf of German monopolies depending on foreign trade, but also at the behest of American "finance capitalism," to which, as mentioned before, he was claimed to be closely linked and which allegedly hoped to retain, with his help, access to the German market.)

Actually, Schacht was forced out because *Hitler* insisted on the attainment of economic self-sufficiency as a precondition of the success for any war he might start. If Hitler incorporated some Farben proposals into the Four-Year Plan he introduced at that time, by which autarky was to be expedited, he did so because he found the proposals useful, not because he was Farben's mouthpiece, as DDR scholars claim. Similarly, Göring did not become Farben's spokesman but acted on Hitler's instructions, and in his own interest as the Luftwaffe's commander-in-chief, when, as plenipotentiary of the Four-Year Plan, he overruled Schacht in favor of the dye trust's stepped-up production program for synthetic gasoline and other substitute products.[44] Neither does Farben's exceptionally strong representation on the staff of the Four-Year Plan confirm the East German conclusions. This personal union—the result of the ensuing reordering of economic priorities—did indeed prove highly profitable to Farben; as a result the dye trust enjoyed favored treatment in the assignment of orders and the allocation of

---

[44]See Paterna et al., *Deutschland*, pp. 221ff., Gossweiler, "Übergang," pp. 110ff.; Eichholtz, *Geschichte*, vol. 1, pp. 42–43, in which assumptions on Farben's role suddenly are turned into facts. That the great bourgeoisie considered Hitler, Göring, and other Nazi leaders "its" men, Pätzold (in Paterna et al., *Deutschland*, p. 177) also concludes from the fact that the bourgeoisie never discussed the question of whether these Nazi potentates were the best representatives of its interests—hardly a suitable topic for discussion in the country of the ubiquitous Gestapo.

manpower and raw materials. But the authority of the Farben officials was confined to the realm of production, and they had no voice in policy-making. Moreover, it is still a matter of controversy whether Farben's attainment of its special position did not actually weaken rather than strengthen business's overall standing. Because Farben's emergence was the result of a bitter competitive struggle with heavy industry, some Western historians have concluded that the dye trust's ascendance created a rift between the contending camps that weakened further what leverage they had vis-à-vis the political leadership. Eichholtz, however, rejects this view, and his data suggest that the existing tensions did not preclude continued cooperation among the rivals.[45]

The government, on the other hand, intruded increasingly on the domain of production. In 1933–1934 Farben could reject with impunity the manufacture of synthetic rubber on the grounds that it was uneconomical, and in 1936 it went into large-scale production only when the government shielded it against all financial losses. Similarly, the government paid its tribute to private enterprise when it returned to it the companies the Brüning government had been forced to acquire during the Depression. Yet later that year, when Hitler decided on the speedy attainment of autarky against the advice of Schacht and others, he warned, as mentioned before, that if private enterprise could not meet such a task, the state would know how to solve it. Accordingly, when the mining and steel industries thought the exploitation of low-grade iron ores too uneconomical, Göring organized his own Hermann Göring Works and forced private industry to underwrite part of the capital—without any voting rights or discernible prospects of profit. The Volkswagen project had a similar history, except that in this case labor rather than business provided much of the capital. To DDR historians, however, these steps serve merely as further illustrations of the continued interlacing of business and government.[46]

In keeping with this view, East German analyses of the governmental and military changes made by Hitler in February 1938

[45]See *GdA*, vol. 5, p. 170; Eichholtz, *Geschichte*, vol. 1, pp. 39ff., 48ff., as compared to Petzina, *Autarkiepolitik*, pp. 116ff.; Schweitzer, *Big Business*, p. 538ff.; Mason, "Primacy of Politics," pp. 181, 185, 189; Martin Broszat, "Soziale Motivation und Führer-Bindung des Nationalsozialismus," *VfZ* 18 (1970): 397–98; Esenwein-Rothe, *Wirtschaftsverbände*, pp. 82ff. On the relegation of the industrialists to the production area, see also Hitler's memorandum on the Four-Year Plan, reprinted in *VfZ* 3 (1955): 209; Göring in IMT, vol. 27, pp. 161–62; Radkau, in Hallgarten and Radkau, *Industrie*, p. 312.

[46]Bracher et al., *Machtergreifung*, pp. 825–26; Petzina, *Autarkiepolitik*, pp. 99–100, 102ff.; Neumann, *Behemoth*, pp. 301ff.; Paterna et al., *Deutschland*, pp. 233–35; Hitler, in his memorandum, *VfZ* 3 (1955): 209; Horst Handke, "Zur Rolle der Volkswagenpläne bei der faschistischen Kriegsvorbereitung," in *Der deutsche Imperialismus*, vol. 2, pp. 133ff., especially pp. 148–49; also Paul Kluke, "Hitler und das Volkswagenprojekt," *VfZ* 8 (1960): 341ff.

again are traced back to monopolist inspiration. Although the relentless drive for armaments and autarky kept the economy in constant turmoil, the most aggressive sectors of German "finance capitalism"—among them I. G. Farben, the electrical concerns, Krupp, Flick, and Mannesmann—are pictured as having pressed for an acceleration of the preparations for war. These demands were opposed, however, by monopolist groups around Schacht and Thyssen, who worried about the economic and diplomatic repercussions of excessive haste and who urged greater caution.

Among military leaders, General von Blomberg, the war minister, and General von Fritsch, the head of the army, voiced corresponding misgivings when Hitler acquainted them with the "war plans and territorial goals of German imperialism" (*Sachwörterbuch*), at a conference in November 1937 (recorded in the now famous Hossbach memorandum). In this dispute, the advocates of all-out preparations for war and conquest among the monopolists are claimed to have emerged as the victors: they secured the further centralization of the fascist state apparatus needed to launch the war they demanded. Hitler assumed direct command of the armed forces and appointed as head of the army General Walther von Brauchitsch, who, as Markus claims (without any documentation), was acceptable not only to his most aggressive fellow generals but also to the politically decisive sector of German finance capitalism. Similarly, two pliant Nazis, Joachim von Ribbentrop and Walther Funk, became foreign and economic ministers, respectively. The monopolist march toward war and conquest, it is argued, continued at an accelerated pace.[47]

Further corroboration for this interpretation is found in the seizure by German concerns of Austrian, Czech, and other foreign enterprises. Yet here, too, the subordinate role of business to the government is apparent: no acquisition could be effected without governmental approval. Often, moreover, the most valuable firms went to the Hermann Göring Works; in Czechoslovakia the Göring Works helped themselves to the lion's share while even such favorites as I. G. Farben had to content themselves with much smaller accessions. Marxists, of course, would maintain that the Göring Works were merely another monopoly. The point is that it was one

[47]See Markus, in Paterna et al., *Deutschland*, pp. 256ff.; *GdA*, vol. 5, 196ff.; *Swb*, vol. 1, pp. 279, 798. Gerhard Förster and his collaborators, in their study of the Prusso-German general staff, claim that the coalescence of military and monopolist interests was greatly helped by the acquisition of large amounts of corporate shares by military commanders and staff officers and by the appointment of these men to influential and "probably highly profitable" positions on boards of directors of industrial concerns (Förster et al., *Der preussisch-deutsche Generalstab: 1640–1965* [Berlin (East), 1966], pp. 251–52, 255).

endowed with governmental authority, to which the others had to submit.[48]

The anti-Semitic barbarities of the Nazi regime are also considered part of the monopolist strategy, for they allowed such entrepreneurs as Krupp, Flick, Mannesmann, and the major banks to acquire choice Jewish enterprises. The expropriation of Jews also aided the monopolists in consolidating the petty bourgeois mass basis on which the fascist dictatorship rested: it helped to corrupt great numbers of artisans and small businessmen by allowing them to take over the stores and plants of Jewish competitors. Anti-Semitism finally is found to have served the interests of monopoly capitalism as part of its war preparations: the mounting persecutions were to inure the population to the brutalities of total war and the inhumanities perpetrated upon conquered peoples. Viewed by Marxists as but another capitalist weapon in the class struggle, racial anti-Semitism, which places the Jew beyond "redemption" because of his alleged biological inferiority, is seen as differing little from religious anti-Semitism, which offers "salvation" through religious conversion and with it escape from persecution.

Contrary to the evidence, Marxists view aggressive anti-Semitism as a great-bourgeois rather than a petty-bourgeois phenomenon. Thus, the middle class, along with the working class, is largely absolved of any responsibility for the anti-Jewish barbarities of the regime (which, to be sure, is not meant to preclude individual legal responsibility for criminal actions). All in all, the emphasis on the manipulative aspects of the anti-Jewish policies and the unwillingness of DDR authors to discuss in detail the sufferings inflicted upon the victims of these policies leave the reader with a rather inadequate picture of the magnitude of the perpetrated crimes and the immensity of the human tragedies caused by that holocaust.[49] Conversely, DDR authors have complained about the disproportionate attention paid to Nazi anti-Semitism in "bourgeois" accounts of the period.[50]

With monopolists seen as the driving force behind all such

---

[48]See Eichholtz, *Geschichte*, vol. 1, pp. 53ff.; Paterna et al., *Deutschland*, pp. 271ff.; Mottek et al., *Studien der Geschichte*, vol. 3, p. 325, as compared to *TWC*, vol. 7, pp. 1400ff., vol. 9, pp. 477ff.; Obermann, in *Der deutsche Imperialismus*, vol. 2, pp. 487–88; Kuczynski, *Geschichte*, vol. 6, pp. 24ff., 87ff., vol. 16, pp. 141ff. On the Göring Works see ibid., vol. 6, p. 38, as compared to Petzina, *Autarkiepolitik*, pp. 104ff.

[49]See Kuczynski, *Geschichte*, vol. 6, p. 40; Paterna et al., *Deutschland*, pp. 302ff. (but see also Wilhelm Treue on the actual motives of Hermann Abs, one of the Deutsche Bank directors mentioned in Paterna, in *Tradition* [1971]: 296ff.); *GdA*, vol. 5, pp. 73, 215; Streisand, pp. 369–71; Drobisch et al., *Juden unterm Hakenkreuz* (Frankfurt, 1973), pp. 69ff., 83, 134ff., 224–25, 239–40.

[50]*Unb. Verg.*, p. 335.

war-oriented activities, DDR historians have no doubts concerning
the responsibility of the "monopoly bourgeoisie" for the war that
broke out a year later. Not only are East German scholars convinced that the banking and industrial magnates knew that German rearmament aimed at aggression—as Marxists they are also
satisfied that these circles were the initiators of that war in their
insatiable quest for markets and raw materials. DDR researchers
have amassed huge amounts of documents on this issue—not in
order to prove their thesis, but to confirm it. On the whole, however, the material demonstrates only that the industrialists readily
took up the manufacture of arms as a profitable business proposition. Only a few scattered documents contain proposals for war on
the part of the arms manufacturers. Even in these cases most of the
authors of the letters and memoranda in question were associating
themselves with the plans of the Nazis rather than initiating plans
of their own.[51]

On the other hand, the East German documentations refute
the assumption of some Western historians that industrialists involved in arms production did not know they were until far into
1935–1936, thanks to the elaborate camouflage of all rearmament
measures until that time. Moreover, few of the participants have
denied their conscious participation in rearmament, although most
have insisted that they cooperated in the belief that such rearmament was to serve solely defensive purposes. The War Crimes
Tribunals set up after the Second World War accepted these pleas
on the grounds of insufficient proof to the contrary. The historian
is bound by less exacting standards of evidence. Thus, he may
doubt that men who played key roles in arms production could be
unaware of the incongruity between Germany's feverish armament
and the dilatory countermeasures of her alleged enemies, and thus
profess ignorance of the aggressive intent of German rearmament.
Many of them, moreover, had long had their own plans of economic expansionism and as economic imperialists had little difficulty accommodating to the Nazis' military imperialism. Nazi
military aggressiveness, in turn, drew strength from this economic

[51]The most important of these documentary collections is Eichholtz and Schumann,
Anatomie des Krieges. The only documents suggesting aggressive intentions on
the part of the industrialists are nos. 31 (p. 117) and 38 (p. 130); the second of these
includes a possibly Freudian slip, "zur Vorbereitung der Industrie auf den [!] Krieg"
("in order to prepare industry for the [!] war"). See also Hermann Röchling's letter
to Göring, Mar. 27, 1937, in T. R. Emessen, *Aus Görings Schreibtisch* (Berlin [East],
1947), pp. 73ff., frequently cited by DDR authors; memoranda on war by Arnold
Rechberg, reprinted in *JfG* 14 (1976): 407ff., with Rechberg, who had inherited a few
potash shares, described as a monopolist and spokesman of the potash industry
(ibid., pp. 399–400). On Rechberg's actual standing as an unwelcome interloper, see
Eberhard von Vietsch, *Arnold Rechberg und das Problem der politischen West-
Orientierung nach dem ersten Weltkrieg* (Koblenz, 1958), pp. 92ff.

imperialism and used it, in central and southeastern Europe, to further its own aggressive purposes. In this context, the West German historian Joachim Radkau suggests, some banking and industrial circles may also have provided "impulses" that helped trigger the annexation of Austria and the Sudetenland and the occupation of the remaining Czech state. (If, conversely, some industrial export drives seemed to force government policy into channels contrary to its general foreign policy objectives, as Radkau also has claimed, the discrepancy was more apparent than real. As he rightly notes, industrial efforts to capture parts of the Latin American and Chinese markets, in which the United States and Japan, respectively, had staked out special claims, offended two countries with which Germany should have maintained good relations in order to pursue undisturbed her European objectives. Yet Radkau's own documentation suggests that the German government did not support these export campaigns simply for the sake of I. G. Farben or Krupp, but because of the badly needed raw materials and foreign exchange these exports produced.)[52]

If, then, the banking and industrial leaders were not the initiators of war, they clearly served as accomplices, and as such they played a crucial role in the preparations for war. DDR historians object rightly to the overriding attention paid by many non-Marxists to the person of Hitler, which is apt to obscure the responsibility of others for the crimes of the Nazi era. At the same time, their insistence that Hitler's role was historically of little significance compared to the role of the "monopoly bourgeoisie" is even more misleading.

As for the type of war for which preparations were being made, DDR analysts find it particularly suited to the specific needs of the German monopolists. The strategy of localized *Blitzkriege*, with its stress on surprise and the concentration of power, was to offset Germany's inferiority in human and material resources. At the same time, the argument runs, the anticipated short duration of such lightning wars rendered unnecessary the imposition of the kind of sacrifices that preparations for a long war required. Actually, as Radkau has pointed out, the strategy of lightning wars appealed to Hitler, with his penchant for quick crushing blows, but

---

[52]See Sauer, in Bracher et al., *Machtergreifung*, p. 802; IMT, vol. 22, pp. 554–56; TWC, vol. 8, pp. 1117ff.; but see also IMT, vol. 22, p. 555, vol. 7, p. 1522; Bracher, *Die deutsche Diktatur* (Cologne, 1970), pp. 363–64; and Radkau, in Hallgarten and Radkau, *Industrie*, pp. 320ff., 342ff., 357, 360ff. There is some evidence that business leaders were told by Hitler of his war plans in March 1939 (Eichholtz and Schumann, *Anatomie*, doc. no. 88, pp. 204–5). For an East German analysis of the Western preoccupation with Hitler personally and the consequences of that preoccupation, see, for example, Eichholtz and Hass, "Zu den Ursachen," des zweiten Weltkriegs . . . ," *ZfG* 15 (1967), pp. 1155ff.

it did not suit industry, because this type of war called for brief stepped-up arms production that just as abruptly dropped off once the lightning campaign had come to an end.[53]

DDR scholars stress rightly, however, that even under the less exacting Blitzkrieg preparations, workers were subjected to much exploitation; their meager and slow pay increases were disproportionately poor, compared with the growth of production and the rapidly expanding profits of the major concerns. If Western analysts make much of the fact that civilian investment as late as 1938 exceeded that in military production, basic industries, and transportation, such data lose in significance if it is kept in mind that civilian investment in 1938 still did not equal that of 1929. As the English labor historian Timothy Mason has written, "The National Socialist regime clearly succeeded, for the sake of rearmament, in achieving a relative intensification of economic exploitation that is without parallel in the 1930s." (This conclusion is not refuted by the increased sales of radios, kitchen appliances, and furniture and of coffee, tobacco, and alcoholic beverages, frequently cited as proof of the workers' improved living standards; most of these items were bought by the middle class, including white-collar employees, who derived greater benefits from the economic upswing than did the workers.) On the testimony of both the Nazi party and the German Labor Front (the body dealing with workers' concerns), discontent among the working class remained widespread, and pressures for more adequate pay and working hours grew rather than abated as time went on. As Timothy Mason also has shown, it was these pressures that kept the government from curtailing the production of consumers' goods, although civilian output interfered seriously with arms production.[54]

Anti-Fascist Resistance as Class Struggle

Even without Mason's findings, of which they have taken scant notice so far, DDR authors are convinced, of course, that fascist totalitarianism could never suppress the class struggle, the motor

[53]Radkau, in Hallgarten and Radkau, *Industrie*, pp. 420, 425.
[54]See Eichholtz, *Kriegswirtschaft*, vol. 1, pp. 20, 26–27; Mottek et al., vol. 3, pp. 320, 324–25; Kuczynski, *Geschichte*, vol. 6, pp. 155ff.; see also Mason, *Sozialpolitik im Dritten Reich* (Opladen, 1977), p. 147ff., 229ff. (quotation on p. 232), 246, 282ff., 315ff. On the other hand, see Burton H. Klein, *Germany's Economic Preparations for War* (Cambridge, MA, 1959), pp. 14–16; Alan S. Milward, *The German Economy at War* (London, 1965), pp. 12ff.; Schoenbaum, *Hitler's Social Revolution*, pp. 97ff.; Schweitzer, *Big Business*, pp. 391ff.; Berenice A. Carroll, *Design for Total War* (The Hague, 1968), pp. 179ff.

power of the historical process. They therefore consider it one of their major tasks to trace the continuing operation of that struggle. For them, the fight against terror, racism, and war thus was essentially a class struggle against monopoly capitalism and imperialism, the breeding grounds of fascism. In a wider perspective, moreover, antifascist resistance is seen as but another phase in the worldwide transition from capitalism to socialism. In this struggle, the politically conscious part of the working class assumed the iniative under the leadership of the Communist party. That party alone, it is noted, took up the fight against the fascist regime from the very first moment and was also the only one to develop a scientific program of action. Admittedly, its efforts were of limited effectiveness, but it is the quality of its efforts that is considered important.[55] (Despite such reservations, DDR authors still tend to attribute exaggerated importance to the party's activities.)

In this scenario, the middle class once again recedes into the background as misled and confused. It did not understand that its real enemies were the monopolists and militarists, not the Jews or the French, let alone the Communist party, which was fighting for the true interests of the nation. Whatever discontent the middle class felt, then, was directed "objectively" against "Hitler fascism." It thus receives attention only insofar as that discontent was mobilized against the regime and as middle-class elements joined in the class struggle against monopoly capitalism.[56]

Large amounts of material have been gathered to support these claims. The approach to this task, however, has undergone some significant changes in the course of time. Until about 1960, East German authors paid special attention to the exploits of individuals and individual resistance groups within the Communist movement. Their main concern was to illustrate the dedication and heroism of the Communist fighters on German soil and to contrast their struggle with the inaction of all other parties. At the same time, the emphasis on Communist valor and sacrifices was to refute West German assertions that only those whose endeavors culminated in the attempt on Hitler's life on July 20, 1944, were engaged in resistance activities that deserved to be taken seriously.[57] In fact, the

---

[55]See Förster et al., in *ZfG* 18 (1970): suppl., p. 554; Rolf Rudolph, "Die nationale Verantwortung der Historiker in der DDR," ibid. 10 (1962): 276–78. The fact that the Communists were the most persistent anti-Nazi force is also pointed out by some non-Marxist scholars (see Bahne, "Kommunistische Partei," p. 722).

[56]*GdA*, vol. 5, pp. 118–19; Hass et. al., *Deutschland*, vol. 1, pp. 301ff.

[57]See the editorial, in *ZfG* 4 (1956): 668. Communist resistance activities have indeed received little attention in West German studies, and the concept of resistance tends to be identified by them with the Goerdeler-Beck-Stauffenberg group and the *Kreisauer Kreis*, with only the Communist-affiliated "Red Chapel" receiving some attention. Although at first, lack of information may have accounted for this silence (see Rudolf Pechel, *Deutscher Widerstand* [Zurich-Erlenbach, 1947],

preoccupation of DDR historians with this issue was such that at first they explored little else of the Nazi period except for the war. The chapter devoted to the Nazi era in the 1960 survey of East German historiography from 1945 to 1960 deals almost exclusively with Communist resistance exploits.[58]

This approach, however, was found to have pitfalls. As a group of researchers of the SED's Institute for Marxism-Leninism complained a year later, many of the accounts failed to do justice to the leading role of the KPD and its Central Committee. They pictured party and leadership as mere advisers and helpmates, not as the guides who laid the foundation for and directed the activities of the various resistance centers. Again, in the case of groups in which Communists and non-Communists had joined forces, the leading role of the Communists, based on the KPD's scientific program and the good judgment of its Central Committee, was not always made clear. Similarly, the continuity of the Communist efforts was ignored, and subjectivist spontaneity received credit at the expense of socialist purposefulness. The fact was, the critics maintained, that Communist resistance activities were always guided by a centralized leadership and rested on an organizational structure that assured the unity of the struggle. Admittedly, the specific scope of that organization had not yet been fully explored, just as its communication techniques, beyond radio contact, would require more study. At this point, however, what mattered most was to establish the decisive role and indispensability of the party and the sagacity of its leaders. In this context, more attention was to be paid to Pieck and Ulbricht, the future heads of the DDR,

---

pp. 67ff.), the main reason now seems to be the ineffectiveness of the Communist efforts and the remoteness of all Communists from positions of any power and influence (cf. Schulz, *Zeitalter der Gesellschaft*, p. 334; Hans J. Reichhardt, "Möglichkeiten und Grenzen des Widerstandes der Arbeiterbewegung," in *Der deutsche Widerstand gegen Hitler*, ed. Walter Schmitthenner and Hans Buchheim [Cologne, 1966], pp. 183ff.). There is also some confusion about Communist tactics; thus, Pechel (*Deutscher Widerstand*) wondered why the Communists never sought to kill Hitler, apparently unaware that in the Marxist view the asssassination of Hitler, the mere frontman of monopoly capitalists, would not have solved anything.

[58]See Heinz Schumann and Wilhelm Wehling, "Literatur über Probleme der deutschen antifaschistischen Widerstandsbewegung," in "Historische Forschungen in der DDR," *ZfG* 8 (1960): suppl., pp. 381ff., 385. DDR authors did acknowledge the activities of the Christian resistance, but they emphasized at the same time that such activities were carried on only by small groups within the churches and on the whole had little effect, because these groups would not cooperate with other antifascist forces, such as the KPD or the German Popular Front (*Volksfront*) (Schmidt, in *Der deutsche Imperialismus*, vol. 2, p. 413). Most East German accounts of Communist resistance activities, including the many memoirs, are curiously impersonal, conveying little information on the actual life and day-to-day activities of the underground fighters. For one exceptionally descriptive report, see Kuczynski, *Memoiren* (Berlin [East], 1975), pp. 242ff.

whose writings and speeches are praised as the best sources for the
party's key role. In response to such censures, the focus of DDR
research shifted to the activities of the KPD's leadership. Special
efforts were made to demonstrate the consistency of the party's
work in this transitional period from capitalism to socialism, with
both strategy and tactics preparing the ground for the establishment of the DDR, the "first socialist state on German soil."[59]

The emphasis on the leaders' planning activities seemed the
more justified because the localized actions of the rank and file
never caused more than pinpricks to the Nazi regime.[60] Larger-
scale actions, if at all feasible, would have required Social Democratic cooperation, but such cooperation was withheld from the
first day of Hitler's assumption of power, when the Communists
proposed a general strike. Not only were the Social Democrats
distrustful of men who only a few weeks before had denounced
them as social fascists, but the SPD leaders also ruled out all militant actions. Thus, when the SPD and the unions affiliated with it
would not join the KPD in a general strike, the Communists, lacking adequate support in the factories, could not act.[61] (How effective such a strike would have been is a matter of speculation: the
East German assertion that "every chance had existed" to defeat
the regime during the first few days of its rule by concerted mass
action is unconvincing.)[62]

Collaboration with other oppositional forces became still
more imperative as the Gestapo kept decimating the ranks of the
party. The goal of creating a "unity front" (*Einheitsfront*) with the

[59]See Collective of the Historical Division of the Party and the German Workers
Movement at the Institute for Marxism-Leninism at the Central Committee of
the SED, "Zur führenden Rolle der kommunistischen Partei Deutschlands und
ihres Zentralkomitees im antifaschistischen Widerstandskampf," BzG 3 (1961):
547ff., especially pp. 551–52, 562–65; Schumann, "Zur führenden Rolle unserer
marxistisch-leninistischen Partei und ihres Zentralkomitees im Kampf gegen Faschismus und Krieg (1933–1945)," ZfG 10 (1962): 1017ff., especially pp. 1017,
1035–36; Förster et al., p. 561. The Soviet Union, it may be noted, felt a similar
need to reemphasize the guiding role of the Soviet Communist party after first
having extolled on their own merits the exploits of its partisan forces in the war
against Germany.
[60]Schumann, "Zur führenden Rolle," pp. 1017, 1023ff., 1030ff.; Klaus Mammach,
Die KPD und die deutsche antifaschistische Widerstandsbewegung: 1933–1939
(Frankfurt, 1974), pp. 63ff.
[61]See Vietzke, "Zur Strategie," pp. 128ff. On membership figures, see also Bahne,
"Kommunistische Partei," pp. 119 n. 2, 662, 683.
[62]See GdA, vol. 5, p. 20; Streisand, pp. 347ff.; Kuczynski, *Geschichte*, vol. 6, p. 10;
also Kalbe, "Rolle," p. 1026. The assertion is based on Hitler's apparent concern
about a possible general strike, as he expressed it in the first cabinet meeting after
his appointment as chancellor (IMT, vol. 25, pp. 373ff.). How genuine this concern was is not clear; Goebbels suggests in his diary that the Nazis would have
welcomed a Communist rising, presumably in order to crush the Communists at
once (Joseph Goebbels, *Vom Kaiserhof zur Reichskanzlei* [Munich, 1934], entry of
January 31, 1933, p. 254).

Social Democrats was to preoccupy the Communists throughout most of the Nazi period. DDR historians have devoted considerable attention to these endeavors. The initial difficulties could not be resolved, partly because of the continuing distrust of the Social Democrats but also because the SPD leadership still ruled out all forcible actions and, moreover, worried lest any rapprochement with the Communists discredit it as a potential ally of oppositional bourgeois and army circles. Such an alliance would have been ideologically more to the liking of the SPD leaders and also seemed politically more realistic, because effective resistance required collaboration with those who still had access to power.

The Communists, on the other hand, rejected this strategy of inaction. Here East German authors point in particular to the last speech Ernst Thälmann made before the KPD's Central Committee early in February 1933. In this address Thälmann outlined with remarkable prescience the full terror the Nazi regime would unleash upon the Communist party and all other working-class spokesmen. He insisted that the Hitler-Hugenberg government could probably be removed only by forcible action and objected to the "legalist illusions" in which the Social Democrats were indulging. He called, therefore, for continuous mass demonstrations, strikes, and other forms of mass struggles and the unity front of all workers to prepare the way for the overthrow of the regime. Yet, rejecting the optimism of some party members, he also warned that the removal of the fascist dictatorship need not lead immediately to a dictatorship of the proletariat, because the time might not yet be ripe.[63]

As DDR scholars regretfully note, Thälmann's realism did not prevail. Deprived of his guidance after his imprisonment a few weeks later, the bulk of the party leadership tended to underestimate the power of the fascist regime and to overestimate the strength of its antifascist opponents. East German historians are as critical as non-Marxists of the assumption prevalent among Communists at that time that the workers had suffered only a temporary setback, that a revolutionary situation was rapidly developing, and that the dictatorship of the proletariat would soon be established. In its certitude, this faction, whose views could claim also approbation by the Comintern, abandoned all thoughts of a unity front with the SPD leadership.[64]

Only a minority, among whom Pieck and Ulbricht are again singled out, perceived the full gravity of the defeat that the workers

[63]Vietzke, "Die Kapitulation der rechten SPD-Führung vor dem Hitler-faschismus . . . ," *BzG* 3 (1961): 67; Thälmann's speech, in *GdA*, vol. 4, pp. 446–47; "Tagung des ZK der KPD, Februar 1933," *Swb*, vol. 2, p. 645.

[64]See *GdA*, vol. 5, pp. 40, 47–48; Paterna et al., *Deutschland*, pp. 127–29; Mammach, *KPD*, pp. 57ff., Mammach, however, blurs the ambiguous role of the Comintern.

and especially the Communist party had suffered. They insisted on the need for a unity front with the Social Democrats as the precondition of any successful action. It took these "Marxist-Leninists" over a year to assert themselves over their "sectarian, dogmatic" opponents, and that did not occur until the Comintern had changed its own views, under the influence of Georgi Dimitrov, the hero of the Reichstag fire trial, who as a prisoner of the Nazis had observed first hand the power of that regime.[65]

The strategy of the unity front was fully revived only after the Seventh Comintern Congress in July/August 1935 and a KPD conference that was held in Moscow in October 1935 but that was generally known as the Brussels conference, as which it was publicized at the time for security reasons. These gatherings were impressed with the effectiveness of the newly formed French Popular Front of Communists, Socialists, and Radical Socialists, which had taken up the fight against the fascist menace in France. Both meetings sanctioned collaboration with the SPD at all levels on the assumption that that party might now be prepared to turn its back on the great bourgeoisie. Beyond such a unity front, they also called for the formation of a "popular front" (Volksfront), including not only the working class but also all antifascist elements among the peasantry, petty bourgeoisie, and intelligentsia. To attract peasant and bourgeois elements, the appeals dropped any explicit demands for socialization—a concession that could be made the more readily because most workers would not have fought for such socialist goals at the time. Instead, the calls for a Volksfront focused on the restoration of all democratic rights and on a government chosen by the working people (*das werktätige Volk*).

For East German historians, the program is also significant because it opened up the road that eventually led to the creation of the German Democratic Republic. They find further evidence of this continuity in the call of the conference for a united revolutionary working-class party as it materialized later on in the Socialist Unity party. All in all, the Brussels decisions are seen as another step of the Leninist forces toward that inherently inevitable breakthrough to socialism that occurred in Germany's eastern part after the Second World War.[66]

[65] *GdA*, vol. 5, pp. 48, 89–90, 93; Paterna et al., *Deutschland*, pp. 129ff.; but see also the criticisms of Heinz Niemann, "Zur Vorgeschichte und Wirkung des Prager Manifestes der SPD," *ZfG* 13 (1965): 1362 n. 40. On the greater realism of Pieck and Ulbricht, see also Bahne, "Kommunistische Partei," p. 715.

[66] *GdA*, vol. 5, pp. 107ff., 114, 118ff.; "Brüsseler Parteikonferenz der KPD," *Swb*, vol. 1, pp. 294ff.; Paterna et al., *Deutschland*, pp. 188ff., 195ff.; Lewerenz, *Analyse*, pp. 90ff.; Vietzke, "Kapitulation," pp. 68–70, 75; Siegfried Ittershagen et al., "Zur Strategie und Taktik der KPD . . . bis zur Brüsseler Konferenz," *BzG* 5 (1963): 242–43.

Accordingly, the East German accounts point out that the Brussels conference expressly affirmed the merely tactical nature of the unity and popular fronts and the provisional status of the antifascist-democratic state that was to supersede the Hitler regime. In the same vein, the conference resolution called for the eventual establishment of the "soviet power that alone does away with the class rule of the employers [and] builds up socialism." This goal was to be attained with the help of a unified mass party that "acknowledges the necessity of the revolutionary overthrow of the bourgeoisie and the establishment of the dictatorship of the proletariat in the form of soviets."[67]

Lack of success in implementing the conference resolution and forming a unity front with the Social Democrats is blamed on the latter's intransigence. This censure applies in particular to a conference of KPD and SPD leaders in Prague in November 1935. The meeting was held at the suggestion of the Communists to explore the possibilities of interparty collaboration on the leadership level. No agreement was reached—according to the East German accounts because of unacceptable conditions set by the Social Democrats. Pointing to the reaffirmation at Brussels of the dictatorship of the proletariat as the ultimate Communist goal—the Brussels resolution had been published in full in the official KPD journal and thus was known to the Social Democrats—the Social Democrats challenged the Communists' democratic professions and demanded an explicit loyalty pledge and a nonaggression pact barring each party from attacking the other. The Communists, for their part, rejected all such commitments. They wished to retain the right to expose those Social Democrats who were still hoping for a coalition with army and bourgeoisie and who therefore opposed any collaboration between SPD and KPD. They maintained that actual collaboration would be the best demonstration of loyalty and would at the same time preclude all reciprocal attacks. The talks were broken off because the Social Democrats felt that without explicit agreements, they would be no match for the hard-driving Communists. There are also, however, strong indications that they did not really wish to come to an understanding with the Communists. Some subsequent attempts at a unity front at the leadership level proved no more successful. (Collaboration on the local level, in Germany, where immediate tactical goals rather than ultimate principles mattered, was, however, effected on various occasions.)[68]

[67]Conference resolution in Hermann Weber, *Der deutsche Kommunismus: Dokumente* (Cologne, 1963), pp. 323ff.; Arnold Sywottek, *Deutsche Volksdemokratie* (Düsseldorf, 1971), pp. 59–60.
[68]See Paterna et al., *Deutschland*, pp. 242–44; *GdA*, vol. 5, pp. 135–37; "Prager Einheitsfrontverhandlungen 1935," *Swb*, vol. 2, pp. 279–80; Ulbricht's speech at

Although the attempts to form a unity front with the SPD ended in failure, DDR authors view the efforts to set up a popular front "from below" in a more positive light. The fact that Social Democrats joined it as individuals rather than as authorized delegates of their party is played down; much is made, on the other hand, of a few meetings in Paris at which representatives of the KPD joined with a number of Social Democrats and bürgerlich politicians and writers in order to call for the overthrow of the Nazi regime and a joint struggle for the preservation of peace. On the steps to be taken after the overthrow of the Nazis, no agreement, however, was possible. Bürgerlich participants insisted on the establishment of a state modeled after the Weimar Republic, but the Communists warned that in such a state the bourgeoisie would remain in control of the economy, exposing the nation anew to the dangers of monopoly capitalism and imperialism. They would accept only a "democratic republic" whose policies would be determined by the "toiling masses" and whose economic policy would serve the "working people." A resolution of the KPD leadership again made clear that such a democratic republic, while not yet socialist, would pave the way toward socialism. Because of these disagreements the popular front movement, too, was stillborn; yet DDR scholars, forever concerned with pointing up the continuity of the historical process, hail the KPD proposal as another milestone on the road to the German Democratic Republic.[69]

Many East German historians maintain that along with the Brussels directives the campaign for a popular front injected new vigor into resistance activities in Germany. Actually, whether resistance increased and to what extent any increase can be attributed to such outside developments is far from clear. Even those DDR authors who see a connection grant that the resulting revival of anti-Nazi activities had no "mass character." Visible opposition, all accounts are agreed, became increasingly difficult. Because of the ever-present Gestapo, slowdowns and other types of inconspicuous sabotage remained the only outlets for protests. As is also pointed out, it was not only the terror of the Gestapo that impeded resistance; some improvements in living conditions, generous recreational facilities provided by the "Strength Through Joy" program, Hitler's foreign-policy coups, and the impact of Nazi propa-

---

Prague meeting, in *BzG* 5 (1963): 75ff.; Social Democratic minutes of meeting in *Mit dem Gesicht nach Deutschland*, ed. Link (Düsseldorf, 1968), pp. 241ff. See also the contemporary commentaries of Victor Schiff and Erich Kuttner, in ibid., 254–55, 265–67, and the analysis by Günther Plum, "Volksfront, Konzentration und Mandatsfrage," *VfZ* 18 (1970): 428–31; also Sywottek, *Deutsche Volksdemokratie*, pp. 61–62.
[69]Paterna et al., *Deutschland*, pp. 245ff.; "Deutsche Volksfront," *Swb*, vol. 1, pp. 456–58; also Sywottek, *Deutsche Volksdemokratie*, pp. 66–67.

ganda all had their conciliatory effect on the working class. KPD activities thus focused on keeping alive the illegal party organization, disrupted ever anew by the relentless Gestapo, and spreading anti-Nazi news and propaganda by word of mouth, leaflets, and underground newspapers. The latter activities, moreover, supplemented the former, for as Lenin had taught, a newspaper not only communicated news and ideas but also served as an organizing agent around which its collaborators could coalesce.[70]

Even when war appeared imminent, the KPD's warnings had little impact. Paterna notes that "the fear of war on the part of the masses was not so deep-rooted that it could not be converted into new faith in the Hitler regime after the conclusion of the Munich Agreement." On the other hand, it is claimed that new hardships imposed on the working class revived the "economic class struggle" (Eichholtz). Among such burdens are mentioned the extension of the normal work week to 60 hours, the legalization of Sunday labor, the contined wage freeze, the authorization of nationwide labor conscription (*Dienstpflicht*), and the ending of labor mobility. To what extent Communist spadework helped stimulate renewed strikes, slowdowns, and other protests again is hard to determine; DDR authors claim direct credit for it only in a few instances. On many occasions, moreover, no persuasion was needed: in these cases, protests took the form of workers letting themselves be hired away from their jobs by firms willing to pay higher wages in violation of the official wage freeze. "Objectively," this was, as Marxists see it, a form of class struggle on the part of the workers inasmuch as it interfered with capitalist exploitation; but "subjectively," it also tended, as they ruefully note, to reconcile its beneficiaries to the existing order.[71]

To what extent the Hitler regime could appease (and/or terrorize) a considerable part of the working class is revealed, too, in the East German analyses of a new KPD conference that met—officially in Berne, Switzerland, but in reality in Draveil, a small town south of Paris—on January 30–February 1, 1939. Once again, the participants agreed that only the concerted action of the entire working class, aided by oppositional peasant and middle-class ele-

---

[70]See *GdA*, vol. 5, pp. 137ff.; Streisand, p. 377; Hass et al., *Deutschland*, vol. 1, pp. 128–29, as compared to Paterna et al., *Deutschland*, pp. 240ff.; Paterna et al. see no impact of the Brussels conference on resistance activities in Germany. Cf. Sywottek, *Deutsche Volksdemokratie*, pp. 35, 49. Mason (*Sozialpolitik, passim*) has uncovered considerable evidence of worker's resistance—small-scale strikes, slowdowns, poor workmanship, etc.—but has found it impossible to tell to what extent these activities were instigated by Communists. Mammach (*KPD*, pp. 166ff.), on the other hand, credits the KPD, without proof, with the leading role. On Lenin, see Ruge, in *ZfG* 22 (1974): 1389; also *GdA*, vol. 5, p. 531.

[71]Paterna et al., *Deutschland*, pp. 287, 324–25; Eichholtz, *Geschichte*, vol. 1, pp. 26ff.; *GdA*, vol. 5, pp. 231–32; Kuczynski, *Geschichte*, vol. 6, pp. 150ff., 218ff.

ments, could stop the outbreak of war. Yet the tenor of the delib-
erations suggests, as Klaus Mammach notes, that the conference
was guided by the assumption that the war could not be prevented
by working-class opposition and that the Hitler regime could and
would be overthrown only by war.

The program worked out by the Berne conference derived
from the plans proposed at the Brussels meeting. Like the former,
it placed special emphasis on the formation of a united revolutionary Marxist-Leninist mass party, but it now also emphasized the
need for radical social changes—land reform and the takeover by
the state of all industrial and banking monopolies—that would
deprive the great bourgeoisie of its material foundation. Once
again, the KPD is hailed by DDR commmentators as the one oppositional force with a concrete post-Hitler program. As always,
stress is also laid on the continuity between that program and the
measures taken in East Germany after the defeat of the Nazis.[72]

Contrary to the claims of some of these authors, there is no
evidence that the Berne conference raised the effectiveness of the
KPD's antiwar stance. The SPD rejected renewed proposals for
collaboration, and anti-Nazi activity in Germany continued in its
subdued, groping way. "Through unrestrained terror, massive
ideological pressures, and demagogical national and social propaganda, Hitler fascism successfully misled large parts of the German people into chauvinism or rendered them passive," *Geschichte* concludes. Most Germans thus would not see that their
real enemies were the German fascists, who controlled politics
and economy, and the militarists. "The German fascists, therefore, were able to launch the Second World War without en-
countering any major resistance in the country."[73]

Nonetheless, DDR authors can rightly claim that the activities of the KPD were neither senseless nor entirely futile. The
party helped nurture a modicum of opposition even though its
contribution may well have been smaller than these historians are
willing to grant—Timothy Mason has concluded that the continuing resistance of the workers, as it expressed itself in carelessness,
slowdowns, absenteeism, and occasional local strikes, was primarily an emotional, "pre-political" reaction, not attributable to political efforts. Yet even if Communist activities produced few tangible
results, the remarkable array of Communist underground pam-
phlets, newspapers, leaflets, and stickers provided moral encour-

---

[72]*GdA*, vol. 5, pp. 216ff.; Paterna et al., *Deutschland*, pp. 308ff.; "Berner Parteikonferenz der KPD," *Swb*, vol. 1, pp. 265–66; Mammach, "Die Berner Konferenz,"
BzG 7 (1965): 979.
[73]Paterna et al., *Deutschland*, pp. 326ff.; Paterna, "Zum Kampf der KPD gegen die
Vorbereitung des zweiten Weltkrieges . . . ," *BzG* 6 (1964): 581ff.; *GdA*, vol. 5,
pp. 226ff. (quotation on pp. 235–36).

agement and a sense of communality as a counterweight to feelings of isolation and impotence.

The East German literature concedes that the Communists cannot claim sole credit for whatever was done in resisting the Nazis, but it insists that among the various resistance groups the Communists played the most important role in this struggle. This accounts for the minimal attention paid to other resistance groups, such as, for example, the (Protestant) Confessional Church. As for the oppositional forces gathered around the former mayor of Leipzig, Carl Goerdeler, which had access to such levers of power as military and high bureaucrats, their efforts are dismissed as constituting mere tactical disagreements within the ruling class. The Goerdeler group, it is claimed, objected only to the foreign-policy risks involved in the Nazis' expansion program and was just as imperialist-minded as the clique backing Hitler, though anxious to avoid war in acquiring new lands. Genuine resistance had to be antifascist and anti-imperialist, and this the great-bourgeois Goerdeler circle was not. Obviously this one-dimensional picture of the Goerdeler group is of little help in determining the comparative significance of the KPD in the spectrum of anti-Nazi activities. This much, however, any assessment of that role must conclude—that the KPD was the only anti-Nazi Resistance group active from the first to the last day of the Nazi era and that its underground fighters opposed the Nazis with great courage and dedication and at an enormous cost to themselves.[74]

Foreign Policy as Preparation for War

Nazi foreign policy is easily fitted into the framework of fascist imperialism in the East German studies. Its first task was to erode the Versailles Treaty; this done, it served to prepare the ground for aggressions and annexations in Spain, Austria, and Czechoslovakia, and for the invasion of Poland. Here Marxist analyses differ little from non-Marxist ones, at least as to means and ends; they part ways, of course, in their attribution of ultimate responsibility for the initiation of these policies.[75]

[74]Mammach, KPD, pp. 261–62; Streisand, pp. 380ff.; "Antifaschistischer Widerstand," Swb, vol. 1, p. 72; as compared to Mason, Sozialpolitik, pp. 312ff. On the Goerdeler circle, see Hass et al., Deutschland, vol. 1, pp. 153, 244–45; Ruge, "Zu den Auseinandersetzungen in der herrschenden Klasse des faschistischen Deutschlands 1936," JfG 10 (1974): 549.

[75]Förster et al., in ZfG 18 (1970): suppl., p. 577; Hella Bünger, "Die herrschenden Kreise in Grossbritannien und der deutsche Faschismus im Jahre 1933," WZ Berlin 22 (1973): 119.

In tracing the course of Nazi foreign policy, DDR authors note, again in agreement with non-Marxist scholars, that its immediate assignment was to conceal the full scope of its plans, for these plans aimed as much at the imperialist Western powers as at the USSR and its socialist order. Such secrecy was essential because "Hitler fascism" could launch its rearmament only with the tolerance of the West. This the Hitler regime secured by presenting itself as an anti-Communist bulwark, both at home and abroad: the "ruling circles" in Britain and France welcomed its assumption of power, because, as Markus puts it, they were greatly concerned about the imminent victory of socialist production relations in the USSR. Nazi imperialism was expected to help destroy the Soviet Union and crush all revolutionary and democratic movements in Europe. The transition from capitalism to socialism could thus be stopped and the worldwide rule of imperialism restored.[76]

Germany's early steps on the foreign policy stage and Western responses to these moves are found to fully bear out these theses. The German withdrawal from the League of Nations, in October 1933, produced no noticeable Western reaction, because, Kurt Pätzold explains, the international armament trusts hoped to profit from Germany's rearmament. Moreover, any German aggression was expected to turn east against Soviet Russia—a misapprehension that was carefully nurtured by the Hitler regime. In the same vein, the West viewed the German-Polish nonaggression pact of January 1934 as an anti-Soviet move on the grounds that Poland had been given to understand that it would later obtain the Ukraine. Its real purpose of driving a wedge between France and her eastern and southeastern allies was largely ignored.[77]

In these analyses, foreign policy is depicted as the concern of a small group of monopolist spokesmen whose narrow material interests dictated the decisions they made. It is an interpretation that in modified form some non-Marxist Western historians, too, have adopted.[78] Yet appeasement was not a policy imposed on un-

---

[76]Gossweiler, in Paterna et al., *Deutschland*, pp. 20, 132; *GdA*, vol. 5, p. 77; Bünger, "Herrschenden Kreise," pp. 116–17. On the U.S.A., see Peter Schäfer, "Kollektive Sicherheit oder Appeasement-Politik," *WZ Berlin* 22 (1973): 89ff.

[77]See Pätzold, in Paterna et al., *Deutschland*, p. 87; Streisand, p. 360; Anderle, *Die Grosse Sozialistische Oktoberrevolution und Deutschland* (Berlin [East], 1967), vol. 1, p. 417. The efforts of French Foreign Minister Louis Barthou to draw the Soviet Union into the French alliance system are explained as an attempt of a more flexible segment of the French bourgeoisie to set aside temporarily its enmity to the Soviet Union in order to check fascist Germany. The reactionary elements of the monopoly bourgeoisie, according to this interpretation, were forced to tolerate Barthou's policy because they had been compromised by an abortive fascist rising in February 1934 (Paterna et al., *Deutschland*, pp. 153–54; Köller and Töpfer, *Frankreich*, vol. 2, pp. 309–10).

[78]A. L. Rowse, *Appeasement* (New York, 1961), especially pp. 114ff.; Martin Gilbert and Richard Gott, *The Appeasers* (London, 1963).

willing nations by a business-oriented upper class preoccupied with the preservation of the extant social order. The fact is that appeasement enjoyed widespread support among all classes. This support sprang from its own indigenous sources—especially from a reluctance to give up the comforts of a peace-oriented economy, from a deep-seated aversion to war, or, in the case of France, from the demoralizing diffidence that weighed on that nation and kept it from making any move without British support. These facts are almost wholly ignored in the class-focused analyses of East German historians; only one author, dealing with the United States, acknowledges the existence of pacifist isolationism as an autochthonous mass phenomenon. For the rest, the masses—as always, when they are not siding with "progress"—are pictured as confused and manipulated and now also as terrorized into acquiescence.[79]

On the other hand, tribute is paid to the Soviet Union for demanding as early as 1933 a policy of collective security against any fascist aggression. In pursuit of this goal, it is noted, the USSR gave immediate support to a French proposal, in 1934, for an eastern "Locarno" Pact, whereas Poland, Germany, and in the end Britain as well rejected the plan. Similarly, the USSR entered the League of Nations and concluded military assistance pacts with both France and Czechoslovakia, pacts that these countries, in sharp contrast to such Soviet cooperation, ratified only reluctantly. Because of the anti-Communist stance of the ruling groups in the West, these measures failed to restrain the German imperialists.[80]

The Comintern, too, is praised for its flexibility. Abandoning its earlier position, it concluded that to rescind the Versailles Treaty would merely aid fascist imperialism. Consequently, it now opposed the return to Germany of her lost territories. Such transfers, it argued, would subject the populations affected, both German and non-German, to fascist terror and would merely strengthen the German fascists. True to their principles, Communists could support only national movements that would weaken or overthrow imperialist powers. Yet, despite all these efforts, DDR scholars note, the Western monopolists won out. The Saar Basin, for one, was returned to Germany in accordance with the Versailles Treaty. In fact, East

[79]Schäfer, "Kollektive Sicherheit," p. 92; Paterna et al., pp. 324ff.; *Grundriss,* pp. 455–56.
[80]See "Kollektive Sicherheit," *Swb,* vol. 1, p. 937; Paterna et al., *Deutschland,* pp. 123, 148, 153–54, 159; Peter Reuther, "Die ... europäische Sicherheit und das Ostpakt-Problem ... 1934," *WZ Berlin* 17 (1968): 175ff. Suprisingly, Markus, in Paterna et al., *Deutschland,* p. 276, seems to believe that the Soviet obligation to come to Czechoslovakia's aid only if France honored its obligation was a precautionary clause insisted upon by Moscow. Actually that reservation was inserted at Czechoslovakia's insistence in order to stress the greater importance of its ties with the West. See Jiri S. Hajek, in *Die Hintergründe des Münchener Abkommens* (Berlin [East], 1959), p. 22.

German accounts give the impression that the return of that region was the result more of monopolist manipulations than on an internationally supervised plebiscite.[81]

Germany's next moves took her further along the road to aggression. DDR analyses of these steps—open rearmament, remilitarization of the Rhineland, intervention in the Spanish civil war—add little to what non-Marxist research has disclosed about these actions as stepping-stones on the road to war.[82] The East German discussions put much greater stress, on the other hand, on the role of the "ruling groups" in the Western countries. These circles are charged with virtually approving all the violations of international law of which the "Hitler fascists" were guilty. Again, the documentation, if there is any, is highly selective and ignores all evidence to the contrary; as so often the conclusions assume that the "monopoly bourgeoisie" by definition was shrewd and deliberate and fully aware of the consequences of its actions.[83]

The accounts grant, however, that after some time the British monopoly bourgeoisie became alarmed at the intrusions of the German imperialists into areas of Western concern. Yet, as these studies also point out, it was not so much Hitler's support of Mussolini during the invasion of Ethiopia that perturbed British businessmen or his intervention in Spain, to which they reacted only half-heartedly, but the German penetration of the British and American overseas market, the dumping of exports, and the reduction of imports, in keeping with the drive toward autarky. Yet, unrelenting in their anti-Communism, the "ruling cliques" persisted in their determinaton to resolve their difficulties with the fascist bloc at the expense of the Soviet Union. To this end, DDR authors charge, they were prepared to abandon central, eastern, and southeastern Europe, as well as the USSR, to the fascist aggressors.[84]

---

[81]See Paterna et al., *Deutschland*, pp. 145ff.; *GdA*, vol. 5, pp. 63–64, 503–4; Markus, "Die deutsch-französischen Auseinandersetzungen um das Saargebiet: 1933 bis 1935," *WZ Berlin* 22 (1973): 103ff.; documentation in *BzG* 11 (1969): 65. On the Comintern, see Thomas Weingartner, *Stalin und der Aufstieg Hitlers* (Berlin [West], 1970), 244–46, 265.

[82]Of course, greater attention is paid to the "monopolist" impact on developments, although again the role of the monopolies as initiators rather than subsequent profiteers is never illustrated. See, for example, Marion Einhorn, *Die ökonomischen Hintergründe der faschistischen deutschen Intervention in Spanien 1936–1939* (Berlin [East], 1962).

[83]Ample testimony to the contrary is available in the diaries and memoirs of leading insiders, such as Viscount Templewood (Sir Samuel Hoare), (*Nine Troubled Years* [New York, 1954]; Sir Neville Henderson, *Failure of a Mission* [New York, 1940]; Thomas Jones, *A Diary with Letters* [London, 1954]).

[84]See Streisand, pp. 365–67, 371–73, 374–75; Paterna et al., *Deutschland*, pp. 230, 263; *GdA*, vol. 5, p. 151; Heinz Lindner, "Die Deutsch-Französische Erklärung vom 6. Dezember 1938," *ZfG* 16 (1968): 884–85. On the importance of economic rivalries, see also the study by the West German historian Bernd-Jürgen Wendt, *Appeasement 1938: Wirtschaftliche Rezession und Mitteleuropa* (Frankfurt, 1968).

There is no suggestion in the East German literature that the Western distrust of the USSR sprang from reasons other than mere hatred of Communism. No mention is made of the fact that the purges of the Red Army then under way raised serious questions about Russia's usefulness as an ally. Other considerations that led Western governments, rightly or not, to avoid a confrontation with Hitler—the status of their economies, threats from Italy and Japan—are similarly disregarded. Granted that anti-Communism was their main reason for rejecting an alliance with Soviet Russia, the claim that they gave Hitler a free hand in eastern Europe in order to launch him on a collision course with the USSR remains unproven. The documentation gathered by DDR researchers does, however, suggest that Britain and France had no objection to Germany's eastward expansion if in this way they could purchase peace for themselves. This was not the same as propelling Germany into a war against Russia, but from the Marxist perspective the difference admittedly must seem minor.[85]

The moves against Austria, the Sudetenland, and rump Czechoslovakia in 1938–1939 and the Western reactions to these moves thus form part of the East German scenario of fascist expansionism as aided and abetted by its counterparts in the West. The Soviet Union, in turn, is singled out as the one country trying to stem the tide of Nazi imperialism and continuing to urge, in vain, the creation of a collective-security system. Markus and, by implication, *Sachwörterbuch* even claim that the USSR was prepared to send military aid to Czechoslovakia regardless of what the West would do in case of a German attack, but they offer no evidence to support this assertion.[86]

[85]A typical example of East German assessments of Western policy can be found in Lindner, "Erklärung," pp. 884ff. The representative character of Lindner's study extends to the selective and often untenable interpretation of his sources. How little Britain and France cherished the prospect of abandoning southeastern Europe to the Germans, if only for economic reasons, is shown by Wendt, *Appeasement.* This is also implied, if not directly admitted, by Paterna et al., *Deutschland,* p. 294.

[86]Markus, in Paterna et al., *Deutschland,* pp. 286, 291–92, 294–95, 298; also, implicitly, "Münchener Abkommen," *Swb,* vol. 2, p. 121. On the question of Soviet help to Czechoslovakia, none of the contemporary accounts available to me mention any promises of military aid beyond existing treaty commitments or obligations resulting from Russia's league membership. Most Marxist accounts, if they deal with this issue at all, are notably ambiguous about it (I. K. Kobljakov, in *Der deutsche Imperialismus,* vol. 2, pp. 567–68; I. I. Minz, in *Hintergründe,* p. 79). Vaclav Kral (*Das Abkommen von München 1938* [Prague, 1968], p. 23) does not raise it at all. There are some vague allusions to it in *New Documents on the History of Munich,* published by the Czechoslovak Ministry of Foreign Affairs (Prague, 1958), doc. nos. 29, 33, 37, 48, 55. Hass et al. (*Deutschland,* vol. 1, p. 116) quote Soviet President M. I. Kalinin as saying in April 1938 that the treaties between the USSR, Czechoslovakia, and France "did not bar any of the parties from providing help without waiting for France." The authors also state, without

The DDR accounts of the Munich crisis differ in one respect, however, from the analyses of preceding developments. Whereas earlier no note had been taken of the overwhelming popular antiwar sentiment in Britain and France, the demand in both countries, during and after the Munich crisis, for determined resistance to any further German aggression is stressed and even overstressed. In this same vein, the antiwar mood displayed by many Germans is praised. On the other hand, the opposition to Hitler that emerged in conservative political and military circles is discounted as unimportant. Once again, the participants are dismissed as monopolists and militarists who disagreed with the "Hitler clique" merely on tactics, not on ultimate goals.[87]

DDR authors find the progressive impact of the masses borne out also by the emergence of mass pressures in Britain and France after the total subjection and breakup of rump Czechoslovakia by Germany in March 1939. As the result of these pressures, they note, the British government pledged aid to Poland and later to Rumania and Greece, should the independence of these countries be threatened. After considerable delay, the British and French governments also initiated talks with the Soviet government on joint resistance to further German aggression. Even so, the East German studies complain, these spokesmen of the monopoly bourgeoisie outwitted the hapless masses. The pledge to Poland referred only to her independence, not her territorial integrity, and left the door

---

documentation, that the Soviet government was willing during the critical weeks to aid Czechoslovakia without the Western powers and the League of Nations if Czechoslovakia would fight, but it also quotes Foreign Commissar Litvinov as stating at a league meeting on September 21, 1938, at the height of the crisis, that, "We intend to fulfill our treaty obligations jointly with France and give help to Czechoslovakia through all accessible channels. Our military administration is ready to take part at once in consultations with representatives of the military authorities of France and Czechoslovakia in order to take the measures required by the situation." The reference to "all accessible channels" concerned the fact that Soviet Russia had access by land to Czechoslovakia only by way of Rumania and Poland, neither of which would let Soviet land forces move across its territory (Rumania, however, was apparently williing to let Soviet planes cross its air space). Another official statement similar to Litvinov's was retrospectively published by the government newspaper *Izvestia* in October 1938 (ibid., pp. 118, 119, 121). The known statements asserting outright the existence of firm Soviet pledges of help regardless of the West's attitude were all made after the event, most of them long afterwards. See also Boris Celovsky, *Das Münchener Abkommen von 1938* (Stuttgart, 1958), pp. 374ff., 441–43.

[87]See Paterna, et al., *Deutschland*, pp. 202–3, 257–58, 288–89; *Grundriss*, p. 461. On the fickleness of British public opinion during the Munich crisis, see A.J.P. Taylor, *English History: 1914–1945* (New York, 1965), pp. 427–30. On the merely tactical nature of the military opposition to Hitler in 1938, see also the study of the West German historian Müller, "Ludwig Beck: Ein General zwischen Wilhelminismus und Nationalsozialismus," in *Deutschland in der Weltpolitik des 19. und 20. Jahrhunderts*, Immanuel Geiss and Bernd-Jürgen Wendt (Düsseldorf, 1973), pp. 513ff.

open to Germany's recovery of formerly German territories. Accordingly, Britain kept holding out to Berlin generous economic and colonial rewards and the eventual cession of Danzig and the Polish Corridor in return for the preservation of peace.[88]

The British are found deceitful, too, in their negotiations with the Soviet government. At the very time at which these negotiations took place, they sought to conclude a nonaggression pact with the Germans. As further evidence of bad faith, DDR authors point to the recurrent talks of British and German businessmen on the division of world markets and price and currency agreements—clear proof to any Marxist observer that these rival monopoly camps sought to adjust their conflicting interests in preparation for an assault on socialist Soviet Russia. The purpose of the Western-Soviet negotiations thus was open only to one interpretation—the Western powers looked on any agreement with the Soviet Union as merely a last resort, in which they would use the USSR against Germany but would not assume themselves any responsibilities toward the Soviet Union or take any other steps to meet the latter's defense needs. Hence, too, the Western rejection of an unconditional support of all states bordering on the Soviet Union, which would have allowed the Kremlin to send toops into or through these countries, even against their will, in the event of a direct German attack on these states or in case of an indirect act of aggression by internal subversion. Marxist historians are all the more critical of the Western refusal to ignore the objections of Poland and the Baltic states to the Soviet proposal because the Western powers had not hesitated to ignore the wishes of the Czech people a year before.[89]

In the end, the Soviet Union decided to throw in its lot with Nazi Germany. Late in August 1939, it concluded a nonaggression pact with the latter. DDR authors argue that the pact was viewed by Moscow as imposed by necessity, not as a preferred alternative; they insist—and the evidence bears them out—that the Soviet government signed the pact only after all possibilities of reaching an accord with the Western powers had been exhausted and that it was fully aware of the unreliability of the Nazi regime as a treaty partner.[90] At the same time, East German scholars present with

[88]Paterna et al., *Deutschland*, pp. 337ff.; Horst Schützler, "Die politischen Verhandlungen der Sowjetunion mit Grossbritannien und Frankreich . . . 1939," *ZfG* 7 (1959): 1720–21.

[89]See Paterna, et al., *Deutschland*, pp. 338–39, 343–44; Streisand, pp. 386–87. Their work is based largely on the research of Soviet and Czech historians; see the pertinent contributions to *Der deutsche Imperialismus*, vol. 2.

[90]See, for example, the protocol of the Anglo-French-Soviet military discussions, reprinted in *Deutsche Aussenpolitik* (1959): 541ff., 674ff.; also Hass et al., *Deutschland*, vol. 1, p. 158.

considerable persuasiveness the Kremlin's case for coming to terms with the Germans: Germany was poised for war against Poland—a war into which the USSR might have been drawn without such a pact, and it would have gone without allies ready to come to its aid. Moreover, such an attack would have come while the USRR was already engaged in border fights with Japan in the Far East. These clashes might have been stepped up by Japan into a full-scale war in case of a German attack with the possible support of the imperialist United States, Britain, and France. Finally, the pact prevented the creation of an anti-Soviet, four-power bloc of Germany, France, Britain, and Italy and thus left the imperialist camp divided.

For Marxist historians, then, the pact's true historical import lies in the fact that it guarded the Soviet Union against encirclement and a two-front war. By thus protecting the one extant socialist state, it is pointed out, the pact served the interests of the toilers throughout the world as it served the cause of peace and democracy. If war nonetheless broke out, it did so not because of the pact but because of the unwillingness of the imperialist Western powers to work for peace in cooperation with the USSR. As DDR authors put it, the pact admittedly did not check the aggressiveness of German fascist imperialism and militarism, but this, as these same authors argue, only the Germans themselves could have brought about—by the overthrow of the Hitler regime. They failed to do so, despite intense Communist efforts to arouse them; thus, the German fascists, unchecked by the Western powers as well, were able to start their war. Yet the war began, thanks to the pact, "not, as strong groups of world imperialism had hoped, as a crusade against the Soviet Union, but as an imperialist war between fascist Germany and the Western powers."[91]

The Imperialist War

This assessment of the war that broke out on September 1, 1939, is not, however, wholly unqualified. Some differences from other imperialist conflicts are noted. Unlike fascist German imperialists,

[91]See Paterna et al., *Deutschland*, pp. 345–47; *GdA*, vol. 5, pp. 233ff.; "Deutsch Sowjetischer Nichtangriffspakt 1939," *Swb*, vol. 1, pp. 475–77; Werner Basler, in *Der deutsche Imperialismus*, vol. 2, pp. 627–28; Anderle, *Grosse Sozialistische Oktoberrevolution*, vol. 1, pp. 431–32 (quotation on p. 432), 615 n. 334. No mention is made anywhere of the secret supplementary protocol by which Poland was to be partitioned between the two powers, and Finland, the Baltic states, and Bessarabia were assigned to the Soviet sphere of interest. On the justification of the subsequent partition of Poland and the incorporation into the Soviet Union of the Polish Ukraine and Byelorussia, see below, page 437.

some authors point out, the Western powers contented themselves with the consolidation and expansion of their position without resorting to the mass spoliation and extermination of entire peoples. Moreover, the imperialist character of the war was modified by the fact that for Poles and Czechs the conflict turned at once into a fight for national liberation. From the outset, then, it contained elements of a "just, antifascist struggle."

For antifascist movements in Germany as in other countries, in this view, the war also offered an opportunity to intensify the fight against fascism and the antinational policies of rapacious monopoly capitalism. In this sense a class conflict, this fight drew its social thrust from the working class, with the Communists playing a leading role, as did the socialist Soviet state, which by its very existence challenged a capitalist order already weakened by its recurring crises. As the conflict wore on, it became in this view increasingly an antifascist war of emancipation, although it never divested itself wholly of its imperialist features.[92]

The accounts of the war's early phase point out the feebleness of all liberation attempts. Imperialism held sway, and the Nazi spoliation of Poland and the brutalities perpetrated upon the Polish people are depicted as illustrations of the excesses of which imperialism was capable. DDR authors are almost more interested, however, in illustrating the imperialist stance of the Western powers than in discussing the atrocities of the Nazis. Thus the "phony war" is viewed by East German authors as a modified sequel to the prewar appeasement tactics of Britain and France. The inaction of those countries serves as proof of their continuing hope of turning Germany against the USSR. To support these claims, attention is called to Western peace soundings during that period. No mention, however, is made of the fact that all Nazi peace efforts failed because the Western powers would not accept the territorial status quo on which Hitler insisted, nor would they have any dealings personally with him—this latter stance being a pointless posture from the Marxist perspective, because Hitler played but a subordinate role in the Marxist scenario.

East German authors also see Anglo-French imperialist intrigues behind the Soviet-Finnish war that broke out in November 1939. Arguing that the war was to secure some Finnish border areas for the Soviet Union in order to strengthen the defenses of Leningrad, DDR analysts claim that that conflict was a defensive act on Moscow's part. According to them, it was provoked by Finnish reactionaries, who, encouraged by London and Paris, blocked a negotiated transfer. The expulsion of the USSR from the League of

[92]Bleyer et al., *Deutschland*, pp. 23ff.; *GdA*, vol. 5, pp. 241ff.; Förster et al., in *ZfG* 18 (1970): suppl. pp. 580–81; *Grundriss*, p. 464.

Nations on the grounds of aggression, Western military and economic help to the Finns, and the assembling of an Anglo-French expeditionary force to be dispatched to their aid thus can be marshalled as evidence of the continuing unjustified anti-Soviet stance of the Western powers. So can plans for an attack from Mideastern bases on the Caucasian oilfields. That these latter plans were meant to cut off oil deliveries to Germany and were abandoned on the grounds that they would harm Russia rather than Germany is not mentioned, however. Still, the charges of an implicit anti-Soviet bias on the part of the Western powers were not unfounded, but, as the failure of all mediation attempts demonstrated, they were not gestures of appeasement addressed to Berlin. Britain and France could well defend their anti-Soviet activities on the grounds that the USSR was a de facto ally of Germany.

On the other hand, whereas DDR authors take the Western powers to task for these alleged offenses, they ignore the substantial appeasement practiced in turn by the USSR. Soviet shipments of war-essential materials to Germany clearly were meant to keep the Nazis at bay, as was Moscow's support of Hitler's peace offer after the Polish campaign, although that offer stipulated his right to retain all conquered lands. If these policies are mentioned at all, they are justified as furthering the socialist development of the USSR and strengthening its defenses.[93]

As for the Soviet occupation of eastern Poland after the defeat of that country, that move is not justified on legal and historical grounds; rather, DDR authors applaud the move as an effort to protect that area from enslavement by Nazi imperialism and to liberate it at the same time from exploitation by Polish bourgeois and estate owners, in response to the alleged wishes of the peoples of these areas. Similarly, Moscow is claimed to have acted merely in response to the unanimous votes of popular elected assemblies in both the Western Ukraine and Western Byelorussia when it let these regions join the Soviet states of the Ukraine and Byelorussia and, through them, the Soviet Union.[94]

The German invasion of Denmark and Norway and the subse-

[93]*Swb*, vol. 2, pp. 100, 119–20, 474; Bleyer at al., *Deutschland*, pp. 34ff.; *Abriss*, p. 65; Taylor, *English History*, pp. 467ff.; E. L. Woodward, *British Foreign Policy in the Second World War* (London, 1962), vol. 1, p. 30; Andreas Hillgruber, "Der Zweite Weltkrieg," *SDG*, vol. 6, p. 878.

[94]See Bleyer et al., *Deutschland*, pp. 32–33; Hass et al., *Deutschland*, vol. 1, pp. 184–86. Similar developments in Lithuania, Latvia, and Estonia in 1940 are nowhere mentioned in these accounts. For a brief analysis, picturing the Communization of the three countries as a matter of lawful popular self-determination made possible by the presence of Soviet troops that prevented domestic or foreign bourgeois interference, see Roswitha Czollek, in a review of a Soviet study, *The Socialist Revolution of 1940 in Lithuania, Latvia, and Estonia, ZfG* 27 (1979): 366–68.

quent campaigns against France and the Low Countries are viewed as implementations of long-held plans of the German imperialists and militarists. These moves were to subdue the rival monopoly capitalists of western Europe and crush the revolutionary working-class movement and all other progressive forces of that area. The success of the attacks was predicated on the element of surprise and on the assumption that the Western powers would persist in their policy of appeasement. In this manner, the German forces made up for their materiel inferiority (which ultimately would help bring about their inevitable defeat) and succeeded in their foolhardy venture. Yet, if the Germans owed their victory to their reckless bravado, the French contributed to that success by the "class" character of their defense. "Clerical-fascist" circles are charged with persistently sabotaging any effective defense measures. In the end, the ruling reactionary groups preferred to come to terms with the Germans rather than call the whole nation to arms and turn the imperialist war into a people's war for national independence, freedom, and democracy. (How such mass mobilization was to be carried out and what it was to accomplish against German airplanes and tanks is not explained.) One author, Gerhart Hass, even claims that the class-centered stance of the ruling groups did more to cause France's defeat than did the victories of the Germans. The Germans thus could conclude an armistice that "enabled German imperialism to despoil France and turn it into a source of supplies for Germany's armament industry."[95]

The hope of the Hitler regime to come to terms with the British was not realized because, as DDR authors see it, British imperialism was unwilling to tolerate the predominance of the German imperialists on the European continent. Unlike their French counterparts, the British imperialists also had the will and the strength to reject the role of a junior partner of German imperialism. At the same time, the British masses insisted on an active resistance. No mention is made of Churchill, except for occasional references to him as a representative of the militant sector of Brit-

[95]See Hass, in Bleyer et al., *Deutschland*, pp. 63ff.; Köller and Töpfer, *Frankreich*, vol. 2, pp. 331ff.; Streisand, pp. 388–89. Although East German accounts on the whole pay little attention to the military aspects of the Western campaigns, the events at Dunkirk have been analyzed with considerable care. The failure to pursue the retreating British right to the sea is attributed, not to an arbitrary decision of Hitler, but to military miscalculations and to the lack of equipment. The analyses thus are meant to disprove, once again, the "myth" of Hitler's solitary key role. At the same time, they demonstrate the discrepancies between German means and goals, confirming the East German thesis of the inherent inevitability of Germany's eventual defeat. See Bleyer et al., *Deutschland*, pp. 66–67; "Dünkirchen-Affäre," *Swb*, vol. 1, p. 511; Hass et al., *Deutschland*, vol. 1, pp. 323ff.; Olaf Groehler, "Menetekel Dünkirchen," *ZfG* 9 (1961): 1225ff. (The suggestive title of this article obviously was to indicate that Dunkirk already heralded Germany's inevitable defeat.)

ish imperialism; if credit for the successful repulsion of the German Luftwaffe is given at all, it is given to the British masses rather than to the Royal Air Force.

Actually, as Ernst Stenzel, a military historian, argues expressly and as other authors imply, the real reason for Germany's failure to invade Britain was that the decision to attack the Soviet Union had already been made. The military leadership was therefore unwilling to commit the troops needed for a successful invasion of Britain, because all available forces had to be saved for the projected assault on the USSR. That the invasion was called off as unfeasible is conceded by only a few authors; most of them dismiss this point as irrelevant, if they bring it up at all, because it did not affect the long-planned attack on the Soviet Union. Following Stenzel, *Sachwörterbuch* concludes that "the existence of the Soviet Union, against which English politicans had tried to turn German fascism, lastly saved Britain from a takeover by fascist German imperialism during the Second World War." Because the Battle of Britain is considered inconsequential, no DDR historian has wondered what the effect of a British surrender on the future course of the war and in particular on the German campaign against the USSR might have been. (As it was, Britain's successful resistance forced Germany to fight British countermoves in the Balkan Peninsula and to delay the invasion of Russia by several possibly crucial weeks.) Some East German authors do not even mention the battle. For Stenzel, the importance attributed to the "so-called Battle of Britain" is in itself significant; he views it as an effort to deprecate the decisive role played by the Soviet Union in defeating "Hitler fascism" and thus prepare the ground psychologically for a third World War, from which the West German "successors of Hitler," in alliance with the Western powers, were expected to emerge as the victors. Others, while not going as far, also see the importance attributed to that battle as a deliberate attempt to downgrade the far more decisive role of the USSR.[96]

The military events of those months, however, are viewed as mere backdrops to the developments that matter most in the Marxist perception—the establishment of a German-dominated "New Order" in Europe. With the reordering of the political, social, economic, and cultural life of the defeated countries, the old goal of German imperialism—continental hegemony—came to fru-

[96]See Bleyer et al., *Deutschland*, pp. 101ff.; "Unternehmen Seelöwe," *Swb*, vol. 2, pp. 671–72; Ernst Stenzel, in *Der deutsche Imperialismus*, vol. 3, pp. 281ff.; Anonymous, in *ZfG* 8 (1960): 691; *Grundriss*, p. 468; Hass et al., *Deutschland*, vol. 1, pp. 354ff. Streisand (p. 388) and *GdA* 5 (pp. 271, 275) make no mention of the Battle of Britain. The best non-Marxist account on this issue is Hillgruber, *Hitlers Strategie: Politik und Kriegsführung, 1940–41* (Frankfurt, 1965), pp. 144ff., especially pp. 166ff., 170–72, 207ff.

ition. In the characteristic fashion of a state-monopolist system, it is noted, plans for annexations and acquisitions were drawn up by government, business, and military groups, and an extensive literature deals with these plans as illustrations of the excesses of which state-monopolist capitalism is capable. At the same time, the "New Order" was to provide the springboard for the destruction of the socialist Soviet state, the basic "class" goal of German imperialism. With Soviet lands and resources incorporated into the "New Order," the German imperialists would then challenge the American and Asian economies in their quest for world rule. The strategic plans of the armed services, aiming at the conquest of the USSR and the Balkan countries; the seizure of Gibraltar and Portugal, with its island possessions, North Africa, and the Suez Canal; and projected campaigns against Iraq, Iran, and Afghanistan expressed the objectives of the monopolists and various agencies of the government. These aims, Gerhart Hass maintains, are revealed with great candor in the so-called "peace plan" of I. G. Farben; that plan "not only establishes the [dye's trust] complete agreement with the goals pursued by the political leadership of Hitler Germany but [also] shows who were the real beneficiaries of the war, in whose interest it was launched, and how these forces determined the main directives of the expansionist policies. It was the task of the political and military authorities of the state-monopolist ruling apparatus to look for the ways and means by which to attain these goals and assure their realization."[97]

Once again, the reasoning rests on a *post hoc, ergo propter hoc* argument by which the fact that the war proved beneficial to major business concerns serves as proof that it was launched on their behalf. Yet as before, the evidence collected by East German researchers fails to bear out any such claims, except by way of highly contrived interpretations.[98] To a Marxist, they do not seem so, of course, because in his perception all imperialist planning grew objectively out of the very existence of German monopoly capitalism, and for this reason the wars by which these plans were achieved are

[97]See Hass, in Bleyer et al., *Deutschland*, pp. 69ff. (quotation on p. 75); "Neuordnung Europas," *Swb*, vol. 2, pp. 182–83; Eichholtz, *Geschichte*, vol. 1, pp. 162ff.; Hass et al., *Deutschland*, vol. 1, pp. 385ff., 419ff. The Farben "peace plan" is reprinted in Eichholtz (*Geschichte*, vol. 1, pp. 248ff.).

[98]For a particularly bizarre misinterpretation of one such source—Hitler's first speech to the Reichswehr generals in February 1933—see Eichholtz, *Geschichte*, vol. 1, p. 157. Hitler said on that occasion, after having discussed the need for German rearmament, that it would have to be decided later whether a rearmed Germany ought to use its newly gained power to secure new export markets or to conquer new living space in the east. To Eichholtz this meant that Hitler had not yet decided which of the expansionist plans the monopolies had submitted to him would be carried out first.

the responsibility of the monopolies. The large chunks of the captured economies that banks and industrial enterprises acquired—with the encouragement and active help or at the behest of the government—merely serve to bear out this argumentation.[99]

If it cannot be said that the war against France and the Low Countries was launched for the sake of I. G. Farben or Vereinigte Stahlwerke, it is true on the other hand that the government relied on the large banks and industrial enterprises to help it dominate and exploit the conquered lands. This was to be done by way of control or outright purchase of key enterprises in the occupied countries. Yet, in carrying out this mandate, German bankers and industrialists in their rapacity created so inequitable an order that it would never have attained stability but would have had to depend permanently on Nazi terror for its survival. Nurturing that terrorism, it would have helped to keep the occupied lands in a state of perpetual warfare, to that extent bearing out the Marxist analyses of the war-generating propensities of the German monopolies.[100]

At the same time, the large industrial concerns are found to have used the military successes to further consolidate their domination of the domestic economy. A first significant move in that direction is seen in the creation of a Reich Office for Economic Development (Reichsamt für Wirtschaftsausbau), which deprived Economics Minister Walther Funk of his war-related economic functions. Karl Krauch, an I. G. Farben director, was made head of the new agency. Krauch and his many fellow Farben officials in the new agency (who all remained on the Farben payroll) thus were no longer confined to the technical sphere of production, as they had been in earlier posts on the Four-Year Plan Staff. They now had a considerable say in its planning as well, much to the benefit of the dye trust. In the words of the West German economic historian

[99]See Bleyer et al., *Deutschland*, pp. 73ff.; Eichholtz, *Geschichte*, vol. 1, pp. 144ff.; Eichholtz and Schumann, *Anatomie des Krieges*, pp. 224ff.; *GdA*, vol. 5, pp. 538–39; Pätzold, review, *ZfG* 26 (1978): 252. For the actual objectives of the Farben plan, see Eichholtz, *Geschichte*, vol. 1, pp. 251–52, 255–57. By a similar misinterpretation, requests submitted by heavy industry to the economics ministry in anticipation of a new commercial treaty with Norway are alleged to have been made in expectation of the conquest of Norway, with the army high command "translating" these demands into plans for military conquests. See Fritz Petrick, "Das wirtschaftliche Okkupationsprogramm . . . beim Überfall auf Dänemark und Norwegen (1940)," *ZfG* 22 (1974): 742–43, and the actual version of the document on which he bases his argument, in *Anatomie der Aggression*, ed. Hass and Schumann (Berlin [East], 1972), p. 41. On the other hand, Fritz Klein (in *ZfG* 23 [1975]: 488) acknowledges that DDR researchers have so far failed to show how entrepreneurial objectives were shaped into governmental policies. (The "how" is revealing: Klein takes for granted that such shaping took place; only the manner in which this occurred remains to be determined.)

[100]Radkau, in Hallgarten and Radkau, *Industrie*, pp. 399ff., 409ff., 414–15.

Dieter Petzina, whose own researches bear out the East German conclusions, "state apparatus and private industry were hardly distinguishable any more in [this] sector."

DDR authors also find evidence of a strengthened monopolist position in the formation of a ministry of armaments and munitions set up in March 1940 to centralize weapons and munitions production, with the army excluded from both the planning and the production process. The exclusion of the army enabled the armament industries to raise their prices and increase their profits—something the military had so far successfully fought. The new arrangements also gave large concerns further preferment in the allocation of government orders, raw materials, and manpower. Similarly, a Reich Coal Union (Reichsvereiningung Kohle) gave the mining industries a position not unlike that attained by the dye trust in the Office of Economic Development. Altogether, the course of events is found to bear out Lenin's thesis that war serves to accelerate the trend toward state-monopolist capitalism, demonstrating again, as the East German analyses keep stressing, the affinity existing between them. All contrary factors—restraints imposed on big business by governmental and party pressures, which were considerable—are ignored as insignificant or irrelevant.[101]

Given the growing power of the "monopolies," it is a particular source of gratification to DDR authors that the class struggle could not be wholly suppressed. As always, they find it spearheaded by the Communist party and its Central Committee, and they have carefully collected all evidence of such activities—demands for pay raises and overtime pay, work slowdowns and sabotage actions, and especially efforts to erode faith in the government through discussions, distribution of leaflets, underground newspapers, and other informational materials, and the organization of groups that would listen to foreign broadcasts. To coordinate these activities and to provide guidance and inspiration, the maintenance of a party organization with a network of local units, directed by the Central Committee in Moscow, took on special significance. It pursued its work with unflagging determination, despite the relentless efforts of the Gestapo to break it up. How-

[101]See Bleyer et al., *Deutschland*, pp. 94ff.; Eichholtz, *Geschichte*, vol. 1, pp. 108ff.; Eichholtz, "Probleme," pp. 110ff.; Wagner, "Dokumente zur Rolle des Monopolkapitalismus . . . ," *ZfG* 17 (1969): 483–84; Petzina, *Autarkiepolitik*, pp. 121ff. (quotation on p. 123). On price controls imposed by the army, see Thomas, *Geschichte der deutschen Wehr- und Rüstungswirtschaft (1918–1943/45)*, ed. Wolfgang Birkenfeld (Boppard, 1966), pp. 137ff. For restraints imposed on business by Nazi party and government, see Esenwein-Rothe, *Wirtshaftsverbände*, pp. 113–14; Eichholtz, *Geschichte*, vol. 1, p. 139 (no coal price increases for at least two years); Eichholtz and Schumann, *Anatomie des Krieges*, doc. no. 120.

ever, even though DDR authors will not say so expressly, stressing instead the courage and sufferings of the party workers involved, the data they have gathered again make it clear that these endeavors amounted barely to pinpricks. As usual, much of the blame is placed on the Social Democratic leadership, who continued to reject all attempts to form a united front and preferred looking for bourgeois allies; yet, what a united front of Communists and Social Democrats could actually have accomplished is not made clear.

On the other hand, tribute is paid to the resistance activities of other groups and individuals—to the *Kreisau Kreis* of liberal-minded former officials, political leaders, and clergymen and to other like-minded circles, as well as to individual fighters from all social strata. All accounts grant, however, that the basic obstacle to effective oppositional action was the nation's willingness to support the regime; government propaganda, buttressed by military successes, kept the country in a state of confusion concerning its real interests.

The Communists, moreover, faced the additional task of calling for opposition to a regime that the Soviet Union appeared to encourage in its aggression by its continued supply of vital materials. This dilemma, however, is passed over altogether. Instead, great stress is laid on the fact that peace was maintained between the Soviet Union and Germany, which served best the interests of socialism. At the same time, the German government is berated for its duplicity in professing its peaceful intentions while preparing for an attack on the USSR only a few months after the Soviet-Nazi pact had been signed.

DDR authors point out rightly, however, in refutation of West German claims, that there is no indication that the accommodations between Berlin and Moscow imposed restraints on the KPD's anti-Nazi strategy. With the full approval of the Comintern, the party kept up its struggle; any limitations to which its work was subjected were the result of the effectiveness of the Gestapo and the nonresponsiveness of the people. Conversely, the KPD rationalized its acceptance of Moscow's supply of strategic materials to the Nazi war machine by arguing that that machine was directed against Britain and France, two imperialist powers bent on expanding the war and attacking the Soviet Union. Pieck and Ulbricht, in fact, joined the Comintern in rebuking France and Britain for not accepting Germany's peace terms after the Polish campaign, although such acceptance would have left Hitler in power and in possession of all territorial gains. These contemporary reactions, however, are not reported in present-day East German accounts, which charge the Western powers with appeasement rather than warmongering during that period.

No such disagreement exists between contemporary and recent assessments of the Social Democratic position. According to the KPD leadership at that time and current East German scholarship, it was the Social Democrats who aided the Nazis by giving up domestic resistance as hopeless and deciding to wait for Hitler's defeat by the British and French before overthrowing him. This stance was then and is still regarded as greatly mistaken, because it disregarded the "class" aspects of any resistance. As bourgeois-imperialist countries, the Western powers were bound to install another antidemocratic regime after they had defeated the Nazis. Only the German people could, by their own revolutionary action, give themselves a progressive, genuinely democratic government. To prepare for that day the Communists considered their overriding, truly national task; they alone understood the "class" significance of any resistance movement, which in order to be successful had to be directed not only against the terrorist fascist frontmen, but above all against monopoly capitalism and imperialism.[102]

The Attack on the Soviet Union

In the Communist view, this task was greatly facilitated by the Nazi attack on the USSR. For Marxist historians, the real import of that invasion lies in its focus on what they view as the central issue of the transition period from capitalism to socialism—capitalism's resolve to stay in power by undoing the progress of socialism: "The assault on the USSR was an attempt, with military means, to attain the basic class aim of German and world imperialism—the liquidation of the first socialist state." With the Soviet Union drawn into the war, it turned into a just antifascist war of liberation in which all progressive mankind, inspired by the Soviet people, rose to annihilate the fascist aggressor and create conditions that would make possible the peaceful and democratic development of all nations. The Soviet-German front thus became the main front of the war, where its outcome would be decided.[103]

[102]Bleyer et al., *Deutschland*, pp. 24–30, 38–40, 50ff., 119–20; *GdA*, vol. 5, pp. 242, 244ff., 278ff., 530ff.; *Abriss*, p. 65; also see Rudolph, Pätzold, and Weissbecker, in *ZfG* 10 (1962): 276–79, 328–29, who criticize their colleague Walter Bartel for minimizing the role of the Central Committee and questioning the intensity of Communist resistance activities during the Nazi-Soviet pact period. For Pieck's and Ulbricht's position, see their contemporary articles, reprinted in Weber, *Kommunismus*, pp. 356–57, 364–67; for West German analyses, see Sywottek, *Deutsche Volksdemokratie*, pp. 110ff.; Duhnke, pp. 353ff. Duhnke, however, is based partly on questionable sources and all in all is somewhat fuzzy.
[103]Karl Drechsler, "Europapläne des deutschen Imperialismus im zweiten Weltkrieg," *ZfG* 19 (1971): 919–20; Förster, in ibid. 8 (1960): suppl., pp. 408–409; *GdA*, vol. 5, pp. 292–94; Bleyer et al., *Deutschland*, pp. 119, 129ff.

Earlier assessments of the war as an imperialist conflict are not altogether discarded, however. As Marxist analysts see it, the war retained some imperialist features. Not only did the imperialist goals of the Nazis remain unchanged, the Western governments also did not abandon their imperialist aims. They were forced to ally themselves with the Soviet Union to safeguard their survival, protect their interests, and eliminate the dangerous rival that Hitler Germany was. These concerns superseded their fears of the socialist state and caused them to suspend their struggle against it, yet this was merely a temporary accommodation, as such anti-Soviet tactics as the recurrent postponement of a second front in the west made clear. (That the Soviet Union had corresponding reservations about the capitalist West is not mentioned, however.) The Western powers, moreover, wished only to weaken an imperialist rival who had become excessively strong; the Soviet Union, on the other hand, was determined to free the peoples of Europe from the yoke of fascism and create a genuinely democratic, peaceful postwar order. Yet, while DDR authors deplore the ultimate aims of the capitalist Western powers, some at least grant that the United States and Britain made great sacrifices and contributed "essentially" to the victory over the fascist bloc.[104]

In Germany's case, East German research, as always, addresses itself in particular to the "monopolist" role in the war against Russia. Whatever its claims, it has failed to produce evidence linking big business to the decision to turn on the Soviet Union. Dietrich Eichholtz, the leading specialist on this issue, admits this implicitly when he states that the monopolies saw "quite essential" war aims realized with the conquest of France and therefore turned their attention to peacetime planning. He also grants that no proof has "so far" been found of any participation of monopoly spokesmen in the decision to attack the USSR. Nonetheless, he considers it a reasonable assumption that Hitler and "all important monopolist groupings" thought "their" decision to invade the USSR the least risky implementation of their main expansionist goals. By a similar legerdemain, Gerhart Hass assigns to business the role of an accessory after the crucial decisions were made, yet at the same time regards it as the initiator of the Russian campaign. And while he quotes as most ominous a letter written in 1938 by the industrialist Hermann Röchling, who called on Hitler to seize Russian territory up to the Ural Mountains and make

---

[104]See *GdA*, vol. 5, pp. 297–99; also Bleyer et al., *Deutschland*, pp. 131–32. Bleyer et al., however, make no mention of a Western contribution to victory. See also Jürgen Kuczynski, *Der Ausbruch des ersten Weltkrieges und die deutsche Sozialdemokratie* (Berlin [East], 1957), pp. viii–ix; Drechsler et al., "Europapläne"; Hass et al., *Deutschland*, vol. 2, p. 33.

Germany self-sufficient in foodstuffs and raw materials, he cavalierly dismisses the concerns of the Krupp Works in 1940 lest a
German-Soviet war interfere with their business arrangements
with the USSR. Actually, it is clear from all available sources that
businessmen were drawn into the preparations for the Russian
campaign after these were well under way and only in order to help
exploit the Soviet resources. To this task, as the sources show,
they devoted themselves with their accustomed zeal until they
discovered how thoroughly factories and mines had been damaged
by the retreating Red Army, after which they virtually had to be
forced to aid in their reconstruction.[105]

The invasion of the Soviet Union is denounced by all East
German authors as the greatest crime the Nazis committed, not
only against that country, but against the German people as well.
This indictment views the attack as one directed against the only
country that was genuinely friendly toward the German people
and, at the same time, a country that was bound to inflict a disastrous defeat on the Germans because of its superior social order. By
trying to turn the wheel of history back through its attempt to
defeat Soviet Russia, German imperialism thus was bringing upon
itself its own inevitable defeat.[106]

At first, to be sure, a Soviet victory did not seem likely, but
the initial setbacks of the Red Army are attributed to special circumstances, among them Stalin's disregard of warnings against a
forthcoming German attack. These were passed on to him by such
underground groups as the "Red Orchestra," an organization of
KPD functionaries and anti-Nazi officials, a few of them Communists, with good connections to the armed forces. Information was
also provided by the press attaché at the German embassy in Japan,
Richard Sorge, who doubled as a Communist intelligence agent.
(That non-Communist sources, such as the German Abwehr
[counter-intelligence], under Admiral Wilhelm Canaris, and the
British and American governments also sent warnings to Moscow
is either ignored or attributed to the desire to draw the Soviet
Union into the war.)[107] Other explanations are that fascist Germany

---

[105]See Helmut Schnitter, in *Der deutsche Imperialismus*, vol. 3, pp. 220ff.; and
Eichholtz, *Geschichte*, vol. 1, pp. 131–32, 207; Hass, in Bleyer et al., *Deutschland*, pp. 112ff.; Eichholtz and Schumann, *Anatomie des Krieges*, doc. nos. 165ff.,
174ff. See also Petzina, *Autarkiepolitik*, p. 143; Radkau, in Hallgarten and Radkau, *Industrie*, pp. 383ff.; on industry's interest in continued friendly relations
with the Soviet Union, see also p. 393. On the reluctance of industrialists to take
over the badly damaged Soviet enterprises, see Matthias Riedel, "Bergbau und
Eisenhüttenindustrie in der Ukraine unter deutscher Besatzung (1941–1944),"
VfZ 21 (1973): 269ff.
[106]*GdA*, vol. 5, pp. 292–93; Bleyer et al., *Deutschland*, pp. 130–31; *Grundriss*, p. 468.
[107]See *GdA*, vol., 5, pp. 291–92, 295; Bleyer et al., *Deutschland*, p. 164; Streisand,
p. 392. On non-Communist warnings, see Böhm, in *Der deutsche Imperialismus*,
vol. 3, p. 80 n. 4; Hass et al., *Deutschland*, vol. 1, pp. 568–69.

benefited from its control of the resources of large parts of Europe, from the greater battle experience of its armies, and from the failure of the Western powers to undertake any military actions that could have compensated for the temporary inferiority of the Soviet forces. However, the successful resistance of the Red Army in the battle of Moscow a few months later and its repulsion of the Germans from both the capital and the Don River signaled the basic superiority of the Soviet system. This Hitler acknowledged, it is claimed, by assuming for himself command of the army.[108]

For these achievements, specific credit is given to the Soviet Communist party. Aided by the superiority of the socialist order, Marxist-Leninist ideology, socialist consciousness, and socialist patriotism, it is pointed out, the party was able to mobilize the entire Soviet people, reinforce the striking power of the Red Army, and organize the toilers behind the front. Having overcome the effects of the initial political mistakes and military miscalculations, it now led the Soviet people to victory. Victory thus was due not to the mysterious Russian masses or to "Generals Mud" and "Snow," nor was it due to accidental mistakes, Hitler's megalomania, or other "subjective" factors; instead, it followed from "objective" developments that had been under way long before 1941.[109]

A corresponding "objective" pattern is found to be operating in the occupied countries. Their peoples showed a more vigorous fighting spirit after the USSR was drawn into the war. The successful resistance of the Soviet people, the appeal of socialist internationalism, and the transformation of the war from a primarily imperialist one into one in which imperialism and socialism confronted each other all are found to have revived hope among the enslaved nations and to have inspired a more determined resistance against Nazi repression. On the other hand, it is noted, this very fact worried Western imperialists, who viewed the worldwide mobilization of the popular masses as a threat to the capitalist system.[110]

On the interstate level, the anti-Nazi front thus is found wanting. The refusal of the Western powers to open a second front on the continent in 1942 and 1943 becomes in this view a deliberate attempt to weaken the Soviet Union. If arms shipments did not arrive when they were urgently needed, such delays, too, are attributed to sabotage of the Soviet war effort. In the same vein, the West's air war is dismissed as an inadequate substitute for a second front, because it failed to reduce German arms production. Worse, it embittered the German people to the point where they believed

[108]*GdA*, vol. 5, pp. 294ff.; Bleyer et al., *Deutschland*, pp. 134–35, 141–42; Förster et al., *Generalstab*, p. 270.

[109]*GdA*, vol. 5, pp. 295–96; Bleyer et al., *Deutschland*, pp. 132, 142–43, 177; Hass et al., *Deutschland*, vol. 2, p. 279.

[110]*GdA*, vol. 5, p. 297; Bleyer et al., *Deutschland*, pp. 166–67; Böhm, in *Der deutsche Imperialismus*, vol. 3, pp. 79ff.

the unceasing Nazi lies about Allied plans for the total destruction of Germany and fought on with even greater determination. Consistent with this approach, the North African invasion receives scant attention; it is viewed as a militarily inconsequential side show, inspired by imperialist interests more concerned with reestablishing their predominance in the Mediterranean than with ending the Nazi tyranny as quickly as possible.[111]

Because these charges fit readily into the class-struggle concept of the Marxist historian, no attempt has been made to provide any specific evidentiary underpinning. There exists for the Marxist enough prima facie evidence to support these accusations—from the unfulfilled pledges made in 1942 by both Roosevelt and Churchill (with great reluctance by the latter, however) to open a second front in France in the fall of that year and the American military judgment that such a front could have been established, if not in 1942, at the latest in 1943, to the subsequent dealings of the United States and Britain with Vichyites and other fascist collaborators in North Africa, Italy, and Greece. No allowance is made for the military and logistical difficulties that delayed the opening of a second front and that caused the substitution of the North African invasion for a cross-Channel attack, granted even that anti-Communist attitudes, though muted, were strong in Britain and even stronger in the United States. Marxist historians can explain the Western strategy only as the product of the inexorable contest between imperialism and socialism.[112]

The defeat of the Germans at Stalingrad[113] is viewed as the turning point of the war, putting the Nazi forces permanently on the defensive. At the same time, the Stalingrad victory is hailed for bolstering the fighting spirit of the national liberation movements and partisan forces. Pursuing this point, DDR authors regard the dissolution of the Comintern in May 1943 simply as a move in-

[111]Bleyer et al., *Deutschland*, pp. 205ff., 226–27, 242; *GdA*, vol. 5, pp. 298–99; Böhm, in *Der deutsche Imperialismus*, vol. 3, p. 87; Hass et al., *Deutschland*, vol. 2, pp. 187ff., 511ff.

[112]See Trumbull Higgins, *Winston Churchill and the Second Front: 1940–1943* (New York, 1957); Samuel Eliot Morrison, *Strategy and Compromise* (Boston, 1958); Herbert Feis, *Churchill, Roosevelt, Stalin: The War They Waged and the Peace They Sought* (Princeton, 1967); Gabriel Kolko, *The Politics of War* (New York, 1968). Kolko shows (pp. 14–30) that political considerations argued for an earlier rather than a delayed establishment of the Second Front on the continent. Only Higgins suggests (p. 196) that Churchill's conservative, that is, anti-Communist, frame of mind reinforced his opposition, on strategic grounds, to an early cross-Channel invasion. On the convoy issue, see Churchill's own account in his *Second World War* (New York, 1962), vol. 4, bk. 1, ch. 15; vol. 5, bk. 1, ch. 15. On the other hand, DDR authors rightly reject the thesis of some Western historians that the North African campaigns were strategically more significant than the battle of Stalingrad (cf. Kurt von Tippelskirch, *Geschichte des Zweiten Weltkrieges* [Bonn, 1956], p. 268).

[113]The name is still being used by DDR authors, although references to the "battle on the Volga" are more common.

tended to give the national Communist parties greater freedom of action in utilizing this new militancy. (There is no indication in the East German literature that the dissolution was also intended to please the Western powers, as Stalin claimed at the time and as the West assumed.) Finally, it is stressed, the Stalingrad victory brought home to the Western powers the fact that the Soviet Union would not be the disabled country dependent on foreign aid they had hoped for; they knew that they would not be able, after the war, to exert their influence on developments in the "land of socialism" under the guise of providing "assistance."[114]

This realization, DDR historians conclude, strengthened rather than weakened the anti-Hitler coalition, bearing out once again, as they never tire of pointing out, the inevitability of developments. In order to check the rising prestige of the Soviet Union, the Western powers intensified their efforts to defeat Hitler Germany. Their call for the "unconditional surrender" of the Axis powers is seen as a response to the demand of all freedom-loving peoples for the destruction of fascist imperialism and thus helped to consolidate the coalition. The coalition drew further strength, it is noted, from the Anglo-American pledge made at the Teheran conference to stage a cross-Channel invasion in the spring of 1944—to East German historians this was the most important result of that conference and was obtained, they claim, as the result of incessant Soviet pressures and in clear refutation of the earlier Western excuses.

Yet, when in June 1944 the Western powers did invade France, they did so, it is charged, to prevent the Soviet Union from becoming too strong on the Continent. At the same time, and wholly inconsistent with this interpretation, the invasion once again is attributed to pressures from the Soviet Union and the popular masses elsewhere—an explanation in any event applicable at best to the British government, but not to the United States, which had pressed all along for an invasion of France in preference to any Mediterranean campaigns. "The anti-Hitler coalition," Wolfgang Bleyer concludes, "grew stronger in proportion to the growth of the worldwide prestige of the Soviet Union as the leading force and the one carrying the main burden of the war; its victories on the battlefield kept raising that prestige with peoples and governments alike."[115]

[114]See *GdA*, vol. 5, pp. 334ff., 338, 410; Bleyer et al., *Deutschland*, pp. 206–7, 224, 240, 241, 246, 317; Böhm, in *Der deutsche Imperialismus*, vol. 3, pp. 86–87. On the dissolution of the Comintern, see Dietrich Geyer, "Kommunistische Internationale," *SDG*, vol. 3, p. 781; Kolko, *The Politics of War*, p. 36.

[115]Bleyer, in Bleyer et al., *Deutschland*, pp. 241–43, 318; *Grundriss*, p. 472; Böhm, in *Der deutsche Imperialismus*, vol. 3, pp. 87ff.; "Konferenz von Teheran," *Swb*, vol. 1, p. 1020. For non-Marxist analyses of the second-front issue, see Kolko, *The Politics of War*, pp. 20ff.; also Feis, *Churchill*, pp. 115–17, 127ff., 134–35, and *passim*.

"Total War" in Germany

While events took an ominous turn for Germany as a whole, the German arms-producing monopolies are found to have benefited from their country's setbacks. Having so far stayed in the background, the leaders of the arms industries now took open control of the economy. They achieved their dominance through Albert Speer, Hitler's favorite architect, who became the minister of arms production in February 1942.[116] Under Speer's aegis, industry ran to arms production on its own responsibility, and this autonomy, the argument runs, enabled it to virtually control types and amounts of all industrial output, close down middle and small enterprises, exploit labor, both German and foreign, even more ruthlessly, and further increase its profits. State-monopolist capitalism, that fusion of state and big-business power into one omnipotent apparatus of monopolist dominance, thus reached heights never attained before. This concentration of power, notes Bleyer, became the point of departure for the conduct of total war: "The German great bourgeoisie showed that it was determined to continue the war by any available means and to gamble away, without scruples, the existence of the entire nation."[117]

This analysis fits easily into a scenario in which the industrial monopolies are viewed as the moving force behind the war. In its support, some facts can of course be cited. Yet, once again, by arguing from a preconceived thesis rather than from the sources, the overall conclusions derived from this approach rest on that confusion of cause and effect noted already on other occasions.[118] In the streamlining of production by the industrial experts, all of them associated with large enterprises, these large concerns clearly benefited at the expense of the smaller ones; because of their spe-

---

[116]That Speer owed his exceptional powers to the industrialists (Eichholtz, "Manager des staatsmonopolistischen Kapitalismus," *JWG* 3 [1974]:225–26) is an unsubstantiated allegation. See Speer, *Erinnerungen,* (Berlin [West], 1969), pp. 215ff.

[117]Bleyer et al., *Deutschland,* pp. 182ff., 253ff., 261; Bleyer et al., "Totaler Krieg und totale Monopolmacht," *ZfG* 14 (1966): 896ff.; *GdA,* vol. 5, pp. 340–41; Eichholtz, "die Vorgeschichte des Generalbevollmächtigten für den Arbeitseinsatz," *JfG* 9 (1973): 344ff., 364–65, 370; Eichholtz and Schumann, *Anatomie des Krieges,* doc. no. 197, p. 383.

[118]For a striking example of such a misleading analysis, see Bleyer, in *Monopole und Staat,* pp. 183ff.; also see his account in Bleyer et al. (*Deutschland,* pp. 264–65) of the alleged impact of Speer and the industrialist Karl Pleiger on Hitler's decision after the Stalingrad debacle not to withdraw from the Donets Basin, "in the interest of the armaments industry in the occupied territories." For Hitler's own justification of his strategy of nonwithdrawal see Willi A. Boelcke, *Deutschlands Rüstung im Zweiten Weltkrieg* (Frankfurt, 1969), pp. 126–27; also Dorpalen, "Hitler, the Nazi Party, and the Wehrmacht in World War II," in *Total War and Cold War,* ed. by Harry L. Coles (Columbus, OH, 1962), pp. 76ff. This, of course, does not preclude the possibility that Hitler used the industrialists' pleas to bolster his own argument.

cial position, they also managed at times to sabotage the war effort to step up their profits, quite apart from the fact that as an incentive profit margins always remained substantial.[119] Because of their success in increasing production, they also objectively helped to prolong the war. There was never any doubt, however, that Hitler made the basic decisions, even in the area of arms production, as the protocols of Speer's conferences with Hitler make very clear. Nor did the industrialists, or for that matter Speer, ever have full control even of the technical process. Allocation of labor was assigned to a special plenipotentiary, wholly beyond their authority, and the rapidly expanding economic enterprises in the concentration camps also remained outside their jurisdiction.[120]

In keeping with the assumption of monopolist domination, the "final solution" of the "Jewish problem" is also linked to monopolist goals. If prior to the war anti-Jewish activities were viewed as psychological preparations for the enslavement and extermination of peoples defeated in wars to come, the mass killings of the Jews that set in after the attack on the USSR are seen as implementing such an extermination program designed to consolidate German imperialist domination. Accordingly, the anti-Jewish atrocities are considered as merely part of a much vaster plan encompassing entire peoples and ethnic groups. Nor are the Jews viewed as the main target of this overall program; rather, the chief victims of this policy of annihilation are Communists and all proletarian forces, that is, the forces of socialist progress.

Here confirmation is found of the "class character" of imperialist extermination, bearing out the contention that such mass murders are a constituent element of imperialism, not the doings of some individual madmen. The Nazi approach, DDR historians maintain, distinguishes itself only by its unparalleled extent and intensity. They also find wholly consistent with the class nature of the "final solution" that, as defeat appeared imminent, efforts were made to trade Jews for Western supplies on condition that these be used only against the USSR. That such transactions were also proposed to prepare the ground for armistice talks with the West serves as further confirmation of such a thesis. Similarly, the readiness of major industrial concerns to exploit Jews (and other forced laborers)

---

[119]Milward, *The German Economy at War*, pp. 91ff.; Esenwein-Rothe, *Wirtschafts-verbände*, pp. 115, 129–30; Boelcke, *Deutschlands*, pp. 10–11; Eichholtz and, Schumann, *Anatomie des Krieges*, doc. no. 197, p. 383, doc. no. 269, p. 472; Drobisch, "Der Freundeskreis Himmler," p. 324. For an admission by Speer of profit considerations interfering with arms production, see Radkau, in Hallgarten and Radkau, *Industrie*, p. 428.

[120]Boelcke, *Deutschlands, passim*; Eichholtz and Schumann, *Anatomie des Krieges*, doc. no. 188, pp. 371–72; doc. no. 196, pp. 381–82, doc. no. 222, pp. 419–20; Mottek et al., *Studien der Geschichte*, vol. 3, p. 338.

under inhuman conditions can be cited to bear out the charge that
the monopolies, true to their insatiable greed, sought to derive profits from the mass extermination by working the victims to death
rather than have them killed outright.[121] Such may not have been
the thinking of the industrialists—at first they objected to the slave-
labor program, not, to be sure, on humanitarian grounds, but because of its inefficiency[122]—but they learned quickly to live with it
and, in the words of one of the Nürnberg tribunals, "embraced,
adopted, and executed the forced-labor policies of the Third Reich,
thereby becoming accessories to and taking a consenting part in the
commission of war crimes and crimes against humanity. . . . " The
squalid story need not be retold here.[123]

Because these activities are seen as efforts to consolidate the
"class position" of the great bourgeoisie, special attention is paid
to the other side of the class struggle. The actions of the antifascist
resistance are explored with customary thoroughness, city by city,
region by region, as well as in overall surveys. The findings make
clear that such activities differed little from those of the early years
of the war. Barred from the levers of power, the Communists continued their informational and propagandistic work by means of
underground newspapers, leaflets, stickers, chain letters, and word
of mouth. Hideouts and other help were provided to fugitives from
the Gestapo, and some aid was given to such "class brethren" as
prisoners of war and forced laborers. A few strikes could be organized and some sabotage performed, but the extent and effectiveness of such actions are hard to determine. At the same time,
Marxist study groups offered ideological training—an especially
important task, because the KPD was not content with bringing

[121]See Streisand, pp. 370–71; GdA, vol. 5, p. 322; Drobisch et al., Juden, pp. 237ff.,
274ff., 306ff., 331–32, 339–41, 344–45, 360ff. On the actual purposes of the extermination program, see Eberhard Jäckel, Hitlers Weltanschauung (Tübingen,
1969); Hillgruber, "Die 'Endlösung' und das deutsche Ostimperium . . . ," VfZ 20
(1972): 132ff.; and the documentary materials in IMT, vol. 38, pp. 86ff., and VfZ 5
(1957): 194ff.; VfZ 6 (1958); 281ff. These materials also make clear, as does Hillgruber's paper, that the "final solution" was not part of a general extermination
program, but went far beyond the treatment envisaged for non-Jewish peoples.
Nonetheless, Unb. Verg. speaks disapprovingly of an overemphasis (Überhöhung)
on anti-Semitism in Nazi Germany on the part of Western historians (p. 335). As
for industry's role, it is perhaps best summed up by Radkau, in Hallgarten and
Radkau, Industrie, p. 535: "On their own the large industrial concerns would
certainly never have started any persecutions of Jews; but they were the ones who
turned an abstruse petty-bourgeois anti-Semitism into a highly profitable enterprise and a way to penetrate economically the German-occupied territories."
[122]TWC, vol. 8, p. 636; vol. 9, pp. 798–99.
[123]See ibid., vol. 8, p. 1172. Nor did they use forced labor merely under duress;
instead, they asked for it. There were even cases in which they solicited government orders for which they knew only forced labor would be available (ibid., vol.
6, p. 1202; vol. 8, pp. 1180ff.; vol. 9, pp. 839, 1412ff., 1435ff.). See also Joseph
Borkin, The Crime and Punishment of I. G. Farben (New York, 1978), pp. 117ff.,
and numerous documentations in ZfG.

about the defeat of the Nazi regime, but was determined to replace this instrumentality of monopoly capitalism with what it conceived as a genuinely democratic order. Guidance was provided by the party's Central Committee in Moscow through radio contact, emissaries occasionally dropped by parachute, and instructions delivered by sympathizers of neutral citizenship. According to *Deutschland im zweiten Weltkrieg*, some special units were trained in the use of arms in preparation for eventual armed risings against the Nazis.[124]

The East German accounts vividly convey pictures of the enormous difficulties the Communists faced. The obstacles were not only physical ones, such as the constant breakup of cells by the Gestapo, the drafting of party workers into the armed forces, or their sudden transfer to new war-essential projects. Their prospective audience remained as unresponsive as ever. If earlier it had not listened because it was reasonably satisfied with conditions, now it was fear of the Gestapo, illusions about the course of the war, and lethargy that kept it from becoming more active as the war dragged on. Nor did matters change when the deterioration of the military situation became fully apparent. As the East German analyses keep pointing out, feelings of complicity in the Nazi crimes and fears of retribution, readily encouraged by Nazi propagandists, deterred malcontents from joining the resistance and helping to end the war. Although some organizational progress was made beginning in late 1942, overt resistance activities, such as sabotage and strikes, could still be organized only on a limited scale. As late as the first half of 1944, only 12,925 German workers went on strike, compared to 193,024 foreign ones.[125]

DDR historians are especially concerned, however, with difficulties that grew out of tensions within the Communist party itself. They developed from disagreements over the strategy to be followed once the Nazi regime was removed. The Brussels and Berne conferences had stipulated that after the overthrow of the Nazis there would be established, not a dictatorship of the proletariat and a full-scale socialist order, but a popular-front regime, headed by the Communists yet resting on all "democratic" forces,

[124]See "Antifaschistischer Widerstand," *Swb*, vol. 1, pp. 72ff. The failure of one DDR author (Walter Bartel) to point out the inseparable connection between the Nazi defeat and the creation of an antifascist order earned him severe reprimands (cf. Pätzold and Weissbecker, in *ZfG* 10 [1962]: 323, 325). On antifascist resistance activities in general, see also Bleyer et al., *Deutschland*, pp. 144ff., 158–60, 202–3, 308–9; *GdA*, vol. 5, pp. 302ff., 366ff., and *passim*; Kurt Baller et al., "Zur Entwicklung des antifaschistischen Widerstandskampfes unter Führung der KPD in Leipzig/Westsachsen (1939–1945)," *BzG* 13 (1971): 830ff.

[125]Ludwig Einicke, "Die antifaschistische Bewegung und . . . die Niederlage des deutschen Faschismus," *BzG*, 2 (1960): suppl., p. 57; Bleyer et al., *Deutschland*, pp. 50, 375; *GdA*, vol. 5, pp. 366ff.; D. I. Melnikov, in *Der deutsche Imperialismus*, vol. 3, p. 382.

including the "progressive" elements of the bourgeoisie. This was also the strategy prescribed by the KPD's Central Committee in Moscow, and given the prevalent mood of the population, this strategy still seemed sound; further-reaching demands would only have reinforced the prevailing reluctance to actively oppose the regime. Nonetheless, many party members in Germany called for an immediate proletarian dictatorship and all-out socialization.

By the same token, the war-weary nation could be expected to support an antifascist regime only if it stood for an end to the war on all fronts. Yet again there were elements in the party proposing a continuation of the war against the Western powers at the side of the Soviet Union once peace had been made with the latter. Dissension on these issues seems to have been widespread, possibly because of the lack of communications within Germany and with Moscow. Such disagreements, it is noted, rendered the task of making converts even more difficult.[126]

Because of these difficulties, the formation in July 1943 of the "National Committee 'Free Germany,'" composed of German prisoners of war in Soviet camps and organized under Communist auspices and Soviet supervision, receives special attention in the East German literature. (Along with it, the "Free Germany" movement, which the National Committee headed and which had branches in a number of other countries, has been widely explored as a gauge of the strength of the "progressive" German anti-Nazi forces outside Germany.) As a truly "national" organization that drew its membership from all classes, the committee traced its ideological ancestry back to the popular-front strategy of the Comintern and the Brussels and Berne conferences of the KPD. It was to gather all anti-Nazi forces outside Germany under Communist aegis and impress on the nation the need to redeem itself by overthrowing the Hitler regime and thus secure for itself a happier future. DDR authors pass over in silence the committee's efforts to conceal its real objectives in order to attract non-Communists, especially officers captured by the Red Army—to do so, the committee's weekly newspaper, for example, featured the black-white-

[126]See *GdA*, vol. 5, pp. 339–401; Bleyer et al., *Deutschland*, pp. 332–33; Baller et al., "Zur Entwicklung," pp. 839–42. See also the documentary materials reprinted in *VfZ* 20 (1972): 430ff. At the one point at which the question of continuing the war beyond the defeat of the Nazis is brought up in these materials, the German underground authors do diverge from the Moscow leadership (p. 438). On the other hand, contrary to the view of the editor of the documents, Hermann Weber, these particular documents, though in places ambiguous, do not seem to call for the immediate establishment of the dictatorship of the proletariat. Instead, they allow for a period of transition, though apparently for a briefer one than the Central Committee in Moscow had envisaged. For favoring such a delay, the authors were chided by some party members (pp. 428, 435–37, 442–46). That cooperation between the leaders in Moscow and those in Germany may have been closer than can be deduced from these documents, Weber, perhaps unwittingly, suggests himself (pp. 429–30).

and-red colors of imperial Germany, a gambit not mentioned in any account. Yet, what all authors consider historically significant and what they stress is the committee's broad-based popular-front approach as a stepping-stone to the Communists' basic aim of destroying the existing capitalist order and replacing it with a socialist one. In the same vein, they point out the continuity that linked the committee, along with the Brussels and Berne conferences, to the subsequent policies of the German Democratic Republic.

East German research has uncovered some revealing data about the implementation of these plans. The early appeals of the committee were addressed to German commanders on Soviet soil, who were urged to defy Hitler's orders and retreat toward Germany. This approach, it appears, was suggested by some captured officers, who warned that none of the generals would lend their names to appeals calling upon the enlisted men to desert to the Soviet side. Such mass desertions, they argued, would undermine discipline, destroy the army, and create chaos both at the front and at home—consequences that were wholly unacceptable to any military leader. On the other hand, the proposal of a voluntary retreat implied the preservation of the army—the main concern of the generals, but a political risk for the Communists, which the latter, however, were willing to take. Whatever its long-range consequences, any voluntary retreat would weaken Germany's striking power and relieve the immense pressure on the Red Army. The Communists (with the consent of the Soviets) thus called for this tactic in the hope that, backed by some prestigious military names, it might be effective. It was not, and when there were indications of the possible replacement of the Nazis by a military dictatorship (as suggested by hints reaching Moscow about the anti-Nazi conspiracy headed by ex-Mayor Goerdeler and the former chief of the General Staff, Colonel General Ludwig Beck, to overthrow Hitler), it was abandoned and calls went out to the rank and file to give themselves up to the Russians. By that time, one author explains, the German forces were anyway in full retreat and the withdrawal to backward positions would no longer have been a political demonstration.

The East German literature is less explicit on the later phases of the committee's existence. Besides converting prisoners of war to its cause, its main function seems to have been to develop a manpower reservoir for the DDR's future police and armed forces. Some of its members were appointed as local administrators as the Red Army advanced into eastern Germany. The committee itself was dissolved in November 1945.[127]

---

[127]See Bleyer et al., *Deutschland*, pp. 292ff., 344–45; *GdA*, vol. 5, pp. 350ff., 362, 387; Bruno Löwel, "Die Gründung des NKFD im Lichte der Entwicklung der Strategie und Taktik der KPD," *BzG* 5 (1963): 613ff.; Gerhard Leschkowitz, "Zu einigen

An effort has also been made to credit the National Committee with a limited impact at least on some of the military participants in the Goerdeler-Beck plot. Thus, DDR authors maintain, on the basis of admittedly very sparse evidence, that the appeals of the committee confirmed those around Colonel Claus von Stauffenberg in their view that their movement must come to terms with the Soviet Union as well as the Western powers. Similarly, it is claimed, the committee contributed to that group's decision to work with the Communists and restructure postwar Germany along genuinely democratic lines, as opposed to the plans drawn up by Goerdeler, the conservative mentor of the oppositional movement, which culminated in Stauffenberg's attempt on Hitler's life in July 1944. These analyses also note, however, that the Stauffenberg group, like the dominant conservative element, did not accept the necessity or feasibility of a mass rising against the Nazi regime, aiming instead at a palace revolution—in actual fact, the only realistic approach, given the hold the Nazi dictatorship had on the country. Stauffenberg's planting of a bomb in Hitler's headquarters on July 20, 1944, thus is discounted as part of an ill-conceived plot that would not have changed much if the bomb had killed Hitler, because the monopoly bourgeoisie would have remained in command. Nonetheless, Stauffenberg's deed is praised as an "anti-Nazi [though not antifascist] endeavor, designed objectively to remove the Hitler regime."[128]

The National Committee was founded at a time when the Western powers were beginning to draw up plans for the postwar treatment of Germany, and the committee was intended to channel developments in a direction more in accordance with Soviet plans. Over these latter plans a historical controversy has since arisen between East and West; the activities of the committee, which obviously were cleared by the Soviet authorities, if they were not initiated by them, throw some light on the Soviet position.

Western accounts of that position, which are based on the

Fragen des Nationalkomitees "Freies Deutschland,' " ZfG 10 (1962): suppl., pp. 193ff. Leschkowitz, however, claims erroneously that the proposal of a voluntary retreat was made by Field Marshal Friedrich von Paulus, the captured commander at Stalingrad. This assertion is chronologically incompatible with Paulus' belated conversion to the committee cause. On committee members as local administrators, see Stefan Doernberg, Kurze Geschichte der DDR (Berlin [East], 1969), p. 32; Walter L. Dorn, Inspektionsreisen in der US-Zone (Stuttgart, 1973), p. 35.

[128]See "Stauffenberg-Gruppe," Swb, vol. 2, p. 617; Kurt Finker, Stauffenberg und der 20 Juli 1944 (Berlin [East], n.d.), pp. 203ff., especially pp. 213–16; Bleyer et al., Deutschland, pp. 338–39, 362–64; Streisand, pp. 390–91. Because Stauffenberg's opposition was directed against the Nazis, not their alleged monopolist and militarist sponsors, it was considered anti-Nazi rather than antifascist. Only Grundriss, p. 477, refers to Stauffenberg and his associates as antifascist, without, however, explaining its divergent position.

official American minutes of the Teheran conference as well as the personal recollections of various participants in that meeting, picture Stalin as agreeing in principle, though with clear reservations, to the partitioning of Germany, preferably into a large number of rather small states. East German historians, on the other hand, along with their Soviet colleagues, describe Stalin as opposed at all times to any partition of Germany, although even from the official Soviet minutes of the Teheran talks Stalin emerges as neither adamantly opposed to nor very enthusiastic about a breakup of Germany (though there is no indication here of any preference on his part for a multitude of small states).[129]

The overall impression conveyed by the available sources, both Eastern and Western, is that Stalin did not consider a partition of Germany as an effective way of putting an end to German aggressiveness, but that he did not wish to specify at that time what he presumably considered the only constructive solution—that is, the complete overhauling of Germany's socioeconomic system—fearful perhaps lest he jeopardize the Western promise of a second front in France the following spring. He may also have wondered whether too open a stand against the Western proposals might not have undermined his own territorial demands that all German lands east of the Oder River be turned over to Poland—in itself a form of dismemberment. Finally, as has been suggested, a noncommittal attitude allowed the USSR to present itself to the Germans as the defender of a compact Germany, in contrast to the Western powers.[130]

The latter assumption can draw some support from the strategy of the National Committee. The committee's early appeals warned that only an immediate revolt against the Nazi regime would protect Germany against the partitioning of its territory; there were hints that any delay would play into the hands of forces that favored partition and that were beyond the control of the committee and its Soviet sponsor. In the same vein, the commit-

---

[129]For a general review of the dispute, see Günter Moltmann, "Konferenz von Teheran," *SDG*, vol. 3, pp. 810ff. See also official American materials in *Foreign Relations of the United States, Diplomatic Papers: The Conferences at Cairo and Teheran* (Washington, D.C., 1961), pp. 510, 602–4, 847, 879–80; see official Soviet materials in *Deutsche Aussenpolitik* 6 (1961): 1282ff. See also Helmut Hesselbarth, in ibid. 7 (1962): 222; Bleyer et al., *Deutschland*, p. 318; "Konferenz von Teheran," *Swb*, vol. 1, pp. 1020–21; *GdA*, vol. 5, pp. 424, 430–31.

[130]Sywottek (*Deutsche Volksdemokratie*, p. 160) suggests that the differing interpretations may have semantic causes—the English term *dismemberment* means partition both in the sense of breakup of and separation of one or more parts from a territory, as in the case of the Soviet demand that all territory east of the Oder River be turned over to Poland—an ambiguity that Stalin may indeed have created deliberately (see also Vojtech Mastny, "Soviet War Aims at the Moscow and Teheran Conferences of 1943," *JMH* 47 [1975]: 499). On Stalin's position, see also Alexander Fischer, *Sowjetische Deutschlandpolitik im Zweiten Weltkreig: 1941–1945* (Stuttgart, 1975), pp. 68ff.

tee's president, Erich Weinert, emphasized at its first meeting on July 12–13, 1943, that only a government representative of the forces gathered in the committee would preserve the country from chaos and partition (*Zerstückelung*). Similarly, the first manifesto of the committee warned that if the Germans did not overthrow Hitler and end the war by their own efforts, "Hitler could only be removed by the arms of the coalition. This would mean the end of our national freedom and our state, this would mean the partition of our fatherland." Even more significant, the National Committee contined to speak out against partition after the Teheran Conference. In an appeal to "People and *Wehrmacht*," issued in March 1944, it again warned against the growing danger of partition and disenfranchisement, suggesting that the Soviet Union, contrary to Stalin's noncommittal attitude at Teheran, continued to oppose the breakup of Germany. Although no explicit opposition to partition was voiced during the closing months of the war, Ulbricht, the German Communist leader, and Stalin still seemed to adhere to it when they insisted that the cession of eastern Germany to Poland was not tantamount to partition. (At Yalta, on the other hand, Stalin appears to have been as noncommittal, according to the Soviet minutes, as he had been at Teheran. The American minutes, in turn, have him explicitly favoring partition.)[131]

East German historians do not take up the role of the National Committee specifically in the context of Stalin's conduct. To them the statements of the Committee are significant as reflections of the worldwide class struggle: by partitioning Germany the imperialist Western Powers wished to prevent the peace-minded progressive forces from leading Germany towards a genuine mass-based democracy. The USSR, on the other hand, while safeguarding itself against renewed German aggression through the strengthening of Poland at Germany's territorial expense, wished to preserve the rest of Germany as a compact unit for the very purpose of ensuring its progressive development. Similarly, these authors maintain, on the basis of wholly inadequate evidence, that the Western powers, in their imperialist greed, hoped to control more easily Germany's industrial competition by dividing the country up into a number of smaller states. In a similar confusion of basic objectives and incidental results, it is claimed that the Morgenthau Plan, calling for severe limits to Germany's industries, was to serve that same purpose.[132]

[131]Erich Weinert, quoted in Sywottek, *Deutsche Volksdemokratie*, p. 128; manifesto, in Weber, *Kommunismus, Deutsche Volksdemokratie*, p. 389; appeal to "People and *Wehrmacht*," quoted in Sywottek, p. 136; Ulbricht and Stalin, in ibid., pp. 159–60. On Yalta, see *Teheran, Jalta, Potsdam*, ed. Fischer (Cologne, 1968), pp. 106ff.; also Fischer, *Sowjetische Deutschlandpolitik*, pp. 122–25.
[132]Böhm, in *Der deutsche Imperialismus*, vol. 3, pp. 91–92; Janis Schmelzer, in *Der deutsche Imperialismus*, vol. 3, pp. 101ff.

The Defeat of the Nazi Regime

Developments during the last phase of the war are fitted with similar ease into the class-struggle framework. All participants are shown to have acted out the roles assigned to them in that context. In June 1944, the Western powers finally established the second front in France; yet, as all accounts stress, they did so as much in order to contain the influence of the Soviet Union and other progressive forces as in order to defeat German fascism. Nontheless, the subsequent advance of the Anglo-American forces is found to have been unduly slow and inefficient. Tribute is paid, on the other hand, to French and Belgian partisan forces, which liberated large parts of their countries on their own. Because of the West's slow advance, the German-Soviet front, it is noted, remained the main theater of the war, with the larger part of the German forces engaged on that front until the end of the war. Still, the Soviet armies kept advancing rapidly toward Germany.[133]

The German monopoly bourgeoisie reacted to these developments in keeping with its "class interests." Because the Hitler regime could no longer safeguard these interests and in fact was endangering them, the monopolists and their militarist and Junker-agrarian allies wished it removed. For just such a purpose, East Germans authors maintain, they supported the conspiratorial group headed by Goerdeler and Beck. Correspondingly, the "class character" of the plotters revealed itself in their hope that after Hitler had been removed, a new German government led by Goerdeler and Beck would come to terms with the Western powers and concentrate, possibly with the latter's support, on the containment of Soviet Russia.[134]

In the East German view, the Goerdeler-Beck undertaking presented no democratic alternative to the Nazis: as part of the ruling class, the plotters wished to preserve the imperialist system; they feared the masses and wanted to curb them, all of which meant in the Marxist perception that the group offered no alternative whatsoever. West German assessments of the group as a liberation and reform movement accordingly are dismissed as falsifications of the historical record. That except for Schacht and one or two others, no "monopolists" were involved in the plot does not, in the Marxist view, argue against the Goerdeler-Beck group acting "objectively" on behalf of the monopoly bourgeoisie. What mat-

[133]Bleyer et al., *Deutschland*, pp. 349ff.; *GdA*, vol. 5, pp. 409–10; Böhm, in *Der deutsche Imperialismus*, vol. 3, p. 90.
[134]"Verschwörung vom 20. Juli 1944," *Swb*, vol. 2, pp. 724–25; Bleyer et al., *Deutschland*, pp. 358ff., 367, 372–73; *GdA*, vol. 5, pp. 42–43, 413–15; Förster, in *ZfG* 8 (1960): suppl., p. 422; Schleier, in ibid. 15 (1967): 1089.

tered was that Goerdeler's constitutional plans would have assured the survival of that system.[135]

Yet, throughout the entire period, as the East German authors themselves stress, all major industrial and banking concerns continued to cooperate wholeheartedly with the Nazis. DDR historians do not find this surprising, because in their view the monopoly bourgeoisie considered support of the Goerdeler-Beck group as only one of the options open to it to deal with the approaching defeat. Cooperation with the regime was another. This strategy was based on the hope, it is claimed, that "fanatical resistance would convince the Western powers that they were fighting the wrong country," because Russia would meanwhile advance farther toward the West.[136]

Nonetheless, as East German research also has shown, behind the façade of whole-hearted cooperation with the government, businessmen did make plans to blunt the defeat once it was clear that Germany would lose the war. However, the proposals that were worked out for new export drives after the war and for the establishment of a European economic community are denounced as unabashed efforts to preserve German imperialism: even in the face of impending defeat, the plans called for the setting up of the proposed European community under German leadership. In the same vein, other evidence of imperialist brazenness is brought up, though not always documented: threats, blackmail, front men, and organizations were to be used to assure future business abroad, and while on the one hand American business was to be driven from the Latin markets, from which German exports had disappeared because of the war, on the other hand, access to the American domestic market was sought by way of the Bank of International Settlements in Basel, Switzerland, where German, British, and American representatives had worked together throughout the war. That these plans were drafted in collaboration with government officials and at least one high S.S. leader (Otto Ohlendorf) serves as

[135]On the at-best peripheral role of businessmen, see Ritter, *Carl Goerdeler und die deutsche Widerstandsbewegung* (Stuttgart, 1955), pp. 151ff., 316–17, 385, 413, 545 n. 18; Eichholtz and Schumann, *Anatomie des Krieges*, doc. no. 257, pp. 458–59; Speer, *Erinnerungen*, p. 227; see also Speer's exchange with the Ruhr industrialist Albert Vögler, ibid., p. 423. More important, the apologetic biography by Gert von Klass, *Albert Vögler* (Tübingen, 1957), makes no mention of an involvement of Vögler in Goerdeler's plans, nor do the Gestapo protocols indicate any major involvement of businessmen (*Spiegelbild einer Verschwörung*, ed. Heinrich Peter [Stuttgart, 1961]). Of the two industrialists who held themselves in readiness to join a government headed by Goerdeler as chancellor, Ewald Loeser, often described as a Krupp director, actually left Krupp in 1943, partly because he objected to the firm's use of slave labor (*TWC*, vol. 9, pp. 817–18) and was after that associated with a Dutch electrical concern, and Paul Lejeune-Jung held an executive position in the cellulose industry (*Spiegelbild*, pp. 210–11, 259, 541–42).
[136]Förster, in Bleyer et al., *Deutschland*, p. 371.

evidence of the continuity of state-monopolist interpenetration. Wolfgang Schumann also finds it noteworthy that some of the very men who had worked on the plans for a European economic community in 1944–1945 were involved in the creation of the European Economic Community "in the capitalist part of Europe" in the 1950s. The implication is that the same imperialist elements were at work once again when the Common Market was being established.

Correspondingly, the industrialists are found seeking to safeguard their interests at home. They objected to Hitler's scorched-earth policy, which called for the destruction of all production facilities. With the help of Armaments Minister Albert Speer, they obtained a modification of this policy, thus saving a large part of their plants and equipment. Such opposition to the Führer's orders receives, however, scant approval in the East German accounts because it is viewed primarily as evidence of monopolist schemes to resume the exploitation of the workers as soon as the fighting was over. DDR authors find their suspicions borne out by attempts of these same circles to draw up plans creating jobs for the demobilized soldiers at the end of the war lest they fall prey, in their idleness, to radical influences out to destroy the monopolist system.[137]

At the same time, the fine hand of these monopolist groups is seen behind the recurrent efforts to enlist the Western powers in a joint campaign with the Germans against the USSR. To DDR authors, these were no mere impromptu feelers, but the outgrowth of an unrelenting monopolist strategy to rally all imperialist forces against socialist Soviet Russia. Thus they see a continuing thread linking these soundings to the foreign-policy plans of the Goerdeler group and, in a forward projection, to what they conceive as a program for the restoration of German imperialism and militarism in West Germany. That some groups in the United States and Britain would have welcomed the realignment of fronts proposed by the Nazis serves to reinforce the East German thesis.[138]

Turning to the role of the antifascist forces in Germany dur-

---

[137]Karl Drechsler et al., "Europapläne des deutschen Imperialismus im zweiten Weltkrieg," *ZfG* 19 (1971): 922–24; Schumann, " . . . Nachkriegsplanungen des faschistischen deutschen Imperialismus . . . ," *ZfG* 27 (1979): 395ff.; Schumann, "Die wirtschaftspolitische Überlebensstrategie des deutschen Imperialismus . . . ," ibid., pp. 499ff.; Eichholtz and Schumann, *Anatomie des Krieges*, doc. nos. 272–73, pp. 483–84; Eichholtz, "Manager," pp. 231–32. See also Speer, *Errinerungen*, pp. 350, 368; IMT, vol. 41, p. 525.

[138]Förster, "Die antikommunistische Grundlinie in konzeptionellen Vorstellungen des deutschen Imperialismus und Militarismus für ein imperialistisches Nachkriegsdeutschland," *Z.f. Militärgeschichte* 9 (1970): 296ff.; Eichholtz and Schumann, *Anatomie des Krieges*, doc. no. 279, p. 491; Bleyer et al., *Deutschland*, pp. 410ff.; *GdA*, vol. 5, p. 430, 624, 626; Benser, "Die Befreiung Europas vom Faschismus durch die Sowjetunion . . . ," *ZfG* 23 (1975): 367ff.

ing the closing months of the war, the East German accounts find their effectiveness still hampered by fear, corruption, and ideological confusion. Thus, no mass support could be mobilized, and efforts to hasten the end of the war were successful only on a limited scale. In some cases, antifascist groups secured the surrender of a town or a village without a fight; in others, the destruction of public utilities, bridges, and other vital installations could be prevented; in a few instances, antifascist committees disarmed local garrisons and took over power. The regretful conclusion is that the nation as a whole did little to liberate and redeem itself.[139]

The most important work of the KPD leaders in Moscow during the last phase of the war consisted in the preparation of a detailed political and governmental program, designed to facilitate the assumption of power by a Communist-led mass-based regime that would pave the way to the eventual establishment of a socialist order. In their endeavor to show how in developing such a program the party contributed to the inherently inevitable transition from capitalism to socialism, East German authors have discussed these plans at great length. The blueprints, they note, centered on the formation of a "bloc of militant democracy," composed of all "antifascist-democratic" parties and mass organizations, and on launching the country's democratic, that is, toiler-oriented, reconstruction. In these endeavors, the reunited working class could play the important role to which it was entitled as the "most determined, strongest, most democratic and anti-imperialist force." The bloc's policies, however, did not call for any large-scale socialization, in keeping with the Communist assessment of the relative strength at the time of the various classes and the organizational status and class consciousness, or lack of it, of the working class and the other mass forces. On the other hand, the bloc would seek to reinforce the initiative, control, and influence of the popular masses on the course of the inevitable social changes in Germany. By thus furthering progress, it is pointed out, "militant democracy" would also bring Germany closer to socialism.

In the same vein, the KPD impressed upon the population in areas occupied by the Red Army that the measures taken by the local Soviet commanders and Soviet-appointed administrators served the interests of the nation, for the Red Army was a liberating force, and the Soviets, following the precepts of Marxism-Leninism, were acting as the agents of social progress. DDR authors also praise the help that leading officials of other Communist parties, especially Georgi Dimitrov, the former secretary general of the Comintern and now head of the international section of the

---

[139]Bleyer et al., *Deutschland*, pp. 404ff.; *GdA*, vol. 5, 431ff.

Soviet Communist party, were rendering in the drafting of the KPD's blueprints.[140]

Although East German historians praise the Soviet Union as a constructive and progressive force, they have strong reservations about the Western share in the defeat of the Nazis. They keep pointing out that to the last the Soviet forces bore the brunt of the fighting. Britain and the United States, on the other hand, benefited from the continuing Nazi attempts to end hostilities in the west, with German troops being moved from the west to the east to give greater weight to such feelers. The Western powers are, moreover, charged with conducting separate peace negotiations on various fronts, contrary to explicit agreements barring such unilateral moves. If these intrigues did not succeed, it is noted, the credit must go to the Red Army: its rapid advance helped to preserve the anti-Hitler coalition and assured the surrender of the fascist forces on all fronts.[141]

It is true that armistice, not peace, talks were carried on by various Western representatives with Nazi spokesmen. It is also a fact that the United States and Britain were anxious to stem the advancing Soviet tide and keep local Communist forces, as in northern Italy, from seizing power. If the Western stance was class-oriented, however, the Soviet position was no less so, of course, as shown by the importation from Moscow of Communist functionaries into the areas occupied by the Red Army. In Germany's case, KPD groups, descriptively called *Initiativgruppen*, were charged to set up, jointly with the Red Army, antifascist-democratic self-government organs under the leadership of the KPD. The Soviet Union was as determined to see its concept of democracy prevail as the Western powers were to assert theirs.[142]

The defeat of the Nazis, then, signified much more in the Marxist assessments than a military and political victory over the Hitler regime: it pointed up the archaic nature of monopoly capitalism and the superiority of the socialist order. (Western contributions to the victory, never considered of major importance, are ignored altogether in these concluding analyses.) Without the Nazi party, that pretorian guard of the great bourgeoisie, the latter was left even more impotent. The victory of the USSR over "Hitler

---

[140]Bleyer et al., *Deutschland*, pp. 382ff.; *GdA*, vol. 5, pp. 424ff.; Berthold, "Der Kampf gegen das Hitlerregime—der kampf für ein neues demokratisches Deutschland," *BzG* 6 (1964): 1007ff.; Laschitza, "Über Inhalt und Programm eines Blocks der kämpferischen Demokratie," ibid., pp. 1037ff.; documentary materials, in ibid. 7 (1965): 261ff.

[141]Bleyer et al., *Deutschland*, pp. 410ff.; *GdA*, vol. 5, pp. 430–31; Benser, "Befreiung," pp. 367ff.

[142]"Initiativegruppen der KPD," *Swb*, vol. 1, p. 832; Bleyer et al., *Deutschland*, pp. 408–9; *Abriss*, p. 79.

fascism," the main force (*Hauptstosskraft*) behind the imperialist drive against the USSR, thus opened up new possibilities for the advance of the socialist order. The German people had a chance now to give their history a wholly new turn. If to Westerners the outcome of World War II confirmed the viability of parliamentary democracy and the capitalist free-enterprise system, to Marxists it ushered in a new phase in the "general crisis of capitalism," accelerating the transition from capitalism to socialism.[143]

[143]*Grundriss*, pp. 481ff.; Bleyer et al., *Deutschland*, pp. 414ff.; Streisand, pp. 394–95.

9

The Socialist-Imperialist Confrontation

The Breakup of Germany, 1945–1949

The Struggle of the Antifascist-Democratic Forces

IN THE GLOBAL VIEW of the Marxist historian, German postwar developments were part of the worldwide transition from capitalism to socialism. Such interconnections did not, however, entail uniformity, and in Germany's case only one part of the country could make use of the opportunity of moving speedily from the capitalist to the socialist order. Germany's specific evolution is traced to a combination of factors not present in the case of other states that went through a corresponding transition. Unlike Poles, Bulgarians, and Yugoslavs, the German people had contributed little if anything to the defeat of Nazism; apathetic and disoriented, they were ill-prepared to proceed into the socialist order. In addition, again unlike the East European countries, a large part of Germany was occupied by the imperialist Western powers, which were determined to uphold the social and political status quo.

Yet, there were also factors favoring progressive developments. The USSR had emerged with increased power and authority from its victory over "Hitler fascism." Its encirclement by capitalist countries had come to an end; a community of socialist states was about to evolve. Correspondingly, international power relationships began shifting toward this emerging community—a trend that would gain in momentum as more countries broke away from the capitalist system and from Western imperialist influences. No major question of world politics could any longer be solved without the USSR—the era of transition from capitalism to socialism, inaugurated by the Bolshevik Revolution of 1917, had been raised to a new, higher level of the world revolutionary process.[1]

In keeping with this approach, Soviet political activities in eastern Europe are viewed as efforts to further the inevitable progress toward the socialist order. DDR authors reject Western

---

[1]Benser, "Die Befreiung Europas vom Faschismus durch die Sowjetunion und der Beginn des Übergangs vom Kapitalismus zum Sozialismus auf dem Territorium der DDR," *ZfG* 23 (1975): 358ff.; *Grundriss*, pp. 484–86.

charges that these activities were acts of imperialism, designed to "export revolution": such accusations ignored the "class function" of the USSR and denied that the Soviet state was fulfilling its "historical mission" of aiding the inherently inevitable, "lawful," advance toward socialism. As Heinz Heitzer has argued, the USSR ought not to be regarded as an external force, willfully injecting itself into the internal affairs of other countries; instead, given the interdependence between this transitional process on the one hand and the overall condition of the capitalist system and the distribution of power between socialism and capitalism on the other, the contribution of the Soviet Union to this process had to be viewed as a constituent element of the power structure of every country that moves toward socialism. To regard the USSR as intervening from the outside, Heitzer maintains, would also be incompatible with the worldwide scope of the transitional process. It meant also ignoring the common interests of the world proletariat that Marx and Engels already had demonstrated; this communality of interests postulated a commitment to mutual help. "The transition [from capitalism to socialism] cannot be adequately assessed in traditional terms, in the categories of the bourgeois nation-state."[2]

Although DDR authors pay glowing tribute to the help given by the USSR, they also insist that the successful changeover from capitalism to socialism depended ultimately on the determination and actions of the indigenous working-class movements. The functions of the Soviet Union consisted in providing to these movements the freedom to perform their respective missions without interference from foreign or domestic imperialist forces. This task the Soviet Union accomplished fully in the people's democracies of eastern Europe, but less so in Germany, where its direct influence extended only to its own occupation zone. As a result, only that zone could avail itself of the opportunity to destroy German imperialism and militarism when, after the defeat of Nazism, the great bourgeoisie lost control of army, police, and all other instruments of state power and when its centralized state and economic apparatus, too, was breaking up.[3]

This breakdown of bourgeois power occurred in all of Ger-

---

[2]See Buchta, review, ZfG 20 (1972): 1438; Heitzer, "Neue Probleme der Erforschung der Geschichte der DDR," ibid., pp. 957–58; Bartel and Schmidt, "Neue Probleme der Geschichtswissenschaft in der DDR," ibid., pp. 809–10; and on the corresponding Soviet position, Sergei T. Tulpanov, "Die Rolle der SMAD bei der Demokratisierung Deutschlands," ibid., 15 (1967): 249. In the same vein, Palmiro Togliatti, the leader of the Italian Communists, later explained that his party could not carry out any major changes after the war because there was no Red Army in Italy to lend its support (Togliatti, quoted in ibid., 23 [1975]: 1123).

[3]Grundriss, pp. 490, 493; Streisand, p. 400; Benser, "Das deutsche Volk und die Siegermächte," ZfG 20 (1972): 140–41; Bartel and Schmidt, "Neue Probleme," pp. 809–10; Abriss, p. 76.

many, and the survival of imperialism and militarism in the western zones, the East German accounts point out, thus was not inevitable. The Allied Control Council, set up to govern Germany as a whole, issued a series of constructive laws and directives. Pressure exerted by the popular masses longing for peace and democracy also forced the imperialist powers to maintain a measure of cooperation with the USSR. So, it is claimed, did the continuing war with Japan. There were also early portents of imperialist countermoves, however, as at the Potsdam Conference.[4]

The Potsdam Conference, which met in July 1945, again committed the victorious powers to the creation of a united, democratic, antimilitarist Germany. The Soviet Union is given credit for having shown the way to attain this goal: while the Western powers called noncommittally for the decentralization of the German economy, the USSR insisted on including in the agreement demands for the speedy liquidation of trusts, cartels, and other monopolist combinations as the instigators of war and fascism. In the same vein, rather than ask vaguely for the admission to public office of Germans who had "conducted themselves well," it demanded the appointment to all influential positions of persons fully committed to Germany's democratization. Finally, the Soviet delegation called not only for the punishment of those guilty of physical war crimes but also for the prosecution of the ultimate instigators of these crimes, the managers of the industrial and banking monopolies. "Unlike the Treaty of Versailles," *Grundriss* notes, "[the Potsdam Agreement] was directed against the real war culprits and provided for effective measures to assure a democratic development."[5] Such democracy had to be antifascist—that is, antimonopolist—as distinct from bourgeois democracy, which requires only the "formal" criterion of a parliamentary system, without regard to the economic and political roots of fascism and militarism. Thus, American efforts to create democratic institutions safeguarding civil liberties, freedom of press, and the unhampered flow of information are dismissed as demagogic attempts to regain freedom of action for counterrevolutionary bourgeois elements and to enable them to block all revolutionary-democratic changes, the indispensable precondition of any genuine democracy.[6]

[4]See Rolf Badstübner and Siegfried Thomas, *Die Spaltung Deutschlands: 1945–1949* (Berlin [East], 1966), pp. 74ff., who find early East-West cooperation more productive than do most other East German historians (Benser, "Das deutsche Volk," p. 138; Schnabel, *Deutsche Geschichte* [Berlin (East), 1968], vol. 3, pp. 396–97).
[5]Streisand, pp. 402–3; *Grundriss*, p. 506; Badstübner and Thomas, *Spaltung Deutschlands*, pp. 65–66.
[6]See Rolf Leonhardt, "Die Politik der SED zur Festigung des Demokratischen Blocks . . . ," *ZfG* 26 (1978): 493; Ulla Plener, "Die SPD und die Spaltung Deutschlands (1945–1949)," *BzG* 16 (1974): 990; Drechsler, "Politik am Scheideweg: Die

It is these ground rules for "democratic" policies that DDR analysts regard as the key features of the Potsdam Agreement, for progress toward the socialist order was directly related to the manner of the implementation of these rules. Other questions covered by the agreement and of major concern to the West receive less attention. In the East German view, they merely confirmed established facts that were no longer open to debate; others touched on sensitive situations in which Soviet interests overrode German ones.

The question of the German-Polish boundary—the Oder-Neisse Line—thus is mentioned but briefly. All accounts maintain that that line was agreed upon by all participants as a permanent border, with the matter of its "final delimitation" referring merely to its cartographical treatment. Proof for this interpretation is found in both the substance and the phrasing of the agreement: in keeping with the finality of the arrangement, the pertinent passage provided for the transfer of the German population from the "former German territories" east of the Oder-Neisse Line to the various German occupation zones. (In actuality, the wording, to judge by the course of the negotiations, expressed not so much an agreement as the West's resignation to its inability to reclaim these territories for Germany.)

No East German historian questions the justice of the territorial takeover by Poland; quoting Ulbricht, Rolf Badstübner and Siegfried Thomas explain the annexation as a protective measure on Poland's part against a resurgence of the insatiable Prussian Junkers and the recurring inability of the German people to check the forces of militarism and the advocates of a "drive to the east." Other writers justify the transfer as an act of restitution for centuries of aggression inflicted on Poland.[7]

Unlike Western accounts, East German analyses of the Pots-

Konzeption der U.S.A. für die Potsdamer Konferenz," in *Die U.S.A. und Europa: 1917–1945*, ed. Klein et al. (Berlin [East], 1975), pp. 288ff. Western claims that the Soviet Union could be expected to base its implementation of the Potsdam Agreement on the Western understanding of the concept of democracy are untenable. Such expectations had already been disavowed by the difficulties that arose over the implementation of the Yalta Agreement. To what absurdities this assumption can lead the argumentation of a West German political scientist, Peter Rabl, makes clear. Rabl maintains that the term *democracy* as used in the DDR constitution of 1968 and in the Soviet–East German friendship pact of 1964 must be understood in the Western sense because of its express or implied association with the Potsdam Agreement (*Zeitschr. f. Politik* 16 [1969]: 502ff., especially pp. 510–11).

[7]See Streisand, p. 399; Schnabel, *Deutsche Geschichte*, vol. 3, pp. 392–94; "Potsdamer Konferenz 1945," *Swb*, vol. 2, p. 278; Ulbricht, quoted in Badstübner and Thomas, *Spaltung Deutschlands*, pp. 72–73; *Grundriss*, p. 505; *Poland, Deutschland und die Oder-Neisse Linie*, ed. Rudi Goguel (Berlin [East], 1959), pp. 360, 419ff. On the West's resignation, see Herbert Feis, *Between War and Peace: The Potsdam Conference* (Princeton, 1960), p. 233.

dam meeting show little concern for the question of reparations, which took up much of the time of the conference. To secure reparations had been a major objective of the war-ravaged Soviet Union. The United States, on the other hand, was mainly concerned with preventing the further dislocation of the German economy lest it become a burden on the Western powers and drive the Germans into a new radicalism. Nor were the Western powers anxious to have the USSR share in the overall control of the German economy, which a specific reparations agreement, as insisted upon by the Russians, would have required. In the end, the American standpoint prevailed; each power was to obtain reparations from its own zone, with the Soviets to receive an additional share of the reparations secured from the Western zones, because the USSR had suffered the greatest losses. The effect of this arrangement was that it precluded the treatment of Germany as an economic unit, but DDR authors, always reluctant to deal with the reparations issue and the concomitant Soviet exactions that placed so heavy a burden on the precarious East German economy, make no mention of this setback to German unity even though it could have been blamed on the American stance.[8]

On the other hand, the United States and Britain are taken to task for having blocked the organizational unity of Germany that they professed to support: although they could not reject a commitment at Potsdam to establish German central administrative departments in such technical fields as finance, transportation, and industry, they would not agree to an all-inclusive German central administration. (That Stalin, for his part, according to the Soviet minutes of the conference, readily dropped his demand for an overall German government agency is not mentioned.) DDR authors complain that Western objections to such a body were inspired by fears that the preservation of German unity would facilitate the spreading of "anti-imperialist, democratic" ideas, as indeed it was hoped that it would.[9]

Marxist assessments of German developments pay special at-

---

[8]See *Swb*, vol. 2, p. 278; Badstübner and Thomas, *Spaltung Deutschlands*, p. 64. Schnabel, *Deutsche Geschichte*, Streisand, and *Grundriss* do not mention reparations at all. On the partitioning effect of the reparations agreement, see Kolko, *The Politics of War*, pp. 570–71, 573–74; Bruce Kuklick, *American Policy and the Division of Germany* (Ithaca, 1972), pp. 167ff.; Charles L. Mee, *Meeting at Potsdam* (New York, 1975), pp. 191ff., 256. That the Soviet delegation at Potsdam realized that the American reparations program precluded the preservation of Germany as an economic unit is evident from the Byrnes-Molotov conversation of July 29, 1945 (*Foreign Relations of the United States, Diplomatic Papers: The Conference of Berlin, 1945* [Washington, 1960], vol. 2, p. 474).

[9]Schnabel, *Deutsche Geschichte*, vol. 3, pp. 392–94; *Grundriss*, p. 506; *GdA*, vol. 6, p. 64; Badstübner and Thomas, *Spaltung Deutschlands*, pp. 68–70; Drechsler, "Politik," pp. 273–274. For Stalin's position, see *Teheran, Jalta, Potsdam*, ed. Alexander Fischer (Cologne, 1968), pp. 353–54.

tention to the antimonopolist mandate of the Potsdam Agreement on the grounds that the Germans' conversion to democratic and peaceful pursuits was predicated on the liquidation of all monopolist power. The performance of the occupying powers as well as that of the Germans is measured against this commitment; correspondingly, such appraisals also explore the support that the "democratic" forces, specifically the working class and its Communist vanguard, were accorded. The old class structure, it is noted, was still largely intact, and although monopoly bourgeoisie and Junkers were faced with a major crisis, they continued to hold important positions from which they might rise to new power. Only quick action could prevent such a comeback.[10]

Such action, it is noted, was undertaken only in the Soviet occupation zone. In keeping with its "class mandate," and faithful to its Potsdam commitments, the Red Army ordered the smashing of the fascist state apparatus, the dissolution of such key bases of monopolist power as entrepreneurial associations, and the transfer to public ownership of all banks and insurance concerns. Because these measures furthered German national interests, they were carried out jointly by the Soviet military authorities and the German "democratic" forces, both working together as allies in a historic mission that neither, it is stressed, could have carried out by itself. In fact, Stefan Doernberg maintains, the Soviet authorities introduced no changes on their own in their occupation zone. Viewing such changes as an internal German concern, Doernberg notes, they contented themselves with providing the German toilers with the needed freedom of action that the latter had never enjoyed before.

Similarly, Soviet historians and one-time occupation officials have stated that most reforms were prepared by the German "democratic forces" before being issued as Soviet military orders. The available evidence suggests that this was indeed the case. Nor should this come as a surprise. Because the KPD had the determining voice among these forces and called for the destruction of "Hitler fascism" and its monopolist, agrarian, and militarist bases, which the Soviets also demanded, the Germans could be given considerable leeway in mapping the internal policies of the Soviet zone. This also had the advantage of presenting these policies as essentially German and enabling the Soviets to reject Western charges that they were "exporting their revolution." At that, both Soviets and Germans responded only to "objective conditions." Little is said, however, about situations in which Soviet and East

---

[10]Streisand, p. 402; Schnabel, *Deutsche Geschichte*, vol. 3, pp. 394, 396–97; Stefan Doernberg, *Kurze Geschichte der DDR* (Berlin [East], 1969), p. 48.

German interests collided, as in the dismantling of industrial facilities in fulfillment of reparations demands.[11]

In this context, the tortuous path of the German Communist party is the subject of a welter of studies. Given the confusion and demoralization of the German people, the KPD's task of enlisting them in the country's political and economic rehabilitation proved especially difficult. From the Marxist viewpoint, the nation's most dangerous error was to blame its misery on military defeat and foreign occupation rather than on the criminal policies of monopoly capitalism.[12] In its strategy, the party was guided by the programs of the Brussels and Berne conferences and the popular-front policy of the Comintern; the specific plans had been worked out in close collaboration with the Soviet Communist party.[13] This strategy enjoined the KPD, which spoke only for a minority, to secure as broad a basis as possible for its policies and to obtain the support not only of workers but also of farmers and "progressive" bourgeois elements.

[11]See Benser, "Das deutsche Volk," pp. 140–42, 151; Heitzer, "Neue Probleme," pp. 958–59; Heitzer, "Allgemeines und Besonderes der Übergangsperiode vom Kapitalismus zum Sozialismus in der DDR," *JfG* 11 (1974): 22; Heitzer, review, *ZfG* 28 (1980): 263; Doernberg, *Kurze Geschichte*, pp. 32, 52–54; Tulpanov, "Rolle der SMAD," 249–50; Tulpanov, "Das Potsdamer Abkommen," *Deutsche Aussenpolitik* 10 (1965): suppl. no. 1, pp. 51–52; Jakov S. Drabkin, in *WZ Berlin* 19 (1970): 179–80; also letter from Ulbricht to Pieck, May 17, 1945, in *ZfG* 13 (1965): 999–1000; *GdA*, vol. 6, pp. 38–39. On the close relationship between Soviet authorities and KPD leaders, see also Leonhard, *Child of the Revolution* (London, 1957), pp. 287ff., and on the reparations issue, pp. 343–44, 345. It has been argued that the Soviet demand for reparations ran counter to the position the Bolsheviks took after the First World War. At that time, they reneged on their foreign debts on the grounds that these were incurred by imperialist elements for whose actions the Russian people could not be held responsible. Correspondingly, it is said, the Soviet occupation zone, now governed by the Soviet authorities in conjunction with German "anti-imperialist" elements, ought not to have been asked to pay reparations for damages caused by fascist imperialists (J. P. Nettl, *The Eastern Zone and Soviet Policy in Germany: 1945–1950* [London, 1951], p. 302). It should be noted, however, that the Communists had always maintained that the nation as a whole shared responsibility for the Nazi aggression and war crimes, because it helped Hitler to power and later did nothing to prevent the war or hasten its end. See the appeal of the KPD of June 11, 1945, reprinted in Weber, *Kommunismus*, pp. 431ff.; also Ulbricht, cited in Henry Krisch, *German Politics under Soviet Occupation* (New York, 1974), pp. 40–41.

[12]*Grundriss*, pp. 490, 496–97; Schnabel, *Deutsche Geschichte*, vol. 3, pp. 396–97. That the conduct of Soviet soldiers in Germany touched off a large part of the complaints about foreign occupation is rarely mentioned. If it is, these offenses are explained, not unjustifiably, as reactions to years of hardships and sacrifices caused by the Germans (Benser, "Über den friedlichen Charakter der revolutionären Umwälzung in Ostdeutschland," *BzG* 7 [1965]: 190).

[13]German Communist leaders remained in close touch with their Soviet counterparts, and it is not without interest that Ulbricht, the KPD secretary, after his return to Germany, sent a report first to Georgi Dimitrov, in charge of the international section of the Soviet Communist party, before reporting to Pieck, the KPD's chairman, who was still in Moscow (letter from Ulbricht to Pieck, May 17, 1945).

In consequence, the KPD called not for an immediate change-over to a fully socialist order but, in the words of the first proclamation of the party's Central Committee, for the "establishment of an antifascist-democratic regime, a parliamentary-democratic republic with all democratic rights and liberties for the people." It was considered wrong "at the present stage of development" to impose the Soviet system on Germany; the first step had to be the creation of a state that unlike the Weimar Republic was free of militarism and fascism, of monopolies and Junker estates, with representatives of the people in charge of the commanding heights of the economy.[14]

While noting that the KPD left no doubt in its proclamation about the temporary nature of this "antifascist-democratic" regime, East German accounts give the impression, however, that the attainment of full socialism was viewed by the party as a rather remote goal.[15] This may well have been its thinking at the time when Communist aspirations aimed at an undivided Germany whose conversion to socialism would require careful and prolonged preparations. Whatever the intentions, DDR authors proudly point out that, contrary to the assertions of West German writers, there existed at the time not only a policy of the victorious powers vis-à-vis Germany, with Germany a mere pawn of these powers, but also, thanks to the KPD, a German-initiated policy, designed expressly to protect Germany from becoming a helpless pawn.[16]

That this policy was not uncontested within the party's own ranks is rarely mentioned. Yet there were at first widespread calls for an immediate dictatorship of the proletariat and the all-out socialization of the economy. The demands were voiced by party members who had stayed in Germany during the Nazi era and were unfamiliar with the strategy worked out by the Central Committee in Moscow. The call for the immediate socialization of the means of production was also adopted by most of the Antifascist Committees (Antifa-Ausschüsse) that sprang up throughout Germany during the final days of the Nazi regime or upon its collapse. However, Günter Benser is probably right when he states that all party members quickly accepted the strategy of the antifascist-democratic bloc policy once the Moscow leaders presented their

---

[14]KPD Proclamation, in GdA, vol. 6, pp. 40–41.

[15]Benser, in Studien über die Revolution (Berlin [East], 1969), p. 459; Benser and Gerhard Rossmann, "Die Gründung der DDR—Bestandteil der Herausbildung des sozialistischen Weltsystems," BzG 16 (1974): suppl., pp. 6ff.

[16]See Schnabel, Deutsche Geschichte, vol. 3, pp. 398–99; Grundriss, pp. 497–98; GdA, vol. 6, pp. 38ff., especially p. 43. For an illustration of the supranational character of this strategy, see the analysis of the parallel moves of the Italian Communist party in Harald Neubert, "Italien zwischen Demokratie und Reaktion," ZfG 24 (1976): 253ff.

case and that non-Marxists have overrated the significance of the original disagreement.

Still, the rift deserves to be mentioned, if only because of the manner in which the KPD leadership managed to end it. On their arrival in the Soviet zone in April 1945, the KPD's *Initiativgruppen* set out at once to counter the socialization demands by having the Antifa committees transform themselves into administrative organs assisting the Soviet military administration. The committees thus were divested of their political functions, which eased the task of the KPD; at the same time, the committees also were used to replace the old antidemocratic bureaucracy, one of the power bases, it is stressed, of the Nazi regime. In the western zones, on the other hand, Benser notes, the Antifa committees were dissolved altogether—essentially because they were largely Communist-dominated—and no attempt was made to use them to remove the Nazi bureaucracy. Benser also points out that the transformation of the committees in the Soviet zone was clear proof that the Soviet Union did not wish to force its own council (soviet) system upon its zone.[17]

The implementation of the Communist strategy is traced in minute detail in the East German literature. As part of that strategy, the formation of the Social Democratic Party (SPD) and two bourgeois parties, the Christian Democratic Union (CDU) and the Liberal Democratic Party (LDPD), was authorized by the Soviet Military Administration. These parties were to enlist those forces that were not prepared to support the KPD but were in basic agreement with at least some of the latter's immediate objectives. Their cooperation, however, was not obtained without difficulty. DDR authors find the Social Democrats vacillating between premature socialist policies and indefensible reactionary positions: on the one hand, the party wished to hasten the process of nationalizing private business concerns, risking the alienation of parts of the population in both east and west; on the other, its proposed lenient treatment of Nazis and war criminals and its ambivalent attitude towards the bourgeoisie raised questions about the sincerity of its antifascist stance. Given the SPD's numerical superiority, there was, moreover, the danger that such views might prevail in a united working-class party. Under the circumstances, the KPD leadership rejected as inopportune the SPD proposal for a merger of

---

[17]See Benser, "Antifa—Ausschüsse—Staatsorgane—Parteiorganisation," *ZfG* 26 (1978): 791ff.; Benser, review, ibid., p. 76; also *Arbeiterinitiative 1945*, ed. Lutz Niethammer et al. (Wuppertal, 1976). Not all Communists who had stayed in Germany adhered to the all-out socialization line; some underground cells adopted the more flexible Moscow strategy even before the end of the war (Heinz Kühnreich and Karlheinz Pech, "Am Beginn der letzten Phase des Krieges: Ein neues bedeutsames Dokument . . . der KPD in Deutschlands 1944," *BzG* 21 [1979]: 416–17).

the two parties. Instead, it contented itself with a cooperative arrangement by which it was able, with Soviet backing, to direct Social Democratic policies in the desired direction. CDU and LDPD are found even less reliable because both groups represented entrepreneurial and agrarian interests. As such, they also challenged the Marxist axiom that a genuine democracy could be attained only under the leadership of the working class. In effect, the two parties were considered not trustworthy allies but instruments through which some middle-class elements might be induced to support Communist objectives.

To assure the cooperation of all non-Communist parties along these lines, a "Bloc of Antifascist-Democratic Parties" was organized under the KPD's aegis (with this less strident name considered preferable to the more revolutionary sounding "Bloc of Militant Democracy" that had earlier been proposed). This "People's Front," it is stressed, differed radically from the coalitions of the Weimar Republic, in which the parties of the monopoly bourgeoisie had been the dominant element. At the same time, DDR authors reject West German charges that the bloc served as a front for a dictatorship of the KPD, and merely admit that the KPD assumed the leadership of the bloc. The party could play this role, it is explained, because the working class provided the progressive impulses from which were derived the solutions to the existing problems. At the same time, it is granted that the workers' parties enjoyed the special support of the Soviet military authorities—a claim far more applicable to the KPD than to the SPD. This preferred treatment is attributed to the greater democratic potential of these two parties as compared to their bourgeois counterparts.

Still, it was not merely a matter of strong-arm tactics or Soviet protection that made the Communist party the inevitable winner in any intra-bloc disputes: Communist initiative, planning, and tactical skills were clearly superior to those of the SPD, let alone the CDU and the LDPD. East German accounts stress rightly the fact that the KPD was the only party that had prepared any plan of action for the day when the Nazi regime would collapse. This foresight, of course, gave the party an additional initial advantage. [18]

In discussing the bloc's record, DDR historians find it hard to

[18]See Schnabel, *Deutsche Geschichte*, vol. 3, pp. 399ff.; Streisand, pp. 404–6; *GdA*, vol. 6, pp. 53–54, 56ff.; Rudolf Agsten and Manfred Bogisch, "Dokumente zur Gründung der Liberal-Demokratischen Partei Deutschlands," *ZfG* 19 (1971): 1279ff.; Karl Matern, a member of the KPD's Central Committee, quoted in Sywottek, *Deutsche Volksdemokratie*, p. 206. On the role of the KPD vis-à-vis CDU and LDPD, see also Eberhard Krippendorff, "Die Gründung der Liberal-demokratischen Partei in der sowjetischen Besatzungszone 1945," *VfZ* 8 (1960): 301, 303; on the SPD, see ibid., pp. 292–93; also Krisch, *German Politics*, pp. 82–83.

decide whether to stress the consensus that was attained, often only after intense pressures on the two bourgeois parties and to a lesser degree on the SPD, or whether to emphasize the recurring disagreements. The latter, of course, are seen as evidence of the continuing class struggle, in which reactionary great-bourgeois elements sought to misuse CDU and LDPD for their own "class purposes," or petty-bourgeois concerns caused the SPD to assume an antiprogressive stance. In either case, the analyses underscore the importance of the KPD's mission and the measure of its achievements.

The negative attitude of the bourgeois parties and the significance of their opposition are singled out in particular in connection with the sweeping land reform that was launched in the fall of 1945. All estates of more than 100 hectares (250 acres) and all land owned by activist Nazis and "other war criminals"—altogether one third of the arable soil—were confiscated and distributed in small units to peasants, agricultural laborers, and refugees. The KPD insisted that the expropriations be carried out without indemnification; the former owners were to be stripped of their economic resources and reduced to political impotence. CDU and LDPD, on the other hand, acted as "Junker spokesmen" and called for indemnities. Their "class egoism" was such, it is noted, that it took the intervention of the Soviet authorities to put an end to their opposition.

East German accounts of the land reform provide also some new insights into the background of the reforms. Most DDR authors describe the reform as the result of a popular mass movement; Jürgen Kuczynski, more candidly, states that it was a measure introduced from above, partly in order to break the power of the Junkers, partly in order to ensure as efficient a cultivation of the land as possible at a time at which agricultural machinery was in desperately short supply and small-scale farming promised the best results. For this reason, the KPD leadership also rejected suggestions from both the Communist rank-and-file and the Social Democrats to preserve the expropriated estates and turn them into rural cooperatives.

Joining theory to practice, DDR authors also provide a doctrinal justification for their rejection of these proposals. To maintain the seized estates undivided would have meant embarking on a premature socialist program and skipping the bourgeois-democratic phase; on the other hand, the breakup of the large latifundia was an essential, long-overdue part of that phase. Moreover, in the overall context of the transition to the socialist order, it is noted, the reform did constitute a move toward that order, inasmuch as one-third of the land that was seized was retained by public agencies that set up "people-owned" (*volkseigene*) farms. Similarly, machine-tractor stations, taking over the available mechanized equipment, formed the nuclei of future production cooperatives.[19]

Unlike the Soviet Union and KPD, the Western powers are found to have been delinquent in fulfilling their task, accepted by them in the Potsdam Agreement, of de-nazifying and democratizing their occupation zones. No serious attempt was made, it is noted, to break up the industrial and banking monopolies or to institute land reforms to deprive those notorious sponsors of fascism—great bourgeoisie and estate owners—of their economic power. Whatever measures were taken to weaken these groups were temporary in nature and were intended more to hamstring potential competitors than to eliminate the mainsprings of imperialism and militarism. The American preoccupation with reviving the German economy and administrative services, viewing political reforms as a secondary concern, appeared to the Marxist observer as a deliberate attempt to protect and nurse back to health the monopoly-capitalist order. This suspicion appeared to be borne out also by the employment, due to carelessness or emergency pressures, of numerous Nazis in important positions while Communists and Social Democrats were treated with distinct distrust. Similarly, the initial reluctance of the Western powers to readmit political parties is interpreted as an effort to bar the genuinely antifascist forces from exerting any influence in the West. This conclusion could also draw on the fact that Western policies were indeed intended not only to prevent a Nazi resurgence, but also a Communist comeback.[20]

At the same time, the German "monopolists" are found to be hiding behind a newly discovered Occidental (*Abendland*) community, posing as the defenders of Christian values against Communist atheism. Along with "political clericalism," they are charged with diverting the masses from the struggle for a just social order,

[19]See Schnabel, *Deutsche Geschichte*, vol. 3, pp. 411–12; Doernberg, *Kurze Geschichte*, pp. 58–60; *Grundriss*, pp. 508–10; *GdA*, vol. 6, pp. 81ff., 86; Kuczynski, *Die Bewegung der deutschen Wirtschaft von 1800 bis 1946* (Berlin/Leipzig, n.d.), pp. 191ff.; Bartel and Heitzer, "Die Anwendung grundlegender Erfahrungen der Sowjetunion in der DDR," *ZfG* 22 (1974): 924; Christel Nehrig and Joachim Piskol, "Zur führenden Rolle der KPD in der demokratischen Bodenreform," ibid. 28 (1980): 324ff., with interesting details on the playing off of the peasants against the advocates of socialization by the KPD leaders. On the land reform as a reform from above, see also Leonhard, *Child*, pp. 341ff.

[20]Schnabel, *Deutsche Geschichte*, vol. 3, pp. 417–18; *GdA*, vol. 6, pp. 91–92; Kuczynski, *Geschichte*, vol. 6a, pp. 8–11; Horst Heininger, in *Der deutsche Imperialismus*, vol. 5, pp. 207ff. For non-Marxist accounts of Western occupation policies, see John Gimbel, *The American Occupation of Germany: Politics and the Military, 1945–1949* (Stanford, 1968), pp. 13ff.; Dorn, *Inspektionsreisen in der U.S.-Zone* (Stuttgart, 1973), pp. 24, 39, 51, 78ff., and *passim*; Kuklick, *American Policy*, pp. 185ff., 226ff.; F. Roy Willis, *The French in Germany, 1945–1949* (Stanford, 1962), pp. 109ff., 126ff., 147ff., 180ff.; also the symposium, "Westdeutschland zwischen 1945 und 1949," *VfZ* 21 (1973): 166ff.

falsely impressing upon them man's impotence in the face of a tragic destiny, and rejecting the "creative initiative" of the popular masses. They were all the more successful in these endeavors because of the ineffectiveness of the antifascist-democratic forces. The latter's failure to mobilize the substantial support they are shown to have had is blamed both on the repressive tactics of the Western occupation authorities and on the obstruction of the West German SPD. Once again, the SPD sided with the bourgeoisie instead of uniting the working class hand in hand with the KPD.[21]

It was these assaults on the genuinely democratic elements, DDR historians maintain, that caused the breakup of Germany. They regard the split not as inevitable but as an avoidable setback in the international and national class confrontation over the question as to whether the German problem was to be solved on democratic or imperialist terms. In this context, Joachim Streisand set forth what he described as a "realistic" alternative to the imperialist policy of splitting Germany and resurrecting the monopoly-capitalist system in the West: "After the liberation from fascism, the Marxist workers' movement asked, in the spirit of the Potsdam Agreement, that the struggle for democracy be decided in open battle and within a united state in which the working class and its allies would have a determining influence to prevent an imperialist resurgence in the Western zones also." Because this was not done, the resulting split was the responsibility of the Western powers. As another author (Manfred Bensing) has put it, "No party that follows more or less faithfully the laws of the course of developments can ever be the cause of a split."[22]

The merger of KPD and SPD into one workers' party, the Socialist Unity Party (SED), in April 1946, was another move designed to strengthen the working class and to further the advance toward the socialist order. East German accounts give various reasons for the KPD and Soviet advocacy of the fusion just a few months after a corresponding Social Democratic proposal was rejected as premature. On a more general plane, the move is explained as a defense against the antidemocratic stance of the Western powers and the favoritism they showed to "reactionary" elements. This attitude, it is charged, encouraged similar elements in the Soviet zone to try blocking democratic developments in that zone, as in the case of the East German land reform. Some authors also point out that the electoral victories of

[21]Schnabel, *Deutsche Geschichte,* vol. 3, pp. 417ff.; *Grundriss,* pp. 503–4, 514ff.; *GdA,* vol. 6, pp. 100ff.; Thomas, "An der Wiege der BRD-Aussenpolitik," *ZfG* 23 (1975): 21ff.
[22]Badstübner and Thomas, *Spaltung Deutschlands,* pp. 85, 429, 431; Streisand, p. 404; Bensing, *Thomas Müntzer,* p. 17; Bensing, in Kossok, *Studien,* p. 478.

non-Communist parties in Austria and Hungary (both of them partly or wholly occupied by the Red Army) were likewise regarded as ominous warnings.

What was probably more decisive was the continuing growth and increasing self-assertion of the East German SPD and, even more so, of its West German counterpart. This attitude is blamed, as usual, on the opportunism of the SPD leaders, who are charged with serving as spokesmen for the old imperialist forces. The SPD thus could no longer be trusted to help reunite Germany on an antifascist-democratic basis; only a revolutionary unified workers' party, that is, one guided solely by Marxist-Leninist principles, could attain this goal, aided of course by other progressive elements. The hope was that once the SED had been set up in the Soviet zone, the West German masses, too, would insist on the merger of the two parties in their part of the country. The East German accounts make clear, however, that the overriding concern of both KPD and Soviet authorities was to bar from the eastern zone all "imperialist" infiltration by way of the SPD; hence the insistence on the immediate merger of KPD and SPD in that zone; even at the risk of widening the gap between East and West Germany.

Ever anxious to illustrate the "history-making powers of the masses," DDR authors maintain that the speedy accomplishment of the merger in East Germany was due primarily to strong mass pressures. This claim is buttressed by the large numbers of petitions and resolutions that called for the merger. Their spontaneity, however, remains open to question—a doubt that Marxists would dismiss on the grounds that it ignores the inherently inevitable, "objective lawfulness" of these petitions. DDR researchers have also gathered a great many calls for a united party from West German party groups, labor unions, and other organizations. Yet the tenor of these pleas suggests that their authors did not envisage the type of tightly integrated and disciplined Leninist party the Communists planned to establish. Nor does the available evidence bear out East German claims that a *majority* of the workers in the Soviet zone, let alone in the western one, called for a merger.

In support of the latter claim, DDR historians used to point to the results of a poll held by the SPD in Berlin's western sectors. The members were asked whether they favored an immediate merger of the two parties or "fraternal" cooperation between them. By relating the West Berlin "no" vote to the membership figures of *all* of Berlin, that is, including the Soviet sector, a predominantly working-class section in which the SPD membership was disproportionately large, East German authors tried to prove that only a minority was opposed to an immediate KPD-SPD merger and that an even smaller minority opposed an alliance with the KPD. Measured against the West Berlin membership, however, the returns show a clear majority opposed to the merger and a large majority favoring an alliance with the KPD. Once again, however, what was envisaged, as the question was put in the poll, was an alliance based on a "genuine cooperative effort," which precluded the resort to Leninist tactics. More recently, *Abriss* has provided an accurate account of what happened, not without charging, however, that the poll obscured the basic issue by asking not for a straight yes-or-no vote on the merger of the two parties but for a choice between an immediate merger and an alliance.

That there was considerable rank-and-file opposition to the merger in the Soviet zone also, Stefan Doernberg and Günter Benser admit at least indirectly when they complain that the masses had not yet outgrown their bourgeois-indoctrinated anti-Bolshevism. The frequency and intensity of the pressure exerted by the Soviet authorities on wavering SPD leaders also attest to the strength of the opposition. To secure Social Democratic cooperation, moreover, the KPD accepted some basic departures from Leninist principles in the new party's organizational structure. DDR authors lay great stress on the fact that the SED was not built exclusively around the factory cell as its organizational core in keeping with Leninist tenets, but in deference to the Social Democratic tradition allowed the retention of party units organized on a residential basis. Yet, as all accounts also point out, such concessions were regarded as minor flaws soon to be remedied. What mattered was that revolutionary Marxism-Leninism could now extend its control over the entire workers' movement in the Soviet zone and advance more effectively there toward the socialist order. However, the hope was also, as mentioned before, that the newly created Socialist Unity Party of Germany would soon be just that—an all-German party—and would serve to restore a unified Germany on an antifascist-democratic basis, the most favorable terrain for the advance toward socialism. In the words of *Sachwörterbuch* and *Grundriss*, the formation of the SED constituted the "greatest accomplishment in the history of the German workers' movement since the proclamation of the *Communist Manifesto*, the emergence of the revolutionary workers' movement in Germany, and the foundation of the KPD."[23]

[23]See Schnabel, *Deutsche Geschichte*, vol. 3, pp. 427ff.; Horst Lipski, "Die Verwirklichung der Beschlüsse der 'Ersten Konferenz der Sechzig' im Januar und Februar 1946," *BzG* 5 (1963): 214–15; *GdA*, vol. 6, pp. 115ff., 150, 154ff., and *passim*; "Sozialistische Einheitspartei Deutschlands," *Swb*, vol. 2, pp. 529–31; *Grundriss*, pp. 518ff.; Kurt Wrobel, "Kampf . . . westdeutscher Arbeiter um die Aktionseinheit der Arbeiterklasse 1945/1946," *BzG* 2 (1960): 51ff., 61; Günter Uebel and Erich Woitinas, "Zur Entwicklung . . . der SED bis . . . 1950," ibid. 12 (1970): 607–8; Benser, "Bürgerliche und sozialdemokratische Literatur über die Vereinigung

The Class Confrontation Intensifies

Because the merger was to strengthen the working class in its struggle against bourgeois imperialism and its helpmates, opportunism, mass apathy, and illusionism, DDR analyses devote their special attention to the impact that the newly formed SED had on these objectives. Its first major move, it is noted, aimed at the nationalization of all enterprises owned by Nazi and war criminals, in particular of all major concerns because the "monopolists" had been the main war criminals. Most DDR authors, however, pass over the fact that this measure had even less support than the earlier land reform. As Stefan Doernberg puts it, large parts of the working class still lacked class consciousness; thus they did not realize the responsibility of the monopolists for the fascist dictatorship and its wars and were not ready to fight for the nationalization of monopolist concerns. Saxony, an SED stronghold, sanctioned the move in a popular referendum by a three-fourths majority, but in the other states of the Soviet zone the state governments simply promulgated laws, without recourse to a vote, "deriving their authority from countless demands of the toilers and from the results of the referendum in Saxony" (*Deutsche Geschichte*).

Nor did the implementation of the decision prove easy. It was turned over to committees composed of members of the "bloc parties" and union representatives, and here, as DDR authors complain, "reactionary elements" in LDPD and CDU, supported by other opponents of nationalization, tried to keep the number of the concerns to be taken over as low as possible. Some bourgeois opponents even proposed postponing all nationalization measures until an all-German referendum could be held on this issue. In these maneuvers, it is noted, the opposition had the support not only of all imperialist elements in West Germany but also of their lackeys, the rightist SPD leaders.

DDR authors view such opposition as a flagrant violation of the Potsdam Agreement, because Germany, it is stressed again and again, could not be democratized without depriving the imperialist camp of its economic foundation. Tribute is paid to the Soviet authorities for the help given in these endeavors: they implemented the confiscation of Nazi property at a time when the East German authorities were still too weak to enforce such a move.[24]

Local, county, and state elections held in the fall of 1946 are

---

von KPD and SPD zur SED," *ZfG* 24 (1976): 431ff.; *Abriss*, pp. 107ff., especially pp. 115–16, 120–21. For non-Communist accounts of the merger, see Krisch, *German Politics*, pp. 103ff., 184, 209. Krisch, however, sees the merger as primarily a Soviet gambit. See also Sywottek, *Deutsche Volksdemokratie*, pp. 207ff.

[24]Streisand, p. 411; Schnabel, *Deutsche Geschichte*, vol. 3, pp. 437ff.; *Grundriss*, pp. 525–26; *GdA*, vol. 6, p. 166; Helga Kanzig, "Die Politik der SED zur Herausbildung und Festigung ökonomischer Grundlagen der antifaschistisch-demokrati-

hailed as further milestones of antifascist-democratic progress. With the bourgeoisie no longer dominating government and economy and deprived of its hold over press and radio, the elections rank as the first truly democratic ones on German soil. Their democratic character was assured also by the conversion of the police from an instrument of the bourgeoisie into an organ of the people, protecting the people against fascist elements. It was in carrying out this latter task, it is noted in refutation of Western charges of political repression, that government, police, and Soviet authorities would check the activities of the reactionary elements in CDU and LDPD. These forces, *Grundriss* complains, still refused to accept the leadership of the working class and its revolutionary party within the antifascist-democratic bloc. Instead, they tried to break up the bloc and replace it with a bourgeois-dominated coalition—endeavors that were all the more dangerous because even the more cooperative elements in these parties did not fully accept the SED's guiding role. In opposing such tendencies, *Geschichte der deutschen Arbeiterbewegung* adds, the SED did not fight the bourgeois parties as such but merely sought to strengthen the bloc.[25]

The outcome of the elections is acclaimed as an important victory of the working class. In the local elections, the SED received 57 percent of the vote; in the county elections, 50.3 percent; in the state elections, 47.5 percent. What is not mentioned is that the SED majority in the local elections was derived from the rural vote, which was more susceptible to political pressures than was the urban one. This factor is, however, implied in recurring complaints about the continuing "strong economic positions" that capitalist elements still retained. Speaking through the CDU and the LDPD, it is charged, these forces demanded a reexamination of the land reform on the grounds that it had been found counterproductive—a criticism left unanswered by East German authors. CDU and LDPD are also accused of abusing their parliamentary role by calling for an independent judiciary. ("Independent from whom?" was the SED answer. "Perhaps from the people?")[26]

---

schen Umwälzung . . . ," *ZfG* 27 (1979): 807–9, 815–16; Heinz Vosske, "Über die politisch-ideologische Hilfe der KPDSu . . . für die deutsche Arbeiterklasse . . . (1945 bis 1949)," *BzG* 14 (1972): 725ff.; see also, on the relationship between SED and the Soviet military administration, Fritz Reinert, "Der Befehl Nr. 209 der SMAD," *ZfG* 23 (1975): 506–7, 509, although one wishes that his analysis of this relationship had been supported by some direct quotations.

[25]Doernberg, *Kurze Geschichte*, pp. 99–100; *Grundriss*, pp. 527, 531; *GdA*, vol. 6, pp. 172–73. For a CDU account, see Ferdinand Friedensburg, *Es ging um Deutschlands Einheit* (Berlin [West], 1971), p. 137; also Krippendorff, *Die Liberal-Demokratische Partei Deutschlands in der sowjetischen Besatzungszone 1945/48* (Düsseldorf, 1965), pp. 94ff.

[26]Krippendorff, *Liberal-Demokratisch Partei*, pp. 97ff., 106ff.; Ernst Lemmer, *Manches war doch anders* (Frankfurt, 1968), p. 252; *Grundriss*, p. 531; Doernberg, *Kurze Geschichte*, p. 103.

These problems were aggravated by the fact that the SED had internal difficulties that impaired its effectiveness. In the larger Marxist-Leninist framework, this was an even more serious impediment to social progress than any alleged bourgeois threats. As every author points out, the SED still suffered from structural weaknesses and ideological misapprehensions. It was also hampered by dissenting SPD members and by "opportunistic" elements led astray by Western propaganda. Thus, despite a tightened organization and increased ideological training, the SED was not yet the closely integrated Marxist-Leninist party that conditions required. As a recurring complaint has it, even some members of the party directorate did not yet have the ideological firmness expected of them. These members could still wonder at the Second Party Congress in 1947 whether the policy of attacking monopoly capitalism and its Social Democratic camp followers or the promotion of friendship with the USSR should not be suspended temporarily in the interests of restoring the unity of the German state—as if reunification at any price were preferable to the destruction of monopolist capitalism and Social Democratic opportunism.[27]

Parts of the SED's rank and file as well as segments of the working class as a whole are found to have shown similar signs of ideological weakness. To a large extent, these misconceptions could be attributed to the economic difficulties besetting the Soviet zone. Many people believed, it is noted, that the existing shortages had been caused, not by the irrational policies of German imperialism and the manipulations of ruthless entrepreneurs, large landowners, and other reactionary elements, but by the new order and the policies of the Soviet authorities. There is an occasional admission, however, that some of the difficulties were those that "inevitably arise if a new class inexperienced in the direction of state and production takes over the leadership" (Benser and Heitzer). Similarly, it is rarely mentioned that reparation deliveries to the Soviet Union also added to the zone's economic troubles. What is stressed, on the other hand, are the benefits East Germans derived from the plants that were turned over to the Russians as reparations but that were producing for them in East Germany instead of being dismantled and transferred to the USSR. The plants left in East Germany, it is pointed out, provided jobs for German workers and trained them in the basics of socialist economics, while the SED for its part learned how to strengthen the alliance between working class and technical intelligentsia and

[27]Vosske, "Lehren der Novemberrevolution für den ideologischen Verschmelzungsprozess von Kommunisten und Sozialdemokraten in der SED," *BzG* 10 (1968): suppl. no. 2, pp. 105, 114; Gerd Dietrich, "Die internationalistische Arbeit der SED, 1947," *ZfG* 24 (1976): 421–22.

how to do party work in large people-owned industrial enterprises. Summing up, *Geschichte der deutschen Arbeiterbewegung* notes that

> The shortage of almost all essential consumer goods led many to look on the American goods provided by the Marshall Plan as the saving solution. Their misery would not let them see the effects of the Marshall Plan. American goods and credits seemed more important to them than the consolidation of peace and democracy and the preservation of the achievements of the antifascist-democratic revolution. Such moods affected also those members of the SED whose views were not yet sufficiently firm politically and ideologically.

Geschichte praises the "patient political and ideological work" by which the SED sought to convince confused and wavering workers and party members of the imperialist goals of the Marshall Plan and rid these doubters of misconceptions that at times bordered on outright "class enmity."[28]

As the East German accounts make clear, ideological fervor was all the more needed in order to cope with the existing shortages, because productivity could not be raised by an increase of food and clothing supplies, which "reactionaries" insisted was the only way to step up productivity. Although with Soviet help some limited material incentives were offered, what was required above all, for lack of more substantial inducements, was a change of attitude on the part of the masses. To encourage confidence and initiative, the Soviets, it is acknowledged with gratitude, also reduced their reparation claims, returned some confiscated plants to the East German state governments, and promised to bring dismantling to an end. The SED leadership for its part pressed the fight against "saboteurs, speculators, and idlers." Details of this campaign, however, can be gathered only from Western sources, which paint a grim picture of persecutions and mass arrests; these included large numbers of one-time Social Democrats and the expulsion of some 1,700 SED members for abuses of their membership to further their personal ends.

As DDR historians report happily, production soon began to increase and under conditions, they stress, that promised a future free of wars, crises, and oppression. The task now was to extend

---

[28]See *Grundriss*, pp. 526–27, 532, 556–57; Benser and Heitzer, quoted by Streisand, p. 418; Badstübner and Thomas, *Spaltung Deutschlands*, p. 146; *GdA*, vol. 6, pp. 226–27. The actual monetary value of the reparations the Russians received is still a matter of controversy. According to Fritz Selbmann, in charge of industrial planning at the time, reparation deliveries amounted to 3,658 million dollars until the end of 1950—a figure compatible with the amount of 11,470 million Reichsmark, or 2,742 million dollars, that Nettl (*Eastern Zone*, p. 237) has computed for the period until July 1948. The total amount, according to Selbmann, paid by January 1, 1954, when deliveries were ended, was 4,300 million dollars (Selbmann, in *Deutsche Aussenpolitik* 10 [1965]: suppl. no. 1, p. 110–11).

this strategy to all of Germany as the foundation for a united, antifascist-democratic republic. "At a time in which American imperialists reached for the economic and military resources of West Germany and proceeded to cut off permanently the western zones from the German national union (*Nationalverband*), the SED became the warning conscience of the nation."[29]

DDR authors leave no doubt about the urgency of this task. The imperialist Western powers, they complain, working closely with the West German imperialists, were stifling all democratic forces in their occupation zones. Defying the popular will as expressed in parliamentary laws and popular referenda, they vetoed the various plans for socialization adopted in Rhineland-Westphalia, Hesse, Schleswig-Holstein, and Berlin. In the same vein, they prohibited the merger of the KPD and the SPD in the western zones, thus preventing the working class from attaining its unity. Nor did they implement the antimonopoly provisions of the Potsdam Agreement, beyond breaking up a few combines, or initiate any land reform. Monopolists and other war criminals were allowed to hold key positions in government, economy, and political parties, assuring them of continued control of West Germany's policies. By the same token, there was no genuine demilitarization, because industries that could be reconverted to arms production remained in the hands of the very men who had put Hitler into power and launched World War II. Yet none of these measures could have been taken, these censures keep stressing, if the Social Democratic leadership had not also accepted them in its blatant betrayal of the true interests of the working class.[30]

The question of reunification, too, is dealt with as an aspect of this class confrontation, as part of the worldwide struggle between socialism and capitalism. Thus viewed, the issue could be resolved in only two ways—either by the restoration of German unity on a democratic basis, with all this implied in the Marxist sense, or by the split-off of the West German zones from the country's democratic sector in defiance of the lawful course of events. The first alternative, it is noted, was adopted by the USSR and the SED, which took democratizing steps in their zone; the Western powers, on the other hand, pursued the second, with the West German parties leaving all decisions to the United States, Britain,

---

[29]*GdA*, vol. 6, pp. 227ff. (quotation on p. 230); *Grundriss*, pp. 532–33; Doernberg, *Kurze Geschichte*, pp. 103ff.; for details, see Nettl, *Eastern Zone*, pp. 100–101, 103; Fritz Schenk, *Im Vorzimmer der Diktatur* (Cologne, 1962), pp. 20–22.

[30]Streisand, pp. 412ff.; Schnabel, *Deutsche Geschichte*, vol. 3, p. 439; *GdA*, vol. 6, pp. 204, 210; *Grundriss*, p. 540; Kuczynski, *Geschichte*, vol. 7a, pp. 57ff.; also "Westdeutschland," *VfZ* symposium; Hans-Dieter Kreikamp, "Die Entflechtung der I. G. Farbenindustrie . . . ," ibid. 25 (1977): 220ff.; Joseph Borkin, *The Crime and Punishment of I. G. Farben* (New York, 1978), pp. 157ff.

and France. Thus, while Western strategy assigned reunification to the province of foreign policy, taking it out of the hands of the German people, the democratic approach of Soviet Union and SED enabled the Germans to work themselves for the attainment of unity on a democratic foundation, in conjunction with Soviet efforts on their behalf.[31]

Numerous studies recount the Soviet endeavors at the various foreign ministers' conferences that followed the Potsdam Agreement. The calls of Foreign Commissar Vyacheslav M. Molotov for all-German institutions, an all-German antifascist-democratic government, and for all-German elections as first steps toward the formation of an anti-imperialist democratic German republic are contrasted with the delaying tactics of the Western representatives. The efforts of the SED receive corresponding attention; special note is taken of the SED's willingness to delay the transition to socialism in order to facilitate the reunification process. In the same vein, the Antifascist-Democratic Bloc is commended for insisting that an all-German conference, called to Munich in July 1947 to discuss some immediate economic problems, take up the question of German unity before discussing anything else. (No agreement could be reached on this point, and the East German minister-presidents thereupon withdrew from the meeting—another casualty, it is pointed out, of the socialist-imperialist class struggle.) Yet there could never be national unity merely for unity's sake, "without regard to the class situation." An all-German constitution drafted by the SED in 1946 is praised for accordingly calling for the liquidation of all trusts and cartels, the socialization of large concerns, the breakup of landed estates, and the removal of other obstacles to democracy and social justice.

The main interest of DDR authors is focused, however, on the efforts of the SED and the West German KPD, aided by other "progressive" elements in the western zones, to organize mass movements calling for the establishment of a united antifascist-democratic republic. These movements also demanded a unified economic policy and the adoption of the reforms introduced in the Soviet zone. Such appeals, it is claimed, with inadequate evidence, were highly effective in the West German zones until the United States launched a counteroffensive by means of the Marshall Plan.

Yet the forces for progress would not be quieted and kept up

[31]See Benser, "Befreiung Europas," p. 371; Schnabel, *Deutsche Geschichte*, vol. 3, p. 465; Badstübner and Thomas, *Spaltung Deutschlands*, p. 181; Doernberg, *Kurze Geschichte*, p. 120; Kanzig, "Politik der SED," p. 807. Thomas has found, however, that Adenauer, for one, actively supported the "separatist" policies of the Western Powers (Thomas, "An der Wiege der BRD-Aussenpolitik," *ZfG* 23 [1975]: 25ff.).

the struggle for unity. Detailed accounts tell of the SED, always in conjunction with other "progressive' forces, calling a "German People's Congress for Unity and a Just Peace." The meeting drew 2,215 participants, with almost one-third—664—coming from the western zones. It laid the foundation for an all-German movement of "national self-help," and a second congress, gathering on March 17–18, 1948, on the centenary of the Revolution of 1848, made arrangements for a popular referendum on the unity issue in all parts of Germany. An initial registration campaign (*Volksbegehren*) produced 14,776,000 signatures, constituting about 40 percent of all qualified voters—far more, it is stressed, than the 10 percent required by the Weimar Constitution in order to obtain such a referendum. The Western powers, however, held off because they intended to set up a separate West German state.

Actually, the proposal was a pointless gesture. Had the referendum been held, it might conceivably have secured the support of a majority of the voters. Because it would have asked only for support of a law reiterating that Germany was an "indivisible democratic republic," however, it would have aroused unfulfillable hopes, for the term *democratic* still awaited a definition acceptable to both East and West.[32]

To DDR authors, the apparent unwillingness of the West to consult the popular will is further proof of its determination not to allow the establishment of a unified democratic republic. Obviously the ruling classes in the United States, Britain, and France viewed any extension of the antifascist-democratic revolution into their zones as a serious threat to their class privileges. The United States therefore allowed France to block as a threat to her security the creation of the central administrative agencies provided for by the Potsdam Agreement. (Conversely, it might be noted, Americans suspected the Soviets of encouraging France's intransigence.) The British in turn adjusted to American policies, both in order to push back the revolutionary movement on the Continent and in order not to jeopardize their prospects of American financial help.

All subsequent Western, and especially American, moves serve to reinforce these conclusions. A draft treaty submitted by Secretary of State James F. Byrnes to the Council of Foreign Minis-

[32]See Schnabel, *Deutsche Geschichte*, vol. 3, pp. 462ff.; Benser, "Befreiung Europas," Doernberg, *Kurze Geschichte*, pp. 123–24; *GdA*, vol. 6, p. 467; Erich W. Gniffke, *Jahre mit Ulbricht* (Cologne, 1966), p. 241; also Erika Demloff, "Zur Konferenz der Ministerpräsidenten . . . Juni 1947," *BzG* 10 (1968): 884–85. The bulk of the referendum registrations obviously came from the Soviet zone; how many were West German ones is nowhere stated. Because there were 10.75 million qualified voters in the Soviet zone (see Nettl, *Eastern Zone*, pp. 90–91) and assuming that of these 90 percent—that is, 9.7 million—voted, the West German votes amounted to 5.1 million, representing 20 percent of the qualified voters in the three West German zones.

ters in Paris in April 1946 that pledged the four occupying powers to guarantee Germany's continued demilitarization for twenty-five years is dismissed as wholly inadequate because it equated demilitarization with disarmament and failed to deal with the roots of German militarism—capitalism and large-scale land ownership. Another American plan of merging all zones into an economic unit is found equally unacceptable on the grounds that the merger was not to be supplemented with a democratic reorganization of the economy. In the words of Badstübner and Thomas, "It was not the formal elimination of the zonal borders that was the cardinal problem of Germany's economic development, but the democratization of the German economy, which would have enabled the German people to coordinate all resources in the most effective manner [and] to adopt a constructive economic plan of rehabilitation." As it was, the Western proposals left untouched the conditions that had produced Nazism.

A more elaborate proposal, presented by Byrnes in a speech at Stuttgart a few months later, is rejected for the same reason. It reiterated the earlier plans for the demilitarization and economic unification of Germany, but going farther, also wanted to let the Germans establish a federal central government. Once again, it is stressed that these schemes were incompatible with the Potsdam Agreement because they failed to provide for the liquidation of monopolist associations, land reform, and the democratization of the economy and bureaucracy. In the same vein, the creation of a federated German state is dismissed as an attempt of the great bourgeoisie to extend its influence to the East German state: the more numerous bourgeois-dominated West German states would have been able to outvote their East German counterparts in such a government. Indeed, it is charged, these plans were purposely drafted so as to be unacceptable to the Soviet Union, thus providing an alibi for the creation of a separate West German state. Such a split-up in turn was to help stem the revolutionary tide that threatened to carry the democratic attainments of eastern and central Europe to the western parts of the continent.[33]

The Marshall Plan was another weapon in this confrontation. DDR authors attack the plan, as they must, because it too was designed to contain the socialist tide and shore up the declining capitalist system. Equally important, the Marshall Plan was drawing the West German zones more firmly into the Western camp. Going beyond the true aims of the plan, however, East German historians assail it also as preparing the way for the transformation of the Western camp into a military bloc in which West Germany

---

[33]Badstübner and Thomas, *Spaltung Deutschlands*, pp. 147–48, 158–60 (quotation on p. 148); Doernberg, *Kurze Geschichte*, pp. 111–13.

was to serve as the launching pad for an eventual attack on the Soviet Union and the people's democracies. All in all, the plan is denounced as a brazen attempt to impose the hegemony of "U.S. imperialism" on Europe, both east and west.[34]

These assessments of Western policies are of interest primarily because of the light they throw on Soviet and SED policies during the immediate postwar period. Many of the charges have a basis in fact—from the claims of Washington's catering to France's obstruction of the Potsdam Agreement[35] to the assertion that plans for a separate West German state were considered already at that early stage[36] and that altogether the Western powers, and especially the United States, were more concerned with fending off the "democratic revolutionary" tide, that is, Communism, than with "democratizing" and reunifying Germany (just as the USSR was unwilling to reunify Germany under just any conditions). What East German historians fail to see (and from their perspective will not and cannot see) is the fact that this policy was derived not from any aggressive designs on the part of bankers and industrialists but essentially from the defensive impulses of all strata and classes. In addition, although American policies obviously were designed to benefit the United States, they were also expected to improve conditions throughout the world.[37]

Yet, if Marxist accounts simplistically view American policy as a drive for monopolist power and profits, they also make clear that non-Marxist interpretations of Soviet and East German activities are similarly misleading. Such interpretations ignore altogether the ideological elements in the Soviet actions and view them in turn as a mere struggle for power. Thus, Molotov's opposition to the American proposals for German demilitarization and economic reunification has been dismissed as simply obstructive, without regard to the serious concern that the lack of comprehensive economic and administrative reforms in the Western zones aroused in the Russians, given their view of trusts and cartels and their wartime experiences at the hands of the Germans. Neither side, then, was willing to consider the fact that the other was

---

[34]*Grundriss*, pp. 539–40; Schnabel, *Deutsche Geschichte*, vol. 3, pp. 459–60; Streisand, p. 417–18; Gerhard Keiderling, "Der Mythos von der 'sowjetischen Gefahr' und die Gründung der NATO," *ZfG* 24 (1976): 1093ff.

[35]On the reasons for this indulgence, see Kuklick, *American Policy*, pp. 195–96; Gimbel, "Die Vereinigten Staaten, Frankreich und der amerikanische Vertragsentwurf zur Entmilitarisierung Deutschlands," *VfZ* 22 (1974): 272ff.

[36]See John L. Gaddis, *The United States and the Origins of the Cold War* (New York, 1972), p. 328; George F. Kennan, *Memoirs: 1925–1950* (Boston, 1967), p. 258. There is no mention anywhere in the DDR literature of the moment when Soviet Union and SED leadership first considered the need for converting the Soviet zone into a separate state.

[37]Gimbel, *American Occupation*, p. 168; Kuklick, *American Policy*, pp. 227–29.

guided by wholly different social values. Instead, each expected the other camp to ignore these differences and adjust its policies to those of its opponent.[38]

The Splitting of Germany

The major events preceding the breakup of Germany into two separate states have not received the detailed attention in DDR historiography that have been accorded to them by Western historians. To East German scholars, the Western currency reform in June 1948 and the ensuing crisis over Berlin are simply preludes to the long-planned establishment of a West German state. When a separate currency was introduced in the Western zones, Streisand notes, "economic relations between these zones and the Soviet occupation zone [were] severed. The demarcation line along the Elbe and Werra rivers developed practically into a state boundary line. On this basis the political split occurred."[39]

The Soviet reaction, DDR authors insist, was merely protective. By suspending passenger travel between the Western zones and Berlin and between the Western sectors of Berlin and the Soviet zone the Soviet authorities sought to guard the latter against being flooded by the worthless old currency. Freight traffic was allowed to continue, after proper inspection. It was the Western powers that escalated the issue into a major confrontation. They cut off all interzonal trade and fomented a war psychosis in order to scare the West Germans into accepting a separate West German state. Similarly, Western Europe was pressured into forming an anti-Soviet bloc, as it was to emerge a few months later in NATO. East German historians deny that Berlin was being blockaded by the Soviets; they point out that the Soviet Union offered to supply West Berlin with foodstuffs and other necessities (provided they were picked up in Berlin's Soviet sector).[40]

Although the West German currency reform is singled out as the immediate reason for the Berlin blockade, the pressures inflicted on West Berlin, it is noted, also were to remind the Western

[38]See Gimbel, *American Occupation*, pp. 73, 112–13; Gaddis, *United States*, pp. 329–30. Kennan, who acknowledges that Soviet policy was in part determined by ideological considerations, fails to take them into account in his specific analyses of Soviet policy (*Memoirs*, pp. 547ff.).
[39]Streisand, p. 418; also *Grundriss*, p. 549.
[40]See *Grundriss*, pp. 549–51; Schnabel, *Deutsche Geschichte*, vol. 3, pp. 470–71. See also Fritz Selbmann's reminiscences in *BzG* 14 (1972): 260ff. Selbmann was at the time deputy director of the Deutsche Wirtschaftskommission, the East German agency dealing with economic matters in the Soviet zone.

powers that their presence in Berlin was predicated upon the continued existence of a united Germany. With the establishment of a separate West German state, Berlin's role as capital of a united Germany would come to an end and the city's administration would revert to the Soviets, because the Berlin territory was part of the Soviet occupation zone.

This claim is based on a four-power statement issued on June 5, 1945, which speaks of the division of Germany into four occupation zones, seemingly implying that Berlin was to have no special territorial status; there is moreover only a reference to a separate *administration* of Berlin in the document. No mention is made of the original agreement on the occupation of Germany, signed by the United States, the Soviet Union, and Britain on September 12, 1944, which the above-cited agreement of the following June merely implements. The earlier document explicitly states that "Germany is to be divided ... for occupation purposes into three zones [there was no French zone as yet] ... and into the special area of Berlin," making it clear that Berlin was not considered a part of the Soviet zone, but a separate unit—a last remnant of a united Germany. (If East German authors do refer to this agreement, they merely quote its inaccurate title, "Protocol ... Concerning the Occupation Zones in Germany and the Administration of Greater Berlin.") There are occasional references to the fact that at Yalta, too, there was talk only of the division of Germany into occupation zones, but the official communiqué again explains that all discussions proceeded from the original agreement of the preceding September, from which the Western powers derived their originary right to be in Berlin.[41]

For the settlement of the crisis, DDR authors give credit to the Soviet Union, whose determined stance, they claim, forced

[41]See Schnabel, *Deutsche Geschichte,* vol. 3, p. 394; Gerhard Keiderling and Percy Stulz, *Berlin: 1945–1968* (Berlin [East], 1970), pp. 64–65, 157; Gerhard Reintanz, in *Der deutsche Imperialismus,* vol. 5, pp. 451ff.; "Viermächtestatus von Berlin," *Swb,* vol. 2, p. 735; Keiderling, "Die stumpfe Waffe der Nichtanerkennung," *JfG* 12 (1975): 323–24. The various agreements on Berlin are conveniently assembled in Ernst Deuerlein, *Die Einheit Deutschlands* (Frankfurt, 1957), pp. 222, 229, 246. Ferdinand Friedensburg states in his memoirs that a constitution proposed for Berlin by the Communist-dominated city government of Berlin in April 1946 provided that "the area of Berlin is subject to the central authority of Germany (*Zentralgewalt Deutschland*)" (Friedensburg, *Es ging um Deutschlands Einheit,* p. 136). This provision thus considered the Berlin territory as a last remnant of a unified Germany that had not been assigned to any of the occupation zones. In the same vein, all the land over which railroad tracks have been laid in Berlin is still registered, at least in the official records of West Berlin, in the name of the German Reich as the legal owner (Otto Jörg Weis, report on West Berlin, *Frankfurter Rundschau,* Jan. 26, 1980). See also Philip E. Mosely, who participated in the drafting of the various agreements and protocols ("The Occupation of Germany: New Light on How the Zones Were Drawn," *Foreign Affairs* 28 [1949–1950], 589, 591, 593–94, 601).

the West to resolve the conflict. The outcome is hailed as a defeat for the latter on the grounds that the Western powers failed to take over all of Berlin, let alone the Soviet zone, and were also frustrated in their efforts to provoke a war with the Soviet Union. How the retention of the West German currency, the establishment of the West German state, and the continued Western presence in West Berlin is to be reconciled with this assessment is not explained.[42]

DDR authors find that the continuing confrontation with Western imperialism also touched off a marked acceleration of the transition to socialism in the Soviet zone. Thus a Two-Year Plan designed to overcome the economic effects of the war was adopted in June 1948 to offset the lures of the Marshall Plan and present a "democratic alternative" to it. Inroads were made into the retail and wholesale trade, which was still largely in private hands. In the same vein, state control was extended over the entire industrial production, one-third of which was also still privately owned. Thus, whatever chances of a full-scale restoration of capitalism remained at this point—and some authors claim that they still were considerable—were further reduced and the socialist order brought closer.[43]

These changes, it is pointed out, were made under the leadership of the Socialist Unity party. The latter, in turn, could fulfill its task only because it was transforming itself into a new Marxist-Leninist party. It abandoned the parity principle by which each leading position had been filled by both a one-time KPD and SPD member—an arrangement, it is charged, by which "petty-bourgeois," that is, Social Democratic, elements kept exerting their divisive antiprogressive influence. Younger men trained in the Soviet Union were now available to replace the Social Democrats, and in the conversion process many of the latter were removed from their posts. Similarly, the party was built increasingly around the place of work rather than the residence of its members; this reorganization strengthened the factory cells and enabled them to promote more

[42]Keiderling and Stulz, *Berlin*, pp. 200–201; Badstübner and Thomas, *Spaltung Deutschlands*, pp. 344–45.
[43]See *GdA*, vol. 6, pp. 253ff., 286; Schnabel, *Deutsche Geschichte*, vol. 3, pp. 472–75; *Grundriss*, pp. 554–56; 565–68. Whereas DDR authors are vague about the oppositional activities of private entrepreneurs, hinting only at black market activities and illegal transfers of property to the West, Western sources have collected considerable material on large-scale under-cover removals of machinery and other capital assets from the Soviet to the Western zones. This material also shows that during the Berlin blockade East German farmers and businessmen surreptitiously supplied West Berlin with substantial amounts of food and other necessities (W. Philips Davison, *The Berlin Blockade* [Princeton, 1958], p. 196; Manuel Gottlieb, *The German Peace Settlement and the Berlin Crisis* [New Brunswick, n.d.], pp. 175–78, 258 n. 20, 265 n. 58).

effectively the fulfillment of the economic plans and fight sabotage, tardiness, and inefficiency.[44]

Suggestions that these Marxist-Leninist principles were forced upon the German workers as something essentially alien are dismissed as wholly unfounded. As *Abriss,* the official history of the SED, argues in a characteristically circular manner, these developments

> constituted a generally valid precondition of the destruction of impe-
> rialism and militarism, of the transition from capitalism to social-
> ism, the creation of the new society, free of exploitation and repres-
> sion, and its guidance by the working class and its revolutionary
> vanguard. The absorption of the Leninist doctrine of the party consti-
> tuted the decisive link which made possible the advance of the
> working class in the Soviet zone.

What was happening, in other words, was the anticipation of an inevitable process. Waltraud Falk reaches the same conclusion by a somewhat more realistic route. She sees the "generally valid laws" borne out by the "concrete historical course of the East German transition from capitalism to socialism": it demonstrated that so-cialist production relations could not win out unless the power of the state were channeled into a dictatorship of the proletariat. At the same time, she adds, the dialectic of productive forces and production relations required the breakthrough of democratic cen-tralism in the economy. In tightening its reins, once again, then, the SED merely proceeded to implement these laws.[45]

In the larger context of the socialist-imperialist struggle, the consolidation of the Socialist Unity party is also welcomed for enabling the party to fight off more effectively what are described as the sabotage activities of the reactionary segments of the CDU and the LDPD. With the advance toward socialism as the preor-dained goal, efforts of these parties to safeguard the proprietary interests of their entrepreneurial and farming constituencies are condemned as merely obstructive. Accordingly, DDR authors take CDU and LDPD to task for objecting to the inclusion of labor unions and other mass organizations in the Bloc of Antifascist-

[44]See *Grundriss,* p. 566; *Abriss,* pp. 182ff., 197ff.; Schnabel, *Deutsche Geschichte,* vol. 3, pp. 480–81; Uebel and Woitinas, "Zur Entwicklung," pp. 615ff.; Rolf Stöckigt, "Probleme des Übergangs vom Kapitalismus zum Sozialismus—der his-torische Platz der Gründung der DDR," *BzG* 15 (1973): 421, 424. That former SPD members did keep in touch with one another and tried to influence the course of developments is confirmed by Gniffke, *Jahre mit Ulbricht,* pp. 259, 288ff., 294–96, 306–8, 328. What to them seemed a natural consequence of their common background and aspirations was considered a grave offense (factionalism) by Marxist-Leninist standards. See the statement of the First Party Conference of the SED (January 25–29, 1949), reprinted in Weber, *Kommunismus,* p. 445.
[45]*Abriss,* pp. 182–83; Waltraud Falk, "Über den erzieherischen Wert ... der Wirt-schaftsgeschichte," *ZfG* 25 (1977): 1084.

Democratic Parties—a move meant to further curb the "reactionary" influences that still survived in these parties. In the same vein, the LDPD is berated for proposing an increase in consumer goods production to improve the living standards of the East German population. This demand is viewed as a brazen attempt to strengthen the private capitalist sector in which consumer goods industries still predominated. It was all the more dangerous, DDR historians conclude, because the Soviet zone was bound to become dependent on the Marshall Plan countries without a substantial increase in the production of capital goods. "In the last analysis," as *Geschichte der deutschen Arbeiterbewegung* sums up the general view,

> these controversies turned on the queston of whether the Soviet occupation zone ought to subject itself to a blackmailing imperialist policy or carry on the fight for a united democratic German republic. If the toilers of the Soviet occupation zone wished to pursue the great national goals and effectively aid the patriots in the western zones, their own order had to be viable and rest on a secure economic foundation. To this great national need the special class interest of certain capitalist circles had to yield.

However, even if CDU and LDPD were not as cooperative as was expected of them, all authors agree that this was not the time to do away altogether with the capitalist sector of the economy; East Germany was not yet ready, either objectively or subjectively, for a socialist order. Although any restorative efforts of private capital had to be crushed, the capitalist system as such could be defeated according to historical laws only by the greater productivity of the people-owned sector of the economy, as it kept growing through planned investment and accumulation. It is also frankly admitted, however, that the superiority of the economy's people-owned sector had to be "safeguarded" by special measures. Meanwhile, the LDPD and the CDU could still play a useful role by helping their constituencies understand that socialism should be viewed not negatively as the destroyer of the Bürgertum, but positively as an order that fostered the creative potential of the entire people.[46]

While the Soviet zone is pictured as progressing toward greater freedom and social justice, the western zones are portrayed as the hapless victims of the imperialist camp. In this view, the exploitation of the West German toilers continued, as exemplified by the Marshall Plan and the currency reform, both of which favored the industrial bourgeoisie at the expense of the masses. Even

---

[46]*GdA,,* vol. 6, pp. 261–62; *Grundriss,* pp. 553, 565; Doernberg, *Kurze Geschichte,* p. 141; Stöckigt, "Probleme," p. 421; Benser, in Kossok, *Studien,* p. 471; also Krippendorff, *Liberal-demokratische Partei,* pp. 113ff., 155–56.

though strikes and other mass actions did secure some social benefits for the workers, DDR authors find large parts of the working
class being misled into believing that continued economic improvements depended on the inclusion of West Germany in the
imperialist bloc and the creation of a separate West German state.
Thus, when the unions were told that American economic aid
might be jeopardized by their call for the nationalization of all
mining industries, they dropped that demand in disregard of their
own best interests. As a result, it is pointed out, the Western imperialists, aided by the West German bourgeoisie, could pursue their
objectives without interference, except for the warnings of the
West German KPD.

In the same vein, the formation of NATO in the spring of
1949 is described as another aggressive move of the West in the
struggle against the socialist states. No attempt is made to explain,
if only to refute, the Western position that NATO was created as a
protection against what the West considered threatening developments in the East. Yet, in thus imputing aggressive designs to the
West, East German historiography presents but a mirror image of
Western interpretations of what Soviet-bloc historians regard as
protective moves on the part of the Soviet Union.

What is of the greatest concern to DDR authors in this context is the relationship between West Germany and NATO. Although West Germany did not yet become a member of NATO,
DDR authors maintain that by placing the Ruhr's coal and steel
output under Western control, the Ruhr Statute, which was imposed on the West Germans, also put such resources at NATO's
disposal. It is noted, too, that secret military preparations were also
initiated—allegedly against the day when Germany would enter
NATO. These preparations, in turn, are traced back to other activities, such as American-sponsored "history" projects, dealing in particular with the German campaign against Soviet Russia, on which
large numbers of former Nazi generals collaborated.[47]

East German historians see a close connection between the
formation of NATO and that of the West German state. The new
state, they maintain, was created as the vehicle by means of which
a West German army was to bolster the NATO forces at an opportune time. For this reason, it is explained, a new Occupation Statute that adjusted the relations between the West Germans and the
Western occupation powers to the forthcoming establishment of
the West German state reserved to the Western powers the conduct of West German foreign relations. By this arrangement, the

---

[47]*GdA*, vol. 6, pp. 298–300, 323; *Grundriss*, pp. 554, 569, 571; Schnabel, *Deutsche
Geschichte* vol. 3, pp. 484–85, 487; Badstübner and Thomas, *Spaltung Deutschlands*, pp. 263–65, 350–53; Keiderling, "Mythos," pp. 1093ff.

new state would be prevented from pursuing an independent policy of reunification so as to assure its eventual entry into NATO. For the same reason, new Soviet attempts to salvage the unity of Germany on the "democratic-nonmilitarist-nonmonopolist" basis of the Potsdam Agreement were rejected by the Western powers at another foreign ministers' conference in Paris in May 1949. Corresponding efforts of the East German People's Congress addressed directly to the West Germans also were unsuccessful. The imperialist bloc on its part proposed reunification on terms that would have abolished the antifascist-democratic order in East Germany.

As the product of an antidemocratic imperialist scheme, the new state was well designed in the East German view to serve the West German and Western monopoly bourgeoisie. Its constitution, the Basic Law, safeguarded the predominance of the monopolies by the bourgeois principle of the separation of powers, by which the will of the parliament could be ignored by the government—a possibility further enhanced by the exceptionally strong position of the chancellor vis-à-vis the Bundestag—and by exclusionary voting arrangements.[48] Indicative of the expansionist aims of the imperialist bloc, the Basic Law also was to be applicable, as it was put, to territories outside of West Germany.

That a bill of rights was included is viewed as a concession to the antifascist-democratic aspirations of the toilers. Some authors dismiss these rights as merely "formally democratic," others accept them as offering some openings to the pursuit of genuinely democratic endeavors. Yet, even such opportunities, the latter hasten to add, were severely limited because the Occupation Statute enabled the Western powers to resume full control over West German affairs if they deemed such a move indispensable for the security and maintenance of the "democratic" order or for the fulfillment of international commitments toward other countries. In the view of DDR authors, this clause was merely meant to deter any effort on the part of the masses to pursue the struggle for German unification, deprive the monopolists and large landed proprietors of their power, and launch major strikes on behalf of the workers. (That the clause might also have been directed against the reemergence of Nazism would be inconceivable in the Marxist-Leninist view, because Nazism is perceived as a creation of monopoly capitalism, and the American monopoly

---

[48]According to West German electoral law, a political party can be represented in the Bundestag only if it wins at least three seats in direct elections or gets 5 percent of the overall vote. These provisions are to bar small splinter parties from complicating the work of the Bundestag, as happened in the Reichstag of the Weimar Republic. Among those affected by this rule is the small West German Communist party, which has not been able to overcome these hurdles since its reemergence as the *Deutsche Kommunistische Partei* in 1967.

bourgeoisie would not want to deprive itself of a tool that could help it fend off the progress of socialism.) "Four and a half years after the unconditional military surrender of German fascist imperialism, " Badstübner and Thomas conclude, "a state had come into being in West Germany that was designed to carry on the fateful traditions of German imperialist policy. The Federal Republic of Germany had nothing in common with that peaceful, democratic Germany that the decisions of Potsdam and Yalta envisaged." Reflecting the larger Marxist-Leninist view, *Deutsche Geschichte* also points out that

> The West German state was created specifically in order to halt and, if possible, undo the democratic revolution that had already taken hold in large parts of Germany.... [This] state dominated by the imperialist bourgeoisie was not willing to accept the results of the Second World War and sought by all available means to correct them.... From the historical perspective this state was reactionary, politically it was antidemocratic and antinational.

Its creation, *Deutsche Geschichte* sums up, signified the breakup of the organizational unity of the German nation.[49]

These "separatist" maneuverings of the West are contrasted with the East German efforts to prevent the splitting of Germany. It is stressed that the Parliamentary Council that drafted the West German constitution was elected only by West Germans, or more precisely by their various state parliaments, whereas the German People's Council, its East German counterpart, was elected by the second German People's Congress, which consisted of both East and West German delegates. Correspondingly, the constitutions of the two states differed significantly: whereas the Parliamentary Council, because of its narrow composition, could draw up only a constitution designed for West Germany, the constitution prepared by the People's Council was an all-German document that in the end could be enacted only in East Germany because of the separatism of the Western imperialists.

The German Democratic Republic in turn was established, according to the East German accounts, in response to the separatist West German state—at the demand, it is noted, of the East German population, which expressed its wishes in innumerable petitions, resolutions, and manifestoes. Once again it thus was the masses who were implementing the inevitable historical process. In the Marxist-Leninist framework, the creation of the DDR constituted part of the predetermined transitional process from capitalism to socialism. With the establishment of the new "Workers

[49]Schnabel, *Deutsche Geschichte*, vol. 3, pp. 485ff. (quotation on p. 490); *GdA*, vol. 6, pp. 321ff.; *Grundriss*, pp. 569–72; Streisand, pp. 419–20; Badstübner and Thomas, *Spaltung Deutschlands*, p. 424.

and Peasants State," this process entered its socialist phase; accordingly, the constitution proclaimed as people's property all mineral wealth and natural sources of energy as well as all plants utilizing these resources. Further progress was assured by the dominant role of the working class in alliance with peasants and other toilers, the principle of democratic centralism, and the principle of the unity of decision and implementation—the latter principle was the result of the unity of legislative, executive, and judicial powers, with the basic decisions resting in this scenario with the parliament, the *Volkskammer*. "For the first time," *Grundriss* notes, "a German state was created that is developing wholly in accordance with the worldwide laws of social progress. . . . [Its policies] corresponded with the goals of the peoples of the anti-Hitler coalition and the legally binding principles of the Potsdam Agreement and the Charter of the United Nations." And although its formation was part of a worldwide revolutionary process, it also was rooted

> in the heritage of Thomas Müntzer and the German Jacobins, of German classicism and all the revolutionary and humanistic traditions of the German people and carries them on at a higher level. It realizes the goals of Karl Marx and Friedrich Engels, of August Bebel and Wilhelm Liebknecht, of Karl Liebknecht, Rosa Luxemburg, and Ernst Thälmann. It fulfills the bequests of the Communist and Social Democratic resistance fighters, of the antifascists of bourgeois-democratic and Christian circles.

The establishment of two separate states also meant, however, that more than ever the national question, that is, the question of German unity, could be resolved only as part of the class struggle. If in 1949, German *staatlich* unity came to an end, national unity survived only a few years longer in the East German view. With the DDR evolving into a fully developed socialist state, the East Germans became a united socialist nation, facing a class-divided capitalist nation in the Federal Republic. DDR historians are convinced that ultimately, in keeping with the laws of historical progress, West Germany too will become socialist, and under that banner the two states will be reunited. For the time being, however, the history of Germany has come to an end, and its place has been taken by the histories of two entirely different states and nations. Of these, it is claimed, only the German Democratic Republic is the heir to the true German cultural and historical tradition and the herald of its abiding future.[50]

---

[50]*Grundriss*, pp. 574–76, 581–83 (quotation on pp. 581–82); Doernberg, *Kurze Geschichte*, pp. 164–66; *GdA*, vol. 6, pp. 341–44; Streisand, pp. 423–24; Bartel, quoted in *ZfG* 26 (1978): 550. Bartel speaks of the DDR's "own, unmistakeable history." On the Marxist distinction between capitalist and socialist nations, see Dorpalen, "Marxism," pp. 505ff.

10

Conclusion

O NE OF THE MOST striking aspects of DDR historiography, and for that matter of all Marxist-Leninist historiography, is its compactness. In part this cohesion results from the overall direction that guides historical research and writing in East Germany (see Chapter 1). Carefully laid-out plans channel historical scholarship into areas considered ideologically or politically relevant and coordinate and integrate much of the work that is being done. In further implementation of these directives, innumerable conferences are held at which findings are discussed and refined and symposia arranged in which the results are published. How team-minded DDR scholars are is suggested by the titling of a large number of their papers as "A Contribution to the Question of . . . " ("Zur Frage des [der] . . . "), implying that these papers constitute merely bricks for a larger structure.

Yet the compact nature of East German historiography is due not only to party or governmental directives or to the efforts of the historians themselves. On the substantive plane, Marxism-Leninism provides the framework of an all-embracing and integrating theory that fuses social, political, economic, and ideological forces into an overall system. The dialectical approach further accentuates existing interrelationships and interactions, as does the focus on classes rather than individuals as the moving forces of history, which reduces the multiplicity of protagonists.

The certitude of historical laws, finally, weaves the flow of developments into a coherent whole. There are few loose ends and few doubts; everything can be explained, and although explanations often differ, there is never any question of the logic of the course of events. Although climate, geography, and natural catastrophes may put obstacles into men's paths, their reactions to any such difficulties, their determination—or lack of it—to overcome obstacles is ultimately decisive. They always remain the makers of their own history—within the confines of their material and social environment. It was not the Black Death so much as agricultural overproduction that plunged Europe into economic misery in the fourteenth century (see Chapter 2); it was not the silting up of its harbors or the shifting of fishing grounds to the North Sea that caused the decline of the Hanseatic League, but the lack of resourcefulness of its merchants (again, see Chapter 2); no irrational demons drove the Germans to Nazism—the cold-blooded manipulations of the monopoly bourgeoisie did so (see Chapter 7). There is no blind, uncontrollable destiny—any seemingly incomprehensible tragedy is caused by human error, ignorance, or criminality for which man is responsible.

The picture of German history that thus emerges is one of notable simplicity in its basic outline. It is the story of classes striving to expand productivity and attain social progress—moving from the limitations of the feudal system to the liberating élan of competitive capitalism and achieving a breakthrough from repressive monopoly capitalism to socialism in at least one part of Germany. In contrast to non-Marxist accounts, Germany's history thus is presented not as particularly unique, but rather as part of a worldwide historical process. Admittedly, many obstacles had to be overcome, for classes often failed to fulfill the tasks assigned to them by history in this process. In the long run, however, the inherently inevitable growth of production could not be stopped. Thus capitalism gained ground on the feudal order because the feudal nobility increasingly turned capitalist and in this manner compensated for the absence of an aggressive bourgeoisie. Socialism, in turn, triumphed over a particularly ruthless type of monopoly capitalism in eastern Germany thanks to the support of the Soviet Union. Above all, the masses as material producers worked in the service of progress and thus were the ultimate makers of history. Beyond that, they propelled social advances through their class struggles—from medieval peasant risings through heretical movements and from the early bourgeois revolution of the Reformation and the Peasants' War to the revolutions of 1848 and 1918.

In this scenario of direct present-day relevance, the events of 1945 do not constitute a breakdown of continuity. Rather they are perceived as a logical sequel, opening up new opportunities for social progress of which the emergence of the socialist order in East Germany is the preeminent development. This emergence represents another advance in a continuing socioeconomic process and as such is rooted deeply in German history.

The contrast with the West German approach to that history is illuminating. West German historians first tried to come to terms with the German past by dismissing the Nazi era as a passing aberration. That position had to be abandoned, however, in the face of a record that left no doubt about the rootedness of Nazism in German social and political traditions and historical antecedents. As a result, those who grew to maturity in postwar West Germany perceived Germany's pre-1945 history as marked off by a deep incision from post-1945 developments, and they questioned the relevance of that history to their own situation. To the present day, West German historians have been unable to develop an integrated conception of German history. Instead, they have turned their attention to such previously neglected areas as economic and social history, which led them to concern themselves with all strata of German society rather than with mainly the political and social elites, as had been the case before, and to focus their attention on structural and social interrelationships. In the same vein, they took up philosophical and methodological problems concerning the meaning and function of history. If they could not develop a new overall picture of German history, they wanted at least to cleanse that history of myths and taboos and thus assign history an emancipatory role.[1]

The one systematic attempt to inject a new relevance into the historical past was undertaken by a layman, Gustav Heinemann, president of the Federal Republic from 1969 to 1974. In various addresses Heinemann pointed out that German history was not merely one of authoritarianism and repression, but also one of efforts at liberation from oppressive authorities, from which today's West Germans can derive new perspectives. By way of illustration he mentioned some of the very uprisings and revolutions on which the German Democratic Republic bases its historical legitimacy and which he insisted, contrary to the traditional view, were no mere upheavals of mutinous mobs but noteworthy struggles for social and political freedom.[2]

Heinemann was answered by the dean of the West German historians, Theodor Schieder, then president of the Association of German Historians and editor of the *Historische Zeitschrift*, who pointed out that most German protest movements and risings, unlike those of other countries, had had little impact on the course of Germany's history and that to single out such activities as the dominant theme—something that Heinemann had not proposed— would be not only misleading but also potentially dangerous for West Germany's young democracy. In reality, Schieder concluded,

---

[1]Hans Mommsen, "Historical Scholarship in Transition: The Situation in the Federal Republic," *Daedalus* (1971): 485ff.; Wehler, "Geschichtswissenschaft heute," in *Stichworte zur geistigen Situation der Zeit,* vol. 2: *Politik und Kultur* (Frankfurt, 1979), pp. 718ff.; *Der Spiegel,* Jan. 22, 1979, pp. 65ff.; Groh, *Kritische Geschichtswissenschaft in emanzipatorischer Absicht* (Stuttgart, 1973).

[2]Heinemann, "Die Geschichtsschreibung im freiheitlichen demokratischen Deutschland," *Bulletin des Presse- und Informationsdienstes der Bundesregierung,* Feb. 17, 1970, pp. 203–4; Heinemann, "Die Freiheitsbewegungen in der deutschen Geschichte," *GWU* 25 (1974): 601ff.

the historical ground on which that democracy was established was one of false starts and of patchwork adjustments, of catastrophes rather than of major reforms or revolutions.[3] Schieder's was, and is, a widely shared view: Germany's history was one of hard labor, of piecemeal reforms reluctantly introduced from above, and of wars fought for dubious causes; it offers few uplifting vistas into the past, let alone into the future. On this note, the debate petered out, but as has rightly been noted, even this more restrained approach has done away with many restricting preconceptions and has encouraged broader-based and more balanced analyses of Germany's past, duly taking into account social and economic conditions—analyses that are far more in accord with social reality than those of Imperial and Weimar days. In fact, within their own frame of reference these changes have been no less far-reaching than the shifts in interpretation that have occurred in DDR historiography since its break with the "misery concept" of German history (see Chapter 1).[4]

Nonetheless, and in fact not surprisingly, Schieder's reply was assailed by DDR critics as that of an ideological guardian of state-monopolist capitalism, and the reluctance of other historians to follow Heinemann's lead was seen as evidence of the continued prevalence of a class-centered conservatism, little modified by pseudo-liberal forays into social history.[5] However, the East German position, for its part, loses some of its self-confident gloss if the movements it hails as evidence of a progressive strand in German history are measured against the basic Marxist criteria of progress, in the way West Germans have measured these movements against their own scale of values. If from the non-Marxist viewpoint these movements contributed little to the liberalization of German conditions, their impact must be assessed as equally modest by Marxist criteria. With the possible exception of the Revolution of 1848, they provided few, if any, new impulses to the growth of production, the indispensable basis of social progress in the Marxist scenario; in the case of the Peasants' War, which accelerated the spread of "second serfdom," productivity was even set back in some parts of Germany (see Chapters 2, 3, and 5). Thus, because by Marxist tenets it is results rather than intentions that count, these risings hardly deserve the acclamation they have received in the East German literature. If they do receive it, the reason is that intentions are not uniformly discounted (see Chapter

[3]Schieder, "Hat Heinemann recht?" *Christ und Welt*, Feb. 27, 1970.
[4]Günter Moltmann, "What History Means to Us: A Comparison of American and German Attitudes toward History," *German Studies Notes* (Indiana University, 1977), pp. 3–4; Wolfgang J. Mommsen, *Die Geschichtswissenschaft jenseits des Historismus* (Düsseldorf, 1971).
[5]*Unb. Verg.*, p. 126.

1), least of all if they point into what is judged by the norms of Parteilichkeit as the right direction.

Questions also arise concerning the nature and validity of the Marxist historical laws. These laws, as explained, are cause-and-effect relationships that result from necessities dictated by class interests (see Chapter 1). Among these are laws such as the Law of the Correspondence of Production Relations with the Character and Developmental Level of the Productive Forces, the Law of the Class Struggle, the Law of the Succession of Socioeconomic Formations, and the Law of Social Revolution. There are also others, however, based not so much on empiricism as on desired results, such as the Law of the Leading Role of the Working Class and its Marxist-Leninist Party, the Law of the Alliance of the Working Class with Collective Farmers and Other Laboring Strata, the Law of the Planned and Proportionate Development of the National Economy, the Law of the Socialist Cultural Revolution, and the Law of the Cooperation of the Socialist States.[6]

Some of these laws, such as that asserting the necessary correspondence of production relations and productive forces, express certain truths—at least in "tendential" form (see Chapter 1). Others, such as the Law of the Class Struggle, which presents that struggle as the perpetual driving force of social progress in class societies, can be sustained only, and barely at that, by a very generous interpretation of the concept of class struggle (see Chapters 2, 3, and 4); class struggles clearly were not the all-dominant motor power of history.

Similarly, the Law of the Succession of Socioeconomic Formations must allow for major exceptions to be compatible with historical reality (see Chapter 1). Moreover, its application to contemporary developments raises serious questions. In the case of East Germany, for example—as in the case of other East European countries and earlier, for that matter, in that of the Soviet Union—the transition from capitalism to socialism was performed, not because there existed that high level of productivity on which Marx and Engels had predicated the adoption of socialism,[7] but because a political opportunity presented itself to impose the socialist order. Lenin, we recall, argued that the Bolsheviks were adhering to the inherently inevitable sequence of socioeconomic formations and merely reversing the chronological order of some steps in the transition from capitalism to socialism, but this expla-

[6]William H. Shaw, *Marx's Theory of History* (Stanford, 1978), pp. 63, 111–12, with references to MEW, vol. 4, pp. 338–39; Marx, *Grundrisse der Kritik des Politischen Ökonomie* (Berlin [East], 1953), p. 231, among others.
[7]Shaw, p. 63.

nation bypassed the crucial point.[8] The revolutions occurred not because of an objective necessity—productivity could have been restored more effectively under capitalist auspices—but on the basis of a subjective political judgment. (Lenin himself warned his associates that unless they used the opportunity to seize power in November 1917, there might not be another chance to establish a socialist state for a long time to come.) The "objective, scientific" approach thus was superseded by subjective judgments, and the same, of course, happened in Eastern Europe after the Second World War. There, too, social revolutions were imposed from above for political reasons rather than from economic necessity. Indeed, the Western world demonstrated that capitalism still had great potentialities for further development and without such intervention would have grown to new strength in Eastern Europe as well. Had not Marx taught that "no social order ever perishes before all the productive forces for which there is room in it have developed"?[9]

Some laws, however, are wholly untenable, and occasionally, when they are products of an outdated policy, this is admitted. Thus a Stalin-inspired "Law of the Intensification of the Class Struggle during the Introduction of Socialism" is now rejected as wrong.[10] Yet others that run counter to the historical record remain virtually unchallenged. The most important example is the "Law of the Decisive Role of the Popular Masses in History,"[11] whose validity was refuted on many occasions in the course of this study. Yet *Wörterbuch der marxistisch-leninistischen Soziologie* expresses a view shared by most, though not all, DDR historians (see Chapter 1) when it states: "The popular masses . . . are the decisive part of a people. . . . As the carriers of material production, they create the basic conditions for the existence and development of society. They are the makers of history and the main driving force of social progress."[12] Actually their contribution has been far more modest, for by themselves the masses have made history only on rare occasions. Revolutions, of course, are the foremost examples. In addition, the masses have at times helped influence the course of events, and as has rightly been stressed in the DDR literature, no policy can be successful without being at least tolerated by the masses—as long as the masses put up with it (Lenin). Such tolera-

---

[8]Stiehler, *Gesellschaft und Geschichte*, pp. 241–47.
[9]See MEW, vol. 13, p. 9. This is a matter of continuing concern to DDR scholars; see, for example, Günther Rose, "Modernisierungstheorien und bürgerliche Sozialwissenschaften," *ZfG* 29 (1981): 9–10.
[10]Streisand, p. 431.
[11]"Volksmassen," *Swb*, vol. 2, p. 753.
[12]"Volksmassen," *Wörterbuch*, p. 498; also *Grundlagen*, pp. 411, 669.

tion, however, more often than not has been the product of fear, resignation, or apathy and can hardly be called a creative history-making achievement.

Ultimately, this misjudgment of the role of the masses results from a mistaken assessment of their significance as a productive force. They have not been, as *Sachwörterbuch* says, *the* carriers of material production. Such production requires not merely physical labor but intellectual effort as well, and administrators, scientists, and technical experts too, are productive forces, as Marxists themselves acknowledge (see Chapter 1). That because of their class affiliations the latter may belong to the bourgeois camp does not deprive them of their productive function.[13] If they are dependent on physical labor to implement their ideas, physical labor has depended increasingly on their performance, especially in regard to the *growth* of production, the trigger of historical progress. On the other hand, the efforts to picture physical labor as the actual originator of new techniques and inventions (see Chapter 1) carry little conviction. Both logically and historically, the "Law of the Decisive Role of the Popular Masses in History" simply is wrong.[14] DDR historians, however, dismiss such criticism as the result of assessing developments, not on the basis of objective conditions, but subjectively by the extraneous standards of the capitalist order.[15]

All in all, the laws of history, even if assessed as mere tendencies, thus are hardly as reliable a guide as they are presented. Nonetheless, attempts to demonstrate their effective operation have been made with considerable subtlety and resourcefulness, and efforts to refine these arguments never end. Thus, with the laws virtually unchallenged on their home ground, they continue to give Marxist history the aura of a discipline that operates with scientific precision.[16] As Gerhard Brendler has written,

> With the victory of the Great Socialist October Revolution in Russia and the establishment of socialism, Marxism-Leninism (and with it historical materialism) has been confirmed in its basic principles by practical application. With its aid the working class has changed the world and has given a new direction to history. The prognoses based on it have on the whole been borne out. Basically it has become

[13]On this, see also Shaw, *Marx's Theory of History*, p. 22.
[14]This issue is, of course, closely connected with Marx's concept of the division of labor—both into occupational specialization and into physical and mental work—as a phenomenon of class societies that deprives man of his freedom and that would disappear in the communist society (MEW, vol. 3, pp. 31–32, 34–35, 46; vol. 19, pp. 224–25; also Tucker, *The Marxian Revolutionary Idea* [New York, 1969], pp. 18ff.; Rudolf Bahro, *Die Alternative* [Cologne, 1977], pp. 47–48, 83–84, 91–92, 164–65).
[15]Heitzer, review, *ZfG* 28 (1980): 263.
[16]Ruge, *Deutschland* (Berlin [East], 1978), p. 46.

irrefutable. New revolutionary experiences have enriched and broadened earlier tenets; far from disproving them, they have rendered them more precise and added new ones. The fundamental categories of historical materialism are firmly established and can no longer be questioned.[17]

At the same time, the laws of history enable the political leadership to pursue its policies with the authority of science to back them. Marxist-Leninist historiography that expects classes to live up to "the objective role imposed upon [them] by history"[18] provides a ready scholarly underpinning for the suppression of all dissentient voices. The analyses of bourgeois conduct during the Revolution of 1848, which seek to reduce the bourgeoisie to a self-destructing instrument in the service of social progress, point up this parallelism of function (see Chapter 5).

DDR historiography, then, is vulnerable on its own doctrinal and methodological terms, quite apart from those disparities—concerning the respective roles of the individual and the masses, the omnipotence of economic power, the nature of National Socialism, or the uses of evidence, to mention but a few— that separate it from the non-Marxist approach on philosophical, empirical, and methodological grounds. Such divergences, however, do not preclude consensus on individual issues. Thus, the non-Marxist will find new facts and conclusions in the East German interpretations that he can usefully incorporate into his own concept of German history— from the social role of the medieval peasantry (see Chapter 2) to the complexities of the Potsdam Conference (see Chapter 9). In addition, although the concept of the sociopolitical function of religion has long been accepted by most Western historians, though until recently less so by Germans, some of the East German observations on this topic deserve serious consideration as refinements of this pivotal issue (see Chapters 2 and 3).

Similarly, data newly discovered by East German researchers can complement or rectify Western interpretations of events and developments. Findings on the economic ramifications of the Thirty Years War, on the ideological aspects of Bismarck's foreign policy, on the unwieldiness of the Great Depression, or on the affinities between academic and business elites and the Nazis during the Wei-

---

[17]Brendler, "Zum Prinzip," *ZfG* 20 (1972): 290.

[18]See Horst Fielder, "Grundlagen und Erfahrungen der Arbeiterklasse der BRD im Ringen um ein antimonopolistisches Bündnis," *ZfG* 26 (1978): 101. The full statement reads: "Bourgeois ideologues keep asking that the working class renounce its 'claim' to hegemony in the struggle for social progress, for democracy and socialism. However, the hegemony of the working class is an objective requirement of the revolutionary transitional process from capitalism to socialism; it is not an attitude arrogated or invented by the proletariat, but an objective role imposed upon it by history . . . ," and then follows as evidence the statement by Marx in *The Holy Family*, quoted in chapter 1, pp. 34–35.

mar era also contribute useful new insights (see Chapters 3, 6, and 7). Yet although such East German findings undoubtedly will be adopted into non-Marxist historiography, and in some cases, have already been so adopted,[19] there remains, however, an insurmountable ideological barrier that sets limits to any consensus; Marxists regard developments as essentially dictated by the social system within which they occur, whereas the non-Marxist refuses to see history shaped by inevitabilities, even though he has become quite aware of the conditioning power of social forces.[20] Thus Western historians would attribute economic crises or social disorders to human inadequacies or other rectifiable shortcomings that can be remedied by reforms. DDR historians, on the other hand, view such problems as an integral part of the capitalist order and as solvable only through its replacement by a socialist order. Parteilichkeit often conceals this basic position, because by bestowing praises and reprimands it seems to suggest that the actions in question were the result of free decisions. DDR historians, of course, would not see it this way.

The dialectical approach underscores further the conditioning of the individual by society, with his conduct often reactive rather than initiatory and determined by circumstances rather than acts of will. With its stress on interaction and interdependence, this approach may give the non-Marxist historian further cause to reconsider his evaluations of class and individual relationships and to concern himself more with interconnections and cross-influences on human activities and with the interrelationships between politics, economics, and social conditions. In recent years, West German historians have been moving in that direction, under the influence of American, British, and French scholarship rather than Marxist dialectics and as a result of the training of a large segment of the postwar generation of academic historians in British and American universities. However, the continued compartmentalization of political, economic, and social history in such leading symposia as Gebhardt's *Handbuch der deutschen Geschichte* and *Handbuch der Deutschen Wirtschafts- und Sozialgeschichte* suggests that there is still something to be learned from the East German approach.[21]

---

[19]On the East German impact on West German historiography, see also Wohlfeil, in Wohlfeil, *Reformation*, p. 24; Stegmann, Wehler, *Sozialgeschichte Heute*, p. 595; Kopitzsch, in Kopitzsch, *Aufklärung*, p. 13.

[20]W. J. Mommsen, *Geschichtswissenschaft*, pp. 42ff.; Volker Rittner, "Zur Krise der westdeutschen Historiographie," in *Ansichten einer künftigen Geschichtswissenschaft*, ed. Imanuel Geiss and Rainer Tamchina (Munich, 1974), pp. 48ff.; Wehler, in Kocka and Nipperdey, *Theorie*, pp. 30–31.

[21]This demarcation of social from political history has led DDR historians to dismiss West German social history as but another technique of pretending concern for the working class without, however, conceding it its rightful political role (*Unb. Verg.*, pp. 54ff.; Walter Schmidt, "Zur historisch-politischen Konzeption

Similarly, the Marxist emphasis on a fact-oriented rather than an empathetic approach deserves serious consideration. DDR historians argue with Marx that "just as we do not judge an individual on the basis of what he thinks of himself,"[22] historical judgments ought to be focused not on contemporary conceptions and values but on objective criteria, such as social and economic conditions. For the non-Marxist historian, the problem remains, however, how far he may go in this direction. Quantitative history, the application of social-science approaches, has already removed him a significant distance from the individualizing approach of historicism, with its emphasis on the understanding of personal motivations. Although the traditional preoccupation with such motivations may lead to erroneous historical judgments and above all may tempt the historian into the uncritical acceptance of what has occurred, motives, on the other hand, are not as irrelevant even in the Marxist view as Marxists maintain—at least in the case of those of whose positions they disapprove. For it was the complete disregard of SPD motives that led their predecessors to as absurd a conclusion as the equation of Social Democracy with a kind of fascism (see Chapter 7). Moreover, such denigration of motivations also encourages the assumption, encountered repeatedly, that if an event occurred, its occurrence must have been intended (see Chapters 7 and 8). Coupled with the insistence on the law-determined power of social forces, this objectivist approach inevitably also pays less attention to factual evidence. The large number of unsubstantiated assertions that were noted in the course of this study are their own commentary on the consequences of such a perspective.

At the same time, however, DDR historiography is not devoid of moral judgments and keeps pointing out the dichotomy of the historical process by which progress exacted an enormous price in human suffering. Thus, there is a continuous emphasis on the hardships and injustices endured by the laboring classes throughout the ages and forever called back to mind by the term *exploitation*. Yet, following Engels, Marxists concede that the social inequities of slavery, feudalism, and capitalism were a price that had to be paid to advance productivity, the basis of all social progress. However, they will not content themselves, as traditional scholarship long has done, with accepting such inequities as a fact of life, best explained by the scarcity of available goods, and their approach certainly must be taken seriously.

---

des Heidelberger 'Arbeitskreises für Sozialgeschichte,'" *BzG* 9 [1967]: 626ff.; Schleier, "German Democratic Republic," in *International Handbook of Historical Studies*, ed. Georg G. Iggers and Harold T. Parker [Westport, CT, 1980], p. 330).
[22]Marx, in MEW, vol. 13, p. 9.

Yet, if Marxists do not find scarcity a satisfactory explanation of the earlier immiseration, the availability of more abundant supplies in capitalist societies in more recent times is not accepted either as the promise of a better life within that system. It is instead assailed as an attempt to conceal continuing inequities and bribe the exploited into accepting their status in an order that is inequitable by definition. Comparisons of this status with that of the working class in the socialist countries invariably produce results in the latter's favor.[23] (How such conclusions can be reconciled with the ceaseless efforts of the East German regime to shield its citizens against non-Marxist influences is not explained.)

Still, the East German approach, with its stress on past and present injustices, has probably had some impact on West German historians and has provided additional impulses to a more critical outlook on Germany's past. Traditionally, German historians have shied away from a critical probing of their history, rejecting such an approach as merely befouling one's own nest, but the Nazi catastrophe and, once again, American and English influences have brought about significant changes. They were touched off by Fritz Fischer's work on *Germany's Aims in the First World War*, which opened up entirely new lines of investigation. With the door thus opened to a more discerning approach, East German research on the vicissitudes endured by the laboring classes apparently has not been without effect, as increasing references to DDR materials in this area suggest.

Yet DDR historiography offers lessons not only to the historian. Marxism is also, in the words of Marx, the "doctrine of the conditions under which the proletariat is to be liberated."[24] This aspect pervades all phases of East German historiography—from the Middle Ages to the present. As historical developments are subject to laws, there is nothing unique about them, and something may be gleaned even from remote periods to aid today's proletariat or the socialist countries in their class struggles against their class enemies.

To what domestic uses history has been put has been discussed in the preceding chapters. What needs to be added is that over the years the picture of the German past has become a more positive one. The first step was the abandoning of the "misery concept" of German history (see Chapter 1), followed by a shift of attention to the democratic milestones of German developments. Gradually, this picture was touched up further: Luther ceased to be

---

[23]Bartsch et al., *Geschichte*, pp. 160ff.; "Arbeiterklasse," *Wörterbuch*, p. 26.
[24]Engels, quoted in Helmut Fleischer, *Marxismus und Geschichte* (Frankfurt, 1970), p. 153.

a "lackey of the princes," and the "Princes' Reformation" became a "Church Reformation" (see Chapter 3).

The history of Prussia has undergone a similar reassessment. The Prussian nobility, it will be recalled, is no longer seen so much as an obstacle to the rise of bourgeois capitalism, but as a class that assumed some of the functions of the bourgeoisie and, within limits, furthered the rise of capitalism (see Chapter 5). In the same vein, a recent biography of Frederick II, while not belittling the limitations of his enlightened despotism, pays considerable attention to the king's economic policies as proof of the thesis that even measures dictated by narrow class interests may prove of permanent value. Reviewing the book, Klaus Vetter felt that a good word also might have been said about Prussian militarism: granted that it typifies ruthless drill, blind obedience, and pedantry, it nevertheless turned out highly qualified military experts and a superbly trained army with remarkable striking power. "Prussia is part of our past . . . ," Ingrid Mittenzwei muses, "invisible threads link us with that yesterday even if we will always have to approach critically that part of our history."

The historical legitimacy of the German Democratic Republic can thus be shown to rest on an even broader social basis than had been asserted before—a factor of particular importance, as some authors have noted, at a time when the Federal Republic, too, is showing a renewed interest in the Prussian past and allegedly claiming it as its own.[25] Even the bourgeoisie of the nineteenth century has benefited from this shift and has been praised for its efforts, however abortive, to challenge the rule of the feudal nobility.[26]

This change of attitude does not, however, extend to the assessments of the monopoly bourgeoisie. As the "ruling class" in West Germany and in all other nonsocialist Western countries, it remains the relentless class enemy. Nor is there any assumption that the monopolists might have learned something from their experiences in the 1930s and 1940s; because their conduct is rooted, not in personal decisions, but in the monopoly-capitalist system, they cannot change their ways and must keep pursuing

---

[25]Mittenzwei, *Friedrich II. von Preussen* (Berlin [East], 1979), quotation on p. 212; Vetter, review, *ZfG* 28 (1980): 674–76; also Bartel et al., "Preussen," pp. 637ff. West German analyses of Prussia: Sebastian Haffner and Ulrich Weyland, *Preussen ohne Legende* (Hamburg, 1979); Bernt Engelmann, *Preussen: Land der unbegrenzten Möglichkeiten* (Munich, 1979); Wehler, "Preussen ist wieder chic," *Der Monat* (Oct./Nov. 1979): 92ff.; Karl Dietrich Erdmann, "Preussens tiefe Spur," *Die Zeit*, Mar. 7, 1980, p. 20.

[26]Schmidt, "Zu den Problemen der europäischen Revolutionen von 1848–49," *ZfG* 27 (1979): pp. 643, 647.

their competitive quest for markets and profits by repression and exploitation, and ultimately by war. Nobility and nonmonopolist bourgeois, on the other hand, either have ceased to exist as a class or have been reduced to secondary class status. They are therefore no longer the threat to the working class that they used to be and can be treated more leniently. Complementing the opposition to the monopolists is the rejection of West German conceptions of present-day capitalist societies as cooperative associations of business and labor in which contract negotiations, workers' participation in management, and profit-sharing have superseded the class struggle. Such views are condemned as attempts to deceive the workers, neutralize the revolutionary workers' parties, and perpetuate the class rule of the monopoly barons.[27]

Closely connected with these topics is another predominant theme—the need for a revolution to do away with the monopoly-capitalist order and the nature of such a revolution. The point that is persistently made is that reforms are nothing but palliatives; no social order can be rendered more effectual or equitable by mere reforms, because reforms leave the old ruling class in control. This means specifically that the inequities to which the working class is subjected under capitalism can be removed only by a revolution. Such a revolution need not be a violent one, and it can be a drawn-out one, as was the revolution by which the capitalist bourgeoisie superseded the feudal nobility in Germany—a process that has been explored with much ingenuity (see Chapters 5 and 6). A plethora of studies has also dealt with the historical lessons to be learned from earlier revolutions, both successful and unsuccessful, and with the technical preconditions of a successful revolution, such as the leadership role of the Marxist-Leninist party, the need for a coalition of workers with other classes, and the ideological preparation of the masses.

DDR historiography thus throws much light on the goals and values of the German Democratic Republic. This, of course, is not a uniquely Marxist facet; all historical writing, if only in its unspoken assumptions, reflects or stimulates political views and values. In this context, much can also be learned from the East German analyses about such fundamental positions as the Marxist concept of democracy, the presumed perpetuity of the class struggle in class societies, and the reasons why parliamentarism and civil liberties are held in such low esteem. East-West dialogues, which so often have turned out to be exercises in futility, will benefit from a recognition of this divergence of basic concepts, if

[27]*Unb. Verg.*, pp. 54ff.; "Arbeiterklasse," *Wörterbuch*, p. 26.

only by accepting the narrow limits within which such exchanges can be meaningful.

What the East German accounts also show is that despite all official secretiveness on day-to-day moves, there was never any secrecy about basic Communist goals. The Brussels and Berne conferences of the KPD laid the groundwork for the policies that were enacted in the Soviet occupation zone (see Chapters 8 and 9). If not all policies were implemented immediately, the KPD's proclamation of June 1945 made it clear that the delay was only temporary. In the same vein, the terms on which reunification would have been acceptable to the East German (and Soviet) leadership were set forth at the time in elaborate detail. As for the future, the march toward communism is to continue at home, and no doubt is left either that abroad the class struggle against imperialism will continue and, as an inherently inevitable process, indeed must go on.[28]

Thus, as East German historiography is to acquaint its Marxist audience with the social realities of the German past and present and provide guidance toward the future, it may well perform a related function for non-Marxists, too. Western historians ought to look upon the perceptions of the East German historians and the picture they paint as very much a part of present-day social reality, with all its challenges and confrontations.

[28]Bartsch et al., *Geschichte*, pp. 182–83; *Grundriss*, p. 778.

Bibliographical Note

G IVEN THE PROLIFIC OUTPUT of East German historians, a bibliographical survey must limit itself to the listing of a few
essential publications representative of the Marxist-Leninist approach, if it is to remain at all manageable.

Among general surveys of German history, Joachim Streisand's *Deutsche Geschichte in einem Band* (Berlin [East], 1974)
presents a readable, concise summary. Another one-volume work,
somewhat more detailed and more analytical, is *Klassenkampf,
Tradition, Sozialismus: Von den Anfängen der Geschichte des
deutschen Volkes bis zur Gestaltung der entwickelten sozialistischen Gesellschaft in der Deutschen Demokratischen Republik
Grundriss*, ed. Ernst Diehl et al. and published under the auspices
of the Academy of Sciences of the DDR (Berlin [East], 1978). The
most elaborate work to date is the twelve-volume *Lehrbuch der
deutschen Geschichte (Beiträge)* (Berlin [East], 1959ff.), a series of
college textbooks covering the period up to 1945. (In the text, the
individual volumes have been cited by their subtitle *Deutschland
von ... bis ...*). An abbreviated edition, *Deutsche Geschichte*
(Berlin [East], 1965ff.), has been published in three volumes; it carries its story, however, into the 1960s. A new multivolume
Deutsche Geschichte is in preparation.

Of more specialized works, an eight-volume *Geschichte der
deutschen Arbeiterbewegung* (Berlin [East], 1966), a topic of primary interest to Marxists, was written by a group of historians
and other social scientists under the direction of the leadership of
the SED and its then first secretary, Walter Ulbricht. Additional
materials on the German workers' movement can be found in the
forty-volume *Geschichte der Lage der Arbeiter unter dem Kapitalismus* by Jürgen Kuczynski (Berlin [East], 1960ff.), which consists
of textual, statistical, and documentary sections, the greater part
of which deal with Germany. A two-volume encyclopedia, *Sachwörterbuch der Geschichte Deutschlands und der deutschen Arbeiterbewegung* (Berlin [East], 1969–1970), has packed an enor-

mous amount of detailed information into relatively little space. *Die bürgerlichen Parteien in Deutschland: Handbuch der Geschichte der bürgerlichen Parteien und anderer bürgerlicher Interessenorganisationen vom Vormärz bis zum Jahre 1945*, ed. Dieter Fricke et al. (Leipzig, 1968–1969), also is a rich source of information. Hans Mottek (et al.), *Wirtschaftsgeschichte Deutschlands* (Berlin [East], 1964ff.), is a thorough, though rather unsophisticated, account of its topic. The post-1945 period is covered in Stefan Doernberg, *Kurze Geschichte der DDR* (Berlin [East], 1969), and *Geschichte der Sozialistischen Einheitspartei Deutschlands: Abriss*, ed. Gerhard Rossmann et al. (Berlin [East], 1978). *Unbewältigte Vergangenheit: Kritik der bürgerlichen Geschichtsschreibung in der BRD*, ed. Gerhard Lozek et al. and published under the auspices of the Academy of Social Sciences at the Central Committee of the SED, the Academy of Sciences of the DDR, and the *Karl-Marx-Universtät Leipzig* (Berlin [East], 1977), presents a comprehensive critique of West German analyses and interpretations of German history. Philosophical, didactic, methodological, and organizational matters are discussed in *Einführung in das Studium der Geschichte*, ed. Walter Eckermann and Hubert Mohr (Berlin [East], 1979).

The leading historical journal is *Zeitschrift für Geschichtswissenschaft*, a monthly, which covers all aspects of history but gives priority to German history. Every ten years it publishes supplements that provide excellent surveys of East German historical publications—books, articles, documentary materials—brought out during the preceding ten years (*Historische Forschungen in der DDR. Analysen und Berichte*, 1960, 1970, 1980). The journal *Beiträge zur Geschichte der (deutschen) Arbeiterbewegung* deals with the history of the workers' movement and of Marxism and the Marxist parties. *Jahrbuch für Wirtschaftsgeschichte* covers all aspects of economic and social history; *Jahrbuch für die Geschichte des Feudalismus*, *Militärgeschichte* (earlier, *Zeitschrift für Militärgeschichte*), and *Jahrbuch für die Geschichte der sozialistischen Länder Europas* provide materials on their respective fields of specialization. *Jahrbuch für Geschichte* covers all fields of history but also brings out issues focused on a specific topic. Finally, all institutions of higher learning publish a *Wissenschaftliche Zeitschrift*, whose *Gesellschafts- und sprachwissenschaftliche Reihe* frequently contains articles on German history.

Important monographs and symposia on specific topics are cited in the pertinent chapters, and so are articles, whose interminable titles have been reprinted in their full length in most cases as a further bibliographical aid.

A more detailed English-language survey of East German publications can be found in the chapter "German Democratic Republic," by the DDR scholar Hans Schleier, in *International Handbook of Historical Studies: Contemporary Research and Theory*, ed. Georg G. Iggers and Harold T. Parker (Westport, CT, 1980), pp. 325ff.

Selected Bibliography of Books Published since 1978

Evan B. Bukey

1. The Marxist-Leninist Concept of History

Autorenkollektiv, *Wirtschaftsgeschichte: Ein Leitfaden* (Berlin, 1979).

Autorenkollektiv, *Das Handelskapital: Geschichte und Gegenwart* (Berlin, 1980).

Buxhoeveden, Christina. *Geschichtswissenschaft und Politik in der DDR: Das Problem der Periodisierung* (Cologne, 1980).

Hartkopf, Werner. *Die Akademie der Wissenschaften der DDR: Ein Beitrag zu ihrer Geschichte* (Berlin, 1983).

Holzer, Horst. *Evolution oder Geschichte: Einführung in Theorien gesellschaftlicher Entwicklung* (Berlin, 1979).

Mottek, Hans. *Die Krisen und die Entwicklung des Kapitalismus* (Berlin, 1982).

Parthey, Heinrich. *Problem und Methode in der Forschung: Wissenschaft und Gesellschaft* (Berlin, 1978).

Rose, Günther. *Modernisierungstheorien und bürgerliche Sozialwissenschaften: Eine Studie zur bürgerlichen Gesellschaftstheorie und Geschichtsideologie der Gegenwart: Zur Kritik der bürgerlichen Ideologie und des Revisionismus* (Berlin, 1981).

Schleier, Hans. *Geschichte der Geschichtswissenschaft: Grundlinien der bürgerlichen deutschen Geschichtsschreibung und Geschichtstheorien vor 1945* (Potsdam, 1983).

Stiehler, Gottfried. *Dialektik und Gesellschaft: Zur Anwendung der Dialektik im historischen Materialismus* (Berlin, 1981).

Träger, Claus. *Die Herder Legende des deutschen Historismus: Zur Kritik der bürgerlichen Ideologie* (Berlin, 1979).

Weissl, Bernhard. *Kultur und Ethnos: Zur Kritik der bürgerliche Auffassungen über die Rolle der Kultur in Geschichte und Gesellschaft* (Berlin, 1980).

2. The Middle Ages: The Age of the Feudal System

Bentzien, Ulrich. *Bauernarbeit im Feudalismus: Landwirtschaftliche Arbeitsgeräte und -verfahren in Deutschland von der Mitte des ersten Jahrtausends u. Z. bis um 1800* (Berlin, 1980).

Epperlein, Siegfried. *Der Gang nach Canossa* (Berlin, 1978).

Gernentz, Hans Joachim. *Ritter, Bürger und Scholaren: Aus Stadtchroniken und Autobiographien des 13. bis 16. Jahrhunderts* (Berlin, 1980).

Herrmann, Joachim et al. *Deutsche Geschichte. Vol. 1: Von der Anfängen bis zur Ausbildung des Feudalismus Mitte des 11. Jahrhunderts* (Berlin, 1982).

————. *Ökonomie und Gesellschaft an der Wende der Antike zum Mittelalter: Zum Problem der Herausbildung der ökonomischen Grundlagen der Feudalgesellschaft im mitteren und westlichen Europa* (Berlin, 1979).

————. and Sellnow, Irmgard. *Produktivkräfte und Gesellschaftsformation in vorkapitalistischer Zeit* (Berlin, 1982).

Leube, Achim. *Neubrandenburg: Ein germanischer Bestattungsplatz des 1. Jahrhunderts u. Z: Beiträge zur Ur- und Frühgeschichte der Bezirke Rostock, Schwerin und Neubrandenburg* (Berlin, 1978).

Müller-Mertens, Ekhard. *Die Reichsstruktur im Spiegel der Herrschaftspraxis Otto des Grossen: Mit historigraphischen Prolegomena zur Frage Feudalstaat auf deutschem Boden, seit wann deutscher Feudalstaat?* (Berlin, 1980).

Töpfer, Bernhard. *Städte und Ständestaat: Zur Rolle der Städte bei der Entwicklung der Ständeverfassung in europäischen Staaten vom 13. bis zum 15. Jahrhundert* (Berlin, 1980).

Werner, Ernst. *Stadt und Geistesleben im Hochmittelalter: 11. bis 13. Jahrhundert* (Weimar, 1980).

3. From Feudalism to Capitalism:
The Reformation to the Thirty Years War

Harnisch, Hartmut. *Bauern-Feudaladel-Städtebürgertum: Untersuchungen über die Zusammenhänge zwischen Feudalrente, bäuerlicher und gutsherrlicher Warenproduktion und die Waregeld Beziehungen in der Magdeburger Börde und dem nordöstlichen Harzvorland von der frühbürgerlichen Revolution bis zum Dreissigjährigen Krieg* (Weimar, 1980).

Langer, Herbert. *Hortus Bellicus: Der Dreissigjährige Krieg: Eine Kulturgeschichte* (Leipzig, 1978).

Ullmann, Ernst. *Kunst und Reformation* (Leipzig, 1982).

Weinbold, Rudolf (ed.). *Volksleben zwischen Zunft und Fabrik: Studien zu Kultur und Lebensweise werktätiger Klassen und Schichten während des Übergangs vom Feudalismus zum Kapitalismus* (Berlin, 1982).

Wölfing, Günther. *Wasungen: Eine Kleinstadt im Feudalismus vom 9. bis zum 19. Jahrhundert* (Weimar, 1980).

4. From Feudalism to Capitalism: The Age of Absolutism

Blaschke, Karlheinz. *Ereignisse des Bauernkrieges 1525 in Sachsen: Der sächsische Bauernaufstand 1790* (Berlin, 1978).
Dietze, Walter. *Johann Gottfried Herder: Abriss seines Lebens und Schaffens* (Berlin, 1980).
Mittenzwei, Ingrid. *Preussen nach dem Siebenjährigen Krieg: Auseinandersetzung zwischen Bürgertum und Staat um die Wirtschaftspolitik* (Berlin, 1979).

5. The Rise of Bourgeois Capitalism: The Road to Unification

Academy of Sciences. *Preussische Reformen—Wirkungen und Grenzen: Aus Anlass des 150. Todestages des Freiherrn vom und zum Stein* (Berlin, 1982).
Bock, Helmut. *Die Illusion der Freiheit: Deutsche Klassenkämpfe zur Zeit der französischen Julirevolution 1830 bis 1831* (Berlin, 1980).
Bräuer, Helmut. *Gesellenmigration in der Zeit der industriellen Revolution: Meldeunterlagen als Quellen zur Erforschung der Wanderbeziehungen zwischen Chemnitz und dem europäischen Raum* (Karl Marx Stadt, 1982).
Forberger, Rudolf. *Die Industrielle Revolution in Sachsen 1800–1861* (2 vols) (Berlin, 1982).
Förster, Wolfgang. *Bürgerliche Revolution und Sozialtheorie: Studien zur Vorgeschichte des historischen Materialismus* (Berlin, 1982).
Fricke, Dieter (ed.). *Deutsche Demokraten: Die nichtproletarischen Kräfte in der deutschen Geschichte 1830 bis 1945* (Berlin, 1981).
Hildebrandt, Gunther. *Parlamentsopposition auf Linkskurs: Die kleinbürgerlich-demokratische Fraktion Donnersberg in der Frankfurter Nationalversammlung 1848/49* (Berlin, 1975).
Hofmann, Jürgen. *Das Ministerium Camphausen-Hansemann: Zur Politik der preussischen Bourgeoisie in der Revolution 1848/49* (Berlin, 1981).
Kunze, Peter. *Die preussische Sorbenpolitik 1815–1847: Eine Studie zur Nationalitätenpolitik im Übergang vom Feudalismus zum Kapitalismus* (Bautzen, 1978).
Lärmer, Karl (ed.). *Studien zur Geschichte der Produktivkräfte: Deutschland zur Zeit der Industriellen Revolution* (Berlin, 1979).
Nietzold, Roland et al. *. . . unserer Partei einen Sieg erringen: Studien zur Entstehungs—und Wirkungsgeschichte des "Kapitals" von Karl Marx* (Berlin, 1978).
Schmidt, Dorothea. *Die preussische Landwehr: Ein Beitrag zur Geschichte der allgemeinen Wehrpflicht in Preussen zwischen 1813 und 1830* (Berlin, 1981).

Schmidt, Walter. *Wilhelm Wolff: Kampfgefährte und Freund von Marx und Engels 1846–1864* (Berlin, 1979).

Weber, Rolf. *Land ohne Nachtigall: Deutsche Emigranten in Amerika 1777–1886* (Berlin, 1981).

Zwahr, Hartmut. *Zur Konstituierung des Proletariats als Klasse: Strukturuntersuchung über das Leipziger Proletariat währrend der industriellen Revolution* (Berlin, 1978).

6. From Competitive to Monopoly Capitalism: The Empire

Aisin, B. A. and Willibald Gutsche. *Forschungsergebnisse zur Geschichte des deutschen Imperialismus vor 1917* (Berlin, 1980).

Bartel, Horst et al. *Das Sozialistengesetz 1878–1890: Illustrierte Geschichte des Kampfes der Arbeiterklasse gegen das Ausnahmegesetz* (Berlin, 1980).

Baudis, Dieter and Helga Nussbaum. *Wirtschaft und Staat in Deutschland vom Ende des 19. Jahrhunderts bis 1918/19* (Berlin, 1978).

Fricke, Dieter. *Kleine Geschichte des Ersten Mai: Maifeiern in der deutschen und internationalen Arbeiterbewegung* (Berlin, 1980).

Groebler, Olaf. *Der lautlose Tod* (Berlin, 1978).

Gutsche, Willibald. *Der gewollte Krieg: Zur deutschen Verantwortung für die Entstehung des Ersten Weltkrieg* (Cologne, 1984).

Höpfner, Christa and Irmtraud Schubert. *Lenin in Deutschland* (Berlin, 1980).

Kaulisch, Baldur. *Alfred von Tirpitz und die imperialistische deutsche Flottenrustung* (Berlin, 1982).

Klein, Fritz (ed.). *Neue Studien zum Imperialismus vor 1914* (Berlin, 1980).

Löschburg, Winfried. *Ohne Glanz und Gloria: Die Geschichte des Hauptmanns von Köpernick* (Berlin, 1978).

Mühlberg, Dietrich et al. *Arbeiterleben um 1900* (Berlin, 1983).

Seeber, Gustav (ed.). *Gestalten der Bismarckzeit* (Berlin, 1978).

———. and Heinz Wolter. *Mit Eisen und Blut: Die preussisch-deutsche Reichsgründung von 1870/71* (Berlin, 1981).

Steigerwald, Robert. *Bürgerliche Philosophie und Revisionismus im imperialistischen Deutschland* (Berlin, 1980).

Stern, Leo (ed.). *Die Berliner Akademie der Wissenschaften in der Zeit des Imperialismus* (3 vols.) (Berlin, 1975–1979).

Thümmler, Heinzpeter. *Sozialistengesetz Paragraph 28: Ausweisungen und Ausgewiesene 1878–1890* (Berlin, 1979).

7. The Era of State-Monopolist Capitalism: The Weimar Republic

Beyr, Hans. *Die Revolution in Bayern 1918/19* (Berlin, 1982).

Doebler, Edgar and Egbert Fischer. *Revolutionäre Militärpolitik gegen fa-*

schistischen Gefahr: Militärpolitische Probleme des antifaschistischen Kampfes der KPD von 1929 bis 1933 (Berlin, 1982).

Habendank, Hans. *Die Reichsbank in der Weimarer Republik: Zur Rolle der Zentralbank in der Politik des deutschen Imperialismus 1919–1933* (Berlin, 1981).

Hortzschansky, Günter et al. *Ernst Thälmann: Eine Biographie* (Berlin, 1979).

Imig, Werner and Walter Kissljakow (eds.). *Studien zur ideologischen Entwicklung der KPD 1919–1923* (Berlin, 1981).

Kinner, Klaus. *Marxistische deutsche Geschichtswissenschaft 1917 bis 1933: Geschichte und Politik um Kampf der KPD* (Berlin, 1982).

Leidigkeit, Karl-Heinz and Jürgen Hermann. *Auf Leninistischen Kurs: Geschichte der KPD-Bezirksorganisation Halle-Merseburg* (Halle, 1979).

Lozek, Gerhard and Alfred Loesdau. *Zeitalter im Widerstreit: Grundprobleme der historischen Epoche seit 1917 in der Auseinandersetzung mit der bürgerlichen Geschichtsschreibung* (Berlin, 1982).

Materna, Ingo. *Der Vollzugsrat der Berliner Arbeiter—und Soldatenräte 1918/19* (Berlin, 1978).

Niemann, Heinz (ed.). *Geschichte der deutschen Sozialdemokratie 1917 bis 1945* (Berlin, 1982).

Nowak, Kurt. *Evangelische Kirche und Weimarer Republik: Zum politischen Weg des deutschen Protestantismus zwischen 1918 und 1932* (Weimar, 1981).

Ruge, Wolfgang. *Novemberrevolution: Die Volkserhebung gegen den deutschen Imperialismus und Militarismus 1918/19* (Berlin, 1978).

Schumacher, Horst. *Die Kommunistische Internationale (1919–1943): Grundzüge ihres Kampfes für Frieden, Demokratie, nationale Befreiung und Sozialismus* (Berlin, 1979).

Wohlgumuth, Heinz. *Die Entstehung der Kommunistischen Partei Deutschlands* (Berlin, 1978).

8. The Era of State-Monopoly Capitalism: The Fascist Period

Balnk, Alexander and Julius Mader. *Rote Kapelle gegen Hitler* (Berlin, 1979).

Eichholtz, Dietrich and Kurt Gossweiler (eds.). *Faschismusforschung: Positionen, Probleme, Polemik* (Berlin, 1980).

Eschwege, H. (ed.). *Kennzeichen J: Bilder, Dokumente, Berichte zur Geschichte der Verbrechen des Hitlerfaschismus an den deutschen Juden 1933 bis 1945* (Berlin, 1980).

Finker, Kurt. *Graf Moltke und der Kreisauer Kreis* (Berlin, 1978).

Herden, Werner. *Wege zur Volksfront: Schriftsteller im antifaschistischen Bündnis* (Berlin, 1978).

Komitee der Antifaschistischen Widerstandskämpfer der Deutschen Demokratischen Republik, *Aktenvermerk R. u. Ein: Bericht über die*

Solidarität und den Widerstand im Konzentrationslager Mauthausen (Berlin, 1979).

Lozek, Gerhard and Rolf Richter. *Legende oder Rechfertigung? Zur Kritik der Faschismustheorien in der bürgerlichen Geschichtsschreibung: Zur Kritik der bürgerlichen Ideologie* (Berlin, 1979).

Pätzold, Kurt and Manfred Weissbecker. *Hakenkreuz und Totenkopf: Die Partei des Verbrechens* (Berlin, 1982).

Petzold, Joachim. *Generalprobe für Hitler* (Berlin, 1980).

———. *Die Demogogie des Hitlerfaschismus: Die politische Funktion der Naziideologie auf dem Wege zur faschistischen Diktatur* (Berlin, 1982).

Stroech, Jürgen. *Die illegale Presse—eine Waffe im Kampf gegen den deutschen Faschismus: Ein Beitrag zur Geschichte und Bibliographie der illegalen antifaschistischen Presse 1933–1939* (Leipzig, 1979).

9. The Socialist-Imperialist Confrontation: The Breakup of Germany, 1945–1949

Bartel, Horst. *Die wirtschaftlichen Ausgangsbedingungen der DDR: Zur Wirtschaftsentwicklung auf dem Gebiet der DDR 1945–1949/50* (Berlin, 1979).

Hoyer, Lutz. *Revolution—Kleinbürgertum—Ideologie: Zur Ideologiegeschichte der LDPD in den Jahren 1945–1952* (Berlin, 1978).

Neef, Helmut. *Entscheidende Tage im Oktober 1949: Die Gründung der Deutschen Demokratischen Republik* (Berlin, 1979).

Schöneburg, Karl-Heinz (ed.). *Errichtung des Arbeiter-und-Bauern-Staates der DDR 1945–1949* (Berlin, 1983).

Biographical Appendix

Evan B. Bukey

BARTEL, HORST. b Cottbus, Jan 16, 28. d Jun 22, 84. *Educ:* Institute for Social Sciences, ZK SED, Dr Phil, 56. *Prof Exp:* Lecturer, 56–57, Professor for the History of the German Labor Movement, Institute for Social Sciences, ZK SED, 66–69–. *Mem:* Commission of Historians GDR/USSR (Deputy Chairman, German Section), Academy of Sciences, 72–. *Honors & Awards:* Patriotic Service Order (Bronze), 65. *Publ: Marx und Engels im Kampf um ein revolutionäres deutsches Parteiorgan, 1879–1890* (Berlin, 61); (co-ed.) *Die grosspreussisch-militärische Reichsgründung* (Berlin, 71).

BARTEL, WALTER. b Fürstenburg, Mecklenburg, Sep 15, 01, into a working class family. *Educ:* Karl Marx Univ, Leipzig, Dr Phil, 57. *Prof Exp:* Commercial Apprentice, Communist Youth, 20; KPD, 23 (imprisoned, Niederschönfeld, 23); Lenin School, Moscow, 29–32; Inmate, Brandenburg-Görden Penitentiary, 33–35; immigration to Czechoslovakia, 35–39; Inmate, Buchenwald, 39–45; Advisor for party questions to Wilhelm Pieck, 46–53; Teaching Fellow, Karl Marx Univ, Leipzig, 53–57; Director, Institute of Contemporary History, Berlin, 62–70. *Honors & Awards:* Patriotic Service Order (Silver), 64 (Gold), 69; Karl Marx Order, 79. *Mem:* Buchenwald Committee. *Publ: Deutschland in der Zeit der faschistischen Diktatur, 1933–1945* (Berlin, 56); *Die Linken in der deutschen Sozialdemokratie im Kampf gegen Militarismus und Krieg* (Berlin, 58); *Ein Held der Nation: Aus dem Leben Ernst Thälmanns* (Berlin, 61).

BERTHOLD, WERNER. b Leipzig, Sep 15, 23, son of a locksmith and a cook. *Educ:* Karl Marx Univ, Leipzig, Dr Phil, 60, Habil, 67. *Prof Exp:* Graphic artist; Wehrmacht; POW (France), 44–48; Adult Education Lecturer, Leipzig; Associate Professor, Karl Marx Univ, Leipzig, 69–73, Professor, 73–. *Honors & Awards:* National Prize, 79. *Publ:* " . . . *Grosshungern und Gehorchen:" Zur Entstehung und politischen Funktion der Geschichtsideologie des westdeutschen Imperialismus untersucht am Beispiel von Gerhard Ritter und Friedrich Meinecke* (Berlin, 60); *Marxistisches Geschichtsbild: Volksfront und antifaschistisch-demokratische Revolution* (Berlin, 70); (ed.), *Kritik der bürgerlichen Geschichtswissenschaft* (Cologne, 70).

DLUBEK, ROLF. b Leipzig-Plagwitz, Aug 8, 29, son of a miner. *Educ:* Karl Marx Univ, Leipzig, Dr. Phil. *Prof Exp:* Carpenter; Fellow, ZK SED, Fellow, Institute of Marxism Leninism ZK SED, 65– Professor, 66–. *Honors & Awards:* Patriotic Service Order, 66; Banner of Labor Order, 68; National Prize, 81. *Publ:* (ed.) *Die I. Internationale in Deutschland, 1846–1972: Dokumente und Materialen* (Berlin, 64); *"Das Kapital" von Karl Marx in der deutschen Arbeiterbewegung (1867–1878): Abriss und Wirkungsgeschichte* (Berlin, 67).

DOERNBERG, STEPHAN. b Berlin-Wilmersdorf, Jun 21, 24, son of a KPD functionary. *Educ:* Moscow Univ; Institute for Social Sciences, ZK SED, Dr Phil, 59. *Prof Exp:* Lieutenant, Red Army, 42–45; Coworker, Soviet Military Administration, Mecklenburg, 45–46; Foreign Editor, *Tägliche Rundschau*, Berlin, 46–50; Head, General History Division, Institute for Social Sciences, 55–62; Director, Institute of Contemporary History, Berlin, 62–71; Professor, 63; Director, Institute of International Politics and Economics, Berlin, 71–77; Institute of International Relations, Potsdam-Babelsberg, 77–; Editorial Board, *Deutsche Aussenpolitik. Honors & Awards:* Patriotic Service Order (Silver), 64 & 66. *Mem:* GDR Committee for European Security (General Secretary), 70–. *Publ: Die Geburt eines neuen Deutschland, 1945–1949: Die antifaschistisch-demokratische Umwälzung und die Entstehung der DDR* (Berlin, 59); *Kurze Geschichte der DDR* (Berlin, 64).

EICHHOLTZ, DIETRICH. b Danzig, 30. *Educ:* Humboldt Univ, Berlin, Diploma (Economics), 54: Institute for History, Academy of Sciences, Dr rer oec, 59, Habil 68. *Prof Exp:* Assistant, Institute for History, Academy of Sciences, 55–62; Lecturer, Ernst-Moritz-Arndt Univ, Greifswald, 62–66; Central Institute for History, Academy of Sciences, Berlin, 66–. *Publ: Junker und Bourgeoisie vor 1848 in der preussischen Eisenbahngeschichte* (Berlin, 62); *Geschichte der deutschen Kriegswirtschaft: 1939–1945* (Berlin, 69); (ed.) *Deutschland im zweiten Weltkrieg* (6 vols.) (Berlin, 74–).

ELM, LUDWIG. b Greussen, Sonderhausen, Oct 10, 34, son of a worker. *Educ:* Agricultural technical school; Humboldt Univ, Berlin; Karl Marx Univ, Teaching Certificate, 56; Friedrich Schiller Univ, Jena, Dr Phil, 64, Dr sc phil, 71. *Prof Exp:* Agricultural teacher, 48–50; Deputy Secretary, FDJ, Karl Marx Univ, Leipzig, 58–61; Deputy Secretary, SED, Friedrich Schiller Univ, 64–69; Lecturer and Pro-rector, Friedrich Schiller Univ, Jena, 69–; Professor, 70–; People's Chamber, 71–. *Honors & Awards:* Patriotic Service Order. *Publ: Zwischen Fortschritt und Reaktion: Geschichte der Parteien der liberalen Bourgeoisie in Deutschland, 1893–1918* (Berlin, 68); *Der "neue" Konservatismus: Zur Ideologie und Politik einer reaktionären Strömung in der BRD* (Frankfurt, 74).

ENGELBERG, ERNST. b Haslach, Apr 5, 09 son of a bookbinder. *Educ:* Univ Berlin; Univ Munich, Dr Phil, 34. *Prof Exp:* Communist Youth, 28– KPD, 30–; Immigration to Turkey, 34–48; Univ Potsdam & Karl Marx Univ, Leipzig, 48–51; Director & Professor, Institute for History, Academy of Sciences, 60–69; President, National Committee of Historians, GDR, 58–65. *Honors & Awards:* Patriotic Service Order, 59 (Gold), 74; National Prize, 3d Class, 64; Dr h c, Karl Marx Univ, Leipzig, 69. *Publ: Revolutionäre Politik und Rote Feldpost 1878/90* (Berlin, 59); *Deutschland von 1849 bis 1871* (Berlin, 59); *Johann Phillip Becker in der I. Internationale: Fragen der Demokratie und des Sozialismus* (Berlin, 64); *Deutschland von 1871 bis 1897* (Berlin, 65); (ed.) *Probleme der marxistischen Geschichtswissenschaft* (Cologne, 72).

FALK, WALTRAUD. b Berlin, Feb 2, 20. *Educ:* Humboldt Univ, Berlin Diploma (Economics), 52, Dr rer oec, 56, Habil 62. *Prof Exp:* First Secretary, FDJ, Humboldt Univ, Berlin; Director, Institute for Economic History, Humboldt Univ, Berlin, 56–; Dean, Social Sciences. *Honors & Awards:* Patriotic Service Order (Bronze), 74. *Mem:* Urania (Vice President, 76–). *Publ: Kleine Geschichte einer grossen Bewegung: Zur Geschichte der Aktivisten- und Wettbewerbsbewegung in der Industrie der DDR* (Berlin, 66): *Wirtschaft, Wissenschaft, Welthöchstand: Vom Werden der sozialistischen Wirtschaftsmacht DDR* (Berlin, 69).

FRICKE, DIETER. b Frankfurt/Oder, Jun 21, 27. *Educ:* Humboldt Univ, Berlin, Dr Phil, 54, Habil 60. *Prof Exp:* NSDAP, 44–45; Head of Correspondence Studies, Humboldt Univ, Berlin & Potsdam Pedagogical Univs, 52–57; Professor, Weimar, 60–. *Honors & Awards:* Patriotic Service Order, 63; Meritorious Teaching Award, 79. *Publ: Bismarcks Prätorianer: Die Berliner politische Polizei im Kampf gegen die deutsche Arbeiterbewegung (1871–1898)* Berlin, 62); (ed.) *Dokumente zur deutschen Geschichte.*

GERICKE, HORST. b Halle, Sep 15, 23, son of an engineer. *Prof Exp:* Principal and Instructor, Walter Ulbricht Workers and Peasants Technical School, Halle; Professor of Oriental and Ancient Studies, Martin Luther Univ, Halle, 69–. *Publ: Deutschland von der Mitte des 11. Jahrhunderts bis zur Mitte des 13. Jahrhunderts* (Berlin, 64).

GUTSCHE, WILLIBALD. b Erfurt, Aug 8, 26, son of a clerk. *Educ:* Friedrich Schiller Univ, Jena, Dr Phil, 60; Humboldt Univ, Berlin, Habil, 67. *Prof Exp:* Teacher and Director, secondary school, Erfurt, 46–61; Fellow, Central Institute of History, Academy of Sciences, 61–; Professor, 76–; Head, Regional History, Institute of History, Academy of Sciences, 81–. *Honors & Awards:* Banner of Labor Order. *Mem:* Society of Regional History, Cultural League of the GDR (President, 79–). *Publ:* (ed.) *Herrschaftsmethoden des deutschen Imperialismus 1897/98 bis 1917* (Berlin, 77); *Sarajevo* (Berlin, 84); *Der gewollte Krieg: Zur deutschen Verantwortung für die Entstehung des Ersten Weltkriegs* (Cologne, 84).

HEITZ, GERHARD. b Burg-Magdeburg, Mar 28, 25. *Educ:* Humboldt Univ, Berlin, Dr Phil, 53; Karl Marx Univ, Leipzig, Habil, 60. *Prof Exp:* NSDAP, 43–45; Professor, 61–; Professor for Regional and Agricultural History, Univ Rostock, 66–; Board of Editors, *Zeitschrift für Geschichtswissenschaft. Honors & Awards:* Service Medal of the GDR, 63. *Mem:* Academy of Sciences. *Publ: Ländliche Leinenproduktion in Sachsen, 1470–1555* (Berlin, 61); *Der Bauer im Klassenkampf* (Berlin, 75).

HEITZER, HEINZ. b Zwickau. *Educ:* Dr Phil, 56. *Prof Exp:* Lecturer, Deputy Director, Institute for History, Academy of Sciences, Berlin, 56–. *Honors & Awards:* Patriotic Service Order (Silver), 66; National Prize, 3d Class, 79. *Mem:* Academy of Sciences (Corresponding Member, 80–). *Publ: Insurrection zwischen Weser und Elbe: Volksbewegungen gegen die französische Fremdherrschaft im Königreich Westfalen (1806–1813),* (Berlin, 59).

HERMANN, JOACHIM. b Lübnitz, Dec 19, 32. *Educ:* Humboldt Univ, Berlin, Dr Phil, 58. *Prof Exp:* Assistant, Division Head, Institute for Ancient and Early History, Academy of Sciences, Ernst-Moritz-Arndt Univ, Greifswald,

Professor, 69–; Director, Central Institute for Ancient History and Archaeology, Academy of Sciences, Berlin, 70–. *Mem:* Academy of Sciences. *Publ: Tornow and Vorberg: Ein Beitrag zur Frühgeschichte der Lausitz* (Berlin, 66); *Siedlung, Wirtschaft und gesellschaftliche Verhältnisse der slawischen Stamme zwischen Oder/Neisse und Elbe* (Berlin, 68); (ed.) *Die Rolle der Volksmassen in der Geschichte der vorkapitalistischen Gesellschaftsformationen* (Berlin, 75).

HOFFMAN, ERNST. b Aug 2, 12, son of a SPD functionary. *Educ:* Univ Cologne (Natural Science). *Prof Exp:* Communist Youth, 30; KPD, 37–; Imprisoned, 33–37; Immigration to Czechoslovakia and England, 36–45; Central Committee KPD/SED, 45–; Deputy Head, Head of Chair for History of Germany & German Labor Movement, Academy of Sciences, Berlin, 52–; Ordinarius, Humboldt Univ, Berlin, 62–. *Honors & Awards:* Patriotic Service Order (Gold), 72 (Honor Clasp) 77.

KLEIN, FRITZ. b Berlin, Jul 11, 24, son of a journalist. *Educ:* Humboldt Univ, Dr Phil, 52, Habil 68. *Prof Exp:* Wehrmacht, 42–45; KPD, 45–; Deputy Division Head, Museum of German History, Berlin, 52–53; Editor, *Zeitschrift für Geschichtswissenschaft,* 56–57; Fellow, 57–; Division Head, Head of Scientific Field of General History, Academy of Sciences, Berlin 73–; Professor, 70–. *Honors & Awards:* Banner of Labor Order, 69. *Mem:* Cultural League GDR; GDR Committee for Security & Disarmament; Peace Council GDR; Academy of Sciences. *Publ: Die Diplomatischen Beziehungen Deutschlands zur Sowjet-Union 1917–1933* (Berlin, 54); (ed.) *Deutschland im ersten Weltkrieg* (3 vols.) (Berlin, 68–69).

KUCZYNSKI, JÜRGEN. b Elberfeld, Sep 17, 04, son of a prominent labor statistician and writer. *Educ:* Univs Berlin, Heidelberg, Erlangen; Dr Phil (Erlangen), 25; Brookings Institution, Washington, DC, 27–28, *Prof Exp:* KPD, 30–; Economics Editor, *Rote Fahne,* 30–32; Director of Information, Revolutionary Trade Union Organization (RGO), 33–35, Information Officer, KPD, 34–35; Publisher and author (with his father, René Kuczynski), *Finanzpolitischer Korrespondenz,* later *Konjunkturstatistischer Korrespondenz;* Immigration to England, 34–35; Editorial staff, *Labour Monthly,* 41–44; Economic contributor, US Strategic Bombing Survey, 44–45; President, Central Administration for Finance, Soviet Military Administration in Germany, 45–47; President, Society for Study of Culture of USSR; Society for German-Soviet Friendship 47–50; People's Chamber, 50–58; Director, German Economic Institute, Berlin, 49–52; Director, Economic History Division, Institute for History, Academy of Sciences, 56–58; Professor of Economic History, Humboldt Univ, Berlin. *Honors & Awards:* Karl Marx Order, 69; Star of International Friendship in Gold, 79; National Prize of the Academy of Sciences, 70. *Publ: A Short History of Labour Conditions Under Capitalism* (5 vols.) (London, 42–46); *Die Geschichte der Lage der Arbeiter unter dem Kapitalismus* (40 vols.) (Berlin, 60–72); *Studien zu einer Geschichte der Gesellschaftswissenschaften* (10 vols.) (Berlin, 75–78); *Geschichte des Alltags des deutschen Volkes* (Berlin, 80–82); *Gesellschaften im Untergang: Vergeleichende Niedergangsgeschichte vom Römischen Reich bis zu den Vereinigten Staaten vom Amerika* (84); *Memoiren: Die Erziehung des Jürgen Kuczynski zum Kom-*

munisten und Wissenschaftler (73); *Dialog mit meinem Urenkel: Neunzehn Briefe und ein Tagebuch* (Berlin, 83).

KÜTTLER, WOLFGANG. b Altenburg, Apr 8, 36. *Educ:* Friedrich Schiller Univ, Jena, Dr Phil, 66; Academy of Sciences, Berlin, Dr sc phil, 76. *Prof Exp:* Head, Research Office for Methodology and History of the Historical Sciences, Central Institute for History, Academy of Sciences, Berlin, 74–; Editor, *Jahrbuch für Geschichte der sozialistischen Länder Europas,* 69–79. *Publ: Patriziat, Bürgeropposition und Volksbewegungen in Riga* (Berlin, 66); *Lenins Formationsanalyse für Russland vor 1905* (Berlin, 78); *Probleme der geschichtswissenschaftlichen Erkenntnis* (Berlin, 77); (with Ernst Engelberg), *Formationstheorie und Geschichte* (Berlin, 78).

MITTENZWEI, INGRID. b Bochum, May 14, 29. *Educ:* Univ Leningrad, 51–56; Institute for History ZK SED. *Prof Exp:* Head, Division of German History 1648–1789, Academy of Sciences; Professor, 80–. *Honors & Awards:* Service Medal of the GDR, 79. *Publ: Der Joachimsthaler Aufstand 1525: Seine Ursachen und Folgen* (Berlin, 68); *Preussen nach dem siebenjährigen Krieg: Auseinandersetzungen zwischen Bürgertum und Staat um die Wirtschaftspolitik* (Berlin, 79); *Friedrich II. von Preussen: Eine Biographie* (Cologne, 80).

MOTTEK, HANS. b Posen, Sep 26, 10. *Educ:* Univ Freiburg & Berlin, 29–32 (law); Humboldt Univ, Berlin, Dr Phil, 50. *Prof Exp:* Immigration to Palestine, 33–35; Communist Party, 35–; Farm and construction worker in Britain, 36–46; Lecturer, 51–54; Professor, 54–, Economic University, Berlin-Karlshorst. *Honors & Awards:* Patriotic Service Order (Silver), 60; National Prize, 68. *Mem:* Academy of Sciences, 69–. *Publ: Wirtschaftsgeschichte Deutschlands* (Berlin, 64–72); (ed.) *Studien zur Geschichte der industriellen Revolution in Deutschland* (Berlin, 70).

MÜLLER-MERTENS, ECKARD. b Aug 28, 23, into a Communist family. *Educ:* Humboldt Univ, Berlin, Dr Phil, 51, Habil, 56. *Prof Exp:* Karl Marx School, ZK SED; Pedagogical University, Potsdam; Professor, 60–; Departmental Chairman, 63–68, Humboldt Univ, Berlin; Director, Medieval Division, Institute for German History, Academy of Sciences, 68–. *Publ: Das Zeitalter der Ottonen* (Berlin, 55); *Karl der Grosse, Ludwig der Fromme und die Freien: Wer waren die liberi homines der karolingischen Kapitularen (742/743 832)?* (Berlin, 63); *Regnum Teutonicum: Aufkommen und Verbreitung des deutschen Reichs- und Königsauffassung im frühen Mittelalter* (Vienna, Cologne, Graz, 70).

NIMTZ, WALTER. b Stettin, Apr 14, 12, into a working-class family. *Educ:* Karl Marx Party University ZK SED, Dr Phil, 59. *Prof Exp:* Bank employee, Stettin; SED functionary, 46. Director, Museum of German History, Berlin, 62–66; Deputy Director, Institute for History, Academy of Sciences, Berlin, 66–. *Honors & Awards:* Patriotic Service Order (Bronze), 59 (Silver), 66; National Prize, 68. *Publ: Die Novemberrevolution 1918 in Deutschland* (Berlin, 62).

OBERMANN, KARL. b Cologne, Sep 22, 05, son of a factory worker. *Educ:* Sorbonne, Paris, 38–39; Humboldt Univ, Berlin, Dr Phil, 50, Habil, 52. *Prof Exp:* Socialist Youth: SPD, 31–36; KPD, 36–; Immigration to France, 33–41 (interned, 39–41); Immigration to USA, 41–46; Black Mountain

College, North Carolina, 42; Editor, *The German American*, 43–46; Return to Germany, 46; Editor, *Forum*, 47–49; Professor, 50–53, Director, Historical Institute, 52–53, Pedagogical University, Potsdam; Professor, 53–70, Humboldt Univ, Berlin; Director, Institute for German History, Academy of Sciences, 56–70. *Honors & Awards:* Patriotic Service Order (Gold & Silver); National Prize; Banner of Labor Order; Fighter Against Fascism Medal; Service Medal GDR; Honor Pin of the Committee of Anti-Fascist Resistance Fighters; Friedrich Engels Prize. *Mem:* Historical Commission GDR & Czechoslovakia (President, GDR Section); Commission of Historians of GDR & Hungary (President, GDR Section); Historical Commission GDR & USSR/GDR & Poland; Commission Internationale de Demographie Historique. *Publ: Joseph Wedemeyer: Pioneer of American Socialism* (New York, 1947); (Ed.) *Einheit und Freiheit* (Berlin, 53); *Die deutschen Arbeiter in der Revolution von 1848* (Berlin, 53); *Deutschland von 1815 bis 1849: Von der Gründung des Deutschen Bundes bis zur bürgerlich-demokratischen Revolution* (Berlin, 61).

PATERNA, ERICH. b Genschmar, Feb 12, 97, son of a postal clerk. d Apr 22, 82. *Educ:* Teachers College; Humboldt Univ, Berlin, Dr phil, 55, Habil 58. *Prof Exp:* German army (Guard regiment), 16–18; Elementary- and Middle School Teacher, –30; Principal, 30–33, Frankfurt/Oder; SPD, 27–32; KPD, 32–; Inmate, Brandenburg-Görden Penitentiary, 36–40; Bookkeeper for a dairy, 40–45; ZK KPD/SED, 45–; Lecturer, Karl Marx Party Univ, Berlin, 46–53; Professor, Humboldt Univ, Berlin, 52–63, Emeritus, 63. *Honors & Awards:* Patriotic Service Order (Gold); Banner of Labor Order. *Mem:* Urania. *Publ: Da stunden die Bergleute auf* (Berlin, 60).

RUGE, WOLFGANG. b Nov 1, 17. *Prof Exp:* Immigration to USSR; Head, Weimar Republic Division, Central Institute for History, Academy of Sciences, 56–. *Honors & Awards:* Patriotic Service Order (Silver), 68; National Prize, 75. *Publ: Deutschland 1917–1933* (Berlin, 67); *Weimar Republik auf Zeit* (Berlin, 69); *Hindenburg: Porträt einens Militaristen* (Berlin, 74) *Stresemann: Ein Lebensbild* (Berlin, 66).

SCHEEL, HEINRICH. b Berlin, Dec 11, 15, into a working-class family. *Educ:* Humboldt Univ, Berlin, 35–40, Dr Phil, 56. *Prof Exp:* Communist Youth, 32; Wehrmacht, 39–42; Imprisoned as a member of *Rote Kapelle* resistance group, 42–45; Principal, Insel Schafenberg School, West Berlin, 46–49; Lecturer, Pedagogical Univ, Berlin; Member, Division Head, Deputy Director, Institute for History, Academy of Sciences, 56–. *Honors & Awards:* Patriotic Service Order (Silver); Friedrich Engels Prize, 66; Banner of Labor Order, 69; Karl Marx Order, 80. *Mem:* Committee of Historians of GDR/Poland (Chairman); Academy of Sciences (Vice President, 72–). *Publ: Süddeutsche Jakobiner-Klassenkämpfe und republikanische Bestrebungen im deutschen Süden Ende des 18. Jahrhunderts* (Berlin, 62); *Die Mainzer Republik: Protokolle des Jakobinerklubs* (Berlin, 75).

SCHILFERT, GERHARD. b Königsberg, Sep 9, 17, son of a teacher. *Educ:* Univ Königsberg, 37–39; Martin Luther Univ, Halle, Dr Phil, 48, Habil, 51. *Prof Exp:* Wehrmacht, 42–45; KPD, 45–; Lecturer, Univ Rostock, 51–52; Professor, Humboldt Univ, Berlin, 52–. *Honors & Awards:* Service Medal GDR. *Mem:* Historical Society GDR (President, 65–68); Urania. *Publ: Sieg und Niederlage des demokratischen Wahlrechts in der deutschen Revolution 1848/49* (Berlin, 52); *Deutschland von 1648 bis 1789* (Berlin, 59).

SCHLEIER, HANS. b Jan 20, 31. *Educ:* Karl Marx Univ, Leipzig, Dr Phil, 63, Dr sc phil. *Prof Exp:* Research Office, Methodology and History of Historical Sciences, Central Institute for History, Academy of Sciences, Berlin; Editorial Board, *Jahrbuch für Geschichte,* 72–. *Publ: Sybel und Treitschke: Antidemokratismus und Militarismus im historisch-politischen Denken grossbourgeoiser Geschichtsideologen* (Berlin, 65); *Die bürgerliche deutschen Geschichtsschreibung der Weimarer Republik* (Berlin, 75); *Geschichte der Geschichtswissenschaft: Grundlinien der bürgerlichen deutschen Geschichtsschreibung und Geschichtstheorien vor 1945* (Potsdam, 83).

SCHMIDT, WALTER. b Weide/Breslau, 30. *Educ:* Friedrich Schiller Univ, Jena, Dr. Phil, Habil. *Prof Exp:* FDJ, 50–; SED, 52–; Director, Institute for History of the German Labor Movement, ZK SED, 64–; Professor, 65–. *Honors & Awards:* National Prize, 3d Class, 74. *Mem:* Historical Convention GDR (Vice President). *Publ: Illustrierte Geschichte der deutschen Revolution 1848/49* (Berlin, 75).

SCHMIEDT, ROLAND-FRANZ. b Pola, Austria-Hungary, Jul 14, 14, son of a teacher. d. Feb 1, 80. *Educ:* Charles Univ, Prague; Martin Luther Univ, Halle, Dr Phil, 63. *Prof Exp:* Socialist Youth, Austria; Immigration to Czechoslovakia, 34; Wehrmacht (punishment battalion); SED in Saxony; German Pedagogical Central Institute, 49–56; Professor, Friedrich Schiller Univ, Jena, 63–67; Professor, Pedagogical Univ, Dresden, 67–74. *Honors & Awards:* Patriotic Service Order (Silver), 74. *Publ:* (with Alfred Meusel), *Lehrbuch der deutschen Geschichte* (Berlin, 59).

STEINMETZ, MAX. b Frankfurt/Main, Oct 12, 12. *Educ:* Univ Heidelberg, Frankfurt, Freiburg, 32–39, Dr Phil (Freiburg), 39; Friedrich Schiller Univ, Jena Habil, 56. *Prof Exp:* Wehrmacht: National Committee of Free Germany; Antifa School; German Administration of Public Instruction; Guest Lecturer, Humboldt Univ, Berlin; Professor, Friedrich Schiller Univ, Jena, 54–60; Professor, 60–; Head, Institute of German History, Dean of Faculty, 62–68, Karl Marx Univ, Leipzig. *Honors & Awards:* Patriotic Service Order (Bronze), 72; National Prize, 75. *Mem:* Comité International des Sciences Historiques. *Publ: Deutschland 1456 bis 1648* (Berlin, 65).

STREISAND, JOACHIM. b Berlin, Oct 18, 20, son of a bookseller. d Jan 6, 80. *Educ:* Univ Rostock –42; Humboldt Univ, Berlin, Dr Phil; Martin Luther Univ, Halle, Habil, 62. *Prof Exp:* Expelled from Univ Rostock under Nazi racial laws, 42; Inmate in a labor camp, Jena, 44–45; SED, 48– ; Museum of German History, Berlin; Founding member, *Zeitschrift für Geschichtswissenschaft* (Editorial Secretary, 53–56); Specialist, Academy of Sciences, 56–80; Professor, 63–80; Director, Institute for History of the German People, Humboldt Univ, Berlin. *Honors & Awards:* National Prize, 3d Class, 69. *Mem:* Historical Society GDR (President, 68). *Publ: Deutschland von 1789 bis 1815* (Berlin, 58); (Ed.) *Studien zur deutschen Geschichtswissenschaft* (Berlin, 62); *Geschichtliches Denken von der deutschen*

Frühaufklärung bis zur Klassik (Berlin, 64); *Deutsche Geschichte in einem Band* (Berlin, 64); *Kritische Studien zum Erbe der deutschen Klassik: Fichte, W. v. Humboldt, Hegel* (Berlin, 71).

WERNER, ERNST. b Thyssa, Czechoslovakia, Nov 20, 20, son of a sales clerk. *Educ:* Karl Marx Univ, Leipzig, Dr Phil, 52, Habil, 55. *Prof Exp:* Wehrmacht; Student teacher, Dresden; Professor, 57, Rector, 67–69, Karl Marx Univ, Leipzig. *Honors & Awards:* National Prize, 3d Class, 66; Patriotic Service Order, 75. *Mem:* Academy of Sciences; National Committee for Balkan Studies (President). *Publ: Die gesellschaftlichen Grundlagen der Klosterreform im 11. Jahrhundert im Zeitalter des Reformpapstums* (Leipzig, 56); *Die Geburt einer Grossmacht—die Osmanen, 1300–1481: Ein Beitrag zur Genesis des türkischen Feudalismus* (Vienna, 72); *Zwischen Canosa und Worms: Staat und Kirche 1077–1122* (Berlin, 73).

ZSCHÄBITZ, GERHARD. b Riesa, Nov 19, 20, son of a clerk. d Leipzig, Jun 15, 70. *Educ:* Karl Marx Univ, Leipzig, Dr Phil, 56, Habil, 64. *Prof Exp:* Teacher and principal, secondary school, Riesa; Institute for History of the German People, Professor, 66–70, Karl Marx Univ, Leipzig. *Publ: Zur Mitteldeutschen Wiedertäuferbewegung nach dem grossen Bauernkrieg* (Berlin, 58); *Martin Luther: Grösse und Grenze* (Berlin, 67).

Sources: "Personalien," *Zeitschrift für Geschichtswissenschaft* 18–32; Günther Buch, *Namen und Daten: Biographien wichtiger Personen der DDR* (Berlin, 1973) (Second edition, 1982); Bundesministerium für Gesamtdeutsche Fragen, *SBZ—Biographie: Ein Biographisches Nachschlagebuch über die Sowetische Besatzungszone Deutschlands* (Bonn, 1964); and information provided by Hans Schleier, Wolfgang Küttler, Willibald Gutsche, Dietrich Eichholtz, and Georg Iggers.

Index

German History in Marxist Perspective

Andreas Dorpalen was professor emeritus of history at Ohio State University from 1978 until his death in December 1982. He held a Guggenheim fellowship in 1953–1954 and has published numerous articles and books in the field of German studies, including *Heinrich von Treitschke* and *Hindenburg and the Weimar Republic.*

The publisher wishes to thank Professor Georg Iggers for his graceful introduction to this book and to Dr. Dorpalen's work in general, and Professor Evan Bukey for bringing the bibliography up to date and providing many biographies of figures important to the discussion here. A further key contribution has been that of Professor Dorpalen's successor at Ohio State University, Professor Alan Beyerchen, who has assisted the Press in the author's stead through each aspect of the publication process.

The manuscript was edited by Barbara Tilly. The book was designed by Jim Billingsley. The typeface for the text and the display is Trump Medieval. The text is printed on 55-lb. Glatfelter and the book is bound in Joanna Mills Kenneth cloth over binder's boards.

Manufactured in the United States of America.